The Bungling Host

THE BUNGLING HOST

The Nature
of Indigenous
Oral Literature

DANIEL CLÉMENT | Translated by Peter Frost

University of Nebraska Press | Lincoln and London

Originally published as *L'hôte maladroit: la matière
du mythe* (Presses de l'Université Laval, 2014).

Except where noted, all figures are by
Christiane Clément

∞

Library of Congress Cataloging-in-Publication Data
Names: Clément, Daniel, 1951–, author.
Title: The bungling host: the nature of
indigenous oral literature / Daniel
Clément; translated by Peter Frost.
Other titles: Hote maladroit. English
Description: Lincoln: University of
Nebraska Press, 2018.
Identifiers: LCCN 2017052574
ISBN 9781496200877 (hardback)
ISBN 9781496206053 (paper)
ISBN 9781496206688 (pdf)
Subjects: LCSH: Indian mythology. | Folklore—
North America. | Indians of North America—Folklore. |
Animals—Symbolic aspects. | Ethnology—
North America. | Montagnais Indians—Folklore. |
Innu Indians—Folklore. | Myth. |
Bisac: Social Science / Ethnic Studies / Native American
Studies. | Literary Criticism / Native American.
Classification: lcc e98.f6 c6413 2018 | ddc
398.2089/97—dc23. LC record available at https://
urldefense.proofpoint.com/v2/url?u=https-3a_lccn
.loc.gov_2017052574&d=Dwif-g&c=Cu5g146wZdoqV
uKptnsyhefx_rg6kWhlklf8eft-wwo&r=pk0dimnulqAcvC
-qpmo0pfw1iqybGdPdscqprlfx-5y&m=Ud9jtrjbvadkyfkj
7ekzao9d1xcmEhRtdeoAbQdeotM&s=Px4oibaffHkgm
9ptkjfa7p1us4cLhij5ktwrfbuzzqs&e=.

Designed and set in Charis by L. Auten.

My Boléro should bear the inscription:
Ram this right into your head!

—Maurice Ravel

A piece of music too widely known and yet always new
thanks to its simplicity. A melody coils up onto itself
tirelessly and keeps increasing in volume and intensity,
devouring the sound environment and finally engulfing
the melody.

—Maurice Béjart

Contents

Illustrations

TABLES

Introduction

When a young man begins to hunt, his knowledge has been
passed down to him from father to son for generations. . . .
Little by little, by hunting well and by continually increasing the number of his catches, he happens to have strange
adventures. One day, before going off to hunt, he has a
dream: "I meet a young girl who likes me a lot, enough
to make love to me. I undress her and put all of her linen
[clothes] in a heap." In the morning, he goes off to hunt
and sees two caribou: a female and its young one. He kills
them, skins them, and puts all of their meat in a heap. He
covers everything with two hides. He looks, remembers his
dream, and grasps its meaning.

—Mathieu André, "Moi, 'Mestanapeu'"

Analysis of myths, the subject of this book, is like the beginnings
of this young Innu hunter of the eastern Subarctic. Like the hunter,
we have some experience, but we listen to these stories without
initially understanding what they mean. As we learn more about
the cultures from which they originate, we gain new insights that
make up for our initial lack of understanding, first by lifting one
corner of the veil and then by lifting the entire veil that hides the
answer to the puzzle. By comparing the myth with the knowledge
we have learned, we will grasp its full meaning.

We began this search for the meaning of myths many years ago when faced with a serious difficulty: the gap between Native American discourse on myths and the most fashionable analytical approach of our time—structuralism. On the one hand, the Native Americans we knew told us myths they felt to be true, and some would even go so far as to offer proof. On the other hand, according to structuralism, a myth has no meaning in itself and produces meaning only within a system of large constitutive units, which are called mythemes by analogy with the phonemes of a language: "It is in vain that one seeks the meaning of a mythic narrative since it has none in itself; it takes (or produces) meaning only in relation to the system of mythemes it belongs to (and participates in)" (Désveaux 1991, 501).

The difficulty was all the more serious because the starting point of structuralism was close to ours. Claude Lévi-Strauss (1963 [1958]) himself wondered about the apparently unintelligible nature of such narratives: "Some claim that human societies merely express, through their mythology, fundamental feelings common to the whole of mankind, such as love, hate, or revenge or that they try to provide some kind of explanations for phenomena which they cannot otherwise understand—astronomical, meteorological, and the like. But why should these societies do it in such elaborate and devious ways, when all of them are also acquainted with empirical explanations?" (207).

To answer this question, or at least to begin to answer, he wrote his four-volume work, *Mythologiques*. "Elaborate and devious" ways of thinking are explained by the structural logic that is universally at work in the language of myths. The rule is as follows: "In order to solve the problem, we must apply an essential rule of structural analysis: whenever a version of a myth contains a detail that seems anomalous, one asks oneself whether, in deviating from the normal this version is contradicting another, which is usually not far away" (Lévi-Strauss 1992 [1983], 106). Elsewhere, he instead speaks of an unintelligible aspect, to which he applies the same rule: "And so if one aspect of a particular myth seems unintelligible, it can be legitimately dealt with, in the preliminary stage and on the hypothetical level, as a transformation of the homologous aspect of another myth, which has been linked with the same group for the sake of the argument and which lends itself more readily to interpretation" (Lévi-Strauss 1983 [1964], 13).

On top of all this, mythic thought has a double bind, which Lévi-Strauss deduces from his research. The bind is mental and ecological, the first one being recognized as potentially greater than the second (Lévi-Strauss 1992 [1983], 121–37).

Therefore, according to structuralism, human beings are pre-destined by their physical makeup to create myths that have no meaning for them. The opposite conclusion, however, has emerged from systematic, in-depth examination of the mythology of one culture we know well—the Innu culture[1] of the eastern Subarc-tic, as well as from analysis of structuralist interpretations by devotees of Lévi-Strauss. Myths have meaning for their users, and seemingly absurd narratives reveal their rich significance to the extent that one has the knowledge to understand them. What is more, these narratives also seem inherently rational once the elements that drive them have been elucidated. We are far from the structuralist assumptions that self-conscious rationality exists only in our own societies: "But although the myths, considered in themselves, appear to be absurd narratives, the interconnections between their absurdities are governed by a hidden logic: even a form of thought which seems to be highly irrational is thus con-tained within a kind of external framework of rationality; later with the development of scientific knowledge, thought interiorizes this rationality so as to become rational in itself" (Lévi-Strauss 1981, 687). The following pages will also lead to another fact that Lévi-Strauss denies: namely that these absurd interconnections include eminently scientific knowledge.

There is clearly a need for a thorough critique of how structural-ism interprets myths, and this critique must flow from arguments other than the ones that have circulated for at least a quarter of a century. This new critique could be made on linguistic, philosophical, or even psychological grounds. In all such cases, however, its basis must differ from that of structuralism, and it must derive its veracity from examples that leave no room for doubt. In other words, the arguments must not be solely intellectual.

The most important critique of structuralism would probably come from linguistics. Structuralism has certainly borrowed from that field of knowledge (Saussure 1916), and Lévi-Strauss (1996 [1983], 148) himself has admitted to this borrowing, at least partially. After analysis of many myths, it seemed to us that one of these borrowed concepts in particular has not been critiqued, one which is a concept fundamental to structuralism.

We are thinking here about the concept of mytheme, whose existence is based on the concept of phoneme. If a myth is made up of unintelligible statements, one can logically compare each statement to a "voice sound"—a phoneme—which becomes a meaningful signifier only when joined to other "voice sounds." By comparison, a mytheme (from myth + eme) gains meaning only if combined with another mytheme. Mythemes can be brought together within a myth, or they may be introduced from another myth belonging to the same culture or to a neighboring or distant culture, just as vowels and consonants can be brought together in spoken language. The different possible ways of combining them give rise to different signifiers.

On the other hand, if, as we have deduced from our own research, mythemes themselves are signifiers, the comparison between mytheme and phoneme no longer holds, and we have to go back to the drawing board.

In this study, we will consider a mytheme to be a constituent unit in a myth, which is made up generally of a subject and a predicate, but which may also be more elaborate than merely a combination of the two. We will give it, however, a different meaning. For that matter, we have always used it differently. Because a mytheme in itself carries meaning, it is equivalent to a *mythic theme* (from myth + theme), and this term is more in line with our own suppositions.

Another related concept is *etymon*, which is borrowed from etymology (Clément 1992a, 1995a). When one is dealing with a myth, the etymon of a mytheme is what supports and drives this constituent unit, be it natural or social. Use of the term *etymon* became necessary as we sought to distinguish the apparently unintelligible mytheme from its source—from which the mind constructs it.

Now, to admit, even just theoretically, the possibility that mythemes have meaning, in and of themselves, leads to a series of difficulties we should stop to think about. Are the main interested parties themselves aware of the signifiers and, if so, why, as Lévi-Strauss rightly wondered, do they prefer unintelligible ways of expressing themselves?

If we reread it, both questions are answered by the introductory quote. An Innu dreams, experiences an event, and only then does he find out what his dream really means. This is like a mytheme. An Innu told us he had known a myth about a male otter's marriage with a she-wolf and how, in this myth, the otter went about killing the caribou it preyed on by sliding through the animal from the anal orifice to the buccal orifice (or the reverse)—unlike the wolf, which had to expend much more effort to kill its prey. As a young man, he had wanted to see how truthful these unintelligible statements were when he was getting ready to cut up his first caribou. To his great surprise, after wondering which way the otter had truly gone, he noticed that the dorsal aorta and the carotid arteries, once cut open, had on their surface small bumps arranged in pairs that appeared all the way along at equal distances from each other. This pattern looked astonishingly similar to an otter's tracks. The hunter had now figured out the myth. These body parts, the dorsal aorta and the carotid arteries, are named in Innu the same way an otter's tracks are: *kuashkuashkutipeu*, i.e., 'he jumps several times at equal distance.'

This example, in and of itself, would be insignificant. But there are others. Here is one from the hunting experiences of another Innu who recounted a legendary episode that initially seems arbitrary:

> Shortly after, our man again dreamt about his grandfather, Giant Eagle. . . .
>
> In his dream, his grandfather told him: "You will mark your path always by sticking a branch or a bush into the ground by the shore of the lake or the river you will cross." One day while on a journey, he crossed a frozen lake. But about halfway over he remembered the words of caution and turned back, telling himself: "I've again forgotten to mark my path. I've got to pay attention!" He was about to continue when, suddenly, an eagle took him away. (André 1984, 135)

The story continued with him being taken away to the eagle's nest. The Innu then recounted how the man managed to escape, ending with an odd remark on the hunter's transformation: "He went home happy and his wife too was happy. He thought he had become a marten up there, in the eagle's nest, but now he was once more a man . . ." (André 1984, 137).

Why a marten? The hunter himself provided the explanation, at least in part: "And now, I will give the meaning of this legend: When one sees a marten's tracks on the lake, one sees that it backtracks and then crosses. We know this is what the man did: he began to cross, came back, and then completely crossed the lake again. This, the eagle knows, and this makes the marten more afraid" (André 1984, 137). The episode alludes to the marten's fear of open spaces: "Raine (1981) found that during winter martens in Manitoba seldom traveled on frozen lakes" (Strickland and Douglas 1987, 535). Martens are prey of eagles.

The etymon of the mytheme is therefore a marten's behavior on an open surface. But without appropriate knowledge, the mytheme seems gratuitous and obscure (why walk ahead, only to backtrack?). This is actually a way of making the listener think it through.

Here is one last example. This is a scene from another Innu myth known under the name of *How the Summer Birds Were Brought North*. The myth tells how a group of animals who had gone looking for the summers, represented as small birds kept in a bag, managed to free them from their custodians. Among the liberators was a fisher who, pursued by these custodians, barely escaped. But the latter shot an arrow into its tail. Now, three elderly hunters told us they had tried to verify the mythical assertion about the animal's split tail: "When they kill an *utshek* . . . They then checked whether the bone of the tail was split. He says it isn't split. He says it's only the fur there . . . on the end . . . It's as if there were a separation" (Mestokosho, Louis, and Napish, Ekuanitshit, 19.11.85). This example clearly shows, regardless of what the hunters did or did not discover, that the narrative's abnormal elements, by their oddness, are incentives to find out how truthful the stories are. This is exactly the same approach we will take in this book.

To test this approach, we chose the Bungling Host as a set of myths that may offer an appropriate challenge. The choice was not really fortuitous. First known to Native American mythologists under the name of the Bungling Host, this set of episodes belongs to a much larger cycle about a series of adventures attributed to the Trickster, a cunning rule-breaker. The Trickster is represented by different animals depending on the Native American cultures where his presence is attested, including Coyote, Jay, Wolverine, Crow, Rabbit, or even a human being. He is generally zany and clumsy, and his adventures are often associated with origin myths about how societies came to be organized, about how species became different from each other, and so on. Within this cycle, the Bungling Host motif brings together the Trickster and another animal who invites him to a meal. All of the episodes are constructed in the same way: a host who receives the Trickster and makes him a meal, following which the Trickster, once back home, receives the one who had invited him, tries to imitate his way of making food but fails every time, sometimes by hurting or even killing himself.

These episodes are interesting in more than one way. First, they are present in dozens upon dozens of North and South American cultures. From culture to culture, elements get switched around. The Trickster varies, as we said above, and so do the hosts, both of them changing as we go from one society or environment to another. As a whole, however, the narrative is fairly consistent, since the plot is invariable, although the ways of making the food will change according to the animals that receive the Trickster. These episodes thus pose a formidable challenge. If some ways of thinking are elaborate and devious or even unintelligible, the award-winner would undoubtedly be these masterful variants of the Bungling Host. Be it about a deer getting its wife ready to be eaten, a beaver serving its host pieces of its own son, a snake cooking a squash in the embers, ducks excreting rice, or a bison piercing its nose and seasoning a dish being prepared with its own blood, these episodes all seem to top each other off in their weirdness. The challenge is evidently to decipher these narratives and see how they can make sense to their users.

Only the North American episodes of the Bungling Host will be covered in this book, from the American Southwest to the far reaches of the Canadian Subarctic, with examples from all culture areas as defined in contemporary ethnology handbooks and as generally used to classify groups of societies by region: the Southwest, the Plains, the Northwest Coast, the Plateau, the Great Basin, California, the Southeast and Northeast, and the Subarctic.

The Bungling Host was not a favorite subject for Lévi-Strauss, who mentioned it very little, and only to highlight how the Trickster, from slipup to slipup, i.e., from failed imitation to failed imitation, realizes he cannot act like his brothers. His fate is tied more to the fate of humans (Lévi-Strauss 1995 [1991], 49–50).

The subject has, however, been addressed in several articles, including publications by Polly Pope (1967), Rémi Savard (1969), and Dell Hymes (1984), not to mention several other publications that deal with the whole corpus of Trickster episodes (Radin 1956, Savard 1972). It also is the main topic of an important treatise by Mak Jean Faber (1970) that we will discuss later.

Franz Boas (1916, 694–702) seems to have been the first author to try to classify the various episodes, using what the host does as the main criterion. Boas recognized the following types in his own words:

a) The Host Lets Oil Drip Out of His Hands
b) Birds Produce Food by Their Song
c) Birds Produce Salmon Eggs by Striking the Ankle
d) An Animal Cuts Its Hands or Feet
e) Animals Stab or Shoot Themselves
f) Wood Transformed into Meat
g) The Host Obtains Food by Killing His Children
h) Diving for Fish
i) Miscellaneous Incidents

Using the episodes and variants he brought together, Faber (1970) defined twenty-four different types solely on the basis of what the first host does. The host's identity is excluded, as in (f) and (g) above, among others, e.g., "1. heats limbs over fire; 2. lacerates limbs, head; 3. utters sounds"; etc.

Neither Boas nor Faber said anything about what these motifs mean, being more concerned about classifying the episodes and their geographic range. The way they classified the episodes went hand in hand with their disinterest in mytheme content. Faber (1970) went so far as to say that studying the history and geography of these episodes takes precedence over study of their meanings. As a result, the subject was detached from the predicate.

The studies by Pope (1967), Savard (1969), and Hymes (1984) can all be considered linguistic in nature. The first one was closer to the componential analysis prevailing in the United States in the 1960s than to structural analysis. Using several Bungling Host variants, Pope tried to reveal a common model based solely on the events and their sequential appearance in the different variants. Pope claimed she took their content into account, but she is unconvincing. She mentioned only what the host apparently did when presenting her model.

The text by Savard, published in 1969, is very structuralist. It deals with five Innu episodes (eastern Subarctic), which the author tried to explain in relation to each other. We will come back to this text in greater detail in the next chapter.

Hymes (1984) analyzed only one Chinook (Northwest Coast) version of the Bungling Host, insisting on the host's benevolence. He argued that, by identifying the key mythical motif solely with the bungling host himself or by stressing only the second host's failure, the previous analyses ignored the narrative's fundamental message—the providential nature personified by the first host (here, a deer), who receives the Trickster and offers him a meal (here, his own flesh). Other than a certain mystical aspect that runs through his text, Hymes had the great merit of standing apart from his predecessors by looking at the problem from its true perspective. What matters is not the Trickster, but rather what the benevolent host does. By straying from this perspective, all of the previous analysts consequently ignored the content of the motif.

The best-known publication about the Trickster corpus of myths is the one by Paul Radin (1956), which includes a commentary by the famous psychologist Carl Jung. This Trickster cycle is found among the Winnebago (Northeast), and we will subsequently analyze some of its mythemes. Generally, Radin interpreted the Trickster as representing evolution from the animal stage to the human stage. Jung felt the same way: "Radin's Trickster cycle preserves the shadow in its pristine mythological form, and thus points back to a very much earlier stage of consciousness which existed before the birth of the myth, when the Indian was still groping about in a similar mental darkness. Only when his consciousness reached a higher level could he detach the earlier state from himself and objectify it, that is, say anything about it" (Radin 1956, 202). This was where Lévi-Strauss probably derived his thinking when he wrote about the kind of reason that guides the so-called primitive mind and that would later emerge as science.

The publication by Savard (1972), which includes the results of his analysis of the Bungling Host (1969), is devoted solely to the Trickster among the Innu, and his views are fairly close to those of previous authors. Wolverine, who incarnates the Trickster, is described as a precursor of humanity, existing in a general state of non-differentiation: "It seemed to us then that Wolverine, by imitating his younger brothers, was looking in the universe for a niche that could not be found for a character as ambiguous as himself" (Savard 1972, 124).

We will begin our analysis of the various episodes of the Bungling Host motif with emphasis on their content. The apparent message or messages of the myth will be put aside, be it the first host's benevolence or the other's failure to imitate this benevolence. We take it for granted that the Trickster represents a human, as confirmed by several mythologists and by the narrators themselves, as we will see in some variants. Does not the Trickster reproach his wife for having spoiled him so much that he can no longer perform the feats that his brothers can do and that he himself could in the past? Marriage, or rather kinship by marriage, is indeed human.

Our analysis, which is a basic one, i.e., *basic analysis*, seeks to find what is driving the narratives beyond the level of appearances. It will cover a great number of episodes and variants, while not claiming to be exhaustive. Faber (1970) counted 209, and we have found dozens upon dozens more that came out before or after his publication. All of the texts are listed in the appendix, and classified by mytheme type and by culture area.

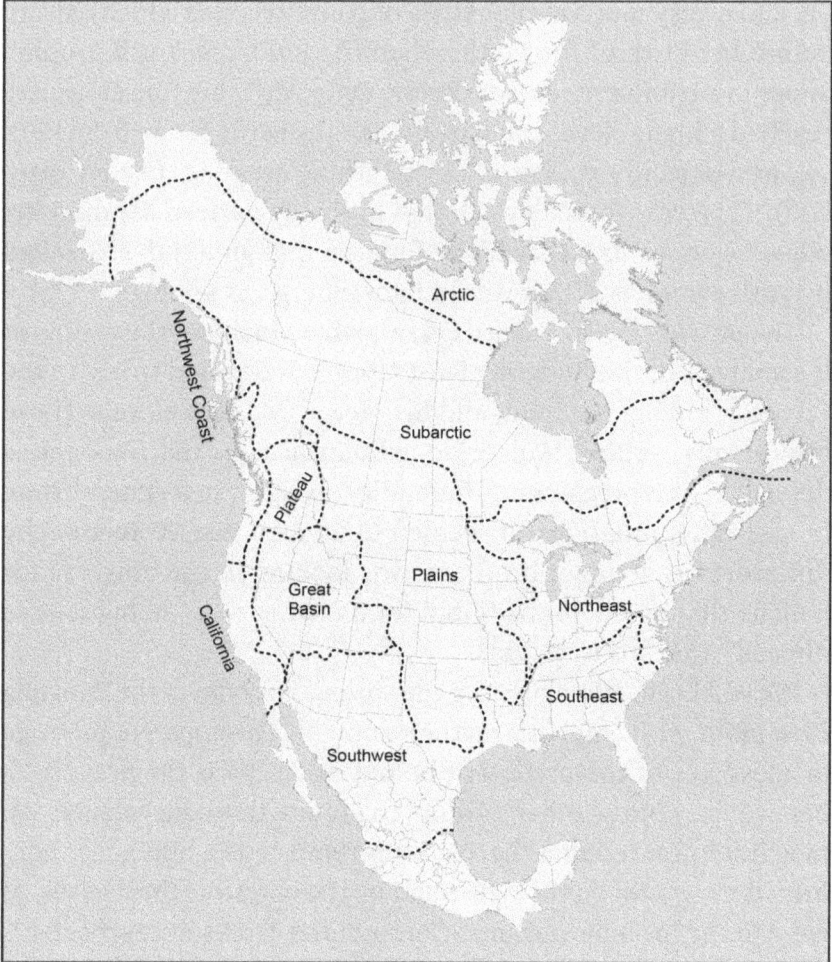

Fig. 1. Map of Culture areas. Archéotec Inc.

The episodes do not appear in any pre-established order, given that only their meanings interest us. Indeed, since each episode or variant has or may have a meaning, it matters little where the analysis begins or ends. Unlike the structuralists, we are under no obligation to look at elements in a neighboring or distant culture to understand a mytheme in a given culture. As a rule, each chapter is devoted to a group of episodes (and sometimes a group of variants) that are specific to a society, or in some cases to a group of societies. These have been selected not so much because explanation is thus made easier by grouping them together as because of a similarity in the relationships underlying the narratives. The common thread linking the chapters is still the Bungling Host motif.

Each chapter is also an opportunity to penetrate further and better understand the culture or cultures under study. Beyond what the first host actually does, all of the mythic episodes contain many ethnographic details about the social and cultural lives of the members of these societies, and these details may help us better place the mythical motif in a specific setting. Each chapter becomes a sort of introduction to the people or peoples the narratives come from.

Above all, and this must be repeated, each of these episodes has been for us a formidable challenge. We were initially as much in the dark as anyone who might hear these "unintelligible" statements. But by taking various approaches, and from one surprise to the next, and from one astonishment to the next, we have untangled the interconnected threads of these statements and discovered, beyond the appearances, the true knowledge of the Aboriginal peoples[2] that is hidden behind these supposedly odd ways of thinking.

The present study is accompanied by nearly fifty illustrations. We wish to express our sincere gratitude to their creator, Christiane Clément, for her extraordinary drawings and to Archéotec Inc. for its precisely drawn maps.

We also thank our editors, Denis Dion from the Presses de l'Université Laval and Matthew Bokovoy from the University of Nebraska Press, for having believed in this project from the very beginning. We thank Thomas McIlwraith, anthropologist, for his encouraging review. Many UNP staff members made this publication simple and enjoyable in the later stages and we deeply wish to extend our gratitude particularly to Heather Stauffer, Andrea Shahan, Ann Baker, and Tish Fobben. We also wish to show our appreciation to Santiago Romero for his permission to use one of his art figures to represent the Trickster on the cover of this book.

The original French version of this book was published thanks to a grant from the Canadian Federation for the Humanities and Social Sciences, via the Award to Scholarly Publications Program, whose funds come from the Social Sciences and Humanities Research Council.

The Bungling Host

1 Caribou Takes In His Wife's Dress (Subarctic)

> "Come on in!" said Caribou. Wolverine entered. . . . Then Wolverine saw his younger brother take a knife and cut his wife's dress. The old male carved off a piece and hung it over the fire . . . . "My wife likewise has food I've never eaten!" thought Wolverine. Caribou roasted this fatty endoderm [*sic*] and offered Wolverine some. "Eat, older brother!" he said. After eating, Wolverine announced: "I'm now going home, younger brother. Come on over whenever you're out of food".
>
> —Rémi Savard, "Carcajou"

The Innu of Quebec-Labrador, from whom come the initial episodes of the Bungling Host, live in the boreal forest of the eastern Canadian Subarctic. Scattered among a dozen or so villages along the shores of the St. Lawrence River or inland in Quebec and Labrador, they form a population of over twelve thousand individuals. Traditionally, the Innu hunted, trapped, fished, and gathered in a relatively specialized ecosystem. They are also known by the older name of "Montagnais," or sometimes "Naskapi."

The corpus of Bungling Host episodes among the Innu first appeared in an article on the subject (Savard 1969) and later in a book by the same author about the Trickster in Innu mythology (Savard 1972). The wolverine plays the Trickster in the myths of the Innu and in those of only a few other Native American cultures:

the Cree, the Malecite, the Mi'kmaq, and the Passamaquoddy—all of them belonging to the Algonquian language family (Fisher 1946). Episodes of the Bungling Host are known solely from the Innu and the Passamaquoddy.

Five episodes of the Bungling Host are attested in the Innu anthropological literature. Some of them have several variants. Wolverine is received by five different hosts, which Rémi Savard (1969; 1972) lists in this order: Beaver, Woodpecker, Osprey, Caribou, and Skunk. These episodes will be presented in full.

The first one features Wolverine as the guest and Beaver as the host:

WOLVERINE IMITATES BEAVER

Wolverine decided to go home, to find his wife. He had two young children. He traveled through a thick forest, along a stream. All of a sudden, Beaver jumped in the water, hitting it with his flat tail. Wolverine said to him: "Younger brother, do I frighten you?"—"I have no reason to be afraid! Do you want to come in?" answered Beaver. Once Wolverine had crawled into Beaver's lodge, his host asked him if he felt hungry. "Yes," answered Wolverine. "I haven't found any food yet!" Beaver invited him to sit down and went to get his son, whom he ordered to sit on the other side. The young beaver obeyed, and his father struck him on the head. He then cooked him for Wolverine. He roasted him very well. "So I've got food too," said Wolverine to himself, "why shouldn't I kill my child when I want to eat?" When the roast was done, Beaver invited him to eat, saying: "Older brother, eat all of the meat carefully, and then give me back the bones." Wolverine agreed and began to eat. While eating, and unbeknownst to his host, he placed one of the claws behind one of the posts along the wall. "I wonder whether he'll notice!" he said. He then announced that his meal was finished, that he had eaten very well, and that this was always so whenever he met his younger brother Beaver. He gave him back the bones, which Beaver hastened to place in the water of the river. The little beaver began to swim, but it seemed impossible for him to make his way. He was seen going this way and that, as if he couldn't control his direction. "Older brother," said Beaver, "you've harmed him!" Wolverine answered: "Ah, yes, it's true. I placed his claw behind the post." The little beaver swam ashore, and he put the missing claw in place above another one. This is why the beaver seems to have a double claw on one of its feet. He put him back in the water, and this time the little beaver could dive in a straight line. "Older brother," said Beaver to Wolverine, "you really thought I wouldn't know?"—"Of course not," answered Wolverine. "I didn't think that. I just forgot and I had placed it behind the post. Say, younger brother, come and see me whenever you're out of food. I'll try to make something for you." Beaver agreed.

Back home, Wolverine built a beaver lodge in a creek. With nothing to eat, Beaver decided to see him: "I wonder how he may help me!" he thought. As for Wolverine he had never stopped waiting. When he saw him arrive, he dove into the water, taking care to slap it with the wooden tail he had made. "Older brother," said Beaver, "do I frighten you?"—"I have no reason to be afraid, come on in!" said Wolverine, thus repeating what Beaver had told him. Beaver entered. Wolverine had two children. "Go and sit down on the other side!" he told his son. The little Wolverine obeyed, not knowing what his father was getting ready to do to him. Wolverine struck his own son, who ducked and got only a glancing blow from his father. Still, his father did strike his son on the side of his eye. The little Wolverine staggered, going round and round. "Older brother," said Beaver, "you're going to kill your son!" And his wife said: "What are you trying to do? You must be trying to imitate someone." Wolverine answered his wife: "There was a time when I could do all of these things. That was before I married you. Since then you've corrupted me!" Beaver went home, Wolverine not being able to offer him anything to eat. (Savard 1972, 74–76)

One cannot overstate how much the beaver (*Castor canadensis*) shaped the encounter between the two worlds, the Old and the New. It was a key trading item and forever marked the history of the Aboriginal peoples, as it marked the history of the Europeans.

A medium of exchange for the former and a source of wealth for the latter, the beaver, more than any other animal, threw Native American nations into unprecedented cultural and economic upheaval. This was especially so with the Innu, who were among the first to encounter the new traders, for better or for worse.

This Innu tale about the beaver, like the following Bungling Host stories, highlights some of the host's morphological and behavioral characteristics. The key ones appear in two ways, either directly in the first part of the episode or indirectly in the second part, when the Trickster foolishly tries to imitate the host.

Thus, the beaver, *amishk*ᵘ in the Innu language, has several defining characteristics that may be seen when it moves about: two alarm signals (diving into the water and slapping it with its tail), an obvious morphological feature (its flat tail), a less obvious one (the double claw on one of its feet), and one relating to its means of locomotion (swimming in a straight line).

Other characteristics appear in Wolverine's attempts at imitation. One is habitat-related (Wolverine builds "a beaver lodge in a creek") and the other is tail-related (he makes a tail out of wood because a real one looks wooden).

Euro-Canadian observers have made similar observations. The beaver has a distinctive lodge. It responds to an intruder's presence ("The beaver, when alarmed, will slap its powerful tail hard on the surface of the water"; Wooding 1982, 183). Its tail has a seemingly wooden-like texture ("The beaver's tail, which on average is about 1½ inches [3.5 cm] thick, is covered with leathery scales"; Wooding 1982, 184). Other defining characteristics could be cited. Some of them (diving into the water, swimming in a straight line) are verifiable but missing from the academic zoological literature, with each culture emphasizing certain characteristics according to the dictates of its perception.

The least obvious one (the double claw on a foot) is specific to beaver feet. Indeed, each back foot has a double claw. According to scientists, the beaver uses this double claw to groom its fur:

"This is in reality a double claw. . . . All in all, it resembles a parrot's beak . . . and it functions the same way as a bird's beak for grooming. The hairs of the fur are combed and aligned by passing this specialized nail through them. . . . The fur, like the plumage, similarly swells up and regains its waterproofing" (Richard 1980, 18–19). Although nails are not considered in Western anatomy to be bones strictly speaking, they are as the Innu see it. Thus, when a character is asked in the myth to put all of the bones back in the water—even the most trivial ones, like nails—this request should be understood with reference to a custom about animal remains. Savard (1972, 92n5), who reported the myth, rightly notes: "There is certainly an allusion to the obligation to put all of the beaver's bones back in the water."

This obligation, which forms part of a religious system, is a means to ensure the reproduction of the species. The system implies that there are animal masters who govern how the species under their respective commands are spread over the land. Bones must be treated with respect—by placing them on scaffolds or in trees for some terrestrial species, or by putting them back in the water for some aquatic or semiaquatic species—in keeping with the expectations of the animal masters who need them to generate new individuals (Armitage 1992, 77–78). Breaking this rule may anger the animal masters, who subsequently will no longer provide the offenders with game animals.

The myth shows that breaking this rule, however slightly, has grave consequences—here, trouble swimming. Thus, it stresses the importance of a rule that cannot be broken without throwing nature into disorder, while at the same time being an original way of teaching young people beaver anatomy.

At least another major beaver characteristic appears in a variant of the episode we have just read. It is about a way of seasoning the meat served to Wolverine, who will in turn imitate dismally: "Beaver observed Wolverine eating the meat of the little beaver. The fat that Beaver gave him, it seemed to Wolverine he had scraped

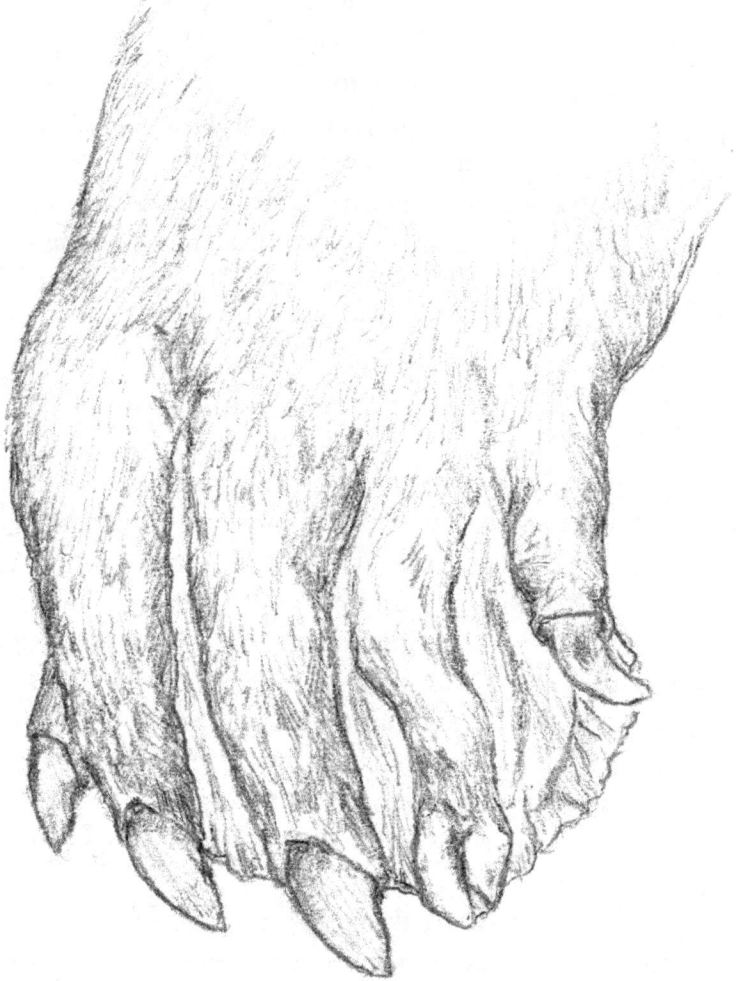

Fig. 2. Double claw on the second toe of a beaver's foot.

it out of his testicles [sic] using some kind of awl" (Savard 1972, 90); and now the imitation: "He [Wolverine] cooked his son and punctured his testicles. But Beaver could not swallow that at all, neither the fat nor their son" (Savard 1972, 90).

The anatomical parts in this extract are not the testicles. Whether male or female, the beaver has two pairs of scent glands in the cloacal area: uîshinaiat and uîtuîa in Innu, or castor sacs and anal glands respectively. Both pairs of glands are palpable from the outside. Beaver testicles are intra-abdominal, very small, and unnamed in Innu. Dissection is necessary to see them.[1]

In his version of the Bungling Host, Savard (1972, 90) does not provide the Innu term and translates it, wrongly as we have seen, as 'testicles'. This mistake is very common and has been made by all contemporary lexicographers (Mailhot and Lescop 1977, 390; McNulty and Basile 1981, 50; Drapeau 1991, 811) and early observers. The Jesuit Louis Nicolas was no better in the seventeenth century: "Beaver testicles, whose medical name is castoreum and which the Indians hunters call ouissinak are excellent for various illnesses" (Gagnon 2011, 342).

Although it is true that the uîshinaiat of some animals—male caribou for example, whose such glands are extra-abdominal—may be the same organ as their testicles, this is not so with the beaver or other species, which have especially large and palpable scent glands in both sexes (Clément 1995b, 90–94).

Whatever the case may be, the glands that Beaver seems to puncture to season his son are most certainly large, either castor sacs or anal glands. The former secrete a yellow liquid that has the consistency of "liquid honey" (Richard 1980, 52), and beavers use it (in Innu, uîshinaiapuî, 'liquid of the gland') to mark their territory. The latter are the size of a nut and "contain a liquid or rather a thick and fatty ointment" (Richard 1980, 54). This liquid, which beavers also use for marking in different contexts, is named in Innu uîtuîapuî: 'the liquid of the anal gland'. This liquid is similar to *pimî*, i.e., a mix of fat and melted bone marrow, which in Innu cooking accompanies a dish of meat.

In the myth, Beaver punctures some sort of gland in his anal or cloacal region and scrapes out a liquid that may be similar to *pimî*, a fatty substance he uses to season the meat he serves to Wolverine. Wolverine wishes to imitate his host but only manages to spoil the meat. The wolverine (*Gulo gulo*) likewise has a pair of anal glands whose odor is surpassed in strength only by the skunk's, which we will talk about later. In addition, this episode also indicates exactly what not to do when skinning a beaver. The Innu say that when skinning a beaver one must at all cost avoid breaking the castor glands; otherwise, the entire carcass will be spoiled: "It's the same thing with the *uîshinaiat*. When one tears them open . . . the taste is everywhere. They say they must be removed right after one kills it, because if one keeps them, all of the meat will taste like the *uîshinaiat*" (Bernard and Menekapo, Ekuanitshit, 14.11.85). If we return to the myth, Beaver tears open his glands, takes out the fat, and offers it to his host. Wolverine can therefore appreciate its smell and flavor, as a hunter would appreciate the taste of *pimî* as a condiment. Conversely, Beaver cannot appreciate the odor of Wolverine's foul-smelling glands, the stench being so nauseating.

This being said, the main mytheme remains to be elucidated. It is a two-part statement. The first part is about how food is obtained and the second is about how the food supply is replenished. The second part matters just as much as the first. But what is the underlying meaning? For a long time, we looked for answers solely in the killing of the little beaver by his father. These answers were always half-satisfactory. There are no real cases of cannibalism among beavers despite marks of battle on their bodies (e.g., tails ripped open); no relationship between the beaver's food, its provisions of wood near its lodge, and some filiation term; the way of killing the beaver by a blow to the head seems in all likelihood to be a hunting technique but provides little insight into the meaning of the mytheme; etc. If, however, we consider the two parts of the statement to be a single continuous whole, the scene makes sense right away. From the standpoint of a hunter and outside observer of life in a beaver habitat (lodge, body of water, provisions, secondary shelters), we can come to only one conclusion: however much the beaver colony declines through dispersal in the spring or for other reasons during the year, such as predation, it is always being replenished. In the twentieth century, an Innu spoke about depopulation in these terms: "Usually, in the spring, the female remains in the lodge to give birth . . . . The parents will keep only the young ones of the year with them until the next spring. Afterwards, the young leave" (Dominique 1989, 37). In a much earlier time, an observer likewise noted how quickly the colony can replenish itself: "Finally in its lodge, the beaver multiplies rapidly in a short time. Where there were only two of them many are seen, and if they are left alone they are seen in troops" (Gagnon 2011, 344).

The young leave the family unit in all likelihood by water, that is, by the only exit from the family lodge—a diving hole that leads into the water. In addition, observers have noted that male beavers regularly left their lodges with used litter shavings pressed against their chests, which they would subsequently throw away on their dump: "In my beaver park, I would see, around twice a month, the male leave with the old litter held against its chest and drop it on its 'dump'" (Richard 1980, 83). Also on the subject of behavior, Innu have noticed that some young beavers could leave the colony, spend a winter alone, and then come back to the original lodge: these beavers are called *upaiuess*, a term also used for young yearling beavers on their own.

These aspects of beaver life feed into the mythical scene: on the one hand, the dispersal of the colony and its replenishment; on the other hand, the male leaving its lodge by the diving hole with something pressed against its chest and the return of young beavers. All of these aspects are condensed into a single continuous image and reinterpreted in a religious context.

Fig. 3. Beaver habitat.

The second Innu episode of the Bungling Host can be analyzed similarly. Here, Woodpecker plays the host for Wolverine. It is a *pâshpashteu*, in the Innu language, which corresponds to several species in Western taxonomy (*Picoides* spp.), including the black-backed woodpecker (*Picoides arcticus*), the American three-toed woodpecker (*Picoides tridactylus*), and others. Wolverine goes to visit this bird, and the meeting proceeds as follows:

WOLVERINE IMITATES WOODPECKER

After living at home for some time, Wolverine began to travel again. Suddenly, he heard someone striking a tree. The sound came from the forest. Wolverine walked toward the sound. It was Woodpecker. "Younger brother," said Wolverine. "I'm hungry." Woodpecker answered he had no reason to be hungry in his presence, and flew to a tamarack. He made a hole in it and brought out a [caribou] rib. "I've never looked for meat in trees!" thought Wolverine. He then began eating the portion of the rib that looked fatty. Before leaving Woodpecker, he said: "Younger brother, come and see me when you need food!" Back home, he made himself a nose with his knife. One day, Woodpecker flew to him and said: "Older brother, I can't find any food." Wolverine answered: "There's no reason for you to be out of food. I've got everything you need." Wolverine climbed a tree, after attaching the knife to his nose, and began to hammer away at the tamarack. But he immediately knocked himself out and fell backwards, even before he could make a hole. His younger brother rushed to help him. As for his wife, she told him over and over: "You must be trying to imitate someone!" And he would reply: "There was a time when I could do all of these things. That was before I married you. Since then, I haven't been able to. You've corrupted me." Before leaving Wolverine, his younger brother said: "Everything we do, to get food, we do it by ourselves." (Savard 1972, 76)

As with the previous episode, this one directly or indirectly describes the woodpecker's defining characteristics. It is astonishingly consistent with what we call the scientific literature. In both cases, the descriptions are identical. The myth tells us about the hard, straight beak—like a knife—and the head that can hammer away without injury, unlike the head of the wolverine, which knocks itself out when making the same movements. The woodpecker also lives in trees, here a tamarack (*Larix laricina*). It is a "meat eater," feeding on insects it gets from trees. Godfrey, a reputed ornithologist, provides a typical description in line with the myth: "Woodpeckers are highly specialized for climbing the trunks and branches of trees and for digging out wood-boring insects. The bill is hard, straight, and chisel-like, ideal for digging holes in either dead or living wood. . . . The skull is extremely thick and heavy, enabling it to withstand the shock of using the head as a hammer" (Godfrey 1966, 238).

Clearly, this in no way explains why Woodpecker pulls a caribou rib out of the tree and not an insect. The Innu nonetheless know, when questioned on the subject, that these climbing birds get a different kind of food from trees, i.e., insects.

Savard, who wrote down this episode, suggests a structuralist explanation based on binary oppositions:

> Let us first settle the easier case of the . . . question (why caribou ribs?) . . .

> We have already seen that some Montagnais beliefs about the caribou make it a being *included* in the terrestrial (caribou pastureland, caribou trails), whereas others downplay the difference between its flesh and the bark of a tree. The caribou species, already present in the story, became therefore privileged to take over the insect role, more specifically to play the role of a form of meat included under the bark. (Savard 1969, 29)

This explanation in all likelihood borrows elements from other stories. In addition, although it seems to explain why Woodpecker feeds on caribou meat instead of insect meat, it fails to explain why the meat comes from the ribs and not from another part of the caribou.

Basic analysis can help us not only to better understand the entire mytheme, but also to grasp its most minor meanings.

For example, why caribou and not insects? The answer must be clear, unambiguous and, above all, meaningful to the listener. We are in a hunting society, and the Bungling Host represents a human. How many times have Aboriginal people told us how the different actors of the myths perceive things differently depending on their standpoint? This may be seen in the tale of the Caribou Man. In this legend, the main character is a human who goes to live with a female caribou and whose perception of caribou changes the longer he lives among them. At first, he sees them as animals gathered together on an expanse of frozen water; his perception then changes and he sees them as a group of humans fishing; next, at the camp, he sees them eating lichen; thereafter, he sees them eating caribou meat; and so on. The same applies to the Bungling Host story, except that the change in perception is not stated explicitly. Wolverine perceives caribou ribs when

Woodpecker pulls insects from the tree. We will later see how this interpretation is corroborated by episodes from other peoples. This clarifies why the meat comes from a caribou, but a longer explanation is needed to understand why it comes from a specific part of a caribou, its ribs.

We first need to study Innu botany. Among the Innu, plants, and trees in particular, are morphologically similar to humans, and this resemblance is stressed in the vocabulary. We find the following botanical terms: the root of a tree, *ushkâtiâpi*, which also means 'leg'; the heartwood of a tree, *uânkanâkanâtuk*[u], which is formed from a morpheme that means 'backbone' (i.e., a tree's backbone); the sapwood, *uînâtshu*, whose initial morpheme, *uîn*, means 'fat' in Innu; and so on. Therefore, a tree has legs, a backbone, and a layer of fat right under its bark, as do many animals. Even in this mythical episode, emphasis is placed on the fattiness of the caribou rib offered to Wolverine, as seen in the two versions recorded by Savard:

> "I've never looked for meat in trees!" thought Wolverine. He then began eating the portion of the rib that looked fatty. (1972, 76)

> Woodpecker fed Wolverine. After eating the fatty caribou rib. (1969, 12)

The caribou rib can now be explained. It is taken from a tree, in the same way that an animal rib can be severed from the backbone to which it is joined. Moreover, the part closest to the bark, the sapwood, is equivalent to the corresponding part of an animal, i.e., its subcutaneous layer of fat.

We will now turn to the third episode, the one where Osprey plays host to the Trickster.

WOLVERINE IMITATES OSPREY

After living at home for some time, Wolverine began to go hunting for game again. Over there, on a tree, an osprey. It dove and brought back a fish to the shore. "Younger brother," called out Wolverine.

"I'm hungry and cannot find food!"—"Very well, older brother, bring me your line!" Wolverine brought him a line, and Osprey began to rise in the air. From there he jumped into the water and was gone from sight for some time. After emerging, he cried out: "Older brother, pull in your line!" Wolverine pulled in his line. Osprey had attached fish to it. Wolverine said: "Younger brother, come and see me whenever you're out of food!" He would try to do as Osprey had done: simply dive into the water and attach fish to the line. Later, Osprey came to Wolverine's home, for he was hungry. "Older brother," he said, "I'm hungry and can't find any food!" He was asking simply to find out. Wolverine had already prepared a place where he could climb up. He went there. But when he was about to jump, the branch broke and he ended up in shallow water. He rushed over to where there was more water. Previously, he had asked his younger brother to give him a line. He disappeared under the water and attached some sticklebacks to the line. "Now, younger brother, pull in your line," he told Osprey. All that he could attach to the line was sticklebacks! Before leaving, Osprey said: "Older brother, I never eat this sort of fish!" Wolverine had not managed to do what he had wished to do. (Savard 1972, 78–79)

This episode about the osprey (*Pandion haliœtus*), *akuâshimesheu* in the Innu language, appears simple at first sight, but some of the details add meaning. Closer examination brings out a fairly important aspect of the Bungling Host. Unlike the previous episode, this one has nothing strange about it. Whereas Beaver kills his own son and Woodpecker pulls caribou ribs out of trees, Osprey merely fishes, and fishing is clearly the main way an osprey feeds itself. Innu know this as much as ornithologists do: "Main foods taken. Live fish at least 99% of prey items recorded in almost every published account; wide variety of species taken" (Poole, Bierregaard, and Martell 2002, 10).

There is no mystery when we compare human food with osprey food. From the standpoint of hunter-gatherers, what Beaver serves his host can be reinterpreted as meat. The same goes for Woodpecker. For Osprey, however, we cannot reinterpret, since he eats exactly the same food as his host—the Trickster, who represents a human and consumes fish.

Since there is nothing strange to explain, we are left with details that seemed secondary in the previous episodes. Their importance now stands out, and we realize how significant they were previously. These details are the differences between humans and animal species, and such differences are accurately spelled out. The myth teaches the listener about zoology, among other things, and highlights the anatomical, morphological, behavioral, and other features of each species.

In this episode, it is said of Osprey that he hunts from treetops ("On a tree, an osprey. It dove"; Savard 1972, 78). Osprey sits on a branch but is light enough for the branch to support him without breaking under his weight. This is not the case with his older brother: "But when he [Wolverine] was about to jump, the branch broke" (Savard 1972, 78). Osprey can also attack from up in the air. This is how he hunts when asked by Wolverine: "Wolverine brought him a line, and Osprey began to rise in the air. From there he jumped into the water" (Savard 1972, 78).

Osprey also fishes in relatively deep water or, at least, he can hurl himself far enough so as not to hurt himself on the riverbank: "He [Wolverine] ended up in shallow water. He rushed over to where there was more water" (Savard 1972, 78). Osprey did not remain long under water, according to the first version recorded by Savard (1969): "After a short while, the bird came back" (12). Osprey selects his prey and does not seem to appreciate sticklebacks (*Gasterosteus aculeatus*; *Apeltes quadracus*; *Ammodytes americanus*).

Is it really necessary to report all of the ornithological observations that support the Aboriginal viewpoint? Ospreys hunt while flying and also from perches: "Prey captures at Nelson were larger . . . and hunting from a perch was used for 26% of all captures" (Steeger, Esselink, and Ydenberg 1992, 470).

The osprey weighs on average 1.5 kilograms (Forbes 1983, n.p.), and a human's weight by comparison is more than enough to break the kind of branch it sits on. The depth of the water where the osprey hunts varies greatly by habitat: "Inland, forages along rivers, marshes, reservoirs, and natural ponds and lakes, where individuals feed in both shallow littoral zones as well as deeper water" (Poole, Bierregaard, and Martell 2002, 10).

The osprey's time under water has also been recorded. It is relatively short: "They hit the water with a resounding splash and occasionally disappear momentarily below the surface. Then, with a few flaps of their powerful wings they clear the water, shrug off the excess water, and continue flying" (Godfrey 1966, 100). Finally, it is said that the osprey usually catches fish that are economically unimportant (Forbes 1983, n.p.).

Scientists have nonetheless calculated the mean weight and mean size of fish caught by ospreys: "Fish captured generally weigh 150–300 g and measure about 25–35 cm in length" (Poole, Bierregaard, and Martell 2002, 12). Savard (1972), who recorded the myth, had some doubts about the fish Osprey said he would not eat: "The translation is uncertain, but it does seem to be the stickleback" (93n18). There are several sorts of sticklebacks in Innu territory, and all of them are fish that measure only 5 centimeters on average (Scott and Crossman 1973). Not surprisingly, the osprey does not deign to eat them, and this message applies also to the Innu: sticklebacks are a very negligible part of their diet.

The mythical episode has a final key element: use of a fishing line and related fishing techniques. This seems in all likelihood to be a reference to an Innu fishing technique for catching several fish in a row, namely longline fishing. Non-Native writers have indeed observed that an osprey can catch more than one fish at once (Forbes 1983, n.p.; Poole, Bierregaard, and Martell 2002, 10).[2] We might add that the osprey catches fish with its feet, which are, not coincidentally, shaped a little like fishhooks: "Soles of feet equipped with sharp horny processes for holding slippery fish" (Godfrey 1966, 99). Finally, when a fish is taken out of the water in an osprey's talons, with its head facing forward, it looks strangely like a fish being likewise reeled in head first: "If successful in catching a fair-sized or large fish, this is carried, in both claws, parallel with the bird's body, head first" (Godfrey 1966, 100).

The fourth and penultimate Innu episode of the Bungling Host features the caribou (*Rangifer tarandus*) as the host. The visit takes place as follows.

WOLVERINE IMITATES CARIBOU

He stayed home until autumn. He suddenly noticed Caribou's fresh tracks and followed them. Caribou abruptly stood up and began to run. Wolverine forced him to go on the frozen lake. Caribou defecated while running. "Younger brother," cried out Wolverine, "do I frighten you? It's me!"—"I have no reason to be afraid," said Caribou, "so come on in older brother!" Wolverine told him he couldn't find any food. "Come on in!" said Caribou. Wolverine entered. The old male caribou said to his wife: "Put the branches back a little on the entrance side. There's wind coming in from there." She began to put the branches back on the entrance side. Then Wolverine saw his younger brother take a knife and cut his wife's dress. The old male carved off a piece and hung it over the fire. The endoderm [*sic*] was very fatty. "My wife likewise has food I've never eaten!" thought Wolverine. Caribou roasted the fatty endoderm [*sic*] and offered Wolverine some. "Eat, older brother!" he said. After eating, Wolverine announced: "I'm now going home, younger brother. Come on over whenever you're out of food!"—"Very well!" answered Caribou. And he thought to himself: "Of course I'll go! I'd love nothing more than to see what my older brother will make for me." Caribou's wife shared her husband's curiosity.

Back home, Wolverine gathered some cones and put them in a mitten. He then waited for his visitor. After a while, the old male Caribou dropped by. Wolverine was camping near a lake. When Caribou got fairly close to him, Wolverine stood up and began to run on the ice parallel to the shoreline and making a curve. While running, he dropped the cones he had gathered. By doing so, he was trying to imitate the old male caribou. Caribou, however, had really defecated! Wolverine couldn't while running. So he left the cones behind him as he ran. "Older brother," said Caribou, "do I frighten you?"—"I have no reason to be afraid!" answered Wolverine. He was repeating what Caribou had replied to him. "Older brother," said Caribou, "I'm hungry!"—"Very well," answered Wolverine, "come on in!" He next asked his wife to put the branches back in the entrance, saying the wind was coming in. She began to put the branches back in the entrance. Then Wolverine took his crooked knife, and he cut his wife's dress. He carved a piece from it such that his wife's anus was visible. She decided to sit down right away. Wolverine took the piece from the dress and hung it over the fire for his younger brother. After a few moments, Caribou began to smell something and ran out. "That's awful, older brother. You're burning something that stinks!" Wolverine's wife could no longer get up from her seat. She said to him: "You must be trying to imitate someone!" This is how Wolverine turned away the one he was supposed to offer a meal, all because of the smell. Caribou went away. (Savard 1972, 79–81)

This episode can be analyzed like the others. The description of Caribou's characteristics, directly or indirectly through Wolverine's laughable conduct, is of some interest. As for the main mytheme, it should be understood as we understood the beaver mytheme.

The myth thus describes certain caribou traits. When an intruder approaches, a caribou may suddenly stand up and begin to run. It may also defecate while running and leave droppings shaped like the cones of conifers. In such a situation, it may seek refuge on a flat, open surface that will let it escape a predator. The female also has a layer of subcutaneous fat on its back.

Caribou behavior has been broadly studied by mammalogists. For example, it is known that caribou are especially sensitive to movement, whereas they respond scarcely or very little to visual, olfactory, or other stimuli in the face of danger:

> It has been noted that the senses of sight, smell, and hearing are more or less inactive as warning agents. . . .

If the animals are insensitive to colour and form, they are sometimes remarkably observant of movement. In August and September, individual bulls have been seen to notice and flee from an inconspicuously dressed, but moving, observer at distances up to a mile [1.4 km]. Sometimes this attention to movement makes the hunting of caribou against open snow backgrounds difficult. (Kelsall 1968, 44–45)

In the myth, the caribou seeks refuge on a frozen surface, which provides an advantage over any predator. In a flat, open landscape, a caribou can easily get away from its fiercest adversary, the wolf. "Caribou, except for the incapacitated and very young, can normally outrun single wolves" (Kelsall 1968, 252). When wolves were seen chasing caribou on the surface of a frozen lake, only one caribou was caught, after it tripped and fell (Kelsall 1968, 253).

Mammalogists do not say whether a caribou defecates while running, but an Innu who commented on the myth leaves no room for doubt: "The translator adds that the caribou often acts this way [Caribou would defecate while running] when it runs away" (Savard 1972, 93n20). Clearly, humans cannot perform such a feat: "By doing so, he was trying to imitate the old male caribou. Caribou, however, had really defecated! Wolverine couldn't while running" (Savard 1972, 79). Caribou droppings may also look like conifer cones with their cracked surface (Murie 1974, 288).

On the other hand, the fatty layer on the animal's back, as referred to in the myth, forms the first proposition of the main mytheme. The mytheme can be understood as two coordinated propositions, as with the beaver episode. For Beaver, the propositions are twofold: Beaver kills his son *and* brings him back to life. For Caribou, the propositions are likewise twofold: first, he carves off a piece from his wife's dress and, second, this action implicitly does not threaten her life. The reality of the second proposition, though unstated, may be shown in several ways. Savard, who recorded the myth, said as much: "Beaver and Caribou find their food very nearby; they feed on their own family members, whom they cook while not causing them to die" (Savard 1969, 18). Aside from a misstatement (in the myth, the host never eats the food he prepares, but rather offers it to a visitor), Savard's comment highlights this key aspect of the mytheme: namely, the absence of any fatal effect on the caribou's wife. This point is more clearly stated in variant tales we will study from other peoples.

Although this mytheme is constructed similarly to the one about the beaver, its enigmatic meaning must be explained at greater length. The myth refers to a body part known as *uatamishkai*. The word was spelled out by Savard (1969) in his first published version of the myth ("According to the translator, what Caribou cooks is his wife's OTIMISKEE"; 13n11), which he later translated as "endoderm," but which is actually the hypodermis or subcutaneous tissue (the endoderm being a part of the fetus). This part is removed and then prepared in various ways: "What has to be roasted, according to the translator, is the fat that lies directly under the skin, and which is removed." The translator adds, "Generally, this fat is dried for preparation of broths" (Savard 1972, 94n23).

Several other details need explaining. The myth focuses on the body fat of Caribou's wife and not Caribou himself because the action takes place in late autumn or winter, when lake and river surfaces are frozen. By then, the male is lean, having used up its fat reserves mainly for the mating season: "Following the rut, in November, adult bulls have little or no visible fat on their bodies" (Kelsall 1968, 41). In contrast, this is when females have the most fat: "They are often fattest just when the bulls are leanest, at the end of the rut" (Kelsall 1968, 41). Innu often prefer "to kill females because they provide more fat" (Dominique 1979, 51). This practice comes up often in myths. The hero Tsheshei kills females, while the other hunters of his group bring back nothing: "Tsheshei told his brother-in-law to wait there with the others, saying he would track the big females alone" (Savard 1979, 50). In a variant of the tale of the Caribou Man, the chief of the caribou allows *female* caribou (and not males) to sit down and be shot by a human hunter (Landriault 1974, 32).

It is also very widespread among the Innu and other Native American peoples to speak of an animal's meat (or fat) as if it were clothing, such as in the Bungling Host episode: "Then Wolverine saw his younger brother take a knife and cut his wife's dress" (Savard 1972, 79). In Innu culture, the same holds true for the black bear (Clément 2012) and the caribou, as in this passage already quoted in the introduction and in other passages:

> One day, before going off to hunt, he has a dream: "I meet a young girl who likes me a lot, enough to make love to me. I undress her and put all of her linen [clothes] in a heap." In the morning, he goes off to hunt and sees two caribou: a female and its young one. He kills them, skins them, and puts all of their meat in a heap. He covers everything with two hides. He looks, remembers his dream, and grasps its meaning. (André 1984, 128–29)

When Wolverine in turn invites Caribou and tries to imitate his way of cooking, we need to understand that Wolverine then cooks part of a real human garment, hence the foul odor.

This being said, the mytheme composed of two coordinated propositions refers to the caribou's annual cycle of body fat. Scientists have noted such a cycle. Females, for example, begin to accumulate fat "a bit later than the bulls" (Kelsall 1968, 41), whose reserves begin to increase around early September. Females are very fat in the late mating season, as we have seen, and remain so much of the winter: "Cows and young animals may carry appreciable amounts of fat until spring if winter feeding conditions are good, but it is lost during spring migration" (Kelsall 1968, 41). In summer, fat deposits vary by area of the body and according to the availability of food and the abundance or scarcity of biting flies, which may keep the animals from resting and feeding adequately (Kelsall 1968, 41). In autumn, the cycle begins anew.

The cycle thus has two key periods: female storage of fat during

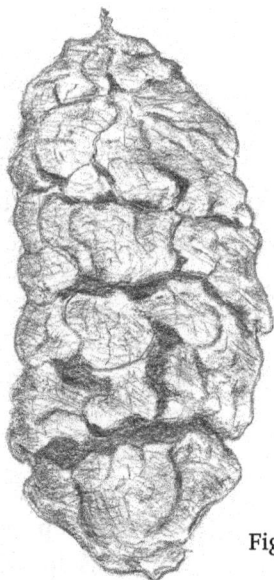

Fig. 4. Caribou droppings.

the winter and massive depletion of fat reserves during spring migration or summer. The fat is especially thick on the back: "The most remarkable layer is over the rump and saddle, sometimes extending over the upper ribs, and along the back of the neck. This layer may be 7.5 cm thick (Jacobi, 1931), and may weigh 39 pounds [18 kg] or more (Stefansson, 1922)" (Kelsall 1968, 41). Remember, in the myth, Wolverine exposed his wife's rear while trying to imitate his brother: "He carved a piece from it such that his wife's anus was visible" (Savard 1972, 81). Caribou, like Beaver, thus has a renewable resource he can offer his host, at least in the myth. In practice, this also means that hunters can feed on a mass of fat that will be replenished at the right time as long as certain rules of respect are followed and as long as the animal masters consent to send forth other individuals that will give themselves up to hunters. This is the reasoning behind the story.

The fifth and last Bungling Host episode features Skunk. This is the striped skunk (*Mephitis mephitis*). It gets its food quite spectacularly, as the myth tells us.

WOLVERINE IMITATES SKUNK

Wolverine stayed home until he ran out of food. He went hunting. On the way he caught sight of his younger brother Skunk. "Younger brother," he said, "I'm hungry and I can't find anything to eat!" Skunk answered: "Build a caribou corral!" When Wolverine finished the corral, his younger brother began to sing. After a while, some caribou arrived. They went into the corral. When it was full, Skunk sprayed them. This is how he killed them. "There you are, older brother, you now have something to eat!" — "Very well," answered Wolverine. He was thoroughly convinced he had enough food. Skunk had killed quite a few. Before going home, Wolverine said to Skunk: "Younger brother, come on over if you're out of food." — "Of course!" answered Skunk.

Back home, he built a corral. His younger brother Skunk decided one day to go and find him. "Older brother," he said, "I can't find any food!" — "Very well," answered Wolverine. His caribou corral was already ready. "I'll try to sort things out for you!" So Wolverine began to sing. The caribou could hear their older brother. "Let's all go and find him," said one. "Anyway he'll never be able to kill us!" So they went on purpose. They knew him well. Tightly packed against each other, they headed to see their older brother. There were very many going into the corral. When it was full, Wolverine closed the entrance and placed himself near the exit. When the caribou went out, he bent over and tried to spray them. Not one of them fell to the ground! When the last caribou showed up — it was a young one, Wolverine's wife struck it on the head with an axe. "There you are, my wife, I've killed one of them. I'm the one who killed it!" — "More like I was the one! fired back his wife. How could you have killed it?" She had killed only one, and he none, even though he had tried to bend over. Skunk said: "Older brother, your corral is first-rate. Would you lend it to me?" — "Of course," answered Wolverine. "I'll lend it to you!" Skunk began to sing and the caribou came around. When the corral was almost full, he blocked its entrance. When the animals began to leave, he stood near the gate and killed them. "Older brother," said Skunk, "you now have what you need to eat. Your corral is first-rate!" He had killed enough caribou to have food to eat. He indeed had enough. (Savard 1972, 81–82)

This episode is the simplest one. The mytheme has only a subject and a predicate: Skunk kills caribou. The food is appropriate for a hunter, as are the caribou ribs served by Woodpecker. In both cases, the hosts Woodpecker and Skunk are known to eat insects, a type of food unsuitable for humans. In Woodpecker's case, a part of an animal's body is removed from a tree, much as one would remove it from a living thing. In Skunk's case, this animal is distinguished the most from other animals by its foul odor, which it uses for defense. Only a fine line separates that use from offensive ones.

The naturalist Ernest Seton aptly describes the power of a skunk's liquid spray: "'A mixture of strong ammonia, essence of garlic, burning sulphur, a volume of sewer gas, a vitriol spray, a dash of perfume musk, all mixed together and intensified a thousand times'" (Seton in Banfield 1974, 339). We should also add that the skunk is quite proficient with its weapon and that it can accurately aim its spray, much like a spear being ably thrown:

> When a skunk decides to spray, it elevates its tail stiffly over its back, everts the anal orifice exposing the twin jets, and by contracting sphincter muscles ejects twin streams of musky fluid. The streams unite about one foot [30 cm] behind the animal and eventually break up into a fine spray, which may be felt five to six yards [4.5 to 5.5 m] away. The skunk possesses uncanny accuracy and can hit an adversary situated a short distance away in any direction— behind, beside, or in front of it—by twisting its rump towards the target. (Banfield 1974, 338)

Skunk's weapon, which he uses to kill caribou, is here used for a form of hunting that used to be practiced at caribou corrals. This large pen was in fact more like a trap that could catch dozens or even more caribou at one time. A caribou enclosure (*menaikan*) (Strong 1930, 5) is a formidable sight: "Another bygone form of hunting (MENIKAN, i.e., 'corral') was practiced in winter once or twice a year and would mobilize forty or so men. A corral 500 feet [150 m] long and 100 feet [30 m] wide would be built under the direction of an old hunter who beforehand had a premonitory dream. The men would drive the herd there and shut them in before killing them at close range with guns" (Mailhot and Michaud 1965, 32). The corral was funnel-shaped and, with the caribou being herded into the far end, the entrance would be closed. The animals would begin to go around in a circle, along the palisade. This technique makes use of the fact that caribou are accustomed to wandering along forest edges.

The animals were next killed by different means: "The use of deer spears and snares, and the practice of driving the animals into a corral where they are clubbed, speared or shot with bow and arrow are among the older aboriginal practices" (Strong 1930, 5). The spear was sometimes mounted with a bone point (Speck 1926, 278). According to the anthropologist Frank Speck (1977 [1935], 202), the cup-and-ball game made from caribou bones symbolizes this hunting technique. In the myths, Skunk is the one who most effectively uses this technique, his foul spray being projected like a spear. In contrast, Wolverine's wife, behaving like a human, uses another technique reported above: bludgeoning the animal with an axe or a club.

In the myth, Skunk also lures the caribou by singing. Innu use singing to locate caribou, with or without other techniques. For example, singing can be combined with the sweat lodge: "There were other ways to locate caribou. . . . One could also find out by the sweat lodge. The person inside the tent would sing and, in this way, could foresee how his hunt would turn out. In this tent, one did not see any fire. One foresaw only when one would kill" (Dominique 1989, 26). Here, the fire is what appears when one plays the drum and sings to find out where the caribou are: "In that time, everyone could find out where the caribou were. One played the drum and sang. During the first song, one saw nothing. Then during the second song, one could see a small flame. If it was intense, that meant the animal was nearby; on the other hand, if the glimmer of light seemed weak, that meant the caribou were very far away" (Dominique 1989, 25).

The songs were of various sorts. Speck reported several examples, including a refrain repeated tirelessly—"Because he who comes [referring to the caribou seen approaching in the dream] looks so fine!"—or these words, which recall a hunting trip farther north—"First time I could eat in the land of the Eskimo, when I danced" (Speck 1977 [1935], 92). The song and the dance were closely intertwined:

> The old people would bring their drums along and over there, at the camp, when we wanted to go hunting, over there, in winter, when we would ask for food (from Papakuassik) we would again use the drum. When we saw the caribou trail, we would sing. When we saw the path made by the caribou, the old people would sing. And we would say to the children and little girls—Dance! (Bacon and Vincent 1979, 20–21)

Apart from singing, Innu can also produce certain sounds like "a growl when the caribou is rutting" (McKenzie in Clément 2012, 464). At this time, a caribou is said to be less wary: "We cry out to it when it's the time when it loses the velvet from its antlers and when the caribou are in heat. It comes to see where the cry comes from. It isn't afraid" (Mestokosho in Clément 2012, 465). This is the behavior we see in the myth when Skunk lures the caribou into his corral by singing (Savard 1969). The striped skunk is known to make a panoply of sounds, including growls: "Skunks utter a variety of sounds: hisses, growls, squeals, and soft cooings" (Banfield 1974, 339).

To complete this portrait, we should examine a detail from a variant of this episode. In this variant, Wolverine prepares food for Skunk before going to the caribou corral: "He prepared fat from his son and asked him to defecate in a recipient. But Skunk couldn't swallow any of that, the excrement being so foul-smelling" (Savard 1972, 91). Savard reports the translator's comment on this mytheme: "According to the translator, the narrator forgot to mention that Skunk had offered Wolverine 'fat' from his son's testicles. Wolverine did the same for his guest" (Savard 1972, 99n82). During fieldwork in 1982 in Ekuanitshit, two elders, Jérôme Napish and Marguerite Mollen, while listing the parts of a striped skunk's body, reported the presence of *uîtuîa* and not the presence of *uîshinaiat*. The *uîtuîa* are the anal glands from which the spray is ejected. The same term also refers to a beaver's anal glands, as we have seen, which are thick and fatty like *pimî*, which is used to liven up meat dishes.

2   Snake Makes a Meal in the Embers (Southwest)

There was a black snake living somewhere. Once Coyote came to his house, and they were visiting. Then it came time to eat. Black Snake had a good sized fire going. When his fire died down he scratched it away, sat in it, and told his wife to cover him up. Some time passed and Black Snake suddenly came out. He went over and told his wife, "You have something roasted there." So his wife went over and scraped the ashes away, and there was a squash. They had a very delicious meal of it and Coyote went away well filled.

—Dean Saxton and Lucille Saxton, "Legends of the Papago"

At the other end of North America, over four thousand kilometers away as the crow flies, in a land as barren as the Canadian tundra, live the Papago, better known today by the name of Tohono O'odham, literally 'the people of the desert.'

They belong to the same language family—Uto-Aztecan—as their inseparable neighbors, the Pima of the Gila River, and have adapted throughout history and prehistory to their ecosystem of southern Arizona and northern Mexico by diversifying their means of survival. The climate left no other choice. With extreme variations in temperature and rainfall (12 to 25 centimeters of rain per year, 12 centimeters of which can fall in one day; 360 days of sunshine per year; temperatures ranging from -10°C in winter to 35°C in the shade during summer), the Tohono O'odham have survived by relying successively on hunting and gathering, livestock raising, and farming.

This versatility is reflected in the three Tohono O'odham episodes we have of the Bungling Host. One refers to mesquite pod gathering, a second to squash growing, and a third to hunting. Twenty-five percent of the traditional Tohono O'odham diet was provided by growing corn, beans, and squash. The most intriguing of the three episodes is the one about squash.

Of these episodes—we will follow here the order of appearance in the classic book by Dean and Lucille Saxton, the husband and wife team of ethnolinguists, about Papago and Pima mythology—only the last two will be quoted in full. The first episode is preceded by a very long introduction, of which only extracts will be presented and which we will now examine.

COYOTE IMITATES BEAN CHILD (PRELUDE-PART 1)

Turtle, they say, was the friend of a little beetle called Mesquite Bean Child and they lived by the ocean. Bean Child was the first to learn the kind of trees which produce good bean pods for food. Now the Desert People eat mesquite beans in many different ways, all known to Bean Child.

Turtle also had saguaro cactus but kept it well hidden. He[1] alone ate the fruit of it every year. . . . He never wandered far. . . .

At that time there were some who always wandered from home to home, looking for something to eat. They had no home of their own and never gathered food, but just lived on what they could beg. Coyote was the worst because he was everyone's "Uncle". . . .

There were also those who like to gossip and were curious. . . . The little woodpecker was especially like that, always eaves-dropping on people and running and telling his friend what he had heard . . . Only Coyote was his friend. . . .

One night Woodpecker snuck out and climbed a tree, keeping hidden. From there he saw Turtle and Bean Child and heard them having a discussion. They were discussing what a good-for-nothing

Coyote was, just a beggar and a liar. . . . When Woodpecker heard this, he ran looking for his friend, Coyote. . . .

When Coyote heard what was being said, he was angry and said, "It won't even be four days until I find out what Turtle eats that he never has to hunt or plant like people . . .".

Sure enough, he went and hid himself near Turtle's house. . . . He went every day. . . . Turtle would be lying there singing. Coyote never understood why the lazy fellow was singing. He would sing like this for the saguaro:

> I've ripened and am standing here.
> Many birds sing many songs and swarm over me.
> They say many different things.
> Many birds sing many songs and swarm over me.

You see, that's how Turtle would sing for his saguaro. That's why the fruit formed and ripened well every year. Turtle sang when it budded, when it blossomed, when the fruit formed, and when it ripened. So, this one saguaro and its branches gave Turtle a good living all year. (Saxton and Saxton 1973, 103–7)

The prelude introduces us to four characters: Bean Child, Turtle, Woodpecker, and Coyote. As is made clear, ties of friendship join Turtle and Bean Child. We need to explain here why the Tohono O'odham bring them together for this story. The turtle is the desert tortoise (*Gopherus agassizii*), the only turtle present in the Mojave and Sonoran deserts. Bean Child is none other than an insect from the Bruchidae family that lives on mesquite pods, particularly *Prosopis vetulina*, on O'odham territory. There are over one thousand known species of bruchids and over twenty-five of them feed on *Prosopis* beans in the New World. Only some species have been studied in detail. The best known, *Algorobius prosopis*, is the most common one in North America. We will come back to it later to discuss its life cycle.

The bruchid and the desert tortoise share so many points in common that a connection between the two was inevitable. Both are herbivores, both live in a desert environment and, last but not least, both have a highly distinctive carapace.

In the Papago language, the prefix *komi-* indicates the presence of a carapace that covers the back of a turtle, a beetle, or some such animal (Saxton, Saxton, and Enos 1998 [1983], 34), hence the names *komikam* for a beetle and *komilch'id* for a turtle. As if that were not enough, a loaf made from mesquite—the tree whose beans are eaten by bruchids—is also named 'turtle' by some in Papago because of its shape: "Some call these loaves *komkĭched* 'turtle' or 'tortoise', in reference to their shape" (Rea 1997, 187).

The other two characters are Woodpecker and Coyote. Many woodpecker species live in the Sonoran Desert, but the Gila woodpecker (*Melanerpes uropygialis*) "is the commonest and noisiest woodpecker in the saguaro stands of southern Arizona" (Philips, Marshall, and Monson 1964, 70). Its name comes from the saguaro cactus (*Carnegiea gigantea*), a favorite nesting spot: "Both Gila Woodpeckers and Gilded Flickers excavate nest cavities into the soft tissues. The cactus seals off the newly exposed tissues with a tough barklike scar" (Rea 1997, 255). Needless to say, in their natural environment, woodpeckers are known for being curious chatterboxes, just as the above myth makes them out to be. At least this is how one may interpret both the continual movements of these birds and the variety of sounds they make:

> Their habit is to fly to a low position on a trunk or branch and then move up it in a series of jerky hops; but woodpeckers can also hop backwards down a vertical surface, or sideways across it. The wings are rounded and flight, although it may be swift, is usually undulating, with a swoop between each wing-beat. . . . Woodpeckers usually have hard harsh notes, often far-carrying, sometimes rapidly repeated to produce "laughing" calls. The alarm note is often a loud rattle. (De Beer et al. 1972, 1964–65)

Coyote is obviously the well-known member of the dog family, *Canis latrans*, whose opportunistic feeding is common knowledge.

It feeds on small rodents, rabbits and hares, larger game animals or livestock, and carrion. Its food also includes some plant items: various fruits, berries, and seeds (Voight and Berg 1987, 349; Rea 1998, 195). Its omnivorous diet, its adaptability (one of the few species whose population has increased and not decreased with the expansion of farms and cities), its large geographic range, its willingness to eat carrion, its predation on livestock—all of these factors predestined it for the Trickster role in Native cultures, including the O'odham culture. The above myth confirms this depiction: it is a "beggar" that lives off the work of others (up to 25 percent of its diet being carrion) and a "liar" or a "good-for-nothing" that very often steals its food (up to 14 percent of its diet is poultry and cattle).

Turtle has a more complex relationship with the saguaro. Turtles and their environment form distinct biocenoses. In the Sonoran Desert, the desert tortoise is associated with stands of saguaros and palo verde (*Cercidium floridum*) more than any other vegetation: "The desert tortoise occurs in a number of plant communities ranging from sparse creosote bush desertscrub in the winter rainfall Mohave Desert to palo verde-saguaro desertscrub in the bi-seasonal Sonoran Desert" ("Desert Tortoise" 2009, 1). Before the 1950s, the population of desert tortoises easily reached several hundred individuals per square kilometer ("Desert Tortoise" 2009, 1–2). Inevitably, the above myth posits the same type of tortoise to saguaro association that has been observed by wildlife specialists and Natives alike. What is more, the desert tortoise's diet encompasses fruits and seeds from a variety of cacti. Not surprisingly, it should eat saguaro fruits and seeds.

Also, according to the same myth, Turtle regularly sings for his saguaro, and his singing is the reason why this cactus bears fruit. Saguaros bloom in May or June—up to a hundred flowers per individual cactus—and the fruits ripen in July. This is the same time of year when the desert tortoises breed (spring to early autumn) or, a year later, lay their eggs (May or June). The desert

Fig. 5. Mesquite of the Sonoran Desert.

tortoise also makes a wide range of sounds ("hisses, grunts, pops, whoops, huhs, echs, bips, etc."; "Desert Tortoise" 2009, 3), which are so diverse one could easily say its song is composed on the fly. Parallel to this fact, the anthropological literature shows that the Tohono O'odham sang songs specially intended for either cultivated or wild plants: "The Papago planted corn, squash, beans, and tobacco, and every stage in the growth of these crops, as well as in that of the wild ones that mature at the same time, was encouraged by singing" (Underhill 1946, 68).

The signature is obvious. When birds arrive in spring, plants also bloom and bear fruit; and the singing of birds may easily be interpreted in rites and myths as efforts to urge plants to develop (see Chapter 4). To take only the example of the saguaro, an ethnobotanist writes about its blooming in these terms: "Blooming time and the arrival of White-winged Doves and Long-nosed Bats correspond. Each flower opens late in the evening, closing the next afternoon. Insects, bats, doves, woodpeckers, and even flycatchers are attracted to these flowers for one reason or another. . . . The Saguaro then puts on a second show, this time to attract seed disseminators: the greenish fruit splits open, revealing the dark red pulp with its mass of black seeds" (Rea 1997, 253).

It is said in the myth that Turtle never goes very far from his saguaro ("He never wandered far"), and it is known to specialists that desert tortoises generally live within a small habitat: "It has been suggested that tortoises rarely move more than two miles from their natal nest in their entire lives" ("Desert Tortoise" 2009, 2). Given that their life expectancy is fifty to eighty years and that a saguaro can live for up to two hundred years, one can understand that in the myth Turtle does not roam very far from his saguaro and that this cactus can feed him with the two thousand seeds from each of its hundred flowers.

The myth also recounts that the events took place near the sea ("and they lived by the ocean"), thus confirming that O'odham territory used to extend as far west as the Gulf of California (Fontana 1983, 126). This is the desert tortoise's geographical range ("Desert Tortoise" 2009, 1). The myth also alludes to close relationships between Bean Child and the mesquite. The relationships will be discussed in detail further on when we comment specifically on the Bungling Host episode.

Following this introduction, the prelude to the tale continues with Coyote trying to figure out Turtle's big secret:

COYOTE IMITATES BEAN CHILD (PRELUDE — PART 2)

One day Coyote . . . saw Turtle coming down from the mountain, carrying a long stick with something in the palm of his hand.

Coyote started out to meet him. While he was still a long way from him he kept saying, "What is that stick for?"

"It's my harvest stick," Turtle kept answering. . . . "Now I've made this so I can bend the mesquite down and eat good beans." . . .

Then Coyote said, "What's that in your hand?" . . . "Ha! Is it some kind of seed? Let me see." . . .

Turtle held out his hand, opening it just a little. . . .

As soon as Turtle opened his hand, Coyote struck it hard from beneath. So, right then, he scattered the seed wherever there's lots of saguaro now. When he had done this, he ran off looking for Bean Child to pay him back for the distressing things he had said about him. (Saxton and Saxton 1973, 108–9)

This second part of the prelude brings us to Coyote's shenanigans, i.e., how he managed to steal the saguaro seeds Turtle was trying to hide from him. It is known that coyotes likewise eat saguaro seeds ("The seeds are important to the diets of birds, ground squirrels, pack rats, coyotes, and others"; Smith 1988, 9–10), hence Coyote's interest in taking them. He also represents humans, who share the same interest. Less known, however, are all of the other elements that help to fit a myth like this one into the setting of a specific culture. For example, Turtle comes down from the mountain and walks around with a long stick. Now, even today, albeit less often, the O'odham still use a *ku'ipad* to dislodge fruits from the tops of saguaro cacti, which may stand up to 15 meters tall. This tool is made of saguaro ribs tied together with a small crosspiece at its far end. Furthermore, Turtle answers Coyote's queries by saying he uses his stick to bend mesquite branches and collect the best pods—a harvesting technique that some desert peoples did use. The Mohave farther north, for example, used a stick to shake these trees and make the pods fall ("In September, dry beans were collected off the ground or shaken from the trees with a long pole"; Hodgson 2001, 178). A neighboring people to the west, the Cocopa, went about their harvesting the same way as Turtle does: "They tested the pods by breaking and tasting them and then pulled down the higher branches to collect the pods using a long, hooked pole" (Hodgson 2001, 179–80). Although such a practice has not been attested among the O'odham, it might have existed among them as well.

For Turtle, this interchangeability of saguaros and mesquites also points to a relationship on another level, namely that the fruits of both species, more than any others, "were the most abundant and accessible resources in the dry season" (Rea 1997, 255). So Turtle's lie to Coyote could go unnoticed, since both plants are not only sources of food but also available at the same time.

The fact that Turtle arrives from a mountain or is coming down one is just as verifiable. Indeed, in palo verde and saguaro stands, one finds turtles on rocky slopes in particular: "Tortoises living in the Sonoran Desert of Arizona occupy entirely different habitats. They are found on the steep, rocky slopes of hillsides" (Berry 2009, 1).

This takes us straightaway to the episode where Bean Child acts as Coyote's host:

COYOTE IMITATES BEAN CHILD

Right then Bean Child understood that Coyote was going to come. He hid his supplies. All that was visible was the foundation of his house. There was no place there where food could be hidden. Bean Child was just sitting there waiting for his uncle to come and discover his fate, and to learn who was a great medicine man. Bean Child remembered that he must get even with him for the sake of his friend. So he was ready, with a basket set up on one side and a pestle on the other side.

Then Coyote came and said, "I tried to go hunting, but killed nothing. Don't you know that when a man gets old he can no longer do what he knew how to do before. Soon he gets hungry and remembers his relatives who are young men and skilled at everything."

Bean Child said, "Ha! Uncle! You're out of luck. Just now my supplies ran out. There's just the bare foundation of my house. Sit down and watch me. Maybe my powers will work and I'll be able to feed you."

When he had said this, he sat right down and started his song:

Even though I'm so small,
I can gather mesquite beans.
With the pod meal I will feed
Anyone who comes to see me.

When he had finished this song of his, he hit himself hard on the forehead with the pestle, but nothing happened. He sang his song again and did the same thing to himself, but nothing happened. When he had done it the fourth time, and hit himself hard on the forehead again, pieces of bean pod poured into the basket. He poured in some water and stirred it hard and gave it to his uncle.

Coyote got very full on this and said, "In the fourth morning, you come and see me. I'll do something to feed you."

So, Bean Child counted the days and on the fourth he left to visit his uncle.

When he arrived Coyote was sitting there with a basket placed on one side and a pestle on the other. Coyote said, "Ha! Nephew! You're out of luck. Just now my supplies ran out. There's just the bare foundation of my house showing. But just sit down here and wait for me. I'll try to use my powers. Maybe they will work and you will eat."

When he had said this, he arose and took the basket on the right and the pestle on the other side and sang his song:

Even though I'm so small,
I can gather mesquite beans.
With the pod meal I will feed
Anyone who comes to see me.

When he had finished, he struck himself hard on the forehead with the pestle, but nothing happened. He sang again.

Bean Child knew Coyote couldn't really make mesquite flour, but he wanted to pay Coyote back for his friend, so he told Coyote, "Ha! Uncle! No bean pod meal can be made that way. You're just tapping yourself. Really hit yourself with all your might, and what you want will happen. Then I won't be hungry at your house."

So he finished the fourth song, and hit himself with all his might. In fact he killed himself and was lying there dead.

But Bean Child knew what to do to make Coyote come back to life. When he accomplished his purpose he went and drew a house around Coyote to hold the power. Then he sat facing him and sang like this:

Spin! Spin! Did I do this to you? No!
One, they say, is an old man above us.
He fell from way up there and did it to you.

Then he finished his song and breathed on him like a medicine man. When he sang the fourth time, Coyote came back to life again. (Saxton and Saxton 1973, 111–15)

Let us prune the story down to size so that the trees will not hide the forest from us. Trimming the details will let us see more clearly.

Bean Child receives Coyote at home and only the foundations are visible, so no food could be hidden there. The O'odham have several types of dwellings, depending on whether the local subgroup is more nomadic or more sedentary. These types sometimes include closed-in houses, open areas with only a roof (or *ramada*), and temporary cooking shelters surrounded only by a corn stalk enclosure. Whatever the type, the harvested or gathered produce was often stored in bins specially designed for this purpose. There were two main types, and each of them could be placed on rooftops, *ramadas*, or in open areas: "There were two kinds of storage bins. One type, called *homda*. . . . These bins might be a yard across and about half as high. Most were placed on rooftops, but some stood free on the ground on a base of more Arrow-weed, protected from livestock by little fences. . . . The other storage basket, called the *vashom*. . . . These jug-shaped baskets might be six feet tall. . . . These baskets stood under the *vatto* (ramada). . . . They held corn, wheat, beans, or already prepared mesquite flour (*vihog chu'i*)" (Rea 1997, 186).

We have already commented on the importance of singing to help crops to grow (here, mesquite harvesting). Bean Child has to repeat his song four times to get the desired effect, and this is but one example in the myth of an omnipresent practice among the O'odham. Their society does everything in fours: four clans coexist; the winter ceremony is held every four years; the sit-and-drink ceremony was held alternately in one of the four villages at the four cardinal points; a ritual was complete only if repeated four times; and so on (Underhill 1946, 51, 136, etc.). "A ceremony or ritual is completed (*am hugith*) by four repetitions or by four days of activity" (Saxton, Saxton, and Enos 1998 [1983], 122).

Thus, in the myth, Coyote likewise hits himself on the forehead four times, just as in the prelude to the episode he boasted that four days would be more than enough for him to find out Turtle's secret.

To bring Coyote back to life, at the end of the episode, Bean Child likewise repeats his song and ritual four times. The healing ceremonies of this myth are corroborated by the anthropological literature. This is what Saxton and Saxton say about the traditional cures that prevailed among the Tohono O'odham: "The cure may include drawing a line around the patient *kihchuth* 'to house or contain (the spirit power)', singing the song or songs for the specific illness (*ne'ichuth*); blowing smoke on the patient (*kummun*)" (Saxton, Saxton, and Enos 1998 [1983], 123).

Even Bean Child's singing can be explained. Without going into the complexity of this subject, let us note the type of words used traditionally by healers. In fact, the words had no relationship to the patient and revealed more about the medicine man than about the patient: "The songs of the medicine man have nothing to do with the patient. They tell of his own dreams. Some men have strange ingenious experiences and some have comic ones. It does not matter what the dream is, so long as it takes the medicine man out of daily life into the realm where power may be captured" (Underhill 1968, 143).

The healer's breath, with or without smoke, was in reality so powerful that a level-headed anthropologist wrote down the following observations: "I have heard stories of people who came back almost from the grave when they smelled that 'holy smoke.'

They believed" (Underhill 1968, 143). This is also what the story suggests when Coyote is brought back to life.

With the details trimmed away, we are left only with the bare bones of the episode: a subject and a predicate, i.e., Bean Child makes mesquite pod meal by hitting himself on the forehead. To understand the mytheme, we have to understand the bruchid's life cycle, which entomologists describe as follows:

> Their life history is usually that the adult female lays eggs on a seed or pod (Figure 1), the first stage larva chews through the egg shell, pod wall and/or seed coat and then into the seed. The first stage larva (Figure 1) is highly modified to enter seeds. . . . Shortly after entering a seed it molts into a legless grub that is very different from the first stage larva and is modified for feeding inside seeds. The larva usually feeds inside one seed. . . . It usually then pupates inside a single seed. . . . After pupation the adult completes a typical round exit hole (Figure 1) that was almost completed by the larva and leaves the seed to begin a new life cycle. (Johnson 1983, 7)

We also have to understand that mesquite pods are gathered before the adult bruchids emerge. Today, beans are no longer considered edible if larvae are present, but it seems that traditionally this additive was thought to improve mesquite flour. It was viewed as a sort of seasoning:

> When stored in the form of whole or dry pods, partially pulverized, they soon became a living mass, since an insect, a species of *Bruchus*, was present in almost every seed. To the Pima or any other tribe of Indians, this made little difference. The insects were not removed but accepted as an agreeable ingredient of the flour, subsequently made from the beans. If reduced to a fine flour soon after gathering, the larvae still remained within the beans and became a part of the meal, forming a homogeneous mass of animal and vegetable matter. (Bell and Castetter 1937, 22–23)

The rest is simple analysis. The mesquite beans were ground into meal, and the larvae were hence pounded while making the same flour: Bean Child was offering himself as food. Stone pestles (Rea 1997, 191) were used because "mesquite seeds are extremely hard" (Hodgson 2001, 181). In the story, this is why Bean Child calls on Coyote to hit himself harder and harder on his forehead.

Once the beans were crushed, water could be added to the preparation, which would be consumed as such in a practically liquid form or as a loaf, depending on how much was added (Hodgson 2001, 184–86).

If we go back to Bean Child's song, it is true that bruchids are very small (*Even though I'm so small*). It is also true that they feed on mesquite and that they have to gather it (*I can gather mesquite beans*). And it is just as true that once crushed they form part of the mesquite flour and feed anyone who comes to pay a visit (*With the pod meal I will feed anyone who comes to see me*).

This takes us back to a point in the opening paragraph of the myth, which we have so far set aside. "Bean Child was the first to learn the kind of trees which produce good bean pods for food." Entomologists generally recognize that legumes, including mesquite, have evolved a strategy of preventing bruchid infestation by producing toxic seeds, which the insects avoid: "According to Janzen (1969), most legumes seem to follow one of two strategies to avoid seed dispersion by bruchids. Some plants produce large toxic seeds that exclude all or almost all seed predators. Other plants produce many small seeds that are fed upon by bruchids but produce so many seeds that some escape the predators" (Johnson 1983, 12–13).

Though not an infallible hypothesis, it may be that the O'odham of earlier times saw a legume with bruchids as a sign that its beans were edible and, conversely, a legume without them as a sign that its beans were inedible: "Nine genera of Bruchidae are known to use *Prosopis* fruits and seeds. Three of these genera are obligately restricted to *Prosopis* while others use fruits of a variety of legumes often found in association with *Prosopis* such as *Acacia, Cercidium*, etc." (Kingsolver et al. 1977, 114). This is the knowledge that Bean Child gained through observation.

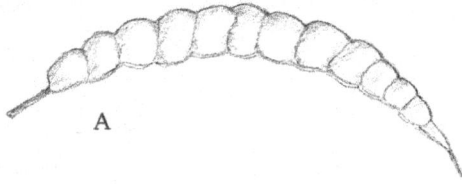

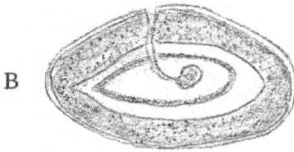

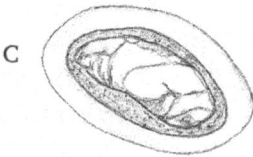

Fig. 6. A. Mesquite bean; B. Cross-section; C. Pupa inside larval feeding chamber.

The initial part of the myth also tells us that "[n]ow the Desert People eat mesquite beans in many different ways, all known to Bean Child." This almost states the obvious. If bruchids remain when beans are being ground to make meal or some other product, it goes without saying that they know all of the ways to prepare mesquite pod meal because they are present at every stage of food preparation right up until the food is eaten.

As a side note, we have here a major difference in perception. Whereas entomologists observe insects feeding on *Prosopis* fruits and seeds and see their presence as a sign of infestation, predation, or parasitism, the Tohono O'odham see only a positive, benevolent relationship, which they even imagine in affectionate kinship terms: bruchids are really the children of mesquite beans.

The second Bungling Host episode is still more fascinating and even very intriguing. We needed much time to see through it clearly, although the mytheme seems simple at first glance: Snake cooks a squash for Coyote in hot sand. This is the full version:

COYOTE IMITATES BLACK SNAKE

They say this happened long ago.

There was a black snake living somewhere. Once Coyote came to his house, and they were visiting.

Then it came time to eat. Black Snake had a good sized fire going. When his fire died down he scratched it away, sat in it, and told his wife to cover him up.

Some time passed and Black Snake suddenly came out. He went over and told his wife, "You have something roasted there."

So his wife went over and scraped the ashes away, and there was a squash. They had a very delicious meal of it and Coyote went away well filled.

Some time passed and Black Snake went to Coyote's house. Again they wanted to eat. Coyote made a good sized fire and curled up in it where there were coals and told his wife to cover him up.

A long time passed as Black Snake was waiting for Coyote. Then he said, "There's something roasted there."

Coyote's wife went over and uncovered her roast. There the poor thing lay, already stiff.

That's the end of the story. (Saxton and Saxton 1973, 116–17)

To understand the mytheme, there is no need to identify the snake species of this episode exactly, but we should still correct the interpretation made by the Saxtons who recorded the story. In the original version (Saxton and Saxton 1973, 116), the term used is *chuk wamad*, from *chuk*, 'black' and *wamad*, 'non-poisonous snake' (Saxton, Saxton and Enos 1998 [1983]). In their dictionary, the Saxtons translate *chuk wamad* as 'black racer snake'. Also named southern black racer snake, this species, *Coluber constrictor priapus*, may be found in Arizona but is extremely rare (only one case reported in 1927; Brennan and Holycross 2009, 114). Moreover, this species does not come in any other color, although an alternate color morph is indicated by a second name, *wegi wamad*, which the Saxtons report for the same snake and which literally means 'red snake'.

These two names in the Papago language seem to point to another colubrid, *Masticophis (= Coluber) flagellum*, which occurs throughout Arizona and includes some individuals that may be completely red or completely black with a variety of striped forms (Brennan and Holycross 2009, 114). It is also a very thin snake whose scale pattern makes it look like a finely braided whip, hence the English vernacular name "coachwhip."

At first glance, this short episode is like most myths of this type: a happy composite of human and animal aspects that are so finely interwoven with each other as to give the impression of an impenetrable mystery. For this reason, we must pull apart each thread of the story line, one by one, as required by basic analysis.

First, a fire is lit and maintained, as humans do when getting ready to cook. Then, once it is put out, the burnt logs are removed and only the embers remain. A meal is placed on the embers, and everything is covered with charcoal. In the myth, Snake acts as both the cook and the meal—as Coyote will try to do likewise—but only Snake leaves a squash behind (or a pumpkin, since the Papago term, *hahl*, means both members of the gourd family). An ethnobiologist describes an identical cooking method that prevailed among the same O'odham: "Fresh greens like amaranth (*Amaranthus palmeri*) and fresh squash were also boiled, but since water was scarce, anything that was juicy enough was roasted. This was the treatment for the flower stalks of aloe and sotol (*Dasylirion wheeleri*) . . . and squash. Ashes were raked out of the fire and the vegetables buried in them" (Castetter and Underhill 1935, 46). As the myth tells us, women—the respective wives of Snake and Coyote—are the ones who pull either a squash or a burnt husband out of the fire. By tradition, cooking was mostly women's work among the Tohono O'odham (Castetter and Underhill 1935, 6).

So why does Snake sit on burning charcoal? Why does Coyote,

by imitating him, coil up like a snake on a similar heat source? The answer is surprisingly simple but requires a bit of thought. Snakes are poikilotherms, i.e., cold-blooded animals. Hence their body temperature varies with the ambient temperature. To regulate their physiological processes, snakes have to adapt themselves by positioning themselves in the shade to cool off or in the sun to warm up. Sunbathing is vital for a process like digestion. They rely, therefore, on external heat sources to raise their body temperature and thus digest more easily: "Digestive processes depend on temperature. . . . The main problem caused by the ingestion of whole prey is its rotting, which would give off lethal toxins. Snakes must steer the right path between enzymic processes and bacterial action. Digestive enzymes reach their optimal level of efficiency around 86° F (30° C), and the snake tries to reach this temperature by active thermoregulation, heating itself in the sun" (Bauchot 2006, 121). This is why the myth has Snake looking for a heat source so he can cook (digest).

But that is not all. We still have to explain why a squash was left behind. Of course, some of the snake's specific characteristics (thinness, black color) might by extrapolation bring to mind the creeping vine of a squash, not to mention that such snakes could be easily found in O'odham fields. Better yet, a snake digesting its prey (and clearly exposed to heat, since the O'odham must have noticed that snakes bask in the sun more often than usual while digesting) could make one think of a creeping vine with a squash-like bulge—as big or deformed as the section of a snake's body with a prey inside (mouse, bird, small tortoise, etc.).

But the myth continues to grow in intensity and reaches its climax only when there appears an element of behavior that seemed insignificant at first. This element comes up only in the initial part of the story about the snake. It is missing, however, from the finale when Coyote tries to imitate the sequence, hence its importance. In the myth, Snake rises abruptly from the embers: "Some time passed and Black Snake suddenly came out." A related behavior

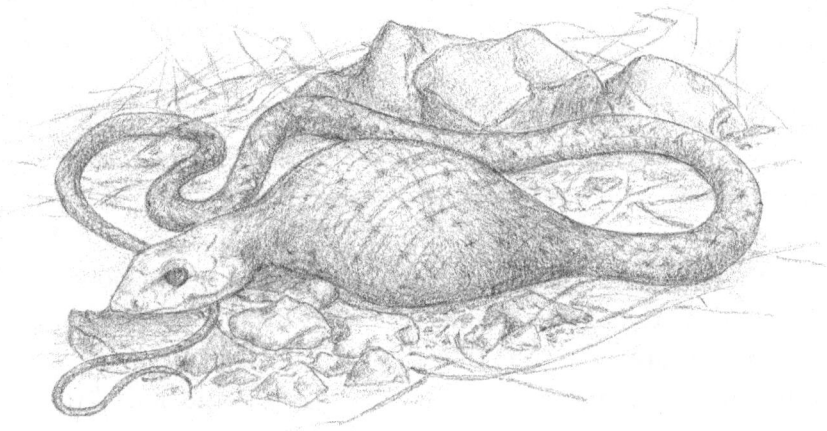

Fig. 7. Snake digesting.

has often been reported by herpetologists and snake breeders. If disturbed while digesting, a snake will readily throw up its prey and make a speedy getaway: "In contrast to the speed at which prey is caught, the long phase of transportation in the mouth requires a sustained effort during which the snake is vulnerable. This is why the snake prefers to regurgitate if disturbed" (Bauchot 2006, 120). The cooking is all done!

And if Coyote coils up in the embers instead of sitting on them, he cannot be digesting anything. When a snake is digesting, it is most often stretched out—at least partly—like the creeping vine and its fruit may suggest: "Small snakes may bask by placing their entire bodies on a warm substrate or in the sun, but large snakes sometimes warm only the portion of their body containing the prey, which is easily identified by the bulge it creates about one-third of the way down" (Mattison 2007, 119).

Finally, the regurgitated prey may likewise evoke the fruit of a squash.

In the third and last Bungling Host episode, Coyote as always vainly tries to imitate the main protagonist, who is now Skunk.

COYOTE IMITATES SKUNK

They say this happened long ago.

Coyote was running along somewhere when suddenly there was a skunk going about hanging up meat to dry.

Coyote came to him and said, "Where did you get the meat, my little brother?"

Skunk said, "A while ago I built a house. When I finished, I stood on top of it and announced that there would be a big meeting at my house. Many people came and crowded into my house. And the wise men spoke.

After a while I said, 'I'm going to stretch a bit.' So I went out and stood in the doorway, stooped over a bit and sprayed them with odor. The people just fell flat. Then I got busy and skinned them and am hanging the meat up to dry."

When Coyote got the idea, he said, "Well, I'm going to run on."

Coyote left and built himself a house. When he finished, he stood on top of it and announced, "My relatives, I've been traveling all over, hearing different things. Come and hear about it."

So the people came from all around and crowded into his house. And the wise men spoke.

After a while, Coyote said, "I'm going out to stretch a bit." So he went and stood in the doorway. He stooped over and tried to spray the people with odor, and then watched them. They ran off in all directions.

One was sitting tight in the doorway. He was stunned because he was asleep. He rushed out and Coyote kicked him and knocked him out.

At dawn, Coyote was walking around hanging meat from his one little victim. Skunk went by and laughed at him!

That's the end of the story. (Saxton and Saxton 1973, 118–20)

This episode is reminiscent of the corresponding episode from the Innu, which appeared in the last chapter. Here, the host is also Skunk, specifically *Mephitis mephitis*, i.e., the striped skunk. It is Arizona's most common species, although one may sporadically or even often encounter other species, such as the hooded skunk

(*Mephitis macroura*), the spotted skunk (*Spilogale gracilis*), and even the hognose skunk (*Conepatus mesoleucus*) (Olin 1982).

Skunks are well known for the musk their anal glands can discharge over long distances with relatively great precision, as already noted with respect to *Mephitis mephitis*: "On the evil side (from the aggressor's point of view) the skunk has one of the most powerful defense mechanisms bestowed on any creature: two rear jets, each capable of spraying a nauseating repellent as far as 20 feet (6 m), and with devastating accuracy" (Wooding 1982, 117). This ability is unique among mammals and has earned it an unchallenged place as best marksman in the eyes of North American Native peoples.

For this reason, as much among the Innu as among the Tohono O'odham, the skunk acts like a hunter. Whereas the Innu compare its projected musk to a spear, the Tohono O'odham most likely associate it with an arrow, since they traditionally used the bow and arrow as a hunting weapon: "The Papagos usually made stone-tipped arrows for war and large game, but wooden-tipped ones for small game" (Castetter and Underhill 1935, 70–71).

The scene in the myth corresponds in every way to a hunt. Thus, the action begins with a speech by the hunting leader, who climbs on to a rooftop: "If the men were to hunt that day, early in the morning before it became light, the *tôpidam* would climb on top of his *o'riski* 'roof house' and make a hunting speech" (Rea 1979, 114).

Each village also had a round house that was similar in type, though larger, where the men would get together to talk things over: "The brush house in which he lived [the head man of the village] was made extra large and was used as a meeting place by the men of the village, who formed an informal council" (Castetter and Underhill 1935, 7).

The Tohono O'odham also used to carry out hunts much like the corral hunting of the Innu. Brush fences would be erected, and rabbits driven into them. The hunters would stand near openings left in the fence and wait to kill their prey. The hunts were preceded by speeches: "Formal orations preceded the actual drive. . . . Prior to the drive, brush fences were erected with a gap at their intersection where the shooters stayed" (Rea 1998, 52). By standing in the doorway to the house, the skunk in the myth acted exactly as these hunters did.

Next, depending on the success of the hunt, the game animals were cut up then and there. The rabbits were immediately cooked in a pit (Rea 1998, 52). In the case of larger animals, which were likewise driven toward a hunter already standing at a strategic point (Rea 1998, 53), the meat was also immediately dried in the form of strips: "The deer meat was usually cut into thin strips and sun-dried on the spot" (Castetter and Underhill 1935, 41). In the myth, Skunk prepares his meat right away once his prey has been killed.

On a final note, skunks are considered by biologists to be omnivorous, although in some regions much of their diet may come from hunting small mammals. Thus, in the American Southwest, it is said of the striped skunk that "its diet consists of small rodents, eggs of ground nesting birds, cactus fruit and whatever insects it may capture" (Olin 1982, 53). An Arizona anthropologist speaks of it as a real hunter: "Skunks are active year-round. . . . they are more active at dusk and during the night. Then they go about hunting for plant material, insects and other arthropods, and even small mammals" (Rea 1998, 224). In the story, Skunk kills people he has invited. It must be said that Native American myths often maintain that all animals used to act as humans do: that is, they spoke, lived in homes, were married, and so on. Such a perspective can help us to interpret this part of the story: the guests are prey, and Skunk is a hunter. This is Skunk's view of things, all the more so because skunks are known for spraying people.

3   The Fire Trap (Grand Basin)

Coyote came to visit Crow. . . . Crow said, "I can't give you much to eat." He thought of how he might get some food for his guest. He took his bow and arrow and some fire, and went out. There were grass and brush growing near his house. These he burned in a circle to trap rabbits and rats. Crow was in the middle of the circle, and as the animals ran toward him, he killed them. He killed many rabbits and rats. When the fire got close to him, he took all the dead animals and jumped over the fire.

—Maurice L. Zigmond, "Kawaiisu Mythology"

This extract comes from the Kawaiisu of the Great Basin, who have been less fortunate demographically than the Papago and have scarcely survived the vagaries of time. In the early twentieth century, their population had already fallen to less than 150 people, only five of whom could still speak their mother tongue (Zigmond 1986, 410; Lewis 2009). They used to number over five hundred, according to the most conservative estimates, and had lived in their native land of the Sierra Nevada for a period of over two thousand years (Zigmond 1986, 399). Today, there remains but one community of the Kawaiisu, the "Kawaiisu Tribe of Tejon" of Bakersfield, California. They still occupy their traditional territory, whose variations in elevation—from 300 meters in the west near the Kern River to 2,500 meters farther east at the top of Piute Peak—partly account for the diversity of the ecosystems they live within and, thus, the breadth of their knowledge about fauna and flora.

The Kawaiisu have successively adapted to environments as different as forest, desert, and prairie. Traditionally, they lived mostly from gathering, while also hunting big and small game.

> The botanical traditions of the Kawaiisu permeated every facet of their culture. Plants played a role not only in diet, medicine, and the manufacture of diverse items, but also in ritual (which was minimal), mythology, and the realm of the supernatural. Lacking agriculture, the Kawaiisu were entirely dependent upon the natural floral growth of the environment as the source of vegetal products. Oak trees . . . produced the acorns that constituted the basic food. . . . Of some 250 taxa to which usage—at times multiple—was attributed, about 120 furnished food and beverage; over 100, medicine; 90, miscellaneous items and services; while 40 had ritualistic, mythological or supernatural associations. (Zigmond 1981, 4)

Very little has been written about the traditional, cultural, and social life of the Kawaiisu. In truth, what we know mostly comes from an anthropologist who conducted several field trips in the 1930s and later in the 1970s. His name was Maurice L. Zigmond, and he wrote a dictionary (Zigmond, Booth, and Munro 1991), an ethnobotanical collection (1981), and miscellaneous articles about mythology (1972, 1980), basket making (1978), and so forth. Our information sources are therefore quite limited.

Nonetheless, we can reconstruct the primary meaning of the myths by using the basic method of analysis we have successfully used so far.

The Bungling Host theme is represented among the Kawaiisu by three different mythemes, which in turn have several variants. The first one is about a snake who receives a visit from Coyote, the Trickster. In the main variant, the host is a colubrid, the same species that among the Papago made a meal in the embers, namely *Masticophis (= Coluber) flagellum*, also commonly known as the coachwhip.

For this mytheme, we have three versions, which do not always specify the kind of snake. We will return to this point later. The main version, reproduced below, had first been provided by Emma Williams, and only her granddaughter's translation had been recorded (Zigmond 1980, 93–101). Later, she provided the anthropologist with another version, this time in Kawaiisu, which belongs to the Numic division of the Uto-Aztecan language family (Zigmond, Booth, and Munro 1991, 161–74). This version was translated by the authors and appears below.

COYOTE AND RED RACER

Red Racer has a winter house and also a sunhouse. Coyote came to visit him. Red Racer saw him as he was coming around the winter house. "Come in! Sit down over there," said Red Racer. They sat and talked until noon. "There is nothing for you to eat because I'm not eating anything," he said. He took his bow and quiver to his desert thorn bush. Coyote stealthily peeked at him through the door. Red Racer put down his bow and his quiver. And then, going under it, he went into it repeatedly, saying "Be tenderloin, be tenderloin." As he said that, his flesh piled up. When he finished he brought it and, arriving, put it down by Coyote.

He pretended not to have seen Coyote doing anything but sitting. "Here, roast it! I usually am doing that while I eat," said Red Racer. Coyote cut off just a little. "Cut lots!" When Red Racer said that, he [said], "Not much, I eat little. And then I usually eat by the children," said Coyote. "Take these leftovers to your house when you go home." Coyote took them when he went home.

He walked along and ate them one by one. He arrived with nothing. Before coming home, "Come visit me! I will give you my star shirt," he said to Red Racer. Coyote said to his children "Go play outside! You will see a Tubatulabal coming this way." A bit later indeed the children saw someone coming. They ran to tell.

"The Tubatulabal is coming, our father," they said, saying that one by one. They sat and talked. As they talked, it became noon. He took his bow and quiver to his desert thorn bush. "I wonder if he will do something too," thought Red Racer.

He just sat with Coyote's wife and talked. Coyote, indeed, going under, went in. He jumped back. "Kikik," he said, trying to go in. "This time I'm going to go in," he thought. All his back was bleeding, but he didn't bring anything. Bleeding, he came outside. There he died. Coyote's wife [said], "Did you do like that when he went to visit you?" [she] said to him. Red Racer [said], "Yes, I did that where he could see. Didn't he bring something? I gave him much tenderloin," said Red Racer to her. "He didn't bring anything," said she, Coyote's wife. "I just came to get that star shirt he was going to give me, he said," said Red Racer. "Nothing, not a thing anywhere did he leave. He lied to you," said Coyote's wife. (Zigmond, Booth, and Munro 1991, 161–74)

Coyote needs no introduction. He plays the Trickster here as elsewhere. In this role, he represents a human or, more simply still, what not to do — behaviors one should avoid.

In the three versions of the myth we have, the snake appears to be the colubrid *Masticophis flagellum*, although its characteristics are not always carefully specified. For example, in the second version, the snake is said to be gray and darker toward its head (Zigmond 1980, 94), a description that suggests the darker color that coachwhips may exhibit: "The dorsal color varies from very light yellow-brown to medium red-brown or gray, becoming lighter posteriorly. On the top and sides of the neck there are very distinct black cross-bands. . . . Frequently these black bands are fused for the greater part of their length . . . and the neck may then appear to be almost entirely black" (Ortenburger 1928, 113). Similarly, the third version (Zigmond 1980, 95) uses the Kawaiisu word *wiigara*, which effectively refers to the coachwhip, although the anthropologist who recorded the story preferred the doubtlessly erroneous translation of 'kingsnake' for *wiigara* (in Kawaiisu, 'kingsnake' is *kaa?yagara*).

We will assume that the snake of the story is a coachwhip, this being the likeliest species. As seen in the last chapter, it lives in a desert habitat and may be found in central California, where the Kawaiisu live: "The true home of this snake is in the deserts of the states mentioned above. It does not seem to be found at any great altitude but rather on the plains floor, open washes, hill slopes, and in northern California also in the coast region" (Ortenburger 1928, 120).

In the myth, Coachwhip lives in a winter house. This term should not mislead us. It is above all a year-round home, although in the summer an outbuilding provides shade and especially a place for work: "In the summer the woman worked in an open, flat-roofed shade house (*havakahni*)" (Zigmond 1986, 401).

In the third version of the myth, the home is described merely as a brush house. Its walls were indeed made out of transverse poles tied to vertical shafts with the intervening space filled with brush (Zigmond 1986, 401).

The myth can therefore happen as easily in summer as in winter, if we ignore some details that point to the spring. Thus, when Coyote arrives, Coachwhip tells him: "There is nothing for you to eat because I am not eating anything" (Zigmond, Booth, and Munro 1991, 162). Colubrids, as we know, do not eat during winter (generally from late autumn to the end of winter), when they withdraw to hibernate. The passage could be interpreted in this sense. As will be seen further on, another detail may likewise place the action in early spring.

Coachwhip invites his guest and, when midday comes, rises and arms himself for hunting. This detail is provided only in the first version—the most complete one. As for the other two versions, it is said, as in the first version, that Coyote sees the host going to his bush. The snake's daytime activities thus seem important. Indeed, coachwhips are known to hunt during the day in full sunlight (Brennan and Holycross 2009, 144), while other snakes try to stay in cooler spots.

This daytime hunter feeds on a variety of animals, including lizards especially and other snakes, mice, birds, various insects, small tortoises, and so on. Such prey can be found under bushes, as may be deduced from the myth. Bushes are hence favorite locations for a coachwhip because they provide refuge for its prey. An observer notes: "Brush fences around the numerous little ranch houses furnished excellent hiding places for this racer. Several of the specimens were found in these fences, where they lay stretched out at full length awaiting their prey. Lizards, to escape their natural enemies, the hawks, sought refuge here, and seldom would a snake have to wait long before securing a meal" (Ortenburger 1928, 118).

The same holds true with bushes, such as the one mentioned in the myth: the thorn bush, which the ethnobotanist Zigmond identifies as the species *Lycium cooperi*. Thorn bushes are found in exactly the same habitats—"alluvial plains and foothill slopes of the Mojavean and Colorado deserts" (Benson and Darrow 1981, 196)—where coachwhip snakes are found.

But why does the colubrid of the story lay down his bow and quiver before crawling into the bush? If he is going to hunt, he will surely need his weapons. Actually, Coachwhip will not be hunting. He is going to make tenderloin. How can this be explained?

We should first point out that a colubrid may crawl under a thorn bush for several other reasons. For example, when a snake like a coachwhip is disturbed, herpetologists know that its immediate response is to hide under a nearby bush: "These rather brightly colored snakes are very difficult to see when in bushes, as, once they reach a desired position, they remain perfectly quiet and are then difficult to distinguish from the numerous branches. It is interesting to note that all the specimens seen took to the bushes when disturbed" (Ortenburger 1928, 119).

But Coachwhip is not really disturbed in the story. To clarify this mytheme completely, we must ultimately look at several interrelated snake behaviors.

The reason is partly hibernation or, more precisely, emergence from hibernation. In fact, to understand the mytheme, we need to see things as the tellers of myth see them, by considering colubrid behaviors that are too repetitive and common to go unnoticed among the Kawaiisu.

First, *Masticophis flagellum* is undoubtedly the most common snake on Kawaiisu territory. Second, like other snakes, it molts many times a year. A young snake first sheds its skin when it is seven days old and, subsequently, up to once a month for as long as it grows. Even an adult snake molts on average three to four times a year. Several factors affect the frequency of molting, including emergence from hibernation: "Frequency of shedding depends on many factors. As shedding is to some extent dependent on growth, young snakes tend to shed more often than adults because they grow more quickly. As their growth rate slows down, so does the frequency of shedding. All snakes shed occasionally, however, even those that have all but stopped growing. In temperate species that go through a resting period, or hibernation, during the winter, shedding often takes place early in the spring almost as soon as they become active" (Mattison 2007, 34).

To this may be added another phenomenon: a snake will feel extremely vulnerable during this period. In the natural state, it will hide or find a quiet place just before molting.

Third, the Kawaiisu, like other neighboring Great Basin groups, used to eat snake. Zigmond (1986) ignores the subject, but the practice is reported among the Shoshone, the Ute, the Paiute, and others (Fowler 1986, 92). "Consumption of snakes, rattlesnakes, and other unidentified lizards and frogs is reported but seems rare other than in the harshest environments" (Fowler 1986, 88). The same author admits, however, that information is lacking on the subject: "Table 5 lists by genus as well as by general category the principal reptile and insect foods of Great Basin people. Data for both of these categories are poorly reported in the literature" (Fowler 1986, 88).

Even less is known about how the same reptiles are cooked. It is nonetheless known that a snake must be skinned before being cooked.

Anatomically, once skinned, a snake looks like a very long piece of meat with a neural arch running down the middle and over the centrum of each vertebra: "Each vertebra has a central portion, or centrum, which is shaped like a short cylinder with one convex and one concave end. These ends articulate on the corresponding ends of the centra that adjoin them. Above the centrum is a neural arch, an arch of bone through which the spinal cord runs" (Mattison 2007, 55).

This is the equivalent of the vertebral column, hence the mythical allusion to tenderloin. In fact, the corresponding Kawaiisu word, *huduku*, refers just as much to the muscle on each side of the column as to the flesh on the back ("meat on the upper back"; Zigmond, Booth, and Munro 1991, 207).

As expected, all of the elements have now come together to explain the mytheme. The action takes place during emergence from hibernation, in the spring, a propitious time when Coachwhip emerges and looks for a quiet spot for molting. Coachwhip heads for the thorn bush and is going through a period of transformation. This is why he sets his hunting weapons aside before crawling under the bush.

The way of crawling under the bush is the high point of the myth and the key to the puzzle. The colubrid goes in and out, sliding its way through the spiny branches of the Desert Bush. In the original text: "And then, going under it, he went into it repeatedly" (Zigmond, Booth, and Munro 1991, 163). Herpetologists will right away recognize here the way snakes shed their old skin. There must always be a rough surface to rub against: "The epidermis is normally shed in one piece, with the snake starting the process by rubbing its snout on a rough object then removing its old skin by crawling through vegetation or against a rock, bark or other rough surface" (Mattison 2007, 34). And what is rougher than a thorn bush?

Fig. 8. A snake's molted skin in the vegetation.

Skinning a snake for cooking can be likened here to molting, where the snake gives up its skin to offer itself as food. The image of snake tenderloin ready to roast is evoked masterfully by the image of a snake that has just molted. The color is resplendent, and to some it even seems iridescent. And the coachwhip, let us not forget, is red in its most widespread color morph: "Because the new skin has not been subjected to the wear that the old one was, the colours of the snake are often much brighter than they were prior to shedding" (Mattison 2007, 34). As final proof of the mytheme's veracity, these molts are found in the vegetation, this being evidence of the snake skinning itself under the bushes and thus exposing the meat on its back for roasting.

As for Coyote's behavior, it is the negative image of Coachwhip's actions. Coyote, as the human he incarnates, cannot offer himself as food. He is not like a snake in this respect. If he ventures too close to the thorn bushes, he will surely scrape his skin. And the injuries may be serious.

In the mytheme, a few secondary aspects remain to be commented on. The first one, which is not documented in the ethnographical literature, is the reason why Coachwhip came to visit Coyote—the star shirt. Explaining this shirt is not, however, essential for us to understand the story. Zigmond's informants described it as a white shirt. It is known that the Kawaiisu used to paint their bodies white for special ceremonies (Zigmond 1986, 403). Such a practice might be related to this shirt. It is also known that other peoples used to give white shirts a special meaning. For example, in the northwest of the Great Basin, Pomo officiants were dressed in this way at ceremonies: "One man, who had special duties, had a shirt designed for him of white material" (Kennedy 1955, 134). During the same ceremonies, all of the dancers were adorned with star-shaped abalone shells (*Haliotis* spp.).

In any case, a scintillating white shirt must have been highly valued in Kawaiisu culture. It could thus be an excellent way to lure guests to Coyote's home who otherwise would not come to visit, knowing full well he could not imitate their way of feeding or offering food. The star shirt reappears in the other two Kawaiisu episodes of the Bungling Host.

Another intriguing aspect of the myth is the name that Coyote's children use to refer to Coachwhip when he comes to visit. He is referred to as a Tubatulabal: "'The Tubatulabal is coming, our father,' they said, saying that one by one" (Zigmond, Booth, and Munro 1991, 168). It is true, as Zigmond (1980, 93) states in a footnote, that the Tubatulabal were northern neighbors of the Kawaiisu and that the two peoples were on good terms with each other. But there is more. Each year, the Tubatulabal and neighboring groups, including the Kawaiisu, would collectively hunt antelope in the San Joaquin valley (Smith 1978, 444). The two peoples also had close trading relations (Zigmond 1986, 399). Furthermore, very precise rules governed funeral customs in the case of intermarriage. Thus, payment must be made to the Tubatulabal parents-in-law if their son or daughter had married a Kawaiisu person and later died. No such custom has been reported for marriages with other neighboring peoples of the Kawaiisu (Zigmond 1986, 404). This kind of rule and others show the esteem held for the Tubatulabal, a feeling that is transposed into the myth, where Coyote shows the same deference to Coachwhip, who visits him and clearly knows how to get food. The Tubatulabal motif, like the star shirt motif, appears again in at least one other Bungling Host episode, given below. This episode features Crow and his host Coyote. A passage from the story is quoted at the start of this chapter.

COYOTE AND CROW

Coyote came to visit Crow. When he entered the house, Crow was seated and told Coyote to sit down. They talked together until noon. Crow said, "I can't give you much to eat." He thought of how he might get some food for his guest. He took his bow and arrow and some fire, and went out. There were grass and brush growing near his house. These he burned in a circle to trap rabbits and rats. Crow was in the middle of the circle, and as the animals ran toward him, he killed them. He killed many rabbits and rats. When the fire got close to him, he took all the dead animals and jumped over the fire.

Coyote was peeking out to see what Crow was doing. Crow roasted all the animals and gave them to Coyote. Crow told Coyote to eat all he wanted. Coyote said, "I don't eat much, but I'll take the rest home to my children." Crow agreed to this. Before he left, Coyote invited Crow to visit him. "When you come," he said, "I'll give you a star shirt."

Coyote put all the animals in his net and started home, but as he went along he ate them one by one until there was none left when he reached home. He told his children to stay outside and watch. "We are going to have company," he said. "You will see him coming." And so they went outside and played. They saw Crow coming. One by one, from the oldest to the youngest, they ran to Coyote and told him, "A Tubatulabal is coming!"

Coyote told Crow to come in and sit down. They talked until noon. There wasn't anything to eat. Coyote took his bow and arrow and some fire and went out. He burnt brush in a circle. He shot the animals as they appeared, but he didn't kill many. He waited until the fire was too close, and when he jumped, he jumped into the fire and was burned to death.

Coyote's wife *kuwaage'bi* (a small bird with red eyes and a red breast) asked Crow if he had done the same thing. Crow said "yes" and told how he had given Coyote meat which Coyote hadn't eaten but said he would take home. "Didn't he bring the meat home?" Crow asked. "No," said *kuwaage'bi,* "he never brought home anything good to eat." Crow asked about the star shirt. The wife said he didn't have any. Coyote had just told him that to make him come.

Then Crow went home. (Zigmond 1980, 97–98)

It is clear that this episode, which we also have in three versions, sums up a form of hunting that prevailed among many peoples of the Great Basin and elsewhere, namely a battue where fire is set to the surrounding vegetation. We call this a trap ("fire trap") because a trap is defined as a means of capturing animals dead or alive or driving them toward one or more hunters. Here, Crow represents the hunter, and he appears in such a context for several reasons. We will come back to them.

Fire-assisted battues are documented among the Shoshone, the Ute, the Paiute, and other Great Basin peoples (Fowler 1986, 79), in addition to the Kawaiisu (Zigmond 1986, 400), although detailed descriptions are hard to come by. Such hunts were also carried out by the Tubatulabal: "Rabbit hunting, a communal affair, was carried out by two techniques: firing the brush cover in various sections of the valley floor and shooting the animals as they attempted to escape" (Smith 1978, 444). In the episode where Coyote visits Crow, it is mentioned in two of the three versions that the game animals are not only rabbits but also rats. In at least one version, however, the animals die by fire and are not necessarily killed while trying to flee: "The fire killed rabbits and rats" (Zigmond 1980, 98). Not knowing better, Zigmond tried to play down the last detail by ascribing it to an omission by his informant: "One step in the story is omitted. The animals are not killed by the fire. See . . . version (A)" (Zigmond 1980, 98n5).

But such is not the case. We have found an even more detailed description of a fire hunt. Though from a people who do not necessarily live next to the Kawaiisu, it is still relevant because it shows how they carry out a similar hunt in a similar environment. These details come from the Jesuit priest Ignaz Pfefferkorn, who worked in Arizona in the Sonoran Desert, an ecosystem much like the Mojave Desert, which lies within traditional Kawaiisu territory. His observations are so evocative and so close to the Kawaiisu mythical episode that one might imagine seeing a live performance of Crow in similar circumstances.

> Above I have stated that in various places in Sonora there are large areas covered with zacatón. This thick brush [grass] is infested with large numbers of rats and mice which the Sonorans [Native Americans] sometimes hunt. Twenty or thirty and sometimes more Sonorans assemble and surround a given circle of brush. They start fires, setting the dry brush ablaze in a circle, and the animals hidden therein are forced to take flight. As the fire advances, the animals retreat more and more to the center and the Indians in turn close the circle on them. In this manner the hunt is continued, until finally a large number of rats and mice is driven together into the center. Of these, the heat has already killed some and burned others; the rest are killed by the Indians with clubs. (Pfefferkorn in Rea 1998, 54–55)

Therefore a fire hunt could target not only rabbits but also rodents. In this account, the hunters worked in a circle, as in the myth, a fact left out of less detailed references to fire hunts. The myth differs only in one detail: Crow waits and stands still in the middle. This detail is important because it stresses how Coyote dies, because he too is in the middle. It is in fact a warning to anyone who, out of thoughtfulness, would let himself be surrounded by the flames of such a fire.

The Jesuit priest goes on and describes how the hunt ends. Again, his account and the myth paint the same picture: "Then the distribution is made. Each Indian fastens to a string by their tails the mice which have fallen to his share. He hangs the string over his shoulder like a bandoleer. Thus attired, shouting and leaping joyously, the entire company returns home, where the game they have brought affords them a splendid feast" (Pfefferkorn in Rea 1998, 55). Crow "leaps" too, and one would imagine him cawing while walking away with his share of the meat.

There are several reasons for Crow being in this particular myth, some being essential and others not. First, a crow—in this case *Corvus brachyrhynchos*—feeds during the day: "In [the] morning, shortly before and after daybreak, [crows] leave roosts in small groups and fly in all directions leading to [their] feeding grounds" (Verbeek and Caffrey 2002, 13). This characteristic would not matter were it not specified in the mythical episode. By comparison, it is not mentioned in the third mytheme, which describes a red-headed bird who visits Coyote and whom we will discuss further on.

Next, Crow is also a hunter of small game, including small mammals. Biologists describe the components of his diet as follows: "*Main foods taken.* Omnivorous. Wide variety of invertebrates (terrestrial and intertidal marine); amphibians; reptiles; small birds and mammals; birds' eggs . . . ; seeds and fruits; carrion" (Verbeek and Caffrey 2002, 6).

Crows also get their food at ground level. "[It] obtains most food on the ground" (Verbeek and Caffrey 2002, 6). In the myth, the host likewise finds its prey on the ground.

Still more crucial to our analysis, scientists have observed that crows are among the first animals to come to a site where there is carrion. "Frequently first species to arrive at bait-sites (road kills and chicken carcasses)" (Verbeek and Caffrey 2002, 8). It is clear that scavengers like crows should be attracted to the flesh of animals that

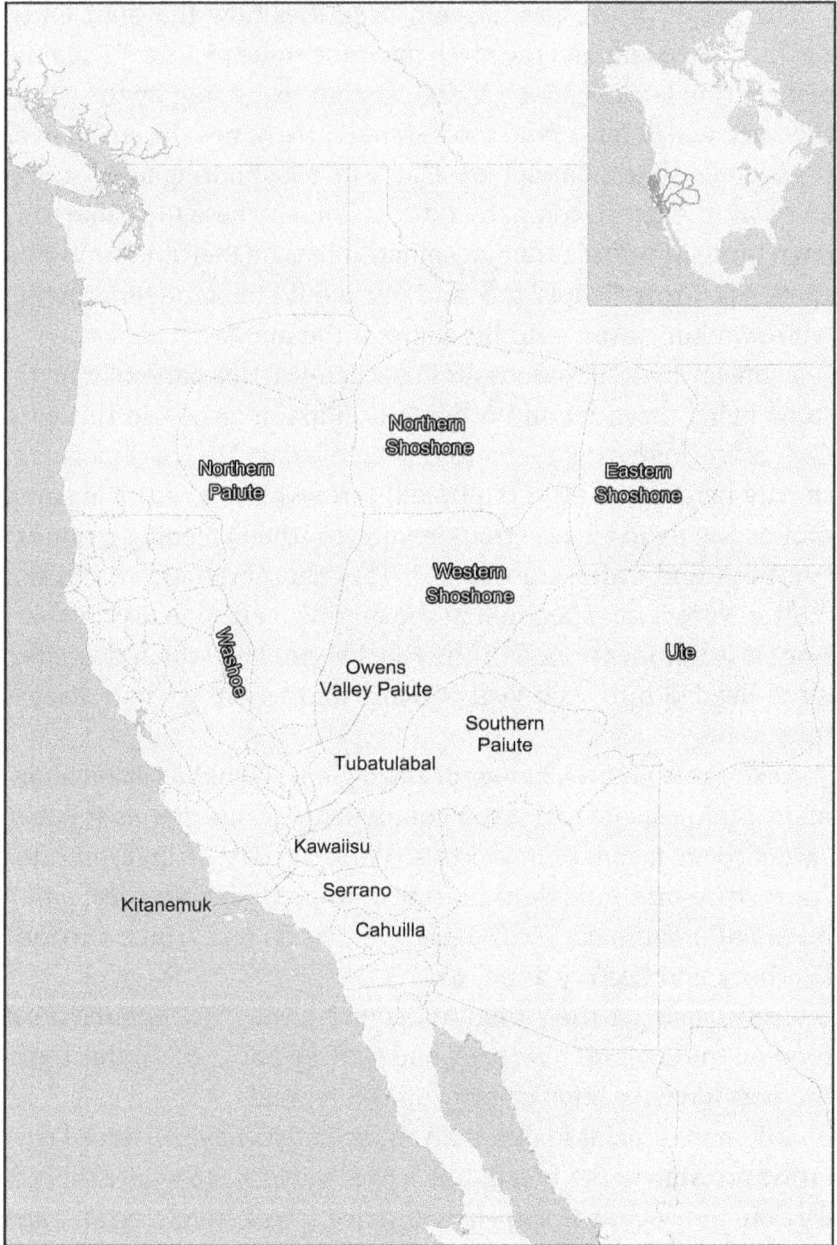

Fig. 9. Map of Location of neighboring peoples of the Kawaiisu.
Archéotec Inc.

have been burned or have died during a fire hunt, and the Kawaiisu must have surely noticed. Not surprisingly, they would view crows as thieves, as do people in other Native American cultures.

If crows are known for plundering the prey of other animals ("Several reports of stealing food from other species"; Verbeek and Caffrey 2002, 16), they should likewise be known for theft of game meat from humans.

Finally, crows often take their food away with their beaks or, occasionally, their feet (Verbeek and Caffrey 2002, 7). This, too, matches Crow's behavior in the myth. Either he jumps with his game meat over the fire, this being almost like flying, as in the first two versions, or he actually flies away and up into the air, as in the oldest version. "Then Crow flew straight up with his bag" (Zigmond 1980, 98).

The eastern neighbors of the Kawaiisu, the Southern Paiute, have a myth that resembles this Bungling Host episode, aside from a few differences. We will give this version in full. It appears to be important because it clarifies how the same story can vary among these peoples:

A HUNTING TRICK IMITATED

A'moyonts thought he would kill some deer, so he burnt heavy brush all round, sat down in the middle and sank underground. The fire burned; after a while he made plenty of snow to cool off the ground, then he came up again. He saw many sheep lying about dead from the fire. He had plenty of meat.

When it was cool, he dragged it to one place. Then Cünā'waBⁱ came and asked, "How did you kill that game?" "Don't say anything, just take any one home that you like." — "Well, how did you kill them?" — "Don't say anything." He continued asking. "Well, I burnt this brush all around and as soon as I had started the fire I sat down in the middle. When it came close to me, I went way down and stayed there a long while. It got too hot, so I made the snow come and when it ceased falling it was cool, so I got it and saw the sheep and deer dead. Thus I killed them."

Cünā'waBⁱ went home and was going to try it. He burnt brush all round and sat in the center. When the fire came close, he thought he would go underground, but he could not go down at all. He could not get out. He was caught in the fire and burnt up. (Lowie 1924, 171–72)

Hence, if the Southern Paiute have a similar Bungling Host episode that nonetheless features a different character from Crow, and different events such as the character sinking into the ground, the appearance of snow, and the killing of a different game animal, there must be reasons for each of these alternate details. This episode does not actually identify the central character, the host A'moyonts. A footnote merely states that he is "a little animal living underground" (Lowie 1924, 171). The term is absent from the Paiute dictionary by Edward Sapir (1992). The same dictionary does, however, translate Cunawab as Coyote.

Although the host's identity is not fully established, it is nonetheless possible to solve the main puzzle of the episode. We know that the fire hunt was common practice among the Native Americans of the Great Basin. There are also reports of big game being hunted in this way: "Northern Paiute in the area of Honey Lake, California, report that small herds of deer were occasionally driven to a low hill and then surrounded by several hunters. The brush around the hill was set afire and the deer moved either to the top of the hill or to an opening in the fire circle. They could then be shot from either vantage point" (Fowler 1986, 79). The deer species they hunted was *Odocoileus hemionus*, the mule deer. In the Great Basin, the bighorn sheep, *Ovis canadensis*, was also prey for all the peoples of the region (Fowler 1986, 80), although anthropologists have not specifically reported it being hunted by means of fire circles. Such hunting does seem to have occurred all the same.

Once again, the myth alludes to a type of hunting done by humans. Nonetheless, because the myth also has a moral purpose—preventing people from being burned accidentally—the story line must have a strategy and a nonhuman hero who can emerge at the end safe and sound. This character cannot be Coyote, who incarnates the human antihero in such circumstances.

The hero is Crow in the Kawaiisu version and a subterranean animal in the Paiute version. In fact, these two animals represent the two ways for an animal to escape from fire, other than running away. Some naturalists have looked into what happens to animals in a forest fire, and they sum up the possibilities as follows: "Deer, foxes, and bobcats run; birds and bats fly; and mice, lizards, snakes and salamanders go underground into burrows or under rocks and fallen logs as a fire approaches" (Moorman et al. n.d., 4). The ruminants in the myth cannot escape. They are surrounded by flames and usually die asphyxiated, as may be surmised from our descriptions of a fire hunt among the Pima, and as the following observer notes: "The majority of animals die from superheated gases that precede the fire front. Their respiratory systems get knocked out. Essentially, they suffocate" ("Angeles National Forest" 2009).

There is no way out for land animals that can only run. The other animals fly away or hide in the ground, as the Paiute episode explains. As for the other elements of the story—the snow that comes, the dragging away of the dead game—one must know the real identity of the central character of the episode to grasp their meaning. But there are good grounds to believe that reasons exist for these elements, as for all of the others.

The interethnic variants show how various real-life possibilities may be exploited from one version of the myth to another, according to circumstances. The Southern Paiute live in a more mountainous environment with heavy snowfall each year. Thus it is not surprising to see such a landscape appear in the myth. The mythical episodes are therefore rooted in the surroundings of the people who create and tell them. This does not mean, however, that differences between different versions are environmentally determined. Far from it, as seen in the variety of possibilities the same myth can exploit in a single environment. Humans know how to draw on their surroundings when they wish to pass on knowledge or teach a lesson.

The same holds true for the third and last Kawaiisu episode about the Bungling Host. This final episode stars a red-headed bird who plays host to Coyote. The way the bird prepares the food is as intriguing as in the previous cases.

COYOTE AND THE RED-HEADED BIRD

Red-headed Bird [unidentified] had a brush house. One day Coyote visited her. She[1] put a pot in the fire and, when the water was boiling, she put her head in it. This is why her head is red.

Soon there were suds like rice in the water, and Red-headed Bird gave them to Coyote. She said, "Eat some, and save a little for your children." Coyote put some of the suds in his net to carry them home. But when he got home, there was none left. He had eaten all of it along the way.

Coyote had invited Red-headed Bird to his house and promised to give her his star-shirt. The next day the Bird came over to visit him. He talked with her a little while. Then he said, "I don't have anything on hand to eat." He went and got a pot, put water in it, and put it on the fire. When the water boiled, he stuck his head in it. His head came off.

Red-headed Bird said to Coyote's wife, "I came to get his star-shirt." Coyote's wife answered, "He has no star-shirt, no nothing."

Red-headed Bird went home. (Zigmond 1980, 101)

This version published by Zigmond (1980, 101) is the only one we know. There are no other variants. It comes from the field notes of an anthropologist, Stephen Capannari, who took them down between 1947 and 1949.

The red-headed bird is unidentified. But Zigmond clarifies its identity in his book on ethnobotany when he explains the etymology of a plant, *Eriophyllum ambiguum* (woolly daisy). The plant bears the name *hu'uyaagahnivi*, which means 'the house of *hu'uyazi*', and the informants used the latter vernacular name for

Fig. 10. House finch.

a red-headed bird (Zigmond 1981, 31). Zigmond adds that the bird was later identified as the house finch, *Carpodacus mexicanus*.

The plant is thus named after the bird because, according to the Kawaiisu, the bird uses parts of the plant to build its nest. The house finch is known to line its nest with woolly materials (Bent et al. 1968, 295–96), and the plant's name, woolly daisy, is sufficiently self-explanatory to justify the Kawaiisu name and the bird's use of the plant.

House finches are also renowned for the coloring of their plumage, in particular the color pattern of the male, whose head, neck, and rump have an intense yellow to red pigmentation. In addition, the redder the male, the more it attracts the females: "Female House Finches prefer to mate with the reddest male available" (Hill 1993, 1–2).

In the mythical episode, the key element is the boiling water.

The aim, when recounting it, is to ensure that the listeners will not injure themselves when cooking with hot water. The other two episodes similarly sought to prevent people from harming themselves, either by slipping their bodies through thorn bushes—as children are wont to do—or by ending up in the midst of a fire through carelessness. Although a snake is not troubled by thorns, although a crow may escape by flying away, although a subterranean animal can burrow into the ground, and although the house finch may not fear hot water because its red head figuratively shows it has survived such an experience, the same is not true for humans, and this is shown by what happens to Coyote in every case.

Making water boil is a human endeavor. In the Great Basin, people traditionally knew how to cook by placing heated stones in a water-filled container (for example, among the Shoshone, "Boiling was done by dropping hot stones into a water-filled basket"; Murphy and Murphy 1986, 295). It may be that the pot placed over the fire in the mythical episode had been introduced post-contact.

In any case, the Kawaiisu cook a variety of seeds in this manner, including some, as in the myth, that swell up like rice in water. We have counted no fewer than thirty-four different species whose seeds are traditionally eaten by the Kawaiisu, in the book of ethnobotany by Zigmond (1981), which describes them. Some of them, especially *Lepidium lasiocarpum* (hairy-pod peppergrass), *Salvia* sp. (commonly known as chia), and *Stipa speciosa* (spear grass, needlegrass), have seeds whose volume increases considerably when placed in water. In particular, Kawaiisu informants themselves compare seeds from the second species to rice: "Boiled, the seeds swell 'like rice.' A cupful will fill a pot" (Zigmond 1981, 66). The plant might be the one that the myth alludes to in very similar terms: "There were suds like rice in the water" (Zigmond 1980, 101). Moreover, house finches feed on this type of seed.

Indeed, the bird is a granivore par excellence, and seeds from herbaceous plants make up over 85% of its diet: "The most thorough study of the house finch's diet was that made by F.E.L. Beal

(1907), who examined the contents of 1206 stomachs and found them to consist in the aggregate of weed seed 86.2 percent, fruit 10.5 percent, animal matter 2.4 percent, miscellaneous 0.9 percent" (Bent et al. 1968, 306).

Stipa speciosa is an herb whose seeds increase in volume when cooked in water, "like rice," and which house finches can feed on in Kawaiisu territory. An observer reports that during the pre-contact period it was undoubtedly the only kind of food available to house finches: "Before the settlement of the Pacific coast region it is evident that the linnet must have subsisted almost entirely upon the seeds of plants growing wild in the valleys and canyons" (Bent et al. 1968, 307). So now two questions remain. What does this bird have to do with water? And why does it bend its head down?

It is surprising perhaps to see just how many papers Euro-American ornithologists have written about the house finch's consumption of water (for example, Bartholomew and Cade 1956; MacMillen and Hinds 1998, etc.). In particular, this bird can consume up to 100% of its weight in water in twenty-four hours when the ambient temperature rises (Bent et al. 1968, 309). Consequently, "its distribution in the desert is clearly related to the presence of surface water" (Bartholomew and Cade 1956, 406).

One observer goes so far as to state that the fact of seeing a house finch is a sure sign of nearby water: "Most numerous about towns and cultivated lands, this species is by no means a stranger to uninhabited wastes and deserts. However, competent observers agree that the sight of a house finch is one of the surest signs that water is near" (Bent et al. 1968, 290).

House finches are associated with water and consume seeds. In some way, they must therefore cook them as a human would. Now, as unusual as it may seem, they can regurgitate their food, a phenomenon that may be observed in the natural state that the story seems to portray when Red-headed Bird lowers her head and seeds remain in the water and swell up "like rice." Indeed, house finches regurgitate by bending their heads down:

On the afternoon of March 19, 1925, a pair alighted on the edge of the table and my attention was soon attracted by a peculiar twittering call given by the female. It was rather unusual, so I watched them carefully and observed the male feed the female regurgitated food several times. His actions were much the same as those of any bird raising partly digested food from its crop; the head was bent sharply downward several times and the pellet was seen to rise up through the gullet. (Bent et al. 1968, 292–93)

Among house finches, the male can thus feed the female in the same way that both parents can regurgitate for their nestlings. This is simply their own way of cooking. The house finch not being excessively shy, this behavior can easily be observed in the natural state, as the last account shows.

From these facts, one may conclude that the episode of the Red-headed Bird has a good share of truth. The etymons of the mytheme are composed of behaviors specific to this kind of bird. As with other Kawaiisu episodes of the Bungling Host, this one teaches people how to avoid harming themselves or others. It also passes on knowledge about the story's central character and its habits.

4 While Bird Sings, Bear Cooks (Northwest Coast)

She [Cwot] planted the spray in the ground and began to sing. Thereupon the spray blossomed forth and berries appeared upon it.

—Charles Hill-Tout, "South-Eastern Tribes"

Bear went out and got two short maple-sticks. He built a fire, and stuck the sticks up close to the fire. Then he raised his foot, and the grease melted and ran down into the grease-pot. When it was full, he gave it to Raven to eat.

—Theresa Mayer, "Quileute Tales"

Franz Boas, an anthropologist of the late nineteenth and early twentieth centuries, is renowned for his work on Native North American cultures, particularly those of the Northwest Coast. He considered the mythemes quoted above—plus a third one about a seal—as being the most widespread and characteristic types of the Northwest Coast: "Perhaps the most widely spread type of these tales [the Bungling Host] is the one in which it is described how the host takes a part of his own body. . . . On the North Pacific coast this type occurs particularly in the form of the seal or bear heating his hands in front of the fire, and letting oil drip out of them into a dish. . . . Characteristic for the North

Pacific coast is also the production of food by the song of a bird" (Boas 1916, 694–95).

If we set aside Seal—to be discussed in the next chapter—a common thread joins Bird, the producer of berries, to Bear, the producer of grease, because both appear in the same mythologies of several Northwest Coast peoples, including the Nootka (or Nuu-chah-nulth), for example (Boas 1895), who occupy the western part of Vancouver Island, in Canada. Also significant is Crow, who incarnates the Trickster among many groups of the same culture area, particularly throughout almost the whole of the central and northern regions of the Northwest Coast (Hymes 1990, 594). Farther south, the role is played by Jay, followed by Coyote.

Both mythemes are so widespread that, after devoting the preceding chapters to the mythologies of different peoples (Innu, Tohono O'odham, and Kawaiisu), we wished this time to study corpuses, each one having a single motif, in order to deepen our overall understanding of the variants that have developed within each corpus. By so doing, we may later understand why some apparently trivial details matter a great deal to those who tell and pass on the myth. We are thinking here of the many variants about Bear, the producer of grease whose hands and feet are interchangeable, whereas the variants about Seal have the grease being produced only from his hands. The difference between the two is paramount because it involves very specific and distinct morphological features, as will be shown further on. By looking at the meaning of a motif, and not its geographic distribution, we may see things in a different light.

The Northwest Coast, or at least part of it, is often said to be North America's tropical rain forest. The climate has favored vegetation that is among the most diverse and extensive north of Mexico. This area is home to many peoples—"It involved 13 of Powell's (1891) linguistic families, represented in at least 45 distinct languages" (Thompson and Kinkade 1990, 30). Over time, these peoples have woven a complex web of relationships with the world of plants, which they still put to many uses: "The Native peoples used plants as sources of food, materials used in technology, medicines, and fuel, and they were concerned about the total vegetation of their environment as it related to the abundance of useful plants and game animals" (Suttles 1990, 21).

In an area where over forty species of fruit-bearing plants are harvested (Suttles 1990, 23), it is hardly surprising to see a mytheme about fruit production. Nor should we be surprised to find the same motif in other stories besides those of the Bungling Host, as Boas observed: "As indicated before, the incident [birds produce food by their song] is not confined to the Bungling Host tale" (Boas 1916, 696). The same goes for other motifs. The Native American mind loves to use and reuse the same themes in new combinations.

The Nootka, for example, integrate this motif into a myth about the Thunderbirds' rapture of the wife of Tlehmamit (Woodpecker). The abduction happens just after the hero's wife has finished preparing a meal of berries for his guests:

THUNDERBIRD AND TLEHMAMIT (EXCERPT)

At last Thunderbird gave up the game since he was unable to win and Tlehmamit invited him for a meal in his house. When they had sat down he told his wife Awip'a-ci'k (Hummingbird?) to prepare a meal. She took a small bowl and modestly and chastely walked behind Thunderbird to her chests and sang, "Berries, berries". Thereupon the bowl filled up at once although it was right in the middle of the winter. The Thunderbirds were very astonished when she served fresh berries to them. . . . So the second brother said to the eldest, "This is a precious woman and she is so beautiful. Let's steal her." (Boas 1974 [1895], 167)

Boas was unsure about the identity of the wife of Tlehmamit (Woodpecker), hence the question mark after his suggestion. Basic analysis can be used to find out who Awip'a-ci'k was. In the natural state, there is an extremely close relationship between woodpeckers and hummingbirds, an association so strong that it may explain the one in the myth. The following observation, from

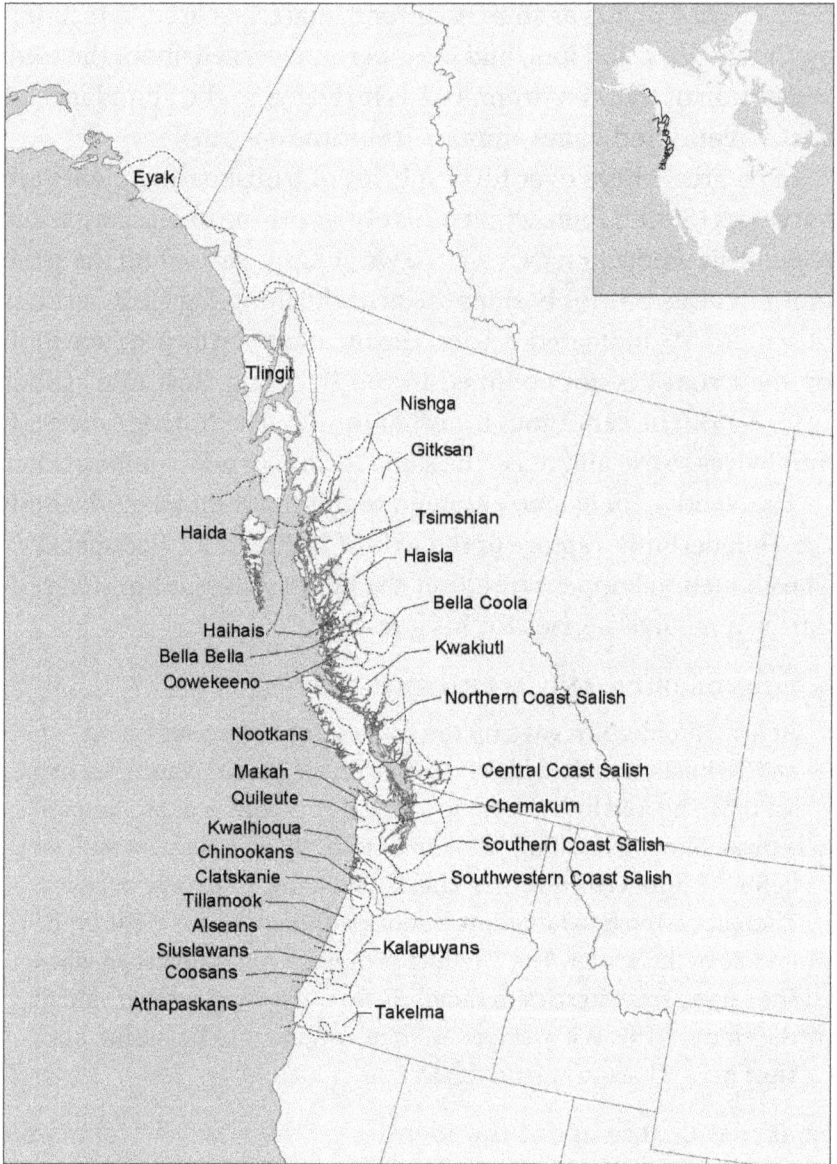

Fig. 11. Map of Geographic distribution of some Northwest Coast peoples. Archéotec Inc.

a document about the ruby-throated hummingbird (*Archilochus colubris*), which inhabits eastern Canada, and not western Canada like the rufous hummingbird (*Selasphorus rufus*), is nonetheless relevant because it can be applied to both species: "Holes made by the Yellow-bellied Sapsucker often release the sap of trees, which is also an important food source. The Ruby-throated Hummingbird is often seen gently buzzing a sapsucker in the expectation of being led to another food source" (De Kiriline Lawrence 2007 [1974]). Other studies show how hummingbirds use sapsuckers feeding sites in California (Sutherland et al. 1982). Hence Hummingbird has enough in common with Woodpecker to be his wife.

The extract from the Nootka myth also tells us about the attraction of rufous hummingbirds to some berry species like the salmonberry (*Rubus spectabilis*). A little further in the myth, Tlehmamit, to recover his wife, uses this berry to attract his wife and rescue her from her abductors: "Woodpecker said [to his ally Heron], 'I'll make a salmonberry bush, you change into a berry on it. When my wife will come to pick you, I'll carry her away'" (Boas 1974 [1895], 168).

Hummingbirds feed on nectar but are also attracted to any brightly-colored fruit, like those of the salmonberry. The next two comments, especially the second, show how hummingbirds are attracted not only to flowers, but also to fruits with vivid colors:

> William H. Kobbé (1900) says that . . . "they are particularly abundant about the flowering salmon berry bushes." (Bent et al. 1964a, 403)

> Mr. W.E. Parrott, of Sergief Island, had a large strawberry patch. . . . Time and again, so he told us, he had seen a hummingbird dash at one of the bright red berries, apparently under the impression that it was a flower, and the bird's bill would be thrust through the fruit, which, of course, was ruined. He had found a number of berries pierced in this way, and was puzzled to account for the damage until he saw a hummingbird in the act. (Bent et al. 1964a, 404)

These details are being presented so that we may clarify all the mysterious aspects of the myths we will present. To come back to the Bungling Host, and in keeping with the Nootka extract, we wish to highlight that the salmonberry appears in most variants when the species of berry served to the guests is specified. The host is never a hummingbird, at least not to the best of our knowledge:

Table 1. "Bird produces berries" versions

HOST	FOOD	TRICKSTER	NATION	SOURCE
Thrush	salmonberry	Born-to-be-the-sun, Raven	Kwakiutl	Boas and Hunt 1906
Thrush	salmonberry and huckleberry	Born-to-be-the-sun	Kwakiutl	Boas 1969 [1910]
Varied Thrush	salmonberry	Raven	Bella Coola	McIlwraith 1948
Thrush	salmonberry	Txämsem	Tsimshian	Boas 1916
Aihoa'qone (bird)	berries	Raven	Bella Coola	Boas 1974 [1895]
Aix'a'xonē' (bird)	salmonberry	Raven	Bella Coola	Boas 1898
Skwit (bird)	salmonberry	Bluejay	Coast Salish	Adamson 1934
Tsia'kwawa (bird)	salmonberry	Bluejay	Coast Salish	Adamson 1934
Cwot (bird)	blackberry	Raven	Salish	Hill-Tout 1907
Bird	salmonberry	Txämsem	Tsimshian	Boas 1902
Dedinye (bird)	huckleberry	Este·s	Dakelh (Carrier)	Jenness 1934
Bird	berries	Raven	Chilcotin	Farrand 1900

In the Bella Coola or Nuxalk variant, the host is the varied thrush (*Ixoreus naevius*). The Trickster is Raven, and the berries are from the salmonberry:

RAVEN AND VARIED THRUSH

Once upon a time Raven went to the home of Varied Thrush.

"I have come to call", he said.

Thrush, a woman, politely invited him to sit down for a meal. Then she took the box which she used for berry-picking, hung it on a projecting rafter outside the house, and began to sing; instantly a few berries appeared in the box. She sang four times, and when she had finished, the receptacle was full. Thrush placed the food before her guest, and Raven ate heartily. When it was time to leave, he picked up the box with what he had not consumed, and invited his hostess to come and collect it the following day.

On the morrow Thrush went to Raven's house, where he invited her to sit down for a meal. Then he made a hole in the corner of the house, placed the same food-box beneath it, and began to sing, imitating his guest's song. A few salmon berries were deceived and entered the receptacle. Again Raven sang, but this time the berries recognized the deception and the box was filled, not with fruit, but guano. Thrush was very angry.

"You tried to steal my method of gathering berries", she burst out.

Then she picked up her box and went home, leaving Raven discomfited. (McIlwraith 1948, vol. 2, 389)

The Bella Coola now occupy a village 120 kilometers inland from the Pacific Ocean, near the mouth of a river of the same name, in southern British Columbia, Canada. The Bella Coola traditionally fished and also hunted several species of marine mammals (seals) and terrestrial mammals (mountain goats). They also gathered wild plant foods: "Over 135 plants species were traditionally used for food, materials, and medicines. . . . Plant foods were numerous and varied" (Kennedy and Bouchard 1990a, 325).

Like the Tohono O'odham we have seen, the Bella Coola attached a special significance to the number four; hence, a song is repeated four times in the myth to get the desired effect. For example, the fourth day after the September full moon, preparations would begin for the special ceremonies held from November to March each year; one of those ceremonies, the *kusuit*, would last four days; the shamans received their powers from a supernatural woman who among other things taught them four songs; Bella Coola cosmology posits the existence of four worlds (sometimes five), which exist one above the other; and so on (Kennedy and Bouchard 1990a).

As in the Nootka variant, the Bella Coola version also refers to a berry container, the former featuring a chest and the latter a box. The Northwest Coast peoples deftly practised the arts of carpentry and woodcarving, and it was indeed common for them to make various containers for gathering or keeping of wild plant foods.

> [Tlingit] The most commonly preserved berries were blueberries, elderberries, strawberries and highbush cranberries. These might be slowly cooked until they could be formed into a cake and dried, or might be put up in a wooden box with grease. (De Laguna 1990b, 212)

> [Kwakiutl or Kwak'waka'wakw] Salmonberries were eaten fresh or boiled, mashed, and dried in cedar wood frames for winter use. The resulting cakes were rolled up and stored in wooden boxes. (Turner and Bell 1973, 291)

> [Nootka] In most instances, the fruits were prepared for storage by drying in cakes, but in the case of crabapples and bog cranberries it is likely that the Nitinaht, like other Northwest Coast groups, stored them in boxes under water or oil. (Turner et al. 1983, 15)

In the Nootka and Bella Coola versions, as in all the other ones, the host is a woman. Clearly, this detail is not unintended. Here, as among the Kawaiisu and other indigenous peoples, cooking is women's work. A comment specific to the Squamish—who form another Northwest Coast culture, this time spread along the coast itself in the area of the present-day city of Vancouver—may easily apply more generally to all of these nations:

Preparation of plant foods by the Squamish was exclusively a woman's job. Indeed, one of the most "desirable" things that a Squamish woman could aspire to be was a "good berry-picker". The Squamish believed that if a female child had a mole on her back that child would be a good berry-picker (because berries were packed in baskets on women's backs). She was given the "nickname" *yeks*, a deliberately altered pronunciation of the term *syek*, "any berry or root already picked or gathered". (Bouchard and Turner 1976, 131–32)

It is worth remembering that the Nootka myth has Hummingbird tirelessly repeating the words "berries, berries" to produce the desired food item. Although the Nootka and the Squamish belong to completely different linguistic and cultural families— respectively the Wakashan and Salishan families—the same doctrine of signatures is at work in both cases. On the one hand, the name "Berry" is given to a young girl who bears the sign of a good berry picker (a birth mark that looks like a berry and makes one think of the berries that a woman carries on her back). On the other, an incantation ("berries, berries") is the signature used to get the desired effect.

Incantations are omnipresent in the variants of the culture area. Very often, they are onomatopoeias that imitate sounds made by the bird. Furthermore, the sounds form the name given to it, as in the following Salish variant:

BUNGLING HOST

Bluejay had a home of his own. One day he asked his cousin Skwik-wi'kʷ, to go with him to visit a certain family. They went up the river to visit Skwit (a bird). They went into the house. In a little while, Skwit told his children to take their baskets and get some salmon-berries. The children kept saying, "Kwit, kwit" and soon had a great many berries. They came home with their baskets full. Bluejay ate as many berries as he could hold. Then he went to his canoe and got in. He called back, "Come to visit me." He reached home.

Next day, Bluejay watched for his visitor. After a while, he saw him coming. Then he told his cousin to clean the seat. Skwit and his children landed. Soon Bluejay told his own children to go out and look for some berries. The five children said, "Kwit, kwit," but they could not find any berries. Then Skwit said to Bluejay, "You are making your children suffer." His children then went out. They said, "Kwit, kwit," and returned with five baskets of berries. They gave them to Bluejay. Then they left. (Adamson 1934, 3–4)

Among some Salish peoples, like the one who provided this legend (Upper Chehalis), myths are very often based on a five-element model: "Like the myths of the Chinookans and others to the south and east, Southwestern Coast Salish myths are characterized by the pattern number five: five brothers, five actions, five objects" (Hajda 1990, 512).

Other Bungling Host versions also link the host's name to the song of the bird that personifies him or her. For example, in a Bella Coola version, the bird is called Aihoa'qone and sings "Aihoaqa'na qa'naqa'na" (Boas 1974 [1895], 404). In a Salish version, the bird is called Tsia'kwawa and its offspring repeat "Tsia'kwawa, kele'tewa" to produce berries (Adamson 1934, 4).

It would be hard at this point to try to identify the bird species—when unspecified—solely by its song as reported in the myths. According to some anthropologists, the bird that produces berries in various Bungling Host versions is the Swainson's thrush (*Catharus ustulatus*), although Thomas McIlwraith (1948, vol. 2, 389), as we have seen, points instead to the varied thrush (*Ixoreus naevius*), whenever it does not appear alternately as a hummingbird in other myths: "L.M. [an informant] points out that the Squamish people believed the Swainson's thrush did help to ripen the salmonberries, by singing its own 'song.' This 'song,' which imitates the sound made by the Swainson's thrush, was recorded . . . and transcribed . . . xwe-xwe-xwe-ní—ye xwe-xwe-xwe-ní—ye" (Kennedy and Bouchard 1976a, 98–99; see

Fig. 12. Swainson's thrush.

also Bouchard and Kennedy 2002, 507n26).The same informant believed the bird's name, Xwet, was onomatopoeic (Kennedy and Bouchard 1976a, 98).

The bird species can vary somewhat, while always being a kind of thrush in the Bungling Host stories, and so can the berry species. In most cases, the stories feature salmonberries, but we have also sporadically encountered huckleberries (*Vaccinium ovatum*; *Vaccinium parvifolium*) and blackberries (*Rubus ursinus*), as in the Salish variant that opens this chapter and appears below in full:

Raven once upon a time went to pay his sister Cwot a visit. She welcomes him, and he bids her call in her children. She goes outside and plucks a spray of blackberry bush and returns to the house with it. She planted the spray in the ground and began to sing. Thereupon the spray blossomed forth and berries appeared upon it. Cwot collects them in a dish and sets them before Raven. He is much gratified and eats his fill of them. After his meal he leaves, telling her as he goes that she must come and see him soon. She promises that she will do so.

Some little time after she went to see him. When she arrived Raven very unctuously bade her welcome. "Come in, come in, dear sister, I am so glad to see you. You will have some dinner with me. What will you have, blackberries, raspberries, salmon berries, or any other kind? I have them all, so take your choice." She replies, "Oh, it doesn't matter what kind; serve me with any that you like." "Very well," returns he, and goes out and plucks, as he had seen her do, a spray of blackberry bush. He brings it into the house and sticks it in the ground and begins to dance and sing. His neighbours hear him and say: "What's up with Raven? Listen to him fooling." Cwot, too, was greatly amused at his antics, and endeavoured to hide her face in her hands to prevent his seeing her smiles. Raven sung and danced a long time, but the berry-spray bore no fruit nor made any growth. After awhile Cwot said to him, "Brother, stand aside and let me try. You don't seem to have the power." Raven was very glad to be relieved of his task. Cwot now sings her mystery song three times. It sounded to him like the song of the "berry-bird."

Immediately the bough began to grow and bloom and the fruit to appear and ripen. "There," said Cwot, "now eat your fill; I don't want any." Raven greedily ate of the berries and took no notice of his crying, hungry children who also wanted some. (Hill-Tout 1907, 348–49)

This last version even has a list of the kinds of berries that might attract a thrush. The bird Cwot again seems to correspond to the berry-bird par excellence—the thrush—because of its song. Ornithologists have listed the fruits consumed by the Swainson's thrush (*Catharus ustulatus*), and their lists include most of the aforementioned ones: "Fruits include elderberries (*Sambucus* sp.), blackberries and raspberries (*Rubus* spp.), twinberries (*Lonicera* sp.), huckleberries (*Vaccinium* sp.) . . . and other wild fruits" (Mack and Yong 2000, 10).

When Raven tries to produce the same kind of berries, the result in some versions is only a pile of dung: guano in the Bella Coola variant already quoted (McIlwraith 1948, vol. 2, 389); unspecified dung in the Chilcotin variant (Farrand 1900, 18), as well as in two other Bella Coola versions (Boas 1974 [1895], 404; Boas 1898, 93); and dust in a Dakelh variant (Jenness 1934, 209). In some versions, Raven even makes a slip of the tongue and thereby reaps what he sows:

> [Chilcotin version] The next time he tried to fill the basket by wishing, he made a slip of the tongue, and, instead of saying "I wish this basket were full of berries!", said, "I wish this basket were full of dung!" and it became full of dung to the top. (Farrand 1900, 18)

> [Bella Coola version] Finally he sang "mɛnk'" and the box was full of excrements. (Boas 1898, 94)

The common raven (*Corvus corax*) likes to seek out and feed on carrion and refuse, being aptly described as "a generalist omnivore eating live meat, eggs, insects, grains, fruit, garbage, and carrion" (Boarman and Heinrich 1999, 5). In the myth, it is quite logical that dung and not berries are produced, all the more so because humans seem to have little use for the bird. For them, it serves no worthwhile purpose. In one of the few papers on Native knowledge about local wildlife, several pages are devoted to the bird's presence in mythology as a Trickster, but no human use is mentioned (Kennedy and Bouchard 1976a, 88–95).

In this analysis, we are now left with the core of the mytheme, namely a bird (more often a thrush) that produces berries (usually salmonberries) by singing an especially onomatopoeic song. According to a Squamish informant, the Swainson's thrush "helped" salmonberries to ripen by singing its song (Kennedy and Bouchard 1976a, 98). Among the Squamish, the plant gives its name to the months of April ("when the salmonberry shoots are collected") and even May ("time of salmonberry") (Bouchard and Turner 1976, 113–14). The Nitinaht of Vancouver Island likewise gave May this name because "the sprouts are ready at this time" (Turner et al. 1983, 124).

Salmonberry sprouts were eaten. They were the first plant foods to be consumed in spring, and their availability after the lean winter months was eagerly anticipated. The Salish of Vancouver Island even held special ceremonies before eating them (Turner and Bell 1971, 88). The sprouts grew so fast, at least according to Natives, that this growth led to a practice that is again consistent with the doctrine of signatures: "It was believed that if a mother chewed up salmonberry sprouts and spat them on the head of her child, he would grow as rapidly as the young shoots" (Turner and Bell 1973, 291). In some variants of the myth, including a Kwakiutl one, the salmonberry develops stage-by-stage, and each stage may be a speeded-up version of how growth is seen in nature. In other words, the rapid growth in the myth is based on real observation: "As soon as this was done, Thrush put on her Thrush mask; and after she had put it on, she sat down by the side of one box and sang the Thrush song. When she sang the Thrush song the first time, the salmonberry bush began to bud; when she sang again, the salmonberry-blossoms opened; when she sang again, they became berries; and when she sang again, they were ripe" (Boas and Hunt 1906, 148). In another Kwakiutl version, Thrush repeats his song to one plant species and then another, the first one being a salmonberry bush and the second a huckleberry bush. It is known that these two species ripen one after the other in July.

The mytheme, a bird that produces berries, undoubtedly owes its etymon to observation of a natural relationship between the arrival of a bird species and the concomitant growth of a plant it feeds on. The mytheme is also closely linked to the song of this species, which is undoubtedly a means to locate salmonberry bushes in addition to being a natural clock that indicates when they appear. The arrow of causality must now be worked out. The most cautious informants say that the thrush "helps" the berries to ripen. The myth itself is less cautious, maintaining that the song of the birds acts on the plant.

Long disparaged as nonsense, the theory that music affects plant growth has been much written about since the 1950s. This literature has been reviewed in an article from a very serious botanical journal:

> The perception and response of plants to sound, more specifically music, has been a part of folklore (see Weinberger and Graefe, 1973) and the source of inspiration for countless primary and secondary school student science fair projects beginning in the 1940s (Klein and Edsall 1965; personal observation). The influence of music, a complex mixture of notes, tones, amplitudes, and harmonics, on plant growth has been the subject of scientific debate for decades. Singh and Ponniah (1955a, b, 1963) reported on the stimulatory influence of music on plant growth in a number of species. Klein and Edsall (1965) reported no influence of a diverse selection of music, from classical to rock and roll, on the growth of *Tagetes erecta*. L. Weinberger and colleagues conducted a number of studies on the influence of both music and single frequency sound, both in the audible and ultrasound range, on plant growth and seed germination and reported that sound can influence plant growth (Weinberger and Measures, 1968; Measures and Weinberger, 1970 . . .). Most recently, Creath and Schwartz (2004) reported music increased the rate of seed germination in zucchini (*Cucurbita pepo* L.) and okra (*Abelmoschus esculentus* (L.) Moench). (Telewski 2006, 1469)

To our knowledge, no one has ever studied how bird song may affect plant development. What Native Americans affirm in the myth is as serious as what Western researchers have debated in scientific papers. One may also go further and ascribe similar intentions to both parties. The latter pursue this avenue of research to learn more about the world and also, very often, for economic gain, insofar as advances will increase productivity. The aim is therefore to find economic applications.

Native people likewise feel a need to explain the world. Nor do they ignore the practical applications of such knowledge. Indeed, one very often encounters cases where they use signatures to try to control the course of events. As for their explanation of the world, it rests on the assumption that nothing is done gratuitously by the living things around us. This is how bird songs are interpreted. If one sees things from a bird's vantage point, its song clearly causes berries to grow and ripen and the entire plant to develop. Otherwise, what use is it? I am a bird. When I arrive in the spring and begin to sing, the salmonberry begins to sprout.

We have already discussed this type of perception or explication where the same phenomena or events are interpreted differently according to one's point of view. Here, Natives give a meaning to Bird and his song, which the Trickster fails to imitate perfectly. The latter represents a human, and a human cannot produce berries by singing. A few berries are tricked by Raven's imitation and come forth in the Bella Coola version already quoted (McIlwraith 1948, vol. 2, 389), but this oddity may easily be put down to the common raven's great talents for mimicry, which almost fool the berries: "Given the great variety of calls ravens make, it is easy to assume some of them are mimics. . . . However, birds reared in isolation can be taught to mimic a variety of sounds, including to say 'nevermore'" (Boarman and Heinrich 1999, 9).

The second major mytheme, which is very widespread in the Northwest Coast culture area according to Boas, is the grease-producing Bear. It can be understood exactly the same way as the first one, i.e., by seeing things from Bear's viewpoint. This viewpoint is supported by a bear behavior we will see further on.

Under this mytheme we have grouped all the episodes, whatever their cultural origin—not only from the Northwest Coast but also from the Subarctic, the Northeast, and other culture areas—which feature a bear who produces grease from his feet and, by extension, from his hands. In so doing, we have not ignored some of the episodes where meat and not grease comes from the same limbs of the animal. The reasons for defining the mytheme in this way will become clear further on.

The Quileute episode is representative of the mytheme in its broad outline. The Quileute, whose current population stands at around five hundred, live in at least two villages within a reservation along the Pacific coast in the United States, in the state of Washington. They are still engaged in fishing, traditionally their main means of subsistence. Part of their diet also came from big game hunting (Powell 1990). This is how they knew about Bear, the host of this episode. Raven is still the Trickster:

RAVEN GOES TO BEAR'S HOUSE

Once upon a time Raven went to Bear's house to get something to eat. After he had been there for a little while, Bear went out and got two short maple-sticks. He built a fire, and stuck the sticks up close to the fire. Then he raised his foot, and the grease melted and ran down into the grease-pot. When it was full, he gave it to Raven to eat, and said, "Raven, what do you want,—dog-meat, or man-meat, or elk-meat?" Raven replied, "I never eat dog-meat or man-meat. I'll take elk-meat."—"All right", said Bear, and he took a big dish and filled it with elk-meat. Raven ate a little and then stopped, because, he said, he wanted to carry the rest home. Before leaving, he told Bear to come to his house on the morrow to get his plate, and then he, Raven, would give him plenty to eat. He went down the river in his canoe. As soon as he was out of sight, he went ashore and ate all the meat. There was only a small piece left in the pot. Then he went home.

Very early next morning Bear went to Raven's house. When he came, Raven built a fire, and then went out and got two short sticks, which he put in front of the fire. Raising his foot, he said to Bear, "What do you want,—dog-meat, man-meat, or elk-meat?" His foot was being burnt to the very bone, and still no grease came out. Seeing this, his wife said, "Now, old man, what are you going to do? Your foot is burning up." Bear watched it all, and laughed fit to die; then he went home and left them. (Mayer 1919, 259)

Table 2. "Bear produces grease" versions

HOST	FOOD	TRICKSTER	NATION	SOURCE
Bear	grease from heel	Wiskedjak (Gray Jay)	Algonquin	Tenasco 1980
Bear	slice of sole	Rabbit	Mi'kmaq	Leland 1884; see Rand 1894
Bear	grease from hands	Raven	Tlingit	Swanton 1909
Bear	grease from feet	Bluejay	Coast Salish	Farrand 1902
Bear	grease from feet	Raven	Quileute	Mayer 1919
Bear	grease from hands	Raven	Nootka	Jones and Bosustow 1981
Bear	grease from hands	Raven	Nootka	Boas 1974 [1895]
Black bear	food from sole	Bluejay	Chinook	Boas 1894
Bear	grease from hands	Raven	Coast Salish	Griffin 1992
Bear	grease from hands	Bluejay	Coast Salish	Adamson 1934
Grizzly bear	grease from hands	Coyote	Coast Salish	Adamson 1934

Bear	meat, grease from hands	Bluejay	Coast Salish	Adamson 1934
Bear	grease from heel	Rabbit	Catawba	Speck 1913
Bear	slice from foot	Rabbit	Passamaquoddy	Mooney 1900
Bear	grease from hands	Raven	Tahtlan	Teit 1919
Black bear	grease from fore-paws	Coyote	Thompson	Hill-Tout 1899
Black bear	grease from hands	Coyote	Thompson	Teit 1898
Black bear	grease from hands	Coyote	Thompson	Teit 1912a

Indeed, Bear is the host. Without the original version, we cannot easily identify the species. One detail, however, seems to indicate a brown bear or grizzly (*Ursus arctos*), which used to be present in the region, at least in its southeastern corner. Bear offers Raven three kinds of meat: man meat, dog meat, and elk meat. The Quileute knew dogs before the contact period and used them for their wool ("*wool-bearing dogs*"; Powell 1990, 433). A dog, like a man, could be attacked by bears, but the grizzly, known for its ferocity, was feared more than the American black bear (*Ursus americanus*), which was also present. Raven, as the Trickster, rejects the first two kinds of meat, because a human would not touch either (except perhaps ceremonially, as reported for dog meat among neighboring peoples), and opts for the meat of an elk (*Cervus elaphus*), a game animal valued by grizzlies and humans alike. Grizzlies, much more than black bears, hunt this member of the deer family: "The grizzlies of the Canadian Rockies are quite carnivorous and hunt moose, elk, mountain sheep, goats, and even black bears" (Banfield 1974, 309).

Our corpus also has a variant where the host is a grizzly (Adamson 1934, 249). It comes from Northwest Coast Native Americans, specifically the Coast Salish of the southwest of this culture area. They also inhabit the state of Washington and are southern neighbors of the Quileute.

Other, more secondary aspects of the mytheme may also be fleshed out. For example, Raven uses a canoe to go down the river. Most Quileute families would overwinter at river mouths and, come summer, move inland and upriver or follow the coast to ancestral hunting, fishing, and gathering grounds. Here, the mountains of the hinterland can be 1,500 to 2,500 meters high. River transport was by means of a dugout canoe, i.e., a boat hollowed out of a cedar trunk. They were made in several sizes—at least six have been recorded—and the model was the Nootka type (Powell 1990, 433).

Another plant use appears in the myth when Bear takes maple sticks and pushes them into the ground near the fire. They are undoubtedly roasting-sticks because elk meat is mentioned a bit further. The Quileute had five main societies, including one for hunters, and each of them held its own ceremonies. Hunting therefore played a major role: "Thought to antedate the introduction of the other groups, the hunter's society is of Quileute origin" (Powell 1990, 433).

Elk meat, like the meat of other big game, was eaten either fresh or dried (or smoked). Anthropological details are lacking on cooking preparation among the Quileute, but unsurprisingly, like many other peoples we know first hand in North America, dried or smoked meat was put on a wooden spit and heated near a fire before being consumed with a bit of grease. For this purpose, grease was highly valued, if not almost a necessity. Finally, we should stress the role of the various maple species in the Northwest Coast: "Next to the conifers, the maples—both *macrophyllum* (broadleaf) and *circinatum* (vine maple)—are perhaps the most useful trees in the Northwest. . . . Reagan gives the word hkats-to-ah-put for the Quileute and says that the tree is very common and the wood widely used" (Gunther 1945, 39–40).

The Quileute episode of the grease-producing bear does not easily fit into the classification that Boas proposed. He divided the similar Bungling Host mythemes about Bear into two categories: (1) the main host (Seal or Bear) lets the grease drip from his hands; and (2) an animal (Bear, Deer, etc.) cuts his hands or feet (Boas 1916, 695–7). In the Quileute variant (Mayer 1919, 259)—which Boas did not know—Bear lets the grease drip from his feet without cutting them. A more important element, for basic analysis: by no means can the species that represents the host be separated from the way it produces food. For this reason, it is paramount—to grasp the meaning of the mytheme or at least to find its source by ascertaining its etymon—to focus on one species, one food, and one body part.

In the case of Bear, the body part is one of its members. In the Quileute episode, his rear member is brought closer to the fire. In the following Nootka episode—a variant that cannot be ignored at this point—his frontal member is brought closer.

BEAR AND RAVEN

Bear invited Raven for a meal. He lit a big fire, put a bowl close beside it and held his hands above it. So grease dripped from his hands into the bowl. Then he roasted salmon, which he served to Raven with grease.

After this Raven invited Bear. When the latter went to Raven's house, he laughed because he knew that he would try to imitate him. Raven made a big fire, placed a bowl close beside it and held his hands above it. He was waiting that grease should drip down, but nothing came out. He turned them and shook them, but no grease came out. His hands were only burned black. Because of this Raven has black wings and feet. (Boas 1974 [1895], 172–73)

The Nootka of Vancouver Island are known for their hunting of marine mammals. In autumn, however, they mainly fish for salmon—sockeye, chinook, and coho (Arima and Dewhirst 1990), hence Bear's use of roasted salmon for the meal he offers to Raven. Fish are very often associated with bears, and with grease, in the Northwest Coast. For example, the Makah, who live immediately next to the Nootka to the south, had this custom: "When a man went fishing he caught one and threw it in the woods, saying 'Oh, Bear, here is your fish'" (Gunther 1936, 114). Among the same people, when the boys of some high-ranking families were training to become hunters, it was notably said that "They ate only dried fish and grease" (Gunther 1936, 116).

In the Nootka myth, Bear roasts the salmon. This takes us back to the way Bear prepared his elk meat in the Quileute variant, i.e., using a roasting-stick. The Squamish used roasting-sticks to cook salmon, and presumably so did the Nootka: "Any salmon, or any 'trout', could be barbecued. The barbecuing sticks used were either single or forked, about three or four feet [1 meter] in length, and made from red cedar (sometimes vine maple could be used for this same purpose)" (Kennedy and Bouchard 1976b, 80). When speaking of the black bear, the same Squamish would likewise say "Bear! He's tyee of the land. He's fisherman" (Kennedy and Bouchard 1976a, 16).

Everyone agrees that bears, be they grizzlies or black bears, love to fish. In the myth, Bear also eats his game meat with grease, a highly popular practice throughout the Northwest Coast, and elsewhere, where Natives would preserve their meat or fish by drying and very often macerating it in oil or grease.

Bear has a special technique to obtain this grease. The last two episodes tell us he can hold his hands or his feet close to a heat source. The next episode, from the Coast Salish, exploits another possibility where he cuts his feet. It provides a counterpart to the Coast Salish episode about the berry-producing bird who received Bluejay.

After his recovery Bluejay set out to visit Bear. He got to Bear's house and went inside. "Sit down, old man," Bear said. After a while Bear got a knife and cut some meat from his feet. There was a lot of fat on Bear. He cooked the meat on a big rock and gave it to Bluejay. Bluejay ate it; it was very good. Then he started home. "Come to my house, come to my house," he called back.

Bear returned Bluejay's visit. After a while Bluejay heated some rocks. Then he sat down and started to cut some flesh off his feet. His poor little feet began to draw up; he had cut through the muscles. "Uh, uh," he peeped like a chicken. Bear worked at Bluejay's feet to heal them and rubbed him to bring his breath back. Then he cut some flesh off his own feet. He had only to rub them a bit to make them normal again. He left the meat for Bluejay and went home. (Adamson 1934, 345)

There are still other possibilities. If one considers all of the episodes where a bear produces grease with one of its limbs, one ends up with the following permutations: a bear (grizzly or black bear) gets grease, meat, or both by (1) warming its feet, (2) warming its hands, (3) cutting its feet, (4) cutting its hands, and (5) piercing its heel (see the summaries of the variants above).

All these possibilities flow from the same paradigm. To understand it, we must also discuss a series of beliefs to the effect that a bear will last through the winter, as we were told by an Innu from Quebec, by feeding "on the skin of its hands, which it eats." Non-Native trappers say the same thing: "Some believe that dormant bears are nourished by 'sucking their paws'" (Matson 1967, 44). The anthropologist Alfred Hallowell (1926, 27–31) found the same belief throughout the eastern Algonquian area, and the anthropologist Frank Speck also reported it among the Innu: "Every person questioned among these bands will confirm the belief that the bear sucks his forepaws while sleeping. They maintain that the proof of this fact is that when the animal is killed in winter (in a winter den) this paw is always at the mouth and that the skin of the sole is raw" (1977 [1935], 99–100). Alberta and British Columbia Natives likewise thought "that the feet of bears are sore and inflamed when they leave their dens in early spring" (Hallowell in Rogers 1974, 672).

It is known that all bear species have forefeet and hindfeet with especially fatty pads, and, even more to the point, that they lose their foot pads during the winter. This takes us back to the mytheme about the caribou that, over a continuous cycle, loses the fat it has on its back and regains it later during the year. The following—a description of the feet of *Ursus arctos*—also essentially applies to *Ursus americanus* (Fig. 13).

> Forefoot. . . . Jutting outward, a blackish, posterior external callus rests on a thick fatty pad. . . . The callus leaves no footprint because it does not touch the ground during walking. Hairless, evenly blackish, perfectly smooth, the palm has the shape of a rectangle with rounded angles; it rests on a thick panniculus adiposus. . . .

> Hindfoot. . . . The heel and the sole strictly speaking form a surface 0.180 [m] long in the male and 0.160 [m] long in the female. It is in reality a huge callus, a little broader at the front end than at the back end, black and rather shiny, with white mottling . . . , smooth in its entirety, and sometimes marked by shallow cracks or grooves especially on old subjects. Underneath, separating it from the tendons and the muscles, lies a thick panniculus adiposus. (Couturier 1954, 66)

Bears have panniculi adiposi and muscles under their forefeet and hindfeet. These are the same parts they use in all the episodes we have seen, either when warming the corresponding limb or when cutting it. There is one ultimate proof that bears use this as a food source: it is gone when they emerge at winter's end: "A recent finding, as reported in the *Journal of Mammalogy* by Lynn L. Rogers, is that black bears shed their foot pads during hibernation. . . . . Mr. Kolenosky, who has pursued this study, writes

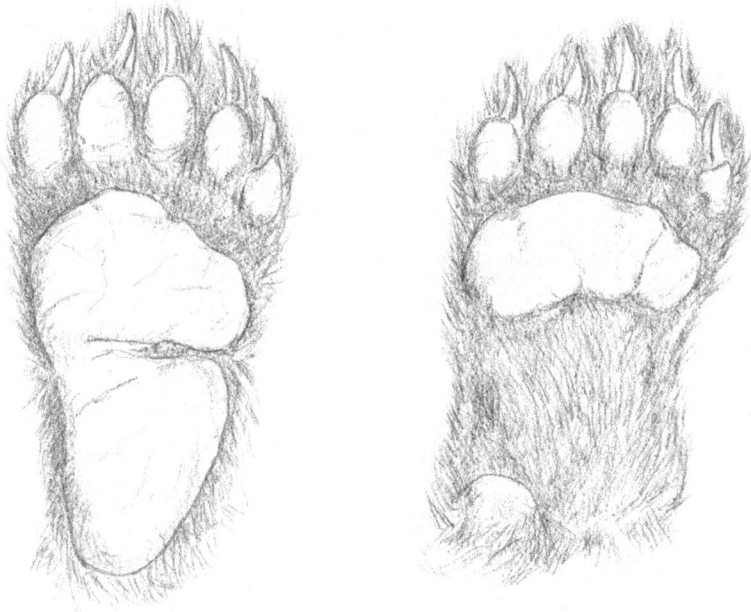

Fig. 13. Feet of the American black bear.

that at the time of shedding 'the pads are quite tender, and this may partially explain the reluctance of bears to move any great distance shortly after spring emergence'" (Wooding 1982, 88). Still skeptical? Read what Lynn Rogers concludes, based on her field observations: "Portions of old foot pads were found in two scats near entrances of dens in the spring of 1972. This suggests that aboriginal reports of bears licking and eating their pads were correct" (Rogers 1974, 673).

The myth of a bear producing grease from its foot is based on real observation of the loss of foot pads by bears. This etymon also enables us to explain why some versions of the mytheme, like the last one we quoted, highlight the bear's ability to recuperate (unlike the Trickster, who even dies in some variants):

[Salish version] He had only to rub them a bit to make them normal again. (Adamson 1934, 345)

[Chinook version] Then he rubbed over the wounds, and they were healed. (Boas 1894, 180)

[Algonquin version] The bear . . . suddenly stabbed his heel! Pure grease flowed out and into the frying pan. He quickly rubbed his heel and the grease stopped. (Tenasco 1980, 64)

Lynn Rogers, in the *Journal of Mammalogy*, also reports cases of bears bleeding because their footpads have been partially lost or improperly detached: "Freshly exposed pads . . . seemed to be sensitive and easily injured. . . . The feet of one bear bled slightly" (1974, 672). Finally, as in the myth, the sensitivity disappears and the epidermis becomes keratinized (Rogers 1974, 672). The bear always manages to heal itself, in a way, and recuperates.

In some variants, the myth is also even more specific about the origin of the grease, which drips not from the hands but from the toes to be precise, as in this Thompson Salish version: "In a little while the Bear's claws began to drip with liquid fat" (Hill-Tout 1899, 578). As one would expect, bear toes also show the presence of calluses (Fig. 13), which bears lose when they lose their other foot pads: "Plantar pads were shed as several pieces; digital pads sometimes were shed as single units" (Rogers 1974, 672).

In addition to enticing us to discover its etymon, the mytheme about the Bear who produces grease sometimes provides us with an odd ending: brief anatomical lessons that are so obvious that they seem to have a role, by reverse logic, of showing everything else to be true. These seals of authenticity, which appear in several other types of myths and which we will henceforth call by this term, apply here either to the host or to the Trickster who, following a successful or unsuccessful performance in the myth, is attributed certain specific characteristics.

[Quinault version] If all this had not happened, there would still be plenty of fat on the bear's feet . . . ; as it is, there is very little. (Farrand 1902, 88)

[Salish version] This is why, today, Raven's hands are thin claws covered with scales. (Griffin 1992, 55)

[Salish version] Today one can still see where Bluejay's hands are cracked open [after having held them over the fire]. (Adamson 1934, 368)

[Nootka version] And that's why ravens have crooked fingers! (Jones and Bosustow 1981, 101)

[Nootka version] Because of this Raven has black wings and feet. (Boas 1974 [1895], 173)

[Thompson version] And thus it is that the Coyote's paws are contracted and bent to this very day. (Hill-Tout 1899, 579)

In an article entirely about explanatory motifs in Native American myths north of Mexico, Thomas Waterman concludes that this element is always an addition to the myth: "The explanations, on the contrary, seem to be purely secondary to the story-plots. . . . In other words . . . , the story is the original thing, the explanation an after-thought" (1914, 41). Actually, as shown earlier, an explanatory motif is used to affirm the truth of the story: if such and such is true, then so is everything stated beforehand.

5   Seal Roasts His Hands (Northwest Coast)

> Raven, who lived in one part of the country, had a sister named Seal, who lived with her large family in another part. One day, Raven determined to visit his sister; so taking his canoe he set out. Upon his arrival, Seal set about preparing a meal for him. She did this by roasting her hands before the fire and catching the oil from them as it dropped into a dish.
>
> —Charles Hill-Tout, "Ethnology of the Siciatl"

Franz Boas (1916, 694) considered the mytheme "Seal roasts his hands" to be characteristic of the Northwest Coast. It is in fact exclusive to this culture area. Even the few transformations it has undergone are confined to the same area and a few very immediate neighboring cultures. It is most often associated with the Bungling Host motif, and sometimes appears in other stories. Its proposition is simple. There is a subject: Seal (or Sea Lion). And there is a predicate: obtaining grease by exposing one's hands to a heat source.

This is not the only way Seal (or Sea Lion) obtains food. In some Bungling Host episodes, Seal kills one of his children, who then comes back to life. In another, Sea Lion cuts himself in the side. In the preceding chapter, we deliberately omitted Bird's or Bear's different ways of getting food—other than by singing or by using feet or hands. Because these different ways are so complex and diverse, they will be presented and studied further on.

Not many of these episodes concern marine mammals like seals and sea lions, and all of them come from the Northwest Coast or nearby. We will thus have less trouble describing and comparing them.

The opening quote comes from the Salish people and is an incomplete version—the recorded story does not mention the guest trying to imitate the host. It is in fact part of another myth. Nonetheless, it does set the general tone of the mytheme by presenting the two main characters: the host, Seal, and the Trickster, here Raven.

The Northern Coast Salish, who provide this variant, live in an area that lies immediately east of Vancouver Island and is separated from it by the Strait of Georgia. This area covers a coastal ecosystem that borders on the more forested inland ecosystems where subalpine tracts may rise to elevations of over 1,000 meters. This may explain why the myth refers to two distinct parts of the country: one that is home to Raven, a species that flies over the land; and another, more marine setting that is home to Seal and his big family. Travel from one to the other was by canoe: "Travel was primarily by water, using a number of canoe types, ranging from narrow, one- or two-man trolling canoes to war canoes designed to carry 20 men" (Kennedy and Bouchard 1990b, 446–47).

The next version is of Bella Coola origin. The Bella Coola inhabit an area north of the Northern Coast Salish (see fig. 11). They, like the latter, focus on freshwater and saltwater resources—fish and marine mammals: "Hair seals and northern sea lions, both killed with harpoons, provided a source of meat and oil as well as skins that were used for moccasins and blankets" (Kennedy and Bouchard 1990a, 325).

This Bungling Host episode, in its original version, is embedded in a larger one that portrays Raven making successive visits to Waterfowl, Young Seal, and Bird. The three visits are followed by three imitations. The first mytheme depicts Waterfowl and will be examined in another chapter (chapter 18). We have already studied the third one, which deals with Bird, the producer of berries.

He returned home and thought what to do next. He was hungry, and was glad when, after a little while, Maxuat!a'laqa (a small water-fowl) invited him to his house. He accepted the invitation, and sat down near the fire. Then Maxuat!a'laqa took a box, held his foot over it, and cut his ankle with a stone knife. At once salmon-eggs fell down into the box, filling it entirely. The Raven ate, and carried home to his sisters what was left over.

On the next morning a woman called K'uela'is ("young seal") invited him to a feast. He sat down near the fire, and she took a dish. She cleaned it, placed it near the fire, and held her hands over it. Then grease dropped down into the dish, filling it entirely. She gave it to the Raven, who ate heartily, and took home to his sisters what was left over.

On the following day, the bird Aix'a'xonē invited him to a feast. He placed a box near the fire and sang: Aix-a.xo-nē xo-nē xo-nē qāx. At once the box was full of salmon-berries. The Raven ate, and carried home to his sisters what was left over.

Now he resolved to invite Maxuat!a'laqa. On the following day the bird came. Then the Raven took a box, put his foot into it, and cut his ankle, but nothing came out of it; and he said to Maxuat!a'laqa, "Go back! I have nothing to give to you." In the evening he made up his mind to invite the young Seal. He felt of his hands all the time, to see if fat were dripping from them. On the next morning he invited her. He placed a mat for her near the fire, took a dish, cleaned it, and placed it on the mat. Then he held his hands over the dish, but not a particle of fat dripped out of them. His hands, however, were burnt to a crisp in the heat of the fire. Then he said to the Seal, "Go back! I have no food for you." Then he invited the bird Aix'a'xonē. He placed a box near the fire, and tried to sing the bird's song; but there was only a single berry in the box. He continued, but did not succeed any better. Finally he sang "mɛnk'," and the box was full of excrements. (Boas 1898, 93–94)

As in the Salish version of the opening quote, Seal's exact identity remains undetermined. It is all the harder to identify its species because we know only the English version of most variants. The word "seal"—the one most often used—refers in English not only to true seals (Phocidae) but also to at least one species of eared seal (Otariidae), the northern fur seal (*Callorhinus ursinus*). If the character is a true seal, the likeliest one is the harbor seal (*Phoca vitulina*), which is the most common Phocidae on North America's Atlantic and Pacific coasts. The harbor seal and the northern elephant seal (*Mirounga angustirostris*) are the only true seals of the Pacific region. But the northern elephant seal "is a rare visitor to our [Canadian] Pacific coastal waters" (Banfield 1974, 380). In all known variants, whenever the actual seal species is identified, a harbor seal is always the one that plays the host (Farrand 1902, 90; Swanton 1905, 133).

Whenever an eared seal is identified, he is always a Steller sea lion (*Eumetopias jubatus*). When not identified, he might also be a northern fur seal (*Callorhinus ursinus*) or a California sea lion (*Zalophus californianus*), which is present near Vancouver Island. The Haida variant, among others, specifies that the host is a Steller sea lion:

RAVEN VISITS SEA-LION AND HAIR-SEAL [= HARBOR SEAL]

After he [Raven] had traveled for a while he came to where Sea-lion lived. And after he had given him some food he roasted his hand, out of which grease dropped. That he gave him to eat. He started off, and when he had traveled for a while came to where Hair-seal lived. Then he, too, roasted his hand in the fire, and grease came out. He gave it to him to eat.

Then he went away and lived in one place for a while. . . . And after he had continued living there for a while Sea-lion and Hair-seal came in. Then he roasted his hand, but it was burned. And they left him. Afterward he came to life again. (Swanton 1905, 132–33)

In the vernacular zoology of Native peoples, the harbor seal and the Stellar sea lion are the two main pinnipeds that are named and used. The Coast Salish, for example, named them respectively *asxw* and *kwexnis*. Both appear in several myths, both were hunted with harpoons, both were cooked the same way, and so on (Kennedy and Bouchard 1976b, 120–27). We therefore assume that either species is the one that usually appears in Bungling Host episodes about a pinniped producing oil or meat.

In the variants seen so far, Seal is sometimes a woman. This is not always so. The host may also be a man, Raven's brother, as in another Salish version: "Raven had a brother, the Seal. He had two children and Seal had one daughter. Once Raven went to Seal and met him sitting by the fire. He was holding up his hands and fat dripped down from them into a bowl" (Boas 1974 [1895], 92–93). Eventually, in a future book, we should examine all of the kinship ties that appear in the myths in order to find their under-lying meanings. With regard to the Bungling Host, these kinship references may have a meaning locally, but for the purposes of studying the mytheme, there seems to be no reason to dwell on this point. All in all, the versions paint a multihued portrait of a host who may be the Trickster's sister or brother or who may have no kinship tie, as in another Salish version:

SEAL INVITES ALL THE ANIMALS

Then Seal invited all the animals. When they had arrived in his house, he held his hands close to the fire and made oil drip out of them, which he served to the people with dried salmon. "Oh," bragged Raven, "I can do that, too." But when he tried, he burned his hands so that big blisters formed which burst and from which water gushed. So he cried again in pain: "Tskān, tskān, tskān, tskān." (Boas 1974 [1895], 124)

This variant also highlights a special culinary practice we encoun-tered while studying Bear the producer of grease, namely the use of animal grease or oil to accompany a meat or dried fish meal.

In the early twentieth century, Northwest Coast specialists were already noting this widespread use of grease or oil among all of these peoples: "Like the other tribes of this region, they [the Squamish] were fond of fish-oils, and particularly salmon-oil. They extracted oil from the sturgeon, the seal, the salmon, and the dog-fish. They stored these oils away in bottles made from the sounds, or air-bladders, of certain fish" (Hill-Tout in Kennedy and Bouchard 1976b, 103). To be more exact, seal oil was produced the following way among the Squamish (but the description holds true for the other peoples): "Seal-oil was obtained through boiling the seal's blubber by means of hot rocks. The oil was "skimmed" from the surface of the boiling mixture and then stored in a seal's air-bladder that had been cleaned and dried. Seal-oil was used as a "dip" for smoke-dried salmon and other dried foods" (Kennedy and Bouchard 1976b, 127).

This practice was so popular that even today the Squamish still have specific terms for it: "*sts'im* which means 'to dip dried salmon into black bear grease or seal-oil'; and *c'im?* which means 'eat grease, take dried salmon and dip it in oil'" (Kennedy and Bouchard 1976b, 127).

Table 3. "Seal produces food" versions

HOST	ACTION	TRICKSTER	NATION	SOURCE
Seal	hands held close to the fire	Raven	Coast Salish	Boas 1974 [1895]
Seal	hands held up near fire	Raven	Coast Salish	Boas 1974 [1895]*
Seal	hands roasted	Raven	Coast Salish	Hill-Tout 1904*
Seal	flippers held above fire	Raven	Bella Coola	McIlwraith 1948
Young seal	hands held over fire	Raven	Bella Coola	Boas 1898

Seal	hands held close to fire	Raven	Bella Coola	Boas 1974 [1895]*
Seal	hands held close to fire	Txämsem	Tsimshian	Boas 1916
Seal	hands held near fire	Txämsem	Tsimshian	Boas 1902
Seal	hands held near fire	Txämsem	Tsimshian	Cove and Macdonald 1987
Young seal	hands warmed	O'ᵉmat	Kwakiutl	Boas 1969 [1910]
Seal	hands roasted	Raven	Kwakiutl	Boas and Hunt 1906
Seal	front feet held up to the fire	Raven	Squamish	Kennedy and Bouchard 1976b
Harbor seal	hands roasted	Raven	Haida	Swanton 1905
Harbor seal	kills son	Bluejay	Coast Salish	Farrand 1902
Sea lion	hands roasted	Raven	Haida	Swanton 1905
Sea lion	own side cut	Bluejay	Coast Salish	Adamson 1934
Seal	kills son	Bluejay	Coast Salish	Adamson 1934
Seal	kills own child	Bluejay	Chinook	Boas 1894
Fish-Oil-Man	hands held over fire	Coyote	Shuswap	Teit 1909
Eagle	hands warmed	Raven	Haida	Swanton 1908*

* Incomplete version

The myth therefore refers to this meal of oil and dried salmon. What is astonishing, however, is the way Seal (or Sea Lion) procures the oil. It is certainly significant that he brings his hands close to a heat source—an allusion to the need to heat seal blubber to make oil from it. There are undoubtedly more allusions. Why does Seal (or Sea Lion) use only his hands when warming a limb and never his feet, as Bear could? Natives recognize that pinnipeds have feet and hands. Scientists make the same distinction, while saying that the hindlimbs do not perform quite the same function in true seals (propulsion mainly) as in eared seals (propulsion in water and locomotion on dry land).

The answer is likewise anatomical and attests to the advanced level of Native knowledge. True seals and eared seals both differ in the composition of their hindflippers and foreflippers. Whereas foreflippers have a rather thick mass of subcutaneous tissue that is palpable to the touch, so thick that some authors even describe it as a fat pad, this is not so with the hindflippers, which are practically reduced to "skin and bones" (pers. comm. Stéphane Lair, Faculty of Veterinary Medicine, University of Montreal): "This is a fatty and fibrous tissue pad between the digits of the foreflipper" (King 1983, 140).

Any remaining doubts? A biologist conducted an experiment whose findings are strangely reminiscent of the mytheme under study: "When a heat lamp is focused on the naked [fore]flipper of a freshly killed seal, the black epidermis soon begins to blister. Before it does so, droplets appear on the surface of the skin in a fairly regular pattern" (Scheffer 1962, 7). The biologist goes on to advance the hypothesis that such droplets are due to sweat gland secretions. This explanation is disconcertingly in line with a Bella Coola variant—which even speaks of exudation: "First he [seal] washed out a box to place near the fire and held his flippers above it so that the grease that exuded from them should drip into the receptacle" (McIlwraith 1948, vol. 2, 388).

Natives have carried out their own experiments and come to

Fig. 14. Harbor seal.

similar conclusions. By observing pinniped foreflippers and hind-flippers, they have figured out how much fatty tissue these limbs respectively have. In particular, they have observed that foreflippers will exude droplets when brought close to a heat source—undoubtedly the origin of our mytheme.

The mytheme thus draws on the concrete lessons of Native experiences, which form the basis of the story. Listeners can always verify these lessons on their own.

On the other hand, the same mytheme has given rise to two distinct groups of permutations that also deserve comment: the Haida group, where Eagle is the host; and the Shuswap group, where the host is a character called Fish-Oil-Man.

The Haida episode is incomplete to the extent that it lacks the part where the guest tries to imitate the host:

GREATEST-EAGLE

After he had left that place, he came to where Greatest-Eagle lived. And he went in to him. And when he got in to him, he told him to sit near by. Then he said to him, "What will you eat, my son? Can you eat the whale which is on the side towards the door?" said he to him. "No," he said to him. "What, then?" said he to him. He said to him, "Your hands." Then Eagle warmed his hands. And grease came out from his hands. (Swanton 1908, 323)

In his classification of the Bungling Host episodes, Boas had included this one under the general theme of a host who lets oil drip from his hands. At first sight, everything in the above extract does seem to include this episode in the same paradigm about a pinniped who warms his hands to get oil. This inclusion, however, is based on an apparent similarity between the two mytheme types, and not on their respective basis. The eagle episode actually evolved out of a completely different etymon. This point is even clearly stated in the story itself, which ends as follows: "Then Eagle warmed his hands. And grease came out from his hands. His hands were stained with grease because he killed whales with his talons" (Swanton 1908, 323).

To take only the bald eagle (*Haliæetus leococephalus*), it is known that it comes flying down on its prey, its talons pointed downward: "To capture live prey, [the eagle] soars overhead to visually locate the item, then suddenly stoops and attempts to capture such items with 1 or both feet" (Buehler 2000, 9). It grabs its prey using its talons, as in the myth. In addition, its diet can include beached whale carcasses, as an inveterate observer of whale behavior attests: "Some [whale] carcasses bloat up, float to the surface and drift onto the shoreline to be consumed by bald eagles, red foxes and hungry grizzly bears emerging from their dens" ("Whale hunting" 2008).

The Haida likewise used beached whales: "The Haida hunted seals (fig. 5), porpoises, sea lions, fur seals, and sea otters, and they used stranded whales" (Blackman 1990, 244). When one has observed an eagle feeding on a beached whale (in the episode of the myth, a whale does lie on the doorstep of Eagle's home), what more is needed to make the eagle the one who killed the whale, at least in the story? And what more is needed to make a permutation from other materials, and change Seal into Eagle, using a situation that looks similar but draws on completely different experiences?

The second mytheme, of Shuswap origin, features Fish-Oil-Man instead of Seal and seems to arise from another phenomenon—local borrowing. To decide whether a mytheme may be called a borrowing, several basic principles must be followed. First, the episode must be an exception to the rule. It must stand out as an anomaly within a corpus of variants on a given theme. Second, basic analysis cannot in any way explain this anomaly only with reference to the local culture. Finally, needless to say, one must show the path the borrowing followed to get to where it is now.

COYOTE AND FISH-OIL-MAN

Continuing his journey, Coyote came to another house, which he entered. It was inhabited by an old man called Fish-Oil-Man. Feeling hungry, and seeing nothing in the shape of food, he wondered what this man could give him to eat. The man made the fire blaze, and placed a wooden dish for catching drippings in front of it. He held his hands over it, with the fingers turned down, and the grease dropped from his finger-ends. When the dish was full, he placed it before Coyote, and asked him to eat. Coyote said, "I can't eat that." And the man answered, "Try it. It is good." Coyote then ate some, and, liking it, he finished the contents of the dish.

Coyote thought, "I will show this fellow that I can do the same thing." So, making the fire blaze, he took the wooden dish, and held his hands above it, in the same way the man had done. His hands shrivelled up with the heat but no grease dropped from them. This is the reason why the coyote has short paws. He cried with pain; and the man threw him outside, saying "You fool! That method belongs to me only." (Teit 1909, 627)

If we examine the available literature on the Shuswap, we cannot in any way retrace this mytheme to an origin within their culture. They seem to have no specific term for an anatomical fish part that would be equivalent to a hand (Hayden 1992), as do other peoples (the Innu term for pelvic, pectoral, and anal fish fins is related to the Innu one for 'hand'; Clément 1995, 497). When fish are being prepared, and in particular salmon, some parts are preferred as sources of oil because of their fatty nature, i.e., the head, the eggs, and the internal organs (Hayden 1992, 239), but not particularly the fins. Nor is there any term for pinnipeds (Kuipers 1974). This should be no surprise, since the Shuswap are Salish of the interior of British Columbia and very far from the Pacific coast. On the other hand, the Shuswap, or Secwepemc, as they say in their language, belong to the same Salishan linguistic and cultural family as do the Coast Salish, who are known to have the mytheme of Seal warming his hands. Moreover, the Shuswap variant comes from the westernmost region of their traditional territory, this being Canoe Creek and Dog Creek, two villages that belong to the geographic division of this territory known as the Fraser River Division. The first European to enter into contact with the members of this nation, Alexander Mackenzie, stayed for a while with a band of the same division that was "en route to the Chilcotin and the Pacific" (Ignace 1998, 215). The Shuswap were nomads par excellence. Pre-contact, they maintained a trading network as much with their immediate neighbors as with those farther away on the Northwest Coast (Ignace 1998, 205).

All of these criteria point to borrowing of a legend. In all likelihood, the mytheme was borrowed from west to east—from the Coast Salish to the Interior Salish, that is, the Shuswap. Among the latter, fishing was very important, salmon in particular being a major resource if not the main one. This change of context may thus explain the permutation. With no word existing for seal, and with fish being boiled for their oil, the motif changed from Seal warming his hands to Fish-Oil-Man warming his hands, all the more so because nothing equivalent to hands existed in the local terminology of fish anatomy. This change was helped along by another cultural trait: the supervision of fish oil production by an old man: "The process of rendering oil was conducted under the supervision of an old man" (Hayden 1992, 297). In the myth, Fish-Oil-Man is an old man. The Trickster's identity likewise changes locally: here Coyote; in the coastal myth, Raven.[1]

In addition to producing grease by warming his hands, Seal has other ways of getting food in these myths, either by killing his own child or by cutting himself in the side. In the first chapter, we have already studied the theme of a host who kills one of his children and brings him back to life after putting the child's bones back in the water. This mytheme has several variations, and in chapter 8 we will discuss one where the protagonist is Mule Deer (Cochiti, Southwest). The mytheme about the seal is slightly different but related. There is no mention of a requirement that Seal must put bones back in the water. This mytheme, too, has variations. The host may alternately be Seal or Red Cod according to the classification by Boas (1916, 698), as well as Sturgeon (Wishram, Plateau), as listed in our inventory (see the appendix).

In the following Salish variant, Seal is the host who offers his own children to Bluejay, the Trickster. We have at least three variants of this mytheme, including two of Salish origin (Adamson 1934; Farrand 1902) and one of Chinook origin (Boas 1894).

BLUEJAY VISITS SEAL

"We'll visit Seal," Bluejay said to his family. When they got there they found six little Seals in front of the fire, along with their father and mother. Soon Seal built a fire of sticks outside. Then he came back inside, got a stick and a hand-axe. He hit his son, the smallest of his six children, over the head. The boy died. He cut the boy's throat, seared his hide, scraped it with a knife, and scalded him as one would a hog. Then he put him in a basket with some hot rocks and boiled him. Bluejay and his family had a grand time, it was sure a nice breakfast; the meat was very good. "Look, look," Bluejay's grandmother suddenly whispered. The little Seal had come to life, although they had already eaten him. There were six little Seals again. The meat was good; it was a good meal. Then Bluejay said,

"It's time to go home now." At the canoe he called back, "Come to my place tomorrow." "All right," Seal answered.

> Seal came to Bluejay's house. He and his wife sat down. Soon Bluejay went out, built a large fire and put some hot rocks in a basket. Then he came back in, hit his smallest son on the head, killed him, cut his throat, cut his head off, and dragged him outside. He seared him, then scraped him and boiled him. Seal ate the smallest of Bluejay's boys. Bluejay looked: his little boy had not come to life at all. He had lost him. He had thought that his son would come to life as Seal's son had. (Adamson 1934, 8)

Here, too, we may apply the explanation for the mytheme about Beaver killing his own son. Two main factors are at work: a widespread belief in the reincarnation of species and observations of animal breeding. As among the Innu, many Northwest Coast peoples believed that animal species would reincarnate as long as certain rules about them were obeyed. Here are a few striking examples:

> [Eyak] Hunters cut the eyeballs of game, so that the animals could not see them, and put the heads, entrails, etc., in appropriate places to insure the animals' reincarnation. (De Laguna 1990a, 194)

> [Tlingit] Certain essential parts (head, bones or vital organs, depending on the species) were interred, returned to the water, or cremated, to insure reincarnation of the animal. (De Laguna 1990b, 209)

> [Tsimshian] Finding their potlatch concerned with the reincarnation of humans and animals. (Suttles and Jonaitis 1990, 86)

In the Salish myth, the same belief can be seen in the return to life of Seal's youngest boy despite a fatal blow from his father. We now come to the second main explanatory factor: the real-life experience that seems to be consistent with this belief. Seals and sea lions—as with the beavers described in the first chapter—continually replenish their populations. They certainly breed once a year, as is widely known. But they are also incredibly numerous when gathering together to breed in what are commonly called rookeries. Such colonies have countless numbers of adult males and females milling about, as well as younger individuals, with births of pups constantly replenishing the herd.

> *Vitulina* seals, for example, are promiscuous and at breeding time congregate in groups of various sizes (. . . sometimes several thousands) made up of mixed sexes and ages. (Wooding 1982, 22)

> Sea lions are highly gregarious: they occupy dense rookeries during the breeding season, swim in herds, and haul out onto rocky islets together during the remainder of the season. The bulls are bellicose. There is a definite social hierarchy on the breeding grounds, with barren cows, bachelor bulls, and yearlings hauling out together at some distance from the breeding colonies. . . . On land there is much bickering between neighbours, much movement of their sinuous necks, and a constant bedlam of roaring bulls, barking cows, and whining pups. (Banfield 1974, 355–56)

For a hunter, killing an animal in a rookery does not seem to endanger the herd in any way, since the population is always being restocked. A hunt in a rookery by Squamish, who are also Coast Salish, may help us to understand the Salish myth—the death blow from Seal's father can be interpreted as an offering by the animal to the human who administers the coup de grâce. In any case, a human (the Trickster) is Seal's guest: "Apparently seals could also be hunted from the shore. The hunters would sneak up to the rookery very carefully, all the while imitating the sound of the seals, and would harpoon the animals where they were laying on the rocks" (Kennedy and Bouchard 1976b, 125). The animal could also be killed by a blow to the head: "Seals were occasionally approached near their rookeries by a hunter disguised in a seal skin and imitating the sound of a seal. The kill was made once the hunter was close enough to use a club or harpoon" (Kennedy and Bouchard 1990b, 445).

Then there are the females, already mentioned, which regularly arrive by sea and increase the population, not to mention the pups continually being born amid this swarming mass of life: "In any case, the [sea lions] males are the first to arrive at the breeding grounds and there they lay claim to well-defined territories and await the arrival of the pregnant females. As the females reach the rookeries, they haul out and . . . are herded to different territories. Within a few days each new arrival gives birth to a single pup weighing 40 to 45 pounds (18–20 kg) . . . . Before the end of the season, as more and more pregnant females arrive, the males are outnumbered by ten to one" (Wooding 1982, 214).

Need we say more? The last few comments are extremely interesting, since in their own way they repeat what the myth says. This seems to be what the episode from the Salish legend tells us: no sooner is one pinniped killed than another takes its place in the colony, often a newborn pup—a cycle of life that is easily observable.

As with Seal's other ways of obtaining food, at least as they appear in the versions we have brought together, the following way has a real-life explanation. Nothing is incidental in these myths—in this case, the Steller sea lion that cuts itself in the side to remove a piece of meat. This happens in a version of Salish origin and goes as follows:

BLUEJAY VISITS SEA LION

Next morning, Bluejay said to his cousin, "Let us visit Sea Lion." They set out and arrived at the place. Just as they opened the door, Sea Lion said, "Hwu . . ." He frightened Bluejay five times; then he let them in. Bluejay was still very frightened. Sea Lion got up; he got a big knife and whetted it on his leg. Then he cut a piece of flesh off his side for Bluejay. Bluejay thought, "Oh, this is terrible—eating this flesh!" He finished the meat, and started home. He called back his usual invitation.

Bluejay was watching for his visitor. After a while, he saw him coming. "Clean a place", he said to his cousin. Bluejay then lay down in bed. Sea Lion opened the door. Bluejay said, "Hwu . . . .

" Sea Lion was not the least bit frightened. Bluejay got out of bed. He whetted his carving knife on his lap. Then he began to feel his side, and cut it. "U . . ", he said and nearly fainted. A little black blood oozed out. Sea Lion said, "Oh, you are hurting yourself." He asked for a knife, cut a piece of his own flesh, and gave it to Bluejay. Bluejay was that much to the good. Then Sea Lion left. (Adamson 1934, 5)

We have looked far and wide for a solution to this puzzle, and yet the answer has been within easy reach. Why does Sea Lion cut his side and not his back, for example, as Caribou does among the Innu, or his ankle, as some bird species do in other Bungling Host episodes? From the Inuit of the Arctic to all of the shore-dwelling peoples of the North Atlantic and North Pacific coasts, we have read through the anthropological literature about how seal meat is cut up. But the literature says little in general about how the cutting is exactly done.

We then read the literature on pinniped anatomy. There we found the answer. Because foreflippers are the sea lion's main means of locomotion, muscle mass is greatly developed in that area: "These different methods of swimming are reflected in the anatomy of the two groups. Otariids need their main muscle mass around their shoulders, since it is by movements of their fore flippers that they swim" (Bonner 2004, 17).

Hence, there is lots of meat all around the foreflippers, including the thoracic region. This is why Sea Lion cut a piece of flesh from that part of his body—a reason that becomes clear and verifiable once the animal has been skinned. As for the rest, we will pass over other details of the myth that nonetheless seem interesting (for example, the sounds made by these animals; the leather that may even be used to sharpen knives, etc.). This chapter is about the way pinnipeds provide humans with food: by offering up their grease.

As with the stories of the preceding chapter—Bird who sings and Bear who cooks—the many versions of Seal warming his hands end with a brief statement that seals the story's authenticity. In their

Fig. 15. Steller sea lion.

own way, the aim is to reassure doubting listeners who wonder about the truth of what they have just heard. The answer is clear: if these statements are true, so is everything that came before.

[Shuswap version] This is the reason why the coyote has short paws. (Teit 1909, 627)

[Kwakiutl version] Therefore the feet of Raven are now this way, because they were shrivelled up. (Boas and Hunt 1906, 160)

[Tsimshian version] For that reason the hands of man are bent (in old age) to this day. (Boas 1902, 48)

[Tsimshian version] People say that in olden times all the joints of man's or woman's fingers had eyes and mouths until Txämsem held up his hands when he invited Chief Seal into his house, and that man's fingers have had no eyes and no mouths since; when people ate food in those days, the fingers also ate. (Boas 1916, 91)

6   Silver Fox Digs Up Yellow Jacket Larvae with His Penis (California)

> Coyote asked, "Son-in-law, how did you catch those yellow-jackets?" Silver Fox said, "I smoked them out with leaves. After smoking them out I dug them up with my penis. When the yellow-jackets came, I did not run. There is lots of meat down in the nest."
>
> —Edward Sapir, "Yana Texts"

A little farther south, the Yana of California's mountainous regions have also adapted the Bungling Host motif—the host is now always the same even though each episode recounts different ways of getting food. To our knowledge, this adaptation is less widespread, being found among a few peoples only, including the Atsugewi, the Serrano, and the Wiyot of California, the Jicarilla of the Southwest, and the Takelma of the Northwest Coast. In all three Yana episodes, gathered by the anthropologist Roland Dixon (in Sapir 1910) and published solely in a version already translated into English, the host is always Silver Fox and the Trickster Coyote.

The Yana have been largely decimated, today numbering a little less than a hundred. They still live in California. Their community, the Redding Rancheria Tribe, encompasses members of two other nations: the Wintu and the Pit-River. In the mid-nineteenth century, there were still at least two thousand Native Americans of Yana nationality, who were then reduced to their current number in the space of two decades after many massacres by the new settlers of America.

The Yana would be a lot less known today were it not for Ishi, a Yahi-Yana survivor of this culture, who lived at the Museum of Anthropology of the University of California between 1911 and 1916. Ishi provided a great deal of information about the traditional life of his people to the anthropologist Theodora Kroeber, who later made him famous in the book *Ishi in Two Worlds* (Kroeber 1961).

The three Bungling Host episodes from the Yana are a formidable challenge. With only an English version available, we can expect trouble identifying the animal and plant species. Furthermore, the literature on the Yana is very poor, as is the literature on other Native Californian peoples, many of whom went extinct before any anthropologist could take an interest in them. Everything written about the Yana goes back eight or nine decades with no realistic possibility of being updated, given the current state of the population. No one speaks the language anymore. Finally, because the same host appears in all three consecutive episodes available to us, we cannot help but wonder what these variants mean specifically. Do they explain the main host's characteristics, as in the other episodes? Or do they simply convey teachings about Yana culture without making any link to animal behavior?

But, upon careful examination, the episodes seem to follow the same model: a judicious mix of animal and human phenomena, where body parts and feeding behaviors are closely linked to cultural practices. The result: a content that only seems absurd and that actually conceals knowledge and skills that remain to be elucidated.

The three Yana episodes are also constructed in such a way that, in at least two of them, the ways of getting food are presented consecutively. The Trickster then attempts his imitations after both have been presented and not after each of them. Such a structure exists in other myths, including the Bella Coola version of the Bungling Host we saw in the last chapter. It thus seems to be relatively widespread and deliberate, since it still appears in Yana variants of the myth now under study. Variants from neighboring peoples, including the Takelma a bit farther north, and the Atsugewi immediately to the northeast, will be studied later on to clarify certain complex aspects of these stories.

The first two Yana episodes, presented below, show Silver Fox getting *cu'nna* from trees, and then grouse by smoking them out. The third episode will be discussed subsequently—an excerpt opens this chapter—and deals with yellow jacket larvae.

SILVER FOX GETS CU'NNA AND GROUSE

By and by another big snow came. Silver Fox made it come. Silver Fox went out; he had a long stick with a crotch at the end to pull down dry branches, and he had a burden basket on his back. Every time he pulled the branches down from a cedar, sweet roots (cu'nna) came down. He carried them home, but did not let Coyote see them. The next day he went out again. There were bunches of something on the pine trees that burned. He set on fire some pine needles and put them on the end of his stick, then held it up to the bunches all about. Then he lay down face down and soon many grouse hit him all over. When they were all down he got up and put them in a brush sack (k'êwatc!i), filled it with the grouse. Coyote was not allowed to see it.

After some time Silver Fox felt sorry for Coyote and let him see the food he had brought back. "Son-in-law, how did you get those roots?" said Coyote. Silver Fox said, "I took a stick, broke off cedar limbs, and down came the roots." Coyote said, "I will go and do the same." Silver Fox said, "I don't look up when I do it." Coyote went, got hit badly, and looked up. He saw no roots, only branches. He went home sick. Fox said, "I did not look up when I was hit and hurt." Coyote saw him bring back grouse. "Son-in-law, how did you kill them?" he asked. Silver Fox told him. Coyote said. "I'll do that too." Silver Fox told him what to do, but Coyote did as before. When four grouse came he said, "Stop! I want to eat." They stopped, only four grouse came. Coyote cooked and ate them. Then he went to another tree and repeated what he had done. He jumped up, could not stand being hit by the grouse. He looked about—there was nothing there. He went home. (Sapir 1910, 211–12)

The first problem with these episodes will be to identify the host exactly. The term "silver fox" usually refers to a color variant of the red fox (*Vulpes vulpes*): "The least common phase is termed the 'silver fox,' which forms 2 to 17 per cent of the population" (Banfield 1974, 299). It sometimes also refers to the gray fox, which is a different species, *Urocyon cinereoargenteus*, whose Latin nomenclature evokes the silver color of part of its coat. A book on Californian fur-bearing animals mentions this possibility: "Other Names . . . Gray Fox, part; Silver Gray Fox, part" (Grinnell et al. 1937, 421). Furthermore, northeast California, especially the Sacramento Valley—well within traditional Yana territory—is mainly home to the gray fox, the red fox being an introduced species in that area:

Two populations of the Red Fox are widely separated in California, one in the higher elevations of the Sierra Nevada and another in some areas of the Sacramento Valley. Only the montane Red Fox is native to California. In the nineteenth century, a population of the eastern Red Fox was introduced into the lowlands of the state. These animals are believed to have descended from foxes that were either released or escaped from the farms, and they most closely resemble Red Foxes from the northern Central Plains states. The Sierran population lives at 1500 m and above. This species is found throughout North America and also Eurasia. (Jameson and Peeters 1988, 144–45)

The gray fox is also the most common and widespread of California's true foxes (Jameson and Peeters 1988, 142). The fox of the myth is therefore the gray fox, *Urocyon cinereoargenteus*, although we will refer often to it by the name in the English translation. This species identification matters because some of its physical and behavioral characteristics will help us to explain several etymons of the story, as we will see later on.

In these episodes, the second major translation problem—and there are others—concerns the species of tree that provides Fox with *cu'nna*. The one episode recorded in English calls it a "cedar." When we looked through the literature on Californian plant life, we found that the term "cedar" may also refer to one of many local species of juniper ("Juniperus, Juniper, Cedar"; Eastwood 1905, 16). Only one true native cedar is listed in the culture area under study, i.e., *Libocedrus decurrens*, which is the Californian incense-cedar (Eastwood 1905, 20). Confusion appears to be widespread in the ethnography of peoples of the American West: "The Kaibab, as seen from items in Sapir's Dictionary, make much use of 'cedar,' though, again, there is only linguistic evidence for the assumption that the plant is of the genus Juniperus" (Zigmond 1941, 94). In his dissertation on the ethnobotany of California and the Great Basin, Maurice Zigmond (1941) provides another example of this misunderstanding when he describes uses of the juniper: "Barrett mentions a Washo winterhouse made of 'cedar' slabs" (96).

More contemporary authors, trained in botany and ethnology and doing research in a neighboring region, say the same thing: "Westerners frequently refer to junipers as 'cedars' even though they are not at all like the true cedars of the genus *Cedrus*" (Dunmire and Tierney 1997, 127).

There is at least one other good reason for considering the "cedar" of the Yana episode to be a juniper—a utilitarian reason. The Californian incense-cedar was certainly put to use, but never as food. For example, the Yana used cedar or pine bark to cover their cone-shaped homes (Johnson 1978, 367), and they used the wood for fire making, turning a stick around and around in it until a flame was ignited (Johnson 1978, 366). But they did not gather the fruit, an oblong cone 3 centimeters long at most with six scales, only two of which had seeds. Other cones were gathered, such as pine cones (Sapir and Spier 1943, 251). In contrast, junipers

(*Juniperus* spp.) produce edible berries of much importance for Native American peoples of the American West: "The eating of juniper berries is indicated in general terms for nearly all of the western states. Aboriginal groups in California, Oregon, Washington, Nevada, Arizona, Utah, New Mexico, and Texas, as well as in British Columbia, are known to have consumed the fruit of a number of species" (Zigmond 1941, 85). The literature on the Yana is sparse and, understandably, not explicit on this point. They likely knew and ate the berries.

Juniper berries are moreover a major component of the gray fox diet, as studies in the American West have shown: "In southwest Utah, fruits were the most important food, followed by mammals (mainly *Odocoileus*, *Thomomys*, *Peromyscus* and *Neotoma*) and arthropods, primarily orthopterans and coleopterans (Trapp, 1978). Seasonally, arthropods dominated the summer diet and fruits dominated the fall and winter diets, with *Opuntia* fruits being most important in the fall and *Juniperus* in the winter and early spring. Juniper berries were also the most frequently eaten food during spring and summer in Arizona" (Fritzell and Haroldson 1982, 4). In California, examination of gray fox stomachs has likewise revealed the presence of juniper berries in the animal's diet (Grinnell et al. 1937, 448).

Clearly, these facts still do not explain why Silver Fox alludes to *cu'nna* as coming from "roots" of trees, and not from berries. Already, however, we see how the myth can have meaning for listeners, since the juniper is used by humans and foxes alike. The context no longer needs explaining. We have only to examine the details.

If we take the episode from the beginning, we see Silver Fox making the snow come. It is not surprising that gray foxes are associated with snow or winter. First, this species has only one seasonal molt, which lasts from summer to autumn, and the quality of its fur is highest during winter: "A single annual molt extends from summer through fall (Grinnell et al. 1937). Stains (1979) indicated that gray foxes were prime from late November to mid-February, with peak primeness occurring in December" (Fritzell 1987, 409). Second, mammalogists have observed that the gray fox becomes much more active in late autumn and winter. Because it is more mobile, one may infer that the signs of its presence are even more visible during this period, a fact observed and then recorded in the myth.

> Home range size of gray foxes varies seasonally. Ranges for both sexes increase in late fall and winter, possibly in response to breeding activity or declining food availability. (Cypher 2003, 523)

> Mobility seems to be greatest in the fall (Richards and Hine, 1953) or winter (Wood, 1954b). (Trapp and Hallberg 1975, 169)

Immediately east of the Yana were the Atsugewi, who omitted this reference to winter in their variant of the same episode, despite living traditionally on a territory much higher in altitude. The Yana lived on the mountain slopes east of the Sacramento Valley, whose annual precipitation could be around 1.5 meters with only a few snowfalls in a region less than 1,200 meters in altitude (Johnson 1978, 362). The Atsugewi lived in the same mountains but at elevations of 1,500 meters or higher, with harsh winters that forced them to stay in permanent villages for around six months (Garth 1978, 236). Although the Atsugewi variant left out this background detail—which we will discuss later—it does include the other elements of the Yana episode:

SILVER-FOX OBTAINS A SORT OF CAMAS

In the morning Silver-Fox went out, and, going up to a cedar tree, pulled off the boughs, which became a sort of camas (?). He brought back a great load of these; and when he got back, as before, Coyote ate all his share at once. He then asked how to get them, and was told to make a long hook and pull the limbs off, but to keep his eyes shut all the time. As in the other cases, Coyote was very successful the first time, and ate all the roots up. When he tried to repeat the plan, however, only big limbs came down, and hit him on the head. (Dixon 1908, 172)

Both variants describe the tool that Fox uses to get his food: in the first case, as "a long stick with a crotch at the end"; in the second, as "a long hook." This tool is said to be used to pull branches down, and even to yank them off. Now, this element of the myth is doubly motivated, first by Yana cultural practices, and second by a body part specific to the gray fox. This body part is observable to the listener, who is thereby assured of the authenticity of what has been told.

The anthropological literature thus refers to the Yana having a "crook for pulling down nuts and firewood" (Gifford and Klimek 1939, 82). It is described as follows: "Pole with short crosspiece lashed on at acute angle. Acorns, pine nuts, and rotten branches pulled down with it." (Gifford and Klimek 1939, 91). The gray fox also has its own hook, i.e., its feet have claws that are so curved that mammalogists see them as a species characteristic, especially in woodlands, which differentiates it from other foxes: "Gray foxes in the forested eastern regions of Mexico were found to have sharper and more recurved claws than those in more arid western regions, where trees are scarce" (Fritzell 1987, 414). These remarkable claws are believed to be a tree-dwelling adaptation that enables gray foxes not only to climb trees but also to move around nimbly from branch to branch. The gray fox is such an agile climber that it is even called the "tree fox," and its arboreal skills are likened to those of squirrels (Seton 1953 [1909], vol. 1, 568).

> Gray foxes are well-known for their tree-climbing behavior. They are adapted anatomically to climbing and have been observed to climb vertical branchless tree trunks to heights of 18 m (60 feet) by grasping the trunk with their forefeet and pushing with their hindfeet (Seton 1929, Terres 1939, Taylor 1943, Leopold 1959). Climbing is also accomplished by jumping from branch to branch (Seton 1929, Grinnell et al. 1937). Gray foxes climb trees to forage

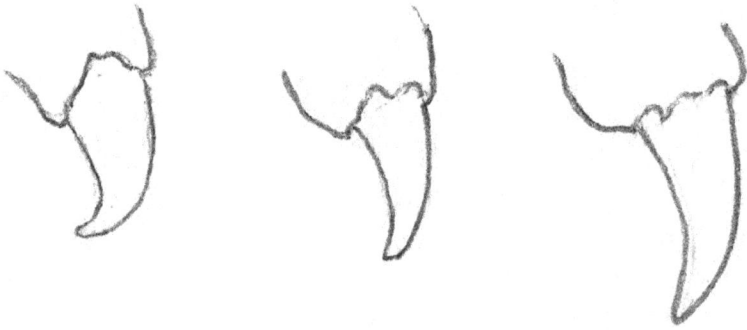

Fig. 16. (from left to right) Claws of the gray fox, the kit fox, and the red fox. Based on Grinnell et al. 1937, 441.

(Grinnell et al. 1937, Gunderson 1961), rest (Seton 1929, Yeager 1938, Leopold 1959), or escape (Terres 1939, Carr 1945). They descend by backing down a vertical tree (Seton 1929) or running headfirst down a sloping tree (Nelson 1930, Yeager 1938). (Fritzell 1987, 414)

Some naturalists have also seen gray foxes try to flee a pursuer by leaping on to the low branches of a tree, such as a juniper: "More often they take to a live-oak or juniper, where the lower branches can be reached at a bound, and then, squirrel-like, hide in the swaying topmost branches" (Seton 1953 [1909], vol. 1, 584).

This great agility has also been noticed by indigenous peoples, who make more than isolated references to it. In another Bungling Host episode, the Atsugewi exploit this possibility by showing how Silver Fox gets pine nuts. The episode intertwines with the one about the grouse we presented earlier in a Yana version. We will return to it later.

SILVER-FOX GETS PINE-NUTS AND GROUSE

Silver-Fox then went out to get some pine-nuts. He climbed a tree and shook the branches, and the nuts fell down already shelled and ready to eat. He filled a basket with them, and brought them in. Coyote had gone to get wood; and when he got back, Silver-Fox divided the pine-nuts, and gave him half. Silver-Fox ate only part of his, and put the rest away; but Coyote ate nearly all night, going out and defecating, and then returning and eating more, until he had finished them. Next morning, Silver-Fox went out and looked for pines having large "witch-brooms" on them. When he found one, he would set fire to it, then walk away looking constantly on the ground, and a grouse would straightway fall out of the tree. Then he placed them in a basket, and brought them back to the house. Coyote wanted to begin eating at once, and helped him with his load. As before, Coyote ate all his share up, whereas Silver-Fox kept most of his.

Next day Coyote asked Silver-Fox how to get pine-nuts. He told him to go to a tree, scrape the brush away, climb up, and then shake the boughs with his foot. Coyote thought he could do this, so went out to try. He was successful, but, on coming down, ate up all the nuts. Then he went to another tree and attempted to repeat the process; but this time no nuts fell, and Coyote himself lost his footing, and was badly hurt by the fall. He came back to the house with his neck bent to one side, and in great pain. Silver-Fox knew all that had been going on, but said nothing. After a while Coyote told him what had happened. The next day Coyote asked how the grouse had been secured, and Silver-Fox told him to set fire to the tree, and then sit with his back to the trunk, and not look up. So Coyote went off to get grouse. He was successful in his attempt, but opened his eyes and looked up, and saw the grouse falling. When he had picked them all up, he cooked and ate them on the spot, and then went to another tree to repeat the process. This time, however, it was burning branches that fell, and they hit him and burned him badly. So he ran back to the house, crying. Silver-Fox gave him some of his food, however. (Dixon 1908, 171–72)

This Atsugewi pine-nut episode can be examined in terms of its main principles, which are likewise twofold. The mytheme is based as much on human actions as on animal characteristics. When Atsugewi men gathered acorns, it is known that they would make them fall to the ground by climbing the trees (Garth 1978, 243).

The Yana did likewise: "The men climbed the trees to shake the acorns down; the women gathered the nuts and shelled them immediately" (Johnson 1978, 365). The same method prevailed for pine-nut harvesting and, though attested only for the Yana, one may infer that it was done by their Atsugewi neighbors as well: "Both sugar pine and digger-pine yield edible nuts. To gather these a family or village would camp out. The men would climb the trees, break off the pine cones, and throw them on the ground. They were then gathered by the women, who pounded the nuts out of them. Digger-pine nuts were mashed and eaten raw" (Sapir and Spier 1943, 251).

The silver fox acts the same way in reality as in the myth. As astonishing as it may seem, some observers have seen gray foxes going into orchards and climbing trees to make the fruit fall down for their young, which would pick them up on the ground: "In Monterey County, W. H. Parkinson once discovered that gray foxes were visiting an orchard, climbing peach trees, and shaking the fruit to the ground. He watched adult foxes climb these trees in the daytime and knock peaches down to young animals below" (Grinnell et al. 1937, 449). An extremely detailed analysis of gray fox stomach contents in the American Southwest revealed the presence of plant material from many plant species, including the ones reported in the above myths, *Pinus*, pine, *Quercus*, oak, and *Juniperus*, juniper, as has been seen (Turkowski 1969, 71). Native Americans too have observed such behavior—getting plant products by climbing trees—or they have noticed plant material in the gray fox's stomach contents, gastrointestinal tract contents, or excrement. All of these clues bear witness to tree-climbing activities. This is how the stories are produced.

At least one other detail seems key to these episodes, one specific to humans only. This is a "burden basket," which is back-mounted in the Yana version of the *cu'nna* episode and which appears also in the Atsugewi pine-nut episode ("He filled a basket with them, and brought them in"). The art of basket-making was highly developed among Californian peoples and, as one may easily expect, some of the many types of baskets were used exclusively to gather nuts and seeds, as among the Yana, where the existence of a "man's burden basket" is attested (Gifford and Klimek 1939, 79), and among the Atsugewi, who made "carrying or seed gathering baskets" (Elsasser 1978, 627, 632).

However, the most intriguing element of these episodes remains the exact nature of the food that Fox obtained and which is associated with roots among the Yana and with camas among the Atsugewi. Actually, the comparison with the camas is unsure. The original English version has a question mark after the word "a sort of camas (?)" and it is not specified whether the doubt was the anthropologist's or the storyteller's. The Yana version uses the term *cu'nna*. Yana dictionaries have no entries for this name of a plant or plant product (Sapir and Swadesh 1960; Merriam 1979). The term for root, *sunna*, could be related. The Yana called the camas (*Camassia* sp.) *k'idi'lla* (Sapir and Spier 1943, 251). Its flowers vary in color from white to blue-violet according to the species (mainly *Camassia quamash* and *Camassia leichlinii*). Its range covers the western United States and western Canada, it can grow up to 80 centimeters tall, and it produces a relatively small bulb measuring between 1 and 5 centimeters. The Yana eat it (Sapir and Spier 1943, 251), as do the Atsugewi (Garth 1978, 243). Once cooked, the tubers become very sweet, so much so that the Native American term for it among the Nootka—who live to the north, on Vancouver Island—was also used for imported figs (Turner et al. 1983, 85).

Although the "roots" that Fox gets from the juniper are not from the camas, the comparison with the camas in the Atsugewi version is not unimportant. One may imagine that the plant product is related in some way to this bulb.

However, before we can figure out this relationship, we must first answer a question. Why "roots" when this product comes from the branches of a juniper? We therefore oriented our line of enquiry using the only certainties we know, namely that we are looking for a plant product that likely comes from a juniper (in particular its branches), was gathered in winter (at least according to the Yana variant), could be eaten fresh (no kind of food preparation is recorded in the myth) as much by humans (Coyote the Trickster) as by animals (the gray fox), and was sweet-tasting, the last element being explicit in the first version ("sweet roots (*cu'nna*)") and implicit in the second one if the allusion to the camas was due to comparable taste.

Then, we found what we were looking for. Among many peoples of the Great Basin and the American Southwest — if not elsewhere — for whom we have sufficient ethnobotanical data, it is reported that they ate the fruit of the mistletoe, including the juniper mistletoe.

The mistletoe is a parasitic plant that may be found on the branches of some trees. In North America, all of these plants belong to the genus *Phoradendron*. Its host species include the oak, the alder, the willow, the ash, the mesquite, the fir, the incense-cedar, the juniper, and others. The mistletoe produces berries, and the Navajos of the Southwest ate juniper mistletoe berries: "Even the profuse, yellow-green mistletoe (*Phoradendron juniperinum*) that often clings tenaciously to juniper branches (but does not really harm the tree) was used among the Navajo. The globular, translucent berries of juniper mistletoe were once eaten fresh, although that's no longer the case today" (Dunmire and Tierney 1997, 129). The neighboring Hopi are said to have used the berries as a substitute for coffee. One may thus infer a stimulating property: "Hough reports the use of the berries [of *Phoradendron juniperinum*] as a substitute of coffee" (Whiting 1939, 72). The Seri of the Southwest described the mesquite mistletoe's white berries as having a sweet taste (Felger and Moser 1991 [1985], 396). Although we have no similar data for juniper mistletoe berries, one may imagine that they too are sweet-tasting. This would explain the association with the equally sweet camas.

Moreover, the fruits of most mistletoe reach maturity from

Fig. 17. Juniper mistletoe (*Phoradendron juniperinum*).

winter to spring. Therefore those of the juniper mistletoe could also be gathered during a certain part of the winter, and this corresponds to the period in the myth, at least the one stated in the Yana version.

The association with roots likewise has an explanation. It is quite plausible to anyone who has seen mistletoe, which are tangled bundles of bushy stems that look like the aerial roots of some trees. Furthermore, the stems have almost nonexistent leaves, which are reduced to 1 millimeter scales along the stems and which make them look more like roots than branches. Of course, the ultimate proof would be to find out how the Yana classified the mistletoe, but this information has eluded us. According to the Native taxonomies used by neighboring peoples of the Great Basin and the Southwest, mistletoe are binomially named as in Western taxonomy, that is, a term for the mistletoe accompanied by one for the host species. This is the case with the Kawaiisu, the Seri, the Pima (Zigmond 1981; Felger and Moser 1991 [1985]; Hodgson 2001), and others. The class to which they belong is not known.

Finally, if we turn to the animals that feed on them, the gray fox is well known to be the canid with the highest consumption of plant foods. Its juniper berry diet during winter is also thoroughly documented. Why would it scorn a berry that grows in the same place? Moreover, it is known that some bird species that overwinter in mountainous regions of the American West and that feed especially on juniper berries also eat mistletoe berries at the same time. This is the case notably with the Townsend's solitaire (*Myadestes townsendi*), whose diet was studied during two consecutive winters in a region not too far from ours (near Flagstaff, Arizona), where mountains rise over 2,000 meters in altitude, at a time when winter was milder than usual and the annual snowfall only 1.50 meters (Salomonson and Balda 1977, 154).

The mytheme of Fox who gets a sweet product from junipers during winter has therefore fulfilled its purpose. Like the others, it has forced us to think as Native Americans do and see what Fox could take away from these trees. The myth has its share of truth, as shown to us by the tangled stems of juniper mistletoe atop the branches, hidden from a ground observer, but made visible by pulling the branches down with a hook. We have only to taste the sweet berries to realize once again that the mytheme makes sense. We have already had the opportunity to see that the gray fox in particular regularly visits junipers and feeds on them year-round.

The second mytheme, which refers to a grouse hunt, has already been presented in two versions, one from the Yana and the other from the Atsugewi. Both versions were recounted jointly with another mytheme. For the only other version we have, from the Takelma, the episode is part of a series of five about Fox and his guest Coyote, during which Fox is fed a quail, a bear, yellow jacket larvae, and salmon (two different episodes). We will look at only the animals that directly concern the subject of this chapter: the grouse and the yellow jackets.

The Takelma are northern neighbors of the Yana and generally assigned by anthropologists to the Northwest Coast culture area, although Edward Sapir, who gathered the following Bungling Host version, saw them as being culturally more Californian. He furthermore believed that the Bungling Host versions we have been studying were of Californian origin (1909a, 79). In fact, the traditional Takelma economy was much closer to that of more southern peoples, with acorns as the main food staple followed by a vegetarian menu (camas bulbs, seeds, and fruits) and a few additions of meat (Kendall 1990, 590). The grouse mytheme features Fox as the host without specifying his species. We will take for granted that he is a gray fox, whose distribution encompasses the state of Oregon, which is home to the Takelma.

COYOTE GOES OUT TO HUNT QUAILS

Houses there were, Coyote and his cousin Fox, and one daughter of Coyote. Fox went out to hunt; quails flew up and lit in the woods, he shot at them, and many he killed. In the evening he returned, brought the quails home. Coyote's daughter was playing in front of the house. Now, 'tis said, Fox returned, carried many quails on his back. "O father, Fox has brought many quails home." — "Squirrel-tongued, ask him, well, in what way he did get them," said Coyote. Next door she ran. "My father says to you, 'In what way did you get them?'" she said. "In what way did I get them? They flew up together into the woods, and underneath them I set fire to the woods. Then I lay down under them belly up, and on my breast they dropped down dead one after another. In that way I killed them," Fox said. Next door returned the little girl. "In the brush I was walking about at random, and quails flew up and lit, and thereupon I set fire to the woods underneath," she said. "Then I lay down under them belly up," she said. "'And on my breast they dropped down dead one after another. In that way I killed them.' That father, did Fox for his part, say."—"S•éhehehe!" he laughed at him. "He even has a little heart, but as for me, my heart is big," he said.

Then the next day came. Then, 'tis said, Coyote went out to hunt, and just the same he did. The quails all flew up together; to the woods he set fire underneath, then under them he lay down belly up, and fragments of fire dropped down on his breast one after another. And one (quail) dropped down on his breast. Coyote now was dead. Then the ants indeed did find him now, and bit him. "C•á! slim-waisted ants! When I, as it seems, was sleeping a short while ago, why did they wake me up?" he said. Now he was restored to life. In the evening he returned, one (quail) he brought home. (Sapir 1909a, 79–80)

In general, the grouse episode raises the same sort of translation problems as does the mistletoe berry one. In particular, in the Yana and Atsugewi versions, we know the game animal solely by the English term "grouse," and there is no Native term that could tell us more about the exact species in question.

In English, "grouse" is sometimes used generically for various species of gallinaceous birds, but it is also applied particularly to some species of the Tetraonidae family. The most common grouse in northern California is the blue grouse (*Dendragapus obscurus*). Its plumage does not match, however, the description in the myth, at least not the one in the basic variant. In the Yana version, Fox goes hunting and sees "bunches of something on the *pine* trees that burned." The pine trees are not burning—rather a "something" that forms bunches. Now, when a bird appears in North American myths, references to fire are used as a way to describe its plumage, as in this Apache episode from the general Trickster cycle that describes a bird and its burning home: "So Coyote started out to the home of Flicker. He sat near Flicker's home. Flicker opened his wings. Coyote said, 'Codi, your house is beginning to burn,' and he started to run. But the bird said, 'No, that is only my wings. Come back'" (Opler 1994 [1938], 276). In a footnote, Morris Opler 1994 [1938], who recorded the myth, explains: "The flicker is the red-shafted one, and Coyote mistakes the red under its wings for fire" (276).

Blue grouse plumage does not in any way evoke an image of fire, but whoever has observed the mountain quail (*Oreortyx pictus*) can see the links between a glistening reddish glow and this quail species that is very common in northern California. It has a reddish-brown patch on its throat and the same color on its sides: "Chestnut throat-patch bordered by narrow black band and adjacent white band. . . . Sides chestnut interrupted with conspicuous vertical white bars" (Gutiérrez and Delehanty 1999, 2). Moreover, the Takelma version explicitly calls the bird a "quail." The mountain quail's geographic range also includes Oregon.

The Atsugewi version puts more stress on the morphological similarity between the bird referent and a witch's broom—a very dense mass of small shoots that grow on the branch of a tree or shrub after infestation by a fungus or virus. Such masses may indeed be taken for gallinaceous birds whose close-fitting plumage blends into the vegetation, and the myth tells the listener to look for witch's brooms, which may in reality be the birds he is hunting. The gallinaceous birds in this Atsugewi version could be grouse, quail, ptarmigan, or others.

But, in fact, the last version points to a quail, as do the other two, especially given the hunting that Native Americans did traditionally. The quail, all species taken together (there is also the California quail, *Callipepla californica*, but it does not have the right plumage), was undoubtedly the bird used the most often in the region that interests us: "Quail were widely utilized by the aborigines of California. In writing of the Pomo, Barrett (1952, 98) states: 'Perhaps no other kind of bird was more esteemed as a food than the quail. Certainly no other land bird was more used'" (Nissen 1977, 217).

In the cultures we have studied, quail hunting is attested at least among the Yana, whose means of capture included snares (Gifford and Klimek 1939, 80). Hunting with fire is also documented among many Californian peoples, although the methods are not always clearly described or lack sufficient detail to identify the smoke-hunting one in the myth:

> The use of fire at night as an aid in hunting quail is also reported. . . . Driver (1937, 111) records the use of fire at night for bird hunting, especially quail, among the Monache, Yokuts, and Bankalachi of the southern Sierra Nevada, but no detail is given as to how this was done. For the Tubatulabal, Voegelin (1938, 13) describes the method as follows: "Lighted torches, made from sticks on which pitch had been smeared, [were] waved under trees where quail were roosting at night; as birds flew down they were easily clubbed." Sparkman (1908, 199) also details this method of capture for the Luiseno: "The valley quail, found in great numbers in the San Luis Rey valley and adjacent country, even to the summit of Palomar, have always been eaten. They were formerly killed with the bow, and were also hunted at night with fire, dry stems of cholla cactus being set on fire and used to attract them; when they flew towards the light they were knocked down with sticks." (Nissen 1977, 225)

Other evidence shows, indirectly, that the Apache used a similar method. In his ethnography of the Walapai, a Southwest people, Alfred Kroeber notably says "the method of building a fire under trees where quail roosted was not used" (1935, 68). He was referring to another anthropologist who had worked among the Havasupai, likewise a Southwest people, and who also reported the same negative finding: "Unlike the White Mountain Apache, the Havasupai do not build fires under trees in which doves and quail roost in order to club the dazed birds" (Spier 1928, 113n1). After enquiring, we have been unable to establish whether Leslie Spier's finding came from his own informants, who would have thus reported a hunting method of another people, the Apache, or whether he himself had looked through the literature to find out.

Nonetheless, the evidence is sufficient to establish that all three versions of the mytheme, whether the Yana, the Atsugewi, or the Takelma, are based on a Native method of hunting quail by smoking them out. The myth therefore corroborates use of this method among these peoples. What about Silver Fox? What does the quail hunting mytheme tell us about traits specific to the gray fox?

A bit of animal behavior will put us on the path to understanding the context of the myth. The relationship between the gray fox and trees has already been established. Remember, the gray fox is so tree-loving that it has been nicknamed the "tree fox." *Urocyon cinereoargenteus* climbs trees, sometimes takes up residence in them by making dens and, what is more, feeds in them. Its arboreal lifestyle may be astonishing.

> Gray foxes climb trees to forage (Grinnell et al. 1937, Gunderson 1961), rest (Seton 1929, Yeager 1938, Leopold 1959), or escape (Terres 1939, Carr 1945). (Fritzell 1987, 414)

> Gray foxes have been found denning in hollow trees 7.6 m (Grinnell et al. 1937) to 9.1 m (Davis 1960) above the ground. (Cypher 2003, 521)

Next in importance in the gray fox diet are birds, including quail (Grinnell et al. 1937, 448; Trapp and Hallberg 1975, 171). On this subject, a biologist calls the gray fox one of the quail's worst enemies. More interestingly, he mentions a scene that Natives undoubtedly know all too well: bunches of feathers from quails that have fallen prey to foxes. "Predatory animals and birds help to account for the high rate of mortality among the young birds [mountain quail], so that, in spite of the large broods hatched, only a few ever reach maturity. Wildcats and gray foxes seem to be their greatest enemies. These animals are also sufficiently agile to capture the old birds as well, for bunches of their feathers are often found" (Bent et al. 1932, 50). The gray fox also eats quail eggs, at least those of one species: "Nelson and Handley (1938) reported on fox behavior in raiding bobwhite quail nests" (Trapp and Hallberg 1975, 171).

Finally, among other tactics, the gray fox, like all other canids, hunts by lying in wait. Hidden from view or not, it will wait for its prey to approach. Foxes can also deceive birds by imitating their cries or by acting in a specific way to arouse their curiosity. Such behaviors have been observed in several fox species, and it would be no surprise if the gray fox acted similarly:

> The fox, who in fables deceives his victims, particularly birds both wild and domestic, with flattery, has been observed luring birds in the wild by several means. An Athabaskan trapper reported hearing a red fox mimic loons in order to entice one to the shore. Noting a similar behavior in Arctic foxes, Reverend Wood writes: "It is found that this animal possesses the power of imitating the cries of the birds on which it loves to feed, and it is probable that it employs this gift for the purpose of decoying its prey to their destruction." Foxes have been observed "rolling" (i.e., summoning them, the way that church bells summon people) for birds, exciting their curiosity by running in circles, and leaping about. (Hufford 1987, 173)

Foxes of all species can be so clever and wily that one cannot help but be awed by the extent of their "powers." A New Jersey farmer, who had a gray fox and three fox cubs tethered in his yard, noticed that his poultry were disappearing for no apparent reason. He set out to solve the mystery. To his surprise, he found that the foxes had worked out a brilliant subterfuge. A fox would push its food to the limit of its chain, and a hen, feeling in security, would come and peck away at the food. With a leap, the fox would pounce on the hen, thus getting a live meal in exchange (Seton 1953 [1909], vol. 1, 590).

All of the elements are now in place. A Native observer can therefore verify first-hand the exactitude of the myth. Knowing on the one hand everything a gray fox can do, and on the other hand its diet of gallinaceous birds, as well as its preference for tree living, he can figure out what has happened on discovering under a tree, most often a pine when identified (Yana and Atsugewi versions), scattered feathers and traces of a fox's presence all around—telltale signs of a fruitful quail hunt. As for the fox being associated with the use of smoke while hunting, this association of ideas can likely be put down to its "powers." Universally, it has a reputation of being one of the wiliest animals ever: "It appears impossible *not* to mention the fox's cunning, which is always referred to by naturalists" (Hufford 1987, 165). When the Innu of the Eastern Subarctic were surveyed to find out how they perceive animals (Clément 1992b; 2012), the findings revealed profound recognition not only of the fox's ruses, but also of its reputed wizard-like if not magical powers. In sum, the clever fox is a widespread stereotype among Native American peoples.

The smoke hunting in the myth may also be merely a reminiscence by some Native groups of quail hunting in the rain—or afterwards in the fog (in a way, a sort of smoke)—when birds with wet plumage were easier to catch, by foxes and humans alike.

> [Pima] Torch hunts were undertaken after days of rain. In a drizzle, Gambel's Quail especially were more flightless and would flock up under the brush. (Rea 2007, 75)

> The Cupeno, Luiseno, Diegueno, and Chemehuevi practiced this method of capture. Drucker (1937a, 47) notes that: "Quail were run down in wet, cold weather when their feathers were too wet for them to fly far." (Nissen 1977, 225)

The third mytheme, quoted in the opening to this chapter, is as intriguing as the other two. Again, as will be seen, it conveys a hidden meaning, which will enable us to retrace the etymon of Fox who digs up yellow jacket larvae using his penis. The Yana version is not set within a larger whole of several mythemes embedded in each other, as were the two preceding mythemes. It is presented continuously, with the Trickster making his imitation right after the host shows his way of getting food:

Coyote asked, "Son-in-law, how did you catch those yellow-jackets?" Silver Fox said, "I smoked them out with leaves. After smoking them out I dug them up with my penis. When the yellow-jackets came, I did not run. There is lots of meat down in the nest. When the sun rises I hold my hand over my eyes and see the yellow-jackets going into their holes." Coyote went out and did so. He saw the yellow-jackets' nest, smoked them, then dug out the nest with his penis. The yellow-jackets began to bite his penis. For a while he stood it, then could not any longer. He rolled on the ground with pain; then he went off. He said, "Son-in-law, I'm sick. The yellow-jackets bit me all over." (Sapir 1910, 212)

Yellow jackets are paper wasps. They mix their saliva with wood particles to construct nests made of a papery material (Powell and Hogue 1979, 337). Some species (*Vespula* spp.) nest on the ground, specifically six different Californian species, and the nests may be as big as 30 centimeters in diameter in late summer (Borror and White 1970, 348). "The colonies may become very large by late summer or fall" (Powell and Hogue 1979, 339).

Yellow jacket larvae were a much-sought-after food of choice in the American West, notably in California among the Pomo, the Achumawi, the Miwok, the Haidu, and others. The Yana, too, enjoyed eating them. As may be easily deduced, the gathering method in the myth was also the one actually in use: "Yellowjackets [were] killed by smudging. Yellowjacket larvae [were] eaten" (Gifford and Klimek 1939, 81).

The Takelma, who also have their own version of the same mytheme, likewise loved eating *Vespula* larvae, and their gathering method—which is still mentioned without ever being described in detail—was identical to the one of the Yana and others: "Outside of such larger game as elk and deer the [Takelma] Indians were fond of grasshoppers . . . and of the white larvæ of the yellow-jacket (*dếl*), the yellowjackets themselves being smoked out of their holes" (Sapir 1907, 260).

The Takelma version differs from the Yana version on a major point: the digging stick (= penis) for digging up larvae becomes a pestle (= penis) for crushing them in order to prepare them for eating.

FOX DIGS OUT YELLOW-JACKETS

And when it dawned, then again Fox went out to hunt, and in the evening he returned.. "*Hẽ+*! Father, Fox has brought home many yellow-jackets."—"Squirrel-tongued, ask of him, 'How did you get them?'" Next door she ran. "'How did you get them?' says my father to you."—"How did I get them? I set fire to them in the earth. Thereupon the yellow-jackets everywhere swarmed up. I dug them out. Then with my penis I squashed them all," he said. Next door she went back. "Father, 'I set fire to them in the earth,' he said," Squirrel- tongued related to her father. "Father, 'I set them on fire in the earth,' he said. 'Thereupon the yellow-jackets swarmed up, then I dug them out, and then I squashed them all with my penis,'", she said. "Cᵋéhehehe! He, for his part, has a small penis, but as for me, I have a big one with me", he said.

The next day came, and just then Coyote again in his turn set fire to them in the earth. Then, 'tis said, the yellow-jackets swarmed up from every side; he dug them out, and all the yellow-jackets he squashed with his penis; now they stung him. One nest he dug out. And he died, and again now the ants bit him. "S'ᵋá! They have waked me up, when, as it seems, I was sleeping a little while ago," he said. One (nest) he brought home. Just in this way he always killed one, then always died. (Sapir 1909a, 81–82)

Among the Yana, the digging stick is described as a "long sharpened pole," made generally from a pole with at least one end hardened by the action of fire (Sapir and Spier 1943, 258). It obviously suggests a penis. And there is more. For example, an observer may notice that a person digging up larvae with a digging stick inserts it into the nest through a circular orifice that forms the entrance, and whose diameter may be up to 3 or 4 centimeters wide, this being fairly suggestive in itself. The comparison becomes extremely hard to avoid if one adds the repeated movements back and forth. The same observations apply just as much to the Takelma version. The anthropological literature tells us little about the exact way of crushing the larvae, but one may imagine the likely back-and-forth movement, not to mention the possibility of a recipient that likewise has an orifice. This possibility is suggested by a way of crushing seeds from, it seems, a sort of sunflower: "Among these was the *làmx*, the seed apparently of a species of sunflower. When the plants were dry the seeds were beaten out by a stick used for the purpose (*mōt!ȍp'*) into a funnel-shaped deer-skin pouch (*ū'ɛxi*) with the mouth wider than the bottom" (Sapir 1907, 259).

If the mytheme—Fox using his penis to dig up yellow jacket larvae—serves to explain a human method of food procurement, what about the relationship between the gray fox itself, as a species, and yellow jackets? There are several ways of looking at this relationship. First, its behavior. The gray fox not only eats insects but also does so in huge amounts. In an area of comparable altitude, flora, fauna, and so on—the High Sonoran Desert—examination of gray fox stomachs revealed that arthropods were present in over 50% of all cases year-round: "Arthropods occurred in 24 of 45 digestive tracts and were found throughout the year. . . . Insects were the most abundant of the major arthropod groups, being represented throughout the year" (Turkowski 1969, 67). For southwestern Utah, a neighboring region, zoologists report that "arthropods dominated the summer diet and fruits dominated the fall and winter diets" (Fritzell and Haroldson 1982, 4).

Yellow jackets are hymenopterans and, although we could find nothing about whether they are part of the fox diet, this seems plausible. At least, an outside observer might think so, given the other insects that the gray fox eats or its other behaviors. First, this fox eats ants crawling on the ground. Second, it sometimes digs into the ground to make itself a den (Seton 1953 [1909], vol. 1, 581, 582; Grinnell et al. 1937, 443). Naturalists note having seen gray foxes looking for insects by scraping rotten wood—where

Fig. 18. Yellow jacket nest.

yellow jackets also make their nests (Powell and Hogue 1979, 339):
"We have seen places where the Gray-fox had been scratching
the decayed logs and the bark of trees in order to obtain insects"
(Seton 1953 [1909], vol. 1, 588).

Last but not least, we wished to verify whether Fox may have
been equipped with his own digging stick. Were we a Native who
had listened to the myth and who was now cutting up a gray fox,
we would examine its genitals more carefully and notice—in the
way Native Americans examine and observe, as discussed in the
introduction to this book—the presence of a baculum or penile
bone (Burt 1960, 15). And although such a bone exists in other
mammals, telling and retelling of the myth would help to maintain the mytheme and all its elements: Fox digging up larvae;
his penis serving as the tool; the digging stick used by members

of Yana society; and the presence of a penile bone in dogs. First impressions can be lasting.

In this mytheme about digging up yellow jacket larvae, two or three details still have to be cleared up. First, no season is specified for the mytheme, it being defined as winter in the preceding cases. One may suppose the summer—the time when yellow jackets are active. Second, in the first Yana version, Fox is speaking truthfully when, after presenting his own method of getting larvae, he exclaims "There is lots of meat down in the nest." The nests do contain a lot of occupants. There are even said to be thousands, up to fifteen thousand individuals in a single nest (Bohart and Bechtel 1957)!

Right after this comment, Silver Fox spells out his own way of locating nests: "When the sun rises I hold my hand over my eyes and see the yellow-jackets going into their holes." The wasps are active from dawn to dusk, never at night. A nest can therefore be found once it comes to life in early morning. An observer has noted a different method among the Achumawi, a people also from northeastern California, who live next to the Yana. The presence of this method shows that several ways exist to find yellow jackets and that the one in the myth could be as valid as this one:

> It was amusing to see them locate a yellow jacket's nest. . . . So Mr. Indian would get a down from the duck . . . and would fasten to its shaft end either a small piece of meat or something sweet. Then Mr. Yellow Jacket would seize hold of the coveted treasure and make a bee line for his home, the down would impede his flight so much that Mr. Indian was enabled to keep close enough to find his nest. Then it would be but short work with fire to clean out their nest. (Neasham 1957, [14])

Of the three Yana mythemes about Silver Fox (as well as the Atsugewi and Takelma variants), we have deliberately left out the anticlimaxes, that is, the consequences of contravening Fox's advice. These little lessons, which we will call the warnings of the myth, have a purpose and are meant to prevent problems—instead of solving them—by showing how an extreme scenario would play out.

The images are indeed extreme and gripping, be they branches that fall and hit the Trickster when he neglects to lower his head while looking for *cu'nna* in the junipers with his hook pole (Yana and Atsugewi versions), or burning branches that also fall down on him— "they hit him and burned him badly"—while he hunts for gallinaceous birds in the pines by smoking them out (Atsugewi version). When the yellow jackets sting Trickster on his penis, the warning is just as dramatic. These wasps are known for inflicting very intense pain on those who bother them: "They are vicious defenders of the nest and deliver extremely painful stings when disturbed" (Powell and Hogue 1979, 339). Just imagine the effect on the genitals, a sensitive area for a man if ever there was one, and the digging stick and penis combination gains even more in intensity and meaning. The warning could not be more effective.

In summary, when we examine the Yana, Atsugewi, and Takelma versions of the mythemes of Fox looking for roots in trees, for gallinaceous birds, and for yellow jackets, we see a close to perfect symbiosis between humans and animals in their many aspects. This is much less so if the stories are taken at face value. Three human methods of food procurement appear in these mythemes, and each of them corresponds not only to a food item of the gray fox—mistletoe berries, quails, and insects—but also to its anatomy and behavior. Its anatomy appears in at least two cases: sharply curved claws to pull down juniper branches; and a penile bone that evokes the image of a digging stick. Its feeding behavior appears in all three cases: the fox feeds on berries found on trees by climbing them; it hunts gallinaceous birds by lying in wait and using much cunning and finesse; and, finally, it digs into soil or rotten wood to get at insects. These combinations of elements make the Silver Fox mythemes real gems that generations of storytellers have honed to perfection through the ages.

7   Wildcat Beats a Blanket (California)

> Coyote went to visit Wildcat. There was not much in the
> house to eat, so Wildcat told his two daughters to bring
> him a blanket, and a little basket. The blanket he folded
> and put across his knee, and the basket he put at his feet.
> Then he beat the blanket, and mesquite dropped out of
> it, and fell into the basket at his feet. So he gave Coyote
> plenty to eat.
>
> —Ruth Benedict, "Serrano Tales"

The Serrano of southern California also have two Bungling Host
myths that feature the same host. This host, Wildcat, provides the
Trickster, Coyote, with a meal, sometimes larvae cooked in ashes,
and sometimes mesquite meal obtained from a beaten blanket.
Both versions pose the same kind of problem as we have seen
previously with the Yana. On the one hand, the anthropological
literature on the Serrano is almost nonexistent. On the other, these
two episodes, which feature the same character as the initial host,
raise a twofold question: do they serve to present characteristics
or behaviors of the cat family, or are they intended only to explain
food preparations that humans alone like to eat?

The Serrano once numbered in the thousands but are now 350
people divided between two southern Californian communities:
the San Manuel Band of Mission Indians and the Morongo Band,
who also include Cahuilla and Cupeno Native Americans. Their

language is for all purposes extinct, and the latest, if not the only, fieldwork on their culture and traditional economy goes back more than three quarters of a century ago (Strong 1929; Benedict 1924; Drucker 1937).

The Serrano used to live mainly by gathering and hunting. The plant foods they gathered were mesquite pods, pine seeds, yucca roots, and the fruits of several cactus species. The animals they hunted included deer, mountain goats, antelopes, rabbits, small rodents, and several bird species—quail most of all (Bean and Smith 1978).

Their traditional territory was east of the present-day city of Los Angeles, in and around the San Bernardino mountains. This land varies a lot in altitude, with elevations reaching 450 meters in desert regions and 3,350 meters in mountainous areas. Most of the villages were however in the zone called the Upper Sonora, below 1,500 meters, with a few campsites in the desert near watering holes.

It is in this setting that the Serrano produced their two myths about the Bungling Host. The first one refers to a food preparation they made from larvae called *pexa'kam*.

WILDCAT COOKS LARVAE IN THE EMBERS

I. Wildcat had two daughters, and he told them to build a fire as if to roast something. Then he went and lay down there himself, and buried himself in the ashes. He told his daughters, "After a while dig up the ashes, and take out the food." So after a while Wildcat's daughters did as they were told. There in the pit were many great roasted *pexa'kam* (green larvae five inches long and big around as a finger; a great delicacy in olden times), and Wildcat came walking up from the other direction, and joined his daughters and Coyote at the feast.

Now Coyote thought this was very easy, so he invited Wildcat to visit him, and he told his daughters to prepare the pit, and he went and lay down in it. Then Coyote's daughters dug up the pit.

But there were no *pexa'kam*. Coyote was cooked in the ashes. So Wildcat went home. (Benedict 1926, 16)

The host is a bobcat (*Lynx rufus* = *Felis rufus*). "Wildcat" is a very widespread alternate name (Anderson and Lovallo 2003, 758; Seton 1953 [1909], vol. 1, 212), as is the literal translation, *chat sauvage,* in Quebec. The animal is well known throughout the southern regions of Canada.

Wildcat has two daughters, a number no more accidental than any other element of these myths. It is the mean litter size of the female throughout the animal's geographic range: "Despite the problems with estimating average litter size, a number of authors have reported means. Anderson (1987) surveyed 21 bobcat studies and found that average litter sizes ranged from 1.7 to 3.6 kittens/litter, with a mean of 2.7" (Anderson and Lovallo 2003, 766). Bobcat females hence give birth to two or three kittens. The kittens remain with their mother until the next breeding season, i.e., for a period of seven months or longer: "Kittens are dependent on their mother until about seven months of age, after which they spend progressively more time away from her, although some mother-young associations may last a year or more" (Sunquist and Sunquist 2002, 194).

That is the backdrop to their behavior. In fact, a female and her kittens really look impressive when they come into view, as described by a naturalist in this account: "'While I was looking at the tree and admiring its beautiful proportions, a full-grown Wild-cat with 2 kittens . . . emerged from a clump of underbrush a few yards below. The old Cat was doubtless giving her young a lesson in woodcraft'" (Seton 1953 [1909], vol. 1, 227). In the myth, this animal likewise teaches human listeners another lesson: how to cook safely.

The lesson first focuses on how to build a roasting pit. Wildcat asks his daughters to make one. Among California's Native peoples, it is known that food preparation was most often woman's work.

In fact, a sexual division of labor ran through all areas of life: "All California Indian tribes distinguished between the statuses and roles of men and women, assigning to each sex special tasks, duties and prerogatives. The pattern of sex dichotomy reveals a remarkable similarity from one end of the state to the other. . . . Most household duties fell to the women. . . . The preparation of food-stuffs—grinding seeds (fig. 3), pounding (fig. 4) and leaching acorns, and the like—as well as their preservation were definitely feminine tasks. Normally women did the cooking" (Wallace 1978, 683).

Native American roasting pits varied somewhat by region, by type of food to be cooked, by materials available, and by other factors. In general, a pit was dug in line with the needs of its user, either an individual or a community, and its bottom covered with hot ashes or fire-heated stones. On this warm bed were laid the food items in successive layers separated (or not) by plant matter (grasses, conifer needles, etc.). All of this was next covered with earth. The Serrano myth refers to the use of ashes. A more or less detailed description has come to us from the Tohono O'odham, who, as we have seen, also inhabited the Sonoran zone, though farther east in Arizona:

> And you could barbecue *chuuwi* [a rabbit] if you wanted, *chuáma*. Won't take long to do. All you got to do is to make a little hole in there and build a fire. . . . Then when your fire goes down a little bit, then you kind of push the ashes and coals away and just lay it right in there. Then cover it back with that ashes, about half way or all the way around. And put a little dirt on top of it, and let it go. If you want to, you can build a little fire on top of it. In about half an hour you're going to have a barbecue. (Frank Jim in Rea 1998, 88)

Roasting pits were used to cook both plants and animals. Their use is attested among the Serrano (Drucker 1937, 9), with all details matching those of the myth. The Yana of California, farther north, similarly collected pine needles to cover the food they cooked:

"The latter [the men] dug the roasting pits, collected firewood and pine needles and placed rocks in the pits over the wood. . . . One man took charge of the actual roasting, placing the various sets of roots belonging to different women each in its own part of the pit . . . and covering them all with the pine needles. Before daybreak he would light the fire and cover the pit with dirt, then allow the roots to cook all day" (Sapir and Spier 1943, 250–51).

Pine needles were widely used throughout North America for roasting pits. In the early nineteenth century, Lewis and Clark saw Nez Perce using them for a pit to cook a bear (Lévi-Strauss 1995 [1991]: 6). The Thompson Salish of British Columbia lined their pits similarly for any food they cooked ("Dry pine needles were placed over fir branches at the bottom of a cooking pit"; Teit in Turner et al. 1990). Other peoples could be cited on this point.

Therefore it is very probable that the Serrano lined their roasting pits with pine needles too. If so, their way of cooking *pexa'kam* can be linked even more strongly to our story and to one of its animal etymons. Indeed, Wildcat has his own "roasting pit," if we may call it that, which may be likened in every way externally to the roasting pit of humans.

This point can be explained with some details on animal behavior. Among other things, bobcats are known to bury their leftover food, be it a large game animal (a deer) or a small one (a rabbit or rodent). A bobcat specialist has described this behavior and the visual result of such food caching—what appears to the eye and what strangely looks like the roasting pit of Native peoples, once completed with its covering of pine needles and soil:

> After feeding on a large kill, the bobcat attempts to hide what remains of the carcass for later feeding. Using its forefeet, it scrapes leaves, pine needles, twigs, dirt, or snow [in this case, in winter] over the carcass (Sunquist and Sunquist 2002). . . . The bobcat remains in the vicinity of its kill, making frequent trips back to feed and to protect the carcass from other bobcats, carnivores, or scavengers. Sometimes a bobcat buries the uneaten portions of its

prey. Young (1978, 106) stated, "Instances have been found where a pile of the intestines of a squirrel were covered with a mound of dust and pine needles scraped from a trail." (Hansen 2007, 44)

There is no doubt that Serrano listeners of our story would recognize these food caches as signs of a bobcat's presence. Hearing this myth, they would also, consciously or unconsciously, link these mounds of buried remains to the roasting pits made by their people.

But we can push the comparison even farther and uncover other relevant etymons of the story, some more important than others. Let us take, for example, the food item that is cooked, the much-loved *pexa'kam*. As stated by the storyteller (or by the person who wrote down the myth), these are "green larvae five inches long and big around as a finger; a great delicacy in olden times." What kind of larvae? We found no adequate answer by looking through the relevant word-lists, whether Serrano or Takic (the linguistic family to which the Serrano language belongs) (e.g., Miller 1967). The Native peoples of California, and the American West in general, consumed all kinds of insects, larvae, and worms, including yellow jacket larvae (as we have seen), caterpillars, grasshoppers, and others. The possibilities are limited, however, by two *pexa'kam* characteristics: their color—green—and their size—12 centimeters. A green-colored invertebrate is in fact eaten by the Tohono O'odham, who live east of the Serrano, and it seems to match the myth's description in other ways: "The worms used were, when young, about an inch long and yellow, but they matured in a few days and turned green. They appeared in quantities just after or during the rainy season on any green growth, especially the amaranth (*Amaranthus palmeri*). Everyone dropped work to gather them, for they were considered a great delicacy" (Castetter and Underhill 1935, 43).

The same authors go on to describe the length of the "worms." They were "gathered by women who pinched off their heads and squeezed out the entrails, leaving the outer portion which was lengthened in the process to a narrow string six inches [15 cm] long" (Castetter and Underhill 1935, 47). They are, in fact, inch-worms of different species that seem to vary with the people who feed on them, such as *Trichoplusia ni,* whose host plant is often a cultigen, or *Hyles lineata,* which lives in symbiosis with a desert plant, *Boerhaavia erecta,* as reported by anthropologists who found similar consumption of caterpillars among the Seri of northwestern Mexico—immediate neighbours of the Tohono O'odham: "Like the Papago [former name of the Tohono O'odham], the Seri gathered caterpillars of the white-lined sphinx moth (*Hyles lineata*), which feed on desert ephemerals during warm weather (Figure 3.5; see *Boerhaavia erecta*). The caterpillar was called *hehe icám,* 'plant its-life', or "plant's live thing." The head was twisted off, the vis-cera stripped out with the fingers, and the "skin" (actually mostly muscle or meat) cooked" (Felger and Moser 1991 [1985], 39).

In everyday English, these caterpillars are indifferently called larvae, worms, or loopers, according to their developmental stage or other criteria. Whatever the actual species, the Tohono O'odham cooked them in the same way that the Serrano myth suggests—in a roasting pit. "The surplus [of worms] was dried and stored but kept better if pit-baked before drying" (Castetter and Underhill 1935, 47).

To return to our comparison, if the Serrano can pull cooked "worms" out of a roasting pit, what exactly can bobcats pull out of their own "roasting pits"? The answer becomes clear if we realize that bobcat "roasting pits," and the carcasses buried in them, very soon attract all kinds of necrophagous insects. Decomposition may occur in as little as one day under extreme conditions: "The remains are cached or covered. . . . Whether the cat stays near the carcass and how long appears to depend on many factors, including the cat's fat reserves. . . . Decomposition rate is also important, as high heat and humidity may render carcasses unpalatable in a day or two" (Sunquist and Sunquist 2002, 189–90). Once decomposition

Fig. 19. Inchworm on a plant.

has begun, necrophagous flies need very little time to invade the carcasses: "Blowflies (Calliphoridae) are the most significant group of arthropods in carrion decomposition. . . . They are among the first insects to arrive at a corpse and their larvae (named maggots) make up the dominant part of the biomass" (Kocarek 2001, 117).

This comparison may seem farfetched. Let us put ourselves, however, in the position of an observer who comes to a bobcat's food cache, notices the covering of soil and pine twigs, which already conjures up the myth, and sees blowfly maggots crawling about. The temptation is strong to see support for the myth and conclude that once again it makes sense. The observer has understood that the myth teaches something by drawing attention to a bobcat behavior.

This etymon would be enough to explain the basis of the mytheme, were it not for a key detail that cannot be separated from it and remains unexplained. The myth states that Wildcat buries himself in the ashes and later reappears from another direction. Of course, it is known that bobcats like burned-over habitats, a behavior they share with other members of the cat family. The reason is simple. A forest fire, whether or not controlled, is followed by successive stages of forest regeneration, which initially attract many herbivores such as deer and rabbits and, consequently, their usual predators: "Some human land-use practices can actually enhance bobcat habitat. In Louisiana and Alabama, bobcats favor open areas in bottomland hardwood forests, which are created by farms, timber cuts, roads, pipelines, and prescribed burning. Such activity maintains areas in early successional stages, resulting in dense growth of briars, vines, and grasses—good habitat for prey species as well as ideal hunting and daytime resting sites for bobcats" (Hansen 2007, 76).

The habitats are so good that a Subarctic Innu hunter preferred this kind of terrain when hunting the Canada lynx (*Lynx canadensis*), which is closely related to the bobcat (*Lynx rufus*) and is quite similar in hunting behavior: "My partner, Ashini, was a specialist on lynx hunting; this was his hobby. During the many years that I knew him he more than doubled the catch of other Indians around. The tract of land he had selected was specially adapted to this, old burned ground, covered with a growth of birch, poplar, balsam and black spruce. In such sections the Northern hare, squirrel, ruffed grouse and spruce partridge abound, and these are the natural food of the lynx" (Comeau 1909, 65).

But this is still not enough. More is needed to explain why the bobcat of our myth literally buries itself in ashes. And there is more to the story's etymon—actually, its double etymon. There are really two distinct phenomena, which, once amalgamated, will clearly solve the puzzle of the Serrano mytheme.

The first one is unrelated to bobcats and has more to do with Serrano customs—as unusual as that may seem. The Serrano had developed female ceremonies that a girl or woman would take part in at certain key points of her life, and during which she would be "roasted" in an earth oven very similar to a roasting pit, except that the bottom was lined with hot sand instead of hot ashes. Ruth Benedict describes the ceremony held at adolescence:

> At adolescence a pit was dug long enough for the girl to lie in, and several feet deep. In this a fire was lighted and rocks put in to heat. When the stones were hot, sand was shovelled in, and raked about till it was evenly warmed. The girl was then brought out, and lay down in the pit, and the hot sand was shovelled over her up to the chin, and a basket-hat placed over her face. When the sand cooled, more sand was heated near by, and thrown on the pit. The girl stayed in the pit usually not more than one day. (Benedict 1924, 380)

Women who had just given birth were likewise "oven-roasted" with their newborn children (Benedict 1924, 381; Bean and Smith 1978, 572).

It is notable that this type of ceremony was only for the women, the men having other initiations that were for them alone. We can therefore clearly say that the Wildcat of our myth is female because, like Serrano women, it too was cooked in a roasting pit. The myth already provided us with a clue when we learned about Wildcat's daughters. In the natural environment, kittens live with their mother and not with their polygamous father: "Like most female cats, the female bobcat is the consummate single parent. The male plays no part in rearing of the young (Bailey 1974; Sunquist 1987; Miller 1991). In fact, the only time the female is tolerant of the male's presence is during breeding" (Hansen 2007, 53).

Therefore, the myth was once again understandable to its listening audience insofar as the latter made a visual association between Serrano women lying down in an earth oven and the female bobcat of the myth. We have only to discuss further the presence of a bobcat in the pit, instead of a human. This is the second phenomenon we mentioned above. To understand it we should consult a myth from another people, the Shawnee of eastern North America, to explain how spots first appeared on the bobcat's fur. Indeed, whatever the habitat, a bobcat's body is covered with dark spots that range from dark brown to almost black: "There are distinct dark brown or black spots covering the back and legs. The white belly fur has distinct black spots" (Hansen 2007, 23). All this is explained in the Shawnee myth:

WHY THE BOBCAT HAS SPOTS

Bobcat was chasing Rabbit and had almost caught him when Rabbit jumped into a hollow tree. Rabbit called out to Bobcat, "I'll stay in here, forever; you'll never eat me!" Bobcat responded, "You'll have to come out; you'll get hungry." Rabbit knew Bobcat was right, so he called out again, saying, "Why don't you make a big fire so you can roast me as soon as I run out?"

Bobcat thought this was a good idea and built a roaring fire. As soon as the fire was hot enough, Rabbit jumped out of the tree, right into the center of the fire, scattering hot coals all over Bobcat's coat. Even though Bobcat jumped into the river and didn't catch fire, his fur was singed dark brown in every place a coal landed, and you can see those spots on his coat even today. (Martin 1994, 25–26)

Must we look for other stories of this sort? There is enough unity in Native American thought from one ocean to the other, certainly in North America, and undoubtedly beyond, to postulate links between this origin myth and the associations one may make between the dark spots on a bobcat's coat and the embers of a fire.

If observed closely while in use, a roasting pit may look like a bobcat's coat when one sees the dark embers showing through, here and there, the fine covering of sandier and lighter-colored soil with hair-like pine needles. We also know how easily a bobcat can melt into its surroundings. Listen to this ethnozoologist describe his trouble making out a bobcat against its natural background in the Sonoran desert: "Walking quietly through the mesquite bosques of the middle Gila, I have at various times had my attention drawn to twin black-and-white objects that slowly resolved themselves first into a large head, then slowly into an entire animal. The carefully camouflaged critter was a resting Bobcat. The soft browns and muted spots blend so well into the desert vegetation, even at close range" (Rea 1998, 230–31).

To return to the myth, there remains only one step for us to show a female bobcat lying down in the roasting pit, and that step is provided by the existence of those women-only ceremonies we have mentioned. Yes, Wildcat did come walking up from another direction, but this detail simply shows the listener that, despite appearances, he never did get roasted in the ashes. The ash-filled layer concealed something other than a bobcat!

Coyote tried to do the same thing and failed because he represents a human, as we argued earlier in the introduction to this book. A human might survive hot sand, but not burning embers.

The mytheme of a bobcat lying down in a roasting pit is an excellent example of successive layers of etymons, where the deepest and primary ones come to light only after we have elucidated the most apparent and secondary ones, which superficially mask the origin of the myth. This mytheme is also revealing when compared with the Tohono O'odham mytheme of the snake in the embers, which we saw in chapter 2. Each of these mythical episodes, though similarly constructed, is explained differently, first by the cultural setting, as perhaps to be expected, and second by the very animals that personify the host. These animals are different and also display different behaviors, as seen in specific details that seem trivial and yet hold much meaning because they are specific to a species. In one case, a snake rises abruptly from the embers; in another, a bobcat lies down but not really because it comes walking up from another direction.

The second Serrano mytheme is perhaps easier to understand. The host, Bobcat, receives the trickster, Coyote, and makes him a meal, this time by beating a blanket. An extract from this myth opens the present chapter.

WILDCAT BEATS A BLANKET

II. Coyote went to visit Wildcat. There was not much in the house to eat, so Wildcat told his two daughters to bring him a blanket, and a little basket. The blanket he folded and put across his knee, and the basket he put at his feet. Then he beat the blanket, and mesquite dropped out of it, and fell into the basket at his feet. So he gave Coyote plenty to eat.

Now when Coyote got home, he invited Wildcat to visit him, and when he had come, he told his daughters to bring him a blanket, and he folded it across his knee; and a basket, and put it at his feet. Then Coyote began to beat the blanket. He beat it till his knee was bruised, and he beat it till his knee swelled up as big as a cooking pot, and he beat it till he was bloody all over, he had hit himself so hard. And no mesquite came.

So Wildcat went home. (Benedict 1926, 16–17)

For the Serrano, mesquite was a staple food, if not the main one: "On the desert mesquite was the standard vegetable food, and was highly valued everywhere in the Serrano territory" (Benedict 1924, 391). There are several sorts of mesquite, but all of them belong to the same genus *Prosopis*. Two species coexist in southeastern California, *Prosopis glandulosa* (Honey mesquite) and *Prosopis pubescens* (Screwbean mesquite). The myth alludes to either of them.

Simply put, mesquite pods were generally processed into flour in two major stages: pounding the pods and winnowing. These stages were universal throughout the region (see also chapter 2):

> [Serrano] It [mesquite] was first pounded coarsely, then winnowed, then pounded to fine meal. (Benedict 1924, 391)

> [Cocopa] Cocopa women and sometimes men pounded the pods to remove the seeds and coarse fiber (Kelly 1977). Further shaking and winnowing separated out the larger pieces to leave the mesquite meal. (Hodgson 2001, 180)

The pods were usually pounded with a pestle or a *metate* (a stationary millstone used with a handheld stone), but we have found at least one reference to the use of a hide for this process. Thus, the Mescalero Apache of the Southwest used *metate* and hides interchangeably: "The Mescalero Apache also grind the seeds of *P. prosopis* into flour which is then used in a sort of pancake. The beans are often boiled, then pounded on a hide or ground on a metate" (Castetter 1935, 45). In California, in the Southwest as a whole and elsewhere, indigenous peoples made blankets from hides. The blankets that appear the most often in the literature were made from woven rabbit skin (McGee 1987, 13)—among the Serrano (Benedict 1924, 388)—or from the tanned hides of large mammals. In all likelihood, mesquite pods were not ground on blankets made from woven rabbit skin. The skin had to be stronger to withstand being repeatedly pounded by probably either a wooden pestle or a stone wheel.

Among the Yana of northern California, the literature notes the use of deer hides for blanket making, as well as skins from rabbits and other mammals like bears. Although we have little comparable data for other peoples of the same culture area, we might infer that the use of such skins was widespread:

> Dressed skins supplied robes and blankets. These were dehaired if desired, fleshed, and tanned with brains soaked in water. Specific names were obtained for several types, although their application is not clear. A dehaired buckskin blanket or robe, comprising only a single skin, was *bat'i'lmi*; a grizzly-bear blanket was *t'e'n'mi*; another, used indifferently as robe or blanket, but made up of three or four deer hides sewn together and with the hair left on was *gā'ninna*; a fourth term, *s'ê'mauna*, is given variously in the notes as a "deer-hide blanket sewn together" and as made from a single hide. . . . Narrow strips of jack-rabbit skins were woven into similar robes and blankets: these were presumably not tanned. (Sapir and Spier 1943, 258)

In any event, the Serrano myth supports this inference. Wildcat gets mesquite from a blanket that is beaten, pounded, and struck, and this blanket can be made only from the hide of a large game animal. There is also a reason why the mesquite, once beaten out of the blanket (= hide) drops into a basket. For example, after mashing the mesquite pods on the *metate* and placing them between two deer hides, Seri women of the Southwest winnowed them in a basket. Serrano women lived a bit farther north but in a similar environment and must have acted similarly: "After the pods were mashed they were placed between deer skins to prevent spoiling in the hot July wind. The pounding continued until all the pods were mashed. The women then placed the pestle across the mortar hole. Mashed pods or pulp were put in a basket and gently winnowed by tapping the basket against the pestle" (Felger and Moser 1991 [1985], 339).

We have here a direct allusion to a deer hide that is used to process mesquite. There is another reason, however, for thinking that the hide (= blanket) in the Serrano myth is a deer hide. This reason will lead us to the etymon of the story.

Fig. 20. Bobcat crouching.

We should first note that bears are in no way preyed upon by bobcats. Deer and rabbits, however, are. We can rule out rabbit skins because, practically speaking, it seems clearly improbable that mesquite pods could be mashed on such a fragile material, as we have already noted.

It is now established that deer are a major prey for bobcats throughout their range, although this finding is a very recent one among specialists who study the carnivore: "Surprisingly, deer is an important food for bobcats. Early researchers believed that most of the deer eaten was carrion obtained as a result of sport hunting or winter starvation (Rollings 1945; Pollack 1951a). It is now known that bobcats regularly kill deer" (Hansen 2007, 39).

This being said, we need to add that, in a desert environment or nearby, both the prey and the predator are found in mesquite forests. The deer feed on mesquite pods, as do other herbivores. This has been reported by an observer studying the mesquite complex among the Cahuilla—the immediate southern neighbors of the Serrano: "Many different kinds of game were found in the vicinity of the mesquite trees. Large game such as deer, antelope, and mountain sheep came to eat the pods" (Bean and Saubel 1963, 63).

We have also described earlier how an observer had much trouble distinguishing a bobcat resting amid mesquite trees. A final account from the Southwest describes the presence of bobcats in the same environment: "Bobcats live in a great variety of habitats in Arizona . . . bobcats occur from the base to the tops of most desert ranges, in mesquite woods" (Hoffmeister 1986, 528).

This still does not explain how Wildcat gets mesquite from a blanket (= hide). Nonetheless, the context already explains a lot by directly linking three things to each other: deer hides as blankets; mesquite as food; and bobcats as predators. It is in this setting that the mytheme will be justified.

We have shown that Wildcat uses a deer hide blanket in the myth. To explain why he acts like a human who beats a hide to get food, we will turn to an Innu myth from the Eastern Subarctic. It is about a mother lynx (*Lynx canadensis*) whose young have been devoured by the Trickster and who receives this unexpected predator while "scraping a caribou hide. She works the hide and then she folds it" (Bacon and Vincent 1979, 66). We have already suggested (Clément 2012, 244) that this element should be seen as referring to a lynx's meticulousness when skinning its prey. Like an Innu woman working a hide, a lynx does not rip the skin of its prey. Zoologists have also noticed this carefulness and have described in these terms how a lynx generally goes about eating its largest prey:

> The lynx first devours the fleshy areas, like the haunches or the shoulders. It breaks only very rarely the bones of the limbs. Once its prey has been largely eaten up, it may gnaw on its ribs. It always abandons the intestines and the rumen to other predators. It neatly skins the hide, without ripping it. But when the animal is to all intents consumed, all of the remains are attached in a single piece: head, paws, and hide are not separated from the body. Dispersed

pieces indicate that other predators have come to feed after it; otherwise, the carcass and the viscera are intact." (Herrenschmidt, Debus, and Madier 1994, 4)

A second comment about the lynx in Eastern Europe, *Lynx lynx*, also implies the same observations. The deer's hide is not torn to pieces: "It eats small prey commencing from the head, leaving the rear portion and viscera. In the case of large prey, for example, roe deer, it eats internal organs (apart from the digestive tract) and flesh. It does not tear the skin into bits nor gnaw at large bones" (Heptner and Sludskii 1992, 631). It is also known that the bobcat in particular, when eating a game animal like a deer, begins most often with the haunches, then hides the carcass, including the head, and never eats the rumen (Sunquist and Sunquist 2002, 189). Sometimes, the material covering the site of the food cache includes many deer hairs, as if the hide had undergone a kind of partial hair removal.

The Serrano myth has thus revealed its etymon—in this case, a composite etymon. In it are embedded two elements. Just as a Serrano woman beats a blanket to get mesquite, Wildcat, whom we now know to be female, gets food for her two daughters from a deer hide. Let us push the comparison further. When we come to the site of a deer kill, we see a carcass with its hide or simply the hollowed-out "shell" of a deer—like an untorn blanket—which the mother bobcat has stripped of its edible meat. Alongside, there is still an uneaten rumen. And what sort of food residues will we find in the digestive system of a deer that has been feeding in a mesquite grove? Intact or half-digested mesquite pods.

As Native observers see it, one may say that Wildcat has removed food from the deer hide and that this food is not only meat but also mesquite pods. One may further say that the meat, by itself, is to mesquite what the deer's hide is to the blanket used by humans. When we discussed several etymons in previous chapters, we looked into how a human mind would filter the way it observes animal behaviors. For example, when Woodpecker pulled caribou ribs out of a tree, the perspective was that of a hunter who could see other species as behaving only like himself—in this case, like a caribou hunter and not like an insect eater. As the Native Americans would say, the Trickster (= human) mentally sees caribou ribs, while in reality these are the insects that Woodpecker feeds on.

The same phenomenon is at work in the Serrano myth. Coyote, the Trickster, sees Wildcat's behavior and wrongly interprets it as a human behavior. When a hide is being beaten, the result can only be mesquite meal. That is what Serrano women end up getting. In reality, a hide provides Wildcat with the kind of food a bobcat wants.

We are speaking of a composite etymon because the myth refers to several possibilities, which may be verified separately or together in the natural state: meat removed from a hide or mesquite pods left in a rumen, or both at the same time.

The mytheme has one little detail, however, that we have forgotten and which now stands out because we have cleared up all of the others. Why did Coyote hurt himself while trying to get mesquite meal from the blanket? To understand the reason, we need to refer to the various positions that Native women take when working with a mortar or a *metate* and which may have a counterpart in bobcat behavior. With these tools in front of her, a woman would most often take one of three positions: sitting on her heels; sitting with her legs stretched out in front; or sitting cross-legged. She would very seldom do the pounding standing up. Now, is it a coincidence that the bobcat also hunkers down when eating (= prepares its food)? "The bobcat, like other small cats, crouches and eats its prey" (Hansen 2007, 44).

This being said, the myth has the host placing the blanket across her knee and the basket at her feet, a position that would have her legs outstretched. We think this is not the case, since the mesquite falls into the basket in front of her. She should instead be squatting on her heels with her knees slightly raised, like a bobcat crouching.

Whatever the case, Female Wildcat does not hurt herself in any way. While pounding the hide with her stone wheel or pestle, she avoids hitting her knee, which is just underneath, and concentrates her efforts on where the mesquite pods should be. In contrast, the Trickster, Coyote, is less focused and less on his guard. He violently pounds the blanket wherever he can and, not surprisingly, hurts his knee.

The Serrano mytheme of Wildcat beating a blanket thus warns people using a mortar or *metate* against possible injuries they might inflict on themselves. Similarly, the roasting pit mytheme stresses the danger of burning oneself (Wildcat cannot burn himself because he has already undergone the test of fire, as seen by the spots on his skin). The danger is greater than in a ceremonial earth oven, where the hot sand seems less of a risk to users than do embers.

The preceding demonstration about the two Serrano mythemes would remain incomplete if we failed to mention here certain ways of perceiving Wildcat-Coyote relations, particularly in this culture and in a few neighboring ones. The Serrano—and the Cahuilla notably—divide the members of their society into many local groups or exogamous clans, each of which is associated with one of two equally exogamous moieties (Gifford 1918; Benedict 1924; Bean and Smith 1978). The eponymous animals of the two moieties were *tukwutam* (Wildcat) and *wahi'?iam* (Coyote). Nonetheless, according to Ruth Benedict (1924, 371), there was no taboo on killing or eating them; nor did the Serrano identify them as totems in their myths.

This information is provided only so that we may better define the context in which the myth was heard and told. Listeners would identify all the more with the characters of the Bungling Host story because the same words were commonly used in their society for its members: "It is undoubtedly significant that no hesitation was shown in assigning to any group [clans] its animal designation.

Even where the proper marriage affiliation had been forgotten, the fact that they were "coyote" or "wildcat" was unclouded" (Benedict 1924, 370). To be more specific, the parallel between a female wildcat with her young, which is crouched down to work the hide of a prey, and a Serrano woman, who is crouched down to pound a hide to make mesquite meal, is rich in meaning, all the more so because many girls or women were named "wildcat." But the parallel ends there. One cannot squeeze more out of it, at least not from these Bungling Host episodes, unless one wishes to speculate. These episodes always have an essentially educational goal, and they inexorably lead their listeners to observe animal behaviors, which in turn corroborate the truth of the myth.

8 Deer Kills Her Children and Puts Their Bones Into the Water (Southwest)

> Somewhere on a mountain dwelt Deer and Coyote. Deer spoke thus. To Coyote he [*sic*] said thus, "Come and visit my house." "All right", said Coyote. . . . She arrived there. She entered. "How are things, friend?" "It is good," said Deer. "Sit down and eat. There is wafer bread and I will kill my two children. Please put down the bones carefully. After you have finished eating I shall take them down to the river." Then she finished eating. . . . Then she carried them down. She arrived below at the river and put them into the river, into the water. Then her children came up and they all went.
>
> —Ruth Benedict, "Tales of the Cochiti"

We have already partly dealt with the mythemes where a host gets food by killing his children, who then come back to life once their bones have or have not been put into water. With Beaver as the main protagonist among the Innu, and Seal among the Salish, we might hastily conclude that water resurrects these species because their habitats are aquatic or semi-aquatic. This series has at least one variant, however, where the main protagonist does not at all live in water.

This variant comes to us from the Cochiti of the American Southwest. Here, the species is a deer, an animal whose habitat and behavior are fully terrestrial. By analyzing this variant, we will better understand the motif and, especially, how a mytheme is fed by a system of meaning whose substrate is not always the natural environment alone, but also cultural practices. Through such practices, humans give meaning to what may seem to have none.

The Cochiti have lived in a New Mexican region between Albuquerque and Santa Fe for several hundreds of years. They number over a thousand today and have inhabited the same pueblo (village) since before the first Europeans came (Lange 1979, 366). Their language is still alive. It belongs to the Keresan cultural and linguistic family, which encompasses seven languages—or dialects, according to some—from seven different pueblos on either side of the Rio Grande: Acoma, Zia, Santa Ana, San Felipe, Santo Domingo, Laguna, and Cochiti.

Although farming has been the Cochiti's economic mainstay for several decades, it apparently has not always been so. In the past, hunting played a very big role, so big that it competed with farming in terms of time and effort:

> In general, Southwestern Pueblo tribes have been pictured as primarily farming peoples. Considering their present economy, this exclusion, or at least minimizing, of hunting might be warranted; considering Pueblo economy in past centuries, however, one gains the impression that the importance of agriculture in relation to hunting has been overemphasized. From literature on Cochiti and other Pueblo tribes and from opinions of Cochiti informants, it seems probable that a half-century ago there would have been an important hunting complex at Cochiti. A century or more ago, there might have been a hunting complex that was a strong competitor of agriculture for man-hours and efforts expended. Goldfrank (1927: 83) noted, "Now, very few people hunt at all, but formerly the animals were a much desired food, and there was an elaborate ritual." (Lange 1959, 124–25)

This former importance of hunting should be kept in mind when we analyze the Cochiti variant about a deer and its Bungling Host. But such analysis has its limits. Our ethnography of hunting traditions remains very fragmentary and insufficient for all of the pueblos, especially because their inhabitants have become more and more reluctant to disclose any kind of cultural information (rites, ceremonial organization, archaeological sites, etc.) (Eggan 1979, 233–34).

Anthropologist Ruth Benedict collected several Bungling Host episodes from the Cochiti. We will analyze only one, which has two versions. The first version, which follows, has been translated from an original Cochiti text provided by anthropologist Franz Boas. The second version, which we will also use, was recorded by Benedict. This Cochiti episode about a deer and its Bungling Host is only the first part of a longer myth, a situation that Benedict herself described as atypical. The second part will be discussed later.

DEER AND COYOTE (PART 1)

Somewhere on a mountain dwelt Deer and Coyote. Deer spoke thus. To Coyote he [sic] said thus, "Come and visit my house." "All right", said Coyote. Then she visited the place where Deer dwelt. They were good friends. She arrived there. She entered. "How are things, friend?" "It is good," said Deer. "Sit down and eat. There is wafer bread and I will kill my two children. Please put down the bones carefully. After you have finished eating I shall take them down to the river." Then she finished eating. Then Coyote stayed there. "Friend, I will carry these bones down to the river." Then she carried them down. She arrived below at the river and put them into the river, into the water. Then her children came up and they all went. They arrived (at the house). Next Coyote wanted to imitate her. "Next you, my friend, visit my house!" Then Coyote killed her children. The deer went there. She arrived. She entered Coyote's house. "How are things, friend?" said she. "It is well, sit down! Eat! Here is wafer bread and I have also killed my children. Put down the bones carefully. Later on I shall carry them to the river." Then Deer finished eating. Coyote carried the bones down to the river. She arrived at the river and put them into the water. She waited, but not at all did her children come out. She had killed them forever. Then she went to the place where she dwelt. She arrived there and she told Deer that her children had not come out. Coyote became angry and pursued Deer. (Benedict 1931, 160–61)

Like its counterpart among the Yana of California, this episode has personal meaning to its audience to the extent that the two central characters, Deer and Coyote, are also the names of exogamous matrilineal clans: "The clans are named after plants, animals, and natural phenomena. . . . No ideas of 'totemic' relationships are involved, and no taboos of food or other usages are observed" (Lange 1979, 371). Deer and Coyote are also clan names in several Southwest pueblos: "Many clans bear the names of mammals, such as Deer, Antelope, Bear, Coyote, and Rat (siyana)" (White 1945, 232). Among the Cochiti in particular, Frederick Hodge (1907–1910, 318) reported the clan names of *shrutsuna* (coyote) and *kishqra* (reindeer?). The term *kishqra* is no longer in use, and the author may have been a bit off in his translation, as suggested by the question mark. As a rule, "reindeer" (*Rangifer tarandus*, which is also caribou) are the only members of the deer family with antlers systematically present in males and females alike. In other species, usually only the males have them. But antlers sometimes occur in the females of some species, such as mule deer (*Odocoileus hemionus*) and white-tailed deer (*Odocoileus virginianus*), both of which exist in New Mexico:

[Mule deer] All but 2 of 17 antlered deer reported as females had poorly developed antlers in velvet. (Anderson and Wallmo 1984, 3)

[White-tailed deer] Normally only the bucks carry antlers, although antlered does are occasionally found. (Banfield 1974, 392)

It may be that Hodge's informants described a kind of deer with antlers in both sexes and that, not knowing about the above two species (or about the absence of reindeer in New Mexico), he translated the Native term by "reindeer"—the quintessential species of the deer family where both males and females have antlers.

Nonetheless, we still have not identified the story's central character, whose name Benedict translated laconically as "deer." As we have noted, New Mexico has two deer species: the mule deer and the white-tailed deer, aside from members of the deer family that are not deer (for example, elk, which used to be present). The story's central character could be either species, but some evidence points to the mule deer as the likeliest one. First, zoologists describe this animal as "the characteristic deer of the mountains and foothills of western North America" (Banfield 1974, 388), by comparison with the white-tailed deer, whose preferred habitats are forest edges, clearings, and plains (Banfield 1974, 393). The Bungling Host myth from Cochiti places the action right away on a mountain. Second, a neighboring people considered the mule deer to be the most common deer in the region, although the white-tailed deer's presence was also attested (Henderson and Harrington 1914, 16–17). From here on, we will assume that the Cochiti host is more likely than not a mule deer.

The myth takes place on a mountain (the mule deer's preferred habitat) near a river where the host will throw the bones left over after her children have been eaten by Coyote. Actually, in the second part of the myth, the action continues farther east and then northeast, where the female mule deer joins an antlered male who will gore and disembowel Coyote, who is still seeking to avenge the death of his own children.

DEER AND COYOTE (PART 2)

The little Deer had already gone ahead. From there eastward they went. They went and crossed the river from there to the northeast side. The deer arrived at some place where there was a buck. The little deer were there already. Then she told the buck: "Coyote pursues me. She became angry because her children did not come out of the river." Then Coyote could not cross the river. There was a big flood. She said to Beaver, "Take me across!" she said to him. "Please, I am pursuing the deer. I will kill her wherever I overtake her." Then Beaver took Coyote across. To some place in the northeast went Coyote. She arrived at the place the buck was. "Where did the Deer Woman go?" said she. "I shall kill her. She killed my children." Then the buck said, "You will not kill her. Now you are going to die." He gored her and took out her intestines. Then he had killed her. (Benedict 1931, 160–61)

The second version, the one recorded by Benedict, is even more explicit. It states where Deer and Coyote live, White Bank, and then names several places along the route taken by Deer while being pursued by Coyote, as seen in the following excerpt:

DEER AND COYOTE (2ND VERSION—EXCERPT)

The Deer came running down the arroyo (just north of Cochiti) and crossed the river near Whirlpool Place. . . . When Coyote came to the river she couldn't get across. She called to Beaver. . . . Beaver came to ferry her over. Old Coyote got into the little boat. As soon as she got in Old Beaver began to tickle Old Coyote. They played with each other. They got to the middle of the river and they had intercourse. Old Coyote asked, "Is the boat getting across the river?" . . . Already they were way down by Santo Domingo (two miles). Coyote jumped out . . . . She ran on after them. . . . As she got on top of La Bajada hill, she saw Deer ahead. She was close to them. . . . She said, "Now I'll catch you!" Father Deer was lying under a big cedar [sic] . . . Father Deer put his antlers through her chest from side to side. . . . So there the Deer were saved. Father Deer went back to his home and Mother Deer and the two children came back from Blue Shell Mountain to their village and they are still living at Cochiti. (Benedict 1931, 162)

All of this is key to understanding how the myth plays out and, consequently, what it means.

We have first identified some of the place names and by drawing on other information, we have learned more about how and where the myth transpires. The two most certain place names are Santo Domingo, which is a Keresan pueblo a few kilometers south of Cochiti, on the Rio Grande's east bank, and the hill La Bajada, an abrupt elevation around 150 meters high and some twenty kilometers northeast of Santo Domingo (Pearce 1988 [1965], 80).

The other place names are less certain. There is a Shell Mountain (elevation 3,097 meters) in Sandoval County, New Mexico, northwest of Cochiti's current location, but is it really the Blue Shell Mountain of the myth? There is also a place named White Rock (elevation 1,940 meters) around twenty kilometers northwest of Santa Fe near White Rock Canyon, where the Rio Grande has carved a valley between white cliffs (hence the name of the rock), but is it really the White Bank of the myth, where Deer and Coyote live?

In any event, we will consider further on whether the last two places could correspond to the similarly-named ones in the second version of the myth. On the other hand, the first version also reports a flood, in all likelihood of the Rio Grande; and to cross the river, Coyote has to get help from Beaver. We have looked through records on annual precipitation in New Mexico and found that flooding does occur along the Rio Grande either because of melting snow between April and June or because of episodic torrential downpours in summer from August to October.

We will now specifically look at the mule deer. In general, this animal has two annual migrations: one in the spring to higher altitudes where melting snow has opened up the land; and another in the fall to flee the accumulation of snow on mountainous terrain:

Seasonal movements exceeding about 15 km or involving migrations from higher elevations (summer ranges) to lower winter ranges are associated, in part, with decreasing temperatures, severe snowstorms, and snow depths that reduce mobility and food supply. . . . The chronology of spring movement from lower (winter ranges) to upper (summer ranges) elevations presumably is an interaction

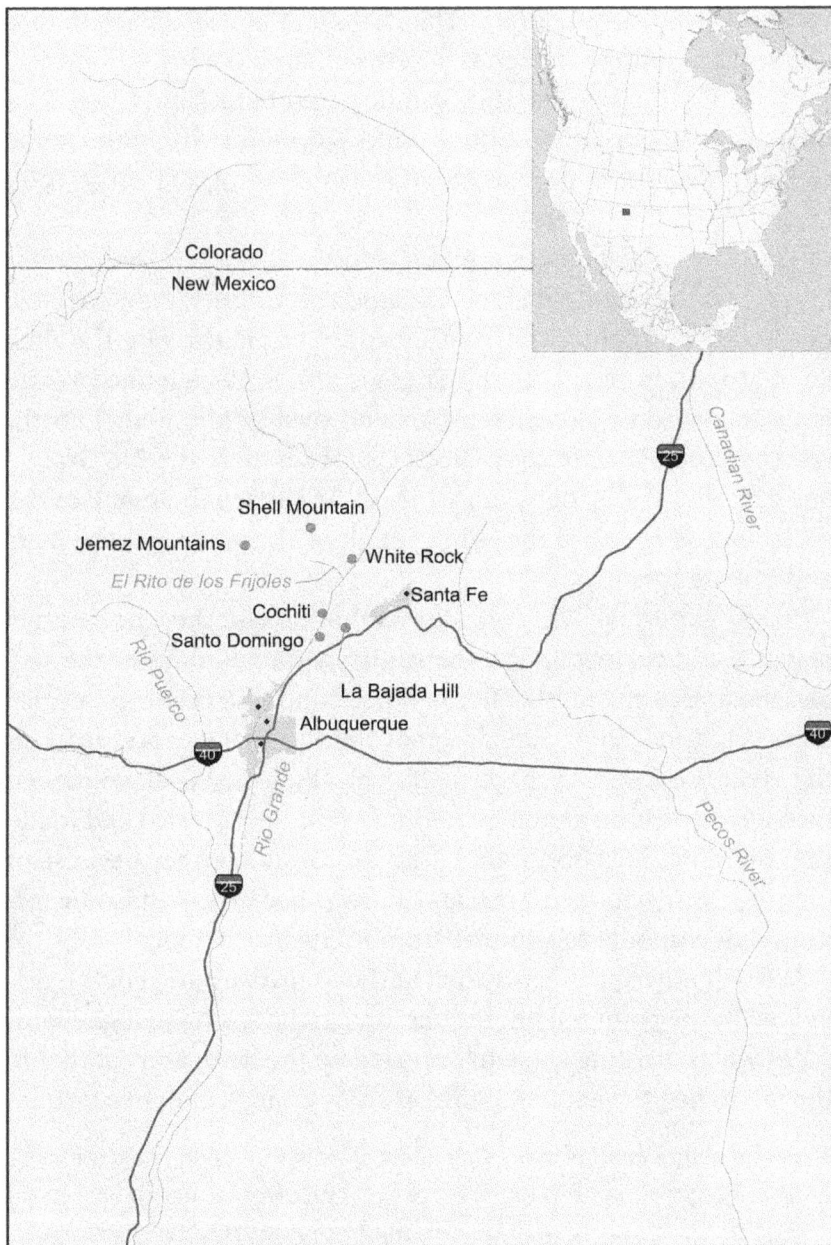

Fig. 21. Map of Place names of the Cochiti myth. Archéotec Inc.

of plant phenology, rate of snow melt, and, perhaps, impending birth period. . . . Mule deer in the arid southwest may migrate in response to rainfall patterns. . . . Autumn and spring migrations may encompass 4 weeks in *O.h. hemionus* . . . or 6 or 7 weeks with delays enroute of about 40 days in *O.h. californicus*. . . . Migratory routes may . . . or may not . . . be confined to major drainages or ridgetops, and may cross other winter ranges enroute to traditional wintering areas. (Anderson and Wallmo 1984, 5)

The spring migration likely takes place around May or June, and the autumn one around September or October (Russell 1932; Seton 1953 [1909], vol. 3, 333–34). Other major events arise from the reproductive cycle, particularly rutting and giving birth. Mule deer give birth within a range of dates from May 16 to early October, with peaks around late June (Anderson and Wallmo 1984, 4). Their litters are two fawns on average (Anderson and Wallmo 1984, 4). The young are weaned around the age of five weeks and may remain with the doe until the next fawning season. Yearlings are definitely rejected by their pregnant mothers at the time of giving birth or just before:

Observations of thousands of does subsequent to the hunt indicate little separation of young from adult does until a new fawning season begins. Even fawns orphaned during the hunt apparently attach themselves to another doe or group of does and fawns. During the fawning season, does with very young fawns seek isolation, and it is common to see them chasing away last year's offspring. Many yearlings apparently become discouraged after repeated chasing and leave their mothers permanently; others return after the does have become more tractable, which usually is not until the new fawns are a few weeks old. Over many years I have observed hundreds of does with newly born fawns and only two of these showed no animosity toward the yearling buck which tagged along. (Robinette 1966, 345)

During this entire period, i.e., from spring to the rutting season, deer live in small independent bands of females and males. It is only when they mate that deer of both sexes come together again: "In spring the does withdraw to bear their fawns. The bucks exercise their dominance only during the autumn rutting season" (Banfield 1974, 389).

With all of this information in mind, we can look again at the Cochiti myth and reconstruct the timeline of events. When the story begins, Deer and Coyote are living on a mountain, which the second version names White Bank (White Rock, which may be the same place, is northwest of Cochiti, as is (Blue?) Shell Mountain, which appears at the end of the second version). According to an informant, members of the Cochiti pueblo would traditionally hunt deer in the Jemez Mountains, likewise northwest of the village: "When the men hunt, they generally go into the Jemez Mountains, where Cochiti have hunted for generations. Despite the availability of trucks and other transportation to areas of more plentiful game, there is little interest in hunting elsewhere. 'We know the Jemez country' seems to express their attitude" (Lange 1959, 138).

However, Charles H. Lange, a Cochiti specialist, says little about the exact time of the deer hunting season (Lange 1953). In a more general text, he refers to two seasons, autumn and winter (Lange 1979, 374, 376), but nothing in principle would confine deer hunting solely to those times of year. Even today, the timing of the hunt is still at the discretion of the one in charge, the "war captain": "At present, there is an occasional communal hunt for deer for the cacique. These are called to the discretion of the war captain, the frequency depending upon the conscience and energy of the individual holding the position" (Lange 1959, 131). Moreover, spring seems to have also been conducive to deer hunting, at least formerly among the Anasazi, who were ancestral to the region's current peoples: "Animal resources also vary seasonally. For example, it is easiest to harvest deer, elk, and antelope during periods when these animals are in large herds, which occurs only when they are moving from higher to lower elevations or back, and during the breeding period; thus the spring and especially the

Fig. 22. A doe and her fawns.

fall would have been the seasons when these animals were most easily taken" (Plog 1979, 111).

In the Cochiti myth, Deer offers her children as a meal to her guest. As seen in previous chapters about Beaver and Seal, this offer could be interpreted as a gift—the game animal gives itself up to the hunter. This idea is very widespread among Native Americans, and is in fact almost universal. We have backed it up a bit with reference to the Innu. In the pueblos of the Southwest, the same idea is reported from the Hopi: "The game animals that are always asked "to give themselves" are mentioned as pets of the Somaikoli society . . . : deer, mountain sheep, antelope, elk, cottontail . . . are pets of the Clouds" (Parsons 1996 [1939], 184). The same author reports a similar idea throughout the pueblos: "Game animals are all impersonated by mask or pelt and addressed with prayer-feathers or prayer-sticks, and by hunters animals are asked to reveal themselves or to 'send their children'" (Parsons 1996 [1939], 197). We have here the full meaning of the myth. Coyote is the hunter who greets the children of Deer, who offers them to him as meat.

This is during hunting season, likely in late winter because the doe is still accompanied by her fawns and because of other reasons, such as the following. At that time the fawns are around ten to twelve months old. Not coincidentally, this is also when a doe seeks isolation and increasingly rejects her young. A hunter may thus see such rejection as a gift. The animal is now confined to its winter range—the snow-free region at lower altitudes—while possibly being still present on mountainous terrain. Remember, Cochiti is at 1,608 meters in altitude—not much lower, for example, than White Rock at 1,940 meters.

This being said, the river where Deer will take her children's bones may be the Rio Grande or a tributary, the Rito de Los Frijoles, whose headwaters rise in the Jemez Mountains—a region that members of the same pueblo had once inhabited before migrating downriver to their current location (Hodge 1907, 317).

The does reject their offspring from the previous year and then give birth. These newborns are represented in the myth as children that come back to life from bones. We will return later to the meaning of this applied metonymy.

Once Deer has given birth to her newborn, two in general, as also reported in the second version of the myth ("Mother Deer and the two children came back from Blue Shell Mountain"), all three of them head east or northeast depending on the versions, while being pursued by Coyote, who is no longer the Trickster of the first part of the myth. In the second part, he has regained his true nature as a predator that preys on deer.

This time of year is characterized, among other things, by a greater vulnerability of fawns: "Fawns are particularly vulnerable to predation" (Geist 1981, 219). A naturalist makes the same point: "Coyotes and other Wolves follow the Mule-deer and drag down those that have been disabled by wounds or sickness; but they do much greater damage by destroying newly born fawns that have been left hidden by their mothers" (Seton 1953 [1909], vol. 3, 352).

As he pursues the doe and her fawns, Coyote is confronted by a flood. The timeline of the myth remains plausible, since the Rio Grande can overflow its banks in May, when the snow melts and the deer migrate. Coyote crosses the waters with Beaver's help, this crossing serving among other things to show how adaptable beavers are to aquatic environments. After all, do not beavers cause flooding? The two of them cross the floodwaters and, in the second version, have sex (beavers are known to have no respect for kinship rules, at least according to our Subarctic Native informants (Clément 2012). Coyote then spots the doe and her fawns to the northeast (first version) or beyond the hill of La Bajada (second version)—an excellent lookout point over the surrounding area, given the lay of the land. He later catches up to them, but they now have the company of an antlered male mule deer. The rutting season can extend from September to March (maximum range of dates), and it is during this time that males and females come together again to form a single band. This is also the time when the males display their finest assets, the dominant males having the most impressive antlers. In sum, the myth condenses the normal timeline but remains faithful to the sequence of events.

In the myth, the male is lying under a "big cedar" (second version). We have already commented in another chapter on the term "cedar," which most often means juniper (*Juniperus* spp.). Indeed, pine-juniper woodlands are characteristic of these regions (Lange 1979, 367). The antlered male ends up goring Coyote, and, although such an event must seldom happen in nature, the myth does serve to remind its audience about two points: first, coyotes attack adult deer only on very rare occasions, and even less often bucks in rut; second, rutting bucks are a danger to flee. Indeed, this is the time of year when they are the most aggressive: "For the coyote and the deer, however, the relationship between the prey and predator is so finely balanced that frequently a single coyote is chased and tormented by its expected prey" (Banfield 1974, 287).

Why does the second version of the myth end with the doe and her fawns returning to Cochiti from Blue Shell Mountain, which is supposedly west of the Rio Grande (if it is Shell Mountain)— like White Bank (if that name is equivalent to White Rock) at the beginning of the story—and not east of the Rio Grande, like the hill of La Bajada? But keep in mind that mule deer generally follow the same spring and autumn migration routes. The myth remains plausible if we assume that some of the action has been left out. The doe and her fawns must have crossed back to the western side of the valley: "We concluded that each deer tended to have a specific home range in summer and another in winter and that migration for a given animal consisted of spring and fall movements between these familiar points. . . . Field observations along migration routes showed that deer tended to use the same trails each year" (Gruell and Papez 1963, 420–21).

The timeline is much less plausible in its sequence of birth and migration. The myth places the former before the latter, while we see the reverse in studies by Western zoology, at least those from Montana in Yellowstone National Park: "Does heavy with young make the journey to summer range with other migrants and arrive there a few days or a few weeks, according to the season, prior to birth of the young" (Russell 1932, 33). This specialist nonetheless answers no to the question he asks immediately after: "Do does seek higher levels in order that their young may benefit by certain favorable conditions of the upper zone?" (Russell 1932, 33). Moreover, the same researcher observed elk sometimes descending to a lower altitude before giving birth (Russell 1932, 33). The same may be true for deer, although evidence is still lacking.

Apart from this detail, the timeline of the myth's events remains convincing, being supported by a chronological sequence of locations that the doe and her fawns have passed through. The chart below summarizes the events, showing the parallels between the yearly cycle in nature and the mythical events.

Table 4. Yearly cycle of deer and mythical events

PERIOD	YEARLY CYCLE	MYTH
Spring	does with fawns only	Deer lives with her children
End of May	yearlings chased away by does	Deer offers children to hunter
Peak period in June (May-Oct.)	fawning (two in general)	children come back to life
May-June	migration	Deer goes to the mountain
April-June	flooding	Coyote impeded by the flooding
Peak period in Nov. (Sept.-March)	rutting season	doe and fawns with males; males are dangerous

This leads us to the core of the mytheme: a big question. Why is there water? Why would Deer, generally thought to be a non-aquatic animal, put her children's bones into the water of a nearby flowing river? The answer, as always, is complex and involves two sets of factors. The first one is a deer's relationship to water and, more precisely, a pregnant doe's relationship to water.

Generally speaking, mule deer are considered to be excellent swimmers (Geist 1981, 173): "They are excellent swimmers and cross straits up to fourteen miles wide between coastal islands" (Banfield 1974, 389).

In arid regions of the Southwest, the presence of mule deer near watering holes is noteworthy. In fact, they seem to depend completely on such sources, in particular when their diet of succulent plants is not enough to meet their need for water: "Mule deer (*Odocoileus hemionus* Rafinesque) in arid regions are dependent upon free water (Wolfe 1978, 367). Mule deer typically are found in close proximity to water sources, particularly during dry periods"

(Rosenstock, Ballard, and Devos Jr. 1999, 304). Wherever artificial water basins have been developed, mule deer populations have always grown noticeably, as have those of other members of the deer family. No such benefit has been shown for other mammals, however, like predators or small game (Rosenstock, Ballard, and Devos Jr. 1999, 302–11).

In particular, a doe will need much more water when pregnant. Several researchers have made this observation:

> Pregnant mule deer have significantly increased water requirements during late gestation, and water requirements are great during lactation. (Short 1981, 111)

> Does visiting catchments consumed more water than did males, perhaps due to increased water requirements associated with lactation. (Rosenstock et al. 1999, 304)

In addition, fawns need as much water if not more. Among mammals, this need is known to be inversely proportional to body size: "The water requirements of mammals, in general, are an inverse function of body size. . . . Conversely, fawns then would have the highest water demand" (Hervert and Krausman 1986, 672).

Indeed, does with very young fawns have been seen drinking at various watering holes by researchers and naturalists alike:

> Tiny tracks in the sands of lake shores and stream banks indicate that very young fawns accompany the mothers to drinking places at night. (Russell 1932, 21)

> El Rito de los Frijoles not only provided the water the Ancestral people needed for cooking and drinking, it attracted game (we came on a mother mule deer and her fawn during our hike), and watered native plants like the aforementioned ponderosa pine and the yucca, which provided soap, food, and fibre. (Willett 2008)

The last observation was made around June along the Los Frijoles valley, through which flows the river of the same name and where Cochiti's inhabitants used to live several centuries ago before moving to their current pueblo. They still go hunting there, the valley being part of the Jemez Mountains.

So the myth mirrors real events. The Cochiti would regularly observe does coming back from bodies of water with their young fawns. This is one of the two etymons of the mytheme.

The second etymon is more intriguing. It belongs not to the realm of nature or animal behavior, but rather to that of humans. To understand it, we first need to know general beliefs about life and death. Like other pueblo-dwelling peoples, the Cochiti firmly believed that the deceased, at least those who were good, would return to the original waters from which the Native Americans first arose. A note by archaeologist and historian Adolph F. Bandelier, who lived in Cochiti in the late nineteenth century, outlines this belief:

> It results from these [words of the songs], that Ma-se-ua is the spirit of Rain who dwells in the lagune of "Skipap". This Lagune is said to be to the North, beyond the "Conejos," and is described to be very round and deep. Many streams flow into it, but it has no issue. Out of this Lagune came forth the Indians and in it dwells "Te-tsha-na," our mother, from which sprang the Indian race. Those who die go to heaven above where God judges them and while the bad ones go to perdition forever, the good ones return to their mother in the said Lagune. . . . There is a singular admixture of Christian and pagan beliefs in this. (Bandelier in Lange 1959, 416)

This belief is strangely echoed by possibly related Cochiti customs about the bear and the eagle, two animals considered with the cougar to be the greatest of all hunters:

> Bear bones are carefully gathered and carried either to the river, where they are thrown in, or to certain shrines located in the surrounding hills. (Lange 1953, 183)

> The eagle's body was thrown into the river. (Lange 1959, 137)

This practice—returning the bones of some animals to the water— was therefore usual among the Cochiti. Since they also ate bears, they may have applied it to other game animals for which it is unattested, including the mule deer. Another piece of evidence is the myth itself, which mentions this practice for mule deer. We find similar treatment of bones in other Bungling Host myths from other peoples, such as the stories about Beaver's children, whose bones are likewise thrown into the water. The Cochiti, like other Native Americans, seem to have believed in the reincarnation of animal species. Broadly speaking, this is one of many beliefs that point to a certain unity of thought among all Native peoples of the Americas.

There may have been other reasons. Among the Acoma, another Keresan people who inhabited a pueblo farther south in the Southwest culture area, the deer was given the ceremonial name, among others, of *tsits*, which means "water" (White 1945, 236). This name was certainly linked to the relationship of deer to water.

Better still, if we look at examples of this Native myth-motif—an animal being resurrected from bones put into water, with various species as the central character (e.g., Beaver, Otter, Salmon, Red Cod; Berezkin 2010)—we also find one example with a deer, not related in this instance to the Bungling Host motif. A Thompson Salish story (Plateau) tells how a hunter goes to live with deer that obtain food by hunting each other. The species survives because their bones are thrown into a river's waters, thus bringing the animals back to life (Teit 1917, 40–43).

What do all of these elements have in common? And what is the origin of this commonality? The answer is a hunting practice. In fact, many indigenous peoples hunted members of the deer family by ambushing them in water. Such hunting was known among the Innu of the Subarctic, who used to wait for caribou near river crossings and then spear them to death in the water when they were most vulnerable. It was also known among the Seri of the Gulf of California coast in northwestern Mexico, who would bludgeon mule deer crossing bodies of water or going through water for other reasons: "The Seri said the deer try to cool off in the water" (Felger and Moser 1991 [1985], 52).

Consequently, if a hunter could hope to find game animals in a body of water or nearby, he would logically look for appropriate ways to get them to make their appearance. With no salt blocks to lure them, such as those used by present-day hunters, and from the standpoint of naturalist thinking, which partly draws on the doctrine of signatures, he might improve his luck at hunting by using a symbol of the animal. Bones were such a symbol. A metonymy (a part standing for the whole) could therefore be applied, i.e., intentionally put into practice. We see the same thing during bingo games today, when people put something down next to them (a bill, a picture, a chip) to symbolize the wealth they desire.

As a matter of fact, this applied metonymy existed among the Salish of the Northwest Coast in British Columbia. On the one hand, they hunted mule deer (*Odocoileus hemionus*), and may still do, by driving them into the water for an easier kill: "The dogs were trained to drive the deer down to the water where they could be killed easily" (Kennedy and Bouchard 1976a, 31). On the other hand, only the bones of deer killed in the water were returned to the river, and not those of animals killed on dry land. The latter bones could be boiled to remove their marrow: "The bones of the deer that had been tracked by dogs were always thrown into the water to ensure the continual return of the deer to the water. The bones of the deer that had been hunted by men alone [called, then killed on dry land] could be boiled" (Kennedy and Bouchard 1976a, 36).

These two practices, which appear together in the same hunting tradition, speak for themselves. Whereas some might see a contradiction between showing respect for animal remains and using them for material purposes (see Savard 1972, 97–98n63), the Native Americans saw none because they applied both practices with the same intent. They used the bones both as a source of food (marrow) and as a means to replenish the food supply (ritual to regenerate animal species).

The Cochiti myth is fundamentally about regeneration, or rather reproduction of species, not to mention the close relationship between humans and game animals. The latter give themselves up to hunters and will not stop doing so, since the annual cycles of mating, pregnancy, and birth flow from the same logic. Hunting is thus justified because it never stops animals from replenishing their numbers.

The myths about Beaver and Seal share the same three premises about game animals: they are, they are not, and they will be. All of these myths with Beaver, Seal, and now Deer, also have an aquatic component, which we have explained in each case. Two of them are also based on a cultural practice about bones (Beaver and Deer), whereas the third one omits this rule (Seal). Several other mythemes mention only the first aspect: the annual reproduction of animal species, with no link to a concomitant cultural practice or a specific habitat. Nonetheless, they are all about the same subject. The following story, of Osage origin (Plains), applies the motif of regeneration to the black bear. It will not be analyzed here. It is presented simply to show that this perception of life is widespread among many Native groups of the Americas.

THE BEAR AND THE WOLF

The Bear and the Wolf once met by a creek. The Wolf said, "Hello, brother." The Bear said, "Hello, brother." "Where do you live?" said the Wolf. The Bear said, "Quite a way along the creek." The Bear said, "Well, I must go. Come over and see me." So the Wolf said, "All right."

Next morning, the Wolf went over to see the Bear. The Bear had some young ones. He killed four of them and cooked them for the Wolf. The Bear said to his wife, "Brother has come." So she prepared the meal for him. The Bear said: "Go ahead and eat your dinner. Swallow no bones, because it would make my young ones crippled." The Wolf said, "All right," but he swallowed two bones, one knee, one wrist, and one ankle. When they were through eating they were talking, and the Bear told his wife to call in his young ones. She did so, and every one was crippled. One was crippled in the rib, another in the wrist, another in the ankle, and another in the knee. The Wolf said, "Brother, I am going; the young ones must be afraid of me." He went, but told his brother, the Bear, to come and see him. The Bear said, "All right."

The next morning the Bear went to see the Wolf. Old she Wolf was with him. When the Bear got there, the Wolf said, "I have not got much to eat, but I will do the best I can." So he cooked four of his young ones. When they were done the Bear began to eat, and the Wolf said, "Brother, do not swallow any bones; it makes my young ones crippled." The Bear said, "All right." He got through eating without swallowing a bone. He handed the dish back, and the Wolf said to his wife, "Well, go and get the young ones." So she went after them, but could not get them back. The Bear said, "Well, brother, I must go; those young ones must be afraid of me." (Dorsey 1904b, 13)

9 Wolf Transforms Two Arrowheads into Mincemeat Puddings (Southwest)

> Soon after this Coyote visited Maitso, the Wolf. The latter took down, from among the rafters of his hut, two of the old-fashioned reed arrows with wooden heads, such as the Navaho used in the olden days; he pulled out the wooden points, rolled them on his thigh, moistened them in his mouth, and buried them in the hot ashes beside the fire. After waiting a little while and talking to his guest, he raked out from the ashes, where he had buried the arrow points, two fine cooked puddings of minced meat.
>
> —Washington Matthews, "Navaho Legends"

Immediately west of the Keresan pueblos along the Rio Grande live the Navajo, formerly known to the conquistadors as *Apache de Nabajo*. The Navajo—a name probably of Tewa origin meaning the 'valley of the cultivated fields'—likely migrated to the Southwest around a thousand years ago (Brugge 1983, 489). They came from the North and belong to the Dene or Athapaskan linguistic family. When the Spanish arrived in New Mexico in the sixteenth century, the Navajo had already given up hunting for a semi-sedentary way of life. They practiced farming but would also leave their fields to hunt or to trade with their neighbors, the pueblo dwellers. Pueblo influence on their culture has been very strong and may be seen in their ceramics, dress, tools, and so on (Brugge 1983, 494). Even the reed arrows of their Bungling Host myth, excerpted above, were of pueblo origin (Brugge 1983, 494).

Our search through the literature turned up two Navajo myths with the Bungling Host motif, available only as free English translations (Matthews 1897, 87–88). In both cases, the Trickster is Mai the Coyote, and the hosts are respectively *Dasáni* the Porcupine and Maitso the Wolf. In the first myth, Porcupine receives Coyote, whom he ends up serving roasted meat, prepared as follows:

COYOTE AND PORCUPINE

From Kintyél, they moved to *To'í'ndotsos* and here, Mai, the Coyote, married a Navaho woman. He remained in the Navaho camp nine days, and then he went to visit *Dasáni*, the Porcupine. The latter took a piece of bark, scratched his nose with it till the blood flowed freely out over it, put it on the fire, and there roasted it slowly until it turned into a piece of fine meat. Porcupine then spread some clean herbs on the ground, laid the roasted meat on these, and invited his visitor to partake. Coyote was delighted; he had never had a nicer meal, and when he was leaving he invited his host to return the visit in two days. At the appointed time Porcupine presented himself at the hut of Coyote. The latter greeted his guest, bade him be seated, and rushed out of the house. In a few minutes he returned with a piece of bark. With this he scratched his nose, as he had seen Porcupine doing, and allowed the blood to flow. He placed the bloody bark over the fire, where in a moment it burst into flames and was soon reduced to ashes. Coyote hung his head in shame and Porcupine went home hungry. (Matthews 1897, 87)

Like other Native American myths, this Bungling Host episode seems puzzling only because it judiciously combines human and animal aspects of morphology and behavior. Coyote represents humans as the Trickster, and his humanness explains all of his actions. He travels between two localities: Kintyél and *To'í'ndotsos*, whose names would have sounded familiar to listeners. Kintyél means 'Big Pueblo' and refers to at least two old, ruined pueblos in New Mexico, one being the famous Chaco Canyon (Matthews 1897, 224n72). The other one remains unidentified.

Coyote has also married a Navajo and lives in her camp. Among the Navajo, matrilocal residence was more common than patrilocal residence: "When a young couple marry, they can live at either spouse's natal unit. There is a preference and an expectation that they will live at the wife's mother's unit" (Witherspoon 1983, 526).

Coyote stays "in the Navaho camp nine days" before leaving. The number nine is important in the Navajo ceremonial system: the universe was created in nine stages (Werner, Manning, and Begishe 1983, 579, 582); the songs of the Holyway ceremonies are sung in a series of two, five, or nine nights (Wyman 1983, 556); and nine songs are recited in one of the hunting rituals, the Wolf Way (Hill 1938, 104–5). We have found no postnuptial rule of this kind, but there may once have been a custom if not a rule to this effect. Navajo ritual is known to be extremely elaborate and impregnates all aspects of personal and social life: "One of the characteristics of Navaho culture is the unusual amount of ritual that has been integrated in the affairs of everyday life" (Hill 1938, 177).

A ritual governing reciprocal visits may also explain the lapse of two days between Coyote's departure and Porcupine's visit—a detail that Coyote seems to stress. Finally, there is something truly human in Coyote's efforts to offer his guest a meal, despite his lamentable failure to imitate Porcupine's way of doing things. Indeed, no one can obtain food by roasting blood-soaked bark.

Porcupine's case is more complex. Here again, the myth proceeds elliptically from an animal aspect to a human one and vice versa. These aspects are so finely juxtaposed that one easily forgets their respective origins. For analysis of this myth, the porcupine has one key anatomical feature: "a blunt muzzle" (Banfield 1974, 233). This is one of the few parts of its body without quills ("There are no quills on the muzzle, legs or underparts of the body"; Gunn 2001 [1977], n.p.).

This blunt muzzle is key to understanding part of the mytheme, as we will explain further on. It is widely viewed as being strange by Native people, and our search through the literature unsurprisingly revealed at least one Native American myth about this "abnormality." The myth comes to us from the Mi'kmaq (Northeast), at the other end of the continent, and explains why the porcupine and the toad look the way they do:

> And knowing all that was in their hearts, he [Glooskap, a Mi'kmaq hero] put on the shape of an old squaw and went into the council-house. And he sat down by two witches: one was the Porcupine, the other the Toad; as women they sat there. Of them the Master asked humbly how they expected to kill him. And the Toad answered savagely, "What is that to thee, and what hast thou to do with this thing?" "Truly," he replied, "I meant no harm," and saying this he softly touched the tips of their noses, and rising went his way. But the two witches, looking one at the other, saw presently that their noses were both gone, and they screamed aloud in terror, but their faces were none the less flat. And so it came that the Toad and the Porcupine both lost their noses and have none to this day. (Leland 1884, 108)

The North American porcupine, *Erethizon dorsatum* is the only living representative of the genus *Erethizon* (Woods 1973), and its range covers Canada, the United States, and part of northern Mexico. We can generally say, then, that a behavior or trait of this species in one region will hold true elsewhere in its range.

Porcupines were hunted by all Native Americans, and by the Navajo no less so. This is clear from the literature: "Porcupines were shot or clubbed. The head and tail were cut off, the animal cleaned, and the quills singed and scraped off. A pit was lined with heated flat rocks. These were covered with wet mud, the porcupine laid in the pit, and another layer of mud and hot stones added. Then the pit was covered with earth and the meat allowed to cook for about an hour" (Hill 1938, 173–74). We see here one of the Navajo ways of killing rodents: bludgeoning them, most likely with a club. It is widespread in many groups and, according to the Natives we have known the longest, the Innu of the Subarctic, it has several advantages. In particular, no bullets are wasted and the skin is not pierced, which helps removing the hairs and the quills more easily.

Navajo cooking also has blood-based preparations like *til* (or *dil*) (Landar 1964, 94). This blood sausage was made with the blood of goats or sheep, and undoubtedly the blood of some game animals. A Navajo recipe gives these details:

dił—Blood sausage

Cut a goat or sheep's throat and catch the blood in a pan. Let stand one-half hour, then squeeze and stir with the hands, discarding the lumpy parts. Add two and one-half cups diced intestines, and other meat. Mix and place in sheep's stomach, tying the holes, or tying in small bundles like sausages. Boil for two hours. (Bailey 1940, 284)

The Navajo cooked as much inside as outside their homes—the ever-popular hogans. Several methods were used: earth ovens, roasting pits, and open fires (Kluckhohn, Hill, and Kluckhohn 1971, 127–34). One documented technique was to roast the meat at the end of a stick, a bit like the bark roasted in the myth: "The ribs of the wildcat were placed on the end of a pointed stick held over the fire (Inf. 7). This was presumably a common method of broiling meat" (Kluckhohn, Hill, and Kluckhohn 1971, 128).

In the myth, Porcupine next serves the meat on a bed of clean herbs: "Porcupine then spread some clean herbs on the ground, laid the roasted meat on these, and invited his visitor to partake." A rule of Navajo etiquette was to set a table on the floor when guests were being received: "The manner of serving guests varies with individual families. Some expect white guests to eat with the family; some serve them first, setting a special 'table' on a blanket on the floor and providing adequate crockery and utensils" (Bailey 1940, 278). It is more than probable that a bed of branches or grasses was once used as a tablecloth. A photo from 1930 and kept in Tucson, Arizona, at the university museum, shows an Apache

Fig. 23. Woman cooking. Based on Photo 18183, Tucson, Arizona State Museum.

woman preparing a meal on the floor in similar conditions (Basso 1983, 468).

We now come to a key point in our argument. Let us begin by saying that many mythemes reflect the ways members of a culture imagine how their hero would perceive or act in a given situation. In the words of people we have interviewed, it is enough to say, "In his own head, the hero perceived things that way."

The Navajo had originally been hunters before they came to the Southwest. This role is played in the myth by Porcupine, although he actually feeds on the cambium layer and inner bark of trees. This type of feeding (porcupines may have others) is transposed here, in this Bungling Host myth, into an act of hunting:

> Animals often return to the same trees to feed, thereby usually damaging these trees. . . . During the winter months their diet consists mainly of the inner bark of trees and of evergreen needles. (Woods 1973, 3–4)

"They feed on the cambium layer and inner bark of trees as well as on the new twigs and buds" (Banfield 1974, 234)

This feeding behavior is so typical of porcupines that one way of finding them in a forest is to look for trees with no bark ("but noisy chewing, cut twigs, and missing patches of bark may advertise its presence"; Gunn 2001 [1977], n.p.). The Innu of the Subarctic even have a special term for tree surfaces that a porcupine has stripped of bark: *uâshâtueua*.

To come back to the myth, we can say that Porcupine's behavior—rubbing his blood onto a piece of bark—refers to several things at once. First, there is an allusion to his short or blunt muzzle. One can almost hear the storyteller softly affirming how he had often seen a porcupine perched in a birch or pine, its head turned toward the tree and bits of bark at its feet. Its muzzle had been worn down by being rubbed so much against the tree.

Second, there is a sort of analogy—the morphological parallels that may be drawn between plants and animals. This has come up previously in at least one of the earlier chapters, particularly the striking example of Woodpecker pulling caribou ribs out of trees. The hunter analogy is projected onto the myth in the heroes' actions, and this projection is reflected in how the heroes feed or prepare meals. A hidden animal behavior is thus taught, and it is up to the listener to seek the truth of the lesson in nature.

Thus, when Woodpecker pulls no other food than caribou ribs from trees, there are several reasons. One is that he is viewed as a hunter. Another is that tree anatomy brings to mind a game animal's anatomy (foot, head, backbone). The Navajo myth works exactly the same way. A tree's bark is associated with an animal's skin, and a tree's cambium with an animal's blood or meat. First, we see Porcupine's bloody muzzle feeding on cambium and scraping the outer bark. Next, we see the blood/cambium/meat from inside the plant or the animal. Finally, we see the end product: a cooked meat roast with its skin (= its bark). Like other species

Fig. 24. Porcupine scraping the bark.

(e.g., grouses), porcupines were eaten with their skin but without their hair and quills, of course.

In other words, tree bark (A) is to animal skin (B) what cambium (C) is to blood (D) and ultimately to meat (Di). The myth cuts out the middle part of the equation, leaving only elements A and D of the story line. The result is thus A (bark) to D (blood) and Di (meat). The logic for this shortcut is simple. Visually, the transfer goes from the outside to the inside, either from bark to cambium or from animal skin to blood and meat—in short, from bark to meat. Porcupine is a hunter and, like Woodpecker, can feed only on animal flesh.

And, as one might expect, this relationship is confirmed by the vocabulary for parts of plants. Like the Innu of the Subarctic, the Navajo named several parts of plants after the corresponding parts of humans and animals:

ANNOTATED LIST OF PLANT PARTS. . . .

Pexetshiin, the base. The base of a tree where it meets the ground. Also said of the feet of a man. . . .

Pikáan, its arm. Used of tree boughs. . . .

Pizit, its liver. The pitch or the inside of a tree. (Elmore 1944, 94–95)

The second Navajo myth, an excerpt from which opens this chapter, features Wolf as the host and Coyote, again, as the Trickster. Since the 1930s, wolves have practically disappeared from the American West (Carbyn 1987, 362). In New Mexico, the prevalent species used to be *Canis lupus*. Judging by Navajo vocabulary, it seems that the total population of wolves was formerly less than that of coyotes (*Canis latrans*) or, at least, less culturally important, since the Native word for coyote (*mai*) is a generic term for the dog family as a whole, which includes the wolf (*maitso* or the 'great wolf') and the kit fox, *Vulpes velox* (*maidotlĭ'z* or the 'blue or grey *mai*') (Matthews 1897, 226n80).

COYOTE AND WOLF

Soon after this Coyote visited Maitso, the Wolf. The latter took down, from among the rafters of his hut, two of the old-fashioned reed arrows with wooden heads, such as the Navaho used in the olden days; he pulled out the wooden points, rolled them on his thigh, moistened them in his mouth, and buried them in the hot ashes beside the fire. After waiting a little while and talking to his guest, he raked out from the ashes, where he had buried the arrow points, two fine cooked puddings of minced meat; these he laid on a mat of fresh herbs and told Coyote to help himself. Coyote again enjoyed his meal greatly, and soon after, when he rose to leave, he invited Wolf to pay him a visit in two days. Wolf went in due time to the house of Coyote, and when he had seated himself the host took two arrow-heads, as Wolf had done, rolled them on his thigh, put them in his mouth, and buried them in the hot ashes. After waiting a while, he raked the ashes and found nothing but two pieces of charred wood where he had placed the arrow-heads. This time he gave no evidence of his disappointment, but sat and talked with his guest just as if nothing had happened, until Wolf, seeing no sign of dinner and becoming very hungry, got up and went home. (Matthews 1897, 87–88)

The etymon of this mytheme will become clear once all of its secondary elements have been clarified. In fact, the myth is constructed so as to create a parallel between wolves and humans in the ways they behave: both are big game hunters.

This kind of comparison between predators and humans is made in other societies, and we have studied it especially among the Innu of the Subarctic (Clément 1987, 59–85). We found that the Innu perceive wolves as being big game hunters on a par with humans, with hunting techniques that seem comparable in every way. The same may hold true for the Navajo, and it is no surprise that they name one of their hunting techniques the Wolf Way (Hill 1938, 101–13). This hunting complex, which has its own songs, rituals, and techniques, appears to be their most important one, the others being also named after animals or aspects of hunting: the Big Snake Way, the Mountain Lion Way, the Stalking Way, the Witch Way, the Arroyo Way, and so on (Hill 1938): "The Wolf Way (na·λé·coh·kehgo) was one of the most popular modes of hunting deer, but used less frequently in hunting elk" (Hill 1938, 101).

Like the Innu, the Navajo borrowed some of their behaviors directly from wolves, as reported by anthropologist Hill:

Now the leader gave further instructions. The hunters were told when calling their partners to use the call of the "hoot" owl, screech owl, coyote, or a whistle like a bird's. "You must never call as a human because you are hunting in an animal's way and must act like animals."

When a hunter killed a deer he gave a wolf call to attract the attention of his partners. "This was because it was told in the myth that the wolf, when running down a deer, gave a call at the kill no matter how hard he ran. This was to invite everyone to come and eat of his meat, crows, coyotes, etc." (Hill 1938, 109)

The same comparison inspires the Bungling Host episode "Coyote and Wolf" with Wolf being compared to a human deer hunter. Equating one with the other leaves things out, as so happens in such storytelling. The known elements are the hunter (a wolf or a human), the hunting weapon (two arrows), and the end product (the cooked meal). The intermediate stages are obviously missing, as shown below. So we have:

$$\text{hunter} \; \rightarrow \; \text{arrows} \; \rightarrow \; | \qquad | \; \rightarrow \; \text{cooked meal}$$

Although the equation works for humans, it makes no sense at face value for wolves unless, as in Native tradition, one sees things as a wolf would (evidently by projecting what we ourselves would perceive in such a situation). To make sense of the myth, we have to replace each human-interpreted element (i.e. as seen by a human) with an animal-interpreted one (i.e. as seen by an animal).

The parallel between humans and hunters has already been made, and we need not dwell on a well-known fact: wolves are renowned predators. Something must be said, however, about the hunting weapon, either the one used by humans or the one used by wolves. The myth states that Maitso the Wolf took down from the rafters of his hut "two of the old-fashioned reed arrows with wooden heads, such as the Navaho used in the olden days." The typical, traditional Navajo hut is called a hogan. This structure of upright posts and crossbeams can take several forms (circular, square, cone-shaped, shelter) and can be covered with various materials (logs, branches, stones, etc.). The rafters seem to be made for storing objects (like arrows) that otherwise might get in the way on the floor and impede daily activities of the hogan's occupants.

The Navajo attribute a mythical origin to their bow and arrow. The origin myth comes from the cycle of The Stricken Twins, which belongs to a ceremonial complex that is called in the Navajo language the Night Chant (*klédze hatál*) (Matthews 1995 [1902], 4). As with other legends, this one relates the adventures of a hero who "through intentional or unintentional misbehavior gets into a series of predicaments requiring supernatural assistance for survival and causing injury or illness calling for ritual restoration" (Wyman 1983, 556).

In this case, mythical divinities named the Holy Ones leave behind their bows and arrows. There are four divinities and four lots of weapons. The heroes are twin brothers who examine the weapons one after another but take only the last lot, which seems best suited to their poverty. These arrows are tipped with wooden points:

> When they came to the fourth lot of weapons the cripple called again to his brother: "Another bow lies on our path with arrows that point to the north"; and the blind boy asked: "How do these appear?" The younger brother answered: "They are rudely formed; the bow is of green cedar from which the leaves have not even been cut off; the arrows are tipped with wood, not stones, and they are trimmed with owl-feathers; they are poor." "Then they are suited for poor people. Let us take them," said the elder. (Matthews 1995 [1902], 241)

The wood for these arrows comes from rosebushes ("arrows of rose"). Other arrows, made from reed, are mentioned in the same origin myth, although the heroes do not take them (Matthews 1995 [1902], 240). And such arrows of composite materials were used in olden times by the Navajo. The literature tells how they were made:

Composite arrows for hunting small games were of cane, *Phragmites communis, tokaa tsoh* (obtained from the Apache country). . . . The cane was gathered, seasoned, and cut to size. If the reed was crooked, the worker heated a stone, spat on it, and placed the crooked portion of the reed on the saliva, bending it straight (AM). The shaft was then smoothed and feathered as above (not feathered, stated PP). The nock was always cut just below a node in the cane. The foreshaft was made of black greasewood or a hardwood and was fitted in the pith channel of the cane. The joint was wrapped for about an inch with sinew. (Kluckhohn, Hill, and Kluckhohn 1971, 38–39)

Wooden arrows (and not reed arrows) had neither a foreshaft nor an arrowhead, the shaft being simply sharpened to a point (Hill 1938, 96) and, according to some informants, also hardened by fire: "The shaft was sharpened to a point with a knife, and fire-hardened in the ashes" (Kluckhohn, Hill, and Kluckhohn 1971, 40).

The arrow of the myth seems to be a composite, like the one described above. The shaft would have come from a species belonging to the genus *Phragmites*, either *P. Communis* (= *P. australis*) or *P. phragmites*, which is also called the common reed. Some details are also known about the species used in making the point:

The most important use of all [for *P. phragmites*], however, was the use of the stems as arrow shafts. (Elmore 1944, 27)

A small stick or twig of sumac is sharpened and driven into the reed (*Phragmites communis*) shaft of an arrow, and fastened there with sinew. The arrowpoint is then secured to this stick. (Elmore 1944, 61)

The sumac is *Schmaltzia trilobata*. The greasewood, mentioned above for making foreshafts, is *Sarcobatus vermiculata*. This plant has extremely hard wood.

This is what we know about the Navajo and their arrows. But what about the wolf? The myth states that Maitso the Wolf looked for his arrows in the rafters of the hut: "When not in use, arrows were kept in the quiver, which hung with the bow from the roof of the hogan. According to Inf. 256, old arrows were stored in a safe place" (Kluckhohn, Hill, and Kluckhohn 1971, 36). He then removed their points: "he pulled out the wooden points." According to what we know about the length of the points, they could measure around 6.5 centimeters. At least, this is the reported length of blunt points for hunting of small game: "Still another type of arrow was used for killing rats and mice. About two and a half inches of the tip of a corncob was forced on to the tip of a wooden pointed arrow. The animals hit with this blunt point were stunned" (Kluckhohn, Hill, and Kluckhohn 1971, 39). In the literature, information on Native archery comes mostly from Ishi, a Yahi-Yana of California and the last survivor of his tribe, whom we discussed in chapter 6. His people made obsidian points that ranged between 2.5 and 7.5 centimeters in length (Pope 1918, 140; fig. 27).

In wolves, the longest teeth are the canines or fangs, which may be as long as 6 centimeters approximately "including the portion imbedded in the jaw" (Mech 1970, 14). The canines are "used in slashing and holding prey" (Carbyn 1987, 360). So they act as arrows, being the first teeth to penetrate and retain the prey. The Navajo are not alone in comparing wolf teeth to arrows, for the same comparison is made by the Innu—the group we first studied and know the most. While explaining a mythical episode about wolves and what they teach the Trickster who accompanies them, a hunter from Ekuanitshit, a community on the north shore of the St. Lawrence, in Quebec, made this comment about a passage that alluded to the arrows of wolves: "Then it, the wolf, he explained to him that the wolves had shot arrows; they used to hunt with arrows. He says that it's the . . . when the wolf kills a caribou, it's with its teeth; it has pointed teeth like an arrow point" (Abraham Mestokosho, Ekuanitshit).

When we first tried to analyze this mythical passage, we thought the comparison alluded to the carnassial teeth of wolves, but after further thought we now believe the allusion may be to the canines, which are more pointed and more comparable in length to arrow points.

In any event, it is not fortuitous that the Navajo myth has Maitso using arrow points to prepare his meal (preparing for a hunt is already part of preparing one's meal). The myth combines human and animal aspects, and it must have enough of both to convince the listener: old arrows come from humans, and arrow points come from wolves, being not only their canines but also their own arrows.

The myth goes on with what at first sight may be a way of preparing food, but which after analysis does not seem to be. Maitso the Wolf rolls his "arrows" (= points) on his thigh, moistens them in his mouth, and finally buries them in the ashes. This mini-mytheme has three distinct elements we need to analyze.

First, Maitso rolls the points (= the arrows) on his thigh. The listener's attention is thus drawn to two things: the perfect smoothness of wolf canines and the same smoothness of arrow points. This is corroborated by the existence of a polishing technique used by the Navajo (the humans), which was to roll arrows on the thigh. The literature again supports this point. In the most complete study of Native American archery, by Saxton Pope, which has already been quoted, we learn that Ishi would sometimes proceed this way: "He sometimes finished the shaft by rolling it back and forth on the thigh with his right palm, while he worked it with a piece of sandstone held in his left hand. By this means he could 'turn' a shaft almost as accurately as if a lathe were used" (Pope 1918, 112).

Second, Maitso moistens the points (= the arrows) in his mouth. We deduce that this detail likewise draws the listener's attention to two aspects, one human and the other animal. We are deducing here because the literature does not tell us enough about the human aspect, although the following explanation is very plausible. According to a specialist, an archer could indeed moisten his arrows before shooting to ensure their elasticity. An arrow drawn back on a bow bends under the pressure and will straighten back into shape only when released. Moistening it makes it more flexible. Besides, some Natives also used their saliva, as stated previously, to straighten crooked sticks of wood to make arrows. Furthermore, a myth told by Ishi mentions a sea-soaked arrow that, once released, flies all the way to the sun:

> By placing the upper end of his braced bow at the corner of his open mouth and gently tapping the string midway between the end and center he caused clear musical notes to be produced. . . . He sang of a great archer who dipped his arrow point in the sea, then in the fire, drew a mighty bow, and shot at the sun. His arrow flew like the north wind, and entering the door of the sun, put out its light. Then all the world became dark, men shivered with cold, and from this time they grew feathers on their bodies to make them warm. (Pope 1918, 110)

As for wolves, their saliva has special characteristics: among others, a lubricating function that enables them to swallow a lot of meat rapidly (Mech 1970, 169). More importantly, like all members of the dog family, wolves always salivate when excited by the prospect of eating. So, in the story, wolves, like humans, also moisten their arrows (= their teeth).

Finally, Maitso buries his points (= his arrows) in the ashes after rolling and moistening them. We have here a metonymy that takes us from hunting to cooking. The arrows of humans, like the teeth of wolves, have pierced their prey. An arrow is to meat what a tooth is to a piece of flesh. One is equivalent to the other, and the fact of placing one (an arrow or a tooth) in the ashes is identical to burying the other (meat) to prepare it for eating. So these pieces of meat, having been impaled on either arrows or teeth, are now being cooked in the embers of a fire. Among the Navajo, cooking in hot ashes was practised. Apart from the widely used earth oven of the Southwest, which the Navajo also used, we have several accounts about meat being prepared directly in the ashes:

> The [deer's] pancreas . . . was turned inside out, buried in the ashes, roasted and eaten. (Hill 1938, 144)

Remove legs, wings, and head of insect [locusts]. Brown the rest in the ashes and eat. (Bailey 1940, 284)

Singe the hair from the [sheep or goat's] head and place it, together with the feet, in a hole in which a fire has burned for an hour. Cover with coals, build a fire on top and bake for about four hours. When done the ashes are removed and the tongue, brains, eyes, and jaw muscles eaten. (Bailey 1940, 283)

Once cooked, the end product in the myth looks like "two fine cooked puddings of minced meat." This kind of cooking is not discussed in the literature. Flora L. Bailey (1940), who wrote a study on Navajo foods and cooking methods, mentions very few game meat recipes. Her information is late, dating from the mid-twentieth century, when the Navajo had long ago given up hunting for crop growing and livestock raising, hence the many recipes for preparing meat from farm animals. The only thing we can say, at least about the human aspect of the mytheme, is that venison could always have been cut up with a view to some of the pieces being eventually minced and used in various dishes.

The wolf is in a quite different situation. On the one hand, it tears its meat to pieces and crushes the bones to make all of the pieces easier to swallow. On the other hand—and this is key—it also buries what remains. In its own way, and from its own standpoint, the wolf makes itself a fine cooked mincemeat pudding: "Much of the cutting and chewing done in feeding is accomplished by the carnassials . . . the fourth upper premolar and the first lower molar. These specialized teeth are much like a pair of self-sharpening shears and function well into cutting tendons and tough flesh" (Mech 1970, 14).

Likewise, in its own way, the wolf will "rake out from the ashes" (in its case = from the ground) the remains of game animals it has buried:

It sets aside a reserve, buries it and stays near its provisions until they have been exhausted. (Bernard 1982, 25)

In some cases, not all the flesh from a carcass is consumed imme-diately. Some large chunks may be buried under the snow or in the ground. (Mech 1970, 189)

After the pack has killed a large animal and initially fed upon it, it may cache the remaining meat in the snow or in a hollow log or stump. If there are pups in the den, the wolves will carry food back and cache it near the den. (Banfield 1974, 292)

Although this burying behavior is exhibited by the wolf only occa-sionally (Carbyn 1987, 368), it must have been noticed by Native peoples. Nature has kept very few secrets from them, at least from those peoples who have lived traditionally in a context of day-to-day survival.

To come back to the mytheme in its entirety, we can now look again at the initial equation and its three elements: hunter → arrows → | | → cooked meal. We are now able to fill in the blanks and pro-vide two parallel, more detailed equations: one for humans, and the other for wolves.

Navajo hunter	→ arrows →	arrows are rolled (polishing)	→ arrows are moistened (elasticity)	→ game animal	→ food removed from the ashes
wolf hunter	→ teeth →	arrows are rolled (smooth canines)	→ arrows are moistened (saliva)	→ game animal	→ food removed from the ground

The two Navajo mythemes about the Bungling Host are therefore constructed in the same way as the ones in the previous chapters. The myth takes us from the human to the animal, and vice versa, while skipping stages, omitting elements from the comparison, and proceeding by metonymy to an end product that looks at first sight disconcertingly strange . . . and impenetrable.

10 Badger Pushes a Stick Down His Throat and Gets Yucca-Juice (Southwest)

So on the fourth morning Coyote started out to visit his friend; and when Badger saw him coming, he said to his grandmother, "Fix up the room, grandmother! My friend Coyote is coming to visit us." So his grandmother got the room fixed up for them, and soon Coyote came in and sat down. "Kyetsanna, happy," said Coyote. "S'imu, sit down!" said Badger. "Now get everything ready for me, grandmother," says Badger; and she went into the other room, and brought back a bowl, which she put down in front of Badger; and then she went into another room and got a long, sharp-pointed stick. Badger pushed the stick down his throat; and when he pulled it up, there ran out into the bowl a whole lot of yucca-juice. "Good!" said Badger. "Now let's eat!"

—Edward L. Handy, "Zuni Tales"

There were once twenty thousand of them. There are now ten thousand. They used to live in five or six distinct villages. They are now confined to one small town. Since 1540, when the Spanish arrived, the Zuni of western New Mexico have suffered many setbacks, including sharp population declines in the eighteenth and nineteenth centuries (down to less than 1,600 inhabitants). But they are still around.

The Zuni—a term referring all at once to a language, a linguistic family, a culture, and a locality of the same name—are undoubtedly one of the most complex societies ever, not only of the American Southwest but also of the whole of North America north of Mexico. Frank Cushing, an anthropologist at the Smithsonian Institution in the United States, summed up this high complexity in one sentence: "The Á-shi-wi, or Zuñis, suppose the sun, moon, and stars, sky, earth, and sea, in all their phenomena and elements; and all inanimate objects, as well as plants, animals, and men, to belong to one great system of all-conscious and interrelated life, in which the degrees of relationship seem to be determined largely, if not wholly, by the degrees of resemblance" (Cushing 1883, 9).

We will sketch out the way the Zuni represent the universe before analyzing their Bungling Host myths. Broadly speaking, this system of representation is as follows.

The world has six directions: north, south, east, west, zenith, and nadir. Each direction has a color, a warrior animal, a "prey animal" or predator, a "game animal", and so on. Zenith and nadir in turn have four upper and four under worlds. Each of the four upper worlds has its own bird species: the crow, the Cooper's hawk, the nighthawk, and the eagle. Each of the four underworlds has its own tree species: the ponderosa pine, the Douglas fir, the aspen, and the cottonwood (Cushing 1883; Stevenson 1904; Tedlock 1979). The following chart sums up these attributes by direction.

Table 5. The six Zuni directions and their attributes

	COLOR	WARRIORS	PREY ANIMALS	GAME ANIMALS
NORTH	Yellow	Mountain Lion	Mountain Lion	Mule deer
SOUTH	Red	Badger	Wild Cat	Antelope
EAST	White	Wolf	Wolf	White-tailed deer

WEST	Blue	Bear	Coyote	Mountain sheep
ZENITH	Multicolor	Eagle	Eagle	Jackrabbit
NADIR	Black	Mole	Mole	Cottontail

The Zuni world is surrounded by oceans, and each ocean has its own mountain and color. The people of this universe come in two kinds: "raw" people and "daylight" or "cooked people." The latter need to eat their food cooked, while the others eat it raw. But these are not the only attributes. In this system, a newborn child is likewise considered to be a "raw person."

We will put aside the system's myriad details: the way it classifies meteorological phenomena (clouds, rainstorms, fog, and dew), birds, snakes, supernaturals, and so on. We will instead focus on the Zuni themselves and their ceremonial organization, i.e., the key elements for understanding the myths presented below: "Equidistant from the four oceans is Zuni itself, also called *?itiwan?a* 'the middle place'" (Tedlock 1979, 501).

Some village homes, in their most isolated rooms, may still have the time-honored *?etto'we*, the ceremonial bundles that the Zuni brought with them on their ancestral journey from the fourth underworld. These sacred bundles include water and seeds, as well as animal fetishes and masks used when different fraternities put on performances: "Taken together, the contents of the sacred bundles constitute a microcosm. At the center of the bundles, at the center of Zuni, there rests a stone on a permanent altar (Bunzel 1932a: 514), and inside this stone beats the heart of the world" (Tedlock 1979, 501).

It goes without saying that the religion of the Zuni is as developed as their system of representation, if not more so. It has everything: the creation of the world; epics; supernatural beings; offerings; prayers; and sacrifices. At the very heart of their practices is ceremonial organization, which encompasses many societies, the most important one being the Kachina Society, essentially devoted to purification rites. Alongside it are fourteen smaller, rather esoteric societies. Two of them are more of concern to us, these being the Wood Fraternity (also known as the Sword Fraternity because one of its two orders is called the Sword Order) and the Great Fire Fraternity. These organizations are placed under the protection of the Beast Priests. They are also among the societies that "have the knowledge of physical and mental powers that exceed ordinary human capacities" (Tedlock 1979, 503). Their members are recruited among people who have had a close brush with death in one way or another (illness, accident, broken taboo). The Wood Fraternity and the Great Fire Fraternity have some members who can push long wooden sticks into their digestive tracts. These are the "sword swallowers." They perform their feats at annual ceremonies, which the anthropological literature has described at length and in great detail (Stevenson 1904).

Only by placing ourselves within this vast amphitheatre of the Zuni's system of representation and their ceremonial complex can we understand the first of the two Bungling Host stories from Zuni oral literature. This myth assigns the role of host to Badger, who swallows "swords" and makes yucca-juice. The guest is played by Coyote—a Trickster, as in many Southwest cultures.

COYOTE AND BADGER TRY SWORD SWALLOWING

Coyote (*susskI*) and Badger (*donacI*) were friends, and went out hunting together one day. They killed so many rabbits, that after they had gotten through hunting, and were coming home, they divided them. When they got home, Badger said, "My friend, come to see me in four days, and we will eat some rabbit-meat." So on the fourth morning Coyote started out to visit his friend; and when Badger saw him coming, he said to his grandmother, "Fix up the room, grandmother! My friend Coyote is coming to visit us." So his grandmother got the room fixed up for them, and soon Coyote came in and sat down. "Kyetsanna, happy," said Coyote. "S'imu, sit down!" said Badger. "Now get everything ready for me, grandmother," says Badger; and she went into the other room, and brought back a bowl, which she put down in front of Badger; and then she went into another room and got a long, sharp-pointed stick. Badger pushed the stick down his throat; and when he pulled it up, there ran out into the bowl a whole lot of yucca-juice. "Good!" said Badger. "Now let's eat!" So they all sat around and ate and drank, and Coyote staid a little while after they had finished. Then he said, "Come to see me in four days." Badger said, "I will come."—"Soanna, good-by! I go," said Coyote. "Ma Lu, well, go!" said the other. In four days Badger went around to see Coyote; and when Coyote saw him coming, he said to his grandmother, "My friend Badger is coming to pay us a visit." So she got the room fixed up, and pretty soon Badger came in. "S'imu, sit down!" said Coyote. Then he told his grandmother to get everything ready for him, just as Badger had done, and she brought him a bowl and a stick. Coyote tried to swallow the stick; but when he tried to pull it out, no yucca-juice came, but there was a bowl of blood instead, and on the end of the sticks was part of Coyote's guts. And Coyote's grandmother started to eat, and Badger pretended to eat, but really didn't. In a little while Coyote died right in front of them. And Badger said, "You can't do that, because you don't belong to the Lewekwe (Sword-Swallowing Fraternity); but I belong to that society; and can do anything." And he went home. (Handy 1918, 459)

For this myth, we have only Edward Handy's English version. His version includes several Zuni terms that we investigated, only to realize they had already been translated in the same text. Take for example: "'Kyetsanna, happy', said Coyote." Here, *kyetsanna*, surely means "to be happy" (*k/ezzana* 'be frisky, behave happily'). In "'S'imu, sit down!' said Badger," the word *s'imu* is the imperative of the verb to sit (*/i:m-u* 'sit down'). In "'Soanna, good-by! I go,' said Coyote," *soanna*, is obviously a loan from the English "so long." Finally, *ma lu*, in "'Ma Lu, well, go!' said the other," corresponds to *ma/* 'well, so' and *lhu:/u* 'go' (Newman 1958, 23, 13, 30). So the Zuni terms in Handy's translation provide no further meaning beyond what he already provides.

The myth begins with a hunting expedition by Coyote (in this case *Canis lutrans*) and Badger (the American badger, *Taxidea taxus*), who are friends and hunting buddies. Although the Trickster represents a human in Bungling Host myths, as we have argued elsewhere, he does show animal traits. This may be seen in the seals of authenticity that bring some versions of this story to a close. This also may be seen in the cooperative effort of the two hunters, which mirrors relationships that naturalists and zoologists have observed in nature.

A coyote and a badger can indeed form a hunting pair, temporarily—and at first sight seemingly more to the benefit of the former than the latter. Many observations have been reported in the literature (Aughey 1884; Hawkins 1907; Cahalane 1950; Lehner 1981; Minta, Minta, and Lott 1992). The technique is simple. While a badger is busy getting a prey out of its burrow or at least going after it, an opportunistic coyote waits at the surface for it to escape from the badger by a secondary exit. In the most complete study on the subject—forty-two badgers followed; 214 cases of coyote-badger associations found—the authors summed up the benefits to both partners:

> A coyote's available hunting habitat increased greatly while hunting with badgers. Relative to open habitat, within brushy habitat (with higher densities of squirrels—Minton, 1990) far more coyotes hunted with badgers than hunted alone. Associated coyotes saved energy and (possibly) time via decreased searching, stalking and chasing. They mostly waited for the opportunity to quickly scramble and capture a squirrel.

> During the several weeks following the emergence of juvenile squirrels in June, badgers sought out burrows containing squirrel litters . . . and associated coyotes captured many more squirrels. . . .

> Predation rates of badgers could not be similarly assessed because squirrels mostly were caught and eaten below ground. However, badgers hunting alone spent far more time above ground than

badgers hunting with coyotes. . . . We interpret the increased time below ground as a direct benefit if that time was spent in consumption, or a decrease in costs if that time was spent more efficiently pursuing prey. (Minta, Minta, and Lott 1992, 815–16)

When these coyote-badger associations were observed in the field, the longest one lasted three hundred minutes. Badgers are essentially carnivores whose prey are underground or burrowing animals, including squirrels and game animals like rabbits, as seen in the Zuni myth: "Jense (1968, unpublished master's thesis, South Dakota State University, Vermillion, S.D.) observed a similar inverse relationship between mice and ground squirrels, but in contrast to the present study he found that consumption of rabbits peaked in spring and summer, when road kills were most plentiful. Our data show that lagomorphs (22% of badger food samples) were taken mostly in January, February, and March" (Messick and Hornocker 1981, 42).

It also seems that a badger will catch rabbits in dens it has abandoned. Rabbits find shelter in such places, and a badger will come back from time to time to look for them: "Species such as cottontail rabbits, which would generally be unavailable to badgers, occupy old dens and occur in the badger's diet" (Lindzey 2003, 686). A watchful coyote may thus take advantage of this situation if a rabbit manages to flee the badger by a secondary exit. In fact, such a possibility is examined in a Zuni myth and may even come from real observation that has never made it into the zoological literature. The myth is named "Coyote and Badger go on a rabbit hunt," and this excerpt echoes the hunting technique described above:

> Coyote (*susskI*) went hunting one day for rabbits. Badger (*donacI*) had gone out too, and they met on the road. Coyote asks the other, "Where are you going my friend?" — "Rabbit-hunting," says Badger. "Good, can I go along with you?" — "Well, yes," says Badger, "you can come along if you can run fast enough to catch the rabbit when

I scare him out of his hole." And Coyote says, "Oh, yes! I can run very fast." So Badger says, "All right! When we find a rabbit in a hole, I will dig down fast, and then crawl in and scare him out and you must catch him." (Handy 1918, 453)

On the other hand, the Zuni were still organizing collective rabbit hunts in the early twentieth century. At that time, an economy based on farming, hunting, and gathering still prevailed (Ladd 1979a, 492), and elements of this economic model are mirrored in the myth. Such a hunt was described in the early twentieth century as having several horsemen closing in from all sides on the panic-stricken rabbits, which quickly succumbed to the specially made sticks raining down on them: "The Indians are very dexterous in the use of the rabbit stick. Not a single rabbit that appeared escaped the weapon. . . . When the rabbit is surprised it starts off in one direction, but finding itself cut off from escape it darts to another point and there meets with a barrier, and so to all points until it becomes utterly bewildered, and it is not remarkable that one of the dozen sticks darted toward it should strike the mark" (Stevenson 1904, 443).

The Zuni also have clans named after animals, including two species of concern to us: the Coyote clan, Suskikwe, literally the 'Coyote clan people', and Tonashikwe, or the 'Badger clan people' (Kroeber 1919, 94; table 2). And the listener identifies completely with the myth, either directly if he belongs to one of the two clans or indirectly because a person's clan membership is known to one and all.

Listeners will further identify with the myth because of other elements that are culture-specific. These and other elements may seem trivial but are nonetheless important because they help make the myth meaningful to its audience. The first element is the lapse of time between Coyote's departure and his return to Badger's home. The second one is a rule of residence. When Badger and Coyote go their separate ways at the beginning of the myth, Badger asks his companion to come back and see him in four days ("My friend, come to see me in four days"); and Coyote, trying to imitate, will later say the same thing ("Then he said, 'Come to see me in four days.'"). Now, four and six are the most common numbers in the rules of rites among the Zuni, in their ceremonial regulations, in their conceptual thinking, and elsewhere. There are four underworlds, four upper worlds, and also many rules like the following:

> [about the Beast Gods] In the afternoon male members of societies offer prayer sticks to the Beast Gods. For four days continence must be observed. . . . The ceremonies in the sick room are continued for four nights, provided the patient lives that long. (Bunzel 1932, 532–33)

> [about death] When a person has been separated from his former daylight existence by four deaths, he finds himself all the way back at the hole where the Zunis emerged from the earth. (Tedlock 1979, 507–8)

In some ceremonies, sticks—named "swords" (in part wrongly, see further)—are swallowed four times (e.g., Stevenson 1904, 505). In other ceremonies, the initiates are each whipped four times (Tedlock 1992, 186). And there are other examples. So the number of days separating Coyote's departure from his return—four—is a familiar number to the Zuni, and this familiarity further helps listeners feel an affinity to the myth as they hear it being told.

The other element is a rule of residence. Badger, like Coyote, lives with his grandmother. This rule underlies not only the family unit but also the whole web of social, economic, and ceremonial relationships: "The mother's household is the social, religious, and economic unit. Normally, it is composed of a maternal lineage segment: an older woman, her sisters, and the married and unmarried daughters to which from time to time are added various male relatives and in-laws. In the 1970s the maternal household was still the social and religious center of the family" (Ladd 1979b, 482). In other words, the children of married daughters can live with their maternal grandmother, at the center of the lineage. This situation is echoed by the myth.

As for the mytheme—Badger shoving a stick down his throat and getting yucca-juice— it is undoubtedly among the most disconcerting ones we have ever encountered. It raises several questions we must address. Since Badger justifies himself in the myth by saying he is a member of the "Sword Fraternity," what is the exact function in Zuni traditional society of sword swallowing as described in the literature? Why does Badger in particular belong to this fraternity? And what is the link between the carnivore Badger and the production and consumption of a plant product, in this case yucca-juice?

First, we should comment on the term the literature uses for this stick—the one a Zuni pushes down his throat. It is the equivalent of "sword" or "saber" (e.g., "sword swallowing" in Stevenson 1904, 445; "Hle'wekwe (Wood Fraternity), or Sword Swallowers", Stevenson 1904, 444; etc.). In Zuni, the word for "sword," *macc'tanne*, is borrowed from Spanish: "The Spanish, or probable Spanish loans are . . . *mačče·tanne* 'sword, bayonet'" (Walker 1979, 511). Although this loanword may go back several centuries, and no Native word appears in the literature, one may doubt whether the Zuni themselves used it for the instrument of this performance. First, the ceremony of a Zuni pushing a stick down his throat seems to have existed since time immemorial, or at least since long before Europeans came to the area. Second, the stick is not a blade. Third, "sword" swallowing does not at all have the same function as swallowing a stick for religious purposes.

The Zuni art of swallowing a stick is very old. Achiyalatopa, a being with wings and a tail of knives instead of feathers, is said to have taught this art to two chief officers of the Hle'wekwe Fraternity (Stevenson 1904, 445). The members of this fraternity had just separated from the other Ashiwi (Zuni) after emerging from the depths of the earth, at a place called Jimikianapiatea. They had scarcely begun their journey to the Middle Place.

After the Ashiwi emerged at Jimikianapiatea, divine beings created the first four fraternities, the fourth one being the Hle'wekwe Fraternity, the 'Wood people' (from *kwe* 'people') (Stevenson 1904, 409). The Hle'wekwe ('Wood people') have only two orders, the Sword (i.e. the sword swallowers), and the Spruce (*Pseudotsuga douglassii*) (Stevenson 1904, 447). An order of the Sword and two orders of the Spruce also exist among the many orders of another fraternity, the Make Hlannakwe or the Great Fire Fraternity, which was created after the Hle'wekwe Fraternity. On the other hand, some Order of the Sword members of the latter Fraternity claim to have been initiated into the secrets of stick swallowing before the members of the Hle'wekwe Fraternity—this being hard to believe if that order was formed after the Hle'wekwe had been. They also claim that the name 'Wood people,' which is also their own name, comes from the wooden composition of the sticks: "Having received the knowledge of sword swallowing from Achiyalatopa (a being with wings and tail of knives) at Shipapolima, Na'ke'e initiated members of his fraternity [Great Fire] into the secrets of sword swallowing, which order he named Hle'wekwe (Wood people), the swords being fashioned of wood" (Stevenson 1904, 409–10).

We will later see that wood may be associated with the Order of the Sword (of either the Hle'wekwe Fraternity or the Great Fire Fraternity) for a reason other than simply the material of the stick. In any event, in this ethnohistorical overview of stick swallowing and its beginnings, we see it began well before the Europeans came, since it appeared soon after the Zuni emerged from the depths of the earth.

Second, calling this stick a sword or a saber is misleading because of the way it is made. The sticks come in several types: the "original," unornamented sticks; the more common ones with a bundle of feathers at one end; and complete trees with one end whittled down to be pushed down a throat. All of these types share some things in common: having a streamlined but somewhat rounded throat end; not having sharp-edged sides; and being pushed down a length (around 40 centimeters) that hardly exceeds two-thirds of the esophagus (next to the heart). By comparison, a sword, without necessarily having cutting edges along its sides, has a pointed end (except for the kind used in fencing), and sword swallowers shove them much farther, as far down as the stomach.

The literature mentions two sorts of original sticks, one being simple and the other zigzag-shaped: "The swords originally used by this fraternity are supposed to have been exactly like the one now used by the Hlem'mosona (sword director), which is asserted to be the original sword presented by Achiyalatopa to the original Hlem'mosona. This sword has a cylindrical handle about 3 inches in thickness, and there are no plumes attached. The zigzag sword carried by the warrior of the fraternity is also declared to be one of the original swords" (Stevenson 1904, 445).

The more common sticks—the ornamented sticks—are described by the literature in even greater detail. These sticks are made of juniper (*Juniperus* sp.), they measure around 40 centimeters, their diameter is around 2 centimeters, and their handles are feathered and detachable: "The blades only are left in charge of the Hlem'mosona, who keeps them, when not in use, in an old cougar skin with not a vestige of hair on it. They are made of juniper, the length from the tip of the middle finger to the elbow, three-fourths of an inch wide, slightly curved, and rounded at the end. They are rubbed with cougar or bear grease and red hematite (see pl. cix). The elaborate feathered handles are stored away in the ceremonial house" (Stevenson 1904, 451). During a ceremony that Matilda Stevenson attended at the turn of the twentieth century, all of the performers held this type of stick in their hands, except for the oldest performer, whose instrument had a sinuous shape and a sharp arrowhead 5 centimeters long and 2.5 centimeters wide: "Though this sword is frequently swallowed to the handle, it is run very cautiously down the throat" (Stevenson 1904, 460). The Zuni also had an Arrow Order (Shotikianna) whose members pushed arrows down their throats during their ceremonies.

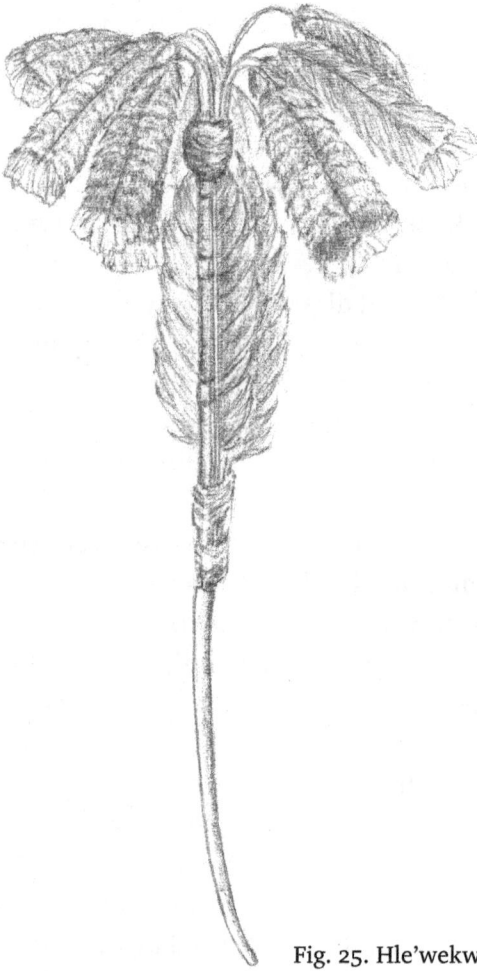

Fig. 25. Hle'wekwe stick. Based on Stevenson 1904.

When complete trees were used as ceremonial sticks for the same ritual, the performers came from the different Spruce Orders (one order, Kialasilo, of the Hle'wekwe Fraternity; two orders, Kialasilo and Posisiski, of the Great Fire Fraternity; Stevenson 1904, 483–85, 515). In the Kialasilo Order of the first fraternity, the trees measured around 3 meters long, and approximately 7.5 centimeters in diameter. The stump end was shoved down the throat, having been first streamlined, and the upper branches were adorned with feathers (from a turkey, an eagle, and each bird of the six directions). A novice was initiated as follows: "Stepping to the middle of the floor, the fraternity father lifts the tree with the sword end pointing downward, passes the top out through the hatchway, and hands the tree to the novice, who, facing south, attempts to swallow the sword" (Stevenson 1904, 485).

These words were written by a skeptical Matilda Stevenson, who had doubted these feats of prowess since her first observations: "Those Indians are so clever at legerdemain that when first observed the sword swallowing was thought to be one of their tricks. To convince herself, the writer induced a member of this order, after long persuasion, to visit her camp and swallow the sword. Great secrecy was observed while the head-kerchief and leather pouch were removed and the sword swallowed, and the Indian to this day feels that he was guilty of a great wrong in swallowing the sword without the ceremony which should attend it" (Stevenson 1904, 505). Some performances were beyond belief: performers swallowing as many as four sticks at once; two partners making each other swallow their sticks; a performer shoving a stick down his throat while dancing; and so on (Stevenson 1904). Also impressive was the swallowing of an entire tree with a tapered end. None of this compares to the sword swallowing of circus acrobats.

There is one last reason for doubting the appropriateness of the term "sword" for a stick (or an entire tree) being pushed down one's throat: the very function of the ceremony. Although this Zuni performance and its Western counterpart may have both arisen as a religious act (the art of swallowing a saber reportedly arose in India over four thousand years ago and was done to show the performer's power and relationship to the world of the gods), fundamental differences already existed at the time of first contact between Natives and Europeans. In the Western world, the practice had become a mere public display of acrobatics; among the Zuni, its highly religious aspects still prevailed.

Furthermore, the Hle'wekwe Fraternity (the Wood People)—which has only two orders, as we have seen, the Order of the Sword and the Order of the Spruce—has no real medical order like some other fraternities have (Stevenson 1904, 417), although unsurprisingly its members are authorized to cure throat illnesses (Stevenson 1904, 447). It is mainly a Sword Fraternity. Nor do the Hle'wekwe have any war-related purpose. Certain other fraternities are devoted to this end, like the War Society of the Bow Priests (Tedlock 1979, 506). So, again, the stick is in no way a sword, which at least formerly was an offensive or defensive weapon.

As a matter of fact, the Hle'wekwe Fraternity holds annual ceremonies where dances, prayers, rites, and performances have only one overriding goal: make the rain and snow come. This may be related to their ancestral northward journey to the Middle Place:

> The Hle'wekwe separated from their people at Hanlipinkia to travel northward in quest of the Middle of the world. The great ones of the Hle'wekwe carried two *et'towe* (rain and crop fetishes). . . . Previous to the separation of the Hle'wekwe from the other Ashiwi these most precious of precious things contained only the seeds of water for rain and vegetation. Some time after the separation, the *et'towe* being placed upon cloud forms of meal on the ground with *telikinawe* (prayer plumes), and prayers being offered for rain, great was the consternation when snow came instead. Never before had the *et'towe* brought snow; never before had the people seen snow; but henceforth these precious seed reeds of the Hle'wekwe were destined to bring the cold rains and snows of winter. (Stevenson 1904, 444)

Snow was key to a good harvest, as the director of the fraternity explained to certain groups who felt otherwise:

> The Ashiwanni were very angry, and the Kia'kwemosi visited the village of the Hle'wekwe and told them he did not wish them to be near. "Should you come and bring your *et'towe* and songs for snows, we should have no corn." The director of the Hle'wekwe replied: "If you have only warm rains your corn will fall over and die after it has come a little above the earth. The earth should be

cooled part of the time with the snows; then the sun's rays will melt the snows and sink them into the earth, and when the warm rains come the corn will be strong." (Stevenson 1904, 446)

The Hle'wekwe were considered so powerful that, if their rites were performed in summer, "the corn would freeze, as their songs and dances are for cold rains and snows" (Stevenson 1904, 447). This was why the Hle'wekwe refrained from depositing prayer plumes except in winter, unlike members of other fraternities who had to deposit them twice a month yearlong (Stevenson 1904, 423). This was also why their annual ceremonies were held only in winter—in January and February.

Members of the Hle'wekwe Fraternity could thus create conditions for better plant growth—rainmaking in general was the purview of other specialists, the Rain Priests—and this power provides insight into the etymon of the mytheme. In the same sort of way as a member of the fraternity, Badger somehow creates conditions for a plant to grow, in this case the yucca, which is metonymized in the myth by the food it typically provides: its juice. This is not the only element, however, that goes into the making of this mytheme, and we need to answer several other questions before we can reveal all of its elements. One thing is nonetheless clear. The term "sword" is misleading both in the nature of this ceremonial instrument and in its function.

That being said, we must still pin down the function of stick swallowing in the ceremonies of the Wood People Fraternity (or other orders). By explaining this function, we will also be led to the reasons why Badger, in particular, belongs to the Hle'wekwe Fraternity.

On their northward journey to the Middle Place, the Hle'wekwe were accompanied by "Beast Gods." These warrior animals were assigned to them as guardians: "When the Hle'wekwe started on their return journey they were provided with Beast Gods as warriors. It has been stated that the Divine Ones visited Shi'papolima and transformed the medicine men into Beast Gods as guardians of the world. The cougar, bear, badger, wolf, shrew, and six snakes for the six regions were appointed to accompany the Hle'wekwe" (Stevenson 1904, 445).

All of these species have one thing in common: they are carnivores. The snake-mammal association visible here is not confined to non-Western societies. A Western medical training manual makes the same mental connection on the basis of similar ways of feeding and, consequently, a similar digestive system: "Flesh eaters such as . . . snakes, hawks, owls, cats and others bolt down their food intact or in large pieces, and its physical reduction is accomplished by muscular and chemical action in the stomach" (Storer et al. 1979 [1943], 89).

This relationship between the carnivorous Beast Gods and the Hle'wekwe was even reflected in the diet that the fraternity members had to adopt on their expedition. The following comment explains the dietary rules that Hle'wekwe ceremony participants had to obey for four days (they had to abstain from "all sweets, beans, squash, dried peaches, and coffee"; Stevenson 1904, 453): "The reason given for abstaining from the foods mentioned above is that during the journey of the fraternity over the northern route to Shi'papolima they subsisted on game, as it was too cold for all fruits of the earth" (Stevenson 1904, 453).

These Beast Gods were also warriors for certain specific reasons. As a whole, predators are recognized by the Zuni as superior to the animals they prey upon: "The Zuñi has chosen above all other animals those which supply him with food and useful material, together with the animals which prey on them, giving preference to the latter" (Cushing 1883, 11). According to the Zuni, this ascendancy comes from both their hearts and their breaths:

> It is supposed that the hearts of the great animals of prey are infused with a spirit or medicine of magic influence over the hearts of the animals they prey upon, or the game animals (K'ia-pin-á-hâ-i); that

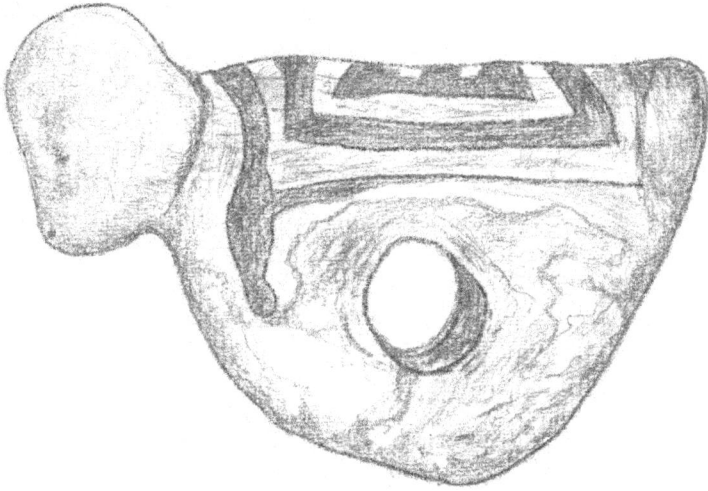

Fig. 26. Badger fetish. Based on Cushing 1883.

their breaths (the "Breath of Life"—Há-i-an-pi-nan-ne—and soul are synonymous in Zuñi Mythology), derived from their hearts, and breathed upon their prey, whether near or far, never fail to overcome them, piercing their hearts and causing their limbs to stiffen, and the animals themselves to lose their strength. . . . Since the mountain lion, for example, lives by the blood ("life fluid") and flesh of the game animals, and by these alone, he is endowed not only with the above powers, but with peculiar powers in the senses of sight and smell. (Cushing 1883, 15)

The power of each Beast God can also be preserved in fetishes. The badger does not escape this rule, as seen in sculptures made in its image.

We emphasize this representation of the power of animals (through their hearts and breaths) because it is omnipresent in the Zuni world—in designs on ancient or contemporary pottery, in petroglyphs, in pictograms, in ritual paintings, and so on. It will also partially explain the mytheme. The term "heart line" is the most common reference to this power. As a Zuni rock art specialist points out, it reflects a conception of the life breath of animals. It can be found as much in depictions of deer (prey) as in those of warrior animals (predators) such as bears and snakes:

> Deer, antelope, and rabbits are frequent and are usually carved in profile. In many cases the deer has a "heart line" from its mouth to its interior (Figure 37d, 74j); in pictographs the heart line is generally red. Similar depictions of deer with heart lines are also found on Zuni pottery water jars (Figure 63). The heart line is a symbolic representation of the source or "breath" of the animal's life. In the rock art, arrows sometimes project from the bodies of the deer as if they had penetrated the heart portrayed at the end of this line (Figure 66). Sometimes pictographs and petroglyphs of bears and horned or plumed serpents also have heart lines. (Young 1988, 82)

Clearly, a person's heart and breath are considered to be signs of life, while death occurs when the heart stops beating and the lungs stop breathing. Conversely, by metonymy, inhaling and exhaling, depending on the circumstances, are synonymous with power. This is why the Zuni believe that breath gives power not only to a warrior animal to mesmerize its prey but also to themselves during their religious ceremonies. Indeed, breath is characteristic of most performances in the various fraternities. This may be seen in two examples from Hle'wekwe Fraternity rites:

> During this prayer all hold their swords with the points upward, and as the prayer closes each draws a breath—all that is good from his sword. (Stevenson 1904, 469)

> At the close of the prayer the swords are carried in a circle over the boxes, brought to the lips, and all that is good in them is inhaled. (Stevenson 1904, 482)

The heart line, representing either cardiac or respiratory functions, also appears in certain designs for Hle'wekwe Fraternity ceremonies. Two works of art interest us specifically: one adorning a wall of the ceremonial chamber where Hle'wekwe ceremonies took place and which anthropologist Stevenson attended; and the other forming the decor of two huge boxes in the center of the courtyard where sword swallowers would perform, as well as other performers of various fraternities (Stevenson 1904, pl. CVIII, CX). In both cases, warrior animals are depicted, and each of them has a heart line. A badger appears on the wall of the ceremonial chamber and, as with the other animals, a stick (or sword) is pushed down its throat with limited ornamentation that seems to be made of feathers that emerge from its mouth.

We have seen above that the most common stick pushed down the throat of a performer of the Hle'wekwe Fraternity (or other orders or fraternities) has feathers at the other end. The only description of the type of feathers used — the description of tree swallowing — mentions the same bird species as for prayer sticks in general (Ladd 1963), i.e., feathers from a turkey, an eagle, and each species that represents the different regions of the world: "When the swords are completed each maker attaches to the top branch of the tree a *la'showannĕ*, composed of a turkey feather, an eagle plume, and feathers from the birds of the six regions" (Stevenson 1904, 484).

Thus the stick swallowed by the Hle'wekwe greatly resembles a prayer stick that has feathers at one end. Some say that the feathers of the latter stick may represent the clothing of the divinities to whom the prayers are offered. "Prayer sticks provide the clothing of the supernaturals. Just as the supernaturals nourish themselves on the spiritual essence of food offered in the fire or the river, they clothe themselves in the feathers of prayer sticks" (Bunzel 1932, 500). Others say that the feathers of the prayer stick are the means by which the prayers are sent to the divine beings. "The sticks designate the god to whom the offerings are made, and the plumes of the eagle and of other birds convey the breath prayers to the gods" (Stevenson 1993 [1915], 57). Nonetheless,

Fig. 27. Wall decoration of the Hle'wekwe. Based on Stevenson 1904, pl. cviii.

one could easily imagine another meaning of the prayer and the swallowed sticks, as a symbol of vegetation that will grow—the ultimate goal of the prayers for cold rain and snow. This may be one of the etymons of the stick swallowing rite for several reasons.

First, in other rites the feathers of some ritual instruments may assume the role of leaves. A ceremonial stick called 'hla'we corresponds to a plant whose stem was "originally white, with foliage of delicate silvery leaves resembling feathers. When the leaves disappeared they were replaced by feathers of the thlai'aluko (sialia arctica)" (Stevenson 1904, 474). The feathers may also represent a flower's petals, such as those of a sunflower: "[A] sunflower which is symbolized by a cluster of yellow feathers supposed to be from the parrot . . . . Each personator of the Uwannami (rain makers) wears the symbol of the sunflower attached to the forelock" (Stevenson 1993 [1915], 59).

Second, the prayer sticks themselves are often "planted" in the ground, as if they were a form of vegetation: "Depending on the individual's religious position, a Zuni must 'plant' prayersticks from 4 to 20 times a year, using from about 16 to 80 prayersticks annually" (Ladd 1963, 28). Whenever a performer swallows his stick down to his heart (as represented by the warrior animals depicted in the ceremonial chamber where the stick follows the heart line), he feeds it with the power in his heart and his breath—the cardiac and respiratory functions that mean life. Absence of vegetation is a sign of winter and, by imitation, life is breathed into these sticks that represent vegetation.

The Zuni themselves believe that blood nourishes the earth. This belief is expressed when they speak about the blood of enemies but it may pervade other aspects of their system of representation: "According to an elderly Zuni woman, the sting of the red ant represents both power to kill the enemies of the Zunis and fertility because the blood of the dead enemy fertilizes the earth. . . . This commentary illustrates a significant connection between death-bringing and life-giving powers. A picture in Stevenson's report of a mural in the meeting place of the Wood Society shows all six Beast Gods plus six snakes colored in the hues characteristic of the six directions" (Young 1988, 134). M. Jane Young makes a link that is similar to the one we have been arguing for, namely that Badger, like other warrior animals—Young also refers to the mural on which Badger is drawn—is as capable of giving death (he is a fierce predator) as he is of giving life. Like other Beast Gods, he can breathe life into the stick he pushes down his throat.

This belief is also reflected in a myth we have found among the western neighbors of the Zuni, the Havasupai. According to the anthropologist Frank Cushing, the Zuni considered the Havasupai to be their "younger brothers" (Cushing 1882, 362). In the company of Zuni guides, he visited the Havasupai and collected their myths, including this one about the origin of their nation. As mankind journeyed up from the four dark cave-plains of earth, their great leader died. Coyote told the people to burn his body and scatter the ashes so that the earth could grow hard. But people had no fire, so Coyote volunteered to fetch it. When he had gone, people were wondering if he would return. The blue-bottle fly came and said he could make fire for them by rubbing his wings against one another, and so he did. The Coyote, who saw from afar the smoke of the fire, was angry and came rushing back just as the body was consumed. Only the heart remained. He grabbed it and ran away with it. He ate only a part of the heart, burying the rest: "Where the Coyote buried the heart a corn plant grew, and upon its stalks were six ears of corn—yellow, white, variegated, black, blue, and red; hence, corn, springing from the heart of man, is his life to this day" (Cushing 1882, 558).

In any event, when a Wood Fraternity actor incarnates a warrior animal and pushes a stick down his throat, we know he is feeding it from his own heart. The stick is actually more than a stick. It is a real living thing. This is why facial features are carved on some of them to represent two eyes and a mouth: "Each tree [to be swallowed] is marked, before it is hewn, with three dots to denote the eyes and the mouth" (Stevenson 1904, 516). Thus, held vertically, with the crown jutting out beyond the hatchway of the ceremonial chamber, the tree, standing upward, becomes more than a stick or even an offering. It is the life one seems to want to breathe into it. The fraternity's very name, the Wood People, now makes sense. They are people who ensure the growth of plants, with trees being undoubtedly the largest and most complete ones—remember, juniper or spruce are used to make the sticks.

So our first question is answered: the stick is swallowed to mimic the growth of a plant. We can now move on to the second question raised by the Zuni version of the Bungling Host: How is Badger linked to the ceremony? In other words, why does he belong to the esoteric fraternity we have been discussing?

We have already mentioned the Beast Gods, whose role was to protect the Hle'wekwe Fraternity on its journey to the Middle

Place. At the fraternity's annual ceremonies, the participants personified each of the Beast Gods except for the fraternity's director, who had to come from the Sandhill Crane clan (sandhill crane; *Grus canadensis*) (Stevenson 1904, 40). Hopefully, his neck was long enough for the job! "The third warrior, who personates the Badger, is of the Badger clan; he carries the other ancient bow and arrows and the same plume offerings as the one who precedes him, the sticks being colored red for the South" (Stevenson 1904, 455).

In the Zuni system, Badger is above all a warrior, and his place in the fraternity is justified, as it were, by proving he is one. We lack Zuni zoological data on this subject, but other sources of information may tell us more. In general, naturalists, zoologists, and other observers of nature know that the badger is one of the fiercest fighters ever:

> The Old World Badger has long been famous as a fighter, and the prairie species [the North American Badger] seems no whit behind its cousin. It is so strong that a man cannot pull it out of its hole if once it gets fairly braced. It is so protected by its thick, loose-fitting hide, that a bulldog may be holding it by the scruff of the neck without in the least shutting off the Badger's wind, or preventing its operating with teeth and energy on any or all four quarters of its preoccupied assailant. Its jaws are so strong that it usually leaves a gash at each bite, and its courage such that it *never* surrenders, no matter how numerous or strong its assailants. It dies fighting to the last. (Seton 1953 [1909], vol. 2, 299)

There is little for us to add. "It presents a ferocious appearance to enemies, emitting aggressive sounds described by Seton" (Long 1973, 3).

The badger is the most formidable of all burrowing animals and endowed with exceptional power—as the Beast God of an esoteric society, it has to be, since one of the defining traits of these societies is the ability to perform feats of exceptional prowess. Medium in size, the badger is effectively known as a remarkable burrowing animal (De Beer et al. 1972, 142–44). Some have even dubbed it "nature's supreme digging machine" (Long and Killingley 1983, 33). Its exploits in this area have no equal. An observer reports having seen a badger disappear completely underground in less than a minute and a half: "The badger dug into the ground and made the most rapid progress in digging of any animal I have ever seen. Although the ground was hard and somewhat crusted with sod, the badger dug himself completely from our sight and plugged the hole behind him with dirt in less than one and one-half minutes" (Long and Killingley 1983, 53). Also reported is the case of a pet badger that even dug through the concrete of its owner's basement floor (Perry 1939) and the case of yet another that escaped from its pursuers by burrowing through a thick asphalt road (Long and Killingley 1983, 45).

The Native Americans know this too. The Tewa of the Southwest, who live next to the Zuni, hold badgers in high esteem for the same reason: "Two of the Indians told with much glee, of the fighting qualities of this animal and its great energy in digging. They told also of how a badger caught one of them by the trousers and held on until it was dragged a long distance to the river and into the water" (Henderson and Harrington 1914, 24).

So the Zuni were right to choose the badger as a Beast God. Its place in the Wood People Fraternity, including the stick swallowing members, is well founded inasmuch as Badger is capable of such phenomenal feats (e.g. digging his way into a hole without hurting himself, as a sword swallower would do by pushing a stick into another kind of hole—his throat—without hurting himself).

This leads us to the last question. What is the link or links that join together all of these elements and that show how Badger can produce and consume yucca-juice? Remember, in the Zuni theological system, each Beast God is assigned a color, a direction, and a season, at least four of them in the last case. Badger is assigned the South as his region, red as his color, and summer as his season. There are reasons for all of these attributes, as there is for his warlike nature. The anthropologist Cushing was undoubtedly one of the first to mention the links that the Zuni make between each of the Beast Gods and various aspects of the environment. The passage about Badger interests us in particular: "To the Badger [Pó-shai-aŋ-k'ia said]: 'Thou art stout of heart but not strong of will. Therefore make I thee the younger brother of Bear, the guardian and master of the South, for thy coat is ruddy and marked with black and white equally, the colors of the land of summer, which is red, and stands between the day and the night, and thy homes are on the sunny sides of the hills,' etc." (Cushing 1883, 17).

Nature signs her work with a flourish. The badger's coat is indeed ruddy, particularly in the subspecies that inhabits Zuni territory: "*Taxidea taxus berlandieri* is fairly reddish too . . . [which] *might* result in part from contact . . . with reddish *jeffersonii* in the west and grayish *taxus* in the east" (Long and Killingley 1983, 96).

Red is also the color of the land where the Zuni live. The red tint of the ground is even more evident in summer, especially in treeless places of the Upper Sonora. This will catch your eyes if you ever travel through the American Southwest: the farther south you go, and the farther away from the mountains, the more vividly red will seem the plateaus, the prairies, and the desert itself.

Badgers are also especially active from spring to autumn, going so far as to fall into a kind of torpor during winter in the northern part of their range. Their association with summer is thus all the more convincing: "Badgers reduced heat loss and limited energy expenditure by remaining inactive within the den during the coldest periods. Efficiency of food use increased, and, in some instances, badgers further reduced their energy expenditures by entering a shallow torpor" (Messick 1987, 593).

The association between badgers, red, and summer seems thus well founded. And even if Western zoological literature is silent on the spatial orientation of badger burrows, they are likely found on sunny hillsides if we are to trust the lengthy experience of Natives. Furthermore, the American badger typically lives in a treeless habitat: "Badgers occupy the treeless habitats of the Transition and Upper Sonoran life zones" (Messick 1987, 590). This is quite logical given the kind of soil it burrows into—"badgers may therefore avoid extremely rocky soils or soils that otherwise prevent digging" (Messick 1987, 591). Its prey also burrow underground.

Now, Zuni territory is typically treeless to the south of the town where they live. An anthropologist, himself a Zuni, describes the vegetation zones around his town. One can guess the rest. What plant do you think grows to the south?

> The geographical limits of this study will be confined to the Zuni reservation which lies along the Arizona border in McKinley and Valencia Counties, New Mexico. In general this area embraces the region drained by the Zuni River and lesser tributaries of the Little Colorado River.
>
> The vegetation of the region follows the main topographical features and is representative of the Upper Sonoran and Transitional ecological life zones. The southern portion of the Zuni basin, where New Mexico joins Arizona, sustains only a meager cover of sagebrush, yucca, a variety of small cacti, and, occasionally along underground water sources, cottonwood and willow. The mesa country and the foothills of the plateau harbor large stands of juniper, pinyon, and a variety of woody shrubs, and along the north facing canyons, where winter snows supply enough moisture, a mixture of juniper, pinyon, oak, and western yellow pine form the cover. In the upper elevations at the northeast end of the reservation, and along the western and southern slopes of the Zuni Mountains, can be found large stands of western yellow pine, spruce, oak, and occasionally aspen. (Ladd 1963, 8)

The most common yucca of the southern Zuni lands, or at least the one the most used, is *Yucca baccata*. In the entire American Southwest, this cactus reaches its highest prevalence in Socorro County, which adjoins Zuni (Webber 1953, 28). *Y. baccata*, which grows notably on prairies, hills, or mountain slopes (Webber 1953,

28), can thrive on rocky or sandy terrain (Webber 1953, 3). It produces many fruits in good times or bad, each one measuring between 70 and 235 millimeters and often weighing between 425 and 500 grams (Webber 1953, 27). Its fruits grow on a central stem that is surrounded by very long leaf blades (30 to 71 centimeters) and has a tapered end. A single *Y. baccata* fruit may fill a recipient up to a liter in volume (Webber 1953, 9): "The yucca most widely used in the Southwest was *Y. baccata* (fig. 23) because its extensive range made it accessible to many groups. . . . The pleasant-tasting, sweet, and nutritious fruits were consumed when they were fully ripened from August through October. Immature fruits are extremely bitter. . . . Native peoples sometimes gathered the immature fruits to ripen in the sun because many fruits were lost due to herbivory by deer, birds, cattle, and insects" (Bell and Castetter 1841)" (Hodgson 2001, 45).

The plant's enemies are long-legged deer and livestock, birds that can fly in, and insects that can climb along stems—characteristics revealing which species are able to get around its defenses. So badgers do not feed on it, although they are known to eat such plants as corn—a fact attested by Western biologists (Long and Killingley 1983, 109) and by the Zuni themselves in a myth about how badgers and other animals ravaging corn fields were trapped (Cushing 1986 [1901], 288). To be sure, badgers prey on at least one animal that feeds on yucca (undoubtedly fallen fruit seeds or leaves). This is *Neotoma albigula*, the white-throated woodrat (Hope and Parmenter 2007). But these details provide us with no worthwhile leads. We have a lead, however, in the way the fruits turn red in the sun—the badger's color par excellence:

First to ripen, first, too, in importance among the fruits, was the datila [*Y. baccata* is also known as the Datil Yucca], called *tsu'-pi-a-we* . . . on account of its blushing color when ripe. Few who have not visited the Southwest in autumn imagine that, dry and sterile though it be throughout most of the year, a fruit rivaling in its size,

Fig. 28. Banana yucca (*Yucca baccata*).

shape, color, and exceeding sweetness the banana, grows there in abundance on the warmer plains. Yellow and red, this long, pulpy fruit hangs in clusters so heavy that they bend or sometimes break the stalks that bear them. (Cushing 1920, 233)

The facts are now all in place to explain the mytheme. Badger swallows a stick because he belongs to the Hle'wekwe Fraternity. In this respect, any other Beast God (Bear, Wolf, Cougar, Mole, Eagle) could have been the Bungling Host who pushes a stick down his throat. But Badger is also a burrowing animal—an expert in holes, if one may say. This part of the mytheme—independently of the second part, which is getting yucca-juice—has therefore its own etymon. Moreover, as we have argued, this practice also seems to be an effort to mimic plants and create optimal conditions (snow and cold rain) for crop growing.

Other reasons explain why Badger was chosen as the most suitable animal to represent stick swallowers. If we were Native Americans, we would say he is the only one of the Beast Gods who so ostensibly bears the mark of a stick swallower. This kind of thinking is omnipresent in Native thought of the Americas, as revealed for instance by the seals of authenticity we have talked about.

Indeed, the American badger does have a distinctive marking that runs vertically down from its head to its shoulders, splitting its body in two: "The face is brownish and is marked with a white stripe which runs from near the snout back across the forehead to the shoulder" (Wooding 1982, 115). In addition, this stripe is so distinct in the subspecies *berlandieri* that it extends down the back and sometimes even farther. It is in fact an identifying mark of this race: "*T.t. berlandieri* is the smallest and is characterized by a long middorsal stripe, often reaching to the tail" (Messick 1987, 588).

Thus, for the Zuni, the badger bears the external mark—the reflection, if one may say—of a stick swallower.

There is more. This burrowing animal is associated with the yucca because of a chain of relationships that the Zuni have formed within their system of representation. Certainly, many chain links separate the badger's reddish coat from the red sandy soil, from the reddening color of yucca fruits, and from the very habitat it shares with this cactus to the south of Zuni and in which they both grow and develop, more so in summer. But this is surely what characterizes the Zuni so well—a tangled web of concepts, all embedded in each other to form a highly complex system.[1]

Still this portrait would remain incomplete if we fail to explain why the badger regurgitates yucca-juice. If we look through the

Fig. 29. American badger (*Taxidea taxus berlandieri*).

literature on animal behavior, we find that regurgitation—for example, by the female to feed her young—is not attested for the American badger but is attested for its cousin, the European badger, *Meles meles* (Howard and Bradbury 1979). This element of the myth may, however, have an etymon in a human practice. Stick swallowers used emetics to get their stomachs prepared, by making themselves throw up before they performed in public (Stevenson 1904), but this human practice does not seem to be the relevant one. Rather, it is the way the Zuni and other peoples had of preparing yucca-juice. One step involved masticating and then discharging the pulp of the fruit. This was an occasion for large gatherings of people that included parents and friends. The best description comes to us from Stevenson, who gives many details about this food preparation (see also Cushing 1920, 234):

> When the boiled fruit becomes cold, the skin is loosened with a knife and pulled off. The fruit is greatly relished when prepared in this way, but is still more highly esteemed as a conserve, which is prepared in the following manner: After being pared the fruit is heaped in large bowls; this part of the work is done by the women of the household assisted by their female friends. They labor industriously throughout the day, and at night the party is joined by male friends and relations, as many as possible sitting around the filled and empty receptacles, while the others sit near by. The fruit is bitten off close to the core containing the seeds, which is cast aside. Then, after being chewed, the fruit is ejected from the mouth into a bowl by those immediately around the receptacle, while the others discharge the fruit into their hands, and, reaching over, place it in the vessel. The chewing continues until late in the night, and when the work is finished a supper is served by the hostess assisted by her women friends. The bowl of chewed fruit, covered with a stone slab, is deposited on the roof for the remainder of the night. In the morning it is emptied into a large cooking vessel balanced over hot embers in the fireplace; no water is used, and the fruit is constantly stirred with a slender rod. When it is sufficiently cooked it is transferred to large bowls; on becoming cold, the mass is made into thick pats about three inches in diameter. These are placed on polished stone slabs and dried in the sun on the roof. About three days are required for the drying process. . . . several pats at a time are [then] taken into the hand and squeezed together; then the mass is worked on polished stone slabs into rolls about 12 inches long and 3½ inches in diameter. . . . When needed, usually a piece the width of four fingers is cut crosswise from the roll, broken into a bowl half filled with water, and then manipulated with the fingers until thoroughly dissolved. The liquid, or syrup, is regarded as delicious. (Stevenson 1993 [1915], 38–39)

As with other mythemes we have analyzed so far, the myth skips the preparation stage and goes directly from regurgitation to end product: the yucca-juice (liquid or syrup). This juice is also red, perhaps darker because of its concentration, but still close enough to the badger's color: "A little slice being hacked off was immersed in two or three quarts of water. When thoroughly soaked, it was stirred, churned, squeezed, and strained, until a dark-red, pasty fluid was formed" (Cushing 1920, 235). As in the Bungling Host myth, yucca-juice was widely used to accompany meat in the American Southwest (Bell and Castetter 1941; Hodgson 2001, 44–51), but the only other people to prepare it through mastication were the Havasupai, the "younger brothers" of the Zuni. "Sometimes the corn preparations are sweetened by chewing and fermentation. The somewhat sweet fruit of the datila, the Spanish bayonet [= *Y. baccata*], is rendered sweeter by a like process" (Cushing 1882, 549).

For anyone listening to the myth, there is still an ultimate way to verify or rather observe its truthfulness. In the myth, Coyote, who incarnates a human being, pushes his stick too far and even pulls back a piece of his guts. The scene is comical and exaggerated, as it should be, but it has an important lesson. On the one hand, Coyote dies following this experience. On the other hand, deaths do sometimes result from public performances. The reason was said to be the "bad heart" of the performers. "While accidents seldom happen from swallowing the sword, death is sometimes the result. This is attributed to a bad heart or to the unfortunate having been touched by another" (Stevenson 1904, 478). In 1915, the ceremony had even been dropped from the annual calendar because it was "in disfavor with the 'American' authorities. M. A. L. has known of the death of two women from the performance" (Parsons 1917, 172). Like many other Bungling Host variants, this one warns against a real danger. "Sword swallowing" is an art, and anyone attempting it without being initiated may pay a heavy price. Conversely, the myth is authenticated when deaths do happen.

For the Zuni, the second Bungling Host mytheme comes to us from another source in the literature. Although it does not refer specifically to any rite of any one fraternity, it is still embedded in the web of relationships by which the Zuni represent themselves theologically and esoterically. It is a story about Woodpecker, who gets food in several strange ways. By explaining at least one of his methods of food preparation, we will be led to examine a second ceremonial complex. Coyote is again the Trickster. This episode was gathered by well-known anthropologist Ruth Benedict, who recorded two variants. We will examine only the first of them, which appears in an English translation from her compendium of Zuni myths.

COYOTE AND WOODPECKER

Next morning Coyote came visiting Woodpecker and he said, "Sit down." Coyote looked at Woodpecker's yellow horns and he said to himself, "They are very pretty." Pretty soon Woodpecker said to his grandmother, "Bring me my quiver." She brought it and he said, "Pull out an arrow." His grandmother pulled one out and gave it to him. He drew it through his mouth and wet it and pushed it into the ashes in the fireplace. He put in another. He said, "Now, we shall have something to eat." He said to his grandmother, "Go up to the roof of the house." She went up and stamped hard on the roof and lots of dust fell down until it covered the floor thickly. Woodpecker said, "This is enough." His grandmother came down and took an abalone shell and dipped up lots and lots of "corn meal". The grandmother urinated and stirred it into the corn meal and made mush. She took the arrows from the fireplace. There were nice big fat prairie dogs all cooked and brown. Woodpecker said, "Come and eat." Coyote ate and ate. He ate all he wanted. When he was through he said, "Thank you." Woodpecker's grandmother took it away and the two men sat and talked and smoked. Coyote said to Woodpecker, "What have you got on your head that shines?" "I have got a bundle of cedar brush that I keep lighted all the time, so that I can see in the dark." Coyote said, "All right. I must go home now. Come to my house tomorrow." "All right." Coyote ran home.

Next morning after the morning meal Woodpecker said to his grand-mother, "I am going to my friend's house today. Coyote is foolish. He will do something foolish today. I like to see people make fools of themselves." Woodpecker went to Coyote's house. Coyote said, "Come in and sit down." He sat down and the two men sat and smoked. Coyote said to his grandmother, "Bring my quiver." He drew out one of the arrows and wet it in his mouth and put it in the ashes in the fireplace. The arrow caught fire and burned up. He burned up all his arrows. Coyote had made two horns of cedar brush and tied them on with yucca over his ears and they were burning slowly. Coyote said to his grandmother, "Bring something to eat." She went to the top of the house and stamped and lots of dirt came down. Coyote said, "That is enough." He dipped it up with a shell and got a jar and urinated and stirred it up into dough. It was just mud. Coyote said, "My friend, let us eat." He took the arrow out of the fireplace and it was just charcoal. He put it in his mouth and his mouth was all black from the charcoal.

Coyote's horns of cedar brush were burning closer and closer to his ears. The fire caught the hair on his back and singed him all over. It made him brown the way he is today. Coyote was in pain but he did not cry out. Woodpecker said, "I must go home now." "All right, come again sometime." As soon as Woodpecker had gone he snatched off the cedar brush horns but his ears were burned small just as they are today. (Benedict 1935, vol. 2, 211–12)

To identify the woodpecker in the story, we can turn to a work of ethno-ornithology by Edmund J. Ladd (1963), himself a Zuni. In his book, he reports the presence, or at least the use, of three woodpecker species in the region: *Asyndesmus lewisi*, the Lewis woodpecker; *Dryobates villosus monticola* (= *Picoides villosus*), the hairy woodpecker; and *Dryobates pubescens* (= *Picoides pubescens*), the downy woodpecker. The first woodpecker has no "horns" (Bent et al. 1964d, 226–37), as stated in the myth. Of the two *Dryobates*, or *Picoides*, according to the latest classification, which resemble each other in many ways, only the hairy woodpecker (Jackson and Ouellet

2002; Jackson, Ouellet, and Jackson 2002) has stripes comparable to the ones described in the myth: "The male has a narrow red patch or 2 smaller lateral patches of red on the back of the crown, readily visible in the field" (Jackson, Ouellet, and Jackson 2002, 1).

This patch is orange-red on juvenile male heads (Jackson, Ouellet, and Jackson 2002, 2), hence the variants reported in the myth (yellow or like burning cedar twigs).

Woodpecker and Coyote each live with their respective grandmothers, as we have already commented on. Two prepared foods are next described in the story: the first one being meat-based (prairie dog); the second one being made from corn (mush). Among the Zuni, as among many Southwest peoples, the meat of a meal was often accompanied by a dish of cooked corn. Both prepared foods will now be examined.

When we study these food procurements and preparations among the Zuni, particularly in the case of corn, we find three reference axes: an animal axis; a human axis; and, given Zuni complexity, an esoteric axis—"One cannot separate Zuni sacred from secular life" (Young 1988, 158).

The peoples of part of the Southwest and the Plains notably hunted prairie dogs (*Cynomys* spp.) in various ways: with bow and arrows; by trapping; by snaring; by drowning and removal with a stick; and so on (Cushing 1920, 598; Hill 1938, 171–72). We will focus on two hunting weapons: the bow and arrow; and the digging stick. To describe how the first weapon was used to hunt prairie dogs, we will turn to this account from the Navajo, although it surely applies to many other peoples, including the Zuni: "Special arrows were used in hunting prairie dogs. These were unfeathered and the points had only one barb. . . . A hunter procured a piece of mica three or four inches square. This was placed in a split stick before the hole so that it reflected the sunlight as far down as possible. When the prairie dog emerged he was blinded by the light, so the hunter could shoot him and pull him out with the barbed arrow" (Hill 1938, 171–72).

A prairie dog is a rodent up to 40 centimeters long. It lives in a colony and makes a burrow whose entrance is around 10 centimeters in diameter. The burrow "falls away in a vertical plunge for ten to fourteen feet" and then at the bottom of the plunge "levels off and proceeds another ten to forty feet" (Banfield 1974, 131). From two to thirty-five individuals live in these quarters that are themselves linked to other similar quarters, forming a network that could stretch over thousands of kilometers. In one Texas region, the prairie dog population four centuries ago is estimated at four hundred million individuals (Banfield 1974, 130). Prairie dogs must have been an abundant game animal of choice for Natives, as could be—and still are—the thousands of insects that woodpeckers dislodge from trees.

The second method for taking prairie dogs is by a digging stick. A description, again from the Navajo, portrays it as follows: "When a large number of prairie dogs were seen bunched about their holes, the hunter stole up and frightened them. In their hurry to escape several would run down the same hole. The hunter then took a digging stick and dug them out" (Hill 1938, 172).

Both methods involve making a deep hole perpendicular to the ground. In the myth, Woodpecker's beak is long and pointed—the hairy woodpecker has a beak proportionately very "long, large, and robust for head size" (Jackson, Ouellet, and Jackson 2002, 2). Coyote sees it as the bird's hunting weapon—like an arrow or a digging stick. Similar things may be said about the way Woodpecker goes about his work. His pecking action aims to make a cavity, which is made deep and also very often perpendicular to the surface being pecked at, i.e., a tree trunk. In other words, a woodpecker's beak is a hunting weapon. It is used to get the insects it eats, just as humans use their weapons to get prairie dogs.

Excavation is means by which wood is chiseled away to reveal a tunnel from which prey might be extracted. . . . In a foraging context, [it] consists of chipping or chiseling small to large holes in bark, into cambium, or into wood of a trunk or branch, live or dead, by digging into those substances with bill. Hairy Woodpecker tends to excavate narrow, deep holes in which to probe for prey . . . . Depths of >5 cm in digging for wood-boring larvae have been recorded occasionally, and a Hairy Woodpecker has excavated for an hour to retrieve a single larva. (Jackson, Ouellet, and Jackson 2002, 9)

To get back to the myth, we see Woodpecker take an arrow out of his quiver, wet it, and then place it in the embers of a fireplace. We have already provided an interpretation of the act of wetting an arrow in the last chapter about Wolf. This act was shown to increase the elasticity when the arrow is being drawn.

On the other hand, as is customary, the myth skips some parts. It takes us directly from the arrow to the end product of the hunt: the cooked game meat. Remember, generally speaking the Zuni roasted their meat over a fire while camping (Stevenson 1904, 368). We have no data on how the Zuni cooked prairie dogs, but the following recipe from the nearby Navajo is consistent with the myth: "Prairie dogs were always cooked in the same way. They were cleaned; the liver, lungs and fat put back in the body cavity; salt added, and the opening pinned up with twigs. Then the hair was singed in an open fire and the animal buried in the ashes to roast" (Hill 1938, 172).

Even more captivating is the second mytheme of this myth: Woodpecker prepares corn mush from earth and urine. Woodpecker sees his grandmother climb onto the roof of the house, begin stamping, and cause a lot of dust to fall down. The dust turns out to be "corn meal." Now, what do woodpeckers do in trees? They climb fairly high (= roof). According to a study, hairy woodpeckers select trees on the basis of height, preferring "larger trees over smaller ones" (Jackson, Ouellet, and Jackson 2002, 8). They then excavate or drum (= stamp), and these operations, in particular the first one, create small chips of wood (= "corn meal") that fall to the ground: "In this manner, sizable chunks or splinters of wood are removed by means of sharp blows of bill and then seized to be tossed aside if they have not already fallen to ground" (Jackson, Ouellet, and Jackson 2002, 9).

The image is certainly apt for anyone who has already seen coarsely ground corn of differently sized pieces. Anyway, the ultimate proof is the equivalence of what one hears: a woodpecker drumming on a tree and a grandmother stamping on a house roof (she could even be beating the corn into meal).

Woodpecker's grandmother then uses an abalone shell to scoop the dust off the ground—the "corn meal." This point has ethnographic value, being consistent with what is known about the shell trade between the Southwest and the Mexican coast (Gulf of California): "Hohokam shell artifacts as well as sherds occur occasionally in Western Anasazi sites" (Plog 1979, 128). These sites correspond geographically to the region where Zuni is located. As for the Hohokam culture, it flourished near the Gulf of California where these farmers of the Sonoran Desert sometimes went for expeditions to gather food, hunt, and do other activities.

The rest of the story is more puzzling. Grandmother Woodpecker urinates and then mixes her organic liquid with the "corn meal" to make mush. Anyone listening to this myth can verify what they have heard. First, a person urinating can sound like a woodpecker hammering away, in particular when the liquid falls onto a resonant material. Remember, in the Zuni language, the term for woodpecker, *tamtununu*, comes from *tununu* (reduplication), a word that means "to make a thudding sound, to make a booming sound, to rumble, etc." (Newman 1958, 39, 44). The last word can thus apply to many types of sounds that are all intermittent and resonant, not only like a woodpecker drumming but also like feet repeatedly stamping on a roof or a stream of urine pattering on a surface.

Corn mush was a basic food not only of the Zuni but also of all Native peoples who grew corn. It was prepared and made ready in various ways. It was used to make all of the breads, pancakes,

cakes, and so on. Clearly, the yellow corn is evoked in the myth by the urine of the same color.

Yet these explanations are not entirely convincing although they partly clarify the mytheme. We need to look elsewhere to find an etymon that leaves no doubt in our mind. If we look at the esoteric side of things, some fraternities did specialize in performing unusual acts (e.g., pushing a stick down one's mouth, bathing under the ice nude and in the middle of winter, etc.). Yes, one of these fraternities, called the Clowns, went in for drinking real or simulated urine. "The Clowns, founded by the opposite-talking *nepayatamu*, know how to drink what is not potable (including urine) and eat what is not edible (including dung) and with great relish at that" (Tedlock 1979, 503; see also Stevenson 1904, 437).

In all this, the most unbelievable act is a ceremony, reported by a Zuni spectator, during which the simulated urine was indeed mixed with corn and then consumed.

> It's embarrassing, but it was for religious doings. Some males dressed like females and stretched out with grinding stones. There were fluteplayers and rain dancers. Ololowishkya had a dingaling made out of a gourd. He peed a sweet syrup into a big pot that had sweet corn in it. He peed to the directions of the earth six times, He made balls of the juice and corn and gave it to everyone. It tasted good. This ceremony was done so there wouldn't be any problem with men's urine. We don't do this now because white people watch. (Young 1988, 142)

Sugar is a diuretic, and a gourd can be very symbolic, here, as a "dingaling"—having lots of liquid, it too must certainly have an effect on the bladder.

The myth can thus be verified from start to finish from any angle. There is the animal angle (woodpecker's pecking sound; chips at the base of trees; larvae and prairie dogs taken from their holes). There is the human angle (living with one's grandmother;

techniques for hunting prairie dogs; methods of food preparation). And there is the esoteric angle (the Clown Fraternity).

If we can coin the term "symbiotic myth"—in this case, a symbiosis between three components—it would certainly apply to these two Zuni versions of the Bungling Host, which have borrowed etymons from different sources, as we have shown. As a Zuni himself said to archaeologist M. J. Young, the myths about his people's past are validated by the real geographical locations that appear in them and that can be located on their land:

> Some Zunis regard their ability to identify points named in the myth with actual geographical locations as a validation of the myth. One man expressed this in the following way: "These so-called legends are all based on actual facts as they are recited in the creation stories—the migrations of our people. So, therefore, all these are based on fact and, this is the part that the whiteman never understood—the missionaries and others." (Young 1988, 146)

This remark can apply just as well to any of the myths. How many times have we heard it from other Native Americans—Innu, Kawaiisu, and others—when they speak about their stories?

This is how we should examine a myth. We need to look for the reasons behind all of its elements—the etymons—which explain why it has meaning both for us and for its users. And for those who want further proof of the myth's assertions, there remain the seals of authenticity, such as geographical locations that may be found and visited. In the last version of the Bungling Host, the one about Woodpecker and Coyote, the end of the story provides two such seals: the coat color of coyotes, as may be seen today; and the size of their ears, which used to be bigger. Both are due to Coyote attaching horns of cedar brush to his head and lighting them. The resulting fire spread to all of the fur on his back while also burning part of his ears.

11 Bison Skewers His Nose (Plains)

Coyote went along. He came to a camp. It was Buffalo's camp. . . . The man said, "Coyote has come to visit us. What shall we do for him? Old lady, go and get some rotten wood and pound it up soft." She did so and gave it to her husband. Buffalo got a stick. He whittled it until it was just the right size to fit in his nose. He pounded the stick on the end, making it soft like a brush. He put the rotten wood before him and stuck the stick up a nostril. Grease ran out of his nose and fell on the wood which changed to meat.

—Morris Edward Opler, "Myths of the Lipan Apache"

In the American West and on the prairie, in the three adjacent culture areas of the Great Basin, the Southwest, and the Plains, there circulate several versions of the Bungling Host where the main character is the continent's largest land mammal: the American bison (*Bison bison*). One of the mythemes is about what he offers his guest—grease—and his peculiar way of getting it—shoving a stick up a nostril and letting the grease run out. We have versions from the Ute (Lowie 1924, 20), the Tiwa (Parsons 1940, 127–28), and the Lipan and Jicarilla Apache (Goddard 1911, 232; Opler 1940, 139; Opler 1994 [1938], 245; Russell 1898, 266). But the bison is not the only mammal to produce grease this way. The same theme appears in other Bungling Host versions, especially those from the above three culture areas, where the host is respectively an elk in another Apache myth (Opler 1994 [1938], 276), a porcupine among the Hopi (Voth 1905, 203), and a condor (or a crow) among the Crow (Lowie 1918, 39). We will see below that while the host changes and that, although at first sight, these versions share a similar mytheme, the etymon is not necessarily the same.

To examine the basic theme (Bison skewers his nose), we will start with a myth from the Lipan Apache, who currently form a tiny population of some thirty or forty families (Opler 2001, 944) on the Mescalero Apache Reservation in New Mexico. This reservation has Apache who speak different dialects, mostly Mescalero but also Chiricahua and Lipan. Originally from Texas, but scattered elsewhere by an American policy of extermination from 1850 to 1900, Lipan survivors found refuge on different American reservations, the one in New Mexico still having the most people from this group. The Lipan traditional economy was based on one main resource, bison, which were hunted especially in autumn and provided an inestimable source of food and also material for clothing, shelter, and tools:

> All parts of the buffalo were utilized. The tongue, entrails, heart, stomach, kidney, udders of the buffalo cow, and the fetal buffalo were eaten. So was the brain, when it was not needed for tanning. The stomach was consumed or used as a water container. From the hide came blankets, robes, tepee covers, parfleches (fig. 3), bulboats, shields, quivers, feather containers, moccasin soles, and carriers. . . . The sinew made excellent bowstrings. From the horn were fashioned spoons, dippers, drinking cups, and ornaments for the ends of the bow. . . . Other rattles were made from the tail or hooves of a young buffalo. The hair was used to ornament shields, was braided for rope, became a component of medicines. . . . Buffalo chips served as fuel, and even the scrotum of the bull was utilized as a bag. (Opler 2001, 945–46)

The bison was for the Apache what the caribou was traditionally for the Innu. It was an indispensable resource for anyone hunting the same resource (to hunt caribou, you need clothes, food, a shelter, tools, and so forth, all of which come from the caribou). This is the perspective for understanding the Lipan myth featuring Bison. It was collected by Lipan specialist Morris E. Opler and belongs to a set of five myths where a host receives a trickster, here Coyote, who then tries to imitate his host. Of the five myths, only the one featuring Bison will be analyzed in this chapter. It was first published in English in 1940.

COYOTE VISITS BUFFALO

Coyote went along. He came to a camp. It was Buffalo's camp. Buffalo turned and looked one way and blew hard. Then he turned the other way and blew also. The buffalo had some children there, yellowish in color.

The man said, "Coyote has come to visit us. What shall we do for him? Old lady, go and get some rotten wood and pound it up soft."

She did so and gave it to her husband. Buffalo got a stick. He whittled it until it was just the right size to fit in his nose. He pounded the stick on the end, making it soft like a brush. He put the rotten wood before him and stuck the stick up a nostril. Grease ran out of his nose and fell on the wood which changed to meat.

Coyote saw this. Coyote ate the meat. Then he said, "My home is just up here a little ways and I want you to come up and visit me too."

As soon as Coyote got back to his camp, he moved it to the place where he had told Buffalo it was.

Buffalo came to the place where Coyote had told him he was camped. Coyote was waiting for him, blowing in imitation of the buffalo. He said, "What shall we do for this old man? Old Lady, get some rotten wood and pound it."

She did so. He prepared the stick as Buffalo had done. He poked it up his nose, but nothing but blood came. He gave himself a nosebleed.

The Buffalo watched. Then he said, "I see you cannot do it though you want to feed me. Give me the stick."

Coyote gave him the stick. He put it up his nose and turned the wood to fat meat as before. "This is the way I feed my children," he said to Coyote, and he left for home. Coyote had failed to do what he had seen Buffalo do. (Opler 1940, 139–40)

As the myth begins, we see how an American bison behaves when a stranger approaches. This behavior stems from two key aspects of its senses of sight and smell. Bison have lateral vision, as may be seen in some circumstances, such as by this zoologist when reporting fighting between males: "Gradually they would draw nearer to each other, their heads slightly at an angle because they cannot see straight ahead when their heads are down. Suddenly they would straighten their heads and the fight would be on" (Garretson 1938, 37). Bison are also known to have a vast repertoire of sounds, including "grunts, bleats, roars, snorts, sneezes, foot stamping, and tooth grinding" (Reynolds, Gates, and Glaholt 2003, 1023). Snorting in particular, which involves exhaling air noisily through the nostrils, seems to be a sign of belligerence in some situations: "Bulls also use snorts and foot stamping as part of their agonistic behavior" (Reynolds, Gates, and Glaholt 2003, 1023). Remember, the Trickster also represents a human in the myth, and Bison, detecting a human presence, responds aggressively.

This response could be all the more aggressive if it corresponded to the behavior of female bison looking for their calves: "When searching for a calf, cows often snort or give a loud grunt similar to their 'threat grunt'" (Reynolds, Gates, and Glaholt 2003, 1023). This possibility interests us because it is supported by the myth, which reports the presence of young bison with the host: "The buffalo had some children there, yellowish in color." The only time young bison have a yellowish coat, distinct from the adult coat, is for a few months after they are born. It later darkens: "A new-born buffalo calf has a bright yellow or tawny coat that is almost pale red on the line of the back, but as the animal grows, the coat darkens and by its first autumn [calves are born from April to June], the calf is almost as dark as its parents" (Garretson 1938, 38–39).

Hence, the myth roughly tells us when the action takes place, since calves are yellowish only during the period from summer to autumn. This being said, it is no surprise to learn that the Lipan preferred hunting bison in autumn: "The mainstay of the food economy was the buffalo hunt. Annual migration brought the buffalo herds south into Lipan territory in the fall 'when the geese were flying,' and the Lipan considered the animals to be fattest and their hides to be at their best then" (Opler 2001, 945).

The rest of the story mentions two prepared foods. One is a powder made by breaking up rotten wood into crumbs. The other is a grease produced by the nose. The two converge in production of a meat dish: "Grease ran out of his nose and fell on the wood which changed to meat."

By now, the story's listeners would have understood that the main etymon is a universal recipe among North American Native peoples, if ever there has been one, namely the recipe for pemmican. Pemmican was meat that had been first dried, then pounded into very small pieces and, finally, mixed with some kind of melted grease, either for consumption or for preservation. The Innu of the Eastern Subarctic made it with dried caribou meat. On the Great Plains it was the fabled "jerky" (= dried bison meat) that was used:

To make jerky less tough, the Indians tried pounding it into shreds: the crushed bits, when dipped into melted grease, were much easier to chew. But the other inconveniences—bulk, dampening in moist air, mold, and decay—remained. All of these difficulties were eventually mastered with the development of pemmican, the product of one of the most effective methods of food processing ever devised.

The processing of pemmican varied slightly from region to region, but the basic steps were the same throughout the Plains Culture Area.

After pulverizing jerky, the Indians packed it into bags sewed from buffalo rawhide, each one about the size of a pillow case. Into these sacs they poured hot liquid marrow fat, which seeped through the contents to form a film around each crumb of meat. . . . A single sack, weighing about ninety pounds, was known as a "piece" of pemmican, and made a convenient parcel for back-packing or portaging. . . . Plain pemmican, if made properly with only dried lean meat and rendered fat, lasted almost infinitely. (McHugh 1972, 89–90)

So pemmican is the etymon of the story. But we can learn more. Two leads are open to us. The first and easiest one is the rotten wood. Bison are herbivores and known for constantly chewing their cud through a process called rumination: "During rumination a bolus may be chewed 38 to 70 times at a rate of about one chew/s" (Meagher 1986, 4). Thus rotten wood is to a bison's cud what crumbling wood is to a bison's chewing. This lead can be taken farther. Bison may be linked to a tree dying back—and hence rotting—since they have a reputation of gashing shrubs with their horns or rubbing themselves against tree trunks (Banfield 1974, 405) often to the point of causing the injured tree species to die off: "Localized stands of trees, particularly those not tightly clumped, may be significantly affected by the horning and thrashing of bison during the rut and at other times of the year. McHugh (1958) estimated that 51% of the lodgepole pine in some areas of Yellowstone Park had been horned by bison" (Reynolds, Gates, and Glaholt 2003, 1038).

Some of the tree species end up dying after such treatment by bison, becoming dead wood and then rotten wood: "There is, indeed, little doubt that the Buffalo have helped to extend the prairies, and to reduce the woodland country by rubbing down the trees" (Seton 1953 [1909], vol. 3, 676).

In the realm of human action, we also see that jerky very plausibly resembles rotten wood, so much so that one author even compares dried meat to a bundle of tree bark, in terms of weight to be sure, but undoubtedly also in terms of appearance: "Although it weighed only one sixth as much as fresh meat, it [jerky] was bulky—rather like a bundle of tree bark" (McHugh 1972, 89).

All in all, the lesson from this part of the mytheme, as from the next part, is Bison's gift to humans—the food of his own flesh. Jerky looks like dried wood but is made from bison meat. This is the meat that the host offers his guest—the human represented by the Trickster.

The second lead is a bit harder to make sense of: the production of grease. It begins with the bison's snout, which of course has two nostrils that are lined inside with serous mucosa, as in all mammals:

> The three parts of the nasal cavities are each covered with tissues that have a specific structure; they can thus be easily distinguished histologically. The name of pituitary is given to the mucosa that wholly lines the nasal cavities and snugly fits the walls, following every bump and hollow.
>
> **Vestibule.**–The vestibule is covered with an epidermis that is an extension of the epidermis of the skin and has sebaceous glands . . . .
>
> **Respiratory region.**–It is covered with a mucosa called the *Schneiderian membrane*, which is locally thick . . . and is characterized by stratified prismatic epithelium . . . with numerous mucous cells lying on a well-developed basal membrane, and numerous serous and mucous glands . . . .
>
> **Olfactory region.**–The mucosa of this region is characterized by the presence of olfactory cells. . . . (Grassé 1973–1996, vol. 16, fasc. 5, 495–96)

In bovines, a subfamily of the bovidae, which includes cattle and bison, the nasal cavities have the same structure and the mucosa is especially thick: "The *nasal mucosa* is thick and the submucosa contains a rich vascular plexus in which the veins are particularly noticeable" (McLeod 1958, 86).

The nasal mucosa is also fatty. The presence of sebaceous glands attests to this fattiness, as do the following descriptions of the nasal cavities of other even-toed ungulates, including a bovid that is closely related to the bison and a cervid, the moose. These descriptions can apply to the bison as well.

> [Saiga antelope, a bovid] These glands occur in vestibular mucosa that has undergone significant fibrofatty elaboration. . . . The mucosa of the alar fold is thick and fatty, as it is in much of the vestibule. (Clifford and Witmer 2004b, 219–23)

> [Moose, a cervid] The nasal vestibule of moose is very large and houses a system of three recesses: one rostral and one caudal to the nostrils, and one associated with the enlarged fibrofatty alar fold. (Clifford and Witmer 2004a, 339)

Now indigenous people love to eat fat and should relish eating a bison's nostrils if these have any fat at all, like those of other even-toed ungulates. This is so. The literature has many references to nostrils as a choice food item when taken from bovines or from various members of the deer family:

> [Buffalo, Plains] The site of the butchering soon became a tumult of Indians cutting and slashing carcasses, shouting clamorously, quarreling and laughing with neighbors. As they worked, most of the participants snacked on raw morsels taken still warm from the slain buffalo, including livers, kidneys, tongues, eyes, testicles, belly fat, parts of the stomach, gristle from snouts, marrow from leg bones. (McHugh 1972, 85)

> [Caribou, Innu] The meat of the head is considered especially good, particularly the tongue and nose. (McGee 1961,67n2)

> [Moose, Mi'kmaq] Most of them were astonished at the trouble he had taken, and, rejoicing to see him, they made him a feast of Moose tongues and muzzles, which they had in abundance. (Le Jeune 1636 in Thwaites 1910, vol. 9, 25)

[Moose, Mi'kmaq] The very long and very wide nose tastes no less exquisite [than the tongue]. When simply flambéed and boiled, it is very delicate. The flesh, or rather a certain very fine, white fat, is so soft and succulent that it delights the palate and fortifies the heart at the same time. It is a little gummy, but not irritatingly so, and the jelly made from it, which is not comparable to that found on the best tables, comes in different colors. (Gagnon 2011, 336–37)

[Deer, Cree] The nose, heart, and tongue of all species of the deer family are considered great delicacies. (Skinner 1911, 29)

The first author specifies that the "gristle" of bison snout was used to quench one's thirst: "The heat of a summer day and the hard work of cutting up the carcasses left the Indians with parched throats. If water was not available, the next best relief came from chewing the gristle of a buffalo's snout" (McHugh 1972, 85). The author is misinterpreting here, for gristle by definition cannot quench any sort of thirst. The author is confusing gristle with mucosa.

This leads us to the way Bison dislodges the mucosa from his nostrils—by making a stick with a rounded, brush-shaped end. We believe this stick could be a tool either to dislodge the mucosa or, by association, to remove the marrow inside long bones. No source confirms this possibility directly, but we do know that some Native Americans had similar cooking utensils. For example, the Navajo made swabs from tree branches to help them eat liquid foods: "These swabs were used in eating any type of liquid food, usually mush, milk, and soup" (Kluckhohn, Hill, and Kluckhohn 1971, 142). The Inuit likewise used special sticks to extract marrow from the bones of some game animals.

We will now turn to what drives the mytheme—its ideological purpose and, concomitantly, its morphological etymons (fat and meat). This purpose is a very widespread belief among aboriginal hunting peoples that game animals ultimately give themselves up to hunters. We have discussed it elsewhere in this book (e.g.,

Fig. 30. American bison.

chapter 8). It likewise prevails in the Lipan myth when, at the end, Bison says, "This is the way I feed my children." We should understand "children" as meaning the Lipan themselves. Their staple was bison flesh and fat.

The mytheme is constructed exactly like the one featuring the bear that gives humans its fat (chapter 4). A bear has a very thick layer of body fat, but the myth focuses on a specific part of its body: the ends of its lower or upper limbs, not only as a metonymy for all of the body fat in general it provides humans, but also, at the same time, as a special anatomy lesson, since its body fat extends to the tips of its toes. For seals and sea lions (chapter 5), the myth is constructed the same way, except that, given pinniped anatomy, only the forelimbs (and not the forelimbs and hindlimbs as in bears) are available for the lesson.

In the same way, the Lipan wished to draw attention to a part of the bison's body—its nostrils and its fibrofatty mucosa—as a metonymy for its entire store of body fat. Because *Bison bison* also has a fatty mass that French adventurers on the Great Plains over the last few centuries customarily called its *dépouille* and which was 2.5 centimeters thick: "The *dépouille* was a fat substance lying along the backbone, next to the hide, running from the shoulder blade to the last rib. This was stripped out and dipped in hot grease for half a minute, then hung up inside the lodge to dry and smoke for a day" (Branch 1929, 49).

This anatomical overview raises a question. If Bison has a thick layer of fat on his back, why is that reality ignored in these Bungling Host myths? By comparison, the Innu of the Subarctic (chapter 1) tell a story about Caribou and the "dress" on his wife's back, which he cuts into parts and offers his guest, the Trickster Wolverine. After analysis, this is linked to a caribou getting leaner and fatter over an annual cycle.

Such a mytheme does in fact exist for bison. The Cheyenne (Plains) have two versions: one where Bison takes fat from the back of his wife's dress; and the other where he takes meat from his own back.

> The man spoke to his wife and said, "Let me have your dress." The woman took off her dress and handed it to him, and the man took it and cut some pieces from it, and threw them in the kettle with the rest of the dress; and after they had cooked for a while, presently he took them out, for they were pieces of fine back fat. (Grinnell 1926, 293)

> A long time ago a man was seen down close to the water, standing on his hands and knees, while a woman was scraping his back with a flesher. When she got through, and the man stood up on his feet, there was a big pile of scrapings—chips shaved off as from a buffalo's hide—and they cooked and ate these. (Grinnell 1926, 292)

If one looks through all of the Bungling Host variants (see the appendix), several have a mytheme where the host gets food from his wife's "dress." These myths are listed in the following chart:

Table 6. "Host gets food from his wife's 'dress'" versions

GAME	CULTURE	MYTHEME
?	Ojibwa (Northeast)	Andahaunahquodishkung gets meat from his wife's back (Radin and Reagan 1928, 78)
Bear	Coast Salish (Northwest Coast)	Bear gets grease by cutting the sole of his foot and meat from his wife's back (Farrand 1902, 87)
Buffalo	Cheyenne (Plains)	[Buffalo] gets grease from his wife's dress at the back (Grinnell 1926, 293)
Caribou	Innu (Subarctic)	Caribou gets grease from his wife's dress at the back (Savard 1972, 79–81)
Deer	Sahaptin (Northwest Coast)	Deer gets meat from his wife's dress which grows out again (Farrand and Mayer 1917, 164)
Elk	Menominee (Northeast)	Elk gets grease from his wife's back (Skinner and Satterlee 1915, 279)
Moose	Ojibwa (Northeast)	Moose gets food by cutting a piece of his wife's garment at the back (Jones 1916, 390)
Mountain sheep	Nez Perce (Plateau)	Mountain sheep gets meat from his wife's dress at the back (Spinden 1917, 182)
Squirrel	Illinois (Northeast)	Squirrel gets meat from his wife's back (Michelson 1917, 494)

Aside from the squirrel, which seems out of place—but which may also reflect an Native American view of the squirrel as a scaled-down "bear" (Clément 2012, 29–42)—these animals are all big game with a lot of meat or fat in their backs, which must have been a major food source for the respective societies that hunted them. Moreover, in the myths, all of these animals undergo permutations that aim, as in the bison's case, to highlight a specific body part that stands in, as a metonymy, for the entire mass of similarly composed body fat or meat, i.e., the same food substance but in a smaller amount. This body part is the snout of the bison and other members of the deer family, the 'hands' or 'feet' of the bear family, and the nose of the mountain goat (Wasco myth; Sapir 1909b, 271). These general points will come up again in the conclusion of this book.

In addition if we look at cultures other than the Lipan, and at their different mythemes about Bison producing meat and grease for his host by skewering his nose, these variants can be explained the same way as the opening myth of this chapter. Four of the five versions we know (three Jicarilla versions, a Ute version, and a Tiwa version) mention the stick he uses to get grease from his nose. The Ute one specifies that the stick is from a willow, a detail that calls to mind the smoothness of the rounded, frayed, brush-shaped stick of the Lipan version. This detail is in the passage where the Trickster tries to imitate his host: "He also bade her cut two willows. She handed them to him. He removed the bark. 'Bring the basket.' He stuck two sticks into his nose, but nothing except blood came from his nostrils" (Lowie 1924, 20).

In some versions, when the Trickster in turn receives the host, he tries to imitate the host's appearance, thus providing the undoubtedly younger audience with a corresponding number of short lessons in animal morphology. In the Jicarilla version (Russell 1898, 266), Coyote adorns his head with a mane of weeds, an appearance that suggests the sometimes shaggy look of bison fur. In other versions, again from the Jicarilla (Goddard 1911, 232) and from the Ute (Lowie 1924, 20), Bison is greeted by the Trickster wearing a bison robe and sporting horns: "When Buffalo came to see Coyote he found him at his home wrapped in a buffalo robe and wearing horns which he had made for himself" (Goddard 1911, 232).

The versions also differ in the way they describe the nostril grease. It may simply be grease with no other detail (Opler 1994 [1938], 275; Goddard 1911, 232). It may be suet, as in the Ute version (Lowie 1924, 20). It may be marrow or even bits of brain, as told by the Tiwa (Parsons 1940, 127–28). These details differ undoubtedly because of the differing cultural settings. In a Jicarilla version, the only one where Bison does not skewer his nose, a part of the nose itself, doubtlessly a fatty one, becomes a tasty side dish: "This he cooked for Fox [the Trickster], and added a choice morsel from his own nose" (Russell 1898, 266).

Similarly, the meat in the different versions does not necessarily come from rotten wood. It does among the Ute ("She brought some of the rotten wood and mashed it up well"; Lowie 1924, 20). Among the Jicarilla, three other possibilities are exploited in three different versions. In one, Bison pulls an arrow out of his back, and with it his kidney and surrounding fat (Russell 1898, 266). In another version, Bison pulls dried meat out of his back, which he grinds into powder; then Coyote imitates him by trying to get the same result from tree bark (Goddard 1911, 232). In the third version, Bison pulls dried meat out of his armpit, and Coyote imitates by again using bark, this time hidden earlier under his own arm (Opler 1994 [1958], 275).

We have already pointed out that jerky (dried meat) resembles tree bark, and this resemblance also appears in the last two versions. The different body parts mentioned (back and sides) should also correspond to body sites from which meat could be cut up into strips and then dried to make pemmican. As for the kidneys, they are among the first morsels to be eaten raw on butchering sites, as we mentioned above. In this sense, they play the role of the snout in other versions.

Finally, several versions describe how a bison exhales noisily through its nostrils when a stranger approaches, as in the opening Lipan version. Snorting is certainly typical of bison.

Even more interesting are the versions that feature another

animal as the host, while having a theme very similar if not identical to the one of grease flowing from a nose. Some details vary, however, and open up new perspectives. As we have already stated, three such versions are known, with Elk, Porcupine, and Condor (or Crow) as respectively the main host. All three will be discussed briefly, more to stress the problems of interpretation due to these permutations and to suggest solutions than to produce a detailed study of each version.

Grease flows from an elk's nose in a myth from the Apache—specifically the Jicarilla, who around the fourteenth century migrated to the Southwest into a region now covered by the state of New Mexico. This version appears in anthropologist Opler's collection of myths right after the one we have just analyzed, where Bison performs the same feats. In that instance, however, dried meat was associated with bark and production of grease from the nose. The two myths were told one after the other. Indeed, the Elk one makes reference to the preceding Bison one:

COYOTE VISITS ELK

So Coyote went to the elk. The elk was lying down. Coyote was sitting close by watching him. When the elk moved his head, Coyote jumped and started to run away.

He said every time, "The oak tree is falling on us!"

Elk told him, "You must not be afraid of me; those are my horns."

Elk put his hand down to his hind leg. He brought some meat out from there. He started to pound it just as Buffalo had done. He, also, put a sharp stick in his nose and let fat drop on the meat. This he gave to Coyote and Coyote ate it.

When Coyote had finished and started to go, he said, "Codi, you come to see me too. I'm a man too and I like to have visitors."

Coyote got busy. On his way home he looked for some spreading branches of oak tree which would resemble horns. He found some and tied them to his head. He waited now for his friend, the elk.

Finally the elk came. As Elk approached, Coyote moved his head. The elk came on undisturbed, but nevertheless Coyote said to him, "Don't be afraid of me; those are only my horns."

Coyote had brought some rotten oak tree wood. He had it under his leg. He pulled it out and started to pound it. Then he put a sharpened stick up his nose and the blood came out. He stirred this up with the meat and offered it to Elk.

Elk said, "I don't eat such food, and you had better not do that; you might kill yourself. I have power and live on power, that's why I can do it."

And Elk did it again to show Coyote. He pounded the meat, drew the fat from his nose, and gave it to Coyote. Then Elk went home. (Opler 1994 [1938], 276)

This Jicarilla myth is constructed exactly the same way as the Lipan myth. The opening lines depict a characteristic trait: the elk's huge antlers: "Adult antlers vary from about 110 to 160 cm (4–5 feet) in length along the beam and about the same in spread" (Banfield 1974, 399). The comparison with an oak, even in texture and coloring, is more than suggestive. It could not have been better said.

The mytheme has the same etymon as the Bison one—production of pemmican. Elk flesh, too, was dried (as was most big game meat in Native American cultures) and then mixed with animal fat. The following comment is about a culture farther south, the Pima of Arizona, but applies to all societies that preserved meat in this way: "Before refrigerators and freezers, the only way of preserving meat was by jerking it. In this dry country, this was commonly done with large game and later with beef" (Rea 1998, 90).

We have sufficiently discussed the snout in members of the deer family—its fat content and how several peoples considered it an exquisite food item. This is seen in the Jicarilla myth.

In sum, the permutation that takes us from Bison in the Lipan version (or in the Jicarilla version that features a bison) to Elk in the other Jicarilla version proceeds smoothly. No new element appears as we go from one to the other, other than the mention of the host's huge antlers in the opening lines of the second version.

When we turn to the versions on the same theme with Porcupine and Condor, we see new elements that should be discussed. The Porcupine version comes from the Hopi of the American Southwest. This excerpt is the first part of the story, when the Trickster visits Porcupine.

THE COYOTE AND THE PORCUPINE (EXCERPT)

At the first named place the Porcupine used to live, a long time ago, while the Coyote was living at the last named place. One time the Coyote went to visit his friend, the Porcupine. "Sit down," the latter said. "All right," the Coyote said, and so they talked together a long time. When it was noon the Porcupine said: "We are going to eat something. You build a fire;" so the Coyote built a large fire. When the Coyote had built the fire the Porcupine said: "Now we are going to have something to eat." So he drew a small pointed stick from his hair on the top of his head and thrust it into his nose. After he had done this repeatedly, blood and fat dropped out of his nose on the fire, where it was roasted. This he handed to the Coyote to eat. So they were eating. "Aha," the Porcupine said: "thus I am preparing food." "Yes," the Coyote said, "we are happy." (Voth 1905, 203–4)

Two details of this myth are key to its meaning: the origin of the tool that Porcupine uses to get fat and blood; and how it should be used ("repeatedly"). Both details are absent from the versions with Bison or other big game. The Porcupine version has no mention, however, of meat being made from some plant substance—rotten wood or bark. When Porcupine produces food for his host, the etymon is not production of pemmican, since only fat and blood are provided, and these are cooked.

The pointed stick taken from the top of Porcupine's head leaves no doubt as to the tool's origin. A North American porcupine (*Erethizon dorsatum*) is characteristically covered with tens of thousands of quills, thirty thousand to be exact, many of which are on the top of its head: "The quill rows are separated from the rows of coat hairs. The quills are located on head, neck, rump, and tail" (Banfield 1974, 233). It is therefore from the hair on the top of his head that Porcupine draws a small pointed stick.

Porcupine then thrusts this quill into his nose. We can infer that no quills were on his face or muzzle, since that part of his body would have been within closest reach. This is indeed so ("There are no quills on the muzzle"; Gunn 2001 [1977], n.p.).

In this way, Porcupine produces the blood and fat that is cooked over the fire. Coyote tries to imitate but fails lamentably and practically bleeds to death:

THE COYOTE AND THE PORCUPINE
(CONTINUATION — EXCERPT)

So the next morning the Porcupine went over to his friend and there sure enough found that the Coyote also had a pointed stick thrust into his hair. . . . So the Coyote pulled out his stick, drew close up to the fire, bent over it, and also began to poke his nose with the stick, whereupon also blood, mixed with fat or tallow, began to come out. It covered the fire, and finally began to flow away, and wouldn't stop. The Coyote's nose was bleeding and bleeding, and finally he became exhausted and fell down. (Voth 1905, 203)

In chapter 9, a similar Navajo myth has already been examined. This is the one with Porcupine, who scratches his nose until blood flows and who roasts a piece of bark until it turns into a piece of fine meat. With what we have just seen, the Navajo myth may have some links with dried meat (bark) cooked with fat to make a specific dish of food.

In any event, the Navajo version and this Hopi one share similar etymons: a meal is made with blood (which may be equivalent to meat); game meat can be roasted over a fire; and there is an association between a porcupine's food, tree cambium, and the blood/meat under its skin. These etymons help explain the how and why of making a meal that in sum represents what a porcupine offers hunters both as an animal and as meat, i.e., part of itself, its fat and blood. They fail to explain, however, a detail we mentioned above: Porcupine repeatedly thrusting a stick up his nose.

In fact, this detail can be explained only by juxtaposing it with Coyote's tragic end when the story closes: he passes out and almost dies trying to imitate his host (but he will revive).

The main etymon of the Hopi mytheme is like a photo negative. The image is inverted. What happens to Coyote bears out the story—it happens to coyotes in general whenever they tangle with a porcupine: "Occasionally the coyote receives the worst of an encounter with a porcupine and gets its jaws filled with quills" (Banfield 1974, 287). Having seen dogs after such encounters, we can add that the quills cover not only the jaws but also the entire front of the head, including the muzzle.

So the myth has the following message. Porcupine quills are dangerous for anyone to handle, whether one is Coyote or the humans he personifies as the Trickster. Only Porcupine can live with them; he who offers his flesh to us. This may be seen in nature whenever animals or humans get jabbed by these nasty quills:

> This second hair is so strongly attached to the skin that it is very hard to pull out; but the porcupine detaches it and throws it with such speed and so rigidly at the dogs that pursue it that it often kills them. And if the hunter is not careful to remove the hairs promptly, all the dogs that are speared with them die; and the hunter himself must take care not to be wounded by these hairs, for the hair is so sharp that it works its way into the flesh without being felt. I have seen hunters crippled for two or three months, until this hair worked its way out on the other side from the first wound. . . . The animal usually lives in holes in rocks or in trees. It is amusing to see young dogs, which have not seen these kinds of animals, cry and run away as if they have been whipped when, trying to bite the animal, they get their mouth full of this hair, and their mouth is bleeding all over. (Gagnon 2011, 313–14)

We will now turn to the last version of the same mytheme, where Condor is the host who produces grease from his nose and meat from the bark he covers with a blanket. This story comes from the Crow, a people of the Plains culture area who live to the north, in a region that corresponds to the present-day American state of Montana.

THE CONDOR AND THE COYOTE (EXCERPT)

When Old-Man-Coyote's wife and child had eaten what he brought home, he went again. He came to another tent, which was yellow and had a black top. He was standing outside the tent. It belonged to the condor. He called in. The condor told him to come in and sit down. When he came in, he told the condor he had been looking for him a long time and was tired. The condor told his wife to bring in some big pieces of bark. When she brought them, the condor covered himself and the bark with a blanket. When the blanket was taken away, the bark had turned into fresh meat. They cooked it over a fire. The condor bade his wife pierce his nose. She did so. The grease came out and it was put into a bowl. He gave the cooked meat to Old-Man-Coyote and he ate it. Old-Man-Coyote told him he was very glad he came there and when he had done eating they smoked together and told stories. When he went home, they gave him more meat and grease from the bird's nose. He told the condor to visit him some time. The bird was called nū'ptɑkō ictsé. He told the condor to come to him any time he wished. (Lowie 1918, 39)

The Crow myth featuring Condor is part of a series of Bungling Host myths. In each one, a different animal is the host and Coyote (Old-Man-Coyote) visits them one after the other. Each animal produces food from a plant substance and from grease using a specific body part. This food production is detailed in the following chart. These details are needed to understand both Condor's place in the series of Crow myths and his place in the series of animals we have examined that produce grease from their noses.

Table 7. Crow Bungling Host series

HOST	MEAT	GREASE	DISH
Owl	pounded bark	pierced eye = grease	grease + bark = meat
Elk	a. pounded bark b. shavings from neck	bark	a. bark → meat or fat b. neck → pudding
Condor	meat	pierced nose = grease	blanket (bark → meat) + grease
Crow	bark	pierced bill = grease	blanket (bark → meat) + grease

Each of these myths operates as explained throughout this book by intentionally highlighting, focusing on, and playing up the specific traits and behaviors of each species that plays the role of host. Conversely, when members of the community hear the myth and see the same traits or behaviors in the real world, they conclude that the myth is true in this respect and, hence, in all other respects. The myth has thus meaning for them.

For example, these four Crow myths give each species its own home: a yellow tent for Owl; a big tent for Elk; a yellow tent with a black roof for Condor; and a black tent for Crow. It is worth noting that Native languages generally had a term for 'yellow' before gaining one for 'brown' and that, during this early stage, the term 'yellow' included a variety of hues from 'yellow' to 'brown' (Berlin and Kay 1969, 18). The respective colors (= external appearance) of Owl's home and Elk's (which also has the dimension of "big") can thus be explained. As for Crow's tent, it is obviously black, and no further comment is needed. Condor's home has a more puzzling color. The California condor (*Gymnogyps californianus*) was known to Crow people—its former geographic range included the western portion of Crow ancestral land (Snyder and Schmitt 2002, 3; Voget 2001, 696). Its head and neck are typically orange or yellow, but these colors change with age, juveniles (2–3 years old) having a completely black coloration that is reduced to black spots here and there on the adult forehead. Intermediate plumage has the following color pattern: "Head blackish with light to moderate freckling and blotching of dull reddish orange to dull yellow on sides of head" (Snyder and Schmitt 2002, 31).

One can therefore say that the condor's home is yellow with a black roof in juveniles, and that such individuals are all the more numerous and observable because a condor's life expectancy is only four years: "The average annual mortality rate of 26.6% documented in the 1980s translates into an average life expectancy of only about 4 yr—less than the normal age of first breeding and far less than the potential life span for the species" (Snyder and Schmitt 2002, 20). The myth might also refer to adults flying in the air and exposing their bottom coloration to view. This ground-level perspective would also create the impression of a yellow tent (the condor's upper chest is yellow-orange) with a black roof (dark wings).

The myth also highlights a specific body part of each host species. This part corresponds to the site from which food is taken. Owl's eyes are pierced to produce fat, and even a non-expert knows that "owl-eyed" means having eyes that typify these birds of prey—big, round, white like grease, and almost bulging. Elk's neck provides scraps of meat that may be used to make pudding. An elk also typically has a mane on its neck: "The hair on the neck is longer and forms a ventral mane" (Banfield 1974, 399). It would be no surprise to learn that one can collect blood after slitting an elk's throat. Native Americans, including the Crow, loved such blood and would use it to make blood pudding, among other dishes (Ehrlich 1937, 324).

The myth reports that Condor's nose and Crow's bill were pierced to get grease. We lack the original version of either myth but we have reason to believe that both referred to the bird's bill. First, in the myth featuring Crow, the host's bill is mentioned when he produces grease ("The Crow told his wife to fix something in his bill and when she had done so, grease came from it") but, when Coyote tries to imitate, the story refers to a nose ("Then he told his wife to pierce his nose. When she did so grease came from his nose"). A crow's bill is typically long ("stout, glossy black bill"; Verbeek and Caffrey 2002, 2), and when the storyteller was reciting the second part, where Coyote is trying to imitate, he may have been thinking of a nose or a muzzle rather than a bill, given how members of the dog family look (and mammals in general).

A condor's bill is likewise very long ("bill elongated and hooked at the end"; Snyder and Schmitt 2002, 2). In fact, birds do not really have noses, only nostrils: "The olfactory organs are like those of reptiles; the vestibule opens externally through the nostrils on the upper side of the bill" (Grassé 1979, tome 2, 95). The nostrils are therefore part of the bill. 'Nose' should be construed as 'bill' in the Condor myth.

With this clarification, we can now fully understand a seemingly trivial detail we passed over without giving any thought. In all of the versions featuring Bison (except the one where the snout itself, or at least part of it, becomes a choice morsel), as well as in the versions with Elk and Porcupine, a stick is always shoved up the host's nostrils. In the Crow versions, either the one with Condor or the one with Crow, the nose (or bill) is <u>pierced</u> rather than skewered: "The condor bade his wife pierce his nose. She did so. . . . The crow told his wife to fix something in his bill" (Lowie 1918, 39). When Coyote imitates Crow's performance, the wording is clear: "Then he told his wife to pierce his nose" (Lowie 1918, 41).

There is a big difference between "inserting a stick up a nose" and "piercing a nose." The first action assumes the presence of a natural hole in the skin; the second does not. In the myths featuring Condor and Crow, the means (piercing the bill) matters as much as the end (producing grease), if not more so. When the listeners have a chance to examine a crow or a condor up close for the first time, they will make a point of verifying right away

Fig. 31. California condor.

where the bill has been pierced, as told in the original myth, thus proving that the myth is true while learning a lesson in bird anatomy: birds have nostrils although these are not as big as in mammals, for example.

There still remain two unsolved problems: the production of grease and the production of meat from bark by Condor or Crow. First, the production of grease. Bison have fat in their nostrils, as we have shown, and were also eaten, unlike birds of prey in general although some, like owls, could be. Owl eyes are white, and this whiteness makes one think of grease. They also contain oil (= grease), hence the mytheme's etymon of eyes producing grease: "In nocturnal birds the rods predominate, though there may be large numbers of cones as well, some of them with pallid, though definitely pigmented, oil-droplets" (Walls 1942, 661).

The grease from Condor's or Crow's bill (or nose) is harder to explain. It may allude to the oil glands at the base of the bird's tail. Birds preen their feathers by using their bill to extract sebum produced by these glands. Could they have an "oily bill?" This is how condors preen themselves: "Preens body- and wing-feathers in usual base-to-tip fashion with bill, often associated with nibbling of oil gland" (Snyder and Schmitt 2002, 9).

Are we extrapolating too much from a single fact? Perhaps, but we have other options. When birds are young, their bills sometimes have white deposits that are left by secretions from their nostrils. These white encrustations appear when the young bird is feeding: "Koford (1953) described a watery nasal secretion associated with feeding to young condors. This discharge, similar to that known in other carnivorous birds, evidently serves to rid the body of excess salt and commonly leaves a whitish deposit around the nares and down the bill as it evaporates" (Snyder and Schmitt 2002, 7).

Keep in mind that Native Americans used to adopt young animals from all kinds of species. The "adoptive parents" would closely examine how their pet animals behaved.

On the other hand, by recounting how a condor or a crow can produce grease, and how bark can turn into meat, these myths strangely resemble a myth from the Northwest we have already explored, about Eagle producing grease with his hands. The reason? The myth tells us. "Then Eagle warmed his hands. And grease came out from his hands. His hands were stained with grease because he killed whales with his talons" (Swanton 1908, 323). Eagles do feed on beached whales, as did the Haida, from whom the myth comes.

Indeed, condors and crows, like Plains Native Americans in general, can act the same way towards carcasses of big game animals. Condors are known to feed almost exclusively on carrion, with fresh carcasses being their top favourite: "California Condors prefer relatively fresh carcasses to ones that have undergone major putrefaction" (Snyder and Schmitt 2002, 7). The diet of the American crow (*Corvus brachyrhundos*) also includes some carcasses but, more importantly, it is known to be one of the first birds to arrive at carrion sites, as an Ontario study has shown: "Frequently first species to arrive at bait-sites (road kills and chicken carcasses)" (Verbeek and Caffrey 2002, 8).

Moreover, condors cannot pierce the thick skin of big game animals, and this must be true for crows as well:

> [Condor] Feeding usually commences with the eyes, tongue, or anal orifice of a carcass, unless the hide of the animal is already penetrated in some other location. Almost all meat ingested is soft tissues, with only a minimum of hide. (Snyder and Schmitt 2002, 6)

> [American Crow] Preferred opened salmon carcasses over intact ones. (Verbeek and Caffrey 2002, 8)

Just as the Haida knew that eagles are drawn to carcasses of beached whales, the unusual sight of numerous condors or crows circling in the sky may have led Native Americans to infer that the carcass of a big game animal was on the ground. Take bison, for example. They were the basis of the Crow food economy ("Buffalo were the major source of meat"; Voget 2001, 698). They also contributed to the diet of condors and crows. And the Plains Native Americans did not scorn eating bison carcasses. Some were even said to prefer this sort of meat: "No matter how their meat was cooked, most Indians preferred it rare. And it did not have to be particularly fresh—many tribesmen favored hanging their cuts of buffalo until decay set in; some became notorious for their fondness for the putrid meat of carcasses conveyed downriver by the spring breakup—apparently they consumed it with relish even when fresh meat was plentiful" (McHugh 1972, 92). And not only Native Americans did so. Such meat was also popular among travellers to the West and new settlers: "Wednesday, April 1st [1801]. The river clear of ice, but drowned Buffalo continue to drift, by entire herds. Several are lodged on the banks near the fort. The women cut up some of the fattest for their own use; the flesh appeared to be fresh and good" (Seton 1953 [1909], vol. 3, 683).

Whenever such an event happened, one might come across a site with carcasses of bison (or other big game) and see condors or crows feeding on the meat, half-hidden by the hides (which they left intact). Let us now return to the myth and take up one last challenge: understanding the gift that Condor and Crow make to humans by turning bark[1] into meat while hiding under a blanket. Blankets come from animal hides—this is known, and we have shown this relationship previously. The Crow are no exception because they too had animal hide blankets: "Sparse furniture included backrests and hide walls that separated bed spaces, where buffalo robes served as mattresses and blankets" (Voget 2001, 700).

In fact, in Crow myths, on several occasions, a blanket (= hide) is turned into the animal species it comes from (or its meat). This would partly explain why meat comes out of a blanket: "In this connection it is interesting to note some miscellaneous cases. There is a boy who, going into the water, is covered by a buffalo robe and is able to turn into a buffalo; in like manner Old Man Coyote, covered with a wolf skin, turns into a wolf" (Ehrlich 1937, 367). But there is also another very simple explanation. As we have reported, condors and crows can be seen feeding half-hidden by the hides of the animals they are scavenging. This is exactly what the myth says: a host under a blanket where he gets meat.

As for encountering bison carcasses on the Great Plains in the past and, consequently, scavenging birds, the likelihood was very high. In 1795, an observer numbered in one day not less than 7,360 buffalo drowned and mired along the river clear of ice and in it (Seton 1953 [1909], vol. 3, 684), not to mention the thousands of bison that Native Americans would kill by driving them off a cliff. Down below, at the bottom, how many scavenging birds were eagerly waiting? "When the cliffs were very high, the herd was merely driven between two converging lines of men and women so as to leap down the precipice and be killed" (Lowie 1922, 211).

Again, the myth seems completely verifiable. It is borne out by observations once they have been made. Condor, however, does not have exactly the same place in the series we have analyzed as Bison does. Seemingly identical, the Condor myths and Bison myths have elements with different meanings, and we have had to elucidate the meanings to understand them. Bison and Condor, each in their own way, provide meat and grease, although the *modus operandi* differs. Bison gives himself up to be eaten, whereas Condor gives up bison meat to be eaten, having nothing interesting of his own. In a hunting society, this may amount to the same thing if we consider the end—rather than the means.

12 White-Tailed Deer Shoots at a Red Clay Bank (Plains)

> Coyote went out again. He came to the camp of the white-
> tailed deer. This deer had his bow and arrow and was shoot-
> ing against a red clay bank. When he hit it, the place where
> the arrow hit turned to a whitetailed doe. He had a slain
> deer there. Deer went over there and dragged the deer over
> and fed Coyote.
>
> —Morris Edward Opler, "Myths of the Lipan Apache"

In 1935, the Apache specialist Morris Edward Opler gathered five Lipan myths on the Bungling Host theme, including the bison one of the last chapter. The same series provides us with the myths of this brief chapter . . . and a new element that gives meaning to the mythemes, namely games.

One myth is about the white-tailed deer (*Odocoileus virginianus*). For the Lipan in their partly mountainous traditional territory, this animal came in close second to the bison in contributing to their social, cultural, and economic life: "The Lipan range included mountain and foothill areas where other game animals were found. As a source of meat deer was second only to the buffalo. Deer was stalked by solitary hunters or by men in pairs or small parties" (Opler 2001, 946).

This story with a white-tailed deer as host first appeared in 1940, as did the one with a bison as host. The only known version is in English:

COYOTE VISITS THE WHITETAILED DEER; THE BUNGLING HOST; COYOTE TRIES TO SPOT HIS CHILDREN LIKE FAUNS

Coyote went out again. He came to the camp of the whitetailed deer. This deer had his bow and arrow and was shooting against a red clay bank. When he hit it, the place where the arrow hit turned to a whitetailed doe. He had a slain deer there. Deer went over there and dragged the deer over and fed Coyote.

This deer had fauns there who were spotted. Coyote asked about this again, but he got the same answer, that the tissue fat was heated and used for spotting them.

Coyote asked Deer to come over to his place too. When he came, Coyote shot at the bank near his home as Deer had done. The arrow stuck in the bank, but nothing else happened. The arrow stayed there.

The deer saw that Coyote was only trying to imitate him. "Give me the arrow," he said, and when Coyote gave it to him, he shot and killed a deer. "This is the way to do it. I feed my children with that," he said. Then Deer went back home.

Coyote tried to make spots on his children again, but he only burned them as before. (Opler 1940, 141–42)

As you may have noticed, this myth refers at least twice to another myth from the Lipan series on the Bungling Host. This other myth, which immediately precedes the current one, is about a mule deer (*Odocoileus hemionus*) and Coyote's attempts to imitate how the deer gets food and how it marks its fawns with their characteristic white spots.

As for the way it gets food, the mule deer obtains fat from its flanks, specifically where its kidneys are. It then mixes this fat with dried meat. Listeners would understand that mule deer have fatty tissues in their kidney region (the parietal peritoneum) and that this animal fat is eaten in a way typical of Native Americans, including the Lipan, i.e. eaten with dried meat.

We are especially interested in this myth because it tells us exactly how the fawns got their spots, thus shedding light on how the fawns of the related white-tailed deer got theirs. Here is the relevant passage from the mule deer myth:

COYOTE VISITS THE MULE DEER (EXCERPT)

Then the coyote said, "How is it that your children are spotted?"

"Oh, I get fat from around the entrails, warm it, and hit my children with it. The hot fat makes the spots."

. . . When Coyote first came home after his visit to the deer, he tried to make his children like the deer children. He took fat and heated it in the fire. Then he beat his children with the fat. But it didn't make the children spotted; it only burned them severely. (Opler 1940, 141)

This passage, which is essentially identical to the other one from the white-tailed deer myth, mentions two aspects of a deer's body: an external, morphological one and an internal, anatomical one. The first aspect is external: the typical white spots of fawns, be they mule deer or white-tailed deer:

[Mule Deer] The fawns at birth are chestnut coloured with rows of white spots on the flanks and back. (Banfield 1974, 390)

[White-tailed Deer] The new-born fawns have bright reddish silky coats, dappled with rows of quarter-sized white spots on flanks and back. (Banfield 1974, 393)

These white spots are paralleled internally by the second aspect: the serous membrane that lines the abdominal cavity—the visceral peritoneum—and which contains all of the organs inside. Some Native Americans liken the membrane to a spider web. This is the case with the Innu of the Subarctic, who describe the peritoneum of another member of the deer family, the caribou, in these words: "It's like a spider web, with its patterns and with its indentations along the edges" (Clément 1995b, 89). Several parallels may thus be drawn between the peritoneum and the white spots that sprinkle a fawn's coat, particularly on its sides. We see the same irregular, indented patterns, the same whiteness—as white as body fat, and the same position on the flanks, the spots on the outside and the peritoneum on the inside. Thus, among mule deer, "the fawns are born . . . carrying a red coat in which there are irregular rows of white spots on the back and sides (with extra spots in between)" (Wooding 1982, 49).

The myth makes one aspect the origin of the other. This is only a stylistic device. The point is not so much to show a relationship of cause and effect—although this mythical relationship does serve as a memory aid—as to teach specific morphological and anatomical traits, highlighted by the myth itself.

A different process gives meaning to the other part of the myth: the mytheme where the white-tailed deer aims his arrow at a red clay bank, kills a white-tailed deer, and later offers the game meat to his guest, Coyote. At work, here, is a way of conceiving relations between humans and animals, in particular the game animals they would hunt. To be understood fully, this mytheme should be examined from three angles, which lead us to three questions. Why does the white-tailed deer kill another member of its species? Why is the killed animal a female? And what is the link between a red clay bank and this animal?

According to the myth, White-Tailed Deer uses a bow and arrow to kill another deer, a female. In the corresponding myth about the mule deer, only arrows are mentioned: "Deer said, 'Here comes Coyote. What are we going to do for him? Well, Old Lady, get me my arrows'" (Opler 1940, 140).

This imagery of a deer using arrows comes, at least in part, from a mental representation that hunters project on to animal societies (animals, even herbivores, hunt their food as humans

Fig. 32. Young white-tailed deer.

do; at least if one were to go and live with them). Such imagery has already been discussed, and we will come back to it a bit further on. There is, however, another hidden meaning, again a morphological one. Bringing it out into the open will require ethnozoographic data, which are lacking for the Lipan, as is the case for most aboriginal societies—among whom such studies can be counted on the fingers of one hand. Nonetheless, we can extrapolate from the few studies that exist and show what this imagery fully means.

Thus, some indigenous peoples make a link between an arrow or an arrowhead and something about the feet of deer and other cervidae. Allusions to this link appear in some myths. For example, an Innu myth tells the story of a young man who goes to live among the caribou (*Rangifer tarandus*) and leaves behind his snowshoes and bow while keeping his arrows. Each arrow is then attached to one of the man's feet by his caribou father-in-law: "He then took his arrows and attached them to his feet" (Michaud, Mailhot, and Racine 1964, 20). Now a caribou—like all members of the deer family—has an interdigital gland between the two hooves of each hind foot (Miller 1982, 927), and each gland is covered with hairs that broaden out—like a mustache to some European observers (Nikolaevskii 1968, 41) or like an arrow or arrowhead to the Innu.

This imagery is not specific to the Innu or to caribou either. Thousands of kilometers to the west, on the Northwest Coast, very similar imagery appears in a Squamish myth about the mule deer (*Odocoileus hemionus*):

> Deer [Mule Deer] is well represented in Squamish mythology. Hill-Tout (1900) tells about the time that the Transformers came upon Deer while he was filing a bone to make an arrow point. When they questioned him as to what he was doing, he replied that he was preparing to kill a nearby chief, so the Transformers grabbed him. They pulled at his ears. . . . Then they took the bone that Deer was sharpening and thrust it into one of his feet—that is why today this bone . . . can be seen in deer's feet. (Kennedy and Bouchard 1976a, 39)

Here, the referent of the myth is undoubtedly the dewclaw—a horny outgrowth above a deer's foot that looks like a bone. Anyway, both the Innu and the Squamish believe that members of the deer family have arrow-like or arrowhead-like body parts, and that such parts furthermore show not only that a human once went to live with them but also that these animals have arrows. Given that all Native American peoples tend to share the same mental constructs in terms of principles and general points, we can extrapolate from these two cases and affirm that such imagery doubtless prevailed among the Lipan as well. Their myths too could endow white-tailed deer and mule deer with the use of bows and arrows.

This being said, we must also understand why, in the myth, Deer kills another deer. This event has two dimensions: a social contract between animals and humans, and how the same event is perceived from two viewpoints—animal and human.

The social contract between animals and humans is simple. In the Lipan story, it works as follows: Deer kills another deer because a human has no power to kill the animal he hunts unless it consents to offer itself up to the hunter. This belief is very old and widespread among Native Americans. It shows up in various ways that often place obligations on the hunter. It is summed up by an anthropologist and specialist in Native Americans of eastern North America, Frank G. Speck:

> There has been no change in these native doctrines since they were first recorded in the seventeenth century in the words of the French priests. "They believe that many kinds of animals have reasonable souls. They have superstitions against profaning certain bones of elk, beaver and other beasts. . . . They pretend that the souls of these animals come to see how bodies are treated and go and tell the living beasts and those that are dead, so that if ill treated the beasts of the same kind will no longer allow themselves to be taken in this world or the next." (Speck 1977 [1935], 72)

We have already mentioned here that other Native peoples think along similar lines. On the Great Plains, for example, the Teton attribute this social contract to the White Buffalo Woman: "The result of the White Buffalo Woman's coming was to formalize the compact between animals and humankind by which animals allowed themselves to be killed for food and also provided sacred and healing powers to people" (De Mallie and Parks 2001, 1071). There is no doubt that the Lipan thought likewise, as seen in the myth of this chapter: Deer feeds his host by offering him the flesh of his own species (a doe).

The second dimension of the mytheme, which overlaps the first one, is the differing perspective of the animal or human spectator. While commenting on an Innu myth about a young man who went to live among the caribou, the anthropologist Adrian Tanner speaks at length on these diverging viewpoints. His text is so clear and precise that it is worth quoting in full:

> This notion that there is a double significance to the events of the hunt is strikingly made use of in a myth which was told to me by Matthew Rich, an Indian from Northwest River, Labrador. The myth, which need not concern us in all the details, is about a young man who married a caribou girl. At the start of the myth the young man is hunting caribou with his family, and the story describes the hunting encounter between the hunters and the caribou from the normal human perspective. However, during the hunt the young man becomes able to see these same events from a different perspective, that is, from the perspective of the caribou. This caribou perspective consists of the transformation of the caribou reality into human terms. The story gives details of how a number of phenomena involving the caribou appear to the young man (caribou reality), and how these same phenomena appear, by contrast, to the young man's family (human reality). For example, the young man sees what to him appears to be a beautiful young woman, while to the hunters this appears as an ordinary female caribou. After the boy marries the caribou girl he joins the other caribou, who to him appear as Indians, living in small hunting groups. Later they all assemble together in a large house. The caribou leader is the father of the caribou girl. During a caribou hunt the hunters and the young man see the same events, but to each they appear quite different. The human beings see the caribou running from the hunters, and when one is shot the animal falls down and dies; but the young man, seeing the same event, sees a person wearing a white cape running away and then throwing off the cape, which the hunter then picks up as the carcass. At another time, what appears to the hunters as the rutting of the caribou in the fall is seen by the young man as a soccer game played by the male caribou. (Tanner 1979, 136–37)

It seems quite logical that the host, despite being an herbivore, offers and even consumes meat in this human-perceived animal reality. One variant of the same Innu myth is very specific: "The caribou place the man in the center of the tent. . . . The caribou speak to the man and feed him good caribou tail, breast, and fat" (Landriault 1974, 28).

This difference in perception is also well described in another myth, this time from the Mi'kmaq (Northeast). A man is the guest of beavers and, on leaving them, receives a gift of meat to take to his human wife: "When he reaches his own wigwam, he drops the load of meat outside, as is the custom, and goes in. His wife is sent out to fetch it in: 'There is a small bundle of something outside,' he says quietly. But when she unwraps it, behold! It is not meat at all. It is *mitiey maskwi*, poplar bark! It is food for beavers, not for humans" (Whitehead 1988, 73).

A similar myth from the Thompson Salish of the Plateau, in the western part of the continent, tells a story identical to the Innu one. A hunter becomes a deer and is given deer meat to eat in the company of his new in-laws. The mytheme this time tells us how the animals revive as part of a cycle of death and regeneration: "Thus these Deer people lived by hunting and killing each other and then reviving. The hunter lived with his wife and her people, and hunted whenever meat was required. He never failed to kill deer, for some of the young deer were always anxious to be killed for the benefit of the people" (Teit 1917, 41).

The same general idea is again expressed by Stephen McNeary about Tsimshian mythology as a whole (Northwest Coast): "In both visual and oral arts there seems to be a pleasure in showing that what appears to be one thing may, from another point of view, be part of something quite different" (1984, 11). Several examples are provided, including a bear's marriage with an indigenous woman who, as long as she lives with him, perceives him as a man, but who, when she comes back to her village, begins to see him as a bear.

Closer to the Lipan, among the Jicarilla, a related myth tells the story of a man who lived among bison. The scenario remains the same. The man, an Apache, sees behaviors that seem human but which are, in reality, animal:

> The Apache let the sun go down. Then he followed the trail of the buffaloes. Darkness came. He was there at the western canyon. He saw five tipis there just like the ones these Indians have. He never thought it was a buffalo camp. He thought it must be the tipis of his own people and that he was lucky to find them so near.

> He came to the first tipi. He looked in. A young woman was in there. She was dressed in buckskin just like a real Apache. She was sitting in a corner pounding dry meat. A fire was burning in the center of the tipi. He went in. (Opler 1994 [1938], 250)

In our myth under study, the Lipan make the same kind of projection. We see Deer kill another deer and offer it to his host—a human represented by the Trickster. As humans, we are only guests of the animals that feed us. This is another way of saying that the host gives up his own flesh to feed his guest.

But why a doe? Why a female deer and not a male? Again, the answer is relatively simple and has already been given. It is known that the females of the deer family, and those of other animals, are fatter than the males at certain times of the year, in particular from late summer to spring calving. The males have a different yearly cycle, being fatter in the summer until the autumn rut, when they get much leaner.

If one is hunting in autumn or winter, the females will be sought more. This is why the Innu, who are better known to us, say they generally prefer "to kill the females because they provide more fat" (Dominique 1979, 51). The same pattern appears in Innu myths: females are killed more often than males, and the gift to humans from members of the deer family, here a caribou, comes from the male caribou's wife and specifically from her back, where the layer of subcutaneous tissue, the hypodermis, is very rich in fat. This point was discussed earlier in chapter 1.

We now turn to the last element of the myth, an odd one to say the least: Deer shooting at a red clay bank. Its etymon comes directly from a game . . . and also from the animal's physical appearance. There being very little on games specifically from the Lipan, we will have to look through the general Native American literature.

Games were played by most if not all North American Native peoples, as shown by an excellent book by Stewart Culin (1907) that has over eight hundred pages on such activities. Games of skill were predominant and evidently included archery. What else in cultures where the bow and arrow were the most common weapons for survival? Archery games were very often played as much by young people as by adults. The targets, the number of players, the stakes, and so on could vary from one culture to the next, or even within a single culture.

Now, among many of these peoples, it was not unusual to aim at a heap of earth large enough to form a bank. On the Great Plains, the Blackfoot and other groups would shoot an arrow into an earth bank and make it the target of the game: "One simple game is opened by a player shooting an arrow into a bank of earth which in turn becomes the target for all. The one placing an arrow nearest the target arrow wins all the arrows shot in the round" (Wissler 1911, 55).

The Thompson Salish of the Plateau in British Columbia had very similar games: "A shooting game was played as follows. A steep sandy bank was generally chosen. Each player had two arrows. An extra arrow was fired at the bank by one of the party, to remain there as a target" (Teit in Culin 1907, 390). The Zuni of the Southwest, not so distant from the Lipan, would bury a grass target under the sand. Arrows were shot at the target, invisible to the naked eye, and then the target was dug up. Success or failure was interpreted as a sign of good or bad fortune:

The name of the game was given as hapoanpiskwaiwe, from ha-po-an, bunch of grass, and pis-kwai-we, shooting. Two men or two boys play it in summer in the cornfields. The target is covered with sand, which is smoothed over so that the ha-po-an does not show. They shoot in turn, leaving the arrows in the ground. Then they pull out the arrows together, and if neither has pierced the target, it is bad luck; but if one has hit the target and lifts it out on his arrow, he is sure to kill deer. (Culin 1907, 398)

This game of fantasy turned a bank of earth into a potential game animal and, if the target was hit, there would be a permutation: the game animal would replace the target. The virtual becomes the real.

The Lipan etymon works the same way. When the host gets a doe from a clay bank, this imagery is certainly inspired by a game of skill that existed throughout North America, given the importance of archery. A bank of earth would also make one think of a real game animal that could blend into the surrounding red earth . . . the summer coloring of a white-tailed deer: "Color varies but normally in summer is reddish fawn on the sides" (Wooding 1982, 53).

No doubt about it. These etymons tell a story that overflows with meaning. They begin with a game and end with a religious belief—a way of representing the universe, where animals and humans are bound by a convention that governs how the former will offer themselves up to the latter for their various needs: food, clothing, tools, and so forth. The famous anthropologist Marcel Mauss likewise pointed to "the mix . . . of religion and play" (2007, 72) as a key to elucidating certain ritual practices that had initially arisen as forms of amusement.

13 Man Kills Bison with His Sharpened Leg (Plains, Plateau)

Nih'ā^{n}ça^n went to visit his friend. When he arrived, his friend said to him: "Come in, come in! Well, my friend, sit down here." Then he went out. Nih'ā^{n}ça^n peeped out and saw him sharpening his leg. When he had sharpened his leg he saw him go unconcernedly out on the prairie. Then he called: "Hoi, hoi, hoi, hoi," and drove out the buffalo. Then Nih'ā^{n}ça^n saw him kick one of them and kill it. Then he pursued another and kicked it and again struck it down. Thus he killed four. Then he came back and skinned them and brought in the meat.

—George A. Dorsey and Alfred L. Kroeber,
"Traditions of the Arapaho"

The mytheme of a man or a woman with a sharpened leg is relatively common among Native Americans, particularly in the western culture areas. It is less commonly associated with the Bungling Host motif. We know only two examples, both from the Plains: an Arapaho myth, excerpted above, and an Assiniboine myth (Lowie 1910, 118).

Bungling Host myths generally have an animal representing the host. With this mytheme, there is only a Man in the Arapaho version and Four Boys in the Assiniboine version. This is rather unusual and poses special problems for analysis. To understand the Arapaho myth, we must examine not only the series it belongs to but also other myths, farther afield, that have a character with a sharpened leg. Although these other myths come mainly from the Plains, some are from the nearby Plateau culture area. One is from eastern North America.

The Arapaho migrated from the north to the Great Plains probably in the early eighteenth century. Their exact origin is uncertain. As a cultural group, they belong to the Algonquian linguistic family and are related to similar groups from the High Plains, like the Blackfoot, the Gros Ventre, the Plains Cree, and others. This culture area is usually divided into two regions: a western one, the High Plains, and an eastern one, the Prairie Plains. The two regions differed greatly in social organization, language, economy, means of subsistence, and so on. The Prairie Plains largely had more sedentary Sioux groups who were both farmers and hunters with greater social complexity. To the west, the High Plains had nomadic groups with hunting-based economies:

> In the High Plains, the historic tribes were nomadic within claimed hunting areas. Each tribe (or, in the case of the larger tribes, subtribe) came together in the early summer for the Sun Dance and other ceremonies, and for tribal bison hunts. In the fall the bands dispersed and wintered in camps along the streams, where wood and water were available. The historic High Plains tribes belonged to a variety of linguistic families, and many had moved into the Plains relatively recently from surrounding areas, including the horticultural areas to the east, the northern forests, and the Great Basin. (Eggan and Maxwell 2001, 974)

In particular, the Arapaho of the High Plains hunted bison, which very largely met their needs for food, clothing, tools, and so on. Their territory was in the Rocky Mountains and the adjacent plains to the east. In the mid-nineteenth century, following a mass influx of settlers and miners, which also killed off the bison in the area, the Arapaho split into two distinct groups. The first group migrated north, becoming the Northern Arapaho who now live on the Wind River Reservation in Wyoming. The second group moved farther south and became the Southern Arapaho who now live in Oklahoma. Two anthropologists, Georges A. Dorsey and Alfred L. Kroeber, worked at the turn of the twentieth century with both groups and in 1903 published a collection of stories, including five Bungling Host myths. The first of the five had Sharpened Leg as the host. It was published only in English and is, in fact, the first of two parts. The title here is the original one.

57.– NIH'Ā^{N}ÇA^N SHARPENS HIS LEG AND DIVES ON THE ICE (PART 1)

Nih'ā^{n}ça^n went to visit his friend. When he arrived, his friend said to him: "Come in, come in! Well, my friend, sit down here." Then he went out. Nih'ā^{n}ça^n peeped out and saw him sharpening his leg. When he had sharpened his leg he saw him go unconcernedly out on the prairie. Then he called: "Hoi, hoi, hoi, hoi," and drove out the buffalo. Then Nih'ā^{n}ça^n saw him kick one of them and kill it. Then he pursued another and kicked it and again struck it down. Thus he killed four. Then he came back and skinned them and brought in the meat. Nih'ā^{n}ça^n ate busily; then, as he started to go home, he said: "Now, my friend you must come to my tent also." Then he went off.

After a time this man went to visit Nih'ā^{n}ça^n, and when he arrived, "Wa^{n}héi, Wa^{n}héi, Wa^{n}héi, my friend! Come, sit down," said Nih'ā^{n}ça^n to him. "Now, my friend," he said again, "sit here and wait for me; I will come back." So Nih'ā^{n}ça^n left the tent, and sitting down on the ground, began to sharpen his leg. After he had sharpened it, he went out on the prairie and alarmed the buffalo, calling: "Hoi, hoi, hoi!" He drove one of them away from the herd and kicked it. But when he had kicked it, he was unable to pull out his leg, and the buffalo dragged him along. After some time his friend said: "I wonder what my friend is doing." He went out and saw him being dragged along by the buffalo. Thereupon he pulled him out, and after he had pulled him out he said to him: "Now, look carefully! This is the way to do it." Then he killed four. He did what Nih'ā^{n}ça^n had wanted to do. After they had eaten, his friend went off, saying to Nih'ā^{n}ça^n: "Now, my friend, it is your turn to come to me." (Dorsey and Kroeber 1903, 112)

The infrastructure of this myth has some Arapaho elements worth discussing: some Native words; a Trickster with a telltale name; and details on hunting and rituals.

There are indeed some words in this myth from the Arapaho language. The first one is repeated four times by the host—*Hoi, hoi, hoi, hoi*—and three times by the Trickster to call out to the bison. This onomatopoeic interjection undoubtedly served to alarm the bison and isolate the more desirable ones (the fat females) from the herd or, at least, to guide them towards a desired location (for example, as close as possible to the camps to minimize the effort of carrying the meat away). This ability to maneuver herds has been recognized for centuries by generations of New World explorers who have crossed the North American prairies: "The hunting strategies of these fifteenth and sixteenth-century buffalo hunters, seen through the few reports of explorers, appear almost unchanged in the reports of the nineteenth-century explorers who traveled buffalo country. What becomes apparent in either sixteenth or nineteenth-century accounts is the ability of the Indian to herd buffalo, to move buffalo when he needed them and where he needed them" (Barsness 1985, 43).

This onomatopoeia is absent from the Arapaho dictionary by Zdenek Salzmann (1983). It is also absent from another version of the same myth published in the Arapaho language and translated word-for-word by Salzmann (1956, 151–53; cf. Salzmann and Salzmann 1950 for a literary translation).

The second Native word is *wa^{n}héi*. It likewise comes in a series, this time a series of three which the Trickster repeats as words of welcome to his visiting friend, Sharpened Leg. In this form, it is absent from the version recorded by Salzmann (1956) but is present in his dictionary under the spelling *wohéi,* which means "o.k.; well"—an exclamation specific to conversations among men (the term reserved for women is *'ine;* Salzmann 1983).

These clarifications may not help us find the etymon of the story, but we should leave no stone unturned in our search not only to understand how the myth is integrated into its original culture but also to uncover its actual meaning.

The Trickster character is named Nih'ā^{n}ça^{n} in the version that opens this chapter (Dorsey and Kroeber 1903). In the following pages, we will use the simplified spelling Nihancan, which appears elsewhere in the literature (Wake 1904), although there are other forms such as Nih$^{?}$óóthoo (Salzmann and Salzmann 1950, 95). The same character appears in the mythology of at least another Plains nation, the Gros Ventre: "Nih'atah . . . is the Gros Ventre culture hero, whose name is also used to mean 'spider' and 'White man'" (Fowler and Flannery 2001, 682). The Cheyenne (Plains) likewise use this word for 'spider' and 'White man' (Wake 1904, 225).

Anthropologists agree on the truly human nature of this Trickster in Arapaho myths. He has no visible spider-like traits, and his name came to mean 'White man' because of a trait ascribed initially to him: an especially pale complexion. In other words, Nihancan is a white man not in a racial sense but rather in the sense of a man with a fair complexion (Dorsey and Kroeber 1903; Wake 1904; Salzmann and Salzmann 1950): "The evil, sensual being whom the Arapaho call Nihancan was regarded as light colored, and his name is now applied to the white people" (Wake 1905, 158).

We have made this point in the other chapters. When used with the Bungling Host motif, the Trickster indeed incarnates a human who stands in opposition to an animal that tries to show him its own way of getting or producing food, a way that is unsuitable for a human. This is as true for Arapaho culture as it is for other Native American cultures.

The Arapaho myth has also another peculiarity: repeated use of a fourfold formula. In the variant collected by Dorsey and Kroeber (1903), which opens this chapter, the interjection *hoi* appears four times for the bison hunt, and the host kills four bison. In the variant collected by Salzmann (1956), Sharpened Leg tells Nihancan not to abuse the power he gives him to kill bison, and not to use it more than four times. The number four seems to hold a special meaning for the Arapaho. Zdenek Salzmann and Joy Salzmann (1950) say it is special in all Native American cultures of North America: "As with most American Indian tribes, *four* is the mystic number of the Arapaho" (1950, 96n18). In reality, this is not so. Our research (see preceding chapters of this book) has convinced us that this sort of mystic number can vary from one culture to the next, e.g., four among the Arapaho, the Tohono O'odham (Southwest) and the Bella Coola (Northwest Coast); five among the Coast Salish (Northwest Coast); nine among the Navajo (Southwest); and four or six among the Zuni (Southwest).

The Arapaho myth that opens this chapter has other extremely important elements (e.g., use of a sharpened leg as a spear to kill bison). Such elements can be explained only by initially or at least concomitantly identifying the host. Is it an animal, as in all of the other Bungling Host myths, or is it a human? If the answer is the latter, we would have an exception to the rule.

The host seems human in the Arapaho series of Bungling Host myths, except for one that explicitly features a kingfisher. The series has five distinct texts, all of them collected by Dorsey and Kroeber (1903, 112–20). The texts were originally numbered and titled as follows:

- No 57 Nih'ā^{n}ça^n sharpens his leg and dives on the ice;
- No 58 Nih'ā^{n}ça^n dives on the ice (variant of No 57, part 2);
- No 59 Medicine-man Kingfisher dives through the ice;
- No 60 Nih'ā^{n}ça^n imitates his host;
- No 61 Nih'ā^{n}ça^n imitates his host.

The last two stories are very different, though having the same title.

If we consider their main themes, the five myths can also be divided into five distinct mythemes:

a. Man kills buffalo with his sharpened leg (No 57, part 1);
b. Man dives under the ice (two: No 57, part 2 and No 58);
c. Kingfisher dives through the ice (No 59);
d. Man turns bark into meat (No 60);
e. Man gets food by calling it (No 61).

In many Native American languages, the term for a male human is related to the term for a male animal. This is so in the Algonquian linguistic family (Hewson 1993). While we do not know the exact rule for male animals in Arapaho, the same principle should apply to that Algonquian language as well. So do not let the term 'Man' mislead when applied by the Arapaho to various hosts. It may in fact refer to an animal, as in other Native American myths. For example, Fish-Oil-Man appears in a Bungling Host myth from the Shuswap (Northwest Coast) (Teit 1909), but this host is known to originate from other myths in which a seal plays the same role (see chapter 5).

Let us prove this point by examining the Arapaho series of Bungling Host myths. Right after the mytheme about a sharpened leg, we come to one about a man who disguises himself as a bird before diving through a hole in the ice. The version we present below is the second part of myth No 57. It picks up where the man who had sharpened his leg invites Nihancan to visit him a second time:

57. – NIH'ĀⁿÇAⁿ SHARPENS HIS LEG AND DIVES ON THE ICE (PART 2)

Then, after a while, Nih'āⁿçaⁿ visited him again. "Waⁿhéi! Come, sit down, my friend," the man told him. After Nih'āⁿçaⁿ sat down, the man said to his wife: "Come, hand me my feathers." Then his wife got them out as readily as if they were lying on top. "Now give me white paint", he said, and his wife gave it to him. "Well, now give me my shoulder belt and my whistle," he said again, and she gave them both. Then, after he had painted himself and put on his wings, he and his friend Nih'āⁿçaⁿ went out together towards the water where there was a round hole in the ice. "Now look at me, my friend," the man said to him and he went up into a tree that was leaning out over the water, and standing there, he made a motion forward four times, at the same time blowing his whistle. As he moved each time, he flapped his wings. The fifth time he plunged headlong through the hole. After a while he emerged with a fish and some ducks. In this way his friend gave Nih'āⁿçaⁿ to eat. When he got up, Nih'āⁿçaⁿ said: "Now you in turn must come to my tent."

Then again after some time his friend visited him in return. When he arrived: "Wukahä, wukahä! Sit down," Nih'āⁿçaⁿ said to him, and gave him a pipe to smoke. Then he said: "Now, old woman, hand me my feathers and my whistle, and white paint and my shoulder belt." "Where are they? I cannot find your things," said his wife to him. "Hurry up. They are over the bed—look for them! Don't be so reluctant," Nih'āⁿçaⁿ said to his wife. After a while she at last found all the ornaments. Then after he had dressed himself, he and his friend both went to the water. "Now, you too look at me, friend," he said to the man. Then he slowly climbed the leaning tree; then he began to do just as the other man had done: he moved his body, flapped his wings, and whistled. Four times he whistled. The fifth time he made a motion to draw back, but fell down head-first and struck the ice in the wrong place and broke his head. "Now you have done it again," his friend said to him. After a while Nih'āⁿçaⁿ became well again. After he recovered, his friend again showed him how to do it. Instead of being given food by Nih'āⁿçaⁿ he procured it for him and gave it to him. (Dorsey and Kroeber 1903, 112–13)

This is of course an osprey (*Pandion halietus*), also called a fish eagle. There is no doubt about it. The bird's North American range includes Arapaho territory (Poole, Bierregaard, and Martell 2002). Under its wings, its body is white: "Mostly white breast (some speckling) and belly, white crown and forehead" (Poole,

Bierregaard, and Martell 2002, 2). Evidently it has wings. And it whistles: "Guard Call, given by both sexes, a series of slow, whistled notes. . . . Y. Prevost . . . suggested these sounds like a whistling kettle taken rapidly off a stove" (Poole, Bierregaard, and Martell 2002, 15).

It eats fish, to be sure, and birds too. This may explain the ducks captured in the myth: "Anecdotal observations of Ospreys with nonfish prey include birds, snakes, voles, squirrels, muskrats (*Ondatra zibethicus*), salamanders, and even a small alligator (*Alligator mississippiensis*)" (Poole, Bierregaard, and Martell 2002, 12).

In the second version of the same myth, the osprey brings beavers back from the water: "The man emerged with a beaver in each hand" (Dorsey and Kroeber 1903, 114). A "beaver" is not far from being a muskrat, especially if very young. On the other hand, as in the next myth, the human Trickster may be projecting his own perceptions onto the osprey's catch.

Finally, although an osprey will snatch its prey very often at the water surface without getting immersed, it will sometimes disappear under water as the myth implies and as naturalists have observed: "Usually it does not go much below the surface, but sometimes it disappears for an instant" (Bent et al. 1961, 367). We have already studied this and other aspects of ospreys in chapter 1, when Wolverine of the Innu suffered a fate similar to that of Nihancan of the Arapaho.

It would be easy for us to go on examining other details (stealth hunting from a perch; balancing before flying away) but the details discussed so far are more than enough to identify the host. Notwithstanding this probable animal identity, the same myth still has at least one human aspect. The Arapaho did fish, as attested by their fishing vocabulary: *nowo'* 'fish'; *nowouunoono* 'fish eggs'; *noyoot* 'fishhook'; etc. It is this human-animal mixture that makes the myth so captivating and meaningful. The human aspects also help the audience identify with the myth, as we have pointed out several times.

The next myth, No 59, is constructed similarly, except that in this case the host's identity is known. He is Medicine-man Kingfisher. To suit his animal role, he is colored differently from the hero of the preceding myth, being painted charcoal black instead of white. The following is only the first part of the myth, the second part being about the Trickster's failed imitation.

59.–MEDICINE-MAN KINGFISHER DIVES THROUGH THE ICE (EXCERPT)

There was once a man (medicine-man), who had camped alone with his wife. One day a friend came to visit them. "Come in!" said the medicine-man to the visitor. So his friend went in and took his seat at the back of the tipi. "My friend, you have come to us at the wrong time, for we have no food to give you," said the medicine-man. Then, turning to his wife, he said: "Old woman, our friend is here; we must get him something to eat. Go over to the lake and see if there is a leaning tree."

So she went over to the lake, which was covered with thick ice, and found in its center a leaning tree. The wife returned and told her husband that there was a leaning tree standing in the center of the lake. The medicine-man then painted his body with charcoal, took his bone whistle and went to the lake with his friend to watch him. He then blew the bone whistle, and at the same time made four leaping motions, the fourth time making a plunge to the ice below in which he made a circular hole, and passing under the ice he brought out two beavers in both hands at the eastern part of the lake. "Well, friend, this is the way I have to furnish you a meal at my tipi," said the man. So they both went to the tipi dragging the beavers. (Dorsey and Kroeber 1903, 115–16)

This medicine-man bird is a kingfisher (*Megaceryle alcyon*). The story's title says as much, as do Dorsey and Kroeber in an end note: "The medicine-man was gifted by a Kingfisher" (1903, 118).

The male kingfisher has greyish blue plumage ("Upper parts greyish blue with wide white collar around neck"; Godfrey 1966,

234). It is present throughout North America (Bent et al. 1964a, 111), and its behaviors are very similar from one region to the next.

Yet the Arapaho describe its plumage as charcoal black. Their language does have a term that means both 'black' and 'dark' (*wo'teen*), and an ashen colour—charcoal—can verge on grey. For the sake of comparison, we questioned Innu from the Subarctic on the color of the same bird, and they described its plumage as dark grey (*uishkushteshiu* 'it is dark grey'; Étienne Louis, Ekuanitshit). It seems that this way of perceiving color holds true for Native Americans from different regions.

The other details of the myth are in line with what any self-respecting naturalist may observe firsthand, except for the "beavers" brought back by the kingfisher. As we have argued, this detail may arise from the Trickster projecting human qualities onto the bird's behaviors. Its fish is his beaver!

Thus, a kingfisher will fish especially by stealth while perched on a branch, a tree trunk, a cliff edge, a rock, in short, any raised position that looks out over an expanse of water where fish may be had: "Its favorite outlook may be the branch of a tree overhanging the water" (Bent et al. 1964a, 111). Western ornithologists have defined its cry as a "harsh rattle" (Godfrey 1966, 235). In any event, the Arapaho describe it more as a whistling sound. And they are not alone. There are many examples throughout North America of this mytheme where a kingfisher gets fish by diving into a body of water and then offers it to the Trickster (see the appendix). These myths include at least another one that likens the kingfisher's cry to the same sound. This is a Sahaptin version from the Northwest Coast: "Kingfisher flew up into a tree, carrying five switches. He whistled and jumped down through the hole in the ice. Before long he came out of the water with a trout on each stick" (Farrand and Mayer 1917, 165). It is worth noting that the sticks of the myth are the same as the ones that Native fishers used to string up their fish. They tellingly resemble a kingfisher's long bill with more than one little fish hanging out.

A kingfisher can likewise dive under the ice during winter. This is confirmed not only by the Arapaho myth but also by many other versions from the Apache, the Sahaptin, the Thompson, the Kutenai, and others (see the appendix). This is furthermore corroborated by more academic naturalists: "They are occasionally seen in winter. . . . Dr. L.H. Walkinshaw writes to me from Battle Creek, Mich.: 'Along open stretches of water, a few kingfishers can be found during the entire winter. I have several dates for Southern Michigan for December, January and February. I have watched them on zero, or near zero, days dive from some dead branch after minnows in the open stream'" (Bent et al. 1964a, 126).

To help Arapaho listeners identify with the myth and its message, human aspects were embedded in the story line. One of them was the medicine-man. Indeed, such people played a key role in Arapaho society: "Powerful curers among the Southern Arapaho were organized into societies according to the spirit-helper: Bears, Beavers, Buffalos, Foxes, Horses, Lizards. These societies accepted apprentices and a doctor could belong to more than one" (Fowler 2001, 844). Another human aspect was fishing, which we have already commented on. The Arapaho may have also prepared themselves for hunting and fishing by disguising themselves in some way (e.g., by wearing an animal hide to fool a game animal), as in many cultures. Other human aspects were the paint of this myth and the shoulder belt and whistle of the preceding one. These too would make listeners think of such preparations for hunting and fishing and further help them identify with the myth. Finally, humans could likewise catch beavers under the ice.

The fourth myth of this Arapaho series makes no explicit reference to the host's identity. This must be deduced from implicit references in the myth. We are thus told that the host gets meat from a piece of bark and mixes it with tallow from his wife's

Fig. 33. Kingfisher diving under the ice.

brain, which he gets by chopping open her skull. The recipe is for tasty pemmican.

60.– NIH'ĀⁿÇAⁿ IMITATES HIS HOST (EXCERPT)

Nih'āⁿçaⁿ went down to the river and came to a tipi where there were a man and wife. When he stopped at the door, he was welcomed and invited to enter. "Well, Nih'āⁿçaⁿ, come in! I am sorry that I cannot give a meal at once. I have just eaten the last food we had," said the man. Nih'āⁿçaⁿ looked at the man and wife carefully.

"Say, my wife, old woman, go and get a slice of bark and bring it inside; also a stick," said the man. So the woman went out and got a piece of cottonwood bark and a small stick and brought them in. "Put the stick into the bark and hold it to the fire!" said the man. The woman [wife] did as she was instructed. The bark turned into tenderloin, well roasted. The wife then took the roasted meat and beat it and placed it in a wooden bowl. "Well, this meat is dry; what shall we have for tallow?" said the wife. The man took the comb and combed his wife's hair, parted the hair in the middle, and after he had parted it, he took a parting hair stick and rubbed it in the red paint bag and made a red streak from her forehead to the back of her neck. "Bring me the axe and then sit down and face toward me," said the man to his wife. So the woman sat down as directed and looked down to the ground. The husband took the axe and raised it, making a motion toward her head three times. At the fourth time, he struck her in the center of her head, and the skull opened along the red painted line or streak. The woman sat still, alive, while the man reached over to her skull and produced the brain and converted it into the tallow. He did not take all of it, but left some. He then gave it to his wife and she mixed it with the dry meat, which made a nice delicious pemmican. The wife dished out the pemmican to the visitor, who ate it. Nih'āⁿçaⁿ watched every movement of the man and wife. (Dorsey and Kroeber 1903, 118–19)

The myth continues with the Trickster's failure at imitation, as in the preceding excerpts. In this particular case, the host can be identified by the way he gets tallow, specifically by the red line that he paints on his wife's head from her forehead to the nape of her neck and which, by reverse logic, proves that everything else in the myth should be true. The myth also teaches a zoology lesson by drawing attention to an animal characteristic.

Then what kind of animal has a red-painted streak? Only one: a bird of the woodpecker family. In the Midwest, the most common species and the one that best fits the description in the myth is the red-naped sapsucker, *Sphyrapicus nuchalis* (NGS 1987): "Adults . . . with some red on nape (posterior to black border of crown) and with the white on back much reduced" (Godfrey 1966, 242).

We know that woodpeckers derive their sustenance from trees, and this behavior is mirrored by the process of bark becoming meat—the reverse of bark giving up insects. We also know about the symbolic similarity between bark and dried meat from a previous myth about bison (chapter 11).

As for the contents of the woman's skull, the listeners would recognize a fatty delicacy that they and other North American Indians loved to eat. "They also mixed warm blood with warm brains" (Barsness 1985, 67), reports an observer about the bison parts eaten raw immediately after a kill. Western Europeans likewise enjoy sweetbread (thymus from a lamb or calf) and consider it a very refined dish.

As for the axe blow to the head, it again evokes a woodpecker hammering away at a tree, and Natives undoubtedly associate the sound with that bird species. For proof, we have a Lipan myth that uses the Bungling Host motif in a similar way and which this time features another woodpecker, the northern flicker (*Colaptes auratus*). Here is an excerpt from the first part of the story:

COYOTE VISITS FLICKER; THE BUNGLING HOST (EXCERPT)

Coyote went on. He went to visit Flicker. Flicker was on an oak tree.

The flicker said, "What shall we feed Coyote? Give me the rock that we use to pound things."

The old woman hunted around and found it. She handed it to her husband. Flicker took it and hit himself on the back of the head. He opened his head and took out pecan nuts.

He gave these to Coyote, saying, "With these I feed my children." (Opler 1940, 140)

There is also a close resemblance between the lobes of a brain and the "lobes" of pecans.

The Arapaho myth about the red-naped sapsucker has human aspects as well, the most obvious one being certainly the production of pemmican. The recipe is even given explicitly: dried meat, pounded and then mixed with fat. Other human aspects are various tools or instruments (roasting stick; axe for chopping; comb to part hair). While on the subject of hair, let us describe how the Arapaho used to style it, particularly the line down the middle: "The Arapaho say that formerly the men parted their hair on each side; while in the middle, over the forehead, they left it standing upright" (Kroeber 1902, 27).

The fifth and last myth of the Bungling Host series from the Arapaho provides fewer clues to the host's identity than do the preceding ones. The clues are in fact reduced to the bare minimum. The myth tells the story of a man whom the Trickster visits, needless to say, and who gets food in the following way. This is the first part of the myth:

61.– NIH'ĀⁿÇAⁿ IMITATES HIS HOST (EXCERPT)

Nih'āⁿçaⁿ arrived at a tent that stood alone. "Well, Nih'āⁿçaⁿ, where are you going?" the man said to him. "My friend, you have come to me at the wrong time, but what I can give you, you shall have to eat, so come in." Then Nih'āⁿçaⁿ went in. "Let the food come down," said the man. "Let the food come down," he said again. "Let the food come down," he said. "Let the food come down," he said the fourth time. When he had called the fourth time, meat of all kinds fell down in front of the tent. "Come, give Nih'āⁿçaⁿ his food," the man said to his wife. (Dorsey and Kroeber 1903, 120)

Among all the Bungling Host myths we know, this myth comes closest to the series of stories where a bird gets berries by singing an incantation. For example, the offspring of the bird Skwit produce berries by repeating "skwit, skwit" (Adamson 1934, 3). These stories were discussed in chapter 4, including the relationship between the birds singing their incantation and the birds getting their berries.

The Arapaho myth may originate in the same belief system, especially because the two myths share another point of convergence. In the Salish variant, the Skwit host asks his children to go and look for berries. In the Arapaho variant, the Trickster similarly asks his children to drop bags of meat in front of the tent when he imitates the call of his host. But his children go to sleep, thus leaving their father to a predictable fate. He fails to imitate his host:

61.– NIH'Ā^NÇA^N IMITATES HIS HOST (CONTINUATION)

He said to his wife: "Hurry, old woman, load your children with food. He is coming to us in order to eat." Then he told his children: "When I call four times all of you drop your bags of food in front of the tent. Listen and remember well what I tell you." Then the man arrived where Nih'āⁿçaⁿ had his tent. "Heii, bring the food," said Nih'āⁿçaⁿ. Four times he call thus. After he had finished saying it four times, his children, however, did not come. "Well, miserable children, I wonder what they are doing," he said, and went outside. Then, behold! his children were fast asleep—although he had said that he was a medicine-man. Having found them, he beat them severely. (Dorsey and Kroeber 1903, 120)

If such is the case, the host must be a bird. This would be no surprise, especially because the animals of this series have all been birds: osprey, kingfisher, and woodpecker.

Nonetheless, the myth also has a human aspect, this time a fundamental, nontrivial, and sacred one. Arapaho religion rests upon a central character, the Pipe Person or Creator, whose power is based essentially on prayer and who thereby formulates ideas that subsequently become real in the material world. The entire belief system hinges on a causal relationship between thoughts and their effects: "In Arapaho belief, thoughts and their expression (for example, in words or in quillwork designs) caused things to happen; this belief underlied prayer and ritual as well as the entire value system" (Fowler 2001, 843).

This view is extremely widespread among the Native peoples of the Americas. Their belief systems or mythologies are mostly, if not wholly, infused with the idea of a cause and effect relationship between making a wish and getting material goods or some other fulfillment. We will cite one example, but there are countless others. The Innu of the Subarctic tell how their hero Tshakapesh uses the power of wishing to make a spruce grow taller and taller until it takes him to the firmament. The same power enables him to raise obstacles in the path of his pursuers. By wishing, he creates the conditions he needs to destroy his enemies (Savard 1985).

This aspect is the human side of the story. It also takes us to the notion of medicine-man—which pervades at least another myth of the Arapaho series—because it is through his special power of praying or wishing that our hero fulfils his desires. The Trickster, who lacks this power, fails.

This takes us back evidently to the first myth of the Arapaho series—the Man with the sharpened leg—and its unresolved questions. Is the host an animal or a human? Does the host's way of getting food contain—as with the other myths—some hidden knowledge of animal behavior? By examining the conclusions we have reached so far, we can come up with a hypothesis. The following chart summarizes what we know from the other myths. It seems that the host of the sharpened leg mytheme may likewise be a bird and that this myth, like the others, may be a puzzling mix of animal and human aspects that hides the true origin of this mytheme.

Table 8. Arapaho Bungling Host series

	ANIMAL FEATURES	ARAPAHO
SHARPENED LEG	?	?
OSPREY	white plumage; whistling	fishing
KINGFISHER	dark plumage; whistling	medicine-man; fishing
WOODPECKER	red line	pemmican; tools; headdress
BIRD (?)	incantation	wishing power

To find out Sharpened Leg's identity in the Arapaho myth, we must also examine the other versions that have a character with a sharpened leg, in the hope of finding one or more enlightening details. We looked through the literature and found another myth that combines both motifs—the Bungling Host and the Sharpened Leg—as well as fourteen myths and variants that have a character with a sharpened leg. Their features are summarized in the next chart.

As we examine these myths and variants, we will use the same basic model to untangle aspects of human societies from aspects of animal behavior or morphology. The main human referents in these myths describe the subject matter of the action (predation or cannibalism), the instrument of the action (spear, awl, etc.); and various background elements, like the kicking game. As for the animal aspects to be examined, they include the species identification of the characters, the signs of animal presence (tracks; sounds), and several special behaviors (modes of locomotion; tree-related habits; accidents).

Table 9. Sharpened Leg myths and variants

	SHARP-LEG	ACTION	OUTCOME	VARIOUS FEATURES
Blackfoot	Woman	kills a man	killed by a warrior	kicking game
Arapaho	Man	kills people	killed and incinerated	
Arapaho	Man	kills people	a man swallows a rock and asks Sharpened Leg to kick him; he breaks his leg and dies	kicking game
Cheyenne	Man	sticks himself in trees	Trickster dies, stuck in a tree	
Arikara	Man	kills son-in-law	dies, stuck in a tree	kicking game; hero springs forward
Crow	Man	pursues his fellow warrior	dies, stuck in a tree	fellow warrior is a squirrel
Gros Ventre	Man	wants to kill a young hero	dies, stuck in a cottonwood-tree	kicking game
Assiniboine	Four boys	hunt big game	Trickster gets caught in a tree	
Assiniboine	Man	plays at killing his comrade and then curing him	gets stuck in a tree	kicking game; turns into different animals

Assiniboine	Man ("Ground-Hog")	pursues his friend (Eagle)	dies, stuck in a tree	
Thompson	Man	stabs his friends when they are asleep		
Thompson	Woman	pierces adults through the neck and children through the belly, and eats their hearts	transformed into stone	tracks like awls, unnoticeable; sharpens her legs under a blanket
Thompson	Man	pierces people's hearts	gets stuck in a tree, killed with arrows, eaten by birds	
Thompson	Man (hermit)	kills people	feet stuck to a post, killed and decapitated, thrown to the dogs	sharpens his legs, covered
Seneca	Trickster	spearing fish	humans fail to imitate Trickster	

Sources: Blackfoot (Wissler and Duvall 1908, 153–54); Arapaho (Dorsey and Kroeber 1903, 257–58); Cheyenne (Kroeber 1900, 169); Arikara (Parks 1991, vol. 1, 91–97; vol. 3, 171–74) ; Crow (Lowie 1918, 212–14); Gros Ventre (Kroeber 1907, 87–88); Assiniboine (Lowie 1910, 118–19, 184–86); Thompson (Teit 1912a, 269, 365–66, 367; 1917, 46); Seneca (Curtin and Hewitt 1918, 283–84).

When we read the Arapaho myth that opens this chapter, we see that the action has a purpose: a bison is killed by Sharpened Leg. Several other myths identify a different game animal, and some have a human or humans being put to death including one case of cannibalism in the Thompson version. In this respect, the most important myth comes from the Assiniboine and thus from the Plains, as does the Arapaho version. It is the only other one with both the Sharpened Leg motif and the Bungling Host motif. Its central characters are four boys who each sharpen one of their legs to hunt big game of varying species (elk, bear, pronghorn antelope) and whom the hero subsequently tries to imitate. The Assiniboine hunted bison and other large mammals: "In addition to buffalo, Assiniboine hunted other game, including elk, deer, bighorn sheep, and antelope. Grizzly bears were occasionally hunted, sometimes in their dens during the winter; killing a grizzly ranked second to killing an enemy and was counted among a man's brave deeds" (De Mallie and Miller 2001, 577–78).

The hero $I^{n}kto^{n}$'mi of the Assiniboine myth meets these boys while they are having fun at different games. They show him these games. The excerpt is confined to the sharpened leg game, since only that game is combined with the Bungling Host motif:

I^{N}KTO^{N}'MI PLAYS AT SHARPENED LEG (EXCERPT)

$I^{n}kto^{n}$'mi was walking through a forest. He heard someone yelling ahead of him. As he approached, he found four boys playing around a pine. . . .

. . . The boys said, "Brother, we will show you something else." $I^{n}kto^{n}$'mi said he would be glad to learn. One of the four boys sat down, and with a knife cut off his feet and began to whittle his legs to a point. Then he jumped into the brush, calling the antelope by name. In the meantime, the other three boys covered up his feet with a robe. They went into the brush and found a dead antelope with a stick through it. Sharpened leg's body was in the animal. He returned to life again, and one of his comrades went through the same procedure, calling an elk. They found, and feasted on, a big male elk. *I^{n}kto^n'mi* was looking at the third boy, who did the same as his companions, calling a bear. The fourth boy jumped into the brush after sharpening his legs and calling an *u^{n}pa'* (?) and the others found a dead *u^{n}pa'*. The boys told *I^{n}kto^n'mi* they would give him the power to perform the same trick whenever he was hungry, but it would always be necessary for someone to be present. . . .

I^{n}kto^n'mi . . . sharpened his knife, whittled off his feet, covered them with his robe and sharpened his legs, although there was no one present. He named the antelope, and leapt into the brush. He found an antelope, came to life again, and ate the meat. He thought he would try again, named the bear, and jumped in, but was caught in a tree. No bear came, and he began to cry. The four boys, who had thought he might get killed, had been tracking him. They found him hanging. "You have done wrong, we'll take your power away. If you whittle your leg again, you will merely have a pointed leg." *I^{n}kto^n'mi* got frightened and never tried the trick again. (Lowie 1910, 117–19)

There are no bison here, unlike the Arapaho myth that opens this chapter. The species of prey therefore matters little to the Bungling Host motif of the Assiniboine myth. Sharpened Leg can hunt a variety of game animals, including other large mammals, like the pronghorn antelope, the elk, the bear, and an unidentified animal in this version, called *u^{n}pa'*. Actually, *u^{n}pa'* is an Assiniboine term to distinguish specifically between female and male elk (Parks and DeMallie 1999). If our corpus of myths is extended to include the one Seneca myth (Northeast) that has a sharpened leg motif, we may conclude that this character can also use his leg to catch fish: "Running after him, they soon came in sight of a creek, in which they saw a man spearing fish. Every little while, raising his foot, he would pull off a fish, for he had sharpened his leg and was using it for a spear" (Curtin and Hewitt 1918, 283).

We need not further discuss hunting of such game animals among these peoples. Perhaps we should now turn to the intertribal wars that appear in many Sharpened Leg myths and the cannibalism in the version from the Thompson of the Plateau. The Thompson were known to be formidable warriors: "There are many stories of battles with the Central Coast Salish, the Shuswap, and the Lillooet (Bouchard and Kennedy 1977, 40–42), which were fought with bows and arrows, clubs, spears, daggers, shields, and armor" (Wyatt 1998, 195). This ferocity of battle is shown by stories where the central character is a cannibal, as in Coyote's mythical fight against the Cannibals and their final destruction: "At last the Coyote changed his song and brought cold and ice. The Cannibal and Kwa'lum could not meet this. They, their daughter, and all the people of the village, were frozen to death" (Teit 1898, 40).

If we look at myths that have only the Sharpened Leg motif, we see that in each of them the subject matter of the action is motivated. What about the instruments used to kill the prey or opponents? No clear answer is given by the Arapaho version that opens this chapter. The Assiniboine version has a puzzling detail, and to which we will come back, about "a dead antelope with a stick through it. Sharpened leg's body was in the animal." When other Sharpened Leg stories specify the weapon implicitly or explicitly, they most often describe a spear, such as what the Seneca used to spear fish, or an awl point, as in most of the Thompson versions. One of those versions describes how the awl point was used: "Xo'lakwa'ka was an old man who sharpened one of his legs to a point. He used it as an awl, and bored skin and wood, with it. He also amused himself by seeing how far he could stick it into earth and trees. When the point became dull, he filed it with a stone. . . . One night he took a desire to try his leg on people" (Teit 1912a, 367).

As weapons for hunting or war, the Native Americans of the Plains and elsewhere could, for instance, use bows and arrows or spears. The latter are the ones that come closest to the myths under study. Spears will interest us in particular for several reasons: first, because they are mentioned explicitly in at least one myth (Seneca); and, second, because of the way they were made and their symbolism.

According to Kroeber, the Arapaho spear—at least the ceremonial one for which he obtained data—had a knife mounted at its cutting end: "At the bottom of the lance is a knife, serving as a spear-point" (Kroeber 1902, 176). The knife itself could be made from a bone, such as a bison shoulder blade, and, "when bone knives were worn down, they were used for awls" (Kroeber 1902, 24). Kroeber does not report any spear-points made from animal bones that correspond to the human one that Sharpened Leg ground to a point, i.e., the shinbone. We do know, however, that the leg bones of many mammals were used as spear-points by many peoples and undoubtedly by the Arapaho as well. Specialists have described how Native Americans in general would make a single spear:

> Another single spear was made from a leg bone of a deer. The spear has a single point. The first step is to cut off the bone ends, leaving the long, straight portion. In the early days these bones were boiled, the meat eaten off them, the ends broken off with rocks, and the marrow sucked out. . . .
>
> In any case, the marrow is removed to leave a hollow bone. One end of the bone is sharpened to a point. Traditionally, a large piece of sandstone was used to grind the point sharp. (Burch 2004, 188–89)

This description echoes, word for word, some Sharpened Leg myths where the main character prepares the bone of his leg by filing it to a point.

> [Arapaho version] Early in the morning one man was hungry. Unable to restrain himself, he cut off the muscle of his calf and cooked it. After he had cooked it, he sharpened his foot. (Dorsey and Kroeber 1903, 257)
>
> [Crow version] Peeping in, he saw his comrade breaking his shinbone and taking the meat from his calves to cook it, as well as the

marrow from his bone. He saw him eat it, then take out his knife and sharpen his shinbone. (Lowie 1918, 213)

For the Thompson, the literature is just as detailed. Awls were still being made from bones when James Teit did fieldwork in British Columbia in the early twentieth century: "Bone awls are still used" (Teit 1900, 186). The Thompson also had bone spear-points. They used them to hunt beaver (Teit 1900, 249) and undoubtedly other game animals.

The Cheyenne are very close physically and culturally to the Arapaho, so much so that anthropological accounts about either are valid for both. They preferred spears for bison hunting, as may also be inferred from the Arapaho myth that opens this chapter: "The methods of hunting seem to have been typical Plains methods, although in hunting buffalo the Cheyenne seem to have used a lance in preference to a bow and arrow when hunting on horseback" (Beals 1935, 4). Use of mammal leg bones is also attested among other peoples like the Navajo, who would make awls from deer leg bones (Kluckhohn, Hill, and Kluckhohn 1971, 413).

As we go from one Sharpened Leg version to the next, a spear-point may thus be replaced with an awl or vice versa, this being consistent with use of the same bones to make various instruments. The Arapaho, as we have said, used their knife blades as spear-points or, once the edges had been worn down, as awls.

Spears as hunting weapons can also help us understand these myths through the symbolism of certain body parts. If we go back to the Bungling Host myth from the Assiniboine, a boy sharpens his leg, and his "body" remains stuck in the killed animal while his amputated foot is kept under a robe and while he still lives at the end. This story line can be juxtaposed with the way Native Americans perceived their spears. The literature on the Assiniboine is silent on the subject, but we have ample data from the Arapaho, whose Bungling Host myth is at least similar in spirit. In both cases, the hero inserts himself into his game animal, and the Trickster, trying to imitate, remains stuck. Some spears were sharpened at the butt end for easier insertion into the ground with the blade end standing up—the right way up, so to speak. This was noted by Alfred Kroeber about certain ceremonial spears: "Like the lances of the following degrees, it is sharpened at the butt-end, by which it is stuck into the ground so that the knife points upward" (Kroeber 1902, 178).

The reason is simple. An Arapaho explained it to the linguist couple Z. and J. Salzmann in the 1950s, while expounding on a myth about a young hero who had killed many bison thanks to his personal power and his spear.

> Although the informant never saw the spear, he was able to describe it vividly. The shaft, about four feet in length, was made of hard wood approximately one inch in diameter and was painted red. One end was provided with a sharp-pointed head about six inches long made of stone; the other was pointed so that the spear could be stuck into the ground, head up. Because of the respect in which the spear was held, it was never laid on the ground. Moreover, its standing position reminded the man to whom it was entrusted that he "should be always on his feet, on his way." The two black-tipped feathers of a white eagle attached to the shaft about one third of the distance from the spearhead were to give eagle power to the spear, and the red fox fur attached about one third of the distance from the opposite end was to give it the cleverness and swiftness of the fox. (Salzmann and Salzmann 1950, 94n14)

A spear is thus represented symbolically as a body with a head and a foot. When the Assiniboine myth describes how the young boy's "body" remains stuck in the game animal, it is actually describing the spear itself. We can infer that the Assiniboine held their spears in great respect, as did the Arapaho. The same myth has the other boys finding a dead antelope that had been run through with a stick. This is again the spear—the boy's body. And the foot kept under a robe is in fact the boy himself, who has been separated from his "body"—the spear.

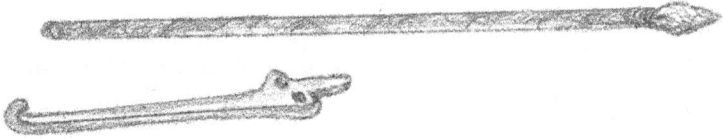

Fig. 34. Atlatl.

This brings to mind a very old hunting weapon used in pre-history by many Native peoples, including Southwest hunting peoples, whose components evoked very realistically a foot (the spear-thrower) and a body (the spear itself). We mean the atlatl. It is well known to archaeologists, and the Assiniboine myth in particular may hark back to use of this weapon in earlier times.

However, the Sharpened Leg stories refer to other aspects of human life which similarly serve to justify them. Several feature a kicking game where the main character asks his traveling companion to play—with the clear intention of not only beating his opponent but also killing him. One example is this Arapaho story:

109.–THE MAN WHO SHARPENED HIS FOOT (EXCERPT)

Two young man were traveling to reach a camp. As night overtook them they came to a pair of brush huts. One of them said, "Let us each use one." The other said, "No, it is not best to do that." Then the one said, "We shall be crowded if we sleep together but we can have all the room we want alone. The shelters must have been put up one for each of us." The fourth time the one who wanted to sleep alone persuaded the other, so that each went into one hut. Then the one who wanted to sleep alone said, "Let us have a kicking match." The other said, "No, we had better go to sleep, for we have to start very early in the morning to reach the camp." He heard his companion strike something and then say again: "Let us have a kicking match." "No, my friend," the other answered, "it is getting late; go to sleep" Then he went out from his shelter slowly and quietly and peeped into the other shelter. His friend was sharpening his leg with an axe. (Dorsey and Kroeber 1903, 258)

The game is mentioned in at least five versions, including a Blackfoot one with a Sharpened Leg motif. Here is how the Blackfoot played it: "A rough game, known as kicking each other, was popular among young men and boys; the usual way was to form two opposing lines and kick each other to see which would give way" (Wissler 1911, 58).

The myths concur in this depiction of the game's brutality. A player was supposed to aim especially for the shinbone, a particularly sensitive area of the leg less padded with flesh. The pain was like a stinging sensation caused by a fine point. The existence of this game may answer questions raised by Clara Ehrlich, who was puzzled by the shinbone's meaning in Crow mythology:

> There seems to be some significance attached to the shinbone, though what it is does not appear clearly. A father beats the shinbone of his son in order to induce him to go on a raid for honors, 137; the broken shinbone of a warrior does not heal readily, 236; a starving man takes the meat from his calves as well as the marrow from his own bone to cook, then he sharpens his shinbone in order to kill and eat his comrade, 213. The Bear Woman warns her sister not to hit her shinbone with firewood, 207. The man who sharpened his shinbone can cut through all the trees except the raven-tree (rough-barked willow?), 213. (Ehrlich 1937, 358)

We are dwelling on this aspect because the kicking game is one of many cultural traits that are recognizable to listeners and which thereby make the story more real to them. One such cultural trait, not to be ignored, is the prowess of the many prairie bison hunters who would actually jump on and ride their prey. This has a bearing on the Sharpened Leg motif, being in the Arapaho myth that opens this chapter—a bison hunt with hunters literally leaping onto bison. As daring as that may seem, the Native Americans—at least some of them—took pride in being able to accomplish such acrobatics: "Out of bravado or necessity, hunters have used strange ways and strange weapons to kill buffalo. Big Ribs, a Northern

Cheyenne, once rode close beside a large bull, sprang from his horse to the buffalo, rode some distance, then leaned over and buried his knife into the flank of the buffalo" (Branch 1929, 47).

The artist George Catlin made similar observations on the Great Plains in the early nineteenth century: "The blinded horsemen . . . were hemmed and wedged in amidst the crowding beasts, over whose backs they were obliged to leap for security, leaving their horses to the fate that might await them" (Catlin in Barsness 1985, 52). In a pictorial book, Catlin even depicted a Native American riding astride both a bison and his horse with a foot on each (Barsness 1985, 55).

In such conditions, hunting accidents were unsurprisingly frequent. We now come to a final human aspect that we cannot ignore either and which has some bearing on the understanding of the Sharpened Leg motif. We are speaking here of the many fractures that afflicted Native Americans—"fractures and dislocations are not rare among them, but they are pretty dexterous in reducing them" (Volney in Vogel 1970, 215). Fractures were treated by means of splints, poultices, and sometimes even amputation.

Many leg fractures seem to have been due to bison hunting in particular: "'Two Bows had been thrown and his leg was broken.' Ely More . . . hunted with the Miamis in 1854 on the day Jimmie Squirrel had the calf of his leg torn off by a bull horn—a thrust which also disembowelled his horse" (Barsness 1985, 62).

Native Americans did resort to amputation, though not on a large scale: "Indians 'are wholly strangers to Amputation,' Lawson wrote, yet he described their amputation of a portion of the feet of captives, and the grafting of skin over the exposed end, which then healed" (Vogel 1970, 192). There may be an allusion to such operations in several Sharpened Leg myths that report the Trickster's pain when his foot is being cut off:

[Arapaho version] As Nih'óóthoo was placing his foot on the log, he saw the man's big knife. He became frightened. And when the man was just about to chop off his foot, Nih'óóthoo cried, "Wait! I have to straighten my foot a little bit." (Salzmann and Salzmann 1950, 96)

[Cheyenne version] Vihuk (White-man) . . . stood on a large log, and the other, with an axe, sharpened his leg, telling him to hold still bravely. The pain caused the tears to come from his eyes. (Kroeber 1900, 169)

All of these cultural aspects contribute to making the myths seem believable to human listeners, including the Arapaho myth that opens this chapter. Also contributing are zoological aspects interwoven with the cultural ones.

Such aspects should also help us identify the host of the Arapaho and Assiniboine myths, as well as the Sharpened Leg character who appears in other stories. If our hypothesis is right, this animal should have certain defining traits that match the ascribed human characteristics or behaviors, or at least most of them. This animal can kill big game or fish, if not literally then at least by projection, as in other cases we have analyzed. Part of its body seems like a spear-point. Its tracks are tiny, like the marks left by an awl, as a Thompson variant describes so well:

Thus she filed her leg-bones until they had fine points like awls. One night, when the people were asleep, she left the house to try her legs. When she walked gently, they made such small holes that her tracks were not noticeable. When she stamped hard on clay, they went in to the knee. She tried them on small trees, and they went right through the wood. She tried them on a large tree, and they went in so far that they stuck, and it was almost daybreak before she was enable to disengage herself. (Teit 1912a, 365–66)

We are also looking for an animal that leaps in the air or onto its prey and that can potentially stay stuck in its prey or elsewhere, as described above in the Thompson variant and in other myths. The animal also makes a sound such as is made when a bone is being sharpened to make a spear blade or when someone is scratching, as Sharpened Leg himself says in some variants when asked what he is doing:

> [Blackfoot version] All this time she was cutting down and sharpening her leg. . . . While she was pounding, the children cried out, "What are you doing?" "Oh!" she said, "I am hacking a bone." (Wissler and Duvall 1908, 153)

> [Thompson version] She always sat in a corner of the house, keeping her legs covered and out of sight while she ground them. The people noticed her always grinding under the blanket, and asked her what she was doing. She answered, "I am scratching my legs." (Teit 1912a, 365)

The most important clue we have to the animal's identity is a Sharpened Leg version that identifies him as a groundhog (*Marmota monax*) and his hunting comrade as an eagle. This is a myth from the Assiniboine:

SHARPENED-LEG

Two young men were living together. One day one of them heard his comrade chopping outside the lodge. He saw that the other man was sharpening his leg to a point, after having chopped off his feet. He was frightened and fled, running for a night and a day. He arrived at some high trees, and climbed one of them. Sharpened-Leg pursued him. When he got to the tree, he espied his comrade, and fell to kicking the trunk. With a dozen kicks he split the tree, so that it tumbled down. He looked for his former comrade, whom he found lying on the ground. "Why did you run away? We used to play together." He kicked his comrade with the point of his leg, and killed him. Then he walked away to some other trees. He began kicking them also, but his leg stuck fast, and he died in this position. When the two men did not return to camp, the father of the one slain went to look for them. He got to their lodge, and then followed their tracks until he reached the corpse of his son and the tree where Sharpened-Leg was caught.

Sharpened-Leg was named Caⁿska' (Ground-Hog) and his comrade Umbis'ka (Eagle). (Lowie 1910, 186)

Now, this myth makes no sense. It is inconceivable that naturalists as seasoned as Native Americans, whose myths are most often nature lessons, could make the groundhog (*Marmota monax*) the victor of a fight against some sort of eagle (unidentified species), when this rodent is actually one of the eagle's main prey items.

Actually, that name was mistranslated by Robert Lowie (or his interpreter). The word *caⁿska'* is a generic term for birds of prey known collectively in English as 'hawks' (pers. comm., Douglas Parks). It is also translated as 'chicken hawk' (Parks and De Mallie 1999), which is yet another generic term for any bird of prey that attacks domestic birds. The word *umbis'ka* has a more precise meaning. It means an eagle, specifically a 'white eagle' (*wamni-*: 'eagle' +*-ska*: 'white'), i.e., a bald eagle, *Haliæetus leucocephalus*.

Despite this rather broad identification, the above Assiniboine myth begins to make sense because some birds of prey have a reputation of attacking eagles and because some calls made by at least one species sound strangely like an object being ground or sharpened.

An observer thus reports about northern harriers (*Circus cyaneus*) that they "have been known to attack and drive away eagles" (Bent et al. 1961, 89). Another naturalist also speaks of a golden eagle (*Aquila chrysætos*) being chased by a red-tailed hawk (*Buteo jamaicensis*): "Mr. Summer has seen a young eagle . . . which was standing on the ground [being] attacked by a red-tailed hawk; the hawk which had been circling in the air, dove at him three times from a height of 300 to 400 feet" (Bent et al. 1961, 309).

Birds of prey may also be attacked by northern goshawks (*Accipiter gentilis*), another bird of prey slightly bigger than northern harriers or red-tailed hawks and present on the Great Plains and in the foothills of the Rockies where the Assiniboine live. Even more interestingly, if you listen to the same goshawk, you will hear it make raspy sounds like a bone or blade being sharpened: "The female's voice may lower slightly in pitch and become harsh and rasping" (Squire and Reynolds 1997, 10).

Although this information does not provide us with the exact species of the Assiniboine myth, we now have a generic identity that can explain the story line: a bird of prey flies through the trees, chasing its companion, here a bald eagle. The bird sharpens its legs (= its talons) and uses this cutting instrument to kill. This is also how a bird of prey kills its prey in nature: swooping down with its talons wide open and with enough speed and momentum to penetrate and inflict death on impact. The puncture holes (= awl marks) are often visible on the prey's body. As for whether a goshawk can kill an eagle, this is an open question. In nature, many kinds of predation have never been recorded and thus remain possible, especially in the case of young eagles.

By identifying the host in this myth, we may have identified the host in all of the other Sharpened Leg myths, including the Arapaho one that opens this chapter. In all of these versions, Sharpened Leg may be a bird of prey. There are several reasons for thinking so. First, in the Arapaho series, we have mentioned that the central character, the host, may be a bird because birds appear in all of the other stories of the series, or at least in three of them with certainty.

Second, it can be shown with other supporting examples that a character may be based on a *generic etymon* and not on a *specific etymon*. We have seen an example in this chapter. Several myths refer to a woodpecker whose species varies from one story to the next, according to the storyteller's culture. The Arapaho myth has a red-naped sapsucker that chops open its wife's head to remove the soft fatty contents, and the Lipan version has a northern flicker that hits the back of its head to get pecans from inside.

Other supporting examples include the following series of characteristics that are shared by all birds of prey that meet the criteria we established when we first tried to identify the host. All birds of prey, be they hawks, harriers, or even eagles, have extremely

Fig. 35. Eagle seizing a prey. After a photograph by V. Zaikin.

sharp talons that can very well be mythically turned into awls, and these talons also leave tiny marks on the ground. All birds of prey leap onto their prey, as seen in several versions, including the Arapaho one that opens this chapter. Most birds of prey, if not all, try to kill, as we have said, by using the force of the impact from their dive to thrust the ends of their legs into the victim. Several birds of prey, including eagles and condors, can also kill very big game animals. A golden eagle, for example, can kill young or adult mountain goats, pronghorn antelopes, deer, and even cattle (Kochert et al. 2002, 10). It swoops down with talons outstretched onto the back of its prey, staying there until death comes: "'Low flight with sustained grip attack' to kill ungulates by landing on victim's back or neck, and riding it until the animal dies" (Kochert et al. 2002, 9). It can also hunt in a group, especially when the prey are big game, as echoed in the Assiniboine version of the Bungling Host when four boys go hunting for pronghorn antelope, elk, and other prey: "Also hunts cooperatively with conspecifics; most cooperative hunting involves large prey (e.g., ungulates, red fox)" (Kochert et al. 2002, 9).

One detail, however, seems to argue against Sharpened Leg being some kind of bird of prey. In several versions, he remains stuck in a tree and eventually dies there. An eagle may indeed sometimes get caught in tangled tree branches and have trouble flying out. The fish eagle, better known today as the osprey, also has a reputation of catching a prey in the water only to get dragged under and drowned: "possibly the large, horny scales on the back of a sturgeon might entrap the claws of an osprey" (Bent et al. 1961, 367). On the other hand, this detail may simply allude to an awl that has been driven too far into a piece of wood for it to be pulled out.

The following chart very succinctly lists the aspects of human culture and animal behavior in the various versions of the Sharpened Leg motif.

Table 10. Sharpened Leg motif: cultural and animal etymons

	CULTURAL ETYMONS	ANIMAL ETYMONS
CHARACTER	Hunter	Bird of prey
WEAPON	Pointed lance	Sharpened claws
SOUND	Filing, whittling	Rasping voice
ACTION	Springing forward	Springing forward
ACCIDENT	Hunting accident	Can get stuck (?)
PREY	Big game, fish, people	Variety of prey

In summary, one may say that cultural and zoological aspects are finely interwoven in the Arapaho myth that opens this chapter, as in the other versions. Sharpened Leg is both a spear that is aimed at a game animal and a bird of prey that swoops down on its prey. This identification is in keeping with all versions of the Sharpened Leg motif. No surprise, then, that the plumes of birds of prey adorn the spears of hunter-warriors in many cultures, endowing these weapons with a predatory power unique to the same birds. This was so among the Arapaho, as seen in a previously quoted passage: "The two black-tipped feathers of a white eagle attached to the shaft about one third of the distance from the spearhead were to give eagle power to the spear" (Salzmann and Salzmann 1950, 94n14). This was also so among the Thompson, who have several myths with the Sharpened Leg motif: "The base of the spear-points was often ornamented with hawk-feathers or hair" (Teit 1900, 263).

14 Black-Mountain-Bear Gets Persimmons by Leaning Against a Tree (Southeast)

At last he grew so hungry that he had to go out for food. He found none, and so he went to visit another one of his friends, for he had many. Black-Mountain-Bear received him graciously when he came to his home and asked him in. Bear said: "I regret that I have no meat to offer you." As he spoke he leaned against a persimmon tree that was weighted down with many ripe persimmons, and as he leaned against the tree the ripe fruit fell to the ground. Bear smiled and asked his friend to eat. Coyote ate many, for he was very hungry.

—George A. Dorsey, "Traditions of the Caddo"

The Southeast culture area has produced very few Bungling Host myths. To be sure, its territories—present-day Texas, Oklahoma, Arkansas, Louisiana, Florida, and other states—went through very severe demographic upheavals with the coming of the first European explorers to the region, particularly the Spanish and the French. The Caddo, whose descendants number some four thousand in Oklahoma, nonetheless have a few Bungling Host stories. The term 'Caddo' applies to a group of communities linked to each other linguistically and culturally and divided into 'confederations,' the Hasinai Confederation being the one most written about. Historically, the Caddo had to endure one challenge from outsiders after another: the religious fanaticism of Spanish missionaries who used every possible means to convert them to the one true religion; the pressures from French traders to make them give up farming and devote themselves solely to fur trapping; and the greed of white settlers who slowly but surely snatched pieces of Caddo territory for their farms, all of this with the blessing of the government (Rogers and Sabo III 2004, 619–22).

Horticulturalists by tradition, the Caddo lived dispersed in hamlets and on small farms to maximize use of their resources (Rogers and Sabo III 2004, 626). Their economy also included hunting and gathering. The latter activities provided the background for Caddo stories on the Bungling Host theme: hunting wild horses; hunting bison and deer, or gathering fruits. There are in fact three Caddo stories of this genre, which we will discuss successively and whose hosts are Cougar, Raven, and Black-Mountain-Bear. An excerpt from the last one opens this chapter. All three myths are known only in English translation, and the Trickster who visits the host is incarnated by Coyote.

The first of the three relates how Cougar kills wild horses to get food for his guest. It also teaches the audience about hunting, whether by animals or by humans. All of the myth titles, including the following one, are by George Dorsey, an anthropologist who worked among the Caddo from 1903 to 1905.

ADVENTURES OF COYOTE (EXCERPT)

[. . .] While Coyote was moving from one place to another he came down to a large lake of clear, cool water, and after he had been there for some time he started off a little way from the lake. While gone he saw some one coming up toward him and, as he was very cowardly, he started to run away. The person was not his enemy, but a friend of his, Mountain-Lion. He called Coyote back, and so he came, and he told his friend that he was very hungry, for he had had nothing to eat for a long while. Mountain-Lion asked him to go along with him, saying that he would find something for him to eat soon. They both went to the lake, and when they came down to the water Mountain-Lion told Coyote that he was going to kill a young horse. In those times there were many herds of wild horses, and at the lake there was a certain place where the wild horses drank. Near the place where the road led to the water there was a large tree, and the horses passed under the tree as they went down to the water. Every day at about noon Mountain-Lion would climb the tree and then pounce down on a young horse and kill him. As Mountain-Lion and Coyote drew near to the tree Mountain-Lion told Coyote to place himself where the wild herd of horses could not see him, and so he did, and Mountain-Lion climbed the tree. Soon Coyote saw dust rise up from the ground and he heard something like thundering, and later he saw many hundreds of horses coming down to the water. As the horses were passing under the tree, Coyote saw Mountain-Lion jump out of the tree and pounce upon a young horse and kill it. Then Mountain-Lion and Coyote both had a fine dinner. That day, after they had eaten, Mountain-Lion told Coyote to continue on his way; but Coyote did not want to leave his friend, and so he asked Mountain-Lion if he could give him power so that he could kill a horse, too, and eat it when he was hungry. Mountain-Lion told him he would. They stayed there until the next day, and at about noon they both went down to the lake again, and went to the tree, and then Mountain-Lion showed Coyote how and what to do when the horses should come. He taught him how to climb the tree, and then he went out to place himself where the horses could not see him.

Soon they began to come from different directions, and as they filed down to the water Coyote picked out a fat young horse, and as they were coming up from the water he jumped on it and killed it. They had another fine dinner, and then Mountain-Lion said to Coyote: "Do not try to kill a three or four year old horse. If you jump on one that is three years old you can not kill him and you may lose your own life. Try to kill one that is one or two years old and you will succeed every time." Coyote left his new friend and went on his way. The next day, while he was alone, he began to get very hungry, and so at about noon he went down to the lake to kill a horse.

While he was on the tree he said to himself: "I wonder if it would be dangerous for me to kill one of the large horses. I may be stronger than Mountain-Lion, and so I will try to kill the largest horse and I will show Mountain-Lion that I am not so small as I look to him." The horses began to go down to the water, and Coyote waited and waited for the chance to jump upon the largest horse in the herd. Finally a large horse came, and when he was right under the tree Coyote jumped upon him. It was but a short time until the horse threw Coyote off from his back, and when Coyote was down on the ground the horse kicked him under the jaws and went off. As Coyote was about to die, Mountain-Lion, who had been watching Coyote all the time, came up to see what was the matter with him, and when he came up to him he saw his jaws to one side. Mountain-Lion asked Coyote what he was laughing about, and asked him if he was able to kill another five-year-old horse. Coyote lay there for a long time before he was able to move. Finally he arose and decided to leave the place, never to return to it. (Dorsey 1905, 87–89)

The cougar of this myth is none other than *Felis concolor*, the largest member of the cat family in North America except for the jaguar, which has been occasionally sighted in the Southwest (Lindzey 1987, 657). It was also the most widespread land mammal in the Americas before the Europeans came but is now for all intents extinct in the eastern United States. A few small populations are still said to persist in Arkansas and Oklahoma, the traditional homeland of the Caddo people (Lindzey 1987, 658).

Cougars preyed on wild horses, whose gregarious behavior is outlined in the myth — each herd numbering in the hundreds and making a thundering sound when on the move. They also had a habit of drinking together, and the herd encompassed individuals of different ages.

The New World was swarming with herds of wild horses soon after the Europeans had arrived. Although horses had disappeared from the New World, they were reintroduced by Europeans in the sixteenth century, and some ran away from their enclosures to form free-roaming bands. By the seventeenth century, white farmers were complaining about the damage to their crops: "Storms and rot soon created passageways through the cow-pen fences, and stallions led their mares and colts off to the woods. In 1670, tobacco planters near Williamsburg complained about invasions by 'bands of wild horses.' Similar complaints echoed along the Maryland frontier a few years later; in 1694, 1695, 1699 and 1712, the legislators of Maryland adopted laws 'to prevent the great multitude of horses in the province'" (Howard 1965, 56).

These populations increased, and some say they reached astronomical proportions: "The two to three million 'wild ones' alleged to have roamed the high-plains and mountains by the end of the Civil War could have carried as much Kentucky-Vermont-Virginia-Tennessee heritage as they did of the vaunted Andalusian blood" (Howard 1965, 221). Several horse breeds were born from the European settlers' lost horses, notably the mustang and the Appaloosa. An Appaloosa appears in the famous book *Codex Canadensis* by the Jesuit Louis Nicolas, who drew pictures of the animals he saw while travelling through North America in the late seventeenth century (Gagnon 2011).

There is no doubt that cougars preyed on wild horses. Even today, they still prey on domestic animals: "Mountain lions take livestock more frequently in the southwestern than in the northwestern United States" (Currier 1983, 4). During the bison golden age, Native Americans likewise lost many of their horses to large predators including cougars, this being notably so with the Blackfoot and undoubtedly other groups as well: "Animal predators killed colts and occasionally some adult horses owned by the Blackfoot in buffalo days. Wolves were the most common colt killers. Bears and mountain lions destroyed both colts and adult animals" (Ewers 1955, 51).

The naturalist Ernst Thompson Seton even spoke of considerable damage by cougars to herds of horses: "The ravages that the Cougar makes among Horse herds are notorious. It is said that

Fig. 36. Appaloosa horse.

in the mountains no Horse can long escape the Cougars" (Seton 1953 [1909], vol. 1, 101). Seton went on to describe how horses could nonetheless protect themselves and which ones were most likely to be killed:

> [Yampah Plateau, Colorado] abounded in mustangs . . . and there they lived and throve in spite of wild beasts and wilder men. . . . And they did not fear the Cougars because the ever-watchful mares keep the keenest lookout. Sign or smell of a Cougar is enough to make them round up into a tight bunch with the colts in the middle, and not the boldest Cougar dare attack them. Only when some headstrong foolish broncho wanders off alone do the Cougars feast on Horse meat. (Seton 1953 [1909], vol. 1, 101–2)

The last comment supports the myth insofar as Cougar—and Coyote, who imitates him in the same way—chooses a similarly isolated prey, since the horses pass one by one under the tree where he is hidden. The literature has very few observations on prey selection by cougars: "Few direct observations of mountain lion captures have been reported" (Dixon 1982, 719). But they are known to choose their prey on the basis of vulnerability, as shown in studies where their prey are members of the deer family. This was undoubtedly also true when they preyed on wild horses: "Mountain lions kill proportionately more old males and very young deer and elk. . . . The older deer are probably more vulnerable because of infirmities, the males are probably more vulnerable because of their solitary habits, and young animals are probably more vulnerable because they are small" (Currier 1983, 4).

Horses reach adulthood around four years of age, sometimes a bit later depending on the breed. This maturation schedule explains Cougar's warning to Coyote against selecting prey that are three, four, or five years old. Stallions, which by definition have reached breeding age, can easily fight off attacks by feline or canine predators: "Thus an all-Europe hybrid developed in the Appalachian highlands of western North Carolina, South Carolina and Georgia. The herds grew fat on the succulent wild pea-vines, buffalo grass and shrubs of the sheltered valleys. Stallions successfully fought off most of the attacks by wildcats and wolves" (Howard 1965, 57).

The cougar's technique of seizing prey, as described in the myth, is not mentioned in Western zoological literature, although this animal is fond of sitting in trees: "The Cougar is perfectly at home in a tree when he chooses to climb" (Seton 1953 [1909], vol. 1, 94). There are also some mentions of hunting by stealth near a body of water: "There are a few—very few—records of a Cougar lying in hiding by a water-hole or on a runway, waiting cat-like for some heedless, hapless Deer to amble within the fatal circle of his amazing spring. James Fullerton tells of two instances that he observed when the Cougar lurked in a high ambush and both times got a Deer" (Seton 1953 [1909], vol. 1, 95).

The naturalist Seton also reported a case of a cougar lying in wait on a cliff for a herd of bighorn sheep to come close enough for it to jump on them (Seton 1953 [1909], vol. 1, 102). Some Native Americans also described cougars using such a technique: "The

Tewa say that the animal crouches or sits waiting for its prey" (Henderson and Harrington 1914, 30). The resemblance to the Caddo myth is striking.

When a cougar attacks a large mammal, it always has to leap onto its back to grab hold and inflict mortal wounds to the neck: "A mountain lion generally brings down larger prey by maneuvering to within about 15 m., then leaping on its back within a few strides and breaking the animal's neck with a powerful bite below the base of the skull" (Currier 1983, 4).

The Caddo myth would have made sense to its human audience in human terms as well. First, many Native peoples, in particular those of the present-day southern United States, consumed horse meat, and not only in time of famine: "The relatively wealthy southern Plains tribes, who could better afford to kill horses for food, were less averse to eating horse meat. Pfefferkorn (1949, pp. 144–45) claimed the Lipan Apache, in the mid-18th century, liked nothing better to eat than the fleshy upper neck of a horse, mule, or burro" (Ewers 1955, 222n67).

The Caddo of the eighteenth century also ate horse meat as much as the flesh of other big game: "But by 1768 we learn through Solís that 'In the woods they live on horses, mules, mares, deer, since there are many, bison which abound, bear, *berrendos* (a species of deer), wild boar, rabbits, hares, dormice, and other quadrupeds'" (Swanton 1996, 135). If they lived on wild horses, they must have been hunting them too. European explorers of the seventeenth to nineteenth centuries observed such captures, while remaining rather silent on the techniques used to hunt for food. The literature describes only captures of wild horses for domestication. We have identified three different methods: throwing a lasso noose at the animal (Ewers 1955, 60); extending a forked pole with a lasso at the end and slipping the lasso over the horse's head (Ewers 1955, 60); and encircling a complete herd. The last method used several hundred men to surround a herd of wild horses and slowly close the circle on the herd. The panic-stricken horses would go running off in all directions and, once exhausted, become easier to approach and lasso (Pike 1932 [1865], 96–97).

In the literature, no mention has been made of capture by leaping from a tree, although such a tactic would have been as possible for a human as for a cougar. It must be said that wild horses were always trained one way or another by a rider mounting the animal. Many Native American experts did so without any accessories, such as a saddle or a surcingle (a strap that fastens around a horse's girth area): "My Oglala and Kiowa informants had no knowledge of the use of either the surcingle or pad-saddle methods by their respective tribes. However, they asserted that riders of those tribes broke horses on dry ground merely by riding them bareback, holding onto the mane with their hands, and maintaining a precarious toehold under the elbows of the horses' forelegs"(Ewers 1955, 64n34).

If some Natives could ride the bison they hunted, as seen in the preceding chapter, some of them would surely have been able to jump onto a wild horse and likewise inflict a death blow to its heart, its lungs, or elsewhere. For this, a colt would have been easier to approach, being less powerful. A stallion, or any adult horse, could in contrast seriously wound its attacker. Even cougars, reputed for their strength and power, did not always escape counterblows from their prey: "Adult lions may be killed by encounters with both prey species and other lions. Once a mountain lion has attacked its prey and is clinging to its back, it may be dislodged by the prey running under low branches, by colliding with trees, or in falls. In some cases the lion is killed directly from injuries sustained in collision with trees or limbs. In other cases, it may be killed by attacks with hooves or antlers of deer or elk after having been stunned by a collision" (Dixon 1982, 720).

This is what the myth teaches. First, even a cougar can get such injuries. Second, if a human jumps onto a horse that is too big, he too may be dislodged and then kicked and trodden underfoot by its hooves. This is of course what happened to Coyote: "It was but a short time until the horse threw Coyote off from his back, and when Coyote was down on the ground the horse kicked him under the jaws and went off." Similar accidents happened to human riders. For example, in Blackfoot country—and probably elsewhere—teenaged boys very often broke in the horses and were forewarned of the risks: "Sometimes a group of boys went to an owner of a large herd and asked him if they could break some of his colts in the water of a nearby pond, lake, or stream. If the owner consented, he pointed out the animals they might break and warned them he would not be responsible if any of the boys were hurt" (Ewers 1955, 61).

Undoubtedly for the same reasons, horses were broken in very young, to avoid accidents as much as possible: "Limited comparative data suggest that it was usual Plains Indian practice to break horses for riding at an early age. The Hidatsa broke them at 1 to 2 years old (Wilson, 1924, p. 150). The Oglala, according to Eagle Bird, broke them before they were 3 years old. Enoch Smoky said the Kiowa broke their horses in their first to third years" (Ewers 1955, 60n32). It seems that adult horses were for all intents untameable.

This first Bungling Host myth from the Caddo is, therefore, relatively simple—no truly puzzling facts, no real surprises. It interests us for other reasons. It more clearly shows the very nature of these mythemes, which amount to lessons. Their oddness varies by myth and by people, acting as a kind of seasoning, so to speak, to spice up the narration and to whet the listener's curiosity. In the case of the Caddo myth, the approach is more direct but no less effective: Coyote, with his smashed jaw, is there to remind everyone about the reality of very painful accidents.

The second Caddo myth is much more mysterious. It relates how Raven gets food by piercing himself with an arrow under the arm and drawing out not only the arrow but also bison meat. This mytheme appears in the first part of a two-episode Bungling Host myth.

COYOTE IMITATES HIS HOST (PART 1)

In the days of old, when animals were like people and talked and visited each other, Coyote and Raven were great friends. One day after Coyote had grown weary of hunting for game and finding none, he went up to the top of the mountain to see his friend Raven. Raven had control of the buffalo and was always seen with the herds. (Now, since the buffalo has gone from the earth, Raven has disappeared and is seldom seen any more.) Raven invited Coyote to enter, and when he saw Coyote weary and sad and silent he arose, took an arrow, shot it up into the air, and then stood waiting for it to come down. It came down and pierced him under the right arm. He drew the arrow out and with it came buffalo meat and fat. He gave the meat to Coyote, who ate heartily. Then Coyote smacked his mouth, arose, and said that he must be going, but before he went he gave Raven an urgent invitation to come over and make him a visit, and Raven promised to come.

When Coyote went home he began making a bow and arrow, and when he had finished them he put them away until Raven should visit him. One day Raven bethought himself of his promise, and so he left his home in haste to pay Coyote a visit. Coyote received him with joy. After they had talked about many things Coyote said: "I have no meat, for I did not expect you, but if you will wait I will soon have some for you." Coyote took his bow and arrow and shot the arrow into the sky, then stood waiting for it to come down. Raven watched him and said never a word. The arrow came down and struck in Coyote's thigh. He ran away screaming with pain and left his guest alone. Raven waited a while and then went home without any meat, but in very high spirits notwithstanding, for Coyote's performance amused him greatly and he chuckled to himself as often as he thought of it. Coyote continued to run until he pulled the arrow out of his thigh; then he took the arrow and broke it to pieces. He never went back to see Raven, and time passed on and none of Coyote's friends saw him, and they all wondered what had become of him. (Dorsey 1905, 93)

This myth first poses the problem of identifying the host's species. The common raven (*Corvus corax*) and the American crow (*Corvus brachyrhynchos*) belong to the same genus and are often mistaken for each other: "In Canada [the Common Raven is] likely to be confused only with the Common Crow. Although much larger than the Crow, size is often deceptive in the field" (Godfrey 1966, 274). In fact, the similarity often misleads observers. Thus, among the Pima of Arizona, where the crow is for all intents extinct, if it ever did exist there, the term for 'raven' is often translated by 'crow' in published myths, anthropological reports, accounts by explorers, and other texts (Rea 2007, 210–15). Furthermore, some cultures have only one term for both species, like the above-mentioned Pima (Rea 2007, 210), the Tewa (Henderson and Harrington 1914, 40), and others. Consequently, some caution is in order, and one has to go beyond the Native terms used in myths and observations and know how to tell the two species apart by their physical traits and behaviors.

In the Caddo myth, the term 'raven' seems validated by at least one reported characteristic: "He went up to the top of the mountain to see his friend Raven." This description matches one of the bird's preferred surroundings: "Habitat. Most often mountainous and wilder hill country" (Godfrey 1966, 275). Although the literature on the Caddo has little to say about Native ornithology, this field of knowledge has been studied in other indigenous groups and can be cited to confirm the species identification. The details in the myth do not look like mere happenstance:

> [Pima] "Ravens go way up there, and can see far, always circling around," offers Culver Cassa. "And they like mountains." (Rea 2007, 211)

> [Innu] "[They are found] everywhere in the woods, inland, on bare hills, in the mountains." (Abraham Mestokosho, Ekuanitshit)

We therefore feel the host of the Caddo myth is indeed a raven.

This being said, the Caddo myth leaves us with an unexpected puzzle. Usually if the host pierces or impales himself in some way to get food or fat from his own body, the reason is that he himself is the game animal. This genre of myth is understood, then, as expressing a widespread Native idea: a game animal gives itself up to a hunter to honor a contract that joins them together. In return, the hunter has to observe certain rules that vary (ritual offering, sharing with others, respect for the remains, no waste, etc.).

This idea appears in many myths, especially those from the Southwest and the Plains. The Lipan Apache (Plains) thus recount how Mule Deer got food for his guest: "He shot an arrow in the air. He stood under it, let it come down on himself and pierce his side. Kidney fat came out. He brought it to camp and mixed it with dry meat" (Opler 1940, 141).

The same thing happens when Deer shoots an arrow into the air in a Yavapai myth (Southwest): the arrow penetrates his back, and he pulls some of his guts out and offers them to his host, Coyote (Gifford 1933, 383). Among the Mohave (Southwest), Beaver similarly removes anal fat from his body: "When Coyote visited Beaver, he had no food. Beaver took his bow, shot up in the air, the arrow fell down and entered his rectum. Beaver turned it around and then pulled it out with fat on the end" (Kroeber 1948, 49). Even closer to the Caddo myth is this episode from the Jicarilla Apache (Southwest), which has a similar Bungling Host theme with Bison as the host: "'What shall I do? I have no food to offer you.' Buffalo was equal to the emergency, however; he shot an arrow upward, which struck in his own back as it returned. When he pulled this out, a kidney and the fat surrounding it came out also. This he cooked for Fox" (Russell 1898, 266).

So why is this idea absent from the Caddo myth? Evidently, Native Americans are not fond of eating the carrion-feeding raven. On the other hand, a raven does give up meat to a hunter, but in another way. It honors its contract indirectly, through a commensal relationship, and this idea is held by many Native peoples who are not necessarily adjacent to each other.

First, the commensalism of *Corvus corax* is supported by non-

Native observers. Arthur Cleveland Bent, an ornithologist, reports this observation about a western subspecies: "Ravens habitually feed on such carrion as dead elk, deer, and small animals; and I believe they follow bears and coyotes at times to benefit by anything they may find or kill" (Bent et al. 1964b, 209). Another ornithologist mentions that the raven "follows wolves and cougars to scavenge on leftovers" (Boarman and Heinrich 1999, 5).

Among the Squamish of the Northwest Coast—ravens were prevalent everywhere in North America until the early twentieth century (Boarman and Heinrich 1999, 3)—this habit of teaming up with a top predator would give rise to a very eloquent legend: "In L.M.'s version of the legend about 'Deer and the Wolf-Children' (cf. section 29, p. 40), Raven is nearby when the Wolf-Children capture their slave, Deer, who has tried to escape from them. As they shake Deer about, Raven hollers out 'I'll have a wonderful meal of your guts, Deer!'" (Kennedy and Bouchard 1976a, 90).

Native naturalists likewise reported such teamwork, some adding that a raven would even help hunters locate their prey. A book on bison hunting mentions such assistance when discussing general Native beliefs about ravens: "Raven spotted game at long distances; he helped man by flying in the direction of game" (Barsness 1985, 78). The Pima of Arizona considered the hunter-raven relationship to be one of companionship:

And I guess my uncle always say that when you are a hunter—like to hunt a lot—you always have him [*hawañ* = usually raven but also crow] as a companion. *Hawañ* is pretty helpful to the hunter in a lot of ways. He can tell where you can find game or whatever. If there is game nearby, you can see him come to the area and even flying close by so you'll know where it's at. And start looking for, down that place [where the raven flies], then you'll find it—deer, Javelina, or whatever. (Rea 2007, 213)

The Koyukon, an Athabaskan people from Alaska, described the bird in exactly the same terms: "If a raven sees people hunting it will occasionally help them find game. It flies overhead, then toward an animal that is visible from above, calling *'ggaagga . . . ggaagga'* ('animal . . . animal')" (Nelson 1983, 83).

All of these Native American observers concluded that such help is always driven by self-interest: "'He does that so he'll get his share from what the hunter leaves behind'" (Nelson 1983, 83; see Rea 2007, 213). The same has been said by more academic ornithologists. Such assistance is extended to all predators, including humans: "Anecdotal evidence suggests ravens may even purposefully attract wolves and hunters to moose and caribou, presumably because they cannot kill and open large prey" (Boarman and Heinrich 1999, 13–14).

Now, if a raven can show humans the way to their prey, it is in a sense giving them food. There is a hunting pair—a raven and a human. One of them shoots an arrow that hits a game animal on its flank, thereby producing food. This reconstituted equation initially had multiple elements, some of which the myth has dropped for simplicity. In particular, the myth has replaced Raven's original action (indicating where game animals are to be found) with the corresponding human action (hunting and killing the game animals with a bow and arrow).

Thus, initially, the relationship was:

Caddo hunter → bow and arrow → game shot in the flank → food

raven   → call and flight → game caught   → food

This relationship has been trimmed down to what we now find in the myth:

raven → [bow and arrow] → [game shot in the flank] → food

The etymon of the mytheme is the help that the commensal gives humans. In this permutation, should we be surprised that some elements of meaning have become interchangeable, like the 'arrow' and the raven's 'cawing' or 'flight'? These elements switch places in a Pima song from the Southwest:

> *The black ravens go flying*
> *Having seen the snapping bow;*
> *Toward it in a narrow line*
> *They go flying.*
> (Rea 2007, 213)

The third Bungling Host myth from the Caddo has Black-Mountain-Bear offering his host, the Trickster, persimmons. The American persimmon (*Diospyros virginiana*) is a persimmon species native to North America and found in the states of the Southeast (Louisiana, Oklahoma, etc.). It stands on average 10 to 24 meters tall but may grow to 35 meters (Keeler 1908). In the autumn, it produces orange-yellow fruits that taste very sweet at maturity. In the Caddo myth, Black-Mountain-Bear gathers them in his own way:

COYOTE IMITATES HIS HOST (PART 2)

At last he grew so hungry that he had to go out for food. He found none, and so he went to visit another one of his friends, for he had many. Black-Mountain-Bear received him graciously when he came to his home and asked him in. Bear said: "I regret that I have no meat to offer you." As he spoke he leaned against a persimmon tree that was weighted down with many ripe persimmons, and as he leaned against the tree the ripe fruit fell to the ground. Bear smiled and asked his friend to eat. Coyote ate many, for he was very hungry. When he had finished he thanked Bear and said that he must be going, but before he went he insisted that Bear come to see him, and Bear promised to come soon.

Coyote wandered all about looking for a persimmon tree. He could not find one with any fruit on it, and so he decided to take one without fruit. He cut the tree down and carried it to his home, where he set it up; then he went out to look for persimmons. He had stolen some from Bear's home, but he had not stolen enough.

When he found more persimmons he took them home, and climbing the tree he placed the persimmons all over the tree, so that they looked as though they had grown there.

Black-Mountain-Bear was out hunting one day, and as he was near Coyote's home he remembered his promise to visit him, and so he ran over to see him. Coyote was glad to see him and asked him in. "I am so sorry I have no meat for you," he said, "but if you will wait I will try to get you something to eat." Coyote began to bump against the tree with his head. He hit harder and harder, but the persimmons would not fall. Finally he arose and shook the tree with his hands, though it embarrassed him to have to do this. He gave the tree a big shake and over it fell, hitting him on the head. He pretended that it did not hurt and went about gathering up the fruit for Bear, though he could hardly see for pain. Bear ate, though he could hardly swallow for laughing, for Coyote's head kept getting bigger and bigger. After a little while Bear said that he must be going, for he was afraid to stay longer for fear Coyote would see him laugh. After he had gone Coyote sat down and held his sore head, but he felt happy notwithstanding, for he had furnished food for Bear. (Dorsey 1905, 93–94)

The third Caddo myth bears a strong likeness to the first one. It is constructed simply and strips this genre of myth down to its barest expression. It thus, again, reveals the storyteller's intent: to convey information. Without the omissions, metonymies, and circumventions, its lessons become clear and relevant, here, among the Caddo, whose diet was much more plant than animal.

Black-Mountain-Bear (*Ursus americanus*) is being very human when he tells his host, Coyote, that for want of meat he will offer something else. Coyote echoes this refrain when Black-Mountain-Bear comes to visit: "I am so sorry I have no meat for you," he said, "but if you will wait I will try to get you something to eat."

These kind words show not only the omnivorous diet of bears and humans, but also the rules of hospitality that prevailed—and still do—among the Caddo. A visitor could not in any way ask his host for food upon arrival and had to accept whatever the host could offer. This custom is very old. The Franciscan Casañas de Jesus Maria had reported it in the late seventeenth century: "It is a habit with them whenever they arrive at a house, never to ask for anything to eat. For it is customary to set whatever a host may have before a visitor as soon as he arrives" (Casañas in Swanton 1996, 174).

Furthermore, in this mainly agricultural society, any game meat was considered a luxury or at least rare enough for the host to plead that he had no meat to offer and would make do with whatever was on hand, namely persimmons.

Black bears eat persimmons, or any fruit for that matter. A study done in Texas, near Caddo traditional territory, has shown the importance of another persimmon species (*Diospyros texana*) in their diet: "In the Serranias del Burro, Coahuila, and Big Bend National Park (BBNP), Texas, plant material was 95% and 93%, respectively, of material found in bear feces (Doan-Crider 1995), and animal material was primarily insect remains. . . . Oaks provide acorns, which are a dominant part of bear diets, wherever they are found. Texas persimmon (*Diospyros texana*), agrito (*Berberis trifoliolata*) and manzanita (*Actostaphylos* spp.) are examples of shrubs providing fruits high in digestible carbohydrates" (Medellin et al. 2005, 396–97).

Nothing has been published on how black bears go about gathering persimmons, although they likely use the same techniques that all bears use to reach or knock down fruits from trees or bushes. One common method is to bend fruit trees over—a frequent cause of damage to vegetation: "Trees that have been bent and broken by feeding bears are common along roads and trails" (Kolenosky and Strathearn 1987, 446).

Thus this detail is key to the myth: a persimmon tree—most probably a sapling—bending under a bear's weight. Furthermore, we encounter an interesting but unrelated detail when Coyote seems to plant a persimmon tree near his home. Persimmons were a common food item among the Caddo and often kept as dried loaves for themselves or for sale to the French or Spanish: "As in other places they make a paste of figs; they make it of persimmons also and keep it for gifts to present and sell to the Spaniards and the French" (Solís in Swanton 1996, 132). This was an old practice. The observation by Brother Solís goes back to the 1760s. Even more interestingly, we learn that the Caddo not only gathered these fruits annually—"Plums, persimmons and cherries were collected" (Rogers and Sabo III 2004, 628)—but also cultivated them. Such farming appears in the historical record, the first account being again by Brother Solís: "They have orchards of various kinds: peaches, plums, persimmons, fig trees, chestnuts, ash [?], pome-granates and other fruit" (Solís in Swanton 1996, 132).

Coyote's behavior is mimicry if not caricature. The Caddo knew how to farm the land, and when and where to plant the various seeds of the plants they grew, the leading ones being corn, sun-flower, members of the gourd family, and tobacco. Unlike Coyote, they did not cut down trees and transplant them near their homes. Nor did they adorn them with fruits. But the etymon of Coyote's technique doubtlessly refers to the existence of orchards and fruit growing. By imitating how a persimmon is planted, Coyote reminds his listeners what not to do and the risks of doing so.

On the other hand, Coyote is true to reality when he looks for fruit-bearing persimmons to transplant but fails to find any. Indeed, in the American Southeast, persimmon trees can vary a lot in their ability to produce edible fruit. This fact is reflected in Coyote's unsuccessful search: "The tree is greatly inclined to vary in the character and quality of its fruit, in size this varies from that of a small cherry to a small apple. Some trees in the south produce fruit which is delicious . . . while adjoining trees produce fruit that never becomes edible" (Keeler 1908, 198).

In sum, the Caddo have given us three Bungling Host myths: one metonymical and two much more direct with no smoke and mirrors. All three come to similar conclusions. A human (or Coy-ote) does not have the same attributes or the same powers as an animal. A human cannot pounce like Cougar, find food like Raven,

Fig. 37. Black bear and persimmon.

or display immeasurable strength like Black-Mountain-Bear, who can bend over a persimmon tree like a reed. Such is life for mortal humans, although some can hope to team up with animals and thereby gain access to their powers. But very few succeed:

> The relationship with the animals is the familiar one of supernatural helper, or, in White Moon's phrase, partner . . . "two are partners with" e.g. bear or panther or screech owl or lightning. . . . "You have the same power as your partner," from him you get your power, and such partners can understand each other. The partnership is established through some *accidental* encounter, not through deliberate seeking, and only certain men, comparatively few, I take it, doctors included, have had such experience. (Parsons 1941, 57–58)

This point is made in the first Caddo myth we saw, when Coyote asks Cougar for his power: "And so he asked Mountain-Lion if he could give him power so that he could kill a horse, too, and eat it when he was hungry."

15 Rabbit Gathers Canes (Southeast)

The Rabbit and the Grizzly Bear had been friends for some time. One day the Rabbit said to the Grizzly Bear, "Come and visit me. I dwell in a very large brier patch." Then he departed home. On his arrival he went out and gathered a quantity of young canes, which he hung up. Meanwhile the Grizzly Bear had reached the abode of the Rabbit, and was seeking the large brier patch; but the Rabbit really dwelt in a very small patch. When the Rabbit perceived that the Grizzly Bear was near, he began to make a pattering sound with his feet. This scared the Grizzly Bear, who retreated to a distance and then stopped and stood listening. As soon as the Rabbit noticed this he cried out, "Halloo! my friend, was it you whom I treated in that manner? Come and take a seat." So the Grizzly Bear complied with the Rabbit's request. The Rabbit gave the young canes to his guest, who soon swallowed them all, while the Rabbit himself ate but one.

—James Owen Dorsey, "Two Biloxi Tales"

We may know little about the Caddo among the peoples of the Southeast, but we know even less about the Biloxi. There is almost no anthropological literature on this Siouan people who originally lived in the vicinity of Biloxi Bay in Mississippi, and migrated to Louisiana in the late eighteenth century. There is nothing aside from several trifling remarks by European explorers of the seventeenth century and in linguistic studies from the late nineteenth century (Dorsey 1894; Dorsey and Swanton 1912). Fortunately, the anthropologist James Owen Dorsey appended several Biloxi-language texts to his Biloxi dictionary, including a Bungling Host myth (Dorsey 1893).

The early twentieth century saw the Biloxi come close to extinction. By 1908 there were no more than six or eight of them, a sharp decline from 420 in 1698 (Brain, Roth, and De Reuse 2004, 593). Today, their descendants live with several other peoples (Tunica, Ofo, Avoyel, and Choctaw) on a shared reservation in eastern Louisiana with a total population of over seven hundred.

The Biloxi myth is doubly interesting. First, the host is a rabbit, and the Bungling Host genre seldom assigns this role to a rabbit or a hare, with the only other example to our knowledge being from the Shoshone (Great Basin). That example succinctly and simply expresses the belief that game animals give themselves up to hunters. This belief is expressed when Jackrabbit cooks another rabbit for his guest.

COYOTE AND JACK-RABBIT

"To-morrow, I am going to my brother-in-law Jack-rabbit," said Coyote. He got there. Jack-rabbit went out. He gathered plenty of dead wood. For a long time, he sat down. He made a fire, cooked a brown rabbit, and gave it to Coyote. Coyote ate, and went home. Jack-rabbit said, "To-morrow, I am going to my brother-in-law Coyote's to eat." Coyote went out and brought in dead wood; but put nothing in the fire to cook for his guest. (Lowie 1909b, 266)

Rabbits could feed humans, represented here by the Trickster character (Coyote), but the reverse was not true. Leporids had never been domesticated.

The Biloxi myth is also interesting because it describes animal behavior. Unlike other Bungling Host myths, which describe only how the host behaves, this one also portrays the behavior of the guest, who is only half-human. Moreover, the host, a kind of rabbit, himself appears in Biloxi mythology as a Trickster. The roles are reversed, and the textual content deviates from the norm of this genre. We will examine these anomalies further on.

The Biloxi myth appears in the literature in its original language with a juxtaposed translation (Dorsey and Swanton 1912, 15–17). A literary translation was published in two different collections of stories (Dorsey 1893, 49–50; Dorsey and Swanton 1912, 17–18).

RABBIT AND GRIZZLY BEAR

The Rabbit and the Grizzly Bear had been friends for some time. One day the Rabbit said to the Grizzly Bear, "Come and visit me. I dwell in a very large brier patch." Then he departed home. On his arrival he went out and gathered a quantity of young canes, which he hung up. Meanwhile the Grizzly Bear had reached the abode of the Rabbit, and was seeking the large brier patch; but the Rabbit really dwelt in a very small patch. When the Rabbit perceived that the Grizzly Bear was near, he began to make a pattering sound with his feet. This scared the Grizzly Bear, who retreated to a distance and then stopped and stood listening. As soon as the Rabbit noticed this he cried out, "Halloo! my friend, was it you whom I treated in that manner? Come and take a seat." So the Grizzly Bear complied with the Rabbit's request. The Rabbit gave the young canes to his guest, who soon swallowed them all, while the Rabbit himself ate but one, that is, the Rabbit minced now and then at one piece of cane while the Grizzly Bear swallowed all the others. "This is what I have always fancied," said the Grizzly Bear, as he was about to depart. Said he to the Rabbit, "Come and visit me. I dwell in a large bent tree."

After his departure, the Rabbit started on his journey to the home of the Grizzly Bear. He spent some time in seeking the large bent tree, but all in vain, for the Grizzly Bear was then in a hollow tree, where he was growling. The Rabbit heard the growls and fled in terror, going some distance before he sat down. Then said the Grizzly Bear, "Halloo! my friend, was that you whom I treated in that manner? Come hither and sit down." So the Rabbit obeyed him. "You are now my guest," said the Grizzly Bear, "but there is nothing here for you to eat." So the Grizzly Bear went in search of food. He went to gather young canes. As he went along he was eating the small black insects which stay in decayed logs. These are called "Bessie bugs" by the white people, and A-kí-di-sīp'-si-wé-di by the Biloxi, from the noise ("Sp! sp!") which they make when they are disturbed. After a long absence he returned to his lodge with a few young canes, which he threw down before the Rabbit. Then he walked in a circle around the Rabbit. In a little while the Grizzly Bear said "Oh!" and turned back toward the Rabbit, before whom he vomited up the black insects which he had devoured. "Swallow these," said he to the Rabbit. "I have never eaten such food," replied his guest. This offended the Grizzly Bear, who said, "When you entertained me, I ate all the food which you gave me, as I liked it very well; but now when I give you food, why do you treat me thus? Before the sun sets, I will kill you and lay down your body." As he spoke thus the Rabbit's heart was beating rapidly from terror, for the Grizzly Bear stood at the entrance of the hollow tree in order to prevent the Rabbit's escape. But the Rabbit, who was very active, managed to dodge, and thus he got out of the hollow tree. He ran at once to the brier patch and took his seat, being very angry with the Grizzly Bear. Then he shouted to the Grizzly Bear, "When they are hunting for you, I will go towards your place of concealment." For that reason it has come to pass ever since that day that, when dogs are hunting a rabbit, they find a grizzly bear, which is shot by the hunter. (Dorsey 1893, 49–50)

To identify the two main characters of the story, we face several problems that can nonetheless be resolved. The original terms are *Tcetkana* and *Oⁿti'* for Rabbit and Grizzly Bear respectively (Dorsey and Swanton 1912, 15). The first term means "The Rabbit, a mythical hero of the Biloxi" (Dorsey and Swanton 1912, 263). He is distinguished from *tcetkan*, a generic word for 'hare' or 'rabbit.' *Tcetkana* seems to represent the Trickster in Biloxi culture, since he acts like one in many myths (playing tricks, creating anomalies, hunting monsters, etc.). He nonetheless seems based

Fig. 38. Swamp rabbit.

on a real animal species if we go by some of the characteristics
in the myth above, namely that he eats canes and lives in brier
patches. In Louisiana, this description matches at least one rabbit
species: *Sylvilagus aquaticus*, the swamp rabbit. Being "the largest
member of the genus" *Sylvilagus* (Chapman and Litvaitis 2003,
102), it may have inspired the character in the myth. Its habitat,
as described by Western biologists, matches the one in the myth:
"Svihla (1929) found the forms and runways of swamp rabbits in
tangled marsh vegetation and brier bushes. Harrison and Hickie
(1931) noted that *S. aquaticus* was closely confined to canebrake
(*Arundinaria gigantia*) communities in Indiana, which by 1930 had
been greatly reduced in size" (Chapman and Feldhamer 1981, 3).

Rabbit's guest is Oⁿti', which Dorsey translated as 'Grizzly Bear.'

John R. Swanton, who edited the manuscript of Dorsey's dictionary, had doubts about this translation: "O^{n}ti', a bear (Dorsey says 'a grizzly bear,' but he must be in error)" (Dorsey and Swanton 1912, 242). The grizzly, *Ursus arctos*, used to range east of the Mississippi into present-day Ohio and Kentucky (Jonkel 1987, 458), hence a little north of traditional Biloxi territory. But some lived closer, in the adjacent state of Texas to the west. It is likely, then, that the Biloxi saw or at least heard about this animal. It is also likely that they included it in their myths because it looked bigger than the black bear (*Ursus americanus*)—which also lived on their territory, and still does (Kolenosky and Strathearn 1987, 444). For the purpose of storytelling, a grizzly would contrast even more with the 'little' swamp rabbit. If Dorsey did err, his error persists in present-day introductory texts on the Biloxi, which report the former existence of several matrilineal clans, including one known as the 'grizzly bear people': "The Biloxi were organized in matrilineal clans, three of which were *ita ayadi* 'deer people', *oti ayadi* 'grizzly bear people' and *naxotoda ayadi* 'alligator people'" (Brain, Roth, and De Reuse 2004, 594).

In any event, the biloxi term definitely means a bear, whatever the species. In his dictionary, Dorsey distinguished between a brown bear and a black bear, but in this case he was referring to the fur color of the black bear, a species that has honey-colored morphs (Banfield 1974, 305): "*o^{n}sidi'*, a 'yellow bear,' a cinnamon bear; *o^{n}t'sŭpi'*, a black bear" (Dorsey and Swanton 1912, 242).

So, in the following pages, we will keep in mind that Rabbit's guest may also be a black bear, and when analyzing the mytheme we may refer to observations of black bear behavior in the traditional environment of the Biloxi.

The mytheme is relatively easy to elucidate. It lacks the strangeness of the other legends seen so far, and its content is less interesting than its form, i.e., the way its elements are interwoven. Here, the etymon merges with its manifestation—Rabbit is literally gathering canes, and a back-and-forth narrative alternates between

Rabbit and Bear, with each of them describing what he perceives in the other, sometimes wrongly. There are in fact gaps between one character's perceptions and the other's reality.

The myth therefore fulfills its main purpose: educating or informing the listener. Here, we learn the following facts about swamp rabbits and bears.

Rabbit lives in a brier patch. He thumps the ground when a stranger comes. He eats canes but only in small amounts. He is terrified by Bear's growling. He flees danger and then stops and sits some distance away. He does not eat insects vomited by Bear. He is very alert and gets away by dodging right and left.

Bear, we learn, is fond of brier patches. He retreats when he senses danger and, when retreating, he likewise stops some distance away, but instead of sitting he stands up to listen. He consumes canes in large amounts. He lives in a hollow tree. He growls. He eats black insects, which he vomits. He can attack a rabbit.

When the story comes to an end, there is also a seal of authenticity. First, however, we should comment on the above descriptions of animal behavior.

Swamp rabbits are found not only in brier patches but also in stands of cane, as we have already noted. Such stands dominated the landscape of the Southeast when settlers came from the Old World: "Extensive stands of cane (*Arundinaria gigantea*) known as canebrakes were a dominant landscape feature in the southeastern United States at the time of European settlement. Hundreds of thousands of hectares were characterized by this ecosystem, which rapidly disappeared following settlement" (Platt, Brantley, and Rainwater 2001, 1).

Swamp rabbits feed on the canes, but only in small amounts, eating only the leaves and new shoots: "Swamp rabbits utilize canebrakes for cover, and they browse foliage and shoots. . . . The local names 'cane cutter' and 'cane jake' reflect the swamp rabbit's affinity for canebrakes" (Platt, Brantley, and Rainwater 2001, 5).

It is also well known that rabbits may thump the ground and

that, when in danger, they flee and then freeze a little farther away. Thumping is a means of communication, as reported for another member of the genus *Sylvilagus*, i.e., *S. floridanus*, also present in Louisiana: "One characteristic sound, thought to be a method of communication, is made by thumping the hind feet" (Wooding 1982, 201). With swamp rabbits, the sound may even be very loud: "Probably all of the Cottontail group do their chief signalling by thumping with the hind feet; we have no observations to show that the Cane-cutter specializes in this department, but the following by Bachman is suggestive: 'Persons who have given us information on the subject of this Hare, inform us, that when first started, and while running, its trampings are louder, and can be heard at a greater distance, than those of any other Hare'" (Seton 1953 [1909], vol. 4, 824).

Similarly, when a swamp rabbit freezes after fleeing some distance from a potential source of danger, we are seeing a behavior of all leporids. This fleeing and freezing behavior has been described for *S. aquaticus* in detail: "Swamp rabbits readily use tree tops, logs and backtracking maneuvers to confuse pursuers. A favorite tactic is to climb onto a large log or tree top, walk its length, then backtrack and leap to the side, moving away at right angles to the previous course. After such behavior, the rabbit frequently travels only a short distance, then sits to watch its backtrail. These sitting spots often appeared to be used more than one time" (Terrel 1972, 292).

In short, a swamp rabbit is very agile. It can easily elude a black bear, using its characteristic agility to dash back and forth. On top of the backtracking manoeuvres, it is known that males and females alike repeatedly rush and jump nimbly in the air during the breeding season:

> *Jump sequence.* — The basic pattern of the jump sequence (Front.) was facing-off, male rush, female jump, facing-off. . . . The per-

Fig. 39. Stand of canes.

formance usually was repeated. The maximum was 30 (in the swamp rabbit) . . . .

The jump sequence was the most complex and variable of the reproductive behaviors. Frequently, it was preceded by male dashes. The speed of the rush and the height of the jump varied and, with the number of consecutive sequences, were good indices to the vigor of the performance. (Marsden and Holler 1964, 14)

Like other rabbits and hares, swamp rabbits are essentially herbivorous. The swamp rabbit's diet includes nothing of animal origin, at least as far as we currently know: "Swamp rabbits feed on a variety of plants. . . . Toll et al. (1960) found that plants were eaten according to their abundance" (Chapman and Feldhamer 1981, 3). In the myth, as in reality, this animal does not accept food of insect origin, such as what Bear offered Rabbit.

Finally, swamp rabbits are very nervous. A growling bear would surely make one of them jump with a start, this animal being always on the alert: "Kept in captivity, they remain extremely wild and nervous and do not become accustomed to their cages, even after months of confinements" (Svihla 1929, 316).

If we turn to bears, whose behaviors are likewise described in detail by the myth, we see the same descriptions by Native and non-Native observers. The myth accurately instructs its audience of future hunters in key points of animal behavior. Yes, the Biloxi used to hunt bears, undoubtedly for food and also for clothing (Dorsey 1894, 269). Everything known about this animal was thus useful for hunting. In the myth, the bear's habitat and diet are spelled out. It prefers briers, and Rabbit exploits this preference to get Bear to come over, by enticingly saying he dwells "in a very large brier patch." In reality, it is quite small. Bears love stands of cane as much as they love brier patches, and either habitat provides them with food. In the past, bears were widely present in cane stands, where their diet included certain greenbrier species (greenbriers encompass several genera of thorny bushes such as *Rosa, Rubus, Smilax,* and others). They ate among others those of the genus *Smilax,* which grows parasitically on canes: "Early writers frequently commented on the abundance of black bears in canebrakes. . . . Bears remained common in northeastern Louisiana canebrakes as late as 1907. . . . Featherstonhaugh (1884) attributed the decline of Arkansas bear populations to widespread canebrake destruction. Black bears feed on cane shoots, culms, and foliage. . . .

Fruits and foliage of greenbrier (*Smilax* spp.), which commonly grows intertwined among culms (Platt and Brantley, 1997), is also an important food" (Platt, Brantley, and Rainwater 2001, 6).

Generally speaking, bears are also very nervous animals. The presence of strangers makes them flee, be they black bears or grizzlies:

> [Black Bear] In many instances, people are not even aware that a bear has been in their vicinity because the bear has moved away as the people approached. Most bears . . . will go to great lengths to avoid people. (Kolenosky and Strathearn 1987, 448)

> [Grizzly Bear] Bears generally go out of their way to avoid humans, so talking, singing, rattling pebbles in a can and making other noises may scare them off. (Wooding 1982, 92)

This is what happens in the story. As soon as he hears Rabbit thump his feet, Grizzly Bear moves away.

Similarly, a bear may stand upright to assess a threat, as Bear does in the myth after moving away, and as several non-Native observers have noticed:

> [Black Bear] Frequently, a black bear will stand on his hindlegs with its nose in the air in an attempt to see over vegetation and detect any unfamiliar odors. (Kolenosky and Strathearn 1987, 443)

> [Grizzly Bear] A bear rearing up on his hind legs is probably taking a more careful sniff to make certain of who or what you are. (Wooding 1982, 93)

The myth states that the retreating bear stops a little farther off to listen. It is known that a bear's sense of hearing is highly developed, much more so than its sight, and this is stressed in the myth. "They [black bears] have a keen sense of smell and acute hearing, but their eyesight is poor" (Banfield 1974, 305).

The bear of the Biloxi myth growls when his guest comes near the hollow tree where he lives. These details are factual. First, growling is a characteristic sound of bears:

[Black Bear] They utter a variety of sounds: squeals, growls, and grunts. (Banfield 1974, 305)

[Grizzly Bear] They growl and roar when fighting. (Banfield 1974, 309)

Second, bear dens are often in hollow trees. As winter approaches, this is where they get ready to hibernate: "In the autumn the black bear seeks the shelter of a cave, rock crevice, hollow log, wind-thrown stump, or merely a mossy hollow under the low, sweeping branches of spruce or fir for its winter den. It drags in some spruce boughs, rotten wood, or heather for bedding" (Banfield 1974, 306).

Also factual is one last element of the myth: bears eat insects. While gathering canes for his guest, Rabbit, Bear stops to eat here and there "the small black insects which stay in decayed logs." In their Biloxi dictionary, Dorsey and Swanton (1912) elaborated on this detail of the myth: "*Akidi' si'psiwe'di*, so called from the noise it makes when caught: 'Sp! sp!'—the 'Bessie-bug' of Louisiana, a small black bug which is found in decayed logs" (171).

In some regions, these insects make up a relatively large pro-portion of a bear's diet. The term 'bessie-bug' corresponds to the passalidæ insect family, which has three species in the United States: "The eastern species forms colonies in well-decayed logs and stumps and is fairly common" (Borror and White 1970, 192). In the Southeast, the species is *Odontotænius disjunctus*. Accord-ing to a Florida study, this insect made up over 11% of the diet of black bears whose stomachs had been analyzed. Some findings convinced the study's author that the bears were selecting some insects over others: "The insects found [in the stomachs] repre-sented a wide range of taxa (Table 1). However, only yellow jackets and bessbugs (*Odontotænius disjunctus*) occurred in more than 2 stomachs. These species are found in subterranean nests (Grissell 1974) or within rotten logs (Borror and White 1970, 192), respec-tively, indicating that bears make a special effort to obtain them as food. Therefore, a preference for yellow jackets and bessbugs may be indicated" (Maehr and Brady 1982, 568).

In the myth, Bear regurgitates the insects he has swallowed. Before doing so, however, he walks in a circle "around the Rabbit." Such a movement if repeated continually might lead to malaise and vomiting in an animal that had overeaten a food item or, at least, eaten one that was difficult to digest. It is harder to explain why the bear of our story regurgitates. Bears do not vomit their food like other animals do to feed their young. This kind of malaise happens only if the bear has been wounded or poisoned, or is simply ill.

In other chapters, we have already stressed the mixed nature of the myths. Human and animal elements get so mixed up that they create a puzzling, truly mythological atmosphere. This particular myth shows that humans too ate insects; at least, one may deduce such consumption by extrapolation, in the absence of any real anthropological literature on the Biloxi. First, it is known that insects were part of the traditional diet of many Native American peoples. Consumption of yellow jackets was relatively widespread, for example among the Yana of California (chapter 6). In the Southeast, they were eaten by the Creek and the Cherokee of Alabama, who were neighbours of the Biloxi:

> [Creek] There is some evidence for the eating of beetles, locusts, fleas, lice, and wasps in the comb. (Walker 2004, 376)

> [Cherokee] Yellowjackets and cicadas were roasted or boiled and served as a soup. (Fogelson 2004, 343)

The mush thrown up by Bear may have resembled the insect soup cited above, and all the more so because some Native American groups are known to have eaten passalidæ. We have come across at least one. This is a Tucanoan people from Amazonia in South America: the Tatuyo of the village of Yapu in Colombia. These Natives ate both the larvae and the adults of a species named *yayaru* in their language and identified as belonging to the passalidæ (Dufour 1987, 386). We got in touch with the specialist who studied this dietary practice to find out whether any rules governed eating of these insects, such as a requirement to cook them or recommended limitations on eating them. The answer was negative, although we learned that they could be eaten either raw or cooked. It is nonetheless instructive in itself that passalidæ are present in the traditional Native American diet. We see that these insects are edible for humans and, thus, the Biloxi too may have harvested them for food.

If they did, this human element is embedded in the myth with Bear's consumption of the same food item. The convergence of the two is confirmed in the myth by a similar fact supported by current studies: canes are eaten not only by bears, as we have seen, but also by humans. Indeed, recent research has shown the great importance of canes in Native American lives of the Southeast: "Cane (*Arundinaria* spp.) was one of the most important plant resources for Native Americans living in the southeastern United States prior to Euro-American settlement. The use of cane permeated virtually every aspect of tribal life. Cane was used to make houses and village structures, military and hunting weapons, fishing gear, furniture and domestic implements, personal adornments, baskets, musical instruments, and watercraft. Medicines were prepared from cane, and parts of the plant furnished food and fuel" (Platt, Brantley, and Rainwater 2009, 271).

In particular, these Native Americans ate seeds, which were "ground into flour that was baked as bread or mixed with water to produce gruel" (Platt, Brantley, and Rainwater 2009, 275). They also ate cane shoots: "Although historic accounts are largely silent on how shoots were prepared, these were presumably eaten raw, steamed, or boiled" (Platt, Brantley, and Rainwater 2009, 275).

It is doubtful that cane shoots were steamed. (Platt, Brantley, and Rainwater have no anthropological training and surely do not know that cooking by boiling, i.e., placing fire-heated stones in some kind of water-filled container, could not have easily been used for steaming). Nonetheless, whether cooked or raw, the Biloxi did likely eat them exactly as in the myth.

Several other elements can help to explain Bear's vomiting.

Of the thirty texts that Dorsey took down from the Biloxi on his visits in 1892 and 1893, two other legends refer to regurgitation (Dorsey 1894, 269; Dorsey and Swanton 1912, 46–49, 107–11). Both legends feature a hero, Tiny Frog and Otter respectively, who, to accomplish his exploits, is first purged using powerful emetics: "One of the biloxi myths is that about a tiny frog, called, *Pěska*, from its cry, "Pěs! Pěs!" This frog, which frequents streams in central Louisiana, is not over an inch long; it has a sharp nose and black skin. Pěskana', the Ancient of this species of frogs, was shut up by his grandmother in order to endow him with superhuman power. Having produced the desired result, partly by means of emetics, she started eastward with him" (Dorsey 1894, 284).

The myth itself is even more explicit than the above summary by Dorsey: "The Ancient of Tiny Frogs was shut up by his grandmother in order to give him superhuman power; and for that purpose she was making him vomit" (Dorsey and Swanton 1912, 48). In the Bungling Host myth, Bear radically changes his attitude after throwing up. Whatever the reason—his self-purging or Rabbit's refusal to accept the food he offers—Bear becomes threatening, and his initially friendly relationship with Rabbit now becomes an antagonistic one. Bear tells Rabbit he will kill him, and this threat is matched by his posture: standing upright and barring the way out of his home.

It is highly probable that the Biloxi conceived the act of vomiting as a purification rite to increase one's personal power. The indigenous Taino of the Caribbean would use a stick to make themselves throw up and thereby purify themselves (Rouse 1992, 14, 119). This human ritual is reflected in the myth and seems to be the main etymon of the bear's regurgitation. The two charts below sum up the concordances between the animal hosts and the reality of this people. The two series of concordances are interlinked and must be separated for analysis. The first one shows the relationship between the Biloxi and rabbits:

Table 11. Biloxi and rabbits

	BILOXI	RABBIT
BRIER	eaten	eaten
CANE	eaten	eaten
VOMIT	not eaten	not eaten

The Biloxi would eat some briers (e.g., *Rubus* spp.) and canes but would not eat vomit. Rabbit likewise. The concordance is perfect.

With the Biloxi and bears, the relationship is a bit more detailed, but it too is very balanced. It can be outlined, in part, as follows:

Table 12. Biloxi and bears

	BILOXI	BEAR
BRIER	eaten	eaten
CANE	eaten	eaten
INSECTS	eaten	eaten

This relationship can have only the following consequence:

$$\text{Biloxi vomiting} \rightarrow \rightarrow \rightarrow \text{Bear vomiting}$$

This relationship is made necessary by an extremely widespread Native American belief: bears are the most human-like of all animals. "To begin with, we may admit that among the animals found in the habitat of the natives of North America and northern Eurasia, the ursine species are distinguished by characteristics which lend themselves more readily to anthropomorphization than those of other animals. . . . In emotional behavior the bears also exhibit a range of facial and bodily expression which is very human. . . . They even resemble human beings . . . and when skinned the human-like proportions of the beast have received repeated comment in primitive and contemporary society alike" (Hallowell 1926, 148–49).

Finally, in passing, we should note that bears are attracted to carrion or anything they can swallow:

> [Grizzly Bear] In some areas, bears feed extensively on carrion found in big game wintering areas. (Jonkel 1987, 465)

> [Black Bear] Black bears are omnivorous and not too selective in their feeding habits. Twigs and leaves are consumed with berries. If they are feeding on garbage, they may consume paper, cardboard, rags, string, and pieces of wood. . . .

> The annual diet consists of approximately 76.7 per cent vegetable matter, 7.4 per cent insects, 15.2 per cent carrion, and 0.7 per cent small mammals. (Banfield 1974, 306)

Is it any wonder that Rabbit—like any rabbit, of course—would not accept Bear's offering of a food item that seemed to him so vile: "I have never eaten such food"?

Above, we mentioned the back-and-forth narrative of the characters in the myth, but we did not develop this point. Indeed, first Bear and then Rabbit naively believes the other's description of where he lives, only to discover the less enticing reality—the description being in fact a subterfuge to get the other to come over. Bear is lured by the idea of visiting "a very large brier patch" where Rabbit claims to live. Bear undoubtedly feels attracted to the heather that grows in such patches, but he seems disappointed on seeing the "very small patch" where Rabbit lives. Evidently, what seems big to a small mammal will seem small to a big one, like Bear.

Reciprocally, Rabbit feels attracted to "the large bent tree" where Bear says he will receive him when in fact Bear is inside a hollow tree when Rabbit comes to visit. Much has been written about the fondness of rabbits for such trees.

> Swamp rabbits customarily deposit fecal pellets on elevated objects, such as logs and stumps, in autumn, winter and spring. Martinson

et al. (1961) evaluated the use of this habit as a sampling technique in Missouri. (Terrel 1972, 290)

In one habit, this Rabbit is said to be peculiar. It affects perches and high lookouts. . . . Thus, Kennicott says: "It generally rests upon logs, stones or other elevations." (Seton 1953 [1909], vol. 4, 824–25)

Sylvilagus aquaticus builds its forms in places where it can detect intruders and have access to vegetation or water for escape. Tops of old trumps covered with vegetation, low crotches of trees, logs . . . were observed to be common form sites for this aquatic rabbit. (Lowe 1958, 120)

So Rabbit is greatly disappointed on finding out that Bear does not live near a bent tree, a habitat he regularly yearns for.

This mutual misunderstanding is instructive. First, it shows us another widespread Native American belief: you can "put yourself in the place" of an animal to understand how it perceives reality or its surrounding world. Second, you can pass on this knowledge by highlighting or contrasting what the same animal likes or dislikes.

As we said, the Biloxi myth ends on a familiar note. There is a seal of authenticity to certify that everything said is true. Here, the seal is Rabbit's revenge. Furious at being threatened, he warns Bear what will happen in the future whenever a hunter and his dogs is chasing a bear: a rabbit will lead them straight to its den.

What better to illustrate Rabbit's words than the following anecdote from a contemporary outdoor magazine, which describes a man hunting rabbits with his dog. He loses his hunting dog, only to find it later in a bear's den.

Trouble started on a bone-chilling February day in Maine when Butch McCormick went out with Dodger, his beagle. Butch was hunting for rabbits. . . .

The dog ran off along a deer trail. Butch ran after him but couldn't find him. . . .

Butch searched all day on Saturday, and then again on Sunday. Finally he found Dodger's tracks. They led to a snow-covered brush pile. Butch went to the pile and called his dog. Dodger nosed out of the pile. But then Butch saw something very strange. A large, black paw reached out from the brush pile and pulled Dodger back in.

Dodger had somehow gotten into a black bear's den. ("Dodger's Den" 1999)

At first simple and trivial in appearance, the Biloxi episode of the Bungling Host becomes more complex the more it is analyzed. This complexity is especially acute when the two protagonists, Rabbit and Bear, provide lessons in animal behavior, and also when their mutual misunderstanding comes to a head, this too being a lesson, albeit a negative one.

All in all, the etymon is easier to grasp here than in the other myths. The Biloxi told this myth to convey knowledge directly with no hidden messages.

16 Squirrel Slits Open His Scrotum (Plains)

Coyote looked up and saw a great big male squirrel, eating pecans. So he called him down and told him that he was hard pressed and wanted something to eat. The squirrel came down. He said: "I can give you something to eat; but you are very tricky. You must do just as I tell you." Coyote said: "All right." So the squirrel stood at the bottom of the pecan-tree. He put one of his legs up against the tree so that his scrotum hung down, and he told the old man to cut his scrotum. He did so, and out poured a quantity of pecans, all ready to eat.

—George A. Dorsey, "Traditions of the Skidi Pawnee"

Immediately northwest of the Biloxi of Louisiana, the Pawnee of Oklahoma offer two Bungling Host variants that pose another special challenge. Originally from Nebraska, where they had lived since time immemorial, the Pawnee had to migrate in 1875 to the state of Oklahoma, where they have lived ever since. Their reservation today has 2,500 members, i.e., around a third of their numbers when the first Europeans arrived. They call themselves in their own language *Chaticks si Chaticks*, which means 'Men of Men' (the word *Pawnee* is Siouan and not Caddoan, the linguistic family of the Chaticks si Chaticks; Parks 2001). Their members were semi-sedentary and divided into four divisions, with each of them having one or more villages. Houses were made of earth, and traditional life alternated between horticulture and hunting, interspersed with gathering of various plant products.

The two Pawnee myths are special in that they are very similar even though the main characters are different. In both myths, the host slits his scrotum to get food—Beaver in the first myth, and Squirrel in the second. From it come two different products: grease and pecans respectively. All of the other details seem to converge: both characters are male; the Coyote Trickster clumsily tries to imitate his host and hurts himself; the host heals Trickster; and so on. Yet the two mythemes—Beaver slits his scrotum to get grease, and Squirrel slits his to get pecans—have completely different etymons, which can be understood only by thoroughly understanding the anatomy of each species.

The first myth is in fact an episode of a cycle whose hero is Coyote. It exists in several versions from the Pawnee (Dorsey 1904c, 245–46, 267–68, 356n267) but is known only in English. The first version, the most detailed one, is as follows:

BEAVER AND COYOTE

They were starving. So he put his raccoon quiver upon his back and went out into the timber to hunt game. He walked along through the timber, and then he would stop and look around, and make a noise: "Hoo! Hoo!" to get the attention of some animal.

While he was standing there he heard some one call to him, speaking to him, who said: "Grandfather, are you here?" Coyote said: "Yes, I am here, grandchild, and I am very hungry, and my children are hungry, and I do not know what to do to get anything for them to eat." He added: "Grandchild, I would like you to help me get something to eat." As it proved, it was a large male beaver. The beaver said: "Grandfather, go and get some dry driftwood that is rotten." Coyote went and got some, and when it was touched it would break easily. The beaver said: "Now come. You must be careful. I know you; you are tricky." The beaver said: "Now cut my scrotum." Coyote cut his scrotum, and there came out a quantity of grease. The beaver now poured the grease over this driftwood; he told Coyote to stir it up, and it turned into pemmican—a little pounded meat mixed with fat. He told Coyote to eat it. Coyote ate it. It was good. He wanted more, but the beaver told him he could not have any more. Coyote begged the beaver to give him the same power, but the beaver would not do it. "You are tricky. You might hurt yourself," said the beaver. Finally the beaver yielded, and told Coyote to do the same thing.

So Coyote went home. When he arrived, he called his children and asked if they were hungry, and they all said, "Yes." He told them that he had learned something; that he wanted something for them to eat. He told the children to go and get a lot of dry driftwood, and they brought it. "Now," said he, "old woman, come here. Get your knife and cut my scrotum." The old woman obeyed, and cut it; and a quantity of grease poured out over the dry driftwood, which all turned into fat meat. He said: "Children, eat it." The children ate it. They ate it all up. Coyote wanted to know what they thought about it. They said that it was fine food to eat. He asked if they wanted any more. They said, "Yes." "Well," he said, "get some more dry driftwood." The old woman got her knife again, cut the old man, and more grease was secured. Then they wanted more again. Coyote got some more, for he wanted them to have plenty. Again the old woman came with her knife and cut his scrotum, and, instead of grease coming out, blood poured out. Coyote began to grow frightened. He yelled and cried and said: "Old woman, you have hurt me." So he got up, ran to where the beaver was, cried, and told the beaver that he had made a mistake; that the old woman had cut him too deep the first time, and made the blood come out. "Yes," said the beaver, "I know you. You have done it too many times." The beaver then got some medicine, poured it on Coyote, healed him, and sent him on. He told him that he should not have the power any more; that his power was taken from him, for he had exercised it too many times. (Dorsey 1904c, 245–46)

This version of the Bungling Host suffers from one major intrinsic problem: an error in translation. We noted this sort of error in chapter 1, and it goes back a very long time—in fact, all the way back to antiquity—namely, the error of confusing the testicles of male beavers with their castor glands. A similar error has been committed in the Pawnee myth.

Indeed, the Pawnee version of the Bungling Host does not refer to a beaver's scrotum, any more than the Innu version refers to a beaver's testicles. The reason is simple and anatomical, as explained in this description:

> It is known that the beaver, whether male or female, has two pairs of glands in its anal region. One is a pair of musk glands, which it uses to mark its territory. The beaver extracts a liquid from them and spreads it on mounds of wood and plant debris it has made along the channels and trails it uses. . . . The other pair of glands it has secretes an oil . . .

> These musk glands have given rise to much confusion. The ancients took them for the animal's testicles—the actual testicles not being apparent from the exterior. To see them, the animal must be dissected. People have taken much time to detach themselves from this belief, as we will see now. (Gagnon 1994, 20–21)

This mistaken belief still haunts lexicographers and anthropologists who study the Innu. We have found another example in an Arikara version of the Bungling Host, which essentially contains the same error as the Pawnee and Innu versions: "Then Beaver lifted his leg up. Then he picked up an awl. Then he took hold of his testicles [*sic*], and then he pricked them. Oh, tallow came out. The liquid flowed onto the kindling. Then it became pemmican. Well, then while he stood there, he put the pemmican into a bowl for Coyote, and now Coyote ate" (Parks 1991, vol. 4, 695). False beliefs can be tenacious, especially longstanding ones.

It is also false to believe that a beaver has a scrotum. Its testicles "are located in the inguinal region under the skin but not in a true scrotum" (Siebold and Stannius 1850, vol. 3, 509). Nor does a beaver have a special pocket for its two pairs of glands. At the very most, these glands distend the skin in the cloacal region by their weight, thus indicating the presence of large organs underneath (up to 10 centimeters or longer for each castor gland, and the size of a big nut for each anal gland; Richard 1980, 52, 44).

As implicitly stated above, the sexes cannot be easily told apart without a thorough examination. This is pointed out by an Innu hunter from the Subarctic: "We can't tell the sex of the animal. There aren't many people who can. It's only once it's killed" (Ab. Mestokosho, Ekuanitshit). A European biologist, and beaver specialist, concurs:

> No *external sexual characteristic* can be used to tell the sexes apart easily. . . . The only certainty is provided by palpation of the sexual organs. For this, you should place the animal on its front feet . . . . Introduce your thumb into the cloaca. . . . Pull the thumb back. If it is a male, you will encounter its penis, whose end is "equipped" with a bone, the baculum, as big as a match. . . . Evidently, a female has no such thing. Although the presence of a baculum is a clear sign, its absence is less so and may only be a simple error by the examiner. . . .
>
> A more elegant, if not more practical, procedure is to observe the cloaca by X-ray imaging. Here again, error is possible if the penis is hidden in the shadow of the backbone. I found out the hard way, having received a "female" identified by this procedure at a well-known zoo. Her persistent intolerance of my male worried me, so I tested her with my thumb . . . only to discover that she belonged to the male sex. (Richard 1980, 14–16)

This point must be stressed to avoid any confusion. The Pawnee myth is misleading, or at least the English version that has come down to us. The main character may seem male, but this detail cannot help us find the etymon of the story because both sexes have very similar-sized pairs of glands in the cloacal region (Richard 1980, 52).

These glands are the ones used in the myth to make pemmican.

Here, beaver behavior may be likened to human behavior. Beavers have their own "meat"—in the myth, "dry driftwood that is rotten." Beavers eat trees, and there are always plenty of fallen trees or shrubs in the water or on land near a beaver colony. A beaver-occupied area is also always strewn with plant debris or wood chips, as attested by the "wood kindling" in the Arikara version of the same motif.

If these pieces of wood are the beaver's "meat" (in other chapters, Natives have likened pulverized wood to dried meat), the "grease" needed to make pemmican comes this time from the beaver's glands. Indeed, beavers are known to spray their musk onto mounds of mud and vegetation (Gagnon 1994, 20; Novak 1987, 296). One beaver family can erect up to one hundred mounds per year (Novak 1987, 296). Hence they must routinely mark such mounds by spraying castoreum (or oil from their anal glands). Such secretions can be smelled by anyone:

> [Castor glands] Upon close examination, fresh paw marks may be seen, and often the oily deposit of musky castoreum may be detected on fresh piles. (Banfield 1974, 159)

> [Anal glands] The anal glands. . . . The Germans call them "oil glands" because they contain a liquid or rather a thick, greasy unguent that has an unpleasant odour to the human sense of smell. (Richard 1980, 54)

This oily liquid must have likewise been noticeable to Natives, as we see when the myth describes the last stage of pemmican making. In his own way, Beaver makes it by adding a liquid to the driftwood, just as grease—often liquid grease—is added to dried and pulverized meat. All of these details serve in fact to draw attention to beaver behavior.

As for the rest, the Pawnee myth borrows materials from concomitant cultural traits, thus providing Pawnee listeners with points of reference they can identify with. When Coyote sets off on his journey, he slides a raccoon quiver over his back. The Pawnee must have

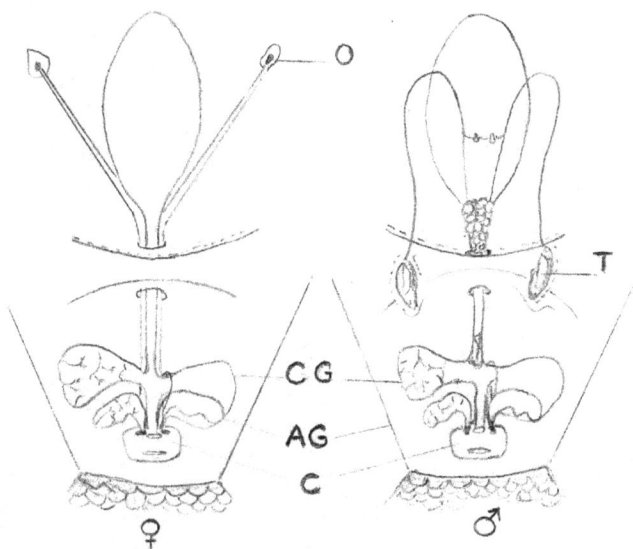

Fig. 40. Cloacal region (beaver). O: ovary; T: testicle;
CG: castor glands; AG: anal glands; C: cloaca.

used the skin of that small carnivore, *Procyon lotor*, as did other peoples, like the Quapaw of Arkansas (Young and Hoffman 2001, 506), the Osage of Arkansas (Bailey 2001, 479), and others who hunted raccoons as much for their fur as for their flesh. In general, Native Americans made quivers from the skin of many small carnivores (badger, marten, etc.). The Yurok of California, for instance, had raccoon quivers: "Throughout the area of fur-bearing animals the pelt of any one of them of sufficient size served as a quiver. . . . The Yurok quiver was made of the skin of the raccoon or marten turned wrongside out and suspended by a string" (Mason 1894, 668).

The same goes for the kinship ties that are established in the myth between Coyote and Beaver, and which make the latter a grandson of the former. On the one hand, many North American mythologies depict the Trickster as an elder to other animal species—unsurprisingly, since it represents a human—and a grandparent was assuredly an elder in Pawnee society. On the other hand, Beaver is a provider for Coyote, as beavers are in the natural state for humans: they provide meat, bones, and skin for dietary, technical, recreational, and ritual needs. In Pawnee society, grandparents played a key role in raising their grandchildren: "Both grandparents were more actively involved in training children than were parents" (Parks 2001, 534). The basic Pawnee social unit was the three-generation family: grandparents and particularly the grandmother, who coordinated the work of members of the group; the women of the next generation, who did most of the housework, while the women of the third generation specifically catered to the needs of the men who lived under the same roof; and finally the oldest men who busied themselves with the social and political life of the village, whereas the youngest men were the most capable hunters and warriors (Parks 2001, 533–34). Consequently, these men of the third generation provided the group with game meat. The situation is echoed in the myth—Beaver being the provider of Coyote—and also is similar in kinship ties—grandchild versus grandparent.

At the end of the story, Beaver uses his medicine to heal the

Trickster. Coyote has a very deep cut in his scrotum. The Pawnee had doctors' societies, and the members of each society had healing powers given by one animal: "At birth every Pawnee child came under the influence of a certain animal who was later to be his guardian. The identity of this animal became known either directly through a vision or, more frequently, by enabling a doctor who had power from that same animal to cure the person when he was ill" (Parks 2001, 537).

Undoubtedly the beaver was among the animals with healing powers, since "all animals, even insects, figured in the mythology of the doctors" (Parks 2001, 537). A traditional Pawnee ceremony in 1911 showed the beaver's importance, particularly in the doctors' societies:

> The first day's activities began with a tobacco offering intended to gain the notice of various deities important to the doctors. The water animals (such as the beaver, otter, and mink), who had been hibernating and whose breath has now broken the ice, were asked to breathe their power into the doctors and the beaver (skin) at the altar. . . .
>
> Three sets of offerings followed: smoke, corn, and meat, the offerings common to all Pawnee ceremonies. The first, and most elaborate, were the smoke offerings. . . . Through this offering, which was made to the beaver at the altar, new life was breathed into the beaver and power also passed from the beaver to the offerer, *Raruhwa:ku.* (Parks and Wedel 1985, 164)

People listening to the myth could identify with Beaver in other ways. A common first name in Pawnee society was 'Beaver': "Children were named by their parents soon after birth. In the selection of names they did not seem to be particularly solicitous, usually taking such as most readily suggested themselves, as *I'-cus* (Turtle), *Ki'-wŭk* (Fox), *Kit'-uks* (Beaver), etc." (Dunbar 1880, 270). Furthermore, the beaver was an emblem for entire clan groups: "These bands were all further divided into sub-bands and families, each of which had its appropriate mark or token. This was usually an animal, as the bear, the eagle, the hawk, the beaver, etc." (Dunbar 1880, 260). Thus, the myth reaches out to real people, in this case, those who are linked to one of its characters, i.e., Beaver.

Furthermore we should not be surprised that castoreum, i.e., the product of the castor glands, was a universal panacea for many peoples. Some even used it as an antiseptic for cuts. The literature on the Pawnee seems silent on this point, but such use is attested elsewhere:

> [Mi'kmaq, Northeast] Lescarbot describes in 1609 the Indian medicine man, Membertou, curing a wound by scarifying it, sucking it and then placing slices of the beaver's stones upon it. . . . It has long had a high repute as a medicine and contains salicin which is antiseptic and eases pain. (Erichsen-Brown 1980, xiii)

> [Innu, Subarctic] Castoreum applied directly to wounds to disinfect. (J. Bellefleur, Nutashkuan)

> [Mohegan, Northeast] For wounds and cuts the Mohegan Indians bandaged on a piece of beaver castor and left it on overnight. (Vogel 1970, 401)

If the Pawnee did use this medication the same way—and we have every reason to think so—the myth would then have been one of the ways to pass on this knowledge.

The second Pawnee story is constructed like the preceding one. This time, the host is Squirrel. We have titled it Squirrel and Coyote, and in the original version it comes after the Beaver and Coyote myth as part of a longer narrative about the Trickster's adventures, as we have already said.

SQUIRREL AND COYOTE

Coyote went home and stayed several days, until he got well. After that he took another trip through the timber. While he was going through a hollow there was a sound of "Hoo! Hoo!" directly above him. Somebody hallooed to him. "Grandfather, is it you?" said the voice. Coyote looked up and saw a great big male squirrel, eating pecans. So he called him down and told him that he was hard pressed and wanted something to eat. The squirrel came down. He said: "I can give you something to eat; but you are very tricky. You must do just as I tell you." Coyote said: "All right." So the squirrel stood at the bottom of the pecan-tree. He put one of his legs up against the tree so that his scrotum hung down, and he told the old man to cut his scrotum. He did so, and out poured a quantity of pecans, all ready to eat. Old Coyote began to eat them. Now he wanted more, but the squirrel would not give him any. Then Coyote wanted him to give him the same power that he had, to make the pecans. So the squirrel told Coyote he could do the same thing that he himself had done, but told him he must not do it often. So Coyote ran to his children and yelled, as he neared the tipi, for the woman to come there, for he was going to make something for them to eat. The woman came out, and went to where Coyote was standing. Coyote removed his breechcloth, lifted his left leg, and rested his foot upon a pecan-tree, so that his scrotum hung down. He told the old woman to get under him, get hold of his scrotum and cut it. She cut the scrotum, and as she squeezed it, pecans, all ready to eat, dropped out. He did this so many times that at last the woman, on cutting him, cut him too deep and hurt him, so that the blood came. He ran back to the place where the squirrels were, and he cried to them for help, and told his grandson that the first time he tried it, his wife cut him too deep, so that he bled. The squirrel cured him and took his power from him, so that he could not do that any more. (Dorsey 1904c, 246–47)

The mytheme "Squirrel slits open his scrotum" appears in one form or another in several other Native American mythologies. In a Dakota (Plains) version, a chipmunk gets rice by cutting open a testicle (Wallis 1923, 90). In an Omaha (Plains) version, Flying Squirrel produces nuts by puncturing his testicles (Dorsey 1890, 558). In several Ojibwa (Northeast) versions, a squirrel gets grease by piercing its testicles (Jones 1916, 390; 1917, 314, 341, 421). In a Menominee (Northeast) version, Red Squirrel gets rice from one testicle and grease from the other (Skinner and Satterlee 1915, 283).

Apart from the beaver that slits open its cloacal region—a mytheme now elucidated—members of the squirrel family seem to be the only animals in all of the Bungling Host versions we have come across (see appendix) whose testicles are a food source. So this mytheme must have originated in something specific to squirrel anatomy or behavior.

The Pawnee myth does not specify the squirrel species. Clearly, it is a tree squirrel, eats pecans, and may be drawn to an intruder's presence, since it comes down from the treetops to interact with Coyote. If we examine how the species of the squirrel family are distributed geographically, we see that two of them can meet the first criterion while being found on Pawnee territory, which has historically stretched across several states of the American Midwest and South (Nebraska and Kansas before 1876; Oklahoma thereafter). They are the eastern grey squirrel, *Sciurus carolinensis* (Koprowski 1994b), and the fox squirrel, *Sciurus niger* (Koprowski 1994a), both of which are tree-dwelling. A contemporary Pawnee dictionary confirms that these two are the only tree-dwelling species with specific names in that language: *ckipistarii'uus* and *ckipispakat* respectively (Parks and Pratt 2008, 293).

> [Grey Squirrel] He is alert and agile, spending much of his time in the trees, which he climbs and descends head first. (Woods 1980, 149)

> [Fox Squirrel] He is the largest and most heaviest of our tree dwellers. (Woods 1980, 155)

The same two species also have a diet that includes nuts, in particular pecans:

> [Eastern Gray Squirrel] Although *S. carolinensis* feed on as many as 97 plants and 14 animal items, 18 plant species account for 87% of the volume while 62% of stomachs contain only one food in Missouri . . . . Squirrels feed heavily on nuts, flowers, and buds of ≥24 oak species, 10 species of hickory and pecan, walnuts, and beech (*Fagus grandifolia*) when available. (Koprowski 1994b, 4)

[Fox Squirrel] Fox squirrels feed heavily on the nuts, flowers, and buds of ≥21 species of oak, 8 species of hickory and pecan (*Carya*), walnuts, beech (*Fagus grandifolia*) and longleaf pine when available. (Koprowski 1994a, 4)

Finally, it is said that at least one of them, the fox squirrel, comes down from the treetops whenever a possible source of danger appears, either to flee or simply to poke fun at the stranger:

At the approach of danger, he will sometimes drop from his tree and try to outrun the intruder. (Woods 1980, 157)

We once spent a riotous half-hour watching two fox squirrels plague a fat Pekinese at the foot of a big soft maple. . . . Hanging upside down on the tree trunk six feet above the ground, one of the squirrels barked, laughed and swore into the raging Peke's face. As this transpired, the second squirrel sneaked around the trunk only a foot or two above the ground, surprising the dog from the flank. [. . .] For over thirty minutes the two squirrels relayed the frothing little dog. (Madson in Wooding 1982, 174)

The Pawnee myth may therefore feature a fox squirrel, and all the more so because it is the larger of the two species.

All male squirrels have a true scrotum. Like all other members of the squirrel family, fox squirrels have intra-abdominal testicles when they are born and the scrotum not yet formed: "In late winter, when spring yearlings and old males breed, summer juveniles have the testes in the abdomen and the scrotum is entirely undeveloped" (Allen 1943, 125). The testicles subsequently descend and take their place behind the penis: "The testes of male fox and gray squirrels descend around 10 months of age; the scrotal sack becomes heavily pigmented, almost black, at 12 months of age. The testes remain descended and are located posterior to the penis" (Flyger and Gates 1982, 212). The testicles later go through annual cycles of seasonal development and regression: "Males [Fox Squirrel . . .] undergo an irregular cycle of testicular development; functional testes are pendant in the scrotum. Two annual peaks in male reproductive activity occur in November-February and May-July; however, functional males are found in all months [. . .]. A period of male sexual quiescence characterized by regressed testes, degenerated glands, and apparent cessation of spermatogenesis usually occurs August-October" (Koprowski 1994a, 3).

When male sexual activity is at its height, the testicles gain weight almost dramatically: "Active testes [in Fox Squirrel] averaged 6.9 g but inactive testes were 0.4 g" (Koprowski 1994a, 3). In addition, the squirrel mating season sees each testicle grow to a size of around 3 centimeters (2.2 to 3.55 centimeters; Mossman, Hoffman and Kirkpatrick 1955, 282). So they are comparable to pecans. Indeed, pecans and testicles can be the same in weight, size, and, probably, configuration. Squirrels eat pecans, and their testicles, being so prominent, are seen as a metonymy for their food. The Pawnee themselves undoubtedly ate pecans, which were very commonly consumed by Native Americans not only at southern latitudes but also at northern ones: "The species, *Carya illinoensis*, was distributed from its original home in the south throughout the northern part of the continent by the Indians who carried the pecans with them on their canoe trips and deliberately planted the biggest and thinnest shelled nuts at the main portages" (Erichsen-Brown 1980, 76). In fact, the pecan tree *Carya illinoensis* has its own name in the Pawnee language: *saahkisiikasa* (Parks and Pratt 2008, 233).

If we turn to the squirrels in other Native American versions of the same motif, we see them getting rice or grease from their testicles. Here, too, the etymons can be easily elucidated. A single example will suffice. In the Menominee (Northeast) version, an American red squirrel (*Tamiasciurus hudsonicus*) provides grease from one testicle and rice from the other: "'Simimik! Simimik! Simimik! Simimik!' sang Squirrel. Suddenly he stopped, and with his knife ripped open one testicle and out poured a lot of wild rice. . . . When Squirrel had finished his ceremony, and his wife had emptied the rice, she ran back under him with the dish. Again

Fig. 41. Male squirrel during the mating season.

Squirrel performed his magic. All at once he stopped and stabbed himself on the other side, and out ran a lot of grease and oil" (Skinner and Satterlee 1915, 283).

First of all, the Menominee harvested wild rice (*Zizania aquatica*), which was one of their food staples: "Early accounts describe the importance of wild rice as a food, and the techniques for harvesting were still used in the early twentieth century" (Spindler 1978, 708). Their name, Menominee, attests to this importance: "The name Menominee . . . derives from the Ojibwa *mano.mini.* . . . , etymologically 'wild rice people'" (Spindler 1978, 723).

Second, squirrels are known to be voracious omnivores, and

Native Americans must have seen them as a serious threat to storage of wild rice harvests. Even today, these rodents are a real pest for farmers: "On forest homesteads they [American red squirrels] are occasionally agricultural pests, stealing corn and grain from cribs and granaries" (Banfield 1974, 140).

Finally, to top it off, the red squirrel's testicles, like those of other members of the squirrel family, when seen in cross-section, look to the naked eye like many little tubes oozing out a viscous fluid. We think right away of rice: a series of tubules stuck to each other, pasty when cooked: "When the tubules are clearly visible to the naked eye abundant sperm is invariably present. The presence of sperm is also indicated when a copious amount of viscous fluid exudes from the tubules when they are severed" (Layne 1954, 243).

We should also mention the grease that also covers the testicles and which increases with seasonal development of the gonads. There are detailed observations for the California ground squirrel (*Spermophilus beecheyi*), which should apply to other squirrels: "The first male examined in 1942, with testes not fully scrotal. . . . Almost no fat deposit was detected on any part of the body. In another individual trapped the same day, the testes were scrotal. . . . Fat deposits on the mesorchium [a residual fold of peritoneum between the testes and epididymis] were heavy" (Linsdale 1946, 308). We rest our case. Squirrel can get "grease" and "rice" from his testicles. Why these two ingredients? The reason may go back to an old Native American dish briefly described by a seventeenth-century Jesuit: "Father Dablon, in the Relation of 1671, says: 'The fat of the buffalo mixed with wild oats [*folle avoine* in the original version, i.e. wild rice] makes the most delicate dish of this country'" (Stickney 1896, 119; see D'Ablon in Thwaites 1910, vol. 55, 197). The Jesuit Claude d'Ablon was referring to the Fire Nation, a term used for all Algonquians on the Lower Peninsula of Michigan, who were eastern neighbors of the Menominee (Clifton 1978, 742). *Folle avoine* was the French term for wild rice.

At the end of the Menominee version, Squirrel heals the Trickster by dressing his wound with dirt: "Squirrel immediately got up and took some dirt which he rubbed on the wound and healed it" (Skinner and Satterlee 1915, 284). The nature of this "dirt" is unknown to us. The Pawnee version does not specify the treatment, but we know that the Pawnee considered all animals to be healers and, presumably, they would have felt the same about Squirrel. Ethno-medical data are lacking, but it would be interesting to know whether testicles from squirrels or other members of the squirrel family were used to dress wounds in some Native American societies, as castor glands were.

If we look at the Pawnee version of the motif with Squirrel as the host, we see that it rests on the same kinship ties (grandparent / grandchild) as does the motif with Beaver. We have already substantiated these ties. Both motifs share one thing that sets them apart from the overwhelming majority of other Native American versions of the Bungling Host. Both have the Trickster doing his imitation with his own family and not with his former host after inviting him over. That sort of storyline is fairly rare. It is absent from the other versions we know from other peoples.

We ascribe this peculiarity to the Pawnee versions being closer to the basic model of the Bungling Host, which is premised on the Trickster representing a human. If these versions are indeed closer, they may convey a meaning that humans get food solely to feed their kind—unlike animals, which feed not only themselves but also humans. Animals make an offering of themselves, which is a belief that we have already discussed and which is openly stated in many societies. Among the Pawnee, it appears in an origin myth whose hero, Patsaa, is instructed by animals in the arts of healing and sorcery. Two or three animals were the enemies of Man and initially wanted to kill and eat the hero, but they were opposed by others who provided Man with their meat: "But the elk (moose, *pax*) at the southwest said, 'Now, you wait. Since you folks could eat him and I can't, I have something to say. I'm the one that supports him and helps him to live.' Just as he got through talking, someone about halfway south, the Beaver, spoke up. 'He's right. I can't eat him either. I also support him and helps him live.' Near the southeast the reindeer said the same thing" (Weltfish 1971 [1965], 404–5).

These deductions are corroborated by another element, generally absent from the other versions (we will see another example in the next chapter). It is a lapse rich in meaning. When Coyote gets ready to slit open his scrotum, he first takes off his breechcloth: "Coyote removed his breechcloth, lifted his left leg, and rested his foot upon a pecan-tree, so that his scrotum hung down." To our knowledge, such an action is never—or at least very seldom—attributed to the main host. This description of a Trickster is rare but in line with the underlying human reality, which differs from the one evoked by cutting up a wife's clothing to feed a guest, as we saw with myths that featured members of the deer family. Clothing as a metonymy for flesh or grease differs from the action of removing a breechcloth.

Pawnee men wore such clothing, as did many other Native Americans: "The main clothes [of the men] were a loincloth, leggings, and moccasins" (Weltfish 1971 [1965], 454). By acting this way, the Trickster shows his real nature in contrast to his hosts, who are real animals and whose behaviors are portrayed either strangely or in a familiar form.

In summary, the two Pawnee myths we have examined seem constructed the same way but are nonetheless based on completely distinct etymons. The first myth, the one with Beaver, teaches its listeners about castor glands. The second myth teaches them about the real testicles or scrotum of a squirrel. In either case, the glands are in the same area of the body. This may confuse some of us, although the presence of castor glands in female beavers should indicate the different origins of these myths. Caution is thus needed when we examine versions of Native American myths that have come down to us. Errors in translation, like the ones we have seen, if not elucidated, may cause serious errors in interpretation.

17 Duck Excretes Rice (Northeast)

On entering in, (he saw) a man that was seated there, likewise a woman and their children. He was addressed: "Welcome! Be seated!" was told Nänabushu. Then up spoke the man: "What have we to offer the guest (to eat)? Well, anyhow, hang up (a kettle of) water!" he said to the woman. . . . And while the man was seated, up he flew, and was heard to say, "Kwänk, kwänk, kwänk!". . . And then yonder upon the cross-pole (above the fire) he alighted, being heard to say, "Kwänk, kwänk!". . . Oh, how strange that when he muted into the kettle, he was saying, "Come on, pay no heed, but keep it stirring!" Truly she stirred it. And while she was stirring it, lo, very full of rice was the kettle there; and it was cooked dry. "All right! now take it off the fire." And then down he flew, alighting. "Now, this is only a way I have whenever I want to eat." It happened to be a Mallard whom he had come to visit.

—William Jones, "Ojibwa Texts"

Rice is produced not just by Squirrel—who, as we saw among the Menominee and the Dakota, slit open his testicles to get wild rice. In those Bungling Host myths where the host gets wild rice, this task is assigned much more often to ducks than to squirrels. As to be expected, these versions come from peoples within the geographic range of wild rice (*Zizania aquatica*), which grows only in the central and eastern parts of North America from the Great Lakes to the St. Lawrence and along the eastern seaboard to Florida. It is most common in those states and provinces with the most inland bodies of fresh water: "The best stands of wild rice are found along the margins of tide water rivers of the Middle Atlantic states, above the saline zone and, more particularly, in the myriad of shallow lakes and ponds, and the numerous sluggish streams broadening occasionally into marshes in northern Minnesota and Wisconsin, and in adjacent areas in Ontario and Manitoba" (Steeves 1952, 112).

Among the Native peoples of the Great Lakes, we know that wild rice gathering mattered the most economically to some Algonquians (Menominee, Potawatomi, Sauk, Fox, Mascoutin, Ojibwa, Ottawa, etc.) and also to some Iroquoians (Wyandot) and Sioux (Dakota) (Jenks 1898). Indeed, this chapter opens with an excerpt from an Ojibwa myth about a rice-producing duck, a motif that most often appears in Ojibwa versions (Radin 1914, 14, 15; Jones 1917, 317–21, 351–57; Speck 1915a, 40–41). We also have variants from the Sauk (Skinner 1928, 148) and the Fox (Jones 1907, 257–59, 261–63), and some elements from those ones will be used in our analysis.

The action of this mytheme is defecation, but not necessarily defecation of rice. In other Bungling Host myths, the final product may be something else: corn in a Plains Cree story (Bloomfield 1934, 299) and berries in a Kwakiutl story from the Northwest Coast (Boas 1969 [1910], 237). In the second myth, the host himself changes. All of these versions can be reduced to three permutations:

duck   → defecation → rice

duck   → defecation → corn

thrush → defecation → berries

The last two will be discussed towards the end of the chapter.

The Ojibwa myth that opens this chapter has come to us in its original language with a translation by the person who took it down. It is part of a series of Bungling Host myths, which, except for this one, we have already commented on: Beaver kills his children and throws their bones into the water (two texts); Skunk shoots animals (two texts); Duck excretes rice (two texts including the following); Kingfisher catches fish with his bill (one text); and Woodpecker pierces a hole (one text). The Ojibwa story of the Duck appears below in full with its original title. The Trickster is personified by Nänabushu (Nanabozho, Manabozho, etc.), the best-known hero of Algonquian mythologies (Fisher 1946, 230–31). His name seems to have no clear origin, although he is sometimes associated with another hero called 'Great Hare.'

NÄNABUSHU AND THE MALLARD

When the morrow was come, then off he went on a hunt for game, but not a thing did he kill. Continually without result did he hunt, and, in spite of all he could do, nothing did he kill. Thereupon very hungry did he become. Then on the morrow away went Nänabushu, it was to wander from place to place visiting (old friends). Once he came upon the footprints of some people, in whose trail he then followed. When some distance farther on he was come, he saw where they lived. On entering in, (he saw) a man that was seated there, likewise a woman and their children. He was addressed: "Welcome! Be seated!" was told Nänabushu.

Then up spoke the man: "What have we to offer the guest (to eat)? Well, anyhow, hang up (a kettle of) water!" he said to the woman.

Truly, then a kettle did the woman hang up. And while the man was seated, up he flew, and was heard to say, "Kwänk, kwänk, kwänk!" (such) was what he uttered. And then yonder upon the cross-pole (above the fire) he alighted, being heard to say, "Kwänk, kwänk!" (such) was the sound he uttered. Oh, how strange that when he muted into the kettle, he was saying, "Come on, pay no heed, but keep it stirring!"

Truly she stirred it. And while she was stirring it, lo, very full of rice was the kettle there; and it was cooked dry. "All right! now take it off the fire." And then down he flew, alighting. "Now, this is only a way I have whenever I want to eat." It happened to be a Mallard whom he had come to visit. After the Mallard was seated, "Come, into a vessel do you put it!" he said to the woman, "and very full do you fill it."

Truly, the woman filled up the bowl.

"All right, Nänabushu, do you eat!"

Nänabushu then began eating. When his desire for food was quite appeased, then he ceased (eating).

"Is that all you are going to eat?"

"And how am I to force (myself) to eat (more)?"

"Nänabushu, therefore then do you take back to them at home the rest of the cooked food. Perhaps to your children do you take it home."

Nänabushu then spoke, saying: "It is now time for me to go back home." And so, when no one was looking, in under the mat he pushed his mittens. When he went outside, then near by did he tarry.

And this was what the man said: "Please do not carry to Nänabushu his mittens."

And so, truly, he did not have them fetched to him. Already was Nänabushu becoming tired of waiting to have them brought to him. Then with a loud voice he called: "I have forgotten my mittens!" He was not harkened to. Then with a louder voice he called. At last, "Well, go take them to him; from afar do you throw him his mittens."

Presently he saw the boys. "Why, come you up close! And so it is a fact that you are without food. I am not hungry. To-morrow let your father come over exactly at noon." Thereupon away then went Nänabushu. When he was come at where he lived, truly pleased were his children to have food to eat, so the same with his wife; thoroughly were they satisfied with food. On the morrow he then waited for his guest, he waited for him at noon. Soon he was come. When he was seated, "What have we to feed the guest? Anyway, hang up the kettle."

To be sure, the wife of Nänabushu hung up the (kettle of) water.

"With much wood do you build up the fire, soon let the kettle boil." Aha! now, while Nänabushu was yet seated, up he sprang, being heard to say: "Kwänk, kwänk, kwänk!" (such) was the sound Nänabushu uttered. It was a great while before Nänabushu was able to mount the cross-pole (over the fire). After he was perched up there on the cross-pole, then with much effort did he grunt in vainly trying to ease himself; he could not do it. But when by and by a lump of solid dung dropped into the kettle, he addressed his wife, saying: "Never mind! But keep it stirring."

Then said the woman: "Mercy sake, vile dog! you will simply ruin our kettle." Accordingly, to her feet the woman quickly rose; immediately down she took the kettle; straightway out of doors she went on her way to empty out the water. After she had cleansed their kettle, then back inside came the woman. Nänabushu was still perched upon the cross-pole (over the fire). He was not able by his own efforts to climb down. Then he spoke to his wife, saying: "Not at all am I able, in spite of my own efforts, to climb down."

Truly very angry was the woman, she was in search of something to use for a club, the woman presently found a stick. While Nänabushu was perched up there, the woman said: "Look and see! for I am going to club him to death who eased himself in the kettle."

When Nänabushu was about to be struck, then from yonder place he fell; he leaped down when she made as if to hit him.

Alas! without cheer there sat the guest. Very anxious was he to eat. Whereupon he said: "Now, forget every thing and hang up your kettle."

Truly, the woman hung up their kettle; presently it began boiling.

At that moment up flew (the guest) from his place, and was heard saying: "Kwänk, kwänk, kwänk," (such) was the sound he uttered. Thereupon he alighted yonder on the cross-pole (over the fire) at the same time that he was heard saying: "Kwänk, kwänk," (such) was the sound he uttered. By him while muting were they addressed: "Never you mind! only do you keep it stirring."

Thereupon, truly, as they kept it stirring, how wondrously full the rice filled (the kettle), and how dry it cooked!

"Now it is time to take it off (the fire)."

Truly off the fire the woman took it.

And so with disappointment forth from the place went their guest. Whereupon then did Nänabushu (and his family) eat. (Jones 1917, 351–57)

Like all of the other myths, this one belongs to a specific cultural context, as shown by several referents. One is the home. The southwestern Ojibwa—who provide the above myth—mainly lived in wigwams: "The most common dwelling was the dome-shaped wigwam. This consisted of a pole framework covered with birchbark and cattail matting" (Ritzenthaler 1978, 748). At the center of the wigwam was a fireplace with a cross-pole set in place below the smoke hole and from which kettles would hang: "The fire place was in the middle of the lodge, being outlined by logs. A short pole was fastened across the smoke hole, and on this pole pieces of meat were hung to dry above the fire. Hooks to hold kettles were commonly made of crotch sticks of green wood and suspended from this pole by strips of green bark" (Densmore 1929, 24).

This is the same cross-pole on which the host and Nänabushu successively alight to produce or try to produce rice. In both cases (Duck's rice-making and the Trickster's failure to imitate), the wife has the job of hanging the kettle, pouring water into it, making the fire, stirring the rice, serving it, and so on. This is the second cultural element, and it refers to a widespread division of labor among Native Americans. The different sex roles are already shown by the traditional seating arrangements of men and women in an Ojibwa wigwam. This social fact appears in the myth and has been described elsewhere in more detail: "The man sat 'cross-legged.' He said this position was the most convenient for a man's work. The woman 'sat on her right foot' with the left foot extending out at one side. She said that in this position a woman could rise easily to 'reach things'" (Densmore 1929, 30).

The myth mentions the sitting position of the Trickster's wife: "to her feet the woman quickly rose" to clean the kettle her husband had just soiled.

The wife also did the cooking in Ojibwa society. As in the myth, she cooked and served the food: "It was said by some informants that only one meal a day was prepared. . . . The meal was cooked and served by the mother, who sat next the door of the lodge" (Densmore 1929, 40).

In another version from the Ojibwa, the host and the guest talked for a long while before Duck offered the Trickster any food: "He [Duck-Bill] was a very pleasant person and set about to make Manabozho as comfortable as he could. The two men told stories for a considerable time. Then Duck-Bill said to his wife, 'Prepare the cooking utensils and get the stones four times their usual heat for cooking'" (Radin and Reagan 1928, 82–83). When the time came for the guest to imitate his host, the storyteller adds: "After their arrival the two men sat and told stories for several hours" (Radin and Reagan 1928, 83).

Indeed, it was customary for Ojibwa to visit each other regularly and carry on long conversations: "Social life was marked by a great penchant for visiting. Besides calling on relatives and friends, there was considerable visiting and conversation before and after religious feasts and ceremonials" (Ritzenthaler 1978, 752).

In the variant that opens this chapter, Nänabushu pretends to have forgotten his mittens. This too is a key cultural element. It refers not only to an everyday piece of clothing but also to a season: winter, the time of year when myths are told: "There was a rich store of folklore. Serious and humorous, that were told in the wintertime both to entertain and to teach ethical precepts" (Ritzenthaler 1978, 757).

In the last chapter, we stressed that the Trickster is actually a human. This is seldom explicit in Bungling Host myths, although the last chapter explicitly reveals his humanness when he takes off a loincloth before slitting his testicles open, as does this chapter when he hides his mittens and pretends to have forgotten them.

This being said, the opening myth of this chapter portrays the host as a mallard even though in most versions the species is not specified beyond the generic term 'duck' or 'waterfowl.' In one variant, the host is identified differently, as an American black duck, *Anas rubripes* (Speck 1915a, 40). A related Ojibwa mytheme, quoted above, calls the host Duck-Bill and describes him taking rice from a field and bringing it back in his mouth (Radin and Reagan 1928, 83). That detail would be trivial had the myth not also specified that this duck feeds on rice, as opposed to a diving duck that feeds on the mud of river and lake bottoms. We learn this at the end of the story when the Trickster, trying to imitate, manages only to bring back mud in his mouth instead of rice:

MANABOZHO CHANGES HIMSELF INTO A DUCK
(EXCERPT)

So Manabozho changed himself into a big clumsy duck and flew off to the rice fields of a distant lake and was soon heard flying back with a buzzing, whizzing voice. He got right over his wigwam and started to descend to light, but not being a duck he lost his balance and fell and nearly killed himself. But he got up and staggered to the tray and spit out what he had brought for the feast from the lake. And lo! It was just sour mud. Quickly it swelled till it filled the tray and had such an odor that instead of throwing the hot stones into it to cook it, his wife took the tray out of the wigwam and threw its content out. —Manabozho had changed himself into a mud-diver instead of a rice duck. (Radin and Reagan 1928, 83–84)

The term 'mud-diver' alludes to the northern shoveler, *Anas clypeata*, which has several related common names (see below). It is indeed a mud-feeding bird.

If we review studies on various ducks and geese and their diet, we can clearly see that the northern shoveler does not eat wild rice, although it ranges over a territory where this plant is known to grow. In a study published in 1911 (Steeves 1952, 137) on the stomach contents of sixteen waterfowl species, no trace of *Zizania aquatica* was found in samples from forty-eight northern shovelers. The largest amounts of wild rice were from mallard stomachs. The results are listed here for the first three species by order of importance:

Table 13. Stomach contents of three waterfowl species

		NUMBER OF STOMACHS EXAMINED	PERCENT OF CONTENTS COMPOSED OF WILD RICE
MALLARD	*Anas platyrhynchos*	209	17.13%
BLACK DUCK	*Anas rubripes*	51	12.05%
WOOD DUCK	*Aix sponsa*	75	11.62%

The northern shoveler's diet has thus a high proportion of mud. One researcher provides some details:

> Popularly the Spoonbill is reputed to feed upon mud and three of the local names of the bird emphasize this belief, namely, "mud duck," "mud lark," and "mud shoveller." With respect to mud, the pure thing itself, can scarcely be considered as nutritious, but the material referred to in common parlance as the pabulum of mud-eaters, is bottom ooze composed largely of more or less decayed

vegetable debris often containing large numbers of minute plants and animals such as diatoms and ostracods. . . . The Spoonbill takes more of this kind of food than other ducks. (McAtee 1922, 381)

Assuredly, after eating "macerated plant debris" (McAtee 1922, 383), a northern shoveler must give off a putrid, muddy smell—quite unlike that of rice-eating ducks, which, as will be seen farther on, are considered true delicacies. This is what the myth seeks to show, among other things.

But there is more. The Trickster has other reasons for his false disguise, and the myth thus highlights other differences between the duck species. Although this Bungling Host variant from the Ojibwa does not clearly identify the host, other than by the common generic name of Duck-Bill, everything points to the duck being a mallard. This would explain two identifying marks of the Trickster's disguise. First, the rice-eating mallard and the mud-eating northern shoveler have something in common that sets both apart from all other ducks and geese of the Great Lakes region—the male's head is entirely green:

"[Mallard] *Adult male*: Green head." (Godfrey 1966, 55)

"[Shoveler] *Adult male (breeding plumage)*: Head and most of the neck, dark green." (Godfrey 1966, 63)

Second, the end of the bill is much broader in the northern shoveler than in any other duck: "Bill longer than head, much wider at end than at base. . . . The long bill is distinctive in both males and females at all seasons" (Godfrey 1966, 63–64).

With these two identifying marks in hand, we can easily imagine how the Trickster may have fooled himself. By nature, he exaggerates everything. So from the mallard he keeps the green color of the head and its bill (Duck-Bill); he chooses the same color but gives himself an inordinately large bill, like a northern shoveler's bill. Both ducks have green heads, and a neophyte could easily mistake one for the other. Finally, the myth reports that

Fig. 42. A flock of ducks in a rice field.

the Trickster looks like a clumsy duck in his disguise, which is a characteristic of the shoveler. Such details—the kind that tells animals apart—matter a lot to Native Americans.

If we go beyond the mytheme that opens this chapter, we have other variants that clearly identify the mallard and which tell us more about the bird, including its behavior. One variant specifically mentions its green head: "Presently the man painted himself with a green color, all around over his head did he put it" (Jones 1917, 317). Further on, for the Trickster: "He had his green paint spread out; in painting himself he colored his head green" (Jones 1917, 319). In the same version, the sounds made before flying off are rendered this way: "'Kwīsh, kwīsh, kwīsh, kwīsh!' (such) was the sound of his voice. Up flew a Mallard that alighted yonder on the cross-pole" (Jones 1917, 317).

The variant that opens this chapter gives no details on the bird's color, and the host, likewise a mallard, is given a different call: "'Kwänk, kwänk, kwänk!' (such) was the sound he uttered" (Jones 1917, 351). Why do we see these differences between two Ojibwa versions gathered by the same anthropologist—two variants that otherwise match?

An author who has written a book about the Ojibwa and wild rice (Vennum 1988) reports the same myths and offers this interpretation of the first variant: "This author interprets painting the body green as the transformation into green, or ripe, rice and the 'kwish' sounds as those made during harvest" (Vennum 1988, 63).

Such an interpretation is open to question. This variant, despite its ambiguity (painting of the entire body or only the head?), nonetheless stresses the greenness of the head in particular. In all of the Bungling Host myths we have analyzed so far, a specific body part is involved when the host paints himself or when the Trickster tries to imitate the host's adornment (e.g., Wolverine trying to imitate Woodpecker by using a sharp object to make himself a bill). It is thus more than probable that the green color in the Ojibwa myth denotes a characteristically green part of the animal. Such is the case, since male mallards typically have green heads. This is not metonymy.

Secondly, in all variants of the mytheme, the vocalizations, whenever reported, are closely associated with the descriptions of the same ducks. In the last variant, the mallard is a male because it has a green head and makes the onomatopoeic sound *kwïsh*. In the variant that opens this chapter, no specific color is mentioned, and the vocalization is *kwänk*. Now, male and female mallards vocalize differently. An ornithologist sums up the difference in a way that recalls how the myths make a contrast between the male with its high-pitched voice and green head and the female with its hoarser voice and non-green head: "A rather loud *quack* is given by the female. The male's voice is similar but softer and higher pitched" (Godfrey 1966, 55).

Ornithologists sometimes describe the male as making a rasping sound (Drilling, Titman, and McKinney 2002, 12), although the onomatopoeias they use to spell out these sounds (*raehb* being the most common one) differ from those of the Native American myth. This would not be the first time. Nonetheless, the *kwänk* is undoubtedly female (the bird has no green head), so the *kwïsh* is most likely male. Moreover, in the only other version where the mallard has no specific color, a hoarse voice is attributed to the host, presumably a female: "[Fox version] 'Hang up the water,' said the Duck to her as he began walking round in a circle. 'Kwän, kwän!' and then he began streaming mute" (Jones 1907, 257; see also 263). The rest is just words. Whoever might see a contradiction in a female mallard asking its wife to prepare the cooking fire is mistaking generic for gender. Although the duck is perceived anthropomorphically in the myth, the lesson is not about its sexual identity but rather about its morphology, behavior, and other traits.

Turning to complementary details that appear in one version or another of the same mytheme, let us return to the details of walking around in a circle, flying off, and alighting above the fire, as well as the wings of ducks. The wings need no comment, being so obvious. They are especially highlighted in an Ojibwa version, where the Trickster breaks one when trying to alight, and the host fixes it for him: "Duck-Bill was tying up Manabozho's broken wing and sprained ankle and making him as comfortable as he could. When he had dressed all the wounds he turned to Manabozho's wife and said, 'Clean out the tray and I will get you something to eat'" (Radin and Reagan 1928, 84).

In the variant that opens this chapter, the host flies off and alights on the cross-pole from which the kettle hangs over the fire. The other variants are very similar: either the Duck "jumps" from where it sits to alight on the rim of the kettle in the Sauk version (Skinner 1928, 148) or it flies up rather brusquely, as in one of many Ojibwa versions: "And while yet seated, and of a sudden, he started forth from the place, uttering: 'Kwīsh, kwīsh, kwīsh,

kwīsh!' (such) was the sound of his voice. Up flew a Mallard that alighted yonder on the cross-pole" (Jones 1917, 317).

It is known that a mallard can fly practically straight up ("[The Mallard] can spring vertically from water surface when alarmed"; Drilling, Titman, and McKinney 2002, 12) and that it can occasionally perch high in the air: "[The Mallard] does not regularly alight in trees, but can perch on elevated sites under special circumstances" (Drilling, Titman, and McKinney 2002, 12).

But the most intriguing detail is one where the duck walks around in a circle before defecating. It is reported only in one of the two Fox versions we know: ""I wonder what we can cook for him?" the Duck said to his wife. 'Hang up the water,' said the Duck to her as he began walking round in a circle. 'Kwän, Kwän!' and then he began streaming mute. All the while the Duck woman kept stirring with the ladle till at last she was hardly able to keep on with the stirring of the rice" (Jones 1907, 257).

The Trickster imitates him point by point: "'I wonder what we should cook for him?' said Wisa'kä. 'Hang up the water,' he said to his grandmother. As he began walking round in a circle, he began a stream of dung. It simply was nothing but his own dung that kept dropping into the water" (Jones 1907, 259). Is walking in a circle a female trait? Remember, the quacking clearly identifies the host in this version as a female mallard. Or is this trait generic, something that all mallards do? The literature describes various circling motions by mallards of either sex:

> I have seen as many as three males in ardent pursuit of one female flying about, high in the air, circling over the marshes in rapid flight and quacking loudly. (Bent et al. 1962, 35)

> The performance usually begins by four or five drakes swimming round a duck with their heads sunk, and their necks drawn back. (Bent et al. 1962, 35)

In the Native American way of thinking, a circular motion is so widely associated with waterfowl locomotion on land, in water, and in the air that it shows up in many major myths. We are thus dealing with a Native expression of knowledge. Such myths are very widespread, particularly among the Algonquians (Fisher 1946), and always feature the Trickster with waterfowl. Some of them tell how the Trickster cunningly captures ducks by inviting them to a *round* dance, during which he kills his guests after telling them to keep their eyes always closed (see Savard 1972 for Innu versions). In other myths, the Trickster joins waterfowl in their migratory flight, and the birds ask him to *circle* with them above the homes of humans (see Fisher 1946, 244 for versions from the Cree, the Ojibwa, the Sauk, and other peoples). Finally, still other myths describe another of the Trickster's tricks for getting waterfowl: he ties their feet together underwater while the birds paddle *around and around* on the surface. This motif appears in the following Ojibwa version: "When the ducks saw Manabozho standing near the shore, they swam toward him and as soon as he saw this, he sent his grandmother ahead to build a little lodge, where they could live. In the meantime, he killed a few of the ducks, so, while his grandmother started out to build a shelter, Manabozho went towards the lake where the ducks and geese were floating around and around" (Radin in Thompson 1966 [1929], 53).

Several of these peoples have also waterfowl-inspired dances that involve going around and around to the sound of music, like this goose dance reported by Leonard Mason, which is not unrelated to the preceding myth: "Always arranged in conjunction with a great feast to ensure good hunting in the months to follow, the dancers mimicked the actions and calls of the birds which were tricked by *wisaketchak*. . . . While men and women join the circling dancers to imitate the wildfowl in actions and calls, a conjurer who sits near the wall sings and beats a primitive rhythm on his drum" (Mason in Meyer 1987, 442).

This takes us to the central motif, the mytheme of rice-excreting Duck. Wild rice was important in Native American societies of the Great Lakes and elsewhere too, a point already shown. It is still gathered today, and several books have been written on it (Jenks 1898; Vennum 1988). It was a staple among the Ojibwa: "The principle vegetable foods were wild rice, corn, and maple sugar. Rice was the staple article of food and was boiled in water or in broth, as well as parched" (Densmore 1929, 39).

Some of these peoples would sow rice (Jenks 1898, 1057). Rice was gathered in autumn, the stalks being sometimes bound into bundles until the grain had ripened, to keep birds of all kinds, including waterfowl, from endangering the future harvest by over-feeding. This was also a way for each family to mark its territory. Each family had its own way of binding the bundles.

Rice was harvested from a boat. Generally, the men moved the canoe with a paddle or a pole, while the women harvested the rice by bending the stalks down with one hand and threshing the seeds into the canoe with the other. There were several ways of doing this, depending on the group:

> Again, as in the tying of the stalks, the canoe is indispensable in the grain-gathering. At times a blanket is spread in the bottom; the canoe is propelled by a paddle, a pole, or a forked stick, sometimes the canoeman propels the canoe from the stern and sometimes from the bow. The grain may be gathered into the canoe by one person, who may hold the stalks in one hand and beat the grain out with a stick, or with two sticks, or sometimes with a paddle; or two persons may gather the rice, one holding the stalks over the canoe while the other beats out the grain with a pole. (Jenks 1898, 1064)

The unhusked rice grains were next dried in the sun or over a fire. Dehusking was done manually. A hole was dug in the ground and covered with a skin. The grains were placed on top, and generally a man stamped on them until the grains separated from their husks. The women next did the sieving with a birchbark tray.

Rice is undoubtedly linked to waterfowl, including mallards and black ducks. First, these birds eat a lot of rice, and a lot is

Fig. 43. Wild rice gatherers.

no overstatement: 17% of their diet according to one study, mentioned above; up to 60% according to the work of an ornithologist
(Stoudt 1944, 109). The proportion must have been higher still in
earlier natural environments. Second, duck hunting always went
together with rice gathering.

> In addition to being an important article of food for himself and
> his family, wild rice served the Indian of former days in another
> way. It attracted vast numbers of wild fowl of every sort, and thus
> brought to him another great food-supply. The fondness which
> these birds evince for wild rice is well known, and to this day in
> northern Wisconsin they can be found in considerable numbers only
> on waters where it abounds. The accounts of early travelers fairly
> teem with descriptions of the vast quantities of birds to be seen

hovering around the *Zizania* and the ease with which they might be killed. The birds were in the finest condition after feeding on the rice, "inexpressibly fat and delicious." The rice not only served as a decoy, but also as a blind, the Indian easily concealing himself in the thick masses and sometimes being able to kill the birds with a club. (Stickney 1896, 120)

This means that when cutting up a duck that had been gorging on rice, one could theoretically find rice grains practically throughout its digestive tract from its mouth to its droppings, including its gizzard, its stomach (= proventriculus) or its cecum.

Wild rice (*Zizania palustris* and *Z. aquatica*) in every stage of its growth is eaten by one or another of the North American ducks and geese, and practically all of them feed on its ripened grain. . . . The seeds are obtained mainly from the bottom in shallow water, where they have fallen into a bed of soft muck to await germination. Germination is often so delayed that grain may sprout at any time up to at least 18 months after ripening. This accounts for the fact that young shoots and germinating seeds of wild rice are found in ducks' stomachs at practically all seasons. (McAtee 1917, 4)

The myths about ducks and rice exploit these possibilities. One of them relates how Duck brings back rice grains in his mouth to feed his guest, the Trickster. A more generic myth portrays rice as a gift that ducks gave to humans.

THE ORIGIN OF RICE

The other tale of the origin of wild rice is taken from a series of experiences of Wenibojo'. One evening he returned from hunting, but he had no game. As he came toward his fire he saw a duck sitting on the edge of his kettle of boiling water. After the duck flew away Wenibojo' looked into the kettle and found wild rice floating upon the water, but he did not know what it was. He ate his supper from the kettle, and it was the best soup that he had ever tasted. (Jenks 1898, 1094)

This myth too is Ojibwa. It brings to mind a similar Kawaiisu myth (chapter 3) about a house finch, and how this little bird ends up above a pot of boiling water with rice-like suds on the surface. In that case too, we showed the bird's close relationship with the seed-bearing plant that it feeds on and which the Kawaiisu likewise consume, not to mention the fact that the bird is always near water.

These two myths are instructive. They undoubtedly tell us something about how humans came to consume rice and other grains. If we replace the pot of boiling water with a body of water in the Ojibwa version, for example, we get the initial vision that Native Americans would have had of ducks feeding on rice. Such feeding may have subsequently been imitated and then developed by cooking. Indeed, in the above myth, Duck produces wild rice but does not cook it. The human does.

The Ojibwa myth likewise brings to mind another myth, this time from the Northwest Coast, where a singing bird becomes a berry "producer" (chapter 4), just as the Ojibwa duck is a rice "producer." In fact, the same idea underlies both mythemes. Do the berries attract the birds or do the birds "attract" the berries? The same goes for ducks and rice. Do rice fields indicate the presence of ducks or do many ducks seen from far off indicate the presence of rice fields? The second interpretation may be justified in two ways. First, Native Americans reverse cause and effect in their myths (and elsewhere) as a rhetorical device—to create a strange atmosphere that helps listeners memorize the knowledge being passed on. Second, ducks can indeed propagate aquatic or semi-aquatic plants, like wild rice.

We will begin with the reversal of cause and effect. Minnesota hunters notice how flocks of ducks and fields of rice tend to go together: "Local veteran hunters believe that wild rice (*Zizania aquatica*) is the most attractive duck food. Ranger Mel Cummins at Cass Lake, stated that this plant is the sole factor in determining whether a big flight of mallards will pass through the Chippewa area. This opinion extends also to the local crop of mallards and other puddle ducks; if the rice crop is poor or lacking, the ducks are thought to leave the area in quest of food elsewhere" (Stoudt 1944, 100). By reversing the last statement word for word, we get what the myth conveys: if ducks are gone from the area, the rice harvest will be poor or nonexistent.

Now, what about waterfowl as propagators of wild rice? No study seems to have directly addressed this question, although there are general studies on ducks as natural plant propagators. When an author studied this possibility in Hawaii and Fiji, he concluded that wild ducks should be considered "flying germinators": "Wild ducks and their kind are active agents in the distribution of the seeds of aquatic plants" (Guppy 1906, 512). Native Americans themselves, after a lifetime of killing and cutting up hundreds of ducks, come to the same conclusions, and such knowledge is conveyed by the myth: "Some Indian people believe that ducks do their share of reseeding. One resident of Mole Lake, Wisconsin, noted: 'Your ducks will eat, will gather rice and then go, probably sit on a lily pad and probably drop a few kernels, just like they're planting too, you know'; Robert Gough, 'Wild Rice and the Sokaogan Chippewa: A Study in Cultural Ecological Adaptation,' unpublished manuscript in Gough's possession" (Vennum 1988, 310n19).

How exactly are the seeds propagated? In zoology, it is known that seed dispersal by birds can be either endozoochorous (transportation via the digestive tract) or epizoochorous (transportation by adhering to the feathers, the feet, or the bill). Here, we are interested in endozoochorous dispersal, and we must say that all studies on the subject tend to show that only a certain percentage of grains or seeds are still intact when excreted by waterfowl and that, of these grains or seeds, only some can germinate. Thus, according to a study by Merel B. Soons et al. (2008, 619–27), grains from twenty-one of the twenty-three plant species ingested by mallards were retrieved from their feces with retrieval percentages ranging from zero to 54%. On average, 32% of the grains germinated. Out of all of the studies we consulted, none were specifically about wild rice, and none showed *Zizania* spp. in their samples (Powers, Noble, and Chabreck 1978; Charalambidou and Santamaria 2002; Soons et al. 2008; etc.).

These studies are therefore inconclusive about dispersal of wild rice by mallards. Nor is this possibility countenanced by the above author—the one who noted that Native Americans believe that waterfowl disperse grains one way or another, and who has also argued that the mallard's green color represents the ripening of rice, without mentioning that this color is typically male. He has denied that the Ojibwa myth that opens this chapter has any real-life basis: "A literal interpretation of these stories is somewhat problematic. Bird droppings scarcely resemble wild rice kernels, cooked or uncooked; furthermore because rice seed, unlike some others, is easily digested by birds, little of it comes through in their excrement—one reason birds play a minimal role, if any, in spreading wild rice" (Vennum 1988, 64).

On the other side of the world, however, native knowledge supports the opposite position, i.e., these stories are based on real life and may be taken literally. Laotian villagers, specifically those living on the Vientiane Plain, have hundreds of names not only for cultivated rice varieties, whose names follow various criteria (provenance, appearance, association with an animal, etc.), but also several specific varieties of wild rice, which are named after the birds that eat them or the bird droppings that contain them. In the case of ducks, one variety is named after the wild ducks that eat it and another, completely distinct variety after the droppings of the same wild ducks, from which this variety grows. These names and their meanings are reproduced here in full (Kuroda et al. 2001, 225):

*Table 14. Local names and meanings of wild rice (*Oryza rufipogon or O. nivara*) and weedy rice on the Vientiane Plain of Laos*

Nyaa khaw kyee nok	*Oryza nivara* or *O. rufipogon*	Rice that comes from bird droppings
Nyaa khaw nok	*Oryza nivara* or *O. rufipogon*	Rice eaten by birds
Khaw maa nyeen	Weedy rice	—
Nyaa khaw kyee nok ped	*Oryza nivara* or *O. rufipogon*	Rice that comes from wild duck (*Anas* spp.) droppings
Nyaa khaw kyee nok khaw	*Oryza nivara* or *O. rufipogon*	Rice that comes from wild pigeon (*Streptopella* spp.) droppings
Nyaa khaw nok ped	*Oryza nivara* or *O. rufipogon*	Rice eaten by *Anas* spp.
Nyaa khaw nok khaw	*Oryza nivara* or *O. rufipogon*	Rice eaten by *Streptopella* spp.

Need we say more? Like Laotian villagers, the Ojibwa of the Northeast of North America made a mental link between the presence of rice and the presence of ducks, and their droppings. Like those same villagers, they undoubtedly noticed under natural conditions (which can differ from those of scientific studies) that rice grains from duck droppings could germinate. They then passed on this knowledge through their myths.

We will now go back to Thomas Vennum—the author who denies that Ojibwa stories about rice and ducks can be taken literally. He is a structuralist and, like any structuralist, he first seeks to show that the myth cannot be understood on its own terms. As we mentioned in the introduction, a myth cannot have any meaning on its own terms for structuralists. Yet Native Americans say their stories are true—these stories we call 'myths.' They see a literal interpretation concealed behind what seems exaggerated and strange, and our book amply supports this conclusion in its entirety.

Vennum continues his analysis:

> Comparison of this bungling host tale with versions of the story collected from the Menominee, neighbors of the Ojibway to the east, helps elucidate the structural meaning of the episode. In the Menominee tale Mallard is replaced by Red Squirrel, who produces wild rice, not by defecating but by slicing open his testicle, from whence pour the rice kernels. He closes the wound and the rice ceases to flow, whereupon he opens the other testicle to let out grease—a typical flavoring for wild rice. When Manabus, the Menominee culture hero, tries the same trick, he produces only blood, prompting him to say, "My wife has spoiled this; she is having her sickness." (Vennum 1988, 64)

The author concludes by evoking structuralism with its classic (and Freudian) oppositions to "explain" the myths: "These stories clearly impart to wild rice (the food) a magical quality, placing it vividly in opposition to menstrual blood, semen, fecal matter, and the like—the realm of Wenabozhoo, the bungler. . . . By contrast, Mallard (or Red Squirrel), in defecating (or spilling semen) to produce wild rice, demonstrates the power to perform magic" (Vennum 1988, 64).

His argument recalls those of Zeno of Elea, the Greek philosopher of antiquity who believed form mattered more than content. He argued that an arrow will never reach its target because it must first cover half the distance separating it from the target, and to cover that half it must first cover half of that half, and so on and so forth. This argument, like structuralism, is based on a denial of meaning.

As for Vennum, his logic is doubtful. Yet these myths have meaning. First, as we showed in the last chapter, there is meaning in the one about a squirrel producing food by slicing open its testicle. This myth can be traced back to an etymon: the cycle of growth and regression of the male gonads, as well as a similarity of shape between the products obtained (rice and, especially in most versions, nuts) and their source (the internal morphology of the testicles themselves). These myths must be analyzed by taking all versions into account, and not just those that confirm one's argument.

Second, as we have shown, the story of rice-excreting Duck likewise has etymons that justify it and give meaning to the audience, and for this we have the support of data from other rice-growing societies. Vennum says there is an opposition between wild rice and fecal matter. How, then, does one explain the duck droppings turning into rice? He is setting up an imaginary opposition. Native Americans themselves could eat fecal matter with their rice. Yes, this has been documented for the inhabitants of Sandy Lake, Wisconsin, who sometimes prepared a rice meal that way: "The Sandy lake Indians, according to Doty, have boiled the excrement of rabbit with their rice to season it, and they esteem it a luxury" (Jenks 1898, 1084). The author also mentioned that the same Natives would take a partridge and, after removing its feathers, with "no further preparation," would pound it to the consistency of jelly and add it to the rice. Although these native dishes may involve other animals than ducks, they show no opposition at all between rice and fecal matter—on the contrary. The same is true for the myth. Interestingly, the Innu of the Eastern Subarctic had a name for rice—wild rice does not grow on their territory, although they might have known about it through trade—and that name referred to fecal matter: *âpûkuhîhimaiha* 'mouse excrement' (McNulty and Basile 1981, 6).

Vennum posits another opposition that raises just as many problems, this time between wild rice and the menstrual periods of the Trickster's wife. Such an assertion seems to disregard the way Native Americans represent menstruation. Indeed, in countless Native societies of North America and elsewhere, it was common to make menstrual huts where women had to live during their periods. The apparent reason was fear of being soiled, and par-ticularly the fear of soiling hunting weapons and even the male hunters themselves. But there were other reasons.

Such huts were present among the southern Ojibwa: "The men-strual hut was a small wigwam, adjacent to the larger ones. Used only by a woman during her period" (Ritzenthaler 1978, 749). The explanations given for the following two groups applied to all Native American societies:

> [Mi'kmaq] Elaborate menstrual taboos were formerly observed, that is, monthly seclusion and prohibition of women's stepping over the legs or weapons of hunters. (Bock 1978, 116)

> [Menominee] During menstruation and following childbirth, women were a threat to the power of the male or small child. A woman was isolated during these periods, using her own utensils, refraining from touching herself or looking up. (Spindler 1978, 714)

These taboos were in fact governed by analogical reasoning. A menstruating woman bleeds and may seem weakened. If she enters into contact with a hunter or his weapons, there will be sympathetic association: either the hunter himself will weaken or his prey will. If a game animal is bleeding and can still move, it is only wounded. It has not been killed.

By evoking his wife's menstrual period, the Trickster, half in earnest, half in jest, is referring to a belief that anyone listening to the story would know. At the same time, he is trying to justify his failed imitation: no rice flowed out of the testicle he sliced open, only blood (like menstrual blood). "Mä'näbus was disgusted. 'An'ääämékút!' he repeated, 'that's all my wife's fault, she was having her monthlies, I have always been able to do it before'" (Skinner and Satterlee 1915, 284).

This refrain is often heard from the Trickster's mouth in Native American myths. What Vennum considers to be an opposition is not at all one. The myth is instead alluding to an explanation—which makes sense in its own way. Moreover, do not Western societies have a customary belief that a woman cannot thicken white sauce or mayonnaise when she is menstruating? Is this inability explained by an opposition between the white sauce (or mayonnaise) and her menstrual blood? Or is this not again a sign of the doctrine of signatures at work? The meaning of a phenomenon belongs to those who experience it, and not to the academic who studies it.

Thomas Vennum's oppositions have no basis and are logically biased. To make sense of the myth, there are only the etymons we have brought to light. This conclusion is also corroborated by the other two myths we set aside when we began our analysis. These are from the Plains Cree and the Kwakiutl of the Northwest Coast, being variants of the same mytheme.

The Plains Cree myth can be understood along the same lines as the variant that opens this chapter. The host could be a mallard if one goes by the sounds it makes: "Quack, quack, quack." In Cree, the only term used is a generic one, *sisip*, which in Algonquian languages is a general category for 'waterfowl': "Sitting on the stone, he said, 'Quack, quack,' like a duck. 'Hey, Old Woman, tip your kettle this way!' Then, while crying 'Quack, quack, quack,' he did this: he lifted his leg and muted into the kettle. Grains of Indian corn fell into the kettle" (Bloomfield 1934, 299).

Mallards, like other ducks, are well known for eating corn: "On or near their breeding grounds in the prairie regions they feed largely on wheat, barley, and corn which they glean from the stubble fields" (Bent et al. 1962, 41). It is even reported that mallards will sometimes feed on "standing corn in flooded areas" (Martin and Uhler 1939, 53).

As with rice, current zoological studies are not conclusive about what happens to corn grains on their way through a duck's gut and into its excrement. In research done solely *in vitro*, the authors reported no trace of cereal grains (rice, corn, etc.) in the excrements of the subjects (Cummings et al. 2008). All of the plants were cultivated species. In addition, we now know that wild rice grains can pass through the gut intact. Finally, another study came to the opposite conclusion with regard to *Zea mays* (corn). Its authors were studying the role of plant dispersal over long distances in Europe, including corn, an introduced species. They found that its distribution is explained by endozoochorous transport via ducks (Brochet et al. 2009, 921, 924).

The main mytheme is constructed identically in the last myth we will study. This Kwakiutl myth features a thrush that produces berries through its anus. Here is the beginning:

Ō'ᵋMĀŁ IMITATES HIS HOSTS (EXCERPT)

Then Thrush-Woman invited (the myth people to a feast). (Ō'ᵋmāł's) tribe entered. Then she pushed (a feather) into her anus, and excrements came out. They were salmon-berries. Then she put them into a dish and placed them before her guests. (Boas 1969 [1910], 237)

These were salmonberries (*Rubus spectabilis*). They were eaten in large amounts by the Kwakiutl (Turner and Bell 1973, 291) and by other peoples of the Northwest Coast. In this book, chapter 4 partly deals with a related mytheme (Bird produces berries by singing) and the close relationship between the growth of berries and the singing of birds. The thrush in these stories was tentatively identified as a Swainson's thrush (*Catharis ustulatus*) or a varied thrush (*Ixoreus nœvius*).

Whatever the case may be, the bird is most often a thrush in all of these myths, and thrushes are known by Natives and non-Natives alike for their berry-based diet. The present mytheme—Thrush excretes berries—is therefore contextually similar to the mytheme of the thrush that produces berries by singing. All the same, the berries are produced in a different way. Setting aside the detail of the feather sticking out of the bird's anus (there are many avenues to follow: feathers molting at the same time that the berries ripen in late summer or very early autumn [Mack and Yong 2000, 23]; continual preening of feathers using the bill; etc.), we can say there is support from ornithologists for the possibility of finding intact berries in the droppings of these birds, or at least berry seeds. Thrushes are indeed described as being endozoochorous dispersers: "When seeds are taken as part of a fruit, particularly a fleshy one, the surrounding pulp is digested and the pits in most instances are either regurgitated or voided in an entirely viable condition and often improved for germination. . . . The more prominent fruit-eating birds include the thrushes, robins, bluebirds" (McAtee 1947, 214).

The three permutations of the generic mytheme—Bird excreting some sort of plant product—can therefore be understood "literally." All of them come from a similar etymon about seed dispersal. However, it would be interesting to pursue a complementary avenue of research for which we currently lack data, namely the relationship between bird droppings and similar-looking Native dishes: rice stew, corn stew, and berry paste. There may be material for a comparative study.

18 Bird Gets Salmon Eggs by Striking His Ankle (Northwest Coast)

This young man was Chief Kingfisher. He had large stores of all kinds of provisions, and gave nearly everything to Txämsem. At last he took a nice dish and stretched his foot out over it. Then he took a smooth stone, struck his ankle, and salmon eggs poured out of it and filled the dish. He placed it before Txämsem, gave him a wooden spoon, and Txämsem ate it all and was very much pleased. He left the house of Kingfisher when he had had enough.

—Franz Boas, "Tsimshian Mythology"

There are several mythemes that each have many versions, enough to require separate analyses. One of these mythemes is about Bird, who may be a kingfisher, a dipper, a snipe, a waterfowl, or another river bird, and who strikes or cuts his ankle or a concomitant body part. In all cases, he gets food—most often salmon eggs—which he generously serves to his guest.

In chapter 5, we deliberately put aside a Bella Coola version because comparison with the other versions seemed necessary to understand its meaning. All of these versions come from the Northwest Coast or nearby, specifically from the lands of the Bella Coola, the Nootka, the Tsimshian, the Salish, the Kwakiutl, the

Haida, and the Chicoltin. These are regions where many Pacific salmon species abound, traditionally providing most of the aboriginal diet. The Tsimshian ate salmon at each meal (Halpin and Seguin 1990, 272).

This chapter opens with a Tsimshian myth. It was collected by Franz Boas in the early twentieth century and belongs to a series of three Bungling Host myths. We have already presented the other two: Seal gets grease from his hands, and Thrush produces berries by singing. The Trickster hero of these tales is Txämsem, a figure related to the raven: "There are two types of Tsimshian myths: those that were known generally and could be told by anyone, such as the Raven cycle (Boas 1916), and those, called *?atáux* that were owned by a particular house. . . . The Raven cycle tells us of the exploits of *txá·msm*, who was known to the Nishga and Gitksan as *wi·két* ('great person' or 'giant'), a trickster and shape-changer" (Halpin and Seguin 1990, 280).

This Tsimshian myth has been published in two versions. The first one appeared in 1902 as a Native-language transcription with a word-for-word translation and a literary translation (Boas 1902, 48–49). In that version, the host is Ts'enk'oä'ts, an unidentified bird. We have chosen to present the second version, which, though published solely in literary translation, clearly identifies the main host—Chief Kingfisher.

TXÄMSEM IMITATES CHIEF KINGFISHER

Again Txämsem went on. He came to a creek, and saw a house in front of him. It was a very nice house. He went toward it; and when he went in, he saw a good-looking young man who was making a hook. When Txämsem entered, the young man looked at him, arose hastily, and spread a new mat on the floor. Then the young man went and fetched a pail of water. He took a nice dish, and roasted a dried salmon. He put it into the dish, and placed it before Txämsem. This young man was Chief Kingfisher. He had large stores of all kinds of provisions, and gave nearly everything to Txämsem. At last he took a nice dish and stretched his foot out over it. Then he took a smooth stone, struck his ankle, and salmon eggs poured out of it and filled the dish. He placed it before Txämsem, gave him a wooden spoon, and Txämsem ate it all and was very much pleased. He left the house of Kingfisher when he had had enough.

Then he thought that he would invite his friend to visit him. Now, Txämsem built a house better than that of young Kingfisher. When he had finished it, he invited Kingfisher, who sat down alongside the fire. Txämsem took a dish, stretched out his foot over the dish, took a smooth stone and struck his ankle. He fell back, and said, "Oh, I am almost dead!" Then young Kingfisher flew away from him, and Txämsem was very much ashamed. His foot was sore and swollen, and he lay there a long time until it became well again. (Boas 1916, 91)

There are today over ten thousand Tsimshian in British Columbia. Their traditional territory extends across the northwest of this Canadian province and beyond, along the Nass and Skeena rivers. The term "Tsimshian" refers to a linguistic and cultural family with four distinct peoples: on the one hand, the Southern Tsimshian and the Coast Tsimshian, who are found along the Pacific; and, on the other, the Nishga and the Gitksan, who live inland to the north. Their economy was centered on fishing different species of salmon, eulachon, herring, and so on. To round out their diet, they hunted mammals and gathered fruits.

The above Tsimshian myth outlines much of Tsimshian culture, with many points of convergence that bring together human and animal elements. The following chart summarizes these juxtapositions, which will be commented on in this chapter. Square brackets indicate shared characteristics that may be inferred.

Table 15. Tsimshian Bungling Host myth:
human and animal elements

	KINGFISHER	TSIMSHIAN
DISTINGUISHING CHARACTERISTICS	distinctive head crest	good-looking young man
HABITAT	close to the water [nest]	near a creek house
ACTIVITY	fisherman (hook)	fisherman
FOOD	fish [food resources nearby]	fish provisions

When Txämsem first catches sight of Kingfisher, he sees a "good-looking young man." Why is this observation made? Surely to link the characteristic beauty of kingfishers to the importance of body ornamentation among the Tsimshian. The kingfisher, *Ceryle alcyon*, is inevitably admired by naturalists, Natives, and non-Natives alike: "Swift, graceful, and picturesque" (Godfrey 1966, 235). First, the bird's head has an especially showy crest of plumes. Second, the plumage is ravishing—spotted dark blue with white or reddish stripes depending on the individual's age or sex. The Tsimshian similarly valued personal beauty. They tattooed their arms and chests, pierced their ears and noses, and adorned themselves with various ornaments (Drucker 1950, 190–91), not to mention the elaborate headgear worn by Tsimshian chiefs during ceremonies (Halpin and Seguin 1990, 275). In the myth, the host, too, is a chief: Chief Kingfisher.

The myth begins with Txämsem coming to a creek and seeing a "very nice house." Later, when his turn comes to imitate Chief Kingfisher, he builds a house better than the Chief's. The first detail is the creek, and kingfishers are undoubtedly associated with water, their habitat being typically aquatic. The belted kingfisher is common in "the vicinity of fish-inhabited water (preferably clear) either fresh or salt: lakes, ponds, rivers, streams" (Godfrey 1966, 234). The Tsimshian, too, always built their villages near water, whether these be winter, spring, or summer villages. They had several good reasons, beginning with availability of drinking water (winter village) and fish (spring and summer villages), the latter resource being the basis of their economy: "Each local group customarily occupied a single winter village, moving in the spring to fishing villages on the lower Nass and in the summers to fishing camps on other rivers" (Halpin and Seguin 1990, 267). Another reason was the need for a way to travel between sites of activity. Such traveling was most often by water: "Transportation between sites for most activities was by canoe, and only in a few areas were there networks of trails. Elsewhere it was, and is, time-consuming and difficult to walk more than a short distance into the bush due to the heavy cover of undergrowth lying over layers of deadfall" (Halpin and Seguin 1990, 269).

We now come to the second detail at the beginning of the myth: the house. The Tsimshian had very sophisticated houses and, although Chief Kingfisher's house is described as being very nice, this initial description likely serves to stress that kingfishers live near water—this is where they nest. His home, in fact, proves to be less grandiose than a human one. In Fort Simpson, well within Coast Tsimshian territory, a traditional house measured on average 15 by 17 meters (50 by 55 feet). Its cedar beam structure was covered with horizontal planks. Its front was very ornate, sometimes with large panels bearing emblematic designs, and sometimes with huge totems at the entrance. There are also reports of planks from winter homes being transported to spring or summer village sites (Halpin and Seguin 1990, 271).

The rivalry expressed in the myth—Txämsem builds a better house—is a cultural trait of the Tsimshian, as it is of many Northwest Coast peoples. A typical manifestation was the famous potlatch, one of their main community ceremonies. A potlatch

Fig. 44. Tsimshian house. Canadian Museum of History.

would take place when a chief of a village (and its inhabitants) invited a neighboring chief (and the inhabitants of his village) to a ceremony where provisions and goods would be given away. A potlatch could take years to prepare because so many goods had to be amassed. The more there were, the more prestigious it would be: "Rivalries and challenges were also typically expressed through crest displays within the *?oix* potlatch framework.... The prestige accorded the potlatch-giver, of course, depended upon the amount of wealth he displayed and gave away" (Halpin and Seguin 1990, 278).

We see the same cultural trait in the stores of provisions that Chief Kingfisher has set aside. These provisions can be explained in two ways. First, the kingfisher's habitat. It always lives near water with plenty of fish. So Chief Kingfisher always has ample provisions within reach. If we start with the widely acknowledged indigenous view of game animals giving themselves up to humans, we can link a kingfisher's presence in a habitat to the presence of a body of water with plenty of fish. In other words, a kingfisher is a sign that fish are nearby and, in this sense, it too can provide humans with meat. The Tsimshian accepted such a principle as true because they believed the converse: game animals could refuse to make themselves available to humans if certain rules were broken (e.g., sexual abstinence as a precondition for some kinds of hunting): "Animals were said to be offended by unclean persons and to refuse to allow themselves to be caught by them" (Halpin and Seguin 1990, 271).

Second, it has already been mentioned that the Tsimshian or, more precisely, their chiefs, accumulated large amounts of provisions to be given away at potlatches. Whether for this purpose or for others, caches were used by this Northwest Coast people: "Other structures included . . . summer houses, sweat lodges, and underground caches" (Halpin and Seguin 1990, 272). They were used to store dried fish, among other things.

Fishing is omnipresent in this myth. The kingfisher, by its very name, is a symbol par excellence. We made this point in chapter 13 while examining an Arapaho myth in which the same bird species dives under the ice. In the Tsimshian story, this bird is seen making a hook. Illustration 33 of the present book shows how a kingfisher, after catching a fish under water, can slip it onto the end of its bill, as one would onto a fish hook. The Tsimshian themselves could also catch salmon using a fish hook: "For fishing, hooks and harpoons are employed" (Boas 1916, 50). On the Northwest Coast, fish hooks were used notably to catch salmon either by trolling or by jigging: "Salmon could be caught in great numbers in traps and dams once they began their migration up river, but they were also successfully caught by trolling with hook, and line in the bays and inlets, especially when they congregated prior to the run" (Stewart 1977, 41).

Kingfishers are also known for fishing alone. This fact, too, is implicit in the myth. The host, Chief Kingfisher, is alone when Txämsem comes to visit. In contrast, numerous Bungling Host myths describe the first host as being with his wife and sometimes with his children. Western naturalists have likewise noticed this propensity of kingfishers: "It prefers to play the role of the lone fisherman" (Bent et al. 1964a, 111).

Kingfishers also consume salmon, just like the Tsimshian. The myth says so, as do non-Native naturalists. If we take one of British Columbia's many salmon species, the coho salmon (*Oncorhynchos kisutch*), it seems to be a known natural predator: "Mergansers, loons, kingfishers, other birds, and some small mammals, may also take numbers of young. All these predators sometimes gorge themselves on young migrating salmon" (Scott and Crossman 1973, 162).

Turning to the Tsimshian, we see that they traditionally prepared salmon for consumption in various ways. The myth mentions at least two of them: the roasted dried salmon that Chief Kingfisher offers his guest, and the salmon eggs he gets from his ankle afterwards.

Franz Boas could not have said it better when he wrote that "the salmon and cedar are the foundations of Northwest coast culture" (Boas 1916, 46). Cedar was so omnipresent in the material culture as to need no demonstration, being used in all aspects of daily life. It appears in the myth in two forms, one of which has been implicitly mentioned: the structural components of homes are made entirely of cedar. Another allusion to cedar is the new mat that Chief Kingfisher hastens to give his newly arrived guest: "Txämsem entered, the young man looked at him, arose hastily, and spread a new mat on the floor." Boas reported the use of cedar bark for this purpose: "The bark of the red cedar is also used extensively for making matting, baskets, and certain kinds of clothing" (Boas 1916, 46). This is the only element of the myth with no animal equivalent. But the myth needs only a few points of convergence to make its point. Not everything has to fit together, and some anthropomorphism is needed.

As for the other foundation of this culture, salmon, it is clear that dried salmon, i.e., preserved through drying and smoking as a winter provision, could be eaten roasted: "He took a nice dish, and roasted a dried salmon." This may be seen in another Tsimshian myth. In *The Four Chiefs and Chief Grizzly Bear*, we are told how a Tsimshian chief on the verge of starvation nonetheless offers his guest, Grizzly Bear, what remains of his stores of fish; and this food was prepared the same way: "He said to his wife, 'See if a dried salmon remains in your box!' Then his wife arose, went to the empty salmon-box, and there was only one large spring salmon left in the box. She took it to the fire and roasted one half" (Boas 1916, 293).

How was salmon roasted? This question cannot be answered by the anthropological literature on the Tsimshian, which is silent on this point. We nonetheless have enough data from neighboring peoples, notably the Coast Salish (Kennedy and Bouchard 1976b, 93) and the Shuswap, who live in British Columbia's interior (Kennedy 1975, 42). The Shuswap example will suffice: "After the smoking process had been completed, the fish was extremely hard. Therefore, it underwent further treatment before being eaten. . . . Smoked fish could also be skewered on a barbecue stick and 'toasted' in front of the fire. This 'toasting' is called *yastsílhen*. As the heat draws the oil to the surface of the flesh, the flesh becomes softer, and therefore, easier to chew" (Kennedy 1975, 42).

The mytheme of this chapter points to the second way to get salmon. A bird—a kingfisher in the variant that opens this chapter—strikes its ankle with a smooth stone and salmon eggs pour out. A smooth stone was probably the most important tool for Native peoples of former times, as noted by this Native American tool specialist: "The first and simplest tools are hammerstones. These are typically water-worn stones from a creek, river, or gravel bed that readily fit the hand and are heavy enough to be used as a hammer to break the chert materials into workable spalls" (Burch 2004, 13–14).

Northwest Coast cultures apparently never developed the art

of hammering a flint stone to make thin, sharp flakes, although pebbles were used as hammers, as Franz Boas reported in his paper on the Tsimshian: "Pecked and battered stone hammers and stone mortars were common" (Boas 1916, 52).

As it happens, water-polished pebbles are found in streams where salmon go to spawn. If we scale down to Chief Kingfisher's size, we see that hammerstones are much like the gravel of salmon spawning grounds. This gravel is dug by females during the spawning season, as has been noted for sockeye salmon (*Oncorhynchos neska*): "The female prepares a nest in streams, in pea-sized gravel, by lying on her side and beating the tail violently up and down" (Scott and Crossman 1973, 168). The eggs are laid in the nest and covered with gravel. They will remain there for several months until they hatch around December or January, the fry emerging only later, in March or May.

This reproductive schedule varies from one species to another. What matters here is that in many of British Columbia's salmon-spawning streams, temperatures remain all winter long above freezing. Although salmon eggs are buried, they are theoretically accessible to many predators, including birds.

The Tsimshian traditionally consumed salmon eggs. We know how they stored fish eggs in boxes or pits (Drucker 1950, 170). Generally speaking, on the Northwest Coast, eggs were removed, either as separated eggs or as egg packets, directly from females while being washed. The eggs could next be smoke-dried or buried for several weeks in a bark container for later use as pancake batter, among other uses (Stewart 1977, 146; Kennedy 1975, 46).

Turning to kingfishers, we need to look at the behavior of related birds to understand the referent of the myth, i.e., a kingfisher gets salmon eggs by striking its ankle, because we lack the necessary ornithological data on this species. No ornithologist seems to have reported fish egg consumption by this bird. Such reports have been made for other species, however, in particular the ones that appear in other versions of the myth. These species are as follows:

Table 16. *"A bird gets salmon eggs by striking its ankle" versions*

	HOST	IDENTIFICATION	SOURCE
Nootka	Water-snipe	?	Sapir and Swadesh 1939, 45
Bella Coola	*Maxuat!a'laqa* Small water-fowl	Small waterfowl	Boas 1898, 93
Bella Coola	*Water-ouzel*	American Dipper *Cinclus mexicanus*	McIlwraith 1948, vol. 2, 386
Kwakiutl (Newettee)	*Kile'qoitsa* A river bird	Shorebird	Boas 1895, 177, 290
Kwakiutl	Water-ouzel	American Dipper	Boas and Hunt 1906, 150
Kwakiutl	Water-ousel	American Dipper	Boas 1969 [1910], 153
Tsimshian	Kingfisher	Kingfisher	Boas 1916, 91
Tsimshian (Nass)	*Ts'enk'oa'ts*	?	Boas 1902, 48-49
Haida	Water ousel	American Dipper	Swanton 1905, 132
Coast Salish (Comox)	*Ma'melaquitsa*	?	Boas 1974 [1895], 76, 124
Chilcotin	Small black water bird	Small black shorebird	Farrand 1900, 18

In addition to the nine versions of this myth listed by Franz Boas (1916, 696), we have added two others published after his research on Northwest Coast Natives. Out of a total of eleven versions, four clearly identify the host as being the American dipper (*Cinclus mexicanus*). A Bella Coola version also refers to the dipper, although Boas (1898, 93) — or his informant — misidentified the main character, *Maxuat!a'laqa*, translating this name as "small water-fowl." Actually, it is not a waterfowl but rather a dipper, as shown by the translation in a contemporary Bella Coola dictionary: "maxwa'alaqa dipper (bird)" (Nater 1990, 73). The same holds true for the Coast Salish version, whose host, *Ma'melaquitsa*, was not identified by Boas (1974 [1895], 76, 124). The word comes from "the Comox term for the bird known as the American Dipper (*Cinclus mexicanus*)" (Bouchard and Kennedy 2002, 197n65). The latter authors go on to say that "this bird's ability to produce fish eggs in the manner described here [by striking his ankle] is widely believed throughout this region" (Bouchard and Kennedy 2002, 197n65). This species identification is supported by a Kwakiutl (Newettee) version collected by Boas (1895, 77, 290), where the bird *Kile'qoitsa* is vaguely described as "a river bird." A more recent translation of Boas' collection of myths, from which this story comes, states that the bird is a dipper: "The Kwakwala term gilíxwi'ca (Boas 'Kilē'qoitsa') refers to the bird identified as the American Dipper (*Cinclus mexicanus*)" (Bouchard and Kennedy 2002, 387n23).

There is also reason to believe that at least two other versions refer to the same bird. The Chilcotin version (Farrand 1900, 18) mentions "a small black water bird" that could be a dipper. The second Tsimshian (Nass) version (Boas 1902, 48–49) has a host named Ts'enk'oa'ts, a term possibly related to *Ts'msmhóon*, which means a "grey diving bird" (a summary definition, among others, of the dipper) in the Coast Tsimshian language (Dunn 1978, 103), which differs from the language of the Tsimshian who live along the Nass River.

We are now left with two versions. One has a kingfisher playing the role of host among the Tsimshian, as we have already seen. A Nootka version has another bird, which Edward Sapir and Morris Swadesh (1939, 45) identify as a water-snipe and which could be the common snipe (*Gallinago gallinago*), this species being the closest match.

Fig. 45. American dipper.

The American dipper is thus the leading bird species, i.e., the one that appears in the most versions (seven if not nine out of eleven). Three lines of non-Native ornithological evidence—for want of Native evidence—amply confirm the choice of this particular species as the main host of the mytheme, thus shedding light on the etymon. To begin with, the American dipper is found solely in the northwest portion of the continent, specifically in British Columbia, which is home to all of the versions of the mytheme. In fact, this bird is an unavoidable sight along the clear-water streams of mountains and valleys, which are sometimes salmon-spawning grounds. It can be easily observed paddling its way through rapids like a little duck or even standing with its feet clutched to streambed stones amidst flowing water: "Its legs and toes are long, and its flexor muscles are very strong, enabling it to hold firmly to the rocks and stones against a strong current, to climb over the slippery rocks, or to swim fast enough for its purposes" (Bent et al. 1964c, 105). Second line of evidence: this bird is known to be fond of salmon eggs. "Unfortunately for the dipper's welfare, it is too fond of the spawn and small fry of salmon and trout, and it is tempted to feed on them freely when and where they are easily available. This habit has made many enemies for the dipper among sportsmen and especially among the managers of fish hatcheries" (Bent et al. 1964c, 103–4).

During one year in the early twentieth century, huge numbers of salmon came to spawn in Northwest Coast streams, and they attracted large numbers of dippers looking for spawn: "In 1924 an enormous salmon run (species unstated) attracted an unusual number of American Dippers to streams in Kitsap Co., WA, where the birds ate salmon eggs; they remained there Sept-Feb" (Kingery 1996, 6).

Final line of evidence: the dipper also has a reputation of being able to dislodge some prey that hide under stones in the water. This ability is sometimes questioned by specialists: "Even the tiny dipper has been accused of robbing spawning-beds. This is manifestly absurd, for the fertile eggs are under gravel which so small a bird is quite incapable of displacing" (Jones 1959, 24).

Yet the above author, a salmon and trout specialist, recognizes its fondness for these eggs, having used spawn as bait ("Nevertheless, dippers are very fond of Salmon eggs"; Jones 1959, 24). On the other hand, many ornithologists would disagree and some go so far as to describe how dippers find and dislodge their prey. It must be said that these birds get most if not all of their food in the water: "The water ouzel obtains most of its food in, on, or under the water of the streams on which it lives" (Bent et al. 1964c, 103). Dippers can move stones to get at numerous insect species, as noted by many researchers:

> It [American Dipper] is very fond of the larvae of the caddicefly, for which it probes around and under the small stones on bottom; there it also finds water-bugs, water-beetles, the larvae of other

insects, aquatic worms, and other forms of animal life that live in such places. (Bent et al. 1964c, 103)

Many stream macroinvertebrates resist predation by moving to underside of rocks . . . hence American Dipper must find prey on or under rocks, which it sometimes moves. (Kingery 1996, 5)

Need we say more? Dippers walk on streambeds, their feet in contact with smooth stones, and they are known to eat salmon eggs. This relationship in the natural environment may be expressed by the following equation:

$$\text{spawn} \; \rightarrow \; \begin{array}{c} \text{smooth stones} \\ \text{(gravel)} \end{array} \; \rightarrow \; \text{American Dipper}$$

The myth takes this equation and plays leapfrog with its elements:

$$\begin{array}{c} \text{smooth stones} \\ \text{(gravel)} \end{array} \; \rightarrow \; \begin{array}{c} \text{American Dipper} \\ \text{(foot)} \end{array} \; \rightarrow \; \text{spawn}$$

Such leapfrogging is consistent with everything we have seen so far. We see here a reversal of perspective.

There remains, however, a secondary point to comment on, namely a complementary relationship involving dipper feet or ankles and salmon egg production. For this, we will return to our discussion in the last chapter on plant dispersal by birds and look at the following data, which may help us better understand our mytheme. The data describe plant dispersal via the lower extremities of birds, a relatively well documented phenomenon: "Some remarkable instances have been noted of the transport of seeds in mud which had become stuck to the feet and legs of shore-birds" (McAtee 1947, 214). These instances should have been noticed by Native Americans. In their oral traditions, such elements of knowledge, however minute, could have easily circulated from generation to generation or even crossed vast distances from people to people. In his study, Waldo McAtee (1947) refers to many academic works in which such instances are reported or examined, notably with respect to wading birds. So can the spawn of fish adhere to the feet of dippers or other birds?

Some ornithologists have studied the various ways that birds spread organisms and have documented ectozoochorous transport by waterfowl like mallards, which likewise may feed on fish eggs:

> It has often been said that teal, mallard, and swans are enemies of Salmon as they are supposed to uproot spawning beds and eat the fertilized eggs and fry. Berry (1933–34) described how he saw swans, teal and mallard poking their bills amongst the stones where Salmon had spawned. He believed that the swans were quite definitely uprooting the redds, but he did not know whether it was for ova or some other food. (Jones 1959, 23)

> In Alaska and on the Pacific coast they [Mallards] feed largely on dead salmon and salmon eggs, which they obtain in the pools on the rivers. (Bent et al. 1962, 41)

Even ducklings join in: "Ducklings <25d old eat mostly animal foods (invertebrates, small crustacea, mollusks, and fish eggs)" (Drilling, Titman, and McKinney 2002, 21).

So there might be more than appears in Franz Boas (or his Bella Coola informant) describing the host in the myth as a "small waterfowl." This is all the more likely given that, in addition to seeds, animal organisms can also attach themselves "to the feathers, bills or legs of waterbirds" (Figuerola and Green 2002, 488). Birds may thus transport the larvae of many sorts of insects, and even eggs: "Seeds and resting eggs that float are obviously more likely to become attached to plumage" (Figuerola and Green 2002, 488).

If mallards can feed on dead salmon in river pools, and on salmon eggs, such eggs may end up getting stuck to their feathers, bill, or feet—perhaps not often, but this sort of thing would happen. Why, then, would not the same thing happen with dippers or other birds that feed on spawn?

In other words, if a Native person simply observes a bird like a dipper walking through running water where salmon spawn and standing on streambed gravel, this observation is already enough to make the story "true" in his or her mind. This is the etymon of the mytheme we wish to understand: Bird gets salmon eggs by striking his ankle. What about the other bird species that personify the host in other versions? The Tsimshian kingfisher poses several problems. First, it might be an error of translation, interpretation, or observation. Our problem would then be solved. As things stand, however, we have no way of knowing, since we lack the Native-language version of that particular myth. The Tsimshian version may have also resulted from observed similarities between the two species: the dipper and the kingfisher. If the original myth is the one where the dipper is the main host, this motif would have spread from one people to another and, in the course of events, another species would have taken over the role. The kingfisher is behaviorally similar to the dipper. It is said that a dipper dives like a kingfisher, is always in or near water like a kingfisher, and feeds alone like a kingfisher: "I have also seen them [Dippers] dive, like kingfishers" (Bent et al. 1964c, 106). Finally, we should repeat that both species, dippers and kingfishers, eat salmon. Kingfishers and dippers alike are seen in salmon-spawning streams. Both can walk or dive underwater to look for food. Their feet or ankles, at least in one case for sure, are therefore in close contact with salmon nests ("redds"). Using their bills, some can push stones aside and onto their ankles or feet to get at salmon eggs. That is how they go about it, according to the way these birds are perceived in the myth.

If we turn to the other bird species that represent the host, we cannot push our analysis further because they have not yet been clearly identified. For example, in the Nootka version, the bird named "water-snipe" may be a "common snipe," the closest matching species. Common snipes and dippers have some traits in common with kingfishers. Both species are solitary, both may be observed along streambanks, and both feed pretty much the same way, by dislodging microinvertebrates strewn over the streambed (Mueller 1999, 5–6). The common snipe's range also covers the Northwest Coast region.

But the comparisons end there. Common snipes prefer stagnant water to the clear water where salmon spawn. They do not consume salmon or trout and are not known to eat fish eggs. To our knowledge, there may have been a translation error, unless this is a case of transposition. Anyway, the American dipper, which appears in most myths on this theme, sufficiently matches the bird of this story to be a convincing etymon.

A related myth is intriguing because the action takes place in a completely different part of the continent, i.e., in the Great Basin area, which covers the states of Utah, Nevada, and others. This Ute myth has other distinctive features. The host is a goose, and the character does not get fish eggs from his ankle; instead, he gets tubers by striking his knees or by cutting his feet. Robert H. Lowie reported two Ute variants of the myth, which he published solely in translation. Here is the first variant:

SÜNĀ'WAVI VISITS WILD GOOSE

Sünā'wavi went to visit Wild Goose. "Have you come to visit me?"—"Yes."—"I have no food." He asked his wife to bring a basket and her digging-stick. He put the basket under his legs and with the knob of the stick he struck his own knee, saying, "sigu'sigigì!" Then he struck his knee hard and wild turnips (sigu') fell into the basket. He did this several times till his basket was full. He told his wife to give them to Sünā'wavi, who ate them. Then he invited Wild Goose.

Sünā'wavi wanted to imitate Wild Goose. Wild Goose said, "I don't know what my relative wants." He arrived and sat down. "I have no food, all my supplies are gone." He bade his wife bring a basket and digging-stick. He put out his leg and said, "sigu'sigigì" striking it hard so he hurt himself. Several times he struck himself, but nothing came out of it. "How did you do it, relative?"—"Give me the basket and digging-stick!" Wild Goose performed the trick, left the food for his hosts, and went home. (Lowie 1924, 21)

The host of this myth is a wild goose. In Utah, the most common species is the Canada goose (*Branta canadensis*), which is known to nest and overwinter there (Mowbray et al. 2002). Thousands of snow geese (*Anser cœrulescens*) may also invade some regions of the state in the spring, long enough for them to stop and feed while on their spring migration to Alaska. An animal word list from the Gosiute—a people related to the Ute and living immediately to the west—mentions only the Canada goose: *nu'gunta*, "goose, Canada (*Branta canadensis*)" (Chamberlin 1908, 87). This does not mean that the referent of the myth can be only this waterfowl species. As will be seen further on, there is reason to believe that the bird of the myth may just as well be a snow goose.

On another note, we can easily identify the tuber produced by the goose of the myth, its English common name being a loan word from a Numic language. The Numic languages include Ute, Paiute, Shoshone (including Gosiute), and others. Thus, the ethnobiologist Ralph V. Chamberlin, who also authored a study about Gosiute botanical knowledge in addition to his zoological study (Chamberlin 1908), identified the term *si'-go* as meaning a member of the lily family, *Calochortus nuttalii*, more commonly called the sego lily: "*Calochortus nuttallii* Torr. and Gray. Sego. *si'-go*. The common name for this attractive lily is taken from the Indian name. In the spring and early summer the bulbs of the sego were formerly much used as food by the Gosiute, constituting a standard source at that time of the year. The bulbs were also dried and preserved for winter use in the usual type of pit or 'cellar'" (Chamberlin 1911, 364).

In yet another study, using information from a Ute-speaker, he concluded that the Gosiute and Shoshone terms are identical (Chamberlin 1909).

The sego lily is the floral emblem of Utah (Dunmire and Tierney

1997, 201) where it abounds. This herbaceous plant grows in semi-desert environments and requires deep sandy soil. It can grow up to 45 centimeters tall (18 inches). Its bulbs develop around 10 centimeters (4 inches) below the surface, and each bulb measures 1 to 2.5 centimeters (3/8 to 1 inch) in diameter. It tastes much like a sweet potato.

Sego lilies were used by very many peoples of the Great Basin and the American Southwest (Paiute, Western Shoshone, Ute, Washoe, Navajo, Hopi, etc.). They were gathered by digging the bulbs up with a digging stick: "Roots and corms of various species were taken everywhere in the region, using another favored Great Basin tool, the hardwood digging stick" (Fowler 1986, 69).

To our knowledge, use of a digging stick is best described in a report on the Navajo, who used it both to plant and to gather bulbs, such as those of the mariposa lily, a plant of the genus *Calochortus* (*Calochortus gunnisonii*) and very similar to the sego lily, to the point of being mistaken for it. Generally speaking, the Navajo had two positions for handling a digging stick: standing up and kneeling down. The position that interests us, kneeling, was well suited for digging up lily bulbs: "In planting, the operator knelt on one knee, scraped away the dry surface soil, and loosened the moist earth beneath. The point of the stick was then forced straight downward and the resulting hole filled with moist soil. Seeds were planted just above the hole, and the loosened soil gave easy access to the roots. Digging sticks of this type were also used to gather the roots of wild plants, among others the tubers of the wild onion and mariposa lily" (Kluckhohn, Hill, and Kluckhohn 1971, 65). These sticks measured around 75 centimeters long and had a beveled blade: "For working in heavy soil, a sharply pointed blade was used; for sandy soil, a broad blade" (Kluckhohn, Hill, and Kluckhohn 1971, 65). Some were pointed at one end and broadened or rounded at the other.

A parallel can be drawn with the different species of geese that pass through or overwinter in the same area. They have a reputation of digging up the soil to get the bulbs or roots of plants, while sometimes consuming other parts (seeds, flowers, leaves, etc.). For this, they have very powerful bills. Snow geese in particular seem to be expert diggers: "Roots are an important food for many grazing species, in particular for Snow Geese *Anser cærulescens* and Magpie Geese. The heavy, thickened bill margin of the Snow Geese is useful for digging out and cutting up the roots of the club-rush *Scirpus* from marshy places, while tubers of the spike-rush *Eleocharis* are the single most important item in the diet of the Magpie Goose" (Kear 1985, 104). Canada geese are also said to have "powerful jaws for grasping and extracting rhizomes and bulbs" (Mowbray et al. 2002, 14).

This propensity to feed on tubers or rhizomes is very well documented. Sometimes, the birds goose-step their way through feeding sites, raising one foot after the other, apparently to loosen the soil.

Digging for roots and stolons of plants is done mainly by those geese with rather elongated bills, but the small-billed geese can find clover stolons which lie only just below the surface. Greenland Whitefronts dig and probe five centimetres (two inches) or more into boggy ground, and find bulbils of plants such as beak-sedge *Rhynchospora*. Greylags, Greater Snow Geese and Whitefronts in North America, all of which feed on the roots and underground tubers of bulrush, often feed in 15–30 cm (6–12 in) of water. Here they can be seen trampling with their feet in order, presumably, to loosen and clear the mud away. (Ogilvie 1978, 95)

The sites they occupy can be devastated. Once a flock of geese have gone over a patch of ground, one can observe the pock marks left by their bills when they were digging up roots or bulbs:

The geese eat several species of bulrush, as well as cordgrass, taking the leaves, the seeds, and digging for the roots. An area that has been heavily used by them is recognisable by the uprooted plants, and broken off leaves and stems, left behind by the feeding birds. In some places the feeding is even more intensive and the geese do not leave what was once a lush marsh of tall plants until it is nothing more than a waste of mud, pock-marked by the holes left by their probing bills. (Ogilvie 1978, 83)

All of the key components are now on the table. We have only to explain how they fit together to make the myth. As with the preceding myth, everything can come down to points of convergence. Geese, like humans, are found where sego lilies grow. Both feed on them. We can at least infer that geese feed on them, using studies that include similar plants. If they do not eat them, they nonetheless eat plants that Natives could see as being "sego lilies for geese."

A human gets this food by kneeling on the ground and using a digging stick to dig it up, a method that necessarily leaves holes in the soil. A goose likewise gets this food by digging it up, however muddy the soil may be, using its own digging stick. The myth compares the edge of its powerful bill to the rounded end of a human's digging stick ("He [Wild Goose] put the basket under his legs and with the knob of the stick he struck his own knee"). This is in opposition to a human, who uses the pointed end of the stick. When the geese fly away, these feeding sites are a mess, being pock-marked by holes due to the churning action of many goose bills. Native Americans must have seen the holes and viewed them as a sign that geese, too, go about their work with their own digging sticks.

The kneeling position is noteworthy. With respect to the myth, it may explain why Goose got salmon eggs from his "knees." The key point is proximity. Fish eggs are under stones and in contact with the feet of dippers. Bulbs are underground and in contact with goose feet and also human knees. If we read the Ute variant about geese, it mentions legs instead of knees: "Next Wolf visited Wild Goose. Wild Goose cut both his legs. Big wild turnips came out and he had his wife cook them for Wolf, who ate them and then invited Goose. When Goose came, Wolf tried to strike himself in the same way but was afraid to do it" (Lowie 1924, 23). In the myth, the Trickster hurts his legs—a reminder perhaps of what may transpire when a digging stick is improperly handled.

Trampling, too, may be key to elucidating the mytheme. According to one report, the Navajo had a technique of gathering wild roots by using a digging stick as one would a paddle (another possible link with the way geese trample the soil): "Wild potatoes were gathered in the fall, about the end of October. They grew to a depth of about six inches, and were dug with a motion like paddling a canoe" (Kluckhohn, Hill, and Kluckhohn 1971, 64).

If we go back to the equation that summarized the preceding mytheme, we see that it applies here too. In the natural environment, the main elements can be related to each other as follows:

$$\text{bulbs} \;\rightarrow\; \text{legs (or knees)} \;\rightarrow\; \text{goose}$$

In the myth, this relationship becomes:

$$\text{legs (or knees)} \;\rightarrow\; \text{goose} \;\rightarrow\; \text{bulbs}$$

It matters little here whether geese are or are not looking for sego lilies in particular. For this, we lack data. What matters is the gathering technique of the myth, which is comparable, on the one hand, to the way humans dig up sego lilies and, on the other, to the way geese dig up roots in general (including perhaps sego lilies).

These two myths can be analyzed similarly although they come from two different contexts. Each of them nonetheless has specific characteristics. The Ute myth unexpectedly likens a digging stick to the edge of a goose's bill. In the Northwest Coast myth, which is found throughout that culture area, use of a smooth stone refers more to the behavior of those bird species that play the host role, and which therefore walk on streambed gravel, than to an instrument that humans might have used to get tasty fish eggs.

19 Muskrat Cooks Some Ice (Northeast)

Wemicus told Muskrat that he was starving and Muskrat said to his wife, "You had better make a fire in the hot sand." So the fire was made, and Muskrat went out with a big sack made out of hide and returned with the sack full of ice, which he dumped into the hot ashes. Wemicus expected that it would explode but it only cooked nicely. Wemicus wondered what it was. Soon Muskrat said, "We are ready now," and they took off the sand and there were a lot of nicely baked potatoes. Wemicus thought that was an easy way in which to live just to get ice for potatoes.

—Frank G. Speck, "Myths of the Timiskaming Algonquin"

The Ojibwa and other nations of the Northeast and the Subarctic have an intriguing Bungling Host myth that seems, at first sight, contradictory and inconceivable. Who would ever think of cooking ice as a substitute for edible tubers? Muskrat is the ice-cooking host and, in all the versions we have found, he is about the only one with this power to transform ice. There must be a reason.

We have five versions of this myth: (a) an Ojibwa version told circa 1893 by a Native from Sault Ste Marie, Ontario, Canada (Bourgeois 1994, 34); (b) a second Ojibwa version recorded by Frank Speck from Lake Temagami, also in Ontario (Speck 1915a); (c) a third Ojibwa version from farther south, from Sarnia in southern Ontario (Radin and Reagan 1928, 76–77); (d) a Winnebago version published by Paul Radin from his ethnographic research in Nebraska and Wisconsin (Radin 1956, 41); and (e) a Dakelh (Carrier) version from the Western Subarctic (Jenness 1934, 209).

The following version, which will be considered the main version, is of Ojibwa origin, from Lake Temagami to be exact. It is one of several episodes from the cycle of Wemicus, the Trickster. This hero experiences many twists and turns of fate, including four Bungling Host adventures: Black duck excretes rice; Muskrat cooks some ice; Woodpecker pulls his food from a tree; and Skunk builds a corral to draw in all sorts of animals, including caribou. These adventures, except for the one with a muskrat host, have already been discussed, and we will reserve a long comment on Woodpecker and his mythemes for the final chapter. Frank Speck's Temagami version has been published only in English.

WEMICUS VISITS MUSKRAT

Soon Wemicus and his family were starving again and Wemicus said, "I must go and see my son-in-law, Muskrat. He lives not far away." "All right," said his wife and Wemicus set out. When he had almost reached Muskrat's home, the little Muskrat children called out, "Our grandfather is coming." Wemicus told Muskrat that he was starving and Muskrat said to his wife, "You had better make a fire in the hot sand." So the fire was made, and Muskrat went out with a big sack made out of hide and returned with the sack full of ice, which he dumped into the hot ashes. Wemicus expected that it would explode but it only cooked nicely. Wemicus wondered what it was. Soon Muskrat said, "We are ready now," and they took off the sand and there were a lot of nicely baked potatoes. Wemicus thought that was an easy way in which to live just to get ice for potatoes.

Next morning Wemicus started out for home and left his mitten behind as he had done with Ninicip. Muskrat's wife sent a child after him and told the child, "Don't go too close to Wemicus. He's always in mischief." Everything happened as before. The child threw the mitten to Wemicus and Wemicus sent an invitation to

Muskrat to come to his home the next day. As Wemicus went on his way he had some potatoes which Muskrat had given him for his family. Half way home he rested and thought he would eat the potatoes, as they looked very good. So he ate every one. "I am the one who works hard," he said to himself. "My family can wait until Muskrat comes." When he reached home he told his wife, "Muskrat is also starving. I brought nothing. Muskrat is coming tomorrow to see us." Next day Muskrat came and they put him on the opposite side of the wigwam. Wemicus said, "We have nothing much, but, wife, make a fire in the hot sand." The wife answered, "I suppose you saw somebody else do something. Don't you try any more mischief." But he made his wife make the fire. He then went out and returned with the sack full of ice, which he dumped on the fire. The sack blew up all over everybody and put out the fire. Then his wife said, "I suppose you saw someone do that again." She made another fire and Muskrat said, "Give me that bag." He went out and brought back the sack full of ice, dumped and buried it in the fire, and, after a while, they got the potatoes. All of them had a good meal. The next morning, before Muskrat left, he got them another bag of potatoes. (Speck 1915a, 41–42)

Wemicus, the Ojibwa Trickster of the Temagami, is the equivalent of Nanabozho, who appears elsewhere in mythologies of the Anishnaabe (the name that the Ojibwa call themselves). Nanabozho is sometimes represented by a hare. Muskrat is the host of the above Ojibwa myth, and he corresponds to *Ondatra zibethicus*, which is one of North America's largest *Muridae*. This rodent lives throughout the continent as far as Alaska, except for arid regions like the Arctic and the American Southwest (Banfield 1974, 199).

In fact, the host is clearly a muskrat in three of the five versions of this myth (two Ojibwa and a Winnebago one). In the Dakelh version, the central character is identified only by a generic title: Rat (Jenness 1934, 209). No Native term is given. The Oblate Father Adrien Morice wrote several detailed publications on the Dakelh, including a dictionary that has the following lexeme: "rat, *tlûn-tco* (—big)" (Morice 1932, vol. 1, 33). He makes this comment: "*Tlûn*, the main root of the present Carrier term for rat, means mouse among their southern neighbours, the Chilcotins; *tlûn-tco*, therefore, corresponds to 'big mouse', and we thus see that the real root of such words is that which has to-day no signification in Carrier" (Morice 1932, vol. 1, 33). A more contemporary dictionary has the same term, written *dlooncho* in this case, and gives it the meaning of "pack-rat." This is the bushy-tailed woodrat (*Neotoma cinerea*). The same book has an entry for muskrat, which is called *tsek'et* (Antoine et al. 1974, 95, 234).

Both species are present on Dakelh traditional territory in northern British Columbia. The first species can be ruled out for several reasons. Although the bushy-tailed woodrat may not hibernate, it is active in winter only under the snow surface (Banfield 1974, 176). Nor does it have truly aquatic or semi-aquatic activities that could link it to the setting of the myth, i.e., getting ice to feed on. It is also much more tree-dwelling than its cousin the muskrat. Finally, a member of the Dakelh nation from Prince George, Nicholette Prince, has identified the host of this myth, which she knows well, as being *tsek'et*, i.e., a muskrat. So when Diamond Jenness wrote "Rat" he meant "Muskrat."

In the southernmost Ojibwa version, from Sarnia, the host is Po.kwis. His species is not identified but, if we consider all of the other versions on the same mytheme—Muskrat transforms ice—he is plausibly a muskrat too. Further on, we will look more closely at the last two versions, which differ from the first three we have discussed in at least one way: the ice is turned into a cooked bird (Dakelh) or a fish (Ojibwa) instead of potatoes. By identifying the etymons behind these actions, we will further corroborate that the host is indeed a muskrat in all five versions.

The muskrat mytheme is always set in winter, since the host lives near a source of ice. The second Ojibwa version provides some details about the muskrat's general habitat, right from the start of the story: "In a few days, when the raccoon meat was all eaten, Nanabozho thought he would go to see the muskrat, who was living with his wife and children at a small lake in the woods. You know the muskrat has a wife to this day. His hut was built over the water and rose above the ice. He built there because he lives on plants that grow in the water" (Bourgeois 1994, 34).

An aquatic environment is undoubtedly typical for muskrats. They always reside near a body of water: "Muskrats live in marshes, ponds, rivers, streams, and lakes, as well as agricultural drainage canals" (Prescott and Richard 1982, 132). They also live in families; the male has a mate and offspring "to this day": "The social unit is a breeding pair that occupies a home range exclusive of other pairs (Errington 1963, Proulx and Gilbert 1983). . . . Juveniles remain on or near their parents' home range at least until autumn and more often until spring. During winter, houses may be shared by a number of individuals considered to be members of a family unit" (Boutin and Birkenholz 1987, 318). In northern Canada, female muskrats have on average two litters per year between March and September (Banfield 1974, 199). The young usually stay with the breeding pair over the winter and until the next spring. This matches the general setting of the myth. In the version that opens this chapter, Muskrat's children rush to welcome their "Grandfather," the Trickster, when they see him arrive.

A muskrat will make several types of shelter. Besides the main lodge, most often built on dry land, and burrows dug into the banks, there are also smaller, temporary lodges on the ice. The myth mentions these feeding huts or "push-ups":

> Another type of lodge is known as a "push-up". A number of these are made throughout the pond by cutting holes in the ice while it is still thin, then pushing mud and underwater vegetation to the surface where it freezes as a mass and eventually becomes covered with snow. The muskrat shapes a chamber inside these little piles and uses each as a place to renew oxygen, to rest from underwater forays, or to munch on aquatic foods. If necessary, muskrats can stay under water for about 15 minutes, but the average time of submersion is 3 to 4 minutes. The "push-ups" enable the animal to

Fig. 46. Muskrat under the ice.

remain within the pond area for as long as it wishes before returning to the main lodge. . . . In winter these little resting lodges are often damaged by moose, deer, elk or caribou. The big animals paw at the mounds as they search for food, with the result that the uncovered holes freeze over rapidly. The muskrats must immediately re-open the holes and rebuild the domes. (Wooding 1982, 188)

The Ojibwa version that opens this chapter has also several cultural aspects we cannot ignore. Such details would have resonated with a Native audience, thus creating conditions for listeners to acknowledge later on the truthfulness of the story's stranger aspects. We thus learn that the home is a wigwam. In a previous chapter (chapter 17), we described the structure of this Ojibwa dwelling, as well as how the family members are spatially distributed inside (e.g., the wife is near the entrance). The version now before us states that the visitor is put "on the opposite side of the wigwam." We have very little data on the way visitors are placed in Ojibwa homes or in similar homes of other groups. Nonetheless, by drawing on personal experience with several Native groups of the Subarctic for periods of several months in a row, in cone-shaped tents or in canvas and log cabins, in particular among the James Bay Cree and the North Shore Innu of the St. Lawrence, we can say that the visitor's position seems to be the one opposite the entrance. That position was invariably assigned to us. Logically, a visitor should be placed there to leave the entrance unobstructed and easily accessible to other members of the hunting group. Women in particular often have to go out to get provisions stored nearby, to tend the cooking fire, and to do other tasks.

There is a second cultural aspect: the Trickster's stratagem to get Muskrat to visit him in turn. He leaves his mittens behind so that they may be brought back to him. He thus tries to extend an invitation without being rejected. The same scenario plays out in the Bungling Host story about the rice-excreting duck (chapter 17), also from the Ojibwa, and in several other versions with the same motif from the Ojibwa, the Winnebago, and others. We still lack ethnographic data on this point but we feel that the Trickster's stratagem reflects a certain Ojibwa or, more broadly, Native way of viewing rules of good conduct. If the Trickster invites his host directly, he may be turned down. His stratagem is to extend the invitation indirectly, i.e., by having children come and bring him the mittens he deliberately left behind. The children can neither accept nor reject his invitation; they can only pass it on to their parents. With no go-between to answer yes or no, the parents have to come and visit. This is also why the host's wife (Speck 1915a, 41) or the host himself, Muskrat, in the other Ojibwa version (Bourgeois 1994, 34), warns the children against getting too close to the Trickster when they return his mittens, given his trickery. They want at all price to avoid feeling obligated to him.

The myth has a third cultural aspect: the kinship ties between the protagonists. These ties very often express obligations that are implicitly or explicitly recognized as such in the myths. In the Ojibwa version that opens this chapter, Muskrat is the son-in-law of Wemicus, and it is well known that a son-in-law must provide his parents-in-law with food. Thus, among the southwestern Ojibwa, a son-in-law would commit to marriage by giving his future parents-in-law a freshly killed big game animal (Ritzenthaler 1978, 752). In the Winnebago version, the Trickster is Kunu: Muskrat's older brother. We have commented elsewhere that the Trickster represents humans, who act collectively as a big brother to nonhuman animals—or as a grandfather, likewise an elder—since humans are responsible for them and assume a role of guardian on their behalf.

These cultural aspects join up with muskrat behavior when the host provides food. In two of the three Ojibwa versions, the food is described as a potato (Speck 1915a, 41) or a similar root: "There is a kind of root a good deal like white potatoes that grows in bayous and ponds" (Bourgeois 1994, 34). The Winnebago version also mentions a root, the "root of the lily-of-the-lake" (Radin 1956, 41). The exceptions are the Dakelh version and another Ojibwa version, where the food is respectively a bird and a fish. As mentioned earlier, we will discuss these exceptions further on.

The two Ojibwa versions and the Winnebago version provide no Native terms that can identify the plant. If we look through the literature on Ojibwa plant foods, we come across the most likely candidate: the broadleaf arrowhead or duck potato, *Sagittaria latifolia*, sometimes called a "lily" and considered to be a "potato" by Natives. This plant with tuber-bearing roots grows in wetlands "totally or partially above water" (Marie-Victorin 1964, 616). The Ojibwa would harvest and eat it: "This is commonly called the 'wild potato,' and grows in deep mud. At the end of the tubular roots are the 'potatoes' which are gathered in the fall, strung, and hung overhead in the wigwam to dry. Later they are boiled for use" (Densmore 1928, 319–20). The plant is also part of the muskrat's diet: "During the summer, the muskrat feeds on leaves, stems, and succulent parts of various aquatic plants: cattails, reeds, sedges, water lilies, arrowheads, pondweeds, and bur-reeds. In winter, it feasts on the submerged portion of the same plants" (Prescott and Richard 1982, 134). Natives, too, know this: "This is one of the Menomini valued wild potatoes and hard to get on their reservation . . . The Indians usually see them in the water, washed out by the current, or see them near the burrow of a muskrat or home of a beaver" (Smith in Erichsen-Brown 1980, 215).

By looking at these junctions between human culture and muskrat behavior, we can answer other questions raised by the myth. Why is ice turned into tubers? Why does a muskrat give food to a human (represented by the Trickster)? First of all, we should mention that at least one version of the myth has the Trickster and the host perceiving the same thing differently. The Trickster sees ice and the Muskrat potatoes: "So she [Muskrat's wife] went out on the Bayou with her axe and brought in some of these potatoes, but to Nanabozho they looked like nothing but lumps of ice" (Bourgeois 1994, 34).

A muskrat's teeth are as sharp as an axe: "The muskrat is equipped with four ¾-inch-long (2 cm), chisel-like incisors which protrude beyond the fleshy, fur-covered lips" (Wooding 1982, 187). It can use them for tasks during the winter both above the ice and below, although the first option is riskier: "Although muskrats do not hibernate, they sleep a great deal during the winter months, and spend the rest of their time in foraging for food in their underwater territory. A typical territory, in both winter and summer, is not much more than 75 to 100 yards beyond the main lodge. In mild weather, if breaks occur in the ice surface, they may move about in the open for short periods, but at such times they are highly vulnerable to attack from predator" (Wooding 1982, 189).

Significantly, Muskrat goes looking for food on the ice, as stated in at least one version. Also significant is his axe—like the one his wife took with her. He then comes back with what seems to be ice, but which is, in reality, food. This paradox may be solved by examining a behavior that not all Western researchers have confirmed. Muskrats seem to lay up food in caches for the coming winter:

> The muskrat does not take as many precautions as does the beaver. It does not store a pile of food for winter. It makes do with moving about under the ice looking for submerged plants. (Vachon 1983, 29)

> It is not thought that muskrats store any significant amount of food for winter use, but sections of stovepipe reed have been found in bank burrows. (Banfield 1974, 199)

Some zoologists have nonetheless discovered more than just reeds in muskrat burrows. Huge stores of provisions can in fact be accumulated for winter:

> These tunnels were packed with tender bulrush roots, sedges, mints, young grass and reeds. The bulk of the store was white and crisp, and very tightly packed. (Carter 1922, 176)

> The most spectacular examples of storage that I have run across were revealed through the digging out or caving in of muskrat burrows in or next to Iowa cornfields. The burrow systems may be stuffed with ear corn. (Errington 1941, 84)

In general, naturalists now admit that muskrats can exhibit such behavior (Erb and Perry 2003, 324).

In any event, Natives have long known about this propensity of muskrats, as told in accounts from at least three different nations (Sioux, Ojibwa, and Meskwaki). In all three cases, these animals always stored arrowhead bulbs for the winter, and Natives were always keen on trying to locate these caches and help themselves to the contents. This was also done by other peoples, like the Seris of the Gulf of California, who would plunder caches of mesquite pods kept by pack rats (*Neotoma* sp.) (Rea 1998, 182).

The earliest account is old. It dates from 1902 and describes the Sioux plundering muskrat caches: "When our people [Sioux]

Fig. 47. Arrowhead bulb.

were gathering the wild rice [in Minnesota], they always watched for another plant that grows in the muddy bottom of lakes and ponds. It is a white bulb about the size of an ordinary onion. This is stored by the Muskrats in their houses by the waterside, and there is often a bushel or more of the *psinchinchal*, to be found within" (Eastmain 1902 in Seton 1953 [1909], vol. 4, 585). Ernest Seton goes on to identify the bulb as an arrowhead: "Evidently, this was the *wapato*, or duck potato, a species of *sagittaria*" (Seton 1953 [1909], vol. 4, 585).

The two other accounts were written by Huron H. Smith, a botanist who worked with the Meskwaki (Fox) and the Ojibwa.

[Meskwaki] The muskrats gather these corms for their winter store of food, and along a stream where these grow one can often find a cache of them. When the Indians find them it saves the trouble of digging them. (Smith 1928, 254)

[Ojibwa] The corms are a most valued food source to the Ojibwe. They will dig them if they cannot get them more easily. Muskrat and beaver store them in large caches, which the Indians learn to recognize and appropriate. It is difficult to dig them out still attached to the plant, because the connection between the roots and the corm is so fragile and small. (Smith in Erichsen-Brown 1980, 215)

The last source is probably the one that inspired this comment by Brother Marie-Victorin in his book *Flore laurentienne*: "In this species [*Sagittaria latifolia*], several internodes of its rhizome broaden into voluminous tubers. These high-starch tubers are an important item in the food of some Indian tribes. They are also harvested by beavers and muskrats, which store them away in caches; the Indians seek out these provisions and take them for themselves" (Marie-Victorin 1964, 617).

Thus Natives would pilfer any arrowhead tubers they found in muskrat caches. This is where muskrats themselves go for provisions in winter, these caches being located outside their actual burrows, i.e., their nests. Such food warehouses may be either in tunnels dug by these rodents or elsewhere, such as "along a stream where these [arrowheads] grow."

In all of these cases, the bulbs are frozen in winter and must be relatively hard to remove from the frozen muck, which may look confusingly similar, both being dark in color. The mytheme is starting to make sense. Its etymon relies on metonymy. Muskrat looks for frozen tubers that may be mistaken for ice. Removing them requires an axe (his teeth). The myth thus replaces the arrowhead

Fig. 48. Muskrat feeding hut.

bulbs with their surrounding matrix of ice, an environment these rodents feel at home in.

muskrat → ice = muskrat → arrowhead

All of this is corroborated by another muskrat behavior. In winter, muskrats never eat food in their burrows (= nests), but instead bring it into feeding huts or "push-ups" they build on the ice: "Food is generally not eaten in the nest, but in some other area that affords protective cover. In winter in northern areas, food is brought into feeding huts and push-ups" (Erb and Perry 2003, 325). We have already mentioned these push-ups, and one of them explicitly appears in an Ojibwa version as the host's home. These are hollowed-out domes of frozen muck, ice, and plant debris that accumulate a blanket of snow as winter progresses. A hunting technique actually involves breaking one open with an axe and setting a trap at the entrance (Vachon 1983, 79). The muskrat will come by right away to repair the damage.

If you break open a push-up, you can always find leftovers from a muskrat's meal, since this is where it feeds, not to mention that the frozen debris forming the dome may include arrowhead plants. These dome-like structures must have been noticed by Natives and mentioned by them in their myths, thus prompting some to find them and thereby become convinced that the myths are true.

Finally, if we go back to the widespread view among Native peoples that a hunted game animal gives itself up to the hunter, these arrowhead tubers taken by Native Americans should likewise be viewed as gifts. Muskrats give humans this food.

What about the two versions that use the same motif but replace the arrowhead tubers with apparently steam-cooked birds (in the Dakelh version) or with fish (in the southern Ojibwa version)? We will start with the Dakelh myth:

ESTE'S VISITS RAT

Este's said to his wife on another occasion, "I am going to visit my brother-in-law Rat." Rat hospitably invited him to enter, then took up his blanket and axe and went outside. Presently he returned with the blanket full of ice, made a hole in the sand of the fire-place, put the ice in the hole and covered it. When he removed the covering after a few minutes, the ice had changed to a cooked bird. Este's ate half of it and said, "I will take the rest home to my wife, and return you the blanket when you come to visit me." Some time later Rat visited him to regain the blanket, whereupon Este's in his turn covered some ice in the fire-place; but when he removed the covering, the ice had melted and extinguished the fire. Rat was so angry that he snatched up his blanket and went home. (Jenness 1934, 209–10)

Although it diverges from the version that opens this chapter, the Dakelh myth likewise highlights the muskrat's ability to work with ice. As we have seen, it can gnaw on ice when making its feeding huts: ("When the pond first freezes over by chewing a hole through the thin ice"; Banfield 1974, 198). Thus, while the Trickster sees only ice, the muskrat sees food. The Innu of the Eastern Subarctic, who are Algonquians like the Ojibwa, sometimes even name these domes of plant debris and ice *umîtshim*, 'its food'—where 'it' means the muskrat (Clément 2012).

This difference in perception also appears in the Dakelh version. Here, the host sees only ice (close view) where Muskrat sees a well-cooked bird meal (far view). It would be hard to explain this replacement of a plant food with meat if the conditions of life had been the same wherever this mytheme is attested. This was not so with the Dakelh. Although this people may have formerly eaten some tubers, it seems that none of these were of aquatic origin and, consequently, could not have been part of the muskrat's diet. We have identified three of them: an unidentified species of fern called *'ah*, whose roots were cooked in a pit paved with heated stones and covered with earth (Morice 1890, 135); a reddish lily (*Tsachœn*) that corresponds to an erythronium (*Erythronium* sp.) (Morice 1890, 135); and another plant, the tiger lily (*Lilium columbianum*): "Tiger lilies were called *teh'ghih'*. Only the bulbs of this plant were eaten" (Bond and Russell 1992, 83).

The first of these plants grows in underbrush, the second in the mountains, and the third in the foothills of the mountains. Moreover, as already mentioned, none of them is known to be eaten by muskrats (Erb and Perry 2003; Willner et al. 1980; etc.).

Had the bulbs of one of these plants been eaten by muskrats and humans alike, this food item could have therefore appeared in the Dakelh myth where the host makes food from ice. The principle would have remained the same: an animal (muskrat) gives itself up (actually, its plant food) to feed humans.

But none of these plants interest muskrats. The Dakelh myth thus falls back on another food item shared by humans and muskrats. As surprising as it may seem, muskrats are known to eat little birds, and in particular those it can get in the water (Seton 1953

[1909], vol. 4, 582; see also Erb and Perry 2003, 324). A hunter even managed to lure a muskrat by imitating a quacking duck:

> My friend was an adept at imitating the quack of a duck. . . . This seemed to me a strange way of coaxing out a Muskrat. . . . But I was mistaken; for, in less than half a minute. . . . I saw a fine, large Muskrat swimming directly toward him. . . .
>
> My friend brought the Rat to shore [once killed]; and, as he threw him down on the snow, he said, "This Rat has evidently been in the habit of catching and eating wounded ducks, and perhaps of pulling down those that were not wounded, and drowning them." (Woods in Seton 1953 [1909], vol. 4, 584)

Another observer made the same discovery. "The feet, bills, and wings of blackbirds (*Agelaius* sp.) and coots (*Fulica americana*) were found in the main chambers of two of the [muskrat] lodges" (Earhart 1969, 186). He attributed the presence of these meal leftovers to the predatory activities of a mink that had moved into the unoccupied lodges. From our standpoint, it matters little whether a mink or a muskrat had caught the birds. Such leftovers would have convinced a Native observer that the myth was true. Bird remains can always be found in muskrat shelters.

It goes without saying that the Dakelh themselves were—and still are—fond of eating birds of all sorts (grouse, waterfowl, etc.). At least in the past, they were known to hunt ducks by the hundreds on lakes the moment the ice was gone: "Taking advantage of the fact that these water fowl are very gregarious and will seldom migrate northwards before the lake [Stuart lake] is free from ice, the natives set common fish nets on the surface of the water and, manning eight to ten canoes at a time, they surround and drive them into the nets. This is a very exciting exercise and at the same time prolific of good results, as a catch of a hundred head at a single drawing of the net is not deemed very marvellous" (Morice 1890, 133).

At this point in time, the temperature is still below freezing. If a muskrat catches a young duck or even another bird, it may very well leave remains in one of its feeding huts—a mound of frozen plant debris and ice. Where an outside observer sees only a mass of ice, the muskrat, once again, sees its own food. Moreover, when asked about her people's version of the myth, a Dakelh informant identified the bird in the story as a swan, *Cygnus* sp. (*ts'un cho*, which means 'big bone'; pers. comm., Nicholette Prince). This kind of bird is a prey species of the muskrat (swans belong to the same family, *anatidae*, that ducks do) and, when seen on ice from afar, may look like a snow-covered mound of frozen plant debris—the sort that a muskrat would build.

The southern Ojibwa version from Sarnia is likewise anomalous and can be analyzed the same way. In this version, Po.kwis fills a bag with ice and later turns it into fish.

MANABOZHO VISITS PO.KWIS (EXCERPT)

Then he went to the lake and filled his bag with ice and started home on the run. As he was running, he heard a gust of wind coming from behind and heard someone say, "Chase him and when you catch him push him down, for he is stealing our fish." Po.kwis ran on and never turned around and when he got to the house, dropped the bag in a well and went inside. He told his wife to go out and get the fish. (Radin and Reagan 1928, 76)

In winter, the Ojibwa fished on the ice of rivers, streams and lakes, as did many other Native groups. Muskrats, too, love fish in summer or winter. This resource contributes to their diet, as has been relatively well documented, and this contribution can be large in some localities, as noted by these zoologists: "Its chief food in winter consists of the roots of aquatic plants—pond lilies, arums, sedges and the like—but in some localities it feeds on mussels and also on carp and other sluggish fish that bury themselves in mud. When ponds are frozen over, muskrats are restricted almost wholly to food accessible under the ice, but in rare cases they leave the water and burrow under the snow in search of the crowns of grasses and sedges" (Stearns and Goodwin 1941, 1–2).

Therein lies the origin of an etymon. But why, in the Ojibwa case, did fish replace edible tubers? Two reasons. First, where the myth comes from, Sarnia, in southernmost Ontario, muskrats might feed more on fish, there being not enough arrowhead tubers for muskrats to store away for winter. Second, fishing was more important to Natives in the Sarnia region than it was farther north, where we find the two other Ojibwa versions: "Fishing may have been more important to the Indians of Southern Ontario and Michigan than hunting or trapping during the nineteenth century" (Rogers 1978, 765). This supports the first reason even more: the greater importance of fishing suggests that fish were relatively plentiful for humans and muskrats alike, and this fact alone might explain the anomalous southern version, just as a greater abundance of arrowhead tubers or suitable bird prey would explain the others.

20   Woodpecker Pulls Eels Out of Trees (Subarctic)

Here lives my story. Rabbit went to visit his friend Woodpecker. When he came to the door, Woodpecker said, "Come
in and sit down!" There was a stump just outside the wigwam.
"I have nothing to eat," said Woodpecker, "but I will go
now and get something for our dinner." Then up the stump
he went, and began to dig worms out of the wood with his
beak. "These," said he, "are eels for our dinner. I always
get them in this way." And when he had enough "eels," he
cooked them, and the two had their dinner.

—Frank G. Speck, "Penobscot Tales"

In general, Bungling Host mythemes follow a recurring pattern.
Each animal is associated with an action that stays the same from
one variant to another or from one Native people to another: Beaver
kills his children, and they come back to life; a big game animal,
either a bovid or a cervid, cuts his wife's dress; Osprey catches
fish; Duck excretes rice; Bear gets grease from his feet; and so on.
There are of course exceptions, derivations, or transformations.
With one animal, however, the exceptions are so numerous that
the pattern no longer applies. This animal is Woodpecker, and
he will need separate study for several reasons. First, by analyzing all of the Woodpecker variants, we can learn how a single
myth operates differently in a range of cultures from its simplest
expression to its most complex. By studying a single myth and its

variants, we can thus confirm what we have already learned in one case after another by studying a single myth and its elements. Whether we are considering variants of a myth or elements of a myth, we learn how myths are constructed and, thus, how to reconstruct intermediate forms, i.e. missing links. It is now time for us to see how each variant forms a unique link in a chain of increasing complexity—and, eventually, disconcerting weirdness.

Second reason: when each variant is placed in its initial social and economic context, it may help us understand how a single mytheme can adapt to the different cultures it has to fit into. The woodpecker is very appropriate for study of these diverse adaptations, since various woodpecker species can be found pretty much all over North America.

Finally, with so many variants of one mytheme, we may have a good example of the unity of Native thought in the New World.

The literature has provided us with four Bungling Host mythemes where Woodpecker is the host. In order of importance, they are:

1) Woodpecker picks food out of a tree;
2) Woodpecker gets food by opening up his head;
3) Woodpecker sets his head on fire;
4) Woodpecker turns an arrow into food.

Some of the myths with these themes—particularly the last three—have come up in other chapters of this book and will be addressed only in passing. All of the above myths emphasize the woodpecker's head, as will be seen below.

The first mytheme is the most widespread one. We have found no fewer than nineteen versions (see the appendix), and undoubtedly there are others. They come from three culture areas: the Subarctic, the Northeast, and the Plains. Specifically, they come to us from the Mi'kmaq (4), the Innu (1), the Penobscot (1), the Ojibwa (8), the Winnebago (1), the Fox (1), the Menominee (2), and the Osage (1). We will start with an Ojibwa version.

This one is very simple and tells us about a behavior we all know: woodpeckers feed on insect larvae by pulling them out of trees with their bills. This version has been published only in English. It comes from Lake Superior and was collected in the early twentieth century. Here it is:

NANIBOZHO VISITS MĒMĒ

Nanibozho once went to visit his brother Mēmē (Red-Headed Woodpecker). Mēmē had his wife heat some water while he went out to get the food. Nanibozho saw his brother light on the side of a tree and pound upon it with his beak. Up the tree Mēmē went, pounding away all the while. At last he gathered a big supply of worms, which he fetched for his wife to cook. When it was done cooking, it was served out to be eaten. Nanibozho found it was delicious. When he started away, he asked that his brother come and visit him some day.

Mēmē once said to his wife, "Let us go visit Nanibozho." She was glad to go, and so off they went. When they were come, Nanibozho had them enter and be seated. Then he bade his wife heat some water while he went out to get some food. He fixed a pointed stick in each nostril and made them fast. He came to a tree, and up he climbed. As he climbed, he pecked, pecking after the manner of Mēmē. The more and harder he pecked, the deeper into his nostrils the sticks were driven, till presently he was knocked out of his head, and down he fell unconscious to the ground.

Mēmē came and revived him. "It is not your nature thus to get food," Mēmē said. So off he flew, and gathered some food from a tree. He fetched it to Nanibozho's, and it was cooked there. The food was good, and all were pleased. (Jones 1916, 391)

Nanibozho is an Ojibwa Trickster, as we have seen. He is sometimes portrayed as being a rabbit. Mēmē, the host, is a red-headed woodpecker (*Melanerpes erythrocephalus*). This species is set apart from other woodpeckers by the color of its head, which is entirely red—as is its neck and throat. Nonetheless, the term "red-headed" is commonly, and wrongly, applied to any woodpecker that is red on only part of its head (cap, whiskers, etc.). Another species might be the host in the above Ojibwa version.

All woodpeckers have large talons and short legs, which they use to climb trees. Their long, hard bills are adapted to the task of drilling holes and pulling insects out of trees, in particular larvae. In several Native languages, the same term applies to worms and other larvae:

> [Tewa] Worms of the most diverse kinds—maggots, larvæ, caterpillars, and almost any worm-like animals—are called *pubœ*. (Henderson and Harrington 1914, 60)

> [Koyukon] Maggot, worm: *gheeno'u*. (Nelson 1983, 267)

> [Squamish] Any "bug" or "worm" of the Class Arthropoda *ts'ekw'*. (Kennedy and Bouchard 1976a, 110)

This is undoubtedly true for the Ojibwa language. The English term "worm" means not only true annelids but also the larvae of any insect. Consequently, when we read that a woodpecker feeds on "worms" in the above Ojibwa myth, we should understand that the narrator may mean larvae, the usual food for this type of bird.

The above Ojibwa myth uses an isological mode of operation, i.e., it posits the equality (iso-) of a mythical signified (Mēmē gets worms by using his bill) and a behavioral signifier (woodpeckers feed on larvae). This is the simplest *modus operandi* of the variants we have:

woodpecker → worm

The above can be transformed to create a second, more complex kind of variant. While still using an isological mode, the myth now explicitly has a comparative element. A typical example is the following Penobscot version, which we excerpted in the opening to this chapter. This version comes to us from Frank G. Speck, who took it down in the early twentieth century and which is likewise published only in English. The Penobscot are an Eastern Abenaki group who traditionally lived in the state of Maine in the United States.

RABBIT TRIES TO OUTDO HIS HOST THE WOODPECKER

Here lives my story. Rabbit went to visit his friend Woodpecker. When he came to the door, Woodpecker said, "Come in and sit down!" There was a stump just outside the wigwam. "I have nothing to eat," said Woodpecker, "but I will go now and get something for our dinner." Then up the stump he went, and began to dig worms out of the wood with his beak. "These," said he, "are eels for our dinner. I always get them in this way." And when he had enough "eels," he cooked them, and the two had their dinner.

Then Rabbit invited Woodpecker to come over and visit him at his house in the brush, and have dinner. When Woodpecker arrived, Rabbit said, "Now I'll go and get our dinner. You sit down and wait." He took a piece of bone with a point to it and tied it to his forehead, as the woodpecker has its beak. Then he tried to climb up a tree near his wigwam, as Woodpecker had done. Up he got a little way by dint of hard scrambling; but his paws slipped, and down he came flat on his back with a thud that drove all the breath out of his body. Up the tree he clawed his way again. This time he got farther, and tried to dig worms ("eels") out of the wood, jabbing in with his bone as he had seen Woodpecker do; but he lost his hold, fell all the way down, and got killed. When Woodpecker saw what had happened, he came out and jumped over the dead Rabbit twice. The second time Rabbit came to life. "Now you go lie down. You are sick. You can't do anything now, you are sick. I'll get the dinner," said Woodpecker to him. Then he went up the tree, dug out the "eels," cooked them, and they had their dinner. (Speck 1915b, 52)

In this version, the woodpecker species is unidentified. Rabbit plays the Trickster role, as he does in many Algonquian cultures. The myth clearly indicates what sort of food a woodpecker eats. It eats worms. The myth also presents, however, an exogenous perception that is actually a projection of human behavior onto the story. Thus, Woodpecker eats his own "eels" as a Native American would, the eels being worms. It must be said that the comparison is helped along by the morphological similarity (soft and long body) between insect larvae and eels.

The Penobscot, of course, fished for eels and did so practically year-round, although they caught them mainly at two times of the year: the spring migration of young fish upriver and the autumn migration back to the sea: "Eels and salmon could be taken in quantity a second time, when they returned to the sea" (Snow 1978, 138).

Among the variants of this Bungling Host myth, we can cite several others with the same mode of operation. We thus have two Mi'kmaq variants (Leland 1884, 210–12; Rand 1894, 302), which tell how Rabbit is offered a tasty insect called *apchel-moal-timpkawal*, a term also meaning a grain of rice.

HOW MAHTIGWESS, THE RABBIT DINED
WITH THE WOODPECKER GIRLS (EXCERPT)

And wandering one day in the wilderness, he found a wigwam well filled with young women, all wearing red head-dresses; and no wonder, for they were Woodpeckers. Now, Master Rabbit was a well-bred Indian, who made himself as a melody to all voices, and so he was cheerfully bidden to bide to dinner, which he did. Then one of the red-polled pretty girls, taking a *woltes*, or wooden dish, lightly climbed a tree, so that she seemed to run; and while ascending, stopping here and there and tapping now and then, took from this place and that many of those insects called by the Indians *apchel-moal-timpkawal,* or rice, because they so much resemble it. And note that this rice is a dainty dish for those who like it. (Leland 1884, 210–11)

This Mi'kmaq word seems to have lost its meaning of insects that woodpeckers feed on. In a recently published dictionary, it means only rice: "*apjelmultimkewey* grain of rice" (DeBlois 1996, 5). A literal translation would be 'we cannot stop laughing,' a reference to the Chinese, who in the eyes of the Mi'kmaq are always laughing when they talk (pers. comm., Stephen Augustine). This word must have entered the myth in the nineteenth century because that was when the first Chinese came to the country. On another note, although nothing in the anthropological literature attests to the practice (Speck and Dexter 1951), the Mi'kmaq used to eat insect larvae. This is at least according to the grandson of Agnès Augustine (1898–1998), who remembers his grandmother saying that such larvae were even very "energizing" (pers. comm., S. Augustine). The myth thus records that humans did use this food source.

The myth also taught its Native audience about woodpecker behavior. By comparing a woodpecker's food to grains of rice, it proceeds analogically like the preceding Penobscot myth where worms take the place of eels. This analogical mode differs from the isological mode in that it introduces a comparison that remains explicit. We thus get successively:

woodpecker → worm

woodpecker → worm like his "eel"
or like his "rice"

A third, more complex mode of operation takes us from comparison to transformation. The food that Woodpecker gets from the tree is changed or transformed into another food that corresponds more, generally speaking, to a food for humans. This new relationship is always clearly spelled out in the myth. There are, however, variations. For example, the worms are pulled out of the tree but are transformed only when they fall to the ground, as in this Menominee version:

MÄ'NÄBUS VISITS HIS LITTLE BROTHER
WOODPECKER (EXCERPT)

Presently, he stopped tapping on the tree, drew out a big white grub which he dropped on the floor. His wife hit it over the head and immediately it became a fat raccoon. Then Woodpecker jumped

Fig. 49. Pileated woodpecker.

down, rubbed his nose, and it changed from an ordinary beak to shining brass or copper, and then, as he continued to rub, Mämäo, the Woodpecker, became a man before the startled gaze of Mä'nä-bus. (Skinner and Satterlee 1915, 284–85)

Raccoons were a favorite source of meat for North American Native peoples. They were hunted wherever they could be found: "Raccoons appear to have been eaten and their fur used in all regions that they occurred (Trigger 1976, 62)" (McGee 1987, 17). Some say they were eaten only when they were fat, as suggested by the myth: "Maria Córdoba said the *vâwook* [raccoon, *Procyon lotor*] was eaten by her people when it was fat—like pork" (Rea 1998, 214).

Whenever raccoons felt in danger, they could seek refuge in trees: "Because of their size and climbing ability raccoons have few natural predators" (Banfield 1974, 315). Such havens would be in trees usually "over ten feet from the ground" (Banfield 1974, 314). Evidently, a good archer can shoot down an animal that has taken refuge at that height. We surmise that the Menominee may have hunted raccoons this way and that the myth's allusion to the falling worm and to the wife hitting it over the head on the ground—the mortal blow—originated in an old hunting strategy, which would be the etymon. Such a conjecture is admirably supported by Woodpecker's beak changing into "shining brass or copper," a clear allusion to an arrowhead!

We have come across several other variants of this sort: a woodpecker hammers away at a tree to get a piece of food, which then, in the air or on the ground, turns into another piece of food that matters more to humans. Here are two examples.

> [Ojibwa] He pecked several holes and pulling out two or three worms, turned them into raccoons, which he dropped into the lodge. (Bourgeois 1994, 33)

> [Osage] The woodpecker then flew to a dead tree nearby and began to peck at it with his bill. In a short time he had a good-size pile of dust on the ground from his pecking. He had his wife put this into a wooden bowl and set it before the coyote. The dust as soon as it was put into the bowl turned into pounded buffalo meat, which the coyote heartily enjoyed. (La Flesche 2010, 147)

The second excerpt describes the transformation of a by-product of woodpecker activity: the little wood chips this bird digs out or drops while making holes. In myths, pieces of wood are often compared to meat, as pointed out in a previous chapter. Here the wood dust looks like minced meat. Furthermore, trees were often viewed by Native peoples as living beings like animals, and their parts named after the parts of a body: the foot of a tree, its head, its backbone (see chapter 1). These analogies between wood and meat had meaning for the people who heard these stories.

The above two excerpts, from the Ojibwa and the Osage, together with the Menominee versions (see also Skinner and Satterlee 1915, 388) show us the third mode of operation in the construction of this Bungling Host myth. The third mode is essentially metamorphological: an analogous product is taken from a tree and turned into a real product, at least real in terms of human needs. Thus, to recapitulate, we have three *modus operandi*:

woodpecker → worm

woodpecker → worm like . . .

woodpecker → worm   → raccoon

The fourth and last mode of operation encompasses the vast majority of Bungling Host myths. If the third mode with its use of metamorphology seems stranger than the first two, the fourth one is stranger still . . . and very conducive to teaching because it motivates the audience to look for the solution to the puzzle and, thereby, understand animal behavior, cultural practices, and so on.

The following Ojibwa myth shows how strangeness may be used to get people to understand woodpecker behavior.

MANABOZHO GOES VISITING

Then the owner of the house, his name was Onwahsahgonaishkung, in the twinkle of an eye, changed himself into a woodpecker, the big woodpecker with the red streak across his cheek "Ceophlœns Pileatus abilticola Bangs" (Northern Pileated woodpecker, or Cock-of-the-woods). Just before he made this transformation, he had told his wife to put on the big tray and prepare to cook a feast to make the stranger welcome. She complained that she had nothing to cook, whereupon Onwahsahgonaishkung said, "Put on the 'pot' and we will have plenty for a feast." So the 'pot' was put on and the stones heated for the cooking process. After he had changed himself into a woodpecker, he flew quickly up the tree-house and nearing its top, began to peck on the bark. Soon a hole opened in the tree above him and a bear and a raccoon tumbled out and fell to the ground and were killed by the fall. (Radin and Reagan 1928, 81)

This myth features another species of woodpecker, the pileated woodpecker (= *Dryocopus pileatus*) and adds another kind of game animal, the bear. Like raccoons, bears will climb trees, and the etymon of this myth undoubtedly originated in bear-hunting strategies (approaching, killing).

The fourth mode of operation is the most widespread one in the woodpecker versions and variants. There are many examples, including some especially complex ones.

> [Winnebago] Then he pecked the pole with his bill exclaiming, "Koko!" Immediately a bear fell down. (Radin 1956, 45)

> [Fox] Up the tree he went a-climbing with a "Kwa-kwa'! Kwa-kwa'!" Right on up he moved. Up there at a great way in the air he tested the tree by the sound of its thump. There in the tree where the honey was he began to peck a hole. It was beautiful honey. He had the skin spread down there on the ground, upon which to let the honey drop. (Jones 190, 271)

The Fox used to collect honey, although the anthropological literature again tells us little: "Women gathered nuts, berries, milkweed, honey, beeswax, and several tubers" (Callender 1978, 637). The myth suggests that one traditional way of finding bee-hives relied on the sound that the hollow portions of trees make when struck—a sign that a bee colony may be present. Here again, the food is up in a tree. Two other myths focus on the similarity between a by-product of woodpecker activity—the little wood chips the bird makes—and a food that humans eat. The referent is truncated, and we have now gone beyond metamorphology. Again this is the fourth mode of operation:

> [Mi'kmaq] Then Woodpecker went out. There was a dry tree-trunk in front of the wigwam, and he went to it and picked a quantity of meal out of it. (Speck 1915c, 65)

[Ojibwa] It happened to be the Red-Head that he was visiting. Now, when (the Red-Head) was come at the meeting of the lodge-poles, he then began pecking. And after a while some corn came pouring into the kettle there, whereupon full of it became their kettle. Down he came hopping; and when (he was come), then back again (was he in) human (form). (Jones 1917, 359)

These two versions have been constructed metonymically, i.e., they replace one element (Woodpecker's diet of worms) with another (a human food) through a meaningful and analogical relation (similarity of shape, of habitat, etc.). The meal and corn are not explicitly compared to wood chips left by a woodpecker. The comparison is implicit. We see the same implicitness in an Innu myth we discussed in the first chapter—likewise metonymical and relatively complex—where Woodpecker pulls not simply caribou meat out of a tree but specifically caribou ribs. To understand this myth, one must first understand the unstated Innu view that trees have animal-like bodies.

For the purpose of analysis, the four modes of operation, can thus be ranked in terms of increasing complexity. Here, the typical food for humans is a raccoon.

[isology]	woodpecker → worm	
[analogy]	woodpecker → worm like . . .	
[metamorphology]	woodpecker → worm	→ turned into a raccoon
[metonymy]	woodpecker → [ ]	→ raccoon

If we put aside this mytheme—Woodpecker pulls food out of trees—there are three other woodpecker mythemes that emphasize something special about the bird's head, as we have already discussed. They are metonymically constructed. The first mytheme has two variants: one from the Arapaho (Dorsey and Kroeber 1903, 118–19) and the other from the Lipan (Opler 1940, 140). The

Arapaho variant has a red-naped sapsucker (*Sphyrapicus nuchalis*) opening up its wife's head and removing the fatty tissue, which will become tallow (for pemmican making). The Lipan variant has a northern flicker (*Colaptes auratus*) opening up its own head to get pecans. In chapter 13, we explained these variants and their underlying etymon: the bird's behavior of pecking at a tree and making a characteristic sound. When this etymon is interpreted metonymically, the woodpecker no longer opens up a tree; it opens up its own head or its spouse's. There is also a morphological correspondence between the interior of a head and the useful products obtained from this interior (brain tissue looks like tallow; the lobes of a brain look like those of a pecan).

The second woodpecker mytheme is exemplified by a Caddo variant. Here, Coyote goes to visit a man who walks around with a "light on his head": "At once Coyote calls out: 'Say, friend, your head is on fire, and you and your house will burn up if you don't look out.'" (Dorsey 1905, 94). What follows is the usual scenario: Coyote invites Woodpecker, puts straw on himself as a headdress, sets it on fire, and his entire fur coat starts burning. Coyote runs off and never comes back. Again, the emphasis is on the bird's head and its special appearance. This is a widespread Native American motif—fire representing a bird's colorful plumage. It appears in a Jicarilla myth, also about a woodpecker (Opler 1994 [1938], 276), and in some myths about other birds that are reddish-colored like woodpeckers, as pointed out in chapter 6.

The third mytheme is about the woodpecker's arrow. This is the starting point for a Zuni myth (Benedict 1935, vol. 2, 211–12) we have already commented on (chapter 10). In short, a hairy wood-pecker (*Dryobates villosus monticola* = *Picoides villosus*) prepares food for his host by wetting two arrows and placing them in the ashes of a fireplace from which he pulls out two fat prairie dogs ready to be eaten. The myth also describes dust falling from a roof, being gathered up, and turning into corn meal. We see here an allusion to the wood chips that a woodpecker makes when drilling into a tree. As for the arrows that become prairie dogs, the meaning definitely works by analogy: an arrow is to a woodpecker's bill as prairie dogs (dug up from holes in the ground with a digging stick) are to larvae (likewise dug out of holes in trees by a comparable technique). A second Zuni version has rabbits instead of prairie dogs (Benedict 1935, vol. 2, 212–13), and rabbits can likewise escape to holes in the ground. In this version, the human food is changed (to sweetbread), as is the means of getting it (by catching the ashes that fall from Woodpecker's burning cedar-bark headdress and then pressing them together to form a loaf). Again, a woodpecker drills and causes something to fall to the ground: fine wood particles. In both versions, the arrow is one element of an equation:

woodpecker → arrow [= beak] → [game] → cooked food

All of this is consistent with a Navajo myth where a wolf's arrows (its teeth) are likewise buried in ashes and turned into meat (chapter 9).

We have thus reviewed all of the Bungling Host myths where a woodpecker is the host. They are all driven by one idea: emphasize a characteristic of the bird's head (or by extension, something done by its head). This may be its bill, its red head, its repeated pecking at trees (enough to split open a head), or the results of its activity (pecking at trees makes wood chips that fall to the ground). More importantly, the different variants and versions help us to understand the myths, including the different modes of operation from the simplest to the most complex—the isological mode, the analogical mode, the metamorphological mode, and the metonymical mode. We will come back to this point in the conclusion.

Conclusion

Languorous, dreamlike, repetitive—such is the vision of Boléro that started off this book and which never left our thoughts while we were writing it. Why? There are many reasons, for there are many points of convergence between this piece by Ravel and the Bungling Host myths. These myths certainly make us dream, as do the Arabic-Spanish melodies that enliven the composer's ballet. A uniform and repetitive tempo is maintained throughout the myths from one culture to another across the North American continent. They coil up on themselves, and they all end on a short, trembling finale when the Trickster comes to grief after failing to imitate his host's ways of getting food so easily.

The dreamy lighting that bathes these myths brings to mind the experience of an Innu hunter who, after dreaming of a maiden who greatly loves him and with whom he has had sex after undressing her, goes hunting and sees his dream come true: he sees two caribou, kills and cuts them up, and places them in a pile, as he did with the maiden's clothing. The Bungling Host myths were analyzed exactly the same way. When confronted with "such elaborate and devious ways" of thinking by means of mythical images—yes, images and not texts—we looked for their meaning using the same approach that many Natives use. For they have no doubt in their minds. These are not myths in the sense that we, Westerners, understand the word. These are distillations of truths that are repeatedly heard through myth-telling and then verified no less often in the daily life experiences from which they are taken and to which they take the listener.

Structuralism initially asks exactly the same questions as we have about these myths and their so-called weird, unintelligible, or absurd elements, but it takes another direction. Its method is indirect; the reality of these myths is denied and "irrefutably" logical arguments are used to ascribe any weirdness to an underlying structure that, through oppositions and transformations, governs how the elements have been expressed. This sort of reasoning is reminiscent of Zeno of Elea, as we said earlier. He likewise began by arguing that the evidence of the senses was fallacious (the evidence of the myths is fallacious) and then, using equally irrefutable logic—so irrefutable that it still has proponents—tried to show the reason for this "non-sense" by using what eerily looks like a system of binary opposition. He used the allegory of Achilles racing against a turtle: Achilles can never catch up to the turtle because during the time he has gone half the distance between himself and the turtle (which gets a head start of one hundred meters), the turtle itself has gone some distance, which Achilles will in turn have to cover, and so on and so on.

It is as if one went about analyzing an obscure poem, as only Gérard de Nerval could write so masterfully, by digressing on the oppositions or transformations at work in these verses when, on the contrary, they conceal a condensed meaning of personal experiences and bookish reminiscences from history, art, astrology, or alchemy. His verses have meaning despite their obscurity and density of thought:

I am the Dark One,—the Widower,—the Unconsoled
The Aquitaine Prince whose Tower is destroyed
My only star is dead,—and my constellated lute
Bears the black Sun of Melancholia
—Gérard de Nerval, "El Desdichado"

Now, the myths we have studied all have meaning despite their apparent weirdness. To discover their meanings, we have had to turn over one stone after another—a *basic analysis* with the sole aim of looking underneath the mythemes and finding their underlying etymons. These are the sources for the themes in the myths, and these are things that exist in real life. All of this strange imagery is clearly based on knowledge of very real and observable natural phenomena. To give only a few examples, such images include the grease of a bear's "hands" and "feet," the subcutaneous fat of a female caribou and other big game, and the fat from the noses of cloven-hoofed mammals and members of the deer family. It also includes a squirrel's testicles, which grow inordinately large during the mating season, an American dipper's feet, with which it wades through a spawning stream and picks up salmon eggs, a wolf's arrows, which it uses to get prey, the eels that a woodpecker pulls out of trees, the paper wasp larvae that a fox gets out of the ground by using its penis, the bean child who knows all about mesquite and its secrets, and on and on. All of these disconcerting images, and more, are begging to be explained.

These Bungling Host myths provide their Native audience with more than knowledge about animal body parts or associated behaviors. Many mythemes can be explained by etymons that relate to plant life, to food-producing techniques, to games, to religious rites, and to much more. Many also outline theories, such as how individual organisms reproduce and, more broadly, how species replenish their numbers. The audience may be introduced to human and nonhuman protagonists who perceive things differently—a difference in perception that often comes up in Native myths, as noticed by other authors who have studied them, particularly Adrian Tanner (1979) among the Cree and Stephen McNeary (1984) among the Tsimshian. In the myths we have studied, the protagonists are a nonhuman host and a Trickster guest, who represents a human, and much of the weirdness in the myths comes from this difference in perception. Whereas the Trickster sees only ice, Muskrat sees the frozen mass of tubers he has gathered; whereas the Trickster can only defecate, Duck can actually "produce" rice by defecating; and so on. Very many myths are also used to teach their audience another belief: hunted animals offer themselves up to hunters either directly or indirectly—through their mates or offspring. This view may be seen in the many myths where a big game animal offers up his wife's "clothing" or where Beaver, for instance, kills his children for the needs of hunters. In this act of giving—for which the hunter always has to pay a price by observing the rules—we may see another theory about the replenishment of species. Nature goes through cycles of regeneration that will bring a beaver's offspring back to life, even if they have been killed, just as the same cycles will bring the offspring of phocids (seals) or cervids (members of the deer family) back to life. These cycles are not only about breeding. Depending on the season, female cervids will have a thicker or thinner layer of subcutaneous fat; which is a fact hunters are aware of when they hunt. Other animals go through other cycles that provide critical information about the animal itself or its natural environment. A squirrel's testicles, for instance, goes through a cycle of growth related to its mating season, followed by shrinkage. There is also the time of year when certain bird species begin to sing, and when berries are produced. We come here to another feature of many myths, namely a reversal of cause and effect, at least as we see things in our societies. Whereas Western scientists will argue that birds are drawn to berries, specifically the color of berries, or that geese and ducks are drawn to ripe grains of rice, Natives will reverse the direction of causality, at least in their myths: birds "make berries appear" by singing, and waterfowl "produce" rice by defecating. Both of these facts are likewise verifiable.

These mythemes deserve a closer look in more analytical ways. To be understood, some of them should be examined and analyzed with all of their component parts; otherwise the conclusions may be incomplete. We are thinking here about Franz Boas, who classified myths by action, thus grouping seal myths and bear myths together with no concern for details, albeit minor ones, that could clarify the meaning and identify the mythemes. For instance, bears can warm their "hands" or their "feet," but not seals (earless or eared seals), which can do so only with their forelimbs, as we have explained. Another example is the beaver mytheme, which has two coordinated clauses and must be studied as such to grasp its full meaning: Beaver kills his children, and they come back to life. The propagation of animal or plant species is finally another source of many Bungling Host myths, and all of the means of propagation are described, including endozoochorous seed dispersal—ducks and geese carrying grains of rice—and epizoochorous seed dispersal—American dippers carrying salmon eggs.

In the first half of the twentieth century, Boas stated that myths could be a better source of information than actual fieldwork—the quintessential method of anthropology: "Boas believed that in a people's myths and tales, references to daily life and the development of plots reflect real practices and values, and that a description based on this material would more accurately portray the culture as the people themselves see it than one based on usual field methods" (Suttles and Jonaitis 1990, 81). Although he consciously exploited mythology in at least one monograph (Boas 1935), it did not really make a good case for this source because it was too limited to the obvious, e.g., material culture as it appears in myths—the tools mentioned, the types of homes, the references to the clothing that people wear, etc. Actually, Boas did not know how right he was. Myths are a storehouse of knowledge—undoubtedly strange knowledge because elements from the natural environment are mingled judiciously with elements from human life. Our book thus opens up a completely new avenue for analysis of myths, an avenue rich in possibilities. We argue that a myth may have elements that only seem nonsensical and which can in fact be analyzed to reveal the underlying etymons and, thus, the myth's meaning. In other words, such analysis is not confined to the Bungling Host motif. We have already shown how to apply it to entire episodes or even entire myths (Clément 1991; 1994).

This evidently takes us to the different modes of operation at work in myths, for we need to answer the question that Claude Lévi-Strauss asked when he wondered why non-Western, Native peoples think in "such elaborate and devious ways when all of them are also acquainted with empirical explanations." We already know that they have knowledge that sometimes exceeds our own, be it in botany (the Hanunóo), in zoology (the Tzeltal), in medicine (various South American peoples), or in other disciplines. So why would they prefer to think metonymically, for example, to the detriment of their own empirical mode of reasoning?

In our own societies, we have come up with fairly arcane and convoluted ways to memorize information that, otherwise, would be very hard to keep in memory. This is the case with the periodic table, which has given rise to all sorts of comic verse, sometimes naughty, where the first letter of each word matches the first letter of each element. For the first eighteen elements (Hydrogen, Helium, Lithium, Beryllium, Boron, Carbon, etc.), this memory aid goes as follows:

Here He

Lies Beneath Bed Clothes, Nothing On, Feeling Nervous.

Naughty Margaret Always Sighs, "Please Stop Clowning Around".

So it becomes funnier, if not easier, to make the connection between words that are hard to remember and other, sillier words that are easier to remember because they are so silly.

The myths we have studied, in particular the strangest ones, operate the same way. They link nonsensical behaviors to precise knowledge. The intention is twofold: mnemonic and, also, pedagogical—the myths impel their audience to verify by themselves the truth of what they heard. This is the principle of validation by personal experience, and it has always been the basis for Native education.

Yet these myths also exhibit modes of operation that are not at all nonsensical. We have called these modes isological, and they co-occur, for instance in the woodpecker myths, with analogical, metamorphological, or metonymical modes. These modes are not confined to the woodpecker myths. The isological mode is visible in other mythemes, such as *Rabbit gathers canes* or *Black-Mountain-Bear gets persimmons by leaning against a tree*. The analogical mode is present, for example, in a version of the mytheme *Muskrat cooks some ice*: "So she [Muskrat's wife] went out on the Bayou with her axe and brought in some of these potatoes, but to Nanabozho they looked like nothing but lumps of ice" (Bourgeois 1994, 34). The metamorphological mode is less common but does appear, such as in a version of a myth where Fox gets camas lilies up in a tree: "In the morning Silver-Fox went out, and, going up to a cedar tree, pulled off the boughs, which became a sort of camas (?)" (Dixon 1908, 172). As for the metonymical mode, it comes up in very many myths. In choosing to present one version or another in this book, we have tended to prefer those that exhibit the metonymical mode. Their weirdness makes them more useful for demonstration. Hence, one will have to look through the appendix, which has all of the myths we have found, to see that the other modes do occur relatively often.

This state of affairs leads to the following observation: the co-occurrence of different modes in myths of the same type. It also leads to a question: when in history did so-called scientific thought arise? Some authors (Jung, Lévi-Strauss; see the introduction) have claimed, with no supporting argument other than the postulate that myths have no meaning, that rational or scientific thought appeared after mythical thought, which by definition is irrational and even absurd ("absurd narratives"), and whose rationality is reduced to an external framework only, in which it is contained. Whereas Lévi-Strauss postulated that scientific thought arose by internalizing an external framework of rationality, Carl Jung spoke more of objectivation of mental processes, including myths. Both positions lead to the same conclusion: one form of thought had to come after the other.

Yet, as we have seen, isological thought is found in myths, i.e., the same kind of thought as the scientific kind—which is its most developed form. Indeed, science developed out of the isological mode. It is based on matching the representation of an object with the object itself—as closely as possible Karl Popper would say—regardless of whether the representation is abstract or concrete. At least, this is how science defines itself. If, however, this kind of thought is present in myths—in the same way that it is present and was present in the traditional lives of Native peoples—it must have co-occurred with the other modes. How could things have been otherwise? After all, isological thought is key to survival.

It is time to conclude. Mythical thought, which operates as much via the isological mode as via other modes—metonymical, analogical, metamorphological, or any other kinds that may in time be revealed—did not precede scientific thought. Scientific thought was already present in mythical thought as one of several modes of operation. It later went through an extraordinary expansion, and it is this later expansion that has misled us. But it did exist earlier, and this earlier existence is shown by the etymons of our mythemes. In a forthcoming book, we hope to extend this research beyond the boundaries of mythology to show how our basic analysis can assist anthropology by revealing the origins of other human practices—rituals, technologies, and even forms of kinship.

Appendix | *Bungling Host Myths*

This appendix includes all of the myths we found in the literature. There are 389. Most follow the same model: a host invites the Trickster to a meal and prepares it in his own way; the Trickster in turn invites the host and tries to imitate his guest's way of preparing the meal but fails each time. We have kept some myths that lack the second part—where the Trickster fails at imitating the host—but which nonetheless belong to the same Bungling Host motif because they meet the main criterion, i.e., a host acts in a specific way.

We have likewise kept some myths where the Bungling Host does not prepare a meal but nonetheless fails to imitate his guest in some other way (headgear, house, etc.).

Whenever an anthropologist has published more than one version from a single campaign of fieldwork, we have indicated the number after the mytheme description. Whenever a myth has been published more than once, the expression *see* appears after the main bibliographic reference and directs the reader to the other reference(s).

MYTHEME	NATION	AREA	SOURCE
Ā'moyonts traps with fire	Southern Paiute	Great Basin	Lowie 1924, 171–72
American Dipper (Water Ouzel) dives for salmon spawn	Lillooet	Plateau	Teit 1912b, 305–6

MYTHEME	NATION	AREA	SOURCE
American Dipper (Water Ouzel) gets salmon eggs by piercing or striking his ankle—2 versions	Bella Coola	Northwest Coast	McIlwraith 1948, vol. 2, 386–88
American Dipper (Water Ouzel) gets salmon roe by driving a stick into his leg	Haida	Northwest Coast	Swanton 1905, 132–33
American Dipper (Water Ouzel) knocks his ankle and salmon roe squirts out	Kwakiutl	Northwest Coast	Boas and Hunt 1906, 150–53
American Dipper (Water Ouzel) strikes the side of his foot and salmon eggs come out	Kwakiutl	Northwest Coast	Boas 1969 [1910], 153–55
Andahaunahquodishkung gets meat from his wife's back	Ojibwa	Northeast	Radin and Reagan 1928, 78–79
Antelope sits with his back close to a fire and grease runs out	Shuswap	Plateau	Teit 1909, 740
Badger cooks fat from his intestines (bull-snakes)—2 versions	Hopi	Southwest	Voth 1905, 205–6, 208–9
Badger pushes a stick down his throat and yucca juice runs out	Zuni	Southwest	Handy 1918, 459
Bald Eagle catches fish	Shuswap	Plateau	Teit 1909, 739
Bald Eagle catches fish in a creek	Osage	Plains	Dorsey 1904b, 15

Bald Eagle gets two turtles, one in each talon	Lipan	Plains	Opler 1940, 142
Bean Child hits himself on the forehead and gets pieces of bean pod	Tohono O'odham	Southwest	Saxton and Saxton 1973, 103–15
Bear (Black) gets fat by holding her hands in front of a fire	Thompson	Plateau	Teit 1898, 40–41
Bear (Black) gets fat by holding his hands in front of a fire—2 versions	Thompson	Plateau	Teit 1912a, 206, 301
Bear (Black) gets meat by cutting his thigh and his feet around his sole	Chinook	Northwest Coast	Boas 1894, 180
Bear (Black) gets ripe fruits by leaning against a persimmon tree	Caddo	Southeast	Dorsey 1905, 93–94
Bear (Black) sits with his back close to a fire and grease runs out	Shuswap	Plateau	Teit 1909, 740
Bear (Grizzly) cuts off a steak from his wife's back	Shuswap	Plateau	Murphy et al. 1999, n.p.
Bear (Grizzly) cuts some meat off his wife's breast and gets grease by holding his hands over the fire	Coast Salish	Northwest Coast	Adamson 1934, 249–50
Bear (Grizzly) sits with his back close to a fire and grease runs out	Shuswap	Plateau	Teit 1909, 740
Bear cooks a piece of his flesh and gets grease from his belly	Natchez	Southeast	Swanton 1929, 254–55

MYTHEME	NATION	AREA	SOURCE
Bear cooks a piece of his own flesh and gets grease from his body	Natchez	Southeast	Swanton 1913, 198
Bear cuts a slice from his foot	Passamaquoddy	Southeast	Mooney 1900, 451
Bear cuts his hand and gets grease by holding it over the fire—3 versions	Coast Salish	Northwest Coast	Adamson 1934, 4–5, 9–10, 368
Bear cuts some fat from his entrails	Yuchi (Creek)	Southeast	Speck 1909, 153
Bear cuts the sole of his foot and turns the piece into meat	Mi'kmaq	Northeast	Rand 1894, 302–3
Bear gets a piece of meat by cutting his thigh	Coast Salish	Northwest Coast	Adamson 1934, 6–7
Bear gets fat by holding his fore-paws close to a flame	Thompson	Plateau	Hill-Tout 1899, 578–579
Bear gets fat by putting his hand close to the fire	Coast Salish	Northwest Coast	Griffin 1992, 55
Bear gets grease by cutting the sole of his foot and meat from his wife's back	Coast Salish	Northwest Coast	Farrand 1902, 87–88
Bear gets grease by holding his hands above a fire	Nootka	Northwest Coast	Boas 1974 [1895], 172–73
Bear [gets grease by holding his hands in front of the fire]	Tahltan	Subarctic	Teit 1919, 220–21

Bear gets grease by raising his foot near a fire	Quileute	Northwest Coast	Mayer 1919, 259
Bear gets grease by slitting the back of his hands, and meat by cutting his thighs	Tlingit	Northwest Coast	Swanton 1909, 6
Bear gets grease by stabbing his heel	Algonquin	Northeast	Tenasco 1980, 64
Bear gets grease by sticking his heel with an awl	Catawba	Southeast	Speck 1913, 320–21
Bear gets lard from his belly	Hitchiti	Southeast	Swanton 1929, 111–12; see Lankford 1987, 224–25
Bear gets leaf lard from his belly	Alabama	Southeast	Swanton 1929, 162–63
Bear gets meat and fat by cutting his feet	Coast Salish	Northwest Coast	Adamson 1934, 345
Bear gets meat by cutting a slice from his own foot	Mi'kmaq	Northeast	Leland 1884, 212–13
Bear gets oil by putting his hand over the fire	Nootka	Northwest Coast	Jones and Bosustow 1981, 100–101
Bear gets oil from his side	Cherokee	Southeast	Mooney 1900, 273–74
Bear kills four of his young ones, and their bones must not be swallowed	Osage	Plains	Dorsey 1904b, 13

MYTHEME	NATION	AREA	SOURCE
Bear picks out a piece of fat from his body	Koasiti	Southeast	Swanton 1929, 210–11
Bear tries to get grease from his toes and from his side	Creek	Southeast	Swanton 1929, 55–56
Bear tries to get grease from his toes and from his side	Creek	Southeast	Mooney 1900, 450–51
Beaver catches fish by jumping with a stick into five holes in the ice	Sahaptin	Northwest Coast	Farrand and Mayer 1917, 167
Beaver consumes his own paws, then restores them by bathing	Pawnee	Plains	Dorsey 1904c, 356n267
Beaver gets grease by shooting an arrow that enters his rectum and pulling it out	Mohave	Southwest	Kroeber 1948, 49
Beaver gets willow branches and mud— 3 versions	Coast Salish	Northwest Coast	Adamson 1934, 4, 8–9, 10–11
Beaver gets wood (salmon berry bush) and mud (elderberries)	Coast Salish	Northwest Coast	Farrand 1902, 88–89
Beaver kills his child, throws the bones into the water and the little beaver runs back—2 versions	Fox	Northeast	Jones 1907, 230–39
Beaver kills his children and they resuscitates when their bones are thrown into the water	Shoshone	Great Basin	Lowie 1909a, 266

Beaver kills his children and throws back their bones into the water	Mohave	Southwest	Kroeber 1948, 48–49
Beaver kills his children, and throws their bones into the water—2 versions	Southern Ute	Great Basin	Lowie 1924, 21–23
Beaver kills his children, throws their bones into the water and they revive	Ute	Great Basin	Smith 1992, 70–71
Beaver kills his son and places his bones into the water—2 versions	Innu	Subarctic	Savard 1969, 10–11; see Savard 1972, 74–76, 90–91
Beaver kills his sons and the Trickster throws their bones into the water	Shoshone	Great Basin	Lowie 1909b, 266
Beaver kills his youngest child, plunges his bones beneath the water and he revives	Omaha	Plains	Dorsey 1890, 557
Beaver kills one of his children, throws his bones in the river and he revives	Kickapoo	Northeast	Jones 1915, 7
Beaver pours grease from his testicles [sic] on kindling and makes pemmican	Arikara	Plains	Parks 1991, vol. 2, 1122–124; vol. 4, 695–696
Beaver prepares willows and mud	Chinook	Northwest Coast	Boas 1894, 180
Beaver scraps off sap from a tree—2 versions	Shuswap	Plateau	Teit 1909, 627–628, 739

MYTHEME	NATION	AREA	SOURCE
Beaver turns a piece of bark and tallow into pemmican	Arikara	Plains	Parks 1991, vol. 1, 659–664; vol. 3, 465–68
Beaver turns driftwood and grease from his scrotum [sic] into pemmican—2 versions	Pawnee	Plains	Dorsey 1904c, 245–46, 267–68
Bee (Bumblebee) gets food by shaking a stalk	Chiricahua	Southwest	Opler and French 1942, 46–47
Bee shakes a hive and honey (grease) drops down	Jicarilla	Southwest	Opler 1994 [1938], 302–3
Bighorn sits with his back close to a fire and grease runs out	Shuswap	Plateau	Teit 1909, 740
Bird (Ā'n'an) gets fat out from his behind with a hook	Coast Salish (Comox)	Northwest Coast	Boas 1974 [1895], 124; see Bouchard and Kennedy 2002, 197
Bird (Aihoa'qōnē) fills a container with berries by singing	Bella Coola	Northwest Coast	Boas 1974 [1895], 404; see Bouchard and Kennedy 2002, 507
Bird (Aix•a'xonē) gets berries by singing	Bella Coola	Northwest Coast	Boas 1898, 93–94
Bird (Cwot) makes berries appear by singing	Coast Salish	Northwest Coast	Hill-Tout 1907, 348–49

Bird (Mā'melaquitsa) gets fish eggs by cutting into his ankle	Coast Salish (Comox)	Northwest Coast	Boas 1974 [1895], 124; see Bouchard and Kennedy 2002, 197
Bird (Skwit) asks his children to get salmon berries	Coast Salish	Northwest Coast	Adamson 1934, 3–4
Bird (Snowbird) turns wood into nuts	Ute	Great Basin	Kroeber 1901, 265
Bird (Ts'enk'oa'ts) gets fish roe by striking his ankle with a stone	Tsimshian	Northwest Coast	Boas 1902, 48–49
Bird (Tsia'kwawa) tells his children to get salmon berries	Coast Salish	Northwest Coast	Adamson 1934, 4
Bird (Waquaqo'li) gets berries by beating his behind	Kwakiutl	Northwest Coast	Boas 1974 [1895], 290; see Bouchard and Kennedy 2002, 387
Bird (Water-bird) gets salmon eggs by tapping his foot with a stone	Chilcotin	Subarctic	Farrand 1900, 18
Bird gets berries by incantation	Tsimshian	Northwest Coast	Boas 1902, 49–50
Bird gets berries by magic	Chilcotin	Subarctic	Farrand 1900, 18
Bird gets berries by singing	Dakelh	Subarctic	Jenness 1934, 209

MYTHEME	NATION	AREA	SOURCE
Bird goes through a hole in the ice and catches either a fish and some ducks or beavers—2 versions	Arapaho	Plains	Dorsey and Kroeber 1903, 112–15
Bird kills her children, prepares a meal (=rabbit), throws out their bones, and they revive—2 versions	Tewa	Southwest	Parsons 1926, 291–93
Bird kills many birds with his arrows	Shoshone	Great Basin	Lowie 1909b, 265–66
Bird makes rice by putting his head in hot water	Kawaiisu	Great Basin	Zigmond 1980, 101
Bird turns a log into prairie dogs	Southern Ute	Great Basin	Lowie 1924, 19
Blowfly goes in the rectum of a deer and cuts off his fat—2 versions	Karok	California	Kroeber and Gifford 1980, 171–73
Blue Jay leaches acorn meal by rubbing it against her elbow	Wiyot	California	Kroeber 1905, 103
Blue Jay puts acorn meal on her feathers and shakes a single feather to get a basket full of meal	Wiyot	California	Kroeber 1905, 102–3
Buffalo gets a kidney and some fat by shooting an arrow which strikes in his own back	Jicarilla	Southwest	Russell 1898, 266
Buffalo gets grease by sticking a stick up his nostril and turns rotten wood into meat with it	Lipan	Plains	Opler 1940, 139–40

Buffalo gets grease by sticking two sticks into his nostrils	Southern Ute	Great Basin	Lowie 1924, 20–21
[Buffalo] gets grease from his wife's dress at the back	Cheyenne	Plains	Grinnell 1926, 293–94
Buffalo gets marrow by sticking his nose with a stick—2 versions	Tiwa	Southwest	Parsons 1940, 127–28
Buffalo gets meat from his back and grease by pushing a stick up each of his nostrils	Jicarilla	Southwest	Goddard 1911, 232
[Buffalo] gets scrapings from his back	Cheyenne	Plains	Grinnell 1926, 292–93
Buffalo pulls out dry meat from under his armpit and fat from his nose with a stick	Jicarilla	Southwest	Opler 1994 [1938], 275
Buffalo sits with his back close to a fire and grease runs out	Shuswap	Plateau	Teit 1909, 740
Caribou cooks his wife's coat or a piece of her—2 versions	Northern Ojibwa	Subarctic	Désveaux 1988, 142–43
Caribou gets grease from his wife's dress at the back	Innu	Subarctic	Savard 1969, 13–14; see Savard 1972, 79–81
Caribou sits with his back close to a fire and grease runs out	Shuswap	Plateau	Teit 1909, 740

MYTHEME	NATION	AREA	SOURCE
Carrion Beetle gets deer by breaking wind	Paiute	Great Basin	Sapir 1930, 410–13
Chipmunk gets rice by cutting off one of his testicles	Dakota	Plains	Wallis 1923, 90
Condor turns bark into meat and gets grease from his nose	Crow	Plains	Lowie 1918, 39, 40
Crane spears salmon	Kwakiutl	Northwest Coast	Boas and Hunt 1906, 157–58
Crow traps with fire— 3 versions	Kawaiisu	Great Basin	Zigmond 1980, 97–99
Crow turns bark into meat and fat, and gets grease from his bill	Crow	Plains	Lowie 1918, 39, 41
Deer cooks his back-fat by standing with his back close to a fire	Lillooet	Plateau	Teit 1912b, 305
Deer cuts a piece of meat from his wife's dress which grows out again	Sahaptin	Northwest Coast	Farrand and Mayer 1917, 164
Deer gets fat by shoving a stick up his nose	Chiricahua	Southwest	Opler and French 1942, 44
Deer gets meat from his own body and blood from his nose	Wishram	Plateau	Sapir 1909b, 144–47
Deer gives his own fat and flesh to the Trickster	Shoshone	Great Basin	Lowie 1909b, 266

Deer kills her two children, puts their bones into the water, and they revive— 2 versions	Cochiti	Southwest	Benedict 1931, 160–62
Deer shoots an arrow in his back and pulls his intestines out	Yavapai	Southwest	Gifford 1933, 383
Deer sits with his back close to a fire and grease runs out	Shuswap	Plateau	Teit 1909, 740
Duck (a small waterfowl) gets salmon eggs by cutting his ankle	Bella Coola	Northwest Coast	Boas 1898, 93
Duck (Black) turns feces into rice	Ojibwa	Northeast	Speck 1915a, 40–41
Duck (children of Sawbill Duck) catches salmon	Coast Salish	Northwest Coast	Farrand 1902, 86–87
Duck (children) catches trout by diving	Chinook	Northwest Coast	Boas 1894, 179–80
Duck (Mallard) defecates rice	Sauk	Northeast	Skinner 1928, 148
Duck (Mallard) defecates rice into a kettle— 2 versions	Ojibwa	Northeast	Jones 1917, 316–21, 350–56
Duck (or children) catches fish by diving— 4 versions	Coast Salish	Northwest Coast	Adamson 1934, 5, 7–8, 249, 344–45
Duck defecates corn	Plains Cree	Plains	Bloomfield 1934, 299–301

MYTHEME	NATION	AREA	SOURCE
Duck defecates in a pail—2 versions	Ojibwa	Northeast	Radin 1914, 14, 15
Duck defecates rice—2 versions	Fox	Northeast	Jones 1907, 256–63
Duck-Bill returns from a field with his mouth full of rice	Ojibwa	Northeast	Radin and Reagan 1928, 83–84
Duck's wife dives and catches a salmon	Quileute	Northwest Coast	Mayer 1919, 259–60
Eagle catches porpoises	Kwakiutl	Northwest Coast	Boas and Hunt 1906, 155–57
Elk brings out meat from his hind leg and fat from his nose with a stick	Jicarilla	Southwest	Opler 1994 [1938], 276
Elk cuts steaks from his own quarter	Jicarilla	Southwest	Russell 1898, 266
Elk gets grease from his wife's back	Menominee	Northeast	Skinner and Satterlee 1915, 278–82
Elk gets meat by cutting a piece of his wife's dress off her back	Nez Perce	Plateau	Phinney 1934, 445–46; see Martin 1950, 20
Elk gets meat by cutting off his wife's sleeve and brings out camas from his own anus	Nez Perce	Plateau	Aoki and Walker 1989, 626–630
Elk [gives food to the Trickster]	Shoshone	Great Basin	Lowie 1909a, 266

Elk sits with his back close to a fire and grease runs out	Shuswap	Plateau	Teit 1909, 740
Elk slices a piece of fat from the back of his wife	Ojibwa	Northeast	Jones 1917, 298–304
Elk takes a piece of meat from his hip	Jicarilla	Southwest	Goddard 1911, 232
Elk turns a stick into intestines filled with meat and feces into camas roots, and cuts a piece of meat off the shoulder of his wife's dress	Sahaptin	Northwest Coast	Farrand and Mayer 1917, 166–67
Elk turns a stick into the marrow gut of an elk and gets camas by sticking a knife up his anus	Nez Perce	Plateau	Spinden 1917, 181–82; see Martin 1950, 20–21
Elk turns bark into meat and fat, and shaves his neck to make pudding	Crow	Plains	Lowie 1918, 39, 40
Elk turns excrement into a duck and a stick into an intestine filled with meat	Sahaptin	Northwest Coast	Farrand and Mayer 1917, 164–65
Fat-Man sits with his back close to a fire and grease runs out	Shuswap	Plateau	Teit 1909, 627
Fish (Red Cod) gets food by cooking ten young virgins and throws their bones into the water	Nootka	Northwest Coast	Boas 1916, 897–900
Fish-Oil-Man gets grease by holding his hands over a fire	Shuswap	Plateau	Teit 1909, 627

MYTHEME	NATION	AREA	SOURCE
Four boys with sharpened legs catch game	Assiniboine	Plains	Lowie 1910, 117–19
Fox (Silver Fox) gets a sort of camas by pulling off the boughs of a cedar tree	Atsugewi	California	Dixon 1908, 172
Fox (Silver Fox) gets cu'nna from cedar branches	Yana	California	Sapir 1910, 211
Fox (Silver Fox) gets grouse by holding up a stick on fire on them	Yana	California	Sapir 1910, 211–12
Fox (Silver Fox) gets grouse by setting fire to a pine tree	Atsugewi	California	Dixon 1908, 171–72
Fox (Silver Fox) gets pine nuts by shaking branches of a tree	Atsugewi	California	Dixon 1908, 171
Fox (Silver Fox) gets yellow jacket [larvae] by smoking them out and digging them up with his penis	Yana	California	Sapir 1910, 212
Fox gets quails by setting fire to the woods	Takelma	Northwest Coast	Sapir 1909a, 79–80
Fox gets salmon by stealing them from people	Takelma	Northwest Coast	Sapir 1909a, 82–83
Fox gets salmon by stringing them with a hazel switch	Takelma	Northwest Coast	Sapir 1909a, 82

Fox gets yellow jacket larvae by smoking them out, digging them up, and squashing them with his penis	Takelma	Northwest Coast	Sapir 1909a, 81–82
Fox is swallowed by a bear, kills him by cutting off his heart, and comes out through his anus	Takelma	Northwest Coast	Sapir 1909a, 80–81
Ghost serves the Trickster food	Coast Salish	Northwest Coast	Adamson 1934, 10
Goat gets meat by butting at a buff with his head	Chiricahua	Southwest	Opler and French 1942, 45
Hawk catches salmon with his talons	Kwakiutl	Northwest Coast	Boas 1969 [1910], 155–57
Kileqoitsa (river bird) cuts his foot and salmon eggs come out	Kwakiutl	Northwest Coast	Boas 1974 [1895], 290–91; see Bouchard and Kennedy 2002, 387
Kingfisher catches fish	Kickapoo	Northeast	Jones 1915, 7–9
Kingfisher catches fish by diving	Omaha	Plains	Dorsey 1890, 558
Kingfisher catches fish by diving into the icy water	Shuswap	Plateau	Murphy et al. 1999, n.p.
Kingfisher catches fish by diving through a hole in the ice	Kutenai	Plateau	Boas 1918, 8–10, 294

MYTHEME	NATION	AREA	SOURCE
Kingfisher catches fish with five switches by jumping through a hole in the ice	Sahaptin	Northwest Coast	Farrand and Mayer 1917, 165–66
Kingfisher catches sturgeon by diving into the water	Sauk	Northeast	Skinner 1928, 148
Kingfisher catches two fish by breaking through the ice	Jicarilla	Southwest	Russell 1898, 265
Kingfisher dives and spears fish with his beak— 2 versions	Penobscot	Northeast	Speck 1915b, 52–54; see Speck 1935, 101–2
Kingfisher dives for fish through a hole in the ice	Thompson	Plateau	Teit 1898, 41
Kingfisher dives for fish through a hole in the ice	Thompson	Plateau	Teit 1917, 6
Kingfisher dives for fish through a hole in the ice— 2 versions	Thompson	Plateau	Teit 1912a, 206, 301
Kingfisher gets fish by diving into the water— 2 versions	Shuswap	Plateau	Teit 1909, 628, 739
Kingfisher goes through the ice and comes out with a fish in his beak	Jicarilla	Southwest	Opler 1994 [1938], 274– 75
Kingfisher goes under the ice and brings out two beavers	Arapaho	Plains	Dorsey and Kroeber 1903, 115–18

Kingfisher harpoons eels with his beak	Innu	Subarctic	Speck 1925, 10–11
Kingfisher harpoons salmon	Kwakiutl	Northwest Coast	Boas 1974 [1895], 290; see Bouchard and Kennedy 2002, 386
Kingfisher jumps into the water and catches fish	Jicarilla	Southwest	Goddard 1911, 231
Kingfisher pulls suckers out of a hole in the ice	Sanpoil	Plateau	Ray 1933, 177–78
Kingfisher sends his children out for fresh salmon	Coast Salish	Northwest Coast	Farrand 1902, 89
Kingfisher spears a fish with his beak	Fox	Northeast	Jones 1907, 263–67
Kingfisher spears salmon	Kwakiutl	Northwest Coast	Boas 1969 [1910], 239
Kingfisher spears salmon	Kwakiutl	Northwest Coast	Boas and Hunt 1906, 158–59
Kingfisher spears some fish through a hole in the ice	Lillooet	Plateau	Teit 1912b, 306
Kingfisher strikes his ankle and salmon eggs pour out of it	Tsimshian	Northwest Coast	Boas 1916, 91
Kingfisher takes a salmon egg from his hair and gets a kettle full of eggs	Quileute	Northwest Coast	Mayer 1919, 260–61

MYTHEME	NATION	AREA	SOURCE
Magpie catches fish by diving through a hole in the ice with his net	Cœur d'Alêne	Plateau	Reichard 1947, 132–33
Magpie gets blood from his nostrils	Ute	Great Basin	Kroeber 1901, 265–66
Magpie nets a deer — 2 versions	Thompson	Plateau	Teit 1912a, 206, 301
Magpie snares a deer	Thompson	Plateau	Teit 1898, 42
Magpie snares a deer	Thompson	Plateau	Hill-Tout 1899, 575–577
Magpie turns a single salmon egg into a kettle full of salmon eggs	Chinook	Northwest Coast	Boas 1894, 178–79
Magpie turns one salmon egg into a pot full of salmon eggs	Coast Salish	Northwest Coast	Farrand 1902, 85–86
Mämäo (Logcock) gets raccoons (=worms) by pecking at a post with his bill	Menominee	Northeast	Skinner and Satterlee 1915, 387–89
Man calls for food and meat drops outside his tepee	Arapaho	Plains	Salzmann 1956, 154–55
Man calls for food and meat falls down in front of his tent	Arapaho	Plains	Dorsey and Kroeber 1903, 120
Man kills buffalo with his sharpened leg	Arapaho	Plains	Dorsey and Kroeber 1903, 112

Man turns bark into meat and gets tallow from his wife by opening her skull	Arapaho	Plains	Dorsey and Kroeber 1903, 118–20
Man with a sharp leg kills a buffalo	Arapaho	Plains	Salzmann and Salzmann 1950, 95–96; see Salzmann 1956, 152–53
Moose cuts a piece of flesh from his wife's shoulder	Chippewa (Ojibwa)	Northeast	Schoolcraft 1856, 45–47
Moose cuts his wife's nose off, turns roots into guts, and gets camas from his backside	Kutenai	Plateau	Boas 1918, 10–11, 294
Moose gets food by cutting a piece of his wife's garment at the back	Ojibwa	Northeast	Jones 1916, 390
Moose sits with his back close to a fire and grease runs out	Shuswap	Plateau	Teit 1909, 740
Mountain Goat shoots himself with two arrows	Southern Ute	Great Basin	Lowie 1924, 24
Mountain Lion kills a horse by springing upon it	Jicarilla	Southwest	Russell 1898, 266–67
Mountain Lion leaps on a horse and kills it	Southern Ute	Great Basin	Lowie 1924, 56–57
Mountain Lion pounces down on a horse and kills it	Caddo	Southeast	Dorsey 1905, 87–89

MYTHEME	NATION	AREA	SOURCE
Mountain Sheep cuts a piece of meat from the front of his wife's dress	Sahaptin	Northwest Coast	Farrand and Mayer 1917, 167–68
Mountain Sheep gets fat meat by shooting himself in the anus	Ute	Great Basin	Kroeber 1901, 264–65
Mountain Sheep gets meat from his wife's dress at the back	Nez Perce	Plateau	Spinden 1917, 182; see Martin 1950, 20–21
Mountain Sheep gets meat from his wife's nose, his wife's sides and his own two sides	Wasco	Plateau	Sapir 1909b, 270–71
Mule Deer gets kidney fat by shooting an arrow and piercing his side	Lipan	Plains	Opler 1940, 140–41
Muskrat gets rice by boiling water	Omaha	Plains	Dorsey 1890, 557–8
Muskrat turns ice into lily-of-the-lake roots	Winnebago	Northeast	Radin 1956, 41–42
Muskrat turns ice into potato-like roots	Ojibwa	Northeast	Bourgeois 1994, 34–35
Muskrat turns ice into potatoes	Ojibwa	Northeast	Speck 1915a, 41–42
Osprey (Fish-Hawk) catches fish	Nez Perce	Plateau	Aoki and Walker 1989, 626–630

Osprey (Fish-Hawk) catches fish by diving through a hole in the ice	Nez Perce	Plateau	Spinden 1917, 183–84; see Martin 1950, 22
Osprey (Fish-hawk) catches fish under the ice— 2 versions	Southern Ute	Great Basin	Lowie 1924, 21, 23
Osprey (Fish-Hawk) catches fish with a string-like thing on his head	Wichita	Plains	Dorsey 1904a, 285–86
Osprey (Fish-Hawk) catches five different kinds of fish by jumping through the ice	Wasco	Plateau	Sapir 1909b, 269–70
Osprey (Fish-Hawk) catches spring salmon	Kwakiutl	Northwest Coast	Boas and Hunt 1906, 153–54
Osprey (Fish-Hawk) turns a stick into a ring of cooked intestine and plunges through a hole in the ice to catch salmon	Nez Perce	Plateau	Phinney 1934, 446–47; see Martin 1950, 22
Osprey catches fish with a line	Innu	Subarctic	Savard 1969, 12–13; see Savard 1972, 78–79
Otter (children) catches fresh salmon	Coast Salish	Northwest Coast	Farrand 1902, 88
Otter catches eels by diving underwater	Mi'kmaq	Northeast	Leland 1884, 208–10
Otter catches fish	Nez Perce	Plateau	Spinden 1917, 182–83

MYTHEME	NATION	AREA	SOURCE
Otter gets fresh salmon out of the water	Shoshone	Great Basin	Lowie 1909b, 266
Otter jumps into a pond and catches eels	Mi'kmaq	Northeast	Speck 1915c, 64–65
Otter plunges in the water and catches eels	Mi'kmaq	Northeast	Rand 1894, 300–301
Owl [gets grease by piercing his eyes]	Shoshone	Great Basin	Lowie 1909a, 266
Owl gets grease by piercing his eyes	Shoshone	Great Basin	Lowie 1909b, 265
Owl gets grease from his eyes and turns pounded bark into meat with it	Crow	Plains	Lowie 1918, 38, 40
Owl jumps on the back of a deer and cuts his throat	Karok	California	Kroeber and Gifford 1980, 194–95
Po.kwis turns ice into fish	Ojibwa	Northeast	Radin and Reagan 1928, 76–77
Polecat lures many deer with acorns and kills them by breaking wind in their direction	Winnebago	Northeast	Radin 1956, 46–49
Porcupine gets blood and grease from his nose	Hopi	Southwest	Voth 1905, 202–4
Porcupine scratches his nose with a piece of bark, blood flows, and he gets meat by roasting it	Navajo	Southwest	Matthews 1897, 87

Prairie Dog gets food by cooking four sticks in the ashes	Jicarilla	Southwest	Russell 1898, 265–66
Prairie Dog whittles four arrows and turns them into fat prairie-dogs	Chiricahua	Southwest	Opler and French 1942, 47
Rabbit (Jackrabbit) cooks a brown rabbit	Shoshone	Great Basin	Lowie 1909b, 266
Rabbit gathers some canes	Biloxi	Southeast	Dorsey 1893, 49–50
Rat turns ice into a cooked bird	Dakelh	Subarctic	Jenness 1934, 209–10
Rattlesnake gets two chickens	Cochiti	Southwest	Benedict 1931, 146–47
Raven gets buffalo meat and fat by piercing himself under the arm with an arrow	Caddo	Southeast	Dorsey 1905, 93
Red Squirrel gets rice from one testicle and grease from another	Menominee	Northeast	Skinner and Satterlee 1915, 282–84
Ring-tailed cat knocks off flesh from his knee with a stone	Yavapai	Southwest	Gifford 1933, 393–94
Robin and Jay make eels for Rabbit	Mi'kmaq	Northeast	Parsons 1925, 83–84
Robin gets worms from a tree and Jay digs up dung to get some worms	Mi'kmaq	Northeast	Parsons 1925, 84

MYTHEME	NATION	AREA	SOURCE
Sea Lion gets food by cutting a piece of flesh off his side	Coast Salish	Northwest Coast	Adamson 1934, 5
Sea Lion gets grease by roasting his hands	Haida	Northwest Coast	Swanton 1905, 133
Seal (Hair Seal) gets grease by roasting his hands	Haida	Northwest Coast	Swanton 1905, 133
Seal (Hair Seal) kills his youngest son and he revives	Coast Salish	Northwest Coast	Farrand 1902, 90–91
Seal gets fat by holding his hands close to a fire	Kwakiutl	Northwest Coast	Boas 1974 [1895], 291; see Bouchard and Kennedy 2002, 387
Seal gets fat by holding his hands close to the fire	Bella Coola	Northwest Coast	Boas 1974 [1895], 404; see Bouchard and Kennedy 2002, 507
Seal gets fat by roasting the back of his hands	Kwakiutl	Northwest Coast	Boas and Hunt 1906, 159–60
Seal gets grease by holding her hands over the fire	Bella Coola	Northwest Coast	Boas 1898, 93–94
Seal gets grease by holding his flippers above a fire—2 versions	Bella Coola	Northwest Coast	McIlwraith 1948, vol. 2, 388–89
Seal gets grease by holding his "front feet" up to a fire	Salish (Squamish)	Northwest Coast	Kennedy and Bouchard 1976b, 123

Seal gets grease by holding his hands close to a fire	Tsimshian	Northwest Coast	Boas 1916, 90–91
Seal gets grease by holding his hands close to the fire	Coast Salish (Squamish)	Northwest Coast	Boas 1974 [1895], 92–93; see Bouchard and Kennedy 2002, 160
Seal gets grease by holding his hands towards the fire	Tsimshian	Northwest Coast	Cove and MacDonald 1987, 20–21
Seal gets grease by warming his hands near a fire	Tsimshian	Northwest Coast	Boas 1902, 46–48
Seal gets oil by holding his hands close to the fire	Coast Salish (Comox)	Northwest Coast	Boas 1974 [1895], 124; see Bouchard and Kennedy 2002, 197
Seal gets oil by roasting his hands before a fire	Coast Salish	Northwest Coast	Hill-Tout 1904, 51
Seal kills his smallest son and he revives	Coast Salish	Northwest Coast	Adamson 1934, 8
Seal kills his youngest son and he revives	Chinook	Northwest Coast	Boas 1894, 181
Seal warms her hands and fat drops out of them	Kwakiutl	Northwest Coast	Boas 1969 [1910], 237–39
Shadow cooks salmon and other food—3 versions	Coast Salish	Northwest Coast	Adamson 1934, 5–6, 9
Shadow cooks salmon for the Trickster	Coast Salish	Northwest Coast	Farrand 1902, 89–90

MYTHEME	NATION	AREA	SOURCE
Shadow has salmon roe for his hosts	Chinook	Northwest Coast	Boas 1894, 181–82
Skunk attracts animals using berries, then shoots at them—2 versions	Fox	Northeast	Jones 1907, 239–55
Skunk gets food by breaking wind	Ojibwa	Northeast	Jones 1917, 320–31
Skunk gets meat by spraying his prey with odor	Tohono O'odham	Southwest	Saxton and Saxton 1973, 118–20
Skunk gives Sitco$^{n'}$ski some of his filth to kill people	Assiniboine	Plains	Lowie 1910, 128
Skunk gives Wolf some ammunition—2 versions	Osage	Plains	Dorsey 1904b, 12
Skunk is imitated by the Trickster who paints his wife and his children with white paint	Kickapoo	Northeast	Jones 1915, 4–7
Skunk kills caribou in a corral by spraying them—2 versions	Innu	Subarctic	Savard 1969, 14–15; see Savard 1972, 81–82, 91–92
Skunk kills game in his enclosure by breaking wind	Ojibwa	Northeast	Speck 1915a, 43–44
Skunk lures caribou with nuts then kills them with his poison	Dakelh	Subarctic	Jenness 1934, 210

Skunk lures game with acorns and kills a buck by turning his buttocks on it— 2 versions	Sauk	Northeast	Skinner 1928, 147– 48, 151
Skunk offers the Trickster something to eat	Kickapoo	Northeast	Jones 1915, 4–7
Skunk shoots a deer with his anus—2 versions	Ojibwa	Northeast	Radin 1914, 14, 16
Skunk stuns animals by breaking wind	Menominee	Northeast	Skinner and Satterlee 1915, 286–88
Skunk takes buffalo in a pound and kills them by breaking wind	Plains Cree	Plains	Bloomfield 1934, 301–9
Skwináuq catches a halibut by fishing under his house	Coast Salish	Northwest Coast	Hill-Tout 1907, 349– 50
Snake gets a squash by covering himself in embers	Tohono O'odham	Southwest	Saxton and Saxton 1973, 116–17
Snake makes tenderloins by going repeatedly under a thorn bush—3 versions	Kawaiisu	Great Basin	Zigmond 1980, 93–95
Snipe catches fish by the gills	Winnebago	Northeast	Radin 1956, 42–44
Snipe strikes his ankle and salmon eggs run out	Nootka	Northwest Coast	Sapir and Swadesh 1939, 45
Squirrel (Flying Squirrel) gets walnuts by piercing his testes	Omaha	Plains	Dorsey 1890, 558

MYTHEME	NATION	AREA	SOURCE
Squirrel gets bear grease by piercing his testes— 3 versions	Ojibwa	Northeast	Jones 1917, 310–15, 340–49, 421–23
Squirrel gets fat by slicing off pieces of his testicles	Ojibwa	Northeast	Jones 1916, 390–91
Squirrel gets meat from his wife's back	Illinois	Northeast	Michelson 1917, 494
Squirrel gets oil by stabbing himself in each flank with an awl	Ojibwa	Northeast	Radin and Reagan 1928, 79–80
Squirrel gets pecans from his scrotum	Pawnee	Plains	Dorsey 1904c, 246–47
Sturgeon butchers his wife, throws her organs into the water and she revives	Chinook	Northwest Coast	Jacobs 1958, 222–26
Thrush gets berries by incantation	Kwakiutl	Northwest Coast	Boas 1969 [1910], 151–53
Thrush gets berries by singing	Bella Coola	Northwest Coast	McIlwraith 1948, vol. 2, 389
Thrush gets berries by singing	Kwakiutl	Northwest Coast	Boas and Hunt 1906, 148–50
Thrush gets berries by singing	Tsimshian	Northwest Coast	Boas 1916, 91–92
Thrush gets berries from her anus	Kwakiutl	Northwest Coast	Boas 1969 [1910], 237

Tortoise gets deer by making them slip off his back	Yavapai	Southwest	Gifford 1933, 392–93
Tzala catches fish by diving through a hole in the ice	Thompson	Plateau	Hill-Tout 1899, 577–578
Warbler sends his wife and children for berries	Coast Salish	Northwest Coast	Farrand 1902, 89
White-Tailed Deer gets doe meat by shooting against a red clay bank	Lipan	Plains	Opler 1940, 141–42
Wildcat eats his own lights (=lungs)	Navajo	Southwest	Parsons 1923, 369
Wildcat gets larvae by burying himself in ashes	Serrano	California	Benedict 1926, 16
Wildcat gets mesquite by beating a blanket	Serrano	California	Benedict 1926, 16–17
Wild Goose gets turnips by striking his own knee— 3 versions	Southern Ute	Great Basin	Lowie 1924, 21–23
Wītcī′gīgits gets piñon nuts by striking a log	Southern Ute	Great Basin	Lowie 1924, 22
Wolf kills deer by shaking his deer-hoof rattles	Sahaptin	Northwest Coast	Farrand and Mayer 1917, 167
Wolf turns arrow points into puddings of minced meat	Navajo	Southwest	Matthews 1897, 87–88
Woodpecker (Flicker) is imitated by Coyote who sets his own head on fire	Jicarilla	Southwest	Opler 1994 [1938], 276–77

MYTHEME	NATION	AREA	SOURCE
Woodpecker digs eels (=worms) out of a tree	Penobscot	Northeast	Speck 1915b, 52; see Speck 1935, 100–101
Woodpecker drives his bill in a tamarack and gets something that turns into a raccoon	Chippewa (Ojibwa)	Northeast	Schoolcraft 1856, 43–45
Woodpecker gathers worms by pounding upon a tree with his beak	Ojibwa	Northeast	Jones 1916, 391
Woodpecker gets a bear and a raccoon by pecking a hole in a tree	Ojibwa	Northeast	Radin and Reagan 1928, 81–82
Woodpecker gets a raccoon (=grub) by striking a tree with his bill	Menominee	Northeast	Skinner and Satterlee 1915, 284–86
Woodpecker gets a raccoon by making a hole in a tree—2 versions	Ojibwa	Northeast	Radin 1914, 14–15, 16
Woodpecker gets a raccoon by pecking in a trunk with his nose	Ojibwa	Northeast	Speck 1915a, 42–43
Woodpecker gets a raccoon by picking a pole with his bill	Ojibwa	Northeast	Radin and Reagan 1928, 77
Woodpecker gets honey by pecking a hole in a tree	Fox	Northeast	Jones 1907, 268–73
Woodpecker gets insects (=rice) by digging them out of an old beech-tree	Mi'kmaq	Northeast	Rand 1894, 301–2

Woodpecker gets pecan nuts by opening up his head at the back	Lipan	Plains	Opler 1940, 140
Woodpecker gets raccoons or corn by pecking a post— 3 versions	Ojibwa	Northeast	Jones 1917, 304–10, 358–62, 423
Woodpecker gets rice by tapping a tree	Mi'kmaq	Northeast	Leland 1884, 210–12
Woodpecker gets three raccoons (=worms) by pecking holes in a stub	Ojibwa	Northeast	Bourgeois 1994, 33–34
Woodpecker gets worms by striking a tree with his nose	Mi'kmaq	Northeast	Parsons 1925, 84
Woodpecker gives something to eat to Coyote, who imitates him by setting his own head on fire	Caddo	Southeast	Dorsey 1905, 94–95
Woodpecker makes a hole in a tree and brings out caribou ribs	Innu	Subarctic	Savard 1969, 11–12; see Savard 1972, 76
Woodpecker pecks at a tree and the fallen dust turns into buffalo meat	Osage	Plains	La Flesche 2010, 147–48
Woodpecker pecks the center pole of his lodge with his bill and a bear falls down	Winnebago	Northeast	Radin 1956, 44–46
Woodpecker picks meal out of a dry tree-trunk	Mi'kmaq	Northeast	Speck 1915c, 65

MYTHEME	NATION	AREA	SOURCE
Woodpecker sets fire to his house	Southern Ute	Great Basin	Lowie 1924, 19
Woodpecker turns an arrow into a rabbit and cedar bark into sweet bread	Zuni	Southwest	Benedict 1935, vol. 2, 212–13
Woodpecker turns arrows into prairie dogs and dust from the roof into corn meal	Zuni	Southwest	Benedict 1935, vol. 2, 211–12
Wood-Tick obtains deer by striking a rock with his staff	Thompson	Plateau	Teit 1912a, 206–7
Wood Worm eats inside a tree	Jicarilla	Southwest	Opler 1994 [1938], 304–5

Notes

INTRODUCTION

1. For the names of peoples, this book generally follows the nomenclature of the *Handbook of North American Indians,* which was published in twenty volumes by the Smithsonian Institution of the United States.
2. The word 'aboriginal' is used in this publication in the generic sense and not in the legal sense (in Canada, it includes Native Americans, the Inuit, and the Métis).

1. CARIBOU TAKES IN HIS WIFE'S DRESS

1. See also Figure 40.
2. The same image is used for the river otter. In a tale about a marriage between an otter and a wolf, the otter is the one who initially provides the couple with food, i.e., fish. "The otter . . . asked her, 'Have you got a piece of line? Give it to me, and I will go to catch some fish for you if you will go and prepare a tent.' The wolf drew out a piece of fishing line and handed it to the otter. The otter went down into the same hole in the ice whence he had come. . . . Soon after, however, the otter came back to the hole with a long string of fish which he had killed and had them all strung on the line" (Turner, *Ethnology of the Ungava,* 166).

2. SNAKE MAKES A MEAL IN THE EMBERS

1. The source text does not specify whether Turtle is male or female. In Native American languages, the masculine or feminine gender is not generally indicated in nouns. We have kept here the gender used in the English translations of the different versions under study.

3. THE FIRE TRAP

1. Feminine gender in the original version.

5. SEAL ROASTS HIS HANDS

1. The explanation of this mytheme rests on one element: fish oil. This is why it has been linked to the mytheme about Seal the producer of oil and not the mytheme about Bear the producer of grease. It may be that the borrowing followed another path or that the mytheme is simply a mixture of two mythemes. The other path is as follows. The origin of Fish-Oil-Man would be Bear who produces fish oil by warming his hands. Because bears catch fish, it seems plausible that Bear would have fish oil at the ends of his hands.

10. BADGER PUSHES A STICK DOWN HIS THROAT

1. Other relationships may still be found. Badgers extract food from the soil. Similarly, they extract juice from their entrails. Yucca-juice can also look like blood.

11. BISON SKEWERS HIS NOSE

1. We assume that in all these versions the bark used by the hosts is inspired by the same etymon as the rotten wood that Bison turns into meat, as the bark that Porcupine feeds on, and so on. For Elk, Owl, Crow, and Condor, this origin must be related to the environment (diet, nesting material, habitat, etc.), which could be eventually examined in greater detail.

Bibliography

Adamson, Thelma. 1934. "Folktales of the Coast Salish." *Memoirs of the American Folk-Lore Society* 27: 1–430.

Allen, Durward L. 1943. *Michigan Fox Squirrel Management.* Lansing MI: Game Division, Department of Conservation.

Anderson, Allen E., and Ollof C. Wallmo. 1984. "Odocoileus hemionus." *Mammalian Species* 219: 1–9.

Anderson, Eric M., and Matthew J. Lovallo. 2003. "Bobcat and Lynx." In *Wild Mammals of North America: Biology, Management and Conservation*, edited by George A. Feldhamer, Bruce C. Thompson, and Joseph A. Chapman, 758–86. Baltimore: Johns Hopkins University Press.

André, Mathieu. 1984. *Moi, "Mestenapeu."* Traduction Montagnaise. Édition Ino.

"Angeles National Forest." 2009. "Angeles National Forest Fire Take Toll on Wildlife." *Los Angeles Times*, September 1: n.p.

Antoine, Francesca, et al. 1974. *Central Carrier Bilingual Dictionary.* Fort Saint James BC: Carrier Linguistic Committee.

Aoki, Haruo, and Deward E. Walker Jr. 1989. *Nez Percé Oral Narratives.* Berkeley: University of California Press.

Arima, Eugene, and John Dewhirst. 1990. "Nootkans of Vancouver Island." In *Handbook of North American Indians*, vol. 7: *Northwest Coast*, edited by Wayne Suttles, 391–411. Washington DC: Smithsonian Institution.

Armitage, Peter. 1992. "Religious Ideology Among the Innu of Eastern Quebec and Labrador." *Religiologiques* 6: 63–110.

Aughey, Samuel. 1884. "Curious Companionship of the Coyote and the Badger." *American Naturalist* 18, no. 6 (June): 644–45.

Bacon, Pipin, and Sylvie Vincent, eds. 1979. *Atanutshe, nimushum. Récits racontés et recueillis par les Montagnais de Natashquan.* French Edition.

Montreal: Conseil Attikamek-Montagnais, distributed by Recherches amérindiennes au Québec.

Bailey, Flora L. 1940. "Navaho Foods and Cooking Methods." *American Anthropologist* 42, no. 2: 271–92.

Bailey, Garrick A. 2001. "Osage." In *Handbook of North American Indians,* vol. 13: *Plains,* edited by Raymond J. DeMallie, 476–96. Washington DC: Smithsonian Institution.

Banfield, Alexander William Francis. 1974. *The Mammals of Canada.* Toronto: University of Toronto Press for the National Museum of Natural Sciences, National Museums of Canada.

Barsness, Larry. 1985. *Heads, Hides and Horns: The Compleat Buffalo Book.* Fort Worth: Texas Christian University Press.

Bartholomew, George A., and Tom J. Cade. 1956. "Water Consumption of House Finches." *Condor* 58, no. 6: 406–12.

Basso, Keith H. 1983. "Western Apache." In *Handbook of North American Indians,* vol. 10: *Southwest,* edited by Alfonso Ortiz, 462–88. Washington DC: Smithsonian Institution.

Bauchot, Roland, ed. 2006. *Snakes: A Natural History.* New York: Sterling.

Beals, Ralph L. 1935. *Ethnology of Rocky Mountain National Park: The Ute and Arapaho.* U.S. Department of the Interior, National Park Service.

Bean, Lowell John, and Katherine Siva Saubel. 1963. "Cahuilla Ethnobotanical Notes: The Aboriginal Use of the Mesquite and Screwbean." Archaeological Survey Annual Report, University of California Department of Anthropology: 53–74.

Bean, Lowell John, and Charles R. Smith. 1978. "Serrano." In *Handbook of North American Indians,* vol. 8: *California,* edited by Robert F. Heizer, 570–74. Washington DC: Smithsonian Institution.

Bell, Willis, H., and Edward F. Castetter. 1937. "Utilization of Mesquite and Screwbean by the Aborigines in the American Southwest." *Ethnobiological Studies in the American Southwest 5, Biological Series 5, no. 2, University of New Mexico Bulletin* 314: 1–55.

———. 1941. "The Utilization of Yucca, Sotol, and Beargrass by Aborigines in the American Southwest." *Ethnobiological Studies in the American Southwest 7, Biological Series 5, no. 5, University of New Mexico Bulletin* 372: 1–74.

Benedict, Ruth. 1924. "A Brief Sketch of Serrano Culture." *American Anthropologist* 26, no. 3: 366–92.

———. 1926. "Serrano Tales." *Journal of American Folk-lore* 39, no. 151: 1–17.

———. 1931. "Tales of the Cochiti." *Bulletin of the Bureau of American Ethnology* 98: 1–256.

———. 1935. *Zuni Mythology.* 2 vols. New York: Columbia University Press.

Benson, Lyman, and Robert Arthur Darrow. 1981. *The Trees and Shrubs of the Southwestern Deserts.* Tucson: University of Arizona Press.

Bent, Arthur Cleveland, et al. 1932. "The Life Histories of North American Gallinaceous Birds." *Smithsonian Institution, United States National Museum Bulletin* 162: 1–490.

———. 1961. *The Life Histories of North American Birds of Prey.* Part 1. New York: Dover.

———. 1962. *The Life Histories of North American Waterfowl.* New York: Dover.

———. 1964a. *The Life Histories of North American Cuckoos, Goatsuckers, Hummingbirds, and Their Allies.* Part 1, 2. New York: Dover.

———. 1964b. *The Life Histories of North American Jays, Crows, and Titmice.* New York: Dover.

———. 1964c. *The Life Histories of North American Nuthatches, Wrens, Thrashers, and Their Allies.* New York: Dover.

———. 1964d. *The Life Histories of North American Woodpeckers.* New York: Dover.

———. 1968. *The Life Histories of North American Cardinals, Grosbeaks, Buntings, Towhees, Finches, Sparrows, and Allies.* New York: Dover.

Berezkin, Yuri. 2010. *Amerindian Mythology with Parallels in the Old World, Classification and Aerial Distribution of Motifs, the Analytical Catalogue.* Manuscript.

Berlin, Brent, and Paul Kay. 1969. *Basic Color Terms: Their Universality and Evolution.* Berkeley: University of California Press.

Bernard, Daniel. 1982. *L'homme et le loup.* Montreal: Libre Expression.

Berry, Kristin. 2009. "Commonly Asked Questions About the Desert Tortoise and Answers." *Tortoise Tracks* 11, no. 1: 1–5.

Blackman, Margaret B. 1990. "Haida: Traditional Culture." In *Handbook of North American Indians,* vol. 7: *Northwest Coast,* edited by Wayne Suttles, 240–60. Washington DC: Smithsonian Institution.

Bloomfield, Leonard. 1934. "Plains Cree Texts." *Publications of the American Ethnological Society* 16. New York: G. E. Stechert.

Boarman, William I., and Bernd Heinrich. 1999. "Common Raven." *Birds of North America* 476, edited by Alan Poole, 1–32.

Boas, Franz. 1894. "Chinook Texts." *Bulletin of the Bureau of American Ethnology* 20: 1–278.

———. 1895. *Indianische Sagen von der Nord-Pacifischen Küste Amerikas.* Berlin: Verlag Von A. Asher.

———. 1898. "The Mythology of the Bella Coola Indians." *Memoirs of the American Museum of Natural History* 2, no. 2: 1–127.

———. 1902. "Tshimshian Texts." *Bulletin of the Bureau of American Ethnology* 27: 1–244.

———. 1916. "Tsimshian Mythology." *Annual Report of the Bureau of American Ethnology* 31: 27–1037.

———. 1918. "Kutenai Tales." *Bulletin of the Bureau of American Ethnology* 59: 1–387.

———. 1935. "Kwakiutl Culture as Reflected in Mythology." *Memoirs of the American Folk-Lore Society* 28: 1–190.

———. 1969 [1910]. *Kwakiutl Tales.* New York: AMS.

———. 1974 [1895]. *Indian Legends of the North Pacific Coast of America.* Translated by Dietrich Bertz. Berlin: A. Asher. British Columbia Indian Language Project.

Boas, Franz, and George Hunt. 1906. "Kwakiutl Texts—Second Series." *Publications of the Jesup North Pacific Expedition* 10, no. 1, *Memoirs of the American Museum of Natural History* 14, no. 1: 1–269.

Bock, Philip K. 1978. "Micmac." In *Handbook of North American Indians,* vol. 15: *Northeast,* edited by Bruce G. Trigger, 109–22. Washington DC: Smithsonian Institution.

Bohart, Richard M., and Robert C. Bechtel. 1957. "The Social Wasps of California (Vespinae, Polistinae, Polybiinae)." *Bulletin of the California Insect Survey* 4, no. 3: 73–102.

Bond, Laurel, and Sandra Russell. 1992. *The Carrier of Long Ago.* Prince George BC: School District 57.

Bonner, Nigel. 2004. *Seals and Sea Lions of the World.* New York: Facts on File.

Borror, Donald J., and Richard E. White. 1970. *A Field Guide to the Insects of America North of Mexico.* Boston: Houghton Mifflin.

Bouchard, Randall T., and Dorothy I. D. Kennedy, eds. 2002. *Indian Myths and Legends of the North Pacific Coast of America, A Translation of Franz Boas' 1895 edition of Indianische Sagen von der Nord-Pacifischen Küste Amerikas.* Vancouver: Talonbooks.

Bouchard, Randall T., and Nancy J. Turner. 1976. *Ethnobotany of the Squamish Indians People of British Columbia.* Victoria: British Columbia Indian Language Project.

Bourgeois, Arthur Paul, ed. 1994. *Ojibwa Narratives of Charles and Charlotte Kawbawgam and Jacques LePique, 1893–1895.* Detroit: Wayne State University Press.

Boutin, Stan, and Dale E. Birkenholz. 1987. "Muskrat and Round-Tailed Muskrat." In *Wild Furbearer Management and Conservation in North America,* edited by Milan Novak et al., 315–25. Ontario: Ministry of Natural Resources.

Brain, Jeffrey P., George Roth, and Willem J. De Reuse. 2004. "Tunica, Biloxi, and Ofo." In *Handbook of North American Indians,* vol. 14: *Southeast,* edited by Raymond D. Fogelson, 586–97. Washington DC: Smithsonian Institution.

Branch, E. Douglas. 1929. *The Hunting of the Buffalo.* New York: D. Appleton.

Brennan, Thomas C., and Andrew T. Holycross. 2009. *A Field Guide to Amphibians and Reptiles in Arizona.* Phoenix AZ: Arizona Game and Fish Department.

Brochet, Anne-Laure et al. 2009. "The Role of Migratory Ducks in the Long-Distance Dispersal of Native Plants and the Spread of Exotic Plants in Europe." *Ecography* 32, no. 6 (December): 919–28.

Brugge, David M. 1983. "Navajo Prehistory and History to 1850." In *Handbook of North American Indians,* vol. 10: *Southwest,* edited by Alfonso Ortiz, 489–501. Washington DC: Smithsonian Institution.

Buehler, David A. 2000. "Bald Eagle." *Birds of North America* 506, edited by Alan Poole, 1–40.

Bunzel, Ruth L. 1932. "Introduction to Zuni ceremonialism." *Annual Report of the Bureau of American Ethnology* 47: 467–544.

Burch, Monte. 2004. *Making Native American Hunting, Fighting and Survival Tools.* Guilford CT: Lyons.

Burt, William Henry. 1960. *Bacula of North American Mammals.* Ann Arbor: University of Michigan Museum of Zoology, 113.

Cahalane, Victor H. 1950. "Badger-Coyote 'Partnerships.'" *Journal of Mammalogy* 31, no. 3 (August): 354–55.

Callender, Charles. 1978. "Fox." In *Handbook of North American Indians,* vol. 15: *Northeast,* edited by Bruce G. Trigger, 636–47. Washington DC: Smithsonian Institution.

Carbyn, Ludwig N. 1987. "Gray Wolf and Red Wolf." In *Wild Furbearer Management and Conservation in North America,* edited by Milan Novak et al., 358–76. Ontario: Ministry of Natural Resources.

Carter, Thomas D. 1922. "Notes on a Saskatchewan Muskrat Colony." *Canadian Field-Naturalist* 36, no. 9 (December): 176.

Castetter, Edward F. 1935. "Uncultivated Native Plants Used as Sources of Food." *Ethnobiological Studies in the American Southwest* I, *Biological Series* 4, no. 1, *The University of New Mexico Bulletin* 266: 1–62.

Castetter, Edward F., and Ruth M. Underhill. 1935. "The Ethnobiology of the Papago Indians." *Ethnobiological Studies in the American Southwest* 2, *Biological Series* 4, no. 3, *University of New Mexico Bulletin* 275: 1–84.

Chamberlin, Ralph Vary. 1908. "Animal Names and Anatomical Terms of the Goshute Indians." *Proceedings of the Academy of Natural Sciences of Philadelphia* 60: 74–103.

———. 1909. "Some Plant Names of the Ute Indians." *American Anthropologist* 2, no. 1: 27–40.

———. 1911. "The Ethno-Botany of the Gosiute Indians of Utah." *Memoirs of the American Anthropological Association* 2, no. 5: 329–405.

Chapman, Joseph A., and George A. Feldhamer. 1981. "Sylvilagus aquaticus." *Mammalian Species* 151: 1–4.

Chapman, Joseph A., and John A. Litvaitis. 2003. "Eastern Cottontail, Sylvilagus floridanus and allies." In *Wild Mammals of North America: Biology, Management, and Conservation,* edited by George A. Feldhamer, Bruce C. Thompson, and Joseph A. Chapman, 101–25. Baltimore: Johns Hopkins University Press.

Charalambidou, Iris, and Luis Santamaria. 2002. "Waterbirds as Endozoochorous Dispersers of Aquatic Organisms: A Review of Experimental Evidence." *Acta Oecologica* 23, no. 3 (June): 165–76.

Clément, Daniel. 1987. "Maikan (le loup)." *Recherches amérindiennes au Québec* 17, no. 4: 59–85.

———. 1991. "L'Homme-Caribou: l'analyse ethnoscientifique du mythe." *Canadian Journal of Native Studies* 11, no. 1: 49–93.

———. 1992a. "Étymons, savoirs et mythèmes: Exemples de récits montagnais." *Culture* 12, no. 1: 9–15.

———. 1992b. "Mâtsheshu (le renard)." *Recherches amérindiennes au Québec* 22, no. 1: 33–43.

———. 1994. "Le poisson-avaleur." *Anthropologica* 36, no. 2: 155–80.

———. 1995a. "Etymons, Knowledge, and Mythical Images as Illustrated with Innu Narratives." *Northeast Anthropology* 50: 109–16.

———. 1995b. *La zoologie des Montagnais*. Paris: Peeters-Selaf, *Ethnosciences* 10.

———. 2012. *Le bestiaire innu, les quadrupèdes*. Québec: Presses de l'Université Laval, Coll. Mondes autochtones.

Clifford, Andrew B., and Lawrence M. Witmer. 2004a. "Case Studies in Novel Narial Anatomy: 2. The Enigmatic Nose of Moose (Arctiodactyla: Cervidae: *Alces alces*)." *Journal of Zoology* 262, no. 4: 339–60.

———. 2004b. "Case Studies in Novel Narial Anatomy: 3. Structure and Function of the Nasal Cavity of Saiga (Arctiodactyla: Bovidae: *Saiga tatarica*)." *Journal of Zoology* 264, no. 3: 217–30.

Clifton, James A. 1978. "Potawatomi." In *Handbook of North American Indians*, vol. 15: *Northeast*, edited by Bruce G. Trigger, 725–42. Washington DC: Smithsonian Institution.

Comeau, Napoléon-A. 1909. *Life and Sport on the North Shore*. Quebec: Daily Telegraph.

Couturier, Marcel A.J. 1954. *L'Ours brun*, Ursus Arctos L. Grenoble: [chez l'auteur].

Cove, John J., and George F. MacDonald, eds. 1987. *Tsimshian Narratives I, Tricksters, Shamans and Heroes*. Ottawa: Canadian Museum of Civilization, Administration, Mercury Series 3.

Culin, Stewart. 1907. "Games of the North American Indians." *Annual Report of the Bureau of American Ethnology* 24: 3–846.

Cummings, John L., et al. 2008. "Dispersal of Viable Row-Crop Seeds of Commercial Agriculture by Farmlands Birds: Implication for Genetically Modified Crops." *Environ. Biosafety Res.* 7: 241–52.

Currier, Mary Jean P. 1983. "Felis concolor." *Mammalian Species* 200: 1–7.

Curtin, Jeremiah, and John Napoleon Brinton Hewitt. 1918. "Seneca Fiction, Legends and Myths." *Annual Report of the Bureau of American Ethnology* 32: 37–819.

Cushing, Frank H. 1882. 'The Nation of the Willows." *Atlantic Monthly* 50: 362–74, 541–59.

———. 1883. "Zuñi Fetiches." *Annual Report of the Bureau of American Ethnology* 2: 3–45.

———. 1920. "Zuñi Breadstuff." *Museum of the American Indian Heye Foundation, Indians Notes and Monographs* 8: 1–673.

———. 1986 [1901]. *Zuñi Folk Tales*. Tucson: University of Arizona Press.

Cypher, Brian L. 2003. "Foxes." In *Wild Mammals of North America, Biology, Management and Conservation*, edited by George A. Feldhamer, Bruce C. Thompson, and Joseph A. Chapman, 511–46. Baltimore: Johns Hopkins University Press.

De Beer, Sir Gavin, et al., 1972. *Encyclopedia of the Animal World.* Sydney, Australia: Bay Books.

DeBlois, Albert D. 1996. *Micmac Dictionary.* Ottawa: National Museum of Man, Canadian Ethnology Service, Mercury Series 131.

De Kiriline Lawrence, Louise. 2007 [1974]. *Ruby-throated Hummingbird.* Hinterland Who's Who no. 43. Ottawa: Canadian Wildlife Service.

De Laguna, Frederica. 1990a. "Eyak." In *Handbook of North American Indians*, vol. 7: *Northwest Coast*, edited by Wayne Suttles, 189–96. Washington DC: Smithsonian Institution.

——. 1990b. "Tlingit." In *Handbook of North American Indians*, vol. 7: *Northwest Coast*, edited by Wayne Suttles, 203–28. Washington DC: Smithsonian Institution.

De Mallie, Raymond J., and David Reed Miller. 2001. "Assiniboine." In *Handbook of North American Indians*, vol. 13: *Plains*, edited by Raymond J. DeMallie, 572–95. Washington DC: Smithsonian Institution.

De Mallie, Raymond J., and Douglas R. Parks. 2001. "Tribal Traditions and Records." In *Handbook of North American Indians*, vol. 13: *Plains*, edited by Raymond J. DeMallie, 1062–73. Washington DC: Smithsonian Institution.

Densmore, Frances. 1928. "Use of Plants by the Chippewa Indians." *Forty-Fourth Annual Report of the Bureau of American Ethnology to the Secretary of the Smithsonian Institution 1926–1927*: 275–397.

——. 1929. "Chippewa Customs." *Bureau of American Ethnology Bulletin* 86: 1–204.

"Desert Tortoise." 2009. *The Desert Tortoise* (Gopherus agassizii), *A Natural History.* Tucson: Arizona-Sonora Desert Museum's Tortoise Adoption Program.

Désveaux, Emmanuel. 1988. *Sous le signe de l'ours, Mythes et temporalité chez les Ojibwa septentrionaux.* Paris: Éditions de la Maison des sciences de l'homme.

——. 1991. "L'analyse des mythes." In *Dictionnaire de l'ethnologie et de l'anthropologie*, edited by Pierre Bonte et al., 500–502. Paris: Presses universitaires de France.

Dixon, Kenneth R. 1982. "Mountain Lion." In *Wild Mammals of North America*, edited by Joseph A. Chapman and George A. Feldhamer, 711–27. Baltimore: Johns Hopkins University Press.

Dixon, Roland B. 1908. "Achomawi and Atsugewi Tales." *Journal of American Folk-lore* 21, no. 81: 159–77.

"Dodger's Den." 1999. "Dodger's Den Mother. A True Story—Dog Gets Into a Bear's Den." *Ranger Rick*, 33, no. 3 (March): 15.

Dominique, Richard. 1979. "Le caribou est un animal indien." *Recherches amérindiennes au Québec* 9, nos. 1–2: 47–54.

———. 1989. *Le langage de la chasse. Récit autobiographique de Michel Grégoire, Montagnais de Natashquan.* Québec: Presses de l'Université du Québec.

Dorsey, George A. 1904a. "The Mythology of the Wichita." *Carnegie Institution of Washington Publications* 21: 1–351.

———. 1904b. "Traditions of the Osage." *Field Columbian Museum Publication 88, Anthropological Series* 7, no. 1: 1–60.

———. 1904c. "Traditions of the Skidi Pawnee." *Memoirs of the American Folk-Lore Society* 8: 1–366.

———. 1905. "Traditions of the Caddo." *Carnegie Institution of Washington Publication* 41: 1–136.

Dorsey, George A., and Alfred L. Kroeber. 1903. "Traditions of the Arapaho." *Field Columbian Museum Publication* 81, *Anthropological Series* 5: 1–475.

Dorsey, James Owen. 1890. "The Çegiha Language." *Contributions to North American Ethnology* 6: 1–794.

———. 1893. "Two Biloxi Tales." *The Journal of American Folk-lore* 6, no. 20, 48–50.

———. 1894. "The Biloxi Indians of Louisiana." *Proceedings of the 42nd Meeting of the American Association for the Advancement of Science 1893:* 267–87.

Dorsey, James Owen, and John R. Swanton. 1912. "A Dictionary of the Biloxi and Ofo Languages." *Bureau of American Ethnology Bulletin* 47.

Drapeau, Lynn. 1991. *Dictionnaire montagnais-français.* Québec: Presses de l'Université du Québec.

Drilling, Nancy, Rodger Titman, and Frank McKinney. 2002. "Mallard, *Anas platyrhynchos.*" *Birds of North America* 658, edited by Alan Poole, 1–44.

Drucker, Philip A. 1937. "Culture Element Distributions V: Southern California." *University of California Anthropological Records* 1, no. 1: 1–52.

———. 1950. "Culture Element Distributions 26: Northwest Coast." *University of California Anthropological Records* 9, no. 3: 157–294.

Dufour, Darna L. 1987. "Insects as Food: A Case Study from the Northwest Amazon." *American Anthropologist* 89, no. 2: 383–97.

Dunbar, John Brown. 1880. "The Pawnee Indians. Their History and Ethnology." *Magazine of American History* 4, no. 4: 241–81.

Dunmire, William W., and Gail D. Tierney. 1997. *Wild Plants and Native Peoples of the Four Corners.* Santa Fe: Museum of New Mexico Press.

Dunn, John Asher. 1978. *A Practical Dictionary of the Coast Tsimshian Language.* Ottawa: National Museum of Man, Canadian Ethnology Service, Mercury Series 42.

Earhart, Caroline M. 1969. "The Influence of Soil Texture on the Structure, Durability and Occupancy of Muskrat Burrows." *California Fish and Game* 55, no. 3: 179–96.

Eastwood, Alice. 1905. "A Handbook of the Trees of California." *Occasional Papers of the California Academy of Sciences* 9: 1–86.

Eggan, Fred. 1979. "Pueblo: Introduction." In *Handbook of North American Indians,* vol. 9: *Southwest,* edited by Alfonso Ortiz, 224–35. Washington DC: Smithsonian Institution.

Eggan, Fred, and Joseph A. 2001. "Kinship and Social Organization." In *Handbook of North American Indians,* vol. 13: *Plains,* edited by Raymond J. DeMallie, 974–82. Washington DC: Smithsonian Institution.

Ehrlich, Clara. 1937. "Tribal Culture in Crow Mythology, *Journal of American Folk-Lore* 50, no. 98: 307–408.

Elmore, Francis H. 1944. *Ethnobotany of the Navajo.* Sante Fe NM: Monographs of the School of American Research 8.

Elsasser, Alfred B. 1978. "Basketry." In *Handbook of North American Indians,* vol. 8: *California,* edited by Robert F. Heizer, 626–41. Washington DC: Smithsonian Institution.

Erb, John, and H. Randolph Perry Jr. 2003. "Muskrats." In *Wild Mammals of North America, Biology, Management and Conservation,* edited by George A. Feldhamer, Bruce C. Thompson, and Joseph A. Chapman, 311–48. Baltimore: Johns Hopkins University Press.

Erichsen-Brown, Charlotte. 1980. *Use of Plants for the Past 500 Years.* 2nd ed. Toronto: Hunter Rose.

Errington, Paul L. 1941. "Versatility in Feeding and Population Maintenance of the Muskrat." *Journal of Wildlife Management* 5, no. 1: 68–89.

Ewers, John Canfield. 1955. "The Horse in Blackfoot Indian Culture." *Bureau of American Ethnology Bulletin* 159: 1–374.

Faber, Mak Jean. 1970. *The Tale of the Bungling Host: A Historic-Geographic Analysis*. Master's thesis, San Francisco State College.

Farrand, Livingston. 1900. "Traditions of the Chilcotin Indians." *Publications of the Jesup North Pacific Expedition* 2, no. 1, *Memoirs of the American Museum of Natural History* 4, no. 1: 1–57.

———. 1902. "Traditions of the Quinault Indians." *Memoirs of the American Museum of Natural History* 4, no. 3: 77–132.

Farrand, Livingston, and Theresa Mayer. 1917. "Sahaptin Tales." In *Folk-Tales of Salishan and Sahaptin Tribes*, edited by James A. Teit et al., 135–179. *Memoirs of the American Folk-Lore Society* 11.

Felger, Richard Stephen, and Mary Beck Moser. 1991 [1985]. *People of the Desert and the Sea: Ethnobotany of the Seri Indians*. Tucson: University of Arizona Press.

Figuerola, Jordi, and Andy J. Green. 2002. "Dispersal of Aquatic Organisms by Waterbirds: A Review of Past Research and Priorities for Future Studies." *Freshwater Biology* 47, no. 3: 483–94.

Fisher, Margaret Welpley. 1946. "The Mythology of the Northern and Northeastern Algonkians in Reference to Algonkian Mythology as a Whole." In *Man in Northeastern North America*, edited by Frederick Johnson, 226–62. Andover MA: Papers of the Robert S. Peabody Foundation for Archaeology, vol. 3.

Flyger, Vagn, and J. Edward Gates. 1982. "Fox and Gray Squirrels." In *Wild Mammals of North America*, edited by Joseph A. Chapman and George A. Feldhamer, 209–29. Baltimore: Johns Hopkins University Press.

Fogelson, Raymond D. 2004. "Cherokee in the East." In *Handbook of North American Indians*, vol. 14: *Southeast*, edited by Raymond D. Fogelson, 337–53. Washington DC: Smithsonian Institution.

Fontana, Bernard L. 1983. "Pima and Papago: Introduction." In *Handbook of North American Indians*, vol. 10: *Southwest*, edited by Alfonso Ortiz, 125–36. Washington DC: Smithsonian Institution.

Forbes, Scott. 1983. *Osprey*. Ottawa: Hinterland Who's Who. Canadian Wildlife Service.

Fowler, Catherine S. 1986. "Subsistence." In *Handbook of North American Indians*, vol. 11: *Great Basin*, edited by Warren L. d'Azevedo, 64–97. Washington DC: Smithsonian Institution.

Fowler, Loretta. 2001. "Arapaho." In *Handbook of North American Indians*, vol. 13: *Plains*, edited by Raymond J. DeMallie, 840–62. Washington DC: Smithsonian Institution.

Fowler, Loretta, and Regina Flannery. 2001. "Gros Ventre." In *Handbook of North American Indians*, vol. 13: *Plains*, edited by Raymond J. DeMallie, 677–84. Washington DC: Smithsonian Institution.

Fritzell, Erik K. 1987. "Gray Fox and Island Gray Fox." In *Wild Furbearer Management and Conservation in North America*, edited by Milan Novak et al., 409–20. Ontario: Ministry of Natural Resources.

Fritzell, Erik K., and Kurt J. Haroldson. 1982. "Urocyon cinereoargenteus." *Mammalian Species* 189, 1–8.

Gagnon, François-Marc. 1994. *Images du castor canadien XVIe-XVIIIe siècles*. Sillery, Québec City: Septentrion.

Gagnon, François-Marc, ed. 2011. *The Codex Canadensis and the Writings of Louis Nicolas*. Montreal: McGill-Queen's University Press.

Garretson, Martin S. 1938. *The American Bison*. New York: New York Zoological Society.

Garth, Thomas R. 1978. "Atsugewi." In *Handbook of North American Indians*, vol. 8: *California*, edited by Robert F. Heizer, 236–43. Washington DC: Smithsonian Institution.

Geist, Valerius. 1981. "Behavior: Adaptive Strategies in Mule deer." In *Mule and Black-Tailed Deer of North America*, edited by Olof C. Wallmo, 157–225. Lincoln: University of Nebraska Press.

Gifford, Edward W. 1918. "Clans and Moieties in Southern California." *University of California Publications in American Archaeology and Ethnology* 14, no. 2: 155–219.

———. 1933. "Northeastern and Western Yavapai Myths." *Journal of American Folk-lore* 46, no. 182: 347–415.

Gifford, Edward W., and Stanislas Klimek. 1939. "Cultural Element Distributions 2, Yana." *University of California Publications in American Archaeology and Ethnology* 37, no. 2: 71–100.

Goddard, Pliny Earle. 1911. "Jicarilla Apache Texts." *Anthropological Papers of the American Museum of Natural History* 8: 1–276.

Godfrey, W. Earl. 1966. *The Birds of Canada*. Ottawa: National Museum of Man, Bulletin no. 203, Biological Series no. 73.

Grassé, Pierre-Paul, ed. 1952–1996. *Traité de zoologie, anatomie, systématique, biologie*. Paris: 17 vols. Masson et cie Éditeurs.

———. 1979. *Abrégé de zoologie*. Paris: 2 vols. Masson.

Griffin, Trenholme J., ed. 1992. *More Ah Mo! Indian Legends from the Northwest*. Surrey BC: Hancock.

Grinnell, George Bird. 1926. *By Cheyenne Campfires*. New Haven: Yale University Press.

Grinnell, Joseph, Joseph Scattergood Dixon, and Jean Myron Linsdale. 1937. *Fur-bearing Mammals of California*. Berkeley: University of California Press.

Gruell, George E., and Nick J. Papez. 1963. "Movements of Mule Deer in Northeastern Nevada." *Journal of Wildlife Management* 27, no. 3: 414–22.

Gunn, Anne. 2001 [1977]. *Porcupine*. Ottawa: Hinterland Who's Who. Canadian Wildlife Federation.

Gunther, Erna. 1936. "A Preliminary Report of the Zoölogical Knowledge of the Makah." In *Essays in Anthropology Presented to A.L. Kroeber*, edited by Robert Harry Lowie, 105–18. Berkeley: University of California Press.

——. 1945. "Ethnobotany of Western Washington." *University of Washington Publications in Anthropology* 10, no. 1: 1–62.

Guppy, Henry Brougham. 1906. *Observations of a Naturalist in the Pacific Between 1896 and 1899*, vol. 2: *Plant Dispersal*. London: MacMillan.

Gutiérrez, Ralph J., and David J. Delehanty. 1999. "Mountain Quail." *The Birds of North America* 457, edited by Alan Poole, 1–28.

Hajda, Yvonne. 1990. "Southwestern Coast Salish." In *Handbook of North American Indians*, vol. 7: *Northwest Coast*, edited by Wayne Suttles, 503–17. Washington DC: Smithsonian Institution.

Hallowell, Alfred Irving. 1926. "Bear Ceremonialism in the Northern Hemisphere." *American Anthropologist* 28, no. 1: 1–175.

Halpin, Marjorie M., and Margaret Seguin. 1990. "Tsimshian Peoples: Southern Tsimshian, Coast Tsimshian, Nishga and Gitksan." In *Handbook of North American Indians*, vol. 7: *Northwest Coast*, edited by Wayne Suttles, 267–84. Washington DC: Smithsonian Institution.

Handy, Edward L. 1918. "Zuni Tales." *Journal of American Folk-Lore* 31, no. 122: 451–71.

Hansen, Kevin. 2007. *Bobcat: The Master of Survival*. Oxford: Oxford University Press.

Hawkins, Albert H. 1907. "Coyote and Badger." *Ottawa Naturalist* 21: 37.

Hayden, Brian, ed. 1992. *A Complex Culture of the British Columbia Plateau: Traditional Stl'atl'imax Resource Use*. Vancouver: UBC Press.

Henderson, Junius, and John Peabody Harrington. 1914. "Ethnozoology of the Tewa Indians." *Bureau of American Ethnology Bulletin* 56: 1–76.

Heptner, Vladimir Georgievich, and Arkadii Aleksandrovich Sludskii. 1992. *Mammals of the Soviet Union*, vol. 2: Part 2, *Carnivora (Hyaenas and Cats)*. Leiden: E. J. Brill.

Herrenschmidt, Véronique, Sylviane Debus, and Monique Madier. 1994. "Le lynx." *Vie sauvage* 27: 1–20.

Hervert, John J., and Paul R. Krausman. 1986. "Desert Mule Deer Use of Water Developments in Arizona." *Journal of Wildlife Management* 50, no. 4: 670–76.

Hewson, John. 1993. *A Computer-Generated Dictionary of Proto-Algonquian.* Ottawa: Canadian Museum of Civilization, Canadian Ethnology Service, Mercury Series 125.

Hill, Geoffrey E. 1993. "House Finch." *Birds of North America* 46, edited by Alan Poole, 1–23.

Hill, Willard W. 1938. "The Agricultural and Hunting Methods of the Navaho Indians." *Yale University Publications in Anthropology* 18: 1–194.

Hill-Tout, Charles. 1899. "Notes on the N'tlaka'pamuq of British Columbia, a Branch of the Great Salish Stock of North America." *Appendix 2 of the Report of the Sixty-ninth Meeting of the British Association for the Advancement of Science:* 500–84.

———. 1904. "Report on the Ethnology of the Siciatl of British Columbia, a Coast Division of the Salish Stock." *Journal of the Royal Anthropological Institute of Great Britain and Ireland* 34: 20–91.

———. 1907. "Report on the Ethnology of the South-Eastern Tribes of Vancouver Island, British Columbia." *Journal of the Royal Anthropological Institute of Great Britain and Ireland* 37: 306–74.

Hodge, Frederick Webb. 1907–1910. "Handbook of American Indians North of Mexico." *Bureau of American Ethnology Bulletin* 30, 2 vols.: 1–1221.

Hodgson, Wendy C. 2001. *Food Plants of the Sonoran Desert*. Tucson: University of Arizona Press.

Hoffmeister, Donald F. 1986. *Mammals of Arizona*. Tucson: University of Arizona Press and the Arizona Game and Fish Department.

Hope, Andrew G., and Robert R. Parmenter. 2007. "Food Habits of Rodents Inhabiting Arid and Semi-Arid Ecosystems of Central New Mexico." *Special Publication of the Museum of Southwestern Biology* 9: 1–75.

Howard, Robert West. 1965. *The Horse in America*. Chicago: Follett.

Howard, Robert West, and Keith Bradbury. 1979. "Feeding by Regurgitation in the Badger." *J. Zool. Lond.* 188: 299.

Hufford, Marry. 1987. "The Fox." In *American Wildlife in Symbol and Story*, edited by Angus E. Gillepsie and Jay Mechling, 163–202. Knoxville: University of Tennessee Press.

Hymes, Dell. 1984. "Bungling Host, Benevolent Host: Louis Simpson's 'Deer and Coyote.'" *American Indian Quarterly* 8, no. 3: 171–98.

———. 1990. "Mythology." In *Handbook of North American Indians*, vol. 7: *Northwest Coast*, edited by Wayne Suttles, 593–601. Washington DC: Smithsonian Institution.

Ignace, Marianne Boelscher. 1998. "Shuswap." In *Handbook of North American Indians*, vol. 12: *Plateau*, edited by Deward E. Walker Jr., 203–19. Washington DC: Smithsonian Institution.

Jackson, Jerome A., and Henri R. Ouellet. 2002. "Downy Woodpecker." *Birds of North America* 613, edited by Alan Poole, 1–31.

Jackson, Jerome A., Henri R. Ouellet, and Bette J. Jackson. 2002. "Hairy Woodpecker." *Birds of North America* 702, edited by Alan Poole, 1–31.

Jacobs, Melville. 1958. "Clackamas Chinook Texts, Part I." *International Journal of American Linguistics* 24, no. 2: 1–293.

Jameson Jr., Everett Williams, and Hans J. Peeters. 1988. *California Mammals.* Berkeley: University of California Press.

Jenks, Albert Ernest. 1898. "The Wild Rice Gatherers of the Upper Lakes." *Annual Report of the Bureau of American Ethnology* 19, part 2: 1013–137.

Jenness, Diamond. 1934. "Myths of the Carrier Indians of British Columbia." *Journal of American Folk-lore* 47, nos. 184–185: 97–257.

Johnson, Clarence D. 1983. *Handbook on Seed Insects of Prosopis species.* Rome: Food and Agriculture Organization of the United Nations.

Johnson, Jerald Jay. 1978. "Yana." In *Handbook of North American Indians*, vol. 8: *California*, edited by Robert F. Heizer, 361–69. Washington DC: Smithsonian Institution.

Jones, Chief Charles, and Stephen Bosustow. 1981. *Queesto, Pacheenaht Chief by Birthright.* Nanaimo BC: Theytus Books.

Jones, John William. 1959. *The Salmon.* New York: Harper.

Jones, William. 1907. "Fox Texts." *Publications of the American Ethnological Society* 1: 1–383.

———. 1915. "Kickapoo Tales." In *Publications of the American Ethnological Society* 9, edited by Truman Michelson, 1–142.

———. 1916. "Ojibwa Texts from the North Shore of Lake Superior." *Journal of American Folklore* 29, 368–91.

———. 1917. "Ojibwa Texts." *Publications of the American Ethnological Society* 7, no. 1: 1–501.

Jonkel, Charles J. 1987. "Brown Bear." In *Wild Furbearer Management and Conservation in North America*, edited by Milan Novak et al., 457–73. Ontario: Ministry of Natural Resources.

Kear, Janet, 1985. *Wildfowl.* New York: Facts on File.

Keeler, Harriet L. 1908. *Our Native Trees and How to Identify Them,* 6th ed. New York: Charles Scriber's Sons.

Kelsall, John P. 1968. *The Migratory Barren-Ground Caribou of Canada.* Ottawa: Queen's Printer.

Kendall, Daythal L. 1990. "Takelma." In *Handbook of North American Indians,* vol. 7: *Northwest Coast,* edited by Wayne Suttles, 589–97. Washington DC: Smithsonian Institution.

Kennedy, Dorothy I. D. 1975. *Utilization of Fish by the Chase Shuswap Indian People of British Columbia.* Victoria: British Columbia Indian Language Project.

Kennedy, Dorothy I. D., and Randall T. Bouchard. 1976a. *Knowledge and Usage of Land Mammals, Birds, Insects, Reptiles and Amphibians by the Squamish Indian People of British Columbia.* Victoria: British Columbia Indian Language Project.

———. 1976b. *Utilization of Fish, Beach-Foods and Marine Mammals by the Squamish of British Columbia.* Victoria: British Columbia Indian Language Project.

———. 1990a. "Bella Coola." In *Handbook of North American Indians,* vol. 7: *Northwest Coast,* edited by Wayne Suttles, 323–39. Washington DC: Smithsonian Institution.

———. 1990b. "Northern Coast Salish." In *Handbook of North American Indians,* vol. 7: *Northwest Coast,* edited by Wayne Suttles, 441–52. Washington DC: Smithsonian Institution.

Kennedy, Mary Jean. 1955. *Culture Contact and Acculturation of the Southwestern Pomo.* HRAF World Cultures 18–024.

King, Judith E. 1983. *Seals of the World.* London: British Museum of Natural History and Oxford University Press.

Kingery, Hugh E. 1996. "American Dipper." *Birds of North America* 229, edited by Alan Poole, 1–28.

Kingsolver, John M., et al. 1977. "*Prosopis* Fruits as a Resource for Invertebrates." In *Mesquite, Its Biology in Two Desert Scrub Ecosystems,* edited by Beryl B. Simpson, 109–22. Stroudsburg PA: Dowden, Hutchinson and Ross.

Kluckhohn, Clyde, Willard W. Hill, and Lucy Wales Kluckhohn. 1971. *Navaho Material Culture.* Cambridge MA: Belknap Press of Harvard University Press.

Kocarek, Petr. 2001. "Diurnal Patterns of Postfeeding Larvae Dispersal in Carrion Blowflies (Diptera : Calliphoridae)." *Eur. J. Entomol.* 98: 117–9.

Kochert, Michael N. et al. 2002. "Golden Eagle." *Birds of North America* 684, edited by Alan Poole, 1–44.

Kolenosky, George B., and Stewart M. Strathearn. 1987. "Black Bear." In *Wild Furbearer Management and Conservation in North America,* edited by Milan Novak et al., 443–54. Ontario: Ministry of Natural Resources.

Koprowski, John L. 1994a. "Sciurus niger." *Mammalian Species* 479: 1–9.

———. 1994b. "Sciurus carolinensis." *Mammalian Species* 480: 1–9.

Kroeber, Alfred L. 1900. "Cheyenne Tales." *Journal of American Folk-lore* 13, no. 50: 161–90.

———. 1901. "Ute Tales." *Journal of American Folk-lore* 16, no. 55: 252–85.

———. 1902. "The Arapaho." *Bulletin of the American Museum of Natural History* 18: 1–229, 279–454.

———. 1905. "Wishosk Myths." *Journal of American Folk-lore* 18, no. 69: 85–107.

———. 1907. "Gros Ventre Myths and Tales." *Anthropological Papers of the American Museum of Natural History* 1, no. 3: 55–140.

———. 1919. "Zuñi Kin and Clan." *Anthropological Papers of the American Museum of Natural History* 18, no. 2: 39–204.

———. 1935. "Walapai Ethnography." *Memoirs of the American Anthropological Association* 42: 1–293.

———. 1948. "Seven Mohave Myths." *Anthropological Records* 11, no. 1: 1–70.

Kroeber, Albert L., and Edward W. Gifford. 1980. *Karok Myths.* Berkeley: University of California Press.

Kroeber, Theodora. 1961. *Ishi in Two Worlds: A Biography of the Last Wild Indian in North America.* Berkeley: University of California Press.

Kuipers, Aert H. 1974. *The Shuswap Language.* The Hague: Mouton.

Kuroda, Yosuke et al. 2001. "Diversity of Wild and Weedy Rice in Laos." In *Rice in Laos,* edited by John M. Schiller et al., 215–34. Los Baños, Philippines: IRRI.

Ladd, Edmund J. 1963. *Zuni Ethno-Ornithology.* Master's thesis, University of New Mexico.

———. 1979a. "Zuni Economy." In *Handbook of North American Indians*, vol. 9: *Southwest*, edited by Alfonso Ortiz, 492–98. Washington DC: Smithsonian Institution.

———. 1979b. "Zuni Social and Political Organization." In *Handbook of North American Indians*, vol. 9: *Southwest*, edited by Alfonso Ortiz, 482–91. Washington DC: Smithsonian Institution.

La Flesche, Francis. 2010. *Traditions of the Osage: Stories Collected and Translated by Francis La Flesche*. Albuquerque: University of New Mexico Press.

Landar, Herbert. 1964. "Seven Navaho Verbs of Eating." *International Journal of American Linguistics* 30, no. 1: 94–96.

Landriault, Martine Marthe. 1974. *Rapports amoureux entre les hommes et les animaux dans la mythologie montagnaise*. Master's thesis, University of Montreal.

Lange, Charles H. 1953. "Culture Change as Revealed in Cochiti Pueblo Hunting Customs." *Texas Journal of Science* 5, no. 2: 178–84.

———. 1959. *Cochiti: A New Mexico Pueblo, Past and Present*. Austin: University of Texas Press.

———. 1979. "Cochiti Pueblo." In *Handbook of North American Indians*, vol. 9: *Southwest*, edited by Alfonso Ortiz, 366–78. Washington DC: Smithsonian Institution.

Lankford, George E., ed. 1987. *Native American Legends, Southeastern Legends*. Little Rock: August House.

Layne, James N. 1954. "The Biology of the Red Squirrel, *Tamiasciurus hudsonicus loquax* (Bangs) in Central New York." *Ecological Monographs* 24, no. 3: 227–67.

Lehner, Philip N. 1981. "Coyote-Badger Associations." *Great Basin Naturalist* 41, no. 3: 347–8.

Leland, Charles Godfrey. 1884. *The Algonquin Legends of New England*. Boston: Houghton Mifflin.

Lévi-Strauss, Claude. 1963 [1958]. *Structural Anthropology*. New York: Basic Books.

———. 1981 [1971]. *The Naked Man*. New York: Harper and Row.

———. 1983 [1964]. *The Raw and the Cooked*. Chicago: University of Chicago Press.

———. 1992 [1983]. *The View from Afar*. Chicago: University of Chicago Press.

———. 1995 [1991]. *The Story of Lynx*. Chicago: University of Chicago Press.

———. 1996 [1985]. *The Jealous Potter*. Chicago: University of Chicago Press.

Lewis, M. Paul, ed. 2009. *Ethnologue: Languages of the World,* 16th ed. Dallas TX: SIL International.

Lindzey, Frederick G. 1987. "Mountain Lion." In *Wild Furbearer Management and Conservation in North America,* edited by Milan Novak et al., 657–67. Ontario: Ministry of Natural Resources.

———. 2003. "Badger, Taxidea taxus." In *Wild Mammals of North America, Biology, Management and Conservation,* edited by George A. Feldhamer, Bruce C. Thompson, and Joseph A. Chapman, 683–91. Baltimore: Johns Hopkins University Press.

Linsdale, Jean M. 1946. *The California Ground Squirrel. A Record of Observations Made on the Hastings Natural History Reservation.* Berkeley: University of California Press.

Long, Charles Alan. 1973. "Taxidea taxus." *Mammalian Species* 26 (June 1973): 1–4.

Long, Charles Alan, and Carl Arthur Killingley. 1983. *The Badgers of the World.* Springfield IL: Charles C. Thomas.

Lowe, Charles E. 1958. "Ecology of the Swamp Rabbit in Georgia." *Journal of Mammalogy* 39, no. 1: 116–27.

Lowie, Robert Harry. 1909a. "Shoshone and Comanche Tales." *Journal of American Folk-lore* 22, no. 85: 265–82.

———. 1909b. "The Northern Shoshone." *Anthropological Papers, American Museum of Natural History* 2: 165–306.

———. 1910. "The Assiniboine." *Anthropological Papers, American Museum of Natural History* 4, no. 1: 1–270.

———. 1918. "Myths and Traditions of the Crow Indians." *Anthropological Papers, American Museum of Natural History* 25: 1–308.

———. 1922. "The Material Culture of the Crow Indians." *Anthropological Papers, American Museum of Natural History* 21, no. 3: 201–70.

———. 1924. "Shoshonean Tales." *Journal of American Folk-lore* 37, nos. 143–144: 1–242.

Mack, Diane Evans, and Wang Yong. 2000. "Swainson's Thrush." *Birds of North America* 540, edited by Alan Poole, 1–32.

MacMillen, Richard E., and David S. Hinds. 1998. "Water Economy of Granivorous Birds: California House Finches." *Condor* 100, no. 3: 493–503.

Maehr, David S., and James R. Brady. 1982. "Fall Food Habits of Black Bears in Baker and Columbia Counties, Florida." *Annual Conference Southeast Association Fish and Wildlife Agencies* 36: 565–70.

Mailhot, José, and Kateri Lescop. 1977. *Lexique montagnais-français du dialecte de Schefferville, Sept-Îles et Maliotenam.* Québec: Ministère des Affaires culturelles, Direction générale du patrimoine, dossier 29.

Mailhot, José, and Andrée Michaud. 1965. *North West River, Étude ethnographique.* Québec: Université Laval, Centre d'études nordiques, Travaux divers 7.

Marie-Victorin, Frère. 1964. *Flore laurentienne.* Montreal: Presses de l'Université de Montréal.

Marsden, Halsey M., and Nicholas R. Holler. 1964. "Social Behavior in Confined Populations of the Cottontail and the Swamp Rabbit." *Wildlife Monographs* 13: 3–39.

Martin, Alexander Campbell, and Francis Morey Uhler. 1939. *Food of Game Ducks in the United States and Canada.* Washington DC: Department of Agriculture Technical Bulletin 634.

Martin, Fran. 1950. *Nine Tales of Coyote.* New York: Harper and Brothers.

Martin, Laura C. 1994. *Wildlife Folklore.* Old Saybrook CT: Globe Pequot.

Mason, Otis T. 1894. "North American Bows, Arrows, and Quivers." *Smithsonian Institution Annual Report for 1893:* 631–80.

Matson, Jerry R. 1967. *The Adaptable Black Bear.* Philadelphia: Dorrance.

Matthews, Washington. 1897. "Navaho Legends." *Memoirs of the American Folk-Lore Society* 5: 1–299.

———. 1995 [1902]. *The Night Chant, a Navaho Ceremony.* Salt Lake City: University of Utah Press.

Mattison, Chris. 2007. *The New Encyclopedia of Snakes.* Princeton: Princeton University Press.

Mauss, Marcel. 2007. *Manual of ethnography.* New York: Durkheim/Berghahn.

Mayer, Theresa. 1919. "Quileute Tales." *Journal of American Folk-lore* 32, no. 124: 251–79.

McAtee, Waldo Lee. 1917. "Propagation of Wild-Duck Foods." *United States Department of Agriculture Bulletin* 465: 1–40.

———. 1922. "Notes on Food Habits of the Shoveller or Spoonbill Duck (*Spatula Clypeata*)." *Auk* 39, no. 3: 380–86.

———. 1947. "Distribution of Seeds by Birds." *American Midland Naturalist* 38, no. 1: 214–23.

McGee, Harold F., Jr. 1987. "The Use of Furbearers by Native North Americans." In *Wild Furbearer Management and Conservation in North*

America, edited by Milan Novak et al., 13–20. Ontario: Ministry of Natural Resources.

McGee, John T. 1961. *Cultural Stability and Change among the Montagnais Indians of the Lake Melville Region of Labrador.* Washington DC: Catholic University of America Press.

McHugh, Tom. 1972. *The Time of the Buffalo.* New York: Alfred A. Knopf.

McIlwraith, Thomas Forsyth. 1948. *The Bella Coola Indians.* 2 vols. Toronto: Toronto University Press.

McLeod, William Max. 1958. *Bovine Anatomy.* Minneapolis: Burgess.

McNeary, Stephen A. 1984. "Image and Illusion in Tsimshian Mythology." In *The Tsimshian and Their Neighbors of the North Pacific Coast*, edited by Jay Miller and Carol M. Eastman, 3–15. Seattle: University of Washington Press.

McNulty, Gerry E., and Marie-Jeanne Basile. 1981. *Lexique montagnais-français du parler de Mingan.* Québec: Université Laval, Centre d'études nordiques, Collection Nordicana 43.

Meagher, Mary. 1986. "Bison bison." *Mammalian Species* 266: 1–8.

Mech, L. David. 1970. *The Wolf: The Ecology and Behavior of an Endangered Species.* New York: American Museum of Natural History, Natural History Press.

Medellin, Rodrigo A. et al. 2005. "History, Ecology, and Conservation of the Pronghorn Antelope, Bighorn Sheep, and Black Bear." In *Biodiversity, Ecosystems, and Conservation in Northern Mexico*, edited by Jean-Luc E. Cartron, Gerardo Ceballos, and Richard Stephen Felger, 387–404. Oxford: Oxford University Press.

Merriam, C. Hart. 1979. *Indian Names for Plants and Animals among Californian and Other Eastern North American Tribes by C. Hart Merriam*, assembled and annotated by Robert F. Heizer. Socorro NM: Ballena.

Messick, John P. 1987. "North American Badger." In *Wild Furbearer Management and Conservation in North America*, edited by Milan Novak et al., 587–97. Ontario: Ministry of Natural Resources.

Messick, John P., and Maurice G. Hornocker. 1981. "Ecology of the Badger in Southwestern Idaho." *Wildlife Monographs* 76: 3–53.

Meyer, David. 1987. "Waterfowl in Cree Ritual—The Goose Dance." In *Proceedings of the Second Congress, Canadian Ethnology Society*, edited by Jim Freedman and Jerome H. Barkow, 433–49. Ottawa: National

Museums of Canada, National Museum of Man, Canadian Ethnology Service, Mercury Series 28.

Michaud, Andrée, José Mailhot, and Luc Racine. 1964. "Un mythe montagnais: l'homme caribou." *Lettres et écritures* 2, no. 2: 19–27.

Michelson, Truman. 1917. "Notes on Peoria Folk-Lore and Mythology." *Journal of American Folk-lore* 30, no. 117: 493–95.

Miller, Frank L. 1982. "Caribou." In *Wild Mammals of North America*, edited by Joseph A. Chapman and George A. Feldhamer, 923–59. Baltimore: Johns Hopkins University Press.

Miller, Wick R. 1967. "Uto-Aztecan Cognate Sets." *University of California Publications in Linguistics* 48: 1–83.

Minta, Steven C., Kathryn A. Minta, and Dale F. Lott. 1992. "Hunting Associations between Badgers (*Taxidea taxus*) and Coyotes (*Canis lutrans*)." *Journal of Mammalogy* 73, no. 4: 814–20.

Mooney, James. 1900. "Myths of the Cherokee." *Nineteenth Annual Report of the Bureau of American Ethnology*, part 1: 3–548.

Moorman, Chris et al. N.d. *Using Fire to Improve Wildlife Habitat*. North Carolina State University, Cooperative Extension Service.

Morice, Adrian Gabriel. 1890. "The Western Dénés, Their Manners, and Customs." *Proceedings of the Canadian Institute for 1888–1889:* 109–74.

———. 1932. *The Carrier Language.* 2 vols. St. Gabriel Modling, Austria: Verlag der Internationalen Zeitschrift "Anthropos."

Mossman, Harland Windfield, Roger A. Hoffman, and Charles M. Kirckpatrick. 1955. "The Accessory Genital Glands of Male Gray and Fox Squirrels Correlated with Age and Reproductive Cycles." *American Journal of Anatomy* 97, no. 2: 257–301.

Mowbray, Thomas B. et al. 2002. "Canada Goose." *Birds of North America* 682, edited by Alan Poole, 1–44.

Mueller, Helmet. 1999. "Common Snipe." *Birds of North America* 417, edited by Alan Poole, 1–20.

Murie, Olaus J. 1974. *Animal Tracks,* 2nd ed. Boston: Houghton Mifflin, Peterson Field Guides.

Murphy, Patricia J., George P. Nicholas, and Marianne Ignace, eds. 1999. *Coyote U: Stories and Teachings From the Secwepemc Education Institute.* Penticton: Theytus Books.

Murphy, Robert F., and Yolanda Murphy. 1986. "Northern Shoshone." In *Handbook of North American Indians*, vol. 11: *Great Basin*, edited by Warren L. d'Azevedo, 284–307. Washington DC: Smithsonian Institution.

Nater, Hendricus Franciscus. 1990. *A Concise Nuxalk—English Dictionary.* Hull: Canadian Museum of Civilization, Canadian Ethnology Service, Mercury Series 115.

Neasham, Ernest R. 1957. *Fall River Valley, a History.* Fall River Mills CA: B. Jenne and E. R. Neasham.

Nelson, Richard K. 1983. *Make Prayers to the Raven: A Koyukon View of the Northern Forest.* Chicago: University of Chicago Press.

Newman, Stanley. 1958. *Zuni Dictionary.* Bloomington: Indiana University Research Center in Anthropology, Folklore, and Linguistics.

NGS [National Geographical Society]. 1987. *Field Guide to the Birds of North America.* Washington DC: National Geographic Society.

Nikolaevskii, L. D. 1968. "General Outline of the Anatomy and Physiology of Reindeer." In *Reindeer Husbandry,* edited by P. S. Zhigunov, 5–57. Transl. from Russian, 2nd rev. ed. Jerusalem: Israel Program for Scientific Translations, reprinted by the U.S. Department of Interior, Bureau of Indian Affairs, Juneau, Alaska.

Nissen, Karen M. 1977. "Quail in Aboriginal California." In *The California Quail,* edited by A. Starker Leopold, 217–28. Berkeley: University of California Press.

Novak, Milan. 1987. "Beaver." In *Wild Furbearer Management and Conservation in North America,* edited by Milan Novak et al., 283–312. Ontario: Ministry of Natural Resources.

Ogilvie, Malcolm Alexander. 1978. *Wild Geese.* Berkhamsted: T. and A. D. Poyser.

Olin, George. 1982. *Mammals of the Southwest Deserts.* Southwest Parks and Monuments Association.

Opler, Morris Edward. 1940. "Myths and Legends of the Lipan Apache Indians." *Memoirs of the American Folk-Lore Society* 36: 1–296.

———. 1994 [1938]. *Myths and Tales of the Jicarilla Apache Indians.* Lincoln: University of Nebraska Press.

———. 2001. "Lipan Apache." In *Handbook of North American Indians,* vol. 13: *Plains,* edited by Raymond J. DeMallie, 941–52. Washington DC: Smithsonian Institution.

Opler, Morris Edward, and David French. 1942. "Myths and Tales of the Chiricahua Indians." *Memoirs of the American Folk-Lore Society* 37: 1–114.

Ortenburger, Arthur I. 1928. *The Whip Snakes and Racers, Genera Masticophis and Coluber.* Ann Arbor: University of Michigan.

Parks, Douglas R. 1991. *Traditional Narratives of the Arikara Indians: Stories of Alfred Morsette.* 4 vols. Lincoln: University of Nebraska Press.

———. 2001. "Pawnee." In *Handbook of North American Indians,* vol. 13: *Plains,* edited by Raymond J. DeMallie, 515–47. Washington DC: Smithsonian Institution.

Parks, Douglas R., and Raymond J. DeMallie. 1999. *Assiniboine Multimedia Dictionary.* Database and manuscript at the American Indian Studies Research Institute, Bloomington Indiana.

Parks, Douglas R., and Lula Nora Pratt. 2008. *A Dictionary of Skiri Pawnee.* Lincoln: University of Nebraska Press.

Parks, Douglas R., and Waldo R. Wedel. 1985. "Pawnee Geography: Historical and Sacred." *Great Plains Quarterly* 5, no. 3: 143–76.

Parsons, Elsie C. 1917. "Notes on Zuni." *Memoirs of the American Anthropological Association* 4, nos. 3–4: 151–327.

———. 1923. "Navaho Folk Tales." *Journal of American Folk-lore* 36, no. 142: 368–75.

———. 1925. "Micmac Folklore." *Journal of American Folk-lore* 38, no. 147: 55–133.

———. 1926. "Tewa Tales." *Memoirs of the American Folk-Lore Society* 19: 1–304.

———. 1940. "Taos Tales." *Memoirs of the American Folk-Lore Society* 34: 1–192.

———. 1941. "Notes on the Caddo." *Supplement American Anthropologist* 43, no. 3, part 2: *Memoirs of the American Anthropological Association* 57: 1–76.

———. 1996 [1939]. *Pueblo Indian Religion.* 2 vols. Lincoln: University of Nebraska Press.

Pearce, Thomas Matthews, ed. 1988 [1965]. *New Mexico Place Names: A Geographical Dictionary.* Albuquerque: University of New Mexico Press.

Perry, Mary Louise. 1939. "Notes on a Captive Badger." *Murrelet* 20: 49–53.

Phillips, Allan, Joe Marshall, and Gale Monson. 1964. *The Birds of Arizona.* Tucson: University of Arizona Press.

Phinney, Archie. 1934. *Nez Percé Texts.* New York: Columbia University Press.

Pike, James. 1932 [1865]. *The Scout and Ranger, Being the Personal Adventures of James Pike of the Texas Rangers in 1859–60.* Princeton: Princeton University Press.

Platt, Steven G., Christopher G. Brantley, and Thomas R. Rainwater. 2001. "Cannebrake Fauna: Wildlife Diversity in a Critically Endangered Ecosystem." *Journal of the Elisha Mitchell Scientific Society* 117, no. 1: 1–19.

——. 2009. "Native American Ethnobotany of Cane (*Arundinaria* spp.) in the Southeastern United States: A Review." *Castanea* 74, no. 3: 271–85.

Plog, Fred. 1979. "Prehistory: Western Anasazi." In *Handbook of North American Indians*, vol. 9: *Southwest*, edited by Alfonso Ortiz, 108–30. Washington: Smithsonian Institution.

Poole, Alan F., Richard O. Bierregaard, and Mark S. Martell. 2002. "Osprey." *Birds of North America* 683, edited by Alan Poole, 1–44.

Pope, Polly. 1967. "Toward a Structural Analysis of North American Trickster Tales." *Southern Folklore Quarterly* 31: 274–86.

Pope, Saxton T. 1918. "Yahi Archery." *University of California Publications in American Archaeology and Ethnology* 13, no. 3: 103–52.

Powell, Jerry A. and Charles L. Hogue. 1979. *California Insects.* Berkeley: University of California Press.

Powell, James V. 1990. "Quileute." In *Handbook of North American Indians*, vol. 7: *Northwest Coast*, edited by Wayne Suttles, 431–37. Washington DC: Smithsonian Institution.

Powers, Kevin D., Robert E. Noble, and Robert H. Chabreck. 1978. "Seed Distribution by Waterfowl in Southwestern Louisiana." *Journal of Wildlife Management* 42, no. 3: 598–605.

Prescott, Jacques, and Pierre Richard. 1982. *Mammifères du Québec et de l'Est du Canada.* 2 vols. Montreal: Éditions France-Amérique.

Radin, Paul. 1914. "Some Myths and Tales of the Ojibwa of Southeastern Ontario." *Geological Survey Memoir* 48, no. 2, *Anthropological Series*: 1–83.

——. 1956. *The Trickster: A Study in American Indian Mythology.* London: Routledge and Kegan Paul.

Radin, Paul, and Albert B. Reagan. 1928. "Ojibwa Myths and Tales." *Journal of American Folk-lore* 41, no. 159: 61–146.

Rand, Silas T. 1894. *Legends of the Micmacs.* New York: Longmans, Green.

Ray, Verne Frederick. 1933. "Sanpoil Folk Tales." *Journal of American Folk-lore* 46, no. 180: 129–87.

Rea, Amadeo, M. 1979. "Hunting Lexemic Categories of the Pima Indians." *The Kiva* 44, nos. 2–3: 113–9.

——. 1997. *At the Desert's Green Edge: An Ethnobotany of the Gila River Pima.* Tucson: University of Arizona Press.

———. 1998. *Folk Mammalogy of the Northern Pimans.* Tucson: University of Arizona Press.

———. 2007. *Wings in the Desert: A Folk Ornithology of the Northern Pimans.* Tucson: University of Arizona Press.

Reichard, Gladys Amanda. 1947. "An Analysis of Cœur d'Alene Indian Myths." *Memoirs of the American Folk-Lore Society* 41: 132–33.

Reynolds, Hal W., C. Cormack Gates, and Randal D. Glaholt. 2003. "Bison." In *Wild Mammals of North America, Biology, Management and Conservation,* edited by George A. Feldhamer, Bruce C. Thompson, and Joseph A. Chapman, 1009–60. Baltimore: Johns Hopkins University Press.

Richard, Bernard. 1980. *Les castors.* Paris: Balland, Collection Faune et Flore.

Ritzenthaler, Robert E. 1978. "Southwestern Chippewa." In *Handbook of North American Indians,* vol. 15: *Northeast,* edited by Bruce G. Trigger, 743–59. Washington DC: Smithsonian Institution.

Robinette, W. Leslie. 1966. "Mule Deer Home Range and Dispersal in Utah." *Journal of Wildlife Management* 30, no. 2: 335–49.

Rogers, Edward S. 1978. "Southeastern Ojibwa." In *Handbook of North American Indians,* vol. 15: *Northeast,* edited by Bruce G. Trigger, 760–71. Washington DC: Smithsonian Institution.

Rogers, J. Daniel, and George Sabo III. 2004. "Caddo." In *Handbook of North American Indians,* vol. 14: *Southeast,* edited by Raymond D. Fogelson, 616–31. Washington DC: Smithsonian Institution.

Rogers, Lynn L. 1974. "Shedding of Foot Pads by Black Bears during Denning." *Journal of Mammalogy* 55, no. 3: 672–74.

Rosenstock, Steven S., Warren B. Ballard, and James C. Devos Jr. 1999. "Viewpoint: Benefits and Impacts of Wildlife Water Developments." *Journal of Range Management* 52, no. 4: 302–11.

Rouse, Irbing. 1992. *The Tainos: Rise and Decline of the People Who Greeted Columbus.* New Haven: Yale University Press.

Russell, Carl Parcher. 1932. "Seasonal Migration of Mule Deer." *Ecological Monographs* 2, no. 1: 1–46.

Russell, Frank. 1898. "Myths of the Jicarilla Apaches." *Journal of American Folk-lore* 11, no. 40: 253–71.

Salomonson, Michael G., and Russell P. Balda. 1977. "Winter Territoriality of Townsend's Solitaires (*Myadestes townsendi*) in a Piñon-Juniper Ponderosa Pine Ecotone." *Condor* 79, no. 2: 148–61.

Salzmann, Zdenek. 1956. "Arapaho II: Texts." *International Journal of American Linguistics* 22, no. 2: 151–58.

———. 1983. *Dictionary of Contemporary Arapaho Usage.* Wyoming: Wind River Reservation, Arapaho Language and Culture Instructional Materials Series 4.

Salzmann, Zdenek, and Joy Salzmann. 1950. "Arapaho Tales 1." *Hoosier Folklore* 9, no. 3: 80–96.

Sapir, Edward. 1907. "Notes on the Takelma Indians of Southwestern Oregon." *American Anthropologist,* 9, no. 2: 251–75.

———. 1909a. "Takelma Texts." *University of Pennsylvania, Anthropological Publications of the University Museum* 2, no. 1: 1–263.

———. 1909b. "Wishram Texts." *Publications of the American Ethnological Society* 2: 1–314.

———. 1910. "Yana Texts." *University of California Publications in American Archaeology and Ethnology* 9, no. 1: 1–235.

———. 1930. "Texts of the Kaibab Paiutes and Uintah Utes." *Proceedings of the American Academy of Arts and Sciences* 65, no. 2: 297–535.

———. 1992. *Southern Paiute and Ute: Linguistics and Ethnography.* Berlin: Mouton de Gruyter.

Sapir, Edward, and Leslie Spier. 1943. "Notes on the Culture of the Yana." *University of California Anthropological Records* 3, no. 3: 239–98.

Sapir, Edward, and Morris Swadesh. 1939. *Nootka Texts.* Philadelphia: University of Philadelphia Linguistic Society of America.

———. 1960. "Yana Dictionary." *University of California Publications in Linguistics* 22: 1–267.

Saussure, Ferdinand de. 1916. *Cours de linguistique générale.* Paris: Payot.

Savard, Rémi. 1969. "L'Hôte maladroit, Essai d'analyse d'un conte montagnais." *Interprétation* 3, no. 4: 5–52.

———. 1972. *Carcajou et le sens du monde.* Québec: Éditeur officiel du Québec, ministère des Affaires culturelles, série Cultures amérindiennes.

———. 1979. *Contes indiens de la Basse Côte Nord du Saint-Laurent.* Ottawa: National Museum of Man, Canadian Ethnology Service, Mercury Series 51.

———. 1985. *La voix des autres.* Montreal: L'Hexagone, Collection Positions anthropologiques.

Saxton, Dean, and Lucille Saxton, 1973. *Legends and Lore of the Papago and Pima Indians.* Tucson: University of Arizona Press.

Saxton, Dean, Lucille Saxton, and Susie Enos. 1998 [1983]. *Dictionary Tohono O'odham/Pima to English, English to Tohono O'odham/Pima.* Tucson: University of Arizona Press.

Scheffer, Victor B. 1962. "Pelage and Surface Topography of the Northern Fur Seal." *North American Fauna* 64: 1–206.

Schoolcraft, Henry R. 1856. *The Myth of Hiawatha and Other Oral Legends.* Philadelphia: J. B. Lippincott.

Scott, William B., and Edward J. Crossman. 1973. "Freshwater Fishes of Canada." *Fisheries Research Board of Canada,* Bulletin 184: 1–966.

Seton, Ernest Thompson. 1953 [1909]. *Lives of Game Animals.* 4 vols. Boston: Charles T. Branford.

Short, Henry L. 1981. "Nutrition and Metabolism." In *Mule and Black-Tailed Deer of North America,* edited by Olof C. Wallmo, 99–128. Lincoln: University of Nebraska Press.

Siebold, Carl Theodor Ernst, and Hermann Strannius. 1850. *Nouveau manuel d'anatomie comparée.* 3 vols. Paris: Roret.

Skinner, Alanson. 1911. "Notes on the Eastern Cree and Northern Saulteaux." *Anthropological Papers of the American Museum of Natural History* 9, no. 1: 1–177.

——. 1928. "Sauk Tales." *Journal of American Folk-lore* 41, no. 159: 147–71.

Skinner, Alanson, and John V. Satterlee. 1915. "Folklore of the Menomini Indians." *Anthropological Papers of the American Museum of Natural History* 13, no. 3: 217–557.

Smith, Anne M. 1992. "Ute Tales." *University of Utah Publications in the American West* 29: 1–175.

Smith, Charles R. 1978. "Tubatulabal." In *Handbook of North American Indians,* vol. 8: *California,* edited by Robert F. Heizer, 437–45. Washington DC: Smithsonian Institution.

Smith, Deborahann. 1988. *Arizona Cactus: A Guide to Unique Varieties.* Frederick CO: Renaissance House.

Smith, Huron H. 1928. "Ethnobotany of the Meskwaki." *Bulletin of the Public Museum of Milwaukee* 4: 189–274.

Snow, Dean R. 1978. "Eastern Abenaki." In *Handbook of North American Indians,* vol. 15: *Northeast,* edited by Bruce G. Trigger, 137–47. Washington DC: Smithsonian Institution.

Snyder, Noel F., and N. John Schmitt. 2002. "California Condor." *Birds of North America* 610, edited by Alan Poole.

Soons, Merel et al., 2008. "Small Seed Size Increases the Potential for Dispersal of Wetland Plants by Ducks." *Journal of Ecology* 96: 619–27.

Speck, Frank G. 1909. "Ethnology of the Yuchi Indians." *University of Pennsylvania, Anthropological Publications of the University Museum* 1, no. 1: 1–154.

———. 1913. "Some Catawba Texts and Folk-lore." *Journal of American Folk-lore* 26, no. 102: 319–30.

———. 1915a. "Myths and Folk-lore of the Timiskaming Algonquin and Timagami Ojibwa." *Geological Survey Memoir* 71, no. 9, *Anthropological Series*: 1–87.

———. 1915b. "Penobscot Tales." *Journal of American Folk-lore* 48, no. 187: 52–58.

———. 1915c. "Some Micmac Tales from Cape Breton Island." *Journal of American Folk-lore* 28, no. 107: 59–69.

———. 1925. "Montagnais and Naskapi Tales from the Labrador Peninsula." *Journal of American Folk-lore* 38, no. 147: 1–32.

———. 1926. "Culture Problems in Northeastern North America." *Proceedings of the American Philosophical Society*: 272–311.

———. 1935. "Penobscot Tales and Religious Beliefs." *Journal of American Folk-lore* 48, no. 187: 1–107.

———. 1977 [1935]. *Naskapi, The Savage Hunters of the Labrador Peninsula.* Norman: University of Oklahoma Press.

Speck, Frank G., and Ralph W. Dexter. 1951. "Utilization of Animals and Plants by the Micmac Indians of New Brunswick." *Journal of the Washington Academy of Sciences* 41, no. 8: 250–59.

Spier, Leslie. 1928. "Havasupai Ethnography." *Anthropological Papers of the American Museum of Natural History* 29, no. 3: 81–392.

Spinden, Herbert J. 1917. "Nez Percé Tales." In *Folk-Tales of Salishan and Sahaptin Tribes*, edited by James A. Teit et al., 180–201. *Memoirs of the American Folk-Lore Society* 11.

Spindler, Louise S. 1978. "Menominee." In *Handbook of North American Indians*, vol. 15: *Northeast*, edited by Bruce G. Trigger, 708–24. Washington DC: Smithsonian Institution.

Squires, John R., and Richard T. Reynolds. 1997. "Northern Goshawk." *Birds of North America* 298, edited by Alan Poole, 1–32.

Stearns, Louis A., and Marvin W. Goodwin. 1941. "Notes on the Winter Feeding of the Muskrat in Delaware." *Journal of Wildlife Management* 5, no. 1: 1–12.

Steeger, Christoph, Hans Esselink, and Ronald C. Ydenberg. 1992. "Comparative Feeding Ecology and Retrospective Performance of Ospreys in Different Habitats of Southeastern British Columbia." *Canadian Journal of Zoology* 70, no. 3: 470–75.

Steeves, Taylor A. 1952. "Wild Rice—Indian Food and Modern Delicacy." *Economic Botany* 6, no. 2: 107–42.

Stevenson, Matilda Coxe. 1904. "The Zuñi Indians: Their Mythology, Esoteric Fraternities, and Ceremonies." *Annual Report of the Bureau of American Ethnology* 23: 3–634.

———. 1993 [1915]. *The Zuñi Indians and Their Use of Plants.* New York: Dover.

Stewart, Hilary. 1977. *Indian Fishing: Early Methods on the Northwest Coast.* Vancouver: Douglas and McIntyre; Seattle: University of Washington Press.

Stickney, Gardner P. 1896. "Indian Use of Wild Rice." *American Anthropologist* 9, no. 4: 115–21.

Storer, Tracy Irwin, et al. 1979 [1943]. *General Zoology.* New York: McGraw-Hill.

Stoudt, Jerome H. 1944. "Food Preferences of Mallards in the Chippewa National Forest, Minnesota." *Journal of Wildlife Management* 8, no. 2: 100–112.

Strickland, Marjorie E., and Carman W. Douglas. 1987. "Marten." In *Wild Furbearer Management and Conservation in North America,* edited by Milan Novak et al., 530–46. Ontario: Ministry of Natural Resources.

Strong, William Duncan. 1929. "Aboriginal Society in Southern California." *University of California Publications in American Archaeology and Ethnology* 26, no. 1: 1–358.

———. 1930. "Notes on Mammals of the Labrador Interior." *Journal of Mammalogy* 11, no. 1: 1–10.

Sunquist, Mel, and Fiona Sunquist. 2002. *Wild Cats of the World.* Chicago: University of Chicago Press.

Sutherland, Glenn D. et al. 1982. "Feeding Territoriality in Migrant Rufous Hummingbirds: Defense of Yellow-bellied Sapsucker (*Sphyrapicus varius*) Feeding Sites." *Canadian Journal of Zoology* 60, no. 9: 2046–50.

Suttles, Wayne. 1990. "Environment." In *Handbook of North American Indians,* vol. 7: *Northwest Coast,* edited by Wayne Suttles, 16–29. Washington DC: Smithsonian Institution.

Suttles, Wayne, and Aldona Jonaitis. 1990. "History of Research." In *Handbook of North American Indians,* vol. 7: *Northwest Coast,* edited by Wayne Suttles, 73–87. Washington DC: Smithsonian Institution.

Svilha, Ruth D. 1929. "Habits of Sylvilagus aquaticus littoralis." *Journal of Mammalogy* 10, no. 4: 315–19.

Swanton, John R. 1905. "Haida Texts and Myths." *Bulletin of the Bureau of American Ethnology* 29: 1–448.

———. 1908. "Haida Texts—Masset Dialects." *Publications of the Jesup North Pacific Expedition* 10, no. 1, *Memoirs of the American Museum of Natural History* 14, no. 1: 274–812.

———. 1909. "Tlingit Myths and Texts." *Bulletin of the Bureau of American Ethnology* 39: 1–451.

———. 1913. "Animal Stories from the Indians of the Muskhogean Stock." *Journal of American Folk-lore* 26, no. 101: 193–218.

———. 1929. "Myths and Tales of the Southeastern Indians." *Bulletin of the Bureau of American Ethnology* 88: 1–275.

———. 1996. *Source Material on the History and Ethnology of the Caddo Indians.* Norman: University of Oklahoma Press.

Tanner, Adrian. 1979. *Bringing Home Animals. Religious Ideology and Mode of Production of the Mistassini Cree Hunters.* Newfoundland: Memorial University of Newfoundland, Institute of Social and Economic Research, Social and Economic Studies 23.

Tedlock, Barbara. 1992. *The Beautiful and the Dangerous: Encounters with the Zuni Indians.* New York: Viking.

Tedlock, Dennis. 1979. "Zuni Religion and World View." In *Handbook of North American Indians*, vol. 9: *Southwest*, edited by Alfonso Ortiz, 499–513. Washington DC: Smithsonian Institution.

Teit, James A. 1898. "Traditions of the Thompson River Indians of British Columbia." *Memoirs of the American Folk-Lore Society* 6: 1–137.

———. 1900. "The Thompson Indians of British Columbia." *Memoirs of the American Museum of Natural History* 2: 163–392.

———. 1909. "The Shuswap." *Publications of the Jesup North Pacific Expedition* 2, no. 7, *Memoirs of the American Museum of Natural History* 4, no. 7: 439–813.

———. 1912a. "Mythology of the Thompson Indians." *Publications of the Jesup North Pacific Expedition* 8, no. 2, *Memoirs of the American Museum of Natural History* 12: 197–416.

———. 1912b. "Traditions of the Lillooet Indians of British Columbia." *Journal of American Folk-Lore* 25, no. 98: 287–371.

———. 1917. "Thompson Tales." In *Folk-Tales of Salishan and Sahaptin Tribes*, edited by James A. Teit et al., 1–64. *Memoirs of the American Folk-Lore Society* 11.

———. 1919. "Tahltan Tales." *Journal of American Folk-lore* 32, no. 124: 198–250.

Telewski, Frank, W. 2006. "A Unified Hypothesis of Mechanoperception in Plants." *American Journal of Botany* 93, no. 10: 1466–76.

Tenasco, Bertha. 1980. *Kitigan-zibi Anicinabe Adisokan.* Maniwaki: River Desert Band.

Terrel, Ted L. 1972. "The Swamp Rabbit (Sylvilagus aquaticus) in Indiana." *American Midland Naturalist* 87, no. 2: 283–95.

Thompson, Laurence C., and M. Dale Kinkade. 1990. "Languages." In *Handbook of North American Indians*, vol. 7: *Northwest Coast*, edited by Wayne Suttles, 30–51. Washington DC: Smithsonian Institution.

Thompson, Stith. 1966 [1929]. *Tales of the North American Indians.* Bloomington: Indiana University Press.

Thwaites, Reuben Gold, ed. 1910. *The Jesuit Relations and Allied Documents, Travels and Explorations of the Jesuit Missionaries in New France 1610–1791.* 73 vols. Cleveland: Burrows Brothers.

Trapp, Gene R., and Donald L. Hallberg. 1975. "Ecology of the Gray Fox (*Urocyon cinereoargenteus*), A Review." In *The Wild Canids: Their Systematics, Behavioral Ecology, and Evolution*, edited by Michael W. Fox, 164–78. New York: Van Nostrand.

Turkowski, Frank Joseph. 1969. *Food Habits and Behavior of the Gray Fox, Urocyon cinereoargenteus, in the Lower and Upper Sonoran Life Zones of Southeastern United States.* PhD dissertation, Arizona State University.

Turner, Lucien. 1979 [1894]. *Ethnology of the Ungava District, Hudson Bay Territory.* Québec: Presses Coméditex.

Turner, Nancy Chapman, and Marcus A. M. Bell. 1971. "The Ethnobotany of the Coast Salish Indians of Vancouver Island." *Economic Botany* 25, no. 3: 335–39.

——. 1973. "The Ethnobotany of the Southern Kwakiutl Indians of British Columbia." *Economic Botany* 27, no. 3: 257–310.

Turner, Nancy Chapman et al. 1983. "The Ethnobotany of the Nitinaht Indians of Vancouver Island." *British Columbia Provincial Museum* 24, *Occasional Papers Series*: 1–165.

Turner, Nancy Chapman, et al. 1990. "Thompson Ethnobotany." *Royal British Columbia Museum, Memoir* 3: 1–335.

Underhill, Ruth. 1946. *Papago Indian Religion.* New York: Columbia University Press.

——. 1968. *Singing for Power: The Song Magic of the Papago Indians of Southern Arizona.* Berkeley: University of California Press.

Vachon, Gaétan. 1983. *Le rat musqué: Mœurs et trappage.* Sainte-Foy, Québec City: G. Vachon.

Vennum, Thomas T., Jr. 1988. *Wild Rice and the Ojibway People.* St. Paul: Minnesota Historical Society Press.

Verbeek, Nicolaas A. M., and Carolee Caffrey. 2002. "American Crow." *Birds of North America* 647, edited by Alan Poole, 1–35.

Vogel, Virgil J. 1970. *American Indian Medicine*. Norman: University of Oklahoma Press.

Voget, Fred W. 2001. "Crow." In *Handbook of North American Indians*, vol. 13: *Plains*, edited by Raymond J. DeMallie, 695–717. Washington DC: Smithsonian Institution.

Voight, Dennis R., and William E. Berg. 1987. "Coyote." In *Wild Furbearer Management and Conservation in North America*, edited by Milan Novak et al., 345–56. Ontario: Ministry of Natural Resources.

Voth, Henry R. 1905. "The Traditions of the Hopi." *Field Columbian Museum Publication* 96, *Anthropological Series* 8: 1–319.

Wake, C. Staniland. 1904. "Nihancan, the White Man." *American Antiquarian and Oriental Journal* 26: 225–31.

———. 1905. "Asiatic Ideas Among the American Indians." *American Antiquarian and Oriental Journal* 27: 153–62, 189–97.

Walker, Willard. 1979. "Zuni Semantic Categories." In *Handbook of North American Indians*, vol. 9: *Southwest*, edited by Alfonso Ortiz, 509–13. Washington DC: Smithsonian Institution.

Walker, Willard B. 2004. "Creek Confederacy Before Removal." In *Handbook of North American Indians*, vol. 14: *Southeast*, edited by Raymond D. Fogelson, 373–92. Washington DC: Smithsonian Institution.

Wallace, Edith. 1978. "Sexual Status and Role Differences." In *Handbook of North American Indians*, vol. 8: *California*, edited by Robert F. Heizer, 683–89. Washington DC: Smithsonian Institution.

Wallis, Wilson D. 1923. "Beliefs and Tales of the Canadian Dakota." *Journal of American Folk-lore* 36, no. 139: 36–101.

Walls, Gordon Lynn. 1942. "The Vertebrate Eye and Its Adaptive Radiation." *Cranbrook Institute of Science Bulletin* 19: 1–785.

Waterman, Thomas T. 1914. "The Explanatory Element in the Folk-Tales of the North-American Indians." *Journal of American Folk-lore* 27, no. 103: 1–54.

Webber, John Milton. 1953. "Yuccas of the Southwest." *U.S. Department of Agriculture, Agriculture Monograph* 17: 1–97.

Weltfish, Gene. 1971 [1965]. *The Lost Universe: The Way of Life of the Pawnee*. New York: Ballantine.

Werner, Oswald, Allen Manning, and Kenneth Y. Begishe. 1983. "A Taxonomic View of the Traditional Navajo Universe." In *Handbook of*

North American Indians, vol. 10: *Southwest,* edited by Alfonso Ortiz, 579–91. Washington DC: Smithsonian Institution.

"Whale Hunting Orcas of False Pass." 2008. *Vancouver Sun,* January 5: n.p.

White, Leslie A. 1945. "Notes on the Ethnozoology of the Keresan Pueblo Indians." *Papers of the Michigan Academy of Science, Arts, and Letters* 31: 223–43.

Whitehead, Ruth Holmes. 1988. *Stories from the Six Worlds: Micmac Legends.* Halifax: Nimbus.

Whiting, Alfred F. 1939. "Ethnobotany of the Hopi." *Museum of Northern Arizona Bulletin* 15: 1–120.

Willett, Ed. 2008. "Notes from an Enchanting Land." *Leader-Post:* n.p.

Willner, Gale R. et al. 1980. "Ondatra zibethicus." *Mammalian Species* 141: 1–8.

Wissler, Clark. 1911. "The Social Life of the Blackfoot Indians." *Anthropological Papers of the American Museum of Natural History* 7, no. 1: 1–64.

Wissler, Clark, and David C. Duvall. 1908. "Mythology of the Blackfoot Indians." *Anthropological Papers of the American Museum of Natural History* 2, no. 1: 1–164.

Witherspoon, Gary. 1983. "Navajo Social Organization." In *Handbook of North American Indians,* vol. 10: *Southwest,* edited by Alfonso Ortiz, 524–35. Washington DC: Smithsonian Institution.

Wooding, Frederick H. 1982. *Wild Mammals of Canada.* Toronto: McGraw-Hill Ryerson.

Woods, Charles A. 1973. "Erethizon dorsatum." *Mammalian Species* 29: 1–6.

Woods, Shirley E., Jr. 1980. *The Squirrels of Canada.* Ottawa: National Museums of Canada, National Museum of Natural Sciences.

Wyatt, David. 1998. "Thompson." In *Handbook of North American Indians,* vol. 12: *Plateau,* edited by Deward E. Walker Jr., 191–202. Washington DC: Smithsonian Institution.

Wyman Leland C. 1983. "Navajo Ceremonial System." In *Handbook of North American Indians,* vol. 10: *Southwest,* edited by Alfonso Ortiz, 536–57. Washington DC: Smithsonian Institution.

Young, Gloria A., and Michael P. Hoffman. 2001. "Quapaw." In *Handbook of North American Indians,* vol. 13: *Plains,* edited by Raymond J. DeMallie, 497–514. Washington DC: Smithsonian Institution.

Young, M. Jane. 1988. *Signs from the Ancestors, Zuni Cultural Symbolism and Perception of Rock Art.* Albuquerque: University of New Mexico Press.

Zigmond, Maurice L. 1941. *Ethnobotanical Studies Among California and Great Basin Shoshoneans.* PhD dissertation, Yale University.

———. 1972. "Some Mythological and Supernatural Aspects of Kawaiisu Ethnography and Ethnobiology." In *Great Basin Cultural Ecology: A Symposium,* edited by Don D. Fowler, 129–34. Desert Research Institute Publications in the Social Sciences 8.

———. 1978. "Kawaiisu Basketry." *Journal of California University* 5, no. 2: 199–215.

———. 1980. *Kawaiisu Mythology: An Oral Tradition of South Central California.* Socorro NM: Ballera Press Anthropological Papers 18.

———. 1981. *Kawaiisu Ethnobotany.* Salt Lake City: University of Utah Press.

———. 1986. "Kawaiisu." In *Handbook of North American Indians,* vol. 11: *Great Basin,* edited by Warren L. d'Azevedo, 398–411. Washington DC: Smithsonian Institution.

Zigmond, Maurice L., Curtis G. Booth, and Pamela Munro. 1991. *Kawaiisu: A Grammar and Dictionary with Texts.* Berkeley: University of California Press.

www.ingramcontent.com/pod-product-compliance
Lightning Source LLC
Chambersburg PA
CBHW022344280326
41935CB00007B/67